PRAISE FOR *VIRGINIA WOOLF*

"Briggs pulls together a high-wire act; biographer and subject seem to commingle on the page, the result being a joint effort of imaginative force." —*The Atlanta Journal-Constitution*

"Briggs has won my mind as well as my heart for her focus on the inner life of Woolf, for her always approachable writing style, for her ambitious mission to inspire casual readers as well as confirmed Woolf fanatics." —*The Denver Post*

"This isn't a quick read; it's a rich and rewarding one." —*The Sunday Oregonian* (Portland)

"Briggs masterfully uses Virginia Woolf's own thoughts and words to gain entrance into the layered world of her life and work." —*The Sun Herald* (Biloxi, MS)

"If you're looking for lucid insight into an intricate mind, a biography that's also a companion to reading Woolf's fiction, Briggs' book is what you want." —*Houston Chronicle*

"An intelligent and well-researched new biography . . . [O]ffers astute insights into both Woolf and her work." —*The New York Times Book Review*

"Happily, the vastly gifted, complex writer who takes shape on these elegantly composed pages is the very genius readers intuit when reading Woolf's resplendent novels and essays. Woolf believed that women writers could 'make the connection between literature and life,' and Briggs has done just that in her sterling interpretation." —*Booklist*

"[A] wonderfully different approach that allows Woolf's writing, not social or historical events, to dictate the overall biographical structure." —*Library Journal*

Virginia Woolf

Night Visitors: The Rise and Fall of the English Ghost Story

This Stage-Play World: Texts and Contexts, 1580–1625

A Woman of Passion: The Life of E. Nesbit, 1858–1924

Reading Virginia Woolf

JULIA BRIGGS

Virginia Woolf

An Inner Life

A HARVEST BOOK · HARCOURT, INC.

Orlando Austin New York San Diego Toronto London

For Anthea

———

www.HarcourtBooks.com

First published in the UK by the Penguin Group.

The Library of Congress has cataloged the hardcover edition as follows:
Briggs, Julia.
Virginia Woolf: an inner life/Julia Briggs.—1st U.S. ed.
p. cm.
Originally published: London: Allen Lane, 2005.
Includes bibliographical references and index.
1. Woolf, Virginia, 1882–1941—Criticism and interpretation. 2. Women
and literature—England—History—20th century. 3. Autobiography
in literature. 4. Self in literature. I. Title.
PR6045.O72Z54359 2005
823'.912—dc22   2005016048
ISBN-13: 978-0-15-101143-8   ISBN-10: 0-15-101143-5
ISBN-13: 978-0-15-603229-2 (pbk.)   ISBN-10: 0-15-603229-5 (pbk.)

Text set in Sabon

Printed in the United States of America

First Harvest edition 2006
A C E G I K J H F D B

Contents

List of Illustrations

Preface

'[E]very secret of a writer's soul, every experience of his life, every quality of his mind is written large in his works, yet we require critics to explain the one and biographers to expound the other'.[1]

In Virginia Woolf's *Orlando*, the narrator/biographer is driven to frenzies of impatience when her subject abandons herself to 'this mere wool-gathering; this thinking; this sitting in a chair day in, day out, with a cigarette and a sheet of paper and a pen and an inkpot. If only subjects, we might complain (for our patience is wearing thin), had more consideration for their biographers!'[2] Though silent, and apparently doing practically nothing, the writer is paradoxically doing exactly what makes her life matter to us, even though her activity, her surrender to 'thought and imagination', may be invisible to an observer.

Woolf's fiction is centrally concerned with the inner life, and finding ways of re-creating that life in narrative. Her first two novels, though more traditional than her later fiction, are preoccupied with dreams – both night dreams and day dreams; she even considered calling the novel that became *Night and Day*, 'Dreams and Realities'.[3] Her first short story written for the Hogarth Press takes place inside the head of a woman sitting by a fire and looking at 'The Mark on the Wall' (as the story is called), while she meditates on the elusive and fragmented nature of experience. Her train of thought is interrupted by a man with a newspaper who identifies the mark, thus extinguishing the rich imaginative potential of uncertainty.[4] Other early stories show how events that occur in the mind – events based on mistaken assumptions, for example[5] – can have the same impact as actual events. From this point on, Woolf's fiction weaves its way in and out of the minds of her characters. Her last novel, *Between the Acts*, creates a series of collisions between mind-acts and actual events.

In his magisterial survey of representation in European fiction, *Mimesis*, the German critic Erich Auerbach argued that Woolf's method of depicting the interior life of a range of characters gestured towards 'a common life of mankind on earth', and he considered this a new and significant development in narrative method.[6] Certainly Woolf's fiction is concerned to acknowledge the interiority, the subjectivity of other human beings. In 1918, she had noted in her diary, 'The reason why it is easy to kill another person must be that one's imagination is too sluggish to conceive what his life means to him – the infinite possibilities of a succession of days which are furled in him, & have already been spent'.[7] In daily life, she was as capable as the next person of ignoring the selfhood of others, but within her fiction, she encourages her readers to extend their sympathies through the use of the imagination, deliberately writing in the tradition of George Eliot, who believed that 'Art is the nearest thing to life; it is a mode of amplifying experience and extending our contact with our fellow-men beyond the bounds of our personal lot'.[8] Both writers share a tradition of women's writing in which moral awareness carries the reader across the boundaries of gender, class and race in the interests of wider sympathy and understanding. In re-creating the interiority of others, Woolf drew, as she had to, on what she knew of her own. She remained a fascinated observer of her own thoughts and also of her own creative process, recording both in her diaries and letters; her late, unfinished autobiographical 'Sketch of the Past' takes a closer look within.

My account is inspired by Woolf's own interest in the process of writing, as well as by a corresponding unease with accounts that (like Orlando's biographer) concentrate too narrowly on her social life, and so underestimate the centrality of her art – the main source of her interest for us. Woolf was evidently a highly sociable person, with a fascinating and gifted circle of family and friends, an engaging companion and an entrancing aunt, yet it was what she did when she was alone, walking or sitting at her desk, for which we now remember her. While the story of her inner life cannot be told (except as another fiction), it is possible to track down a number of the factors that brought her books into being, by following the genesis and process of their writing as reflected in the surviving drafts, and supplementing these with the accounts she gave to friends, or confided to her diary as aids to reconstruction. My aim, ultimately, is to lead readers back to her work with a fresh sense of what they might find there. Although the book has an overall direction, individual chapters are structured in different ways, as seemed most appropriate, though each concludes with an 'aftermath', a history of the book's production and reception after publication. These can, of course, be skipped, as can the endnotes, which list sources and suggest lines of thought that seemed too specialized or speculative to appeal to 'the common reader', for whom my book is primarily intended.

This book inevitably stands upon the achievements of other Woolf scholars, editors, critics and readers – most of these are, I hope, acknowledged in the endnotes. It has taken me several years to write, and I have incurred many debts along the way: the first is to the Arts and Humanities Research Board who, in conjunction with my university, De Montfort, Leicester, enabled me to take a year's research leave from January 1999 to January 2000. I am warmly grateful to the colleagues who made this possible – to Deborah Cartmell, Jane Dowson, Imelda Whelehan and Nigel Wood. I have learned a great deal about Woolf in conversation with friends and colleagues, both here and abroad, and fear that, in the process, I have both borrowed and distorted their ideas without necessarily noticing that I was doing so. I particularly want to thank Michèle Barrett, James Beechey, Kate Benzel, Ted Bishop, Rachel Bowlby, David Bradshaw, Beth Rigel Daugherty, Marion Dell, Diane Gillespie, Kathy Laing, Phyllis Lassner, Jane Liddell-King, Alison Light, Nicola Luckhurst, Vara Neverow, Sybil Oldfield, Merry Pawlowski, Jem Poster, Sue Roe, Anna Snaith, Alice Staveley and Pierre-Eric Villeneuve. I am well aware of how much the kindness of librarians has contributed, and particularly want to thank the incomparable Bet Inglis, formerly of Sussex University Library, who always knew what one needed before one knew oneself; and also Michael Bott of Reading University Library, Dr Isaac Gewirtz,

Curator of the Berg Collection in the New York Public Library, and Karen Kukil, Curator of the Rare Book Room at Smith College, Northampton, Mass.

Special thanks are due to the several close friends who have listened, read and encouraged at every stage: to Jane Marcus, the fairy godmother of Woolf studies; to Nigel Hamilton, who prevented me from writing 'lit. crit.', and invented the 'headstones', to David Stocker, who insisted upon the importance of Roger Fry, and more recently, to Hans Gabler, who with characteristic warmth and generosity, has contributed in so many different ways. I would also like to thank my agent Gill Coleridge, my copy-editor Charlotte Ridings, my publisher Simon Winder and my excellent readers, Stuart Clarke and Mark Hussey, for their full, helpful and constructive comments – the remaining errors are my own. Further, different and loving thanks belong to my nearest and dearest – to Jon and Christina, to Simon and Belle, and to Jeremy, and especially to my sister Anthea, to whom this book is dedicated.

Julia Briggs
De Montfort University, Leicester
2004

I have followed the spelling and punctuation of quotations from Woolf's *Diaries* as transcribed and published by Anne Olivier Bell, with Andrew McNeillie, from her *Letters* as transcribed and published by Nigel Nicolson, with Joanne Trautmann Banks, and from the various other published transcriptions of her drafts cited, unless otherwise stated in the notes. I have transcribed Clive Bell's eccentric spelling as best I could.

Acknowledgements

The author and publishers would like to thank the Society of Authors as the literary representative of the Estate of Clive Bell for permission to quote from his letters and unpublished diary; as the literary representative of the Estate of Katherine Mansfield for permission to quote from Mansfield's review of *Night and Day* and from her letters; as agent of the Strachey Trust for permission to quote from Lytton Strachey's letters; as the literary representative of the Estate of Leonard Woolf for permission to quote from his letters; as the literary representative of the Estate of Virginia Woolf for permission to quote from Woolf's manuscript drafts and their transcriptions, and from her *Collected Essays*, edited by Leonard Woolf.

Extracts from *Sketches in Pen and Ink: A Bloomsbury Notebook* by Vanessa Bell, edited by Lia Giachero and published by the Hogarth Press, are used by permission of the Random House Group Limited, as are extracts from *An Autobiography* by Leonard Woolf, published by the Hogarth Press, and from *The Wise Virgins* by Leonard Woolf, published by Chatto & Windus.

Extracts from *A Passionate Apprentice* by Virginia Woolf, edited by Mitchell Leaska; *The Complete Shorter Fiction of Virginia Woolf*, edited by Susan Dick; *The Essays of Virginia Woolf*, edited by Andrew McNeillie; from *The Diary of Virginia Woolf*, *The Letters of Virginia Woolf* and from *Moments of Being*, all published by the Hogarth Press, are used by permission of the executors of the Estate of Virginia Woolf and the Random House Group Limited.

Thanks to the Harry Ransom Center at the University of Texas at Austin for permission to quote from Clive Bell's letters to Mary

Hutchinson, and to the Henry W. and Albert Berg Collection, the British Library and the University of Sussex Library for permission to quote from material in their collections.

The author and publishers would like to thank the following for illustrations: Henrietta Garnett, and the Victoria University Library at the University of Toronto, for reproductions of book jackets on pp. 27, 56, 82, 107, 128, 159, 185, 215, 237, 267, 303, 336, 368 and 393; the Henry W. and Albert A. Berg Collection of English and American Literature, the New York Public Library, the Astor, Lennox, and Tilden Foundations, and the Society of Authors, for illustrations on pp. 2, 30 and 161; the University of Sussex, and the Society of Authors, for illustrations on pp. 59, 85, 217, 239, 270, 306, 339 and 371; the British Library, and the Society of Authors, for illustrations on pp. 131 and 400–401; and the British Library (Colindale), and the Society of Authors, for the illustration on p. 110.

I

Beginning

How does a writer begin? Virginia Woolf published her first novel, *The Voyage Out*, in 1915, when she was thirty-three, but her life in fiction began with the novel's conception, eight years before, the moment when she embarked on a quest for her own powers – for its title says as much about her own creative journey as it does about the novel's action.

Later Woolf would keep a diary in which she recorded key moments in the genesis of her fictions, providing an outline history of how they came into being, but no such records survive for her first novel. The exact moment of its birth is irrecoverable, yet she plunged herself into it at the very moment when she launched herself as an independent person, obliged to make choices as to how and where she would lead her life. Once begun, the narrative provided a focus for her imagination, a secret centre, a private path that, with occasional gaps and lapses, would guide her for the rest of her life. *The Voyage Out* was a desperate struggle to write, draft succeeding draft, racking her confidence, yet when completed, it proved, as its first reader had promised, 'a work that counts'.[1]

If the precise 'when' is unknown, the 'where' is partly written into the novel itself: all the surviving drafts begin in the heart of London, in 'the streets that lead from the Strand to the Embankment' [p.3],[2] though the exact street is not named. The traffic flows, like a tributary stream, towards the Thames, which in its turn flows into the great oceans beyond (as in Conrad's *Heart of Darkness*), eventually finding the mouths of other rivers – the Tagus, and later the Amazon. Jostled by busy clerks and typists, a married couple are walking down the street arm-in-arm, an image of one of the possible futures that the

Chapter Twenty One.

Halfway up the stairs which led to the upper world,
Rachel felt a hand violently grasping her shoulder.
"Miss Vinrace" said Mrs Flushing. "We met the other
day." "Are you going back? Won't you stay a lunch?.
Sunday! such a a dismal day, & they don't even give one
beer for luncheon here, which at any rate makes me
go to sleep afterwards. I want say, That's what I do miss
here — the meat. Come out with me won't you?, &
then we'll lunch together. It would be awfully kind of
you to stay,"

"I would like to stay" said Rachel. "Except — She looked from
one to another, They were standing new in the hall, & the
congregation still stood about, as though the service still had
power over them. "Everyone looks so respectable" she ventured.
"Aren't they awful?" "& returned Mrs Flushing with a vivid
flash of malice. "English people abroad...." "We
won't stay here, she continued plucking at Rachel's skirt
— & Come up to my room. I've some things to
show you." She bore Rachel past Hewet & Hirst & the
Thornburys & Elliots.   Hewet put out Stepped forward
"Luncheon — " he began.
Miss Vinrace lunches with me " said Mrs Flushing,
& began to pound energetically up the staircase,
as though pursued by the middle classes of England were in
pursuit.   "What did you think of it?"

twenty-five-year-old Virginia Stephen might have imagined for herself. But before the novel was finished, the nature and meaning of marriage would be thoroughly explored, and its promise of 'calm sea and fair voyage' dismantled.

This married couple make their way to Wapping in London's sordid East End, to the docks and the ship that will carry them to South America. In later drafts of this opening scene, the woman dissolves into tears as she reaches the Embankment, while her embarrassed husband recites poetry to himself, and attempts to calm her. But in the earliest surviving version, Geranium Ambrose and his wife discuss the city's corrosive effect upon the soil beneath. He tells her that the earth between the paving cracks was once fertile enough to grow vines. Now it is poisoned, and no living thing could find its way out. For a moment, she imagines Regent Street festooned with vines, but they agree that such grapes would never ripen, or else would be black and bitter. London is a barren and deadening weight of stone, crushing out the impulses of life beneath it.[3]

Such a vision of the city, as a vast environmental disaster, is all too familiar at the beginning of the twenty-first century, yet the Victorians too saw London as a city in decay, physically polluted by its sewers and cemeteries, morally contaminated by social and sexual degradation. The young Virginia Stephen had read Richard Jefferies' *After London* (1885),[4] a post-apocalyptic fantasy, in which a depopulated England has been reclaimed by the wild; society has reverted to small communes in which a feudal aristocracy protects its peasants and slaves from bandit raids, while London itself has been abandoned, as a lethal swamp of poisonous fumes, burning with methane gas and fatal to all forms of life. Virginia later abandoned the fantasy of her original opening (as dialogue, it was stiff and implausible), but her original vision of London as a place of darkness, 'a circumscribed mound, eternally burnt, eternally scarred' [p.11], underpins the opening of *The Voyage Out*, though in later drafts its decay is pictured in terms of visible destitution and social injustice: 'When one gave up seeing the beauty that clothed things, this was the skeleton beneath.' [p.5][5]

At every stage of composition, Woolf's first novel was haunted by a sense of an underworld, of horrors lying beneath the surface: the human suffering that furnishes middle-class comfort; the white hairless monsters, and the ribs of wrecked ships that lurk in the ocean's unplumbed depths,[6] dank tunnels under the Thames, inhabited by deformed and gibbering creatures with long nails – and whatever lies beneath the conscious mind. Social occasions only momentarily distract us 'from seeing to the bottom of things' [p.116]. In the end, the unplumbed depths, the dark and sticky pool of what we fear but cannot understand or deal with, rises and overwhelms the novel's heroine.

The Voyage Out was begun during the summer of 1907 and submitted for publication in March 1913. No one knows exactly how many times it was rewritten. Virginia's husband, Leonard Woolf, recalled that 'she once opened a cupboard and found in it (and burnt) a whole mountain of MSS; it was *The Voyage Out* which she had rewritten (I think) five times from beginning to end'.[7] But why did it take so long to write? For its author, everything seemed to hang on it. Virginia had always known that she would become a writer, perhaps even an important writer. In February 1904, soon after her father's death, she had walked along the down at the edge of the sea at Manorbier, in Pembrokeshire, wanting to write 'a book – a book – But what book?'[8] Once she had embarked upon it, her first novel had to justify her commitment, not just to others, but to herself. She was a perfectionist, and each new draft disappointed her high hopes and increased her fear of failing.

The task she had set herself was, by any standards, a daunting one. For several years before she began, she had been reviewing popular novels, but found herself dissatisfied with their predictable treatments of plot and character – she would continue to experiment with these elements for the rest of her career. She felt particularly impatient with the highly structured, coincidental plotting still current in fiction, and would have no truck with it. Her early readers were troubled by what they took to be gaps or flaws in the novel's design, later recognizable as the signatures of modernism. To cast conventional methods aside required courage and conviction: 'My boldness terrifies me', she admitted.[9]

Another delaying factor was her sheer creativity, a scrolloping fecundity of invention that tempted her to rework her fictions endlessly, making it hard for her to let them go. She was artist enough to judge when the story-telling had to stop, yet the tale-spinning continued inside her head: early characters, like Mr and Mrs Dalloway in *The Voyage Out*, turned up again in later fictions, both published and unpublished.[10]

At each stage of writing, she was reluctant to confine herself to a single approach to the exclusion of others: 'What I wanted to do was to give the feeling of a vast tumult of life, as various & disorderly as possible . . . the whole was to have a sort of pattern and be somehow controlled. The difficulty was to keep any sort of "coherence"', she later explained to Lytton Strachey.[11] The completion of individual drafts further compounded her problems. While it was always possible to rework events from a different point of view, the several approaches did not necessarily sit comfortably with one another. The surviving versions show a process of accretion, accompanied, inevitably, by some loss of focus, direction and consistency. The struggle between her impulse to fantasize and a commitment to social reality continued, and the fantasy element tended to get suppressed, to the lasting regret of her earliest reader, Clive Bell. Then and always, she shared her heroine's commitment to 'the world of things that aren't there [which] was splendidly vigorous and far more real than the other. She felt that one never spoke of the things that mattered, but carried them about, until a note of music, or a sentence or a sight, joined hands with them.'[12]

These lines do not appear in *The Voyage Out* but in an earlier version, which has since been published by Louise DeSalvo under the novel's working title, *Melymbrosia* – an invented compound word, combining the Greek and Latin names for honey and ambrosia (the food of the gods, which conferred immortality) and playing on the name of the Ambroses. Drafts in manuscript or typescript survive from at least four distinct versions, and there are fragments of others: all of them describe a voyage from London to South America undertaken by the couple of the opening scene, eventually named Helen and Ridley Ambrose, with Helen's niece Rachel Vinrace, daughter of the ship's captain. On the voyage they are joined by a reactionary politician, Richard Dalloway and his wife Clarissa. When Clive Bell read 'volume 1', early in 1909 he congratulated Virginia on its brilliance, adding,

'Now, how are you going to finish it? Surely the Dalloways must appear again, & the Mary Jane [the name of the ship, at that stage]? Unless, indeed, you have invented some new, undream't of form?'[13] She had. In chapter VI of the published text, the Dalloways walk out of the novel for good (though they were to make a comeback in *Mrs Dalloway*).

Staying with the Ambroses in their villa at Santa Marina, Rachel meets a group of English visitors at the hotel, including St John Hirst and Terence Hewet, two young men recently down from Cambridge. After a picnic, a dance, a lunch, Rachel, Helen and the two young men make a further voyage inland, up the Amazon, where the jungle's strangeness threatens to engulf them. As Terence and Rachel recognize that they are falling in love, the travellers feel threatened by the unknown and uncontrollable world that surrounds them. Now the structures that human beings construct for themselves, both real and imaginary, begin to look temporary and vulnerable. 'These trees get on one's nerves', Hirst exclaims; 'it's all so crazy. God's undoubtedly mad.' [p.260] Helen is filled with 'presentiments of disaster', and in the earlier draft she remembers a river party where a boat had suddenly capsized:

In the same way then they had been mocked at; now again they had ventured too far.

'At any moment the awful thing may happen', she breathed.

What did their pretence of competence and wisdom amount to? . . . All the disasters in her experience seemed to have come from civilised people forgetting how easily they may die.[14]

Death and love lie beneath the surface of life like monsters on the sea-bed, mysterious forces that at any moment may rise and explode.[15] The inexplicable and inexplicably painful nature of love is examined, and the promise that it may be happily house-trained in marriage (the traditional plot of romance) is rejected. Yet ironically, one meaning of 'the voyage out' for Virginia derived from the kind of stories that her mother may have handed on to her daughters, stories in which romance led to the long voyage of marriage, symbolized by the journey undertaken by the Ambroses in the opening chapter:

We were in a little boat going out to a ship at night . . . The sun had set and the moon was rising over our heads. There were lovely silver lights upon the waves . . . It was life, it was death. The great sea was round us. It was the voyage for ever and ever.[16]

For the young Virginia Stephen, marriage no longer held out the promise it had for her mother's generation; the old ideal was undermined by the merest observation. Within *The Voyage Out*, the Ambroses' marriage, for all its strengths, seems to Terence Hewet morally compromising: 'She gave way to him; she spoilt him; she arranged things for him; she who was all truth to others was not true to her husband, was not true to her friends if they came in conflict with her husband.' [p.229] His insight occurs in the course of a meditation on the several marriages of the hotel guests. He remembers Rachel telling him that men and women bring out the worst in one another and should live separately. Desiring her, and confused by his thoughts, he wonders whether to tell her he loathes marriage – its smugness, its safety, its concessions.

The desire for marriage and its impossibility provide the central theme of *The Voyage Out*. It begins in a style of comedy and social satire inherited from a range of English examples, from Jane Austen to E. M. Forster (Virginia had reviewed *The Longest Journey* and *A Room with a View* while writing her own novel). It tells the familiar story of a young woman launching herself into society, yet marriage, as the expected climax, becomes first a source of doubt and anxiety, and then a disaster, with Rachel's death. The case against marriage is first made with the appearance of the Dalloways, whose gender politics are as suspect as their imperialism – indeed the two are closely connected. While Clarissa assures Rachel that she can see her husband's faults 'more clearly than I see anyone else's' [p.52], she wonders privately 'whether it is really good for a woman to live with a man who is morally her superior, as Richard is mine . . . I suppose I feel for him what my mother and women of her generation felt for Christ' [p.44].

Women and men have been brought up so differently, are constructed so differently, have such different expectations of life, that the very words they use have different meanings. Richard Dalloway, in a moment of intimacy with Rachel, confides to her the importance he has found in 'love', 'a word that seemed to unveil the skies for Rachel.' He tries to explain that he isn't using it in the conventional sense: 'I use it as young men use it. Girls are kept very ignorant, aren't they?' [p.59]

Just what he does mean by 'love' becomes apparent at their next encounter:

The ship lurched. Rachel fell slightly forward. Richard took her in his arms and kissed her. Holding her tight, he kissed her passionately, so that she felt the hardness of his body and the roughness of his cheek printed upon hers. She fell back in her chair, with tremendous beats of the heart, each of which sent black waves across her eyes. He clasped his forehead in his hands.

'You tempt me,' he said. The tone of his voice was terrifying. He seemed choked in fight. They were both trembling. [p.67]

Dalloway's attitudes to sexual as well as public politics ('may I be in my grave before a woman has the right to vote in England!' [p.35]) are here inextricably linked: he takes advantage of Rachel's inexperience and then justifies himself by blaming her for tempting him, in a familiar masculine manoeuvre. Rachel is overcome with conflicting emotions – excitement ('something wonderful had happened' [p.67]); embarrassment at his presence (he refuses to meet her eye at dinner); and panic – his action releases images of sexual and social anxiety lurking beneath the surface of her consciousness, which rise up in the form of nightmares later that night. She dreams that she is walking down a long tunnel leading to a vault, whose walls 'oozed with damp, which collected into drops and slid down'. This quasi-vaginal passage is occupied by 'a little deformed man' [p.68], at once a goblin and an outcast of the city. As when she falls ill, Rachel suffers from bad dreams in which she is simultaneously trapped in the depths of her own body and the lowest places of the city – both sites of the alien, the unknown.

Talking it over with Helen next day, Rachel confronts her own confusion: 'I was a good deal excited . . . But I didn't mind till afterwards; when – . . . I became terrified' [p.71]. Helen silently blames Rachel's father for leaving her in such a state of ignorance, and tries to put Dalloway's kiss into a wider perspective: male sexual desire is common but better ignored, like 'the noises people make when they eat, or men spitting'. Rachel, pursuing her own train of thought, admits to herself and Helen 'I liked him, and I liked being kissed', yet she is appalled at the wave of panic and self-loss induced by sexual desire. She later experiences a similar reaction during a picnic that Terence has organized, when she and he accidentally stumble upon Arthur and Susan (guests at the hotel) 'courting':

They saw a man and woman lying on the ground beneath them, rolling slightly this way and that as the embrace tightened and slackened . . . Nor could you tell from [the woman's] expression whether she was happy or had suffered something . . .

'I don't like that,' said Rachel after a moment. [pp.127–8]

Dalloway's remark, that girls were kept very ignorant, was a constant and constantly reiterated complaint of women at the turn of the century. Rachel suffers 'terrors and agonies . . . Women one sees in the streets, . . . Men kissing one . . . Things one guesses at . . .' [p.202] Talking to Helen, Rachel links the threat of Dalloway's sexuality with the dark world of the city, the prostitutes in Piccadilly, symbolically circling the statue of Eros, and their effect on the lives of young women like herself, forbidden to walk down Bond Street alone because of the risk of being mistaken for one of them – a restraint upon her liberty that she bitterly resents: 'So that's why I can't walk alone! . . . Because men are brutes! I hate men!' [p.72][17]

Prostitution is one visible outcome of male desire, and through its dark consequences for women and its silent exposure of unanswered needs, it troubles Rachel and the novel as a whole, as it had troubled the Victorian social conscience. Evelyn Murgatroyd, the novel's comically gushing 'New Woman', believes that, with a few like-minded friends, she could put a stop to prostitution in six months, if she went to Piccadilly and talked, woman to woman, to its victims, telling them frankly how 'beastly' they were being. For Rachel, prostitution is linked with death through a cheap novel she has picked up, 'whose purpose was to distribute the guilt of a woman's downfall upon the right shoulders' [p.113]. Though the actual novel is not identified, it belongs to a popular format of the day, designed to raise social consciousness and scare young women off the streets through horrific warnings. An earlier draft sets out its stereotypical plot in greater detail: after being raped by her landlord, the working-class heroine is forced into prostitution, until, battered and abandoned, she dies in a cheap lodging house, having lost her baby, and even her identity. At the inquest, she is referred to only as 'Sloper's Sal' and dismissed as 'a loose woman'. The book upsets Rachel, yet she keeps it by her, 'as a reminder of the frailty of the body'. The novel is scarcely mentioned in the published version, yet a sudden recollection of 'Sal's' death prompts Rachel to ask Terence, 'Is it true . . . that women die with bugs crawling across their faces?'[18] [p.284]

Radical critics of patriarchy represented marriage itself as a form of prostitution, which made sexual and domestic slavery appear acceptable by exploiting women's desire for romance and love, while motherhood ensured their continued subjection. Yet as Woolf's novel shows, unmarried women were often just as subject to domestic slavery, being tied to parents or elderly relatives, and required to act as hostesses or housekeepers, to run errands or act as unpaid companions. Marriage might reasonably be preferred because it offered middle-class women greater choice, as well as higher social status (a view reflected in Susan Warrington's delight in her engagement).

If the relationship between Rachel and Terence is to work, they must confront and, if possible, overcome the evident inequalities in love and marriage. In the *Melymbrosia* draft, it is Rachel who despairs of any communication between the sexes, seeing only her own terror and the empty myths of masculinity:

After all . . . what's the use of men talking to women? We're so different. We hate and fear each other. If you could strip off my skin now you would see all my nerves gone white with fear of you . . .

Besides women see the worst of men. How cruel they are at home, how they believe in ranks and ceremonies, how they want praise and management. Even Uncle Ridley who is far better than most wants praise all day long and things made easy by Helen. As for men talking to women as though they were men, no; it's the worst relationship there is; we bring out all that's bad in each other; we should live separate.[19]

But in the published novel, it is no longer Rachel but Terence who describes the way relations between men and women have been undermined by women's exaggerated respect for men, men's bullying, and the neglect and ignorance in which most young women were brought up: 'Doesn't it make your blood boil? If I were a woman I'd blow someone's brains out,' says Terence [p.201].

Why did Virginia transfer her critique of patriarchy from Rachel to Terence? Possibly it seemed out of character or sounded too much of a feminist rant – Rachel appears less experienced and articulate in *The Voyage Out* than she had done in the earlier draft, 'Melymbrosia'. Giving this insight to Terence makes him unusually clear-sighted, but it also suggests that men too might have something to gain from insights which promised a release from the mistakes of the past. His marriage to Rachel will be different, more truthful, more vital, more equal: 'it does seem possible . . . though I've always thought it the most unlikely thing in the world – I shall be in love with you all my life, and our marriage will be the most exciting thing that's ever been done!' [p.281][20] Yet though Terence intends to compensate for the disparities between them, he quickly reverts to stereotypical male behaviour, interrupting her when she is playing the piano, and expecting her to answer their letters of congratulation. His noble resolutions are not translated into practice.[21]

Unless the old order can be changed, marriage threatens to narrow, rather than enhance Rachel's opportunities for psychological growth. And, at this crucial juncture in the novel, when all seems set for a happy (or not so happy) ending, Rachel suddenly falls ill and dies. Our narrative expectations are frustrated and disappointed with an abruptness that seems closer to the randomness of life than the tidier outcomes of fiction. Love and death now seem arbitrary. The predominant mode of social comedy makes Rachel's death even more worrying, more disruptive, its pointlessness confronting and invalidating the plot of romance.

The difficulties of marriage and Rachel's fears of her own sexuality have encouraged critics to interpret her death as at some level self-inflicted or self-willed, even an acknowledgement of the impossibility of intimacy. Certainly as the book draws to its close there is a sense of impasse, in which the novel's critique of marriage and the social system seems pitted against Rachel's own future. Yet against the suggestion that her world has defeated her must be set Rachel's own view of nature as indifferent or even hostile to human life, erupting uncontrollably and to terrible effect. Dreams, nightmares, hallucinations, illness, death all come from somewhere beyond conscious will or choice, however much our state of mind may lay us open to them. We seek to tame them by finding a meaning for them, but the novel itself remains sceptical. As E. M. Forster noticed, the storm on the final pages makes its own comment on the anxieties of the survivors: ' "It can't only be an accident. For if it was an accident – it need never have happened." Primaeval thunderstorms answer Mrs Thornbury. There is no reason.'[22]

Rachel confronts, but fails to answer the question, 'what do young women want or expect from life?' For Jane Austen and the Brontës, and a whole tradition of women's fiction, marriage had provided happy endings. For Virginia Stephen, marriage was all too often a sham and a deception, yet what were the alternatives? And what compensations were there for those who rejected or failed to achieve the pleasures of motherhood and the marriage bed? A profession required training, dedication and self-discipline. One vocation is written into the novel itself – Terence's ambition is to be a novelist, and when he speaks of his aspirations, he seems to speak for his creator: 'I sometimes wonder whether there's anything else in the whole world worth doing . . . there's an extraordinary satisfaction in writing, even in the attempt to write.' [p.204]

The novel charts Rachel's struggle towards selfhood: 'I'm going out to t-t-triumph in the wind', she stutters. 'I can be m-m-myself.' Gazing into the depths of the sea, she is intensely alive to the world beyond, and the deep waters beneath. For a moment, just before she falls ill, she pictures herself 'flung into the sea', and transformed into a swimming mermaid, but as her temperature rises, the deep waters seem to drag her down, until she lies curled up at the bottom of a deep pool.[23] Virginia Stephen survived that dark undertow; writing itself became the raft that would carry her forward.

The novel's bleak and unconsoling view of death was that of a young woman who had seen too much of it at close hand: within eleven years she had lived through four deaths among her closest family, three of them quite as unexpected as Rachel's. In 1895, when Virginia was thirteen, her mother had died suddenly of rheumatic fever. Her half-sister Stella had tried to take her mother's place. Two years later, and newly married, Stella died of peritonitis. '[A]t fifteen to have that protection removed, to be tumbled out of the family shelter, to see cracks and gashes in that fabric, to be cut by them, to see beyond them – was that good?'[24] Virginia wondered, looking back from middle age.

Early in 1904, her father, Leslie Stephen, had finally died of stomach cancer. His death freed the four Stephen children to start again, to leave their childhood home at Hyde Park Gate for a new life at Gordon Square, in the heart of Bloomsbury. Thoby, the eldest, was reading for the bar after a brilliant career at Cambridge; Vanessa was studying painting; Virginia was reading, writing reviews and giving adult education classes at Morley College for Working Men and Women; her younger brother, Adrian, was still at Cambridge. In 1906, the young Stephens, accompanied by Violet Dickinson, an older friend of Virginia's, set out on an ambitious trip to Greece and Constantinople, which went disastrously wrong when first Vanessa, and then Violet fell ill, and Virginia found herself struggling with uncomprehending doctors and boiling milk in a hotel room in Athens. They had 'ventured too far'. Back in London, Thoby, who had gone back early, was also seriously ill, while Vanessa gradually recovered. Only at a late stage did his doctors diagnose Thoby's high temperature and violent diarrhoea as typhoid, for which there was, in any case, no effective treatment at the time. In the third week of November, he grew suddenly worse and died, after a mistaken attempt to operate on him.

As *The Voyage Out* draws to a close, Rachel's friends search for some kind of explanation: 'And yet the older one grows . . . the more certain one becomes that there is a reason. How could one go on if there were no reason?' 'There must be some reason why such things happen . . . Only at first it was not easy to understand what it was'; ' "It seems so inexplicable, . . . Death, I mean" '; 'What did matter then? What was the meaning of it all?'[25]

Before the shock of Thoby's death could be absorbed, Clive Bell, his closest friend from Cambridge, had proposed to Vanessa for a second time, and had been accepted. For Virginia, it seemed as if she had lost them both. The household of four was now reduced to two, with Virginia responsible for Adrian, although she herself felt in need of mothering; in childhood, she had resented the attention her mother gave to Adrian as the baby of the family. She was afraid that she had lost her intimacy with Vanessa for ever, and blamed herself for feeling resentful when Vanessa was so happy. She tried to feel protective to Adrian as a 'poor little boy',[26] admitting 'I cant get reconciled – but we have to go on',[27] and hoping 'I can make a living out of what is left.'[28] At the height of her desolation, friends and relatives tried to cheer her up with assurances that she too would find a husband: 'The world is full of kindness and stupidity.'[29]

A few days after Vanessa's wedding on 7 February 1907, she told Violet Dickinson, 'I am going to write something serious, needing work'.[30] Initially, Clive and Vanessa had planned to find their own home, but then it was agreed that they would take over 46 Gordon Square, so in March, Virginia moved herself and Adrian into 29 Fitzroy Square, accompanied by the family cook, Sophie Farrell, anxious that Virginia wouldn't look after herself ('she's such a harum scarum thing . . . She don't know what she has on her plate'[31]).

It is easy to overlook the determination and self-determination that Virginia showed in the months and years after Thoby's death, partly because she herself was more often aware of her failures than her successes – her loneliness, her impatience with Adrian, and her jealousy of Clive. Letters to her closest friend Violet announced her want of 'Affection. I don't get None',[32] and her desire to be babied, to be 'the most compassionable and soft of Baby Wall[abie]s just climbing on to your bed'.[33] Yet six months later, new energies began to stir in her; her letters hum with suppressed excitement about 'certain manuscripts', about her future as a writer, which suddenly seems to hang in the balance: 'I shall be miserable, or happy; a wordy sentimental creature, or a writer of such English as shall one day burn the pages.'[34]

Her excitement sprang from the writing she was doing each morning, the 'many small chapters that form in my head',[35] as if claiming a fertility of her own, in the face of Vanessa's pregnancy. Though she often felt afraid that she was less sexually attractive than Vanessa, and less suited to marriage ('I see how I shall spend my days a virgin, an Aunt, an authoress'[36]), she had discovered a secret source of joy for herself, a private theatre in her head, and its actors demanded all the attention she could give. 'Why should I intrude upon your circle of bliss?' she asked her preoccupied sister in October. 'Especially when I can think of nothing but my novel.'[37]

As she found a new focus for herself, she began to attract the attention of her brother-in-law Clive, who was as fascinated by the art of fiction as that of painting, and was constructing theories on both. In the immediate aftermath of Thoby's death, she had barely been able to restrain her resentment of him, finding him utterly unworthy of Vanessa (nor was she alone in this): 'When I think of father and Thoby and then see that funny little creature twitching his pink skin and jerking out his little spasm of laughter I wonder what odd freak there is in Nessa's eyesight',[38] she confided to Violet, in an unexpectedly sexual image. But as he began to surface from the first absorbing months of marriage, she softened: 'I think he unfolds.'[39] In August, he drew up a list of French literature for her to read. His favourite, Mérimée's *Lettres à une inconnue*, she had already read in the sick-room, on their disastrous holiday in Greece, but she took up Flaubert's letters.[40] Marriage had made them both feel shut out, but in different ways – Virginia from her intimacy with Vanessa, and Clive from the approval of the Stephen clan – a mutual friendship seemed to offer each of them a way back.

If Virginia kept a daily diary of these years, it has not survived (though her early journals describe holidays, particular landscapes seen and people met[41]). Clive Bell, however, began a diary on 1 January 1908, though by the 25th he had already abandoned it. On 2 January he records, 'Reading Froude's Carlyle, Dante and Virginia's Sarah, first part poor, last part excellent, very penetrating and often exquisite'[42] ('Sarah' might have been the name of her heroine at this stage, but was more probably the name of the ship, later the 'Sarah Jane',[43] and later still, the 'Euphrosyne'). His diary shows how often they met: on the 3rd, 'dinner and talk with AVS'; on the 5th, 'AVS for dinner'; on the 6th, 'Dinner with Virginia; talked a great deal about myself; for the most part true but gave an altogether wrong impression. Must be corrected.' She dined with Clive and Vanessa at Gordon Square on the 8th; they met at a play-reading on the 12th, and at home at Fitzroy Square on the 16th. They met again on the morning and evening of the 17th, when she read a paper ('very beautiful and brilliant, though not thoroughly argued'), and Clive dined at Fitzroy Square on the 24th (the eve of her birthday). He was finally one of the family.

Her need for advice and encouragement opened a channel between them from which Vanessa could be playfully excluded – 'Clive what's that letter about? O these Authoresses!',[44] but the conversation did not run all one way. Clive, too, had plans for a 'magnum opus', a book on aesthetics to be called 'The New Renaissance'. When, in 1928, he dedicated *Civilization* to her, he reminded her that this was 'the book about which I used to chatter in your workroom in Fitzroy Square . . . You alone know that it was the first conceived of all my brood, and that all the rest . . . have in a sense come out of it. Its conception dates from our nonage.'[45]

Their friendship was full of ambiguities: Virginia did not know whether she wanted to attract Clive's attention because she liked him, or in order to detach him from Vanessa, or as a way of reaching out to her. Her letters are full of her love for her sister, but by asking Clive to convey it, she seems to be searching for a place of entry into their relationship, even a place between them, a place that might at least alert one of them to her needs. She urges Clive to kiss her sister 'most passionately, in all my private places – neck –, and arm, and eyeball, and tell her – what new thing is there to tell her? how fond I am of her husband?'[46] Both she and Clive claimed Vanessa's attention. When a son, Julian, was born on 4 February 1908, neither of them could help with the new baby's demands. Both felt they were 'deserters'.[47] On holiday in Cornwall in April, they went for long walks together, described in Virginia's fragment, 'A Dialogue on a Hill'. Here, two travellers set out across a Cornish moor on the first fine day of spring. For those who love it, the scenery provides 'a clearer notion of the nature of Heaven' than 'all the enchantments of the Lotos Isles'. '[T]hey had the whole of the lengthening afternoon before them in which to make their ascent and communicate their minds.' The speakers, Charmides and Eugenia, are a man and a woman, although 'their relationship forbids any motive of another kind to have its effect upon their words'.[48]

But how far did their relationship actually prohibit 'any motive of another kind'? Virginia's 'Dialogue' tails off, leaving the question in the air. 'Do you remember our talk about intimacy and the really exciting moments in life?' Clive wrote to her after their return from Cornwall. 'Did we ever achieve the heights? Sometimes, during the last few days, I have liked to think so.'

Virginia replied, 'I was certainly of opinion, though we did not kiss – (I was willing and offered once – but let that be) – I think we "achieved the heights" as you put it. But', she adds, reminding him of his domestic commitments, 'did you realise how profoundly I was moved, and at the same time, restricted, by the sight of your daily life.'

Clive explained, '[O]n the top of Rosewall, I wished for nothing in the world but to kiss you. I wished so much that I grew shy and could not see what you were feeling'.[49] It was not the only time he was to plead shyness with her, though he was in fact more sexually confident with women than anyone else in their circle, having enjoyed a long affair with a married woman since late adolescence. He was, and liked to be thought of as, the most aggressively heterosexual of Thoby's Cambridge friends. If there was shyness, it must have been catching. In a scene set on the Acropolis written into but later cut from *Jacob's Room*, Woolf groped to define what the lovers had been fumbling for, when they failed to kiss:

Presumably they both wished only for one thing – certainty.

That something survives, still means, yes even in the chasms of dark years the thing we felt . . .

They wanted certainty; separate, they wanted that the thin shell dividing them should break. Once united, something even in the waste of chaos, survives.[50]

Was Virginia disappointed? 'Clive is now shaped like a spade and thick as an oak tree . . . I warm my hands at these red-hot-coal men. I often wish I had married a foxhunter. It is partly the desire to share in life somehow, which is denied to us writers', she wrote to Jacques Raverat in 1925, and in 1930 she told Ethel Smyth that 'when 2 or 3 times in all, I felt physically for a man, then he was so obtuse, gallant, foxhunting and dull that I – diverse as I am – could only wheel round and gallop the other way. Perhaps this shows why Clive, who had his reasons, always called me a fish'.[51] Was she also recalling Clive's attractions, in this second letter? He was certainly 'foxhunting', though not obviously 'obtuse' and seldom 'dull'. By 1922, he had become 'enough of my old friend, & enough of my old lover, to make the afternoons hum'.[52] Richard Dalloway's kiss may register something of the complex of feelings he aroused in her – desire, fear, flattery. The forbidden nature of their relationship was at once a source of guilt and a kind of protection for Virginia, setting limits on how far they could go, while bringing them together regularly and often. A chaste relationship, warmed by Clive's desire for something more, suited Virginia, while Clive was as intrigued as he was tantalized and frustrated.

In choosing Clive as her literary confidant, Virginia had chosen better than she knew – she had realized instinctively that her old friend and supporter Violet Dickinson would not have understood her need to break with traditional narrative style and subject matter. Violet had read Virginia's earliest writings, and had helped her get her first reviews and essays into print, essays written in a formal, impersonal, 'man-of-letters' voice that her father would have recognized and approved of – indeed in April 1908 she dreamed that she was showing her father the manuscript of her novel, but 'he snorted, and dropped it on to a table'.[53] In a different, and more extravagant vein, she had also composed a fantasy life of Violet ('Friendship's Gallery'[54]), in which her friend appeared as an enchanting giantess in a garden of beautiful women. In one way or another, most of Woolf's early writings had focused on women's lives: in addition to that of Violet, she composed a life of Vanessa addressed to her new-born son, but it was stiff and Victorian, tailing off abruptly with the first threat of sexual scandal. Several early short stories also tackle women's lives in contemporary society and history, searching for patterns and directions other than those of conventional romance, as her first novel does.

Clive endorsed her instinct to break free of existing fictional constraints, and was genuinely excited by the boldness of her vision. By August 1908, she had written a hundred pages of 'Melymbrosia', and asked him for his opinion. 'To my apprehension, the wonderful thing that I looked for is there unmistakeably' he told her, praising her power 'of lifting the veil & showing inanimate things in the mystery & beauty of their reality'. He felt that he could detect an essential form, 'beneath the loose draperies . . . a hard, solid, thing, not to be changed and chiselled without splinters'.[55] He recognized from the outset her need for endorsement: all first novelists are assailed by self-doubt, but the search for new forms of expression carries with it a correspondingly greater need for self-confidence. He nourished her with compliments – so much so that she was tempted to discount them.

Sometimes these were poetic, as when he told her to 'reach up to the tall fruit of your imagination and feel it growing warm and ripe'; sometimes oddly predictive, as when he announced her future status (though misjudging how many years she had to achieve it): 'Virginia Stephen, the great contemporary novelist (1882–1972)'.[56] Virginia's belief in her own genius was a family joke, a chance to tease her; 'genius' was a word she clutched to herself as a talisman, but from the first, Clive had recognized and celebrated that quality in her.

The first hundred pages of the novel were written in a rush, in that 'dream like state' that characterized her moments of inspiration. At such times she seemed possessed, or in some kind of trance, but when she reread it, she felt disappointed and 'proceeded to slash and rewrite'.[57] She showed the revised version to Clive in February 1909. 'I don't know that I like the new draft as well as the old', he admitted, feeling that she had 'sacrificed the "inhuman", – the super-natural – the magic which I thought as beautiful as anything that had been written these hundred years'. He encouraged her to concentrate on atmosphere, and not to 'bother much about the characters of your people'. He made one criticism, however, which would exercise her critical faculties till the end of her life: he thought that there was something 'didactic, not to say priggish' in the way that she had drawn such sensitive women and such stupid men: 'an artist, like God, should create without coming to conclusions.'[58]

Clive subscribed to an impersonal aesthetic, in which the artist sought for an ideal form, rather than passing on a value system: Victorian moralizing had had its day. Virginia shared with her contemporaries a passionate commitment to aesthetic form, yet at the same time she recognized that the source of her originality lay in her personal vision, and her fiction wrestled backwards and forwards between an ideal of formal beauty and social comment, between abstraction and instruction, between imagination and history. Meanwhile she replied to Clive, 'Possibly, for psychological reasons which seem to me very interesting, a man, in the present state of the world, is not a very good judge of his sex.'[59] She didn't allow his criticism to weigh with her, for the draft of *Melymbrosia* that followed is often forcefully and explicitly feminist in its critique of society, more obviously so than the published version. But she never forgot his point, and it became one of her inner voices, urging her to be just, to be even-handed, to bear her male readers in mind. It is always more difficult to disagree with a sympathetic reader than a hostile critic, yet 'I think I gather courage as I go on.'[60]

Tired with the long slow haul of the novel, she interrupted herself in 1909 by inventing a brilliant comic fiction inspired by her experiences as a reviewer: 'Memoirs of a Novelist' describes an imaginary biography of a 'silly woman novelist', but its narrator extracts from the deadening clichés of Victorian memoirs a different, tougher and more amusing account of the novelist, creating a tale that displays all the fictiveness of fiction (denied her by the realist mode of *The Voyage Out*). While Clive realized that she had 'discovered a new medium peculiarly suited to your genius',[61] Reginald Smith, the editor of the *Cornhill*, to whom she submitted it, was less perceptive. His rejection damned it in her eyes, and aborted any possible successors.

Clive was the reader she needed, yet their relationship was never easy. They lived close to one another, and the Bells often invited Virginia to spend holidays with them. Both she and Clive were opinionated and sometimes lost their tempers: there were fierce quarrels, in Cornwall, Siena, London. When Vanessa felt especially left out, she talked of moving to Paris – there seemed no other way out of what was at times a painful triangle. Early in 1909, Lytton Strachey noticed Vanessa's uneasiness and, under cover of a role-playing game, asked Virginia exactly what was going on. She avoided giving him a direct answer. Jealousy was the dark side of her worship of Vanessa and she would always be drawn to her sister's lovers. Looking back ten years later, she noted that Clive's admiration for Vanessa 'doesn't make me jealous as once it did, when the swing of that pendulum carried so much of my fortune with it: at any rate, of my comfort.' But she knew it had driven a wedge between them.[62]

Clive was quite as capable of jealousy: any potential suitor might suddenly become a dangerous rival, threatening to marry Virginia and carry her away. He sent her angry, complaining letters, accusing her of favouring Oliver Strachey, and, on one occasion, flared up over her old friend from Morley College, Mary Sheepshanks. As he well knew, his main rival for her attention was Lytton Strachey, whose brilliance, wit and feminine qualities strongly appealed to Virginia. In February 1909, desperate to change his life, Lytton had proposed to her, but then retracted almost immediately: 'I was in terror lest she should kiss me'[63] he confided to his old Cambridge friend, Leonard Woolf, who was working as a British civil servant in Ceylon (now Sri Lanka).

In the summer of 1909, Virginia travelled to Florence with the Bells, but she felt unhappy and came home early. For several months in 1910, she was ill, suffering from headaches, sleeplessness and anorexia, but recovered, and by Christmas had begun to look for a weekend cottage in the country. The next year brought all kinds of change, as Vanessa broke out of the triangle by falling in love with Roger Fry, and then underwent a long breakdown herself. Virginia wrote sympathetically, 'Did you feel horribly depressed? I did. I could not write, and all the devils came out – hairy black ones. To be 29 and unmarried – to be a failure – childless – insane too, no writer.'[64]

As she was writing thus to Vanessa, Leonard Woolf had just arrived home on leave from seven years in the Colonial Service. Lytton had urged Leonard to marry Virginia some months before he had proposed to her himself. Leonard had agreed enthusiastically, but while he was living on the other side of the world, there was little he could do about it. Now he was delighted to be back and once again in the company of Lytton, and Thoby's beautiful sisters. Virginia invited Leonard down to her house at Firle, and on a country walk together they discovered Asheham, a remote Georgian house on the South Downs, which she later rented with Vanessa. She and Leonard quickly became friends. Leonard was intellectually powerful, passionately interested in politics and the arts, and working on his own first novel, *The Village in the Jungle*, a dark and compelling account of the struggle for life at the margins. He fell deeply in love with Virginia. It was a relationship in which she was in control: she liked and admired him but didn't find him physically attractive; this time there was no hidden agenda. Leonard proposed. At first she hesitated, then accepted him. Leonard already possessed the self-discipline that Clive would never acquire. He set himself targets to meet in terms of word counts each day, and encouraged Virginia to create structures around herself. He protected her and worried about her health. She completed the final draft of *Melymbrosia* just in time for their wedding.

They were married at St Pancras Register Office on 10 August 1912 and spent most of their long honeymoon travelling in Europe. 'We've talked incessantly for 7 weeks, and become chronically nomadic and monogamic', she wrote to one friend, and enquired of another, 'Why do you think people make such a fuss about marriage and copulation? . . . I find the climax immensely exaggerated.'[65] The couple returned confirmed as friends, rather than as lovers.

Back in London in October, Virginia spent the next five months redrafting – expanding, tightening and polishing her novel. She worked harder and faster than ever before, and seemed at last to have a clear sense of where it was going. In March 1913 it was submitted to her half-brother, the publisher Gerald Duckworth, who accepted it on the recommendation of the famous reader and talent-spotter Edward Garnett, though a further two years passed before it was published.

Leonard, meanwhile, had completed his second novel, *The Wise Virgins*. Its heroine, inspired by Virginia, writes to turn down the hero's proposal, describing her own conflicting hopes and desires:

It's the romantic part of life that I want; it's the voyage out that seems to me to matter, the new and wonderful things. I can't, I won't look beyond that. I want them all. I want love, too, and I want freedom. I want children even. But I can't give myself; passion leaves me cold . . .

And then there's so much in marriage from which I recoil. It seems to shut women up and out. I won't be tied by the pettinesses and the conventionalities of life. There must be some way out . . .[66]

Leonard had gauged her feelings exactly. But in 1913 she had not yet found her way out – indeed, it seemed that, like Rachel in *The Voyage Out*, she too was being dragged under by deep waters.

THE VOYAGE OUT: THE AFTERMATH

Two thousand copies of The Voyage Out *were published by Duckworth & Co. on 26 March 1915, bound in moss green with gilt lettering on the spine, priced at six shillings and dedicated to Leonard.[67] The reviews that appeared in the following month would have cheered Virginia, had she not been too ill to read or respond to them. Inevitably there were dissenting voices, critics who found its plot disjointed and its characters unreal: 'not very true to life as we live it or see it' (the* Saturday Review*). A reviewer in the* Glasgow Herald *thought it 'most doubtful whether any reader who starts on this "Voyage Out" will ever have the requisite patience to get to its end, as a more wearisome, long-winded, purposeless tale would be hard to find. We should advise careful thought before plunging again into print' – the Woolfs were so much amused by these quotations that they included them in a list of 'press opinions' reprinted at the end of* Jacob's Room, *in* 1922.[68]

Most reviews were more positive, and several recognized its exceptional qualities: The Spectator *hailed it as 'that rarest of things a novel of serious artistic value', praising its 'overwhelming reality' and recognizing Mrs Woolf as 'a consummate artist in writing'.* The Nation *found it 'a very promising first novel', and the* Observer *thought it showed 'something startlingly like genius . . . a wild swan among good grey geese'. The power of the ending was admired even by those who had other reservations about it: '[t]he tragedy of the girl's illness and death is vividly and artistically told' (*Morning Post*); '[t]he pathos of the heroine's death is the more poignant for the restraint with which it is treated' (*Athenaeum*).[69]* The Times Literary Supplement *reviewer found it 'illogical, this sudden tragedy, but it is made almost to seem like the illogic of life; it is so intense that one is desolated by a sense of the futility of life and forgets the failure of design' (as if unconsciously acknowledging its success).[70] The most judicious praise came from Allan Monkhouse, writing in the* Manchester Guardian, *who noted its power of 'finding strangeness even in the world of familiar things' and its 'penetration into certain modes of consciousness', judging it a first novel that displayed 'not merely promise, but accomplishment'.[71]* E. M. Forster, *in a review for the* Daily News, *found the characters lacking in vividness, but thought it attained unity 'as surely as* Wuthering Heights'. *He recognized it as 'a voyage into solitude', and valued its exploratory energy, its confrontation of unanswerable questions, evoking its passionate engagement in terms of a quotation from Dostoevsky's* The Idiot: *'It's life that matters – the process of discovering, the everlasting and perpetual process, not the discovery itself at all.'[72]*

When she eventually read the reviews, Virginia was at once pleased and disappointed by Forster's – she was always to value his judgement and take his criticism seriously. Early in 1916, Lytton Strachey sent his own generous appreciation of the novel:

I don't think I ever enjoyed the reading of a book so much. And I was surprised by it. I had naturally expected wit and exquisiteness – what people call 'brilliance', but it's a wretched word – but what amazed me was to find such a wonderful solidity as well! Something Tolstoyan, I thought – especially that last account of the illness, which really – well! –[73]

Replying, Virginia explained to him that she had aimed 'to give the feeling of a vast tumult of life . . . The difficulty was to keep any sort of coherence, – also to give enough detail to make the characters interesting – which Forster says I didn't do.'[74] Yet if Forster's criticism troubled her, his praise had warmed her: the sentence from Dostoevsky was carefully enshrined in Night and Day, *quoted by Katharine as she walked down the Strand in chapter X and again at the beginning of chapter XI, passages that were probably composed in the late summer or early autumn of 1916.[75]*

The publication of Night and Day *in October 1919 brought renewed interest in her first novel, and by November two American publishers – Macmillan, New York, and George H. Doran – had made competing offers for them both, Doran gaining the contract. In a flurry, Woolf wrote to Lytton asking him if he had noticed 'any special misprints, obscurities or vulgarities in either . . . I have to send the books off on Monday and they say the more alterations the better – because of copyright'.[76] At that time, US copyright law required all English books published in the States to be reset, printed and bound there, so in theory she was at liberty to revise as extensively as she wished. She seems to have assumed that any corrections would make it more difficult to print illegal copies of the English first edition.*

Late in January 1920 she told Saxon Sydney-Turner[77] 'I sent the copy I marked to America, and now they're bringing out a new edition here', asking him to tell her once more the correct opus number of the Beethoven piano sonata referred to in chapter II; she asked another friend, Bob Trevelyan, whether he had noticed 'any special howlers'.[78] Early in February, she spent an hour each day before lunch 'reading the Voyage Out. I've not read it since July 1913.' It seemed to her patchy and inconsistent, 'a harlequinade', 'here simple & severe –

24

here frivolous & shallow – here like God's truth – here strong & free-flowing as I could wish'. Sometimes it embarrassed her, but at other times it impressed her. 'I like the young woman's mind considerably,' she wrote patronisingly of her former self. 'How gallantly she takes her fences – & my word what a gift for pen & ink!'[79] *It's not clear how this revision process differed from the one she had carried out in early December for a second British edition, which never, in fact, appeared. Two copies of the novel with her marked-up corrections have survived, and one at least is probably the source for the American reprint, but nothing more is heard of this further stage of revision.*[80]

Her rereadings led her to make a large number of minor cuts and alterations for the American edition: Clarissa Dalloway's letter goes, and her exclamation, 'Being on this ship seems to make it so much more vivid – what it really means to be English', loses its emphatic 'really'. Rachel's reading of Who's Who, *a reference to Nora in Ibsen's* A Doll's House *and another to the yellow-backed novel describing a woman's descent into prostitution are all cut, and chapter XVI, in which Rachel and Terence talk about their lives and hopes, a chapter already substantially rewritten, was now drastically cut, losing much of the detail of Rachel's life at Richmond and abbreviating Terence's literary ambitions. There were a few additions, mainly to cover transitions where cuts had been made, though not in every case – in the scene where Rachel and Helen discuss Dalloway's kiss, Rachel resents the incursions of patriarchy on her freedom: 'her life that was the only chance she had – a thousand words and actions became plain to her'. Woolf replaced the last nine words with the unforgettable phrase, 'the short season between two silences'.*[81]

Doran published The Voyage Out *in the US on 20 May 1920, at $2.25, and supplied Duckworth with sheets for a second English edition, issued in September 1920, so that, for the next nine years, the only British edition available was the revised American one.*[82] *The US reviews echoed the English reception: the* New York Times *found the story 'painfully lacking, both in coherency and narrative interest . . . one rather wonders what it is all about, for it does not seem to get anywhere in particular', yet Ruth Underhill, reviewing it for* The Bookman, *found depths in its very incompleteness: 'it is not the conventionally emotional scenes by which one is stirred – it is rather those* *reminiscent and elusive moments when both heroine and reader palpitate at the approach to truth.'[83]*

In 1924, *Clive Bell, its first reader, wrote a long review for* The Dial *of all Woolf's work to date. He had been disappointed by* The Voyage Out *on its first appearance, feeling that the unearthly magic of the early drafts had been sacrificed in the long revision process. He told Mary Hutchinson that he found the first two chapters 'very disappointing, costive and rather conventional – quite different from what she read me three or four years ago – but now in the third she is becoming herself and ceasing to be Mrs Wolfe' (in Clive's opinion, Leonard's influence was to blame for this). On finishing it, he added, 'The book's a good one, but nothing more I'm afraid. The psycology and observation are amazing and amazingly witty; but it's all about life and states of mind and nothing about the other thing which you have discovered to be the essence of a work of art. She's an analytical chymist, not God.'[84] Later, writing in* The Dial, *he judged* The Voyage Out *'a remarkable failure . . . it had been writing too long and had grown stiff', while glimpsing within it a highly individual view of the world: 'she had her peculiar vision'[85] – a phrase Woolf seems to echo in the final words of* To the Lighthouse.

In 1921 *George Doran rejected Woolf's collection of short stories,* Monday or Tuesday, *but Harcourt, Brace & Co. made an offer on it, and thereafter Donald Brace became her American publisher. In 1925 he bought back the rights to her first two novels from Doran, reissuing a thousand copies of* The Voyage Out *in the US in 1926 (which pleased and reassured her), and in 1927, Brace supplied Duckworth with a thousand sheets. Half of these were issued in 1927, while the remainder were taken over by the Woolfs' own Hogarth Press in February 1929, when the Press bought back the rights to her first two novels from Duckworth. The Hogarth Press issued a hundred copies with a special cancel title, but the other 400 were pulped in 1932, having been overtaken by the Press's uniform edition of Woolf's works:* The Voyage Out, *issued in September 1929, became the first volume in the new series.[86] For the uniform edition, the Hogarth Press reverted to the original text of 1915, though whether this was a conscious decision on Woolf's part is another mystery: she might have reread it, and preferred her original version, but we do not know. It may have been*

By VIRGINIA WOOLF
THE VOYAGE OUT

There is something greater than talent that marks this book. Cleverness it undoubtedly has. But there are as well its humor, its sense of irony, poignancy of emotion and profound originality which bring it near to genius.

"The Voyage Out" is Mrs. Woolf's first novel. The London *Spectator* says of it: "The Voyage Out" is that rarest of things, a novel of serious artistic value.... Above all, Mrs. Woolf is a consummate artist in writing."

Here indeed is a book which attains unity as surely as "Wuthering Heights", though by a different path. It is absolutely unafraid, with the courage that springs not from naiveté but from education, and it soars straight out of local questioning into intellectual day.

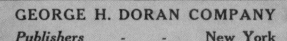

 GEORGE H. DORAN COMPANY
Publishers - - New York

simply a matter of convenience: Richard Kennedy, then working as an assistant at the Press, ordered the wrong size of paper for the first four volumes in the uniform edition, and this may have proved the crucial factor since the uniform edition was reprinted photographically and the new page size was closer to the original English edition than to the first American edition (set on fewer but larger pages).[87] By 1929, Woolf's novels were being published in significantly different versions on either side of the Atlantic – indeed she seems to have adopted a conscious policy of providing variant texts for her American publishers.

Assessments of Woolf's work have often marginalized her first two novels, but when American scholarship began to revalue them in the 1970s, Louise DeSalvo examined the various preliminary manuscripts and typescripts collected in the Berg Collection of the New York Public Library, where most of Woolf's papers had come to rest. In 1982 the Library published DeSalvo's edition of the 1912 draft of the novel under its working title, Melymbrosia, *making it possible to read this penultimate version beside the final text and watch the novelist in the process of acquiring the technical skills that would sustain her through the rest of her career.[88] DeSalvo prefaced her account of that process by quoting from Woolf's own comments on George Meredith's first novel:*

[T]he first novel is always apt to be an unguarded one, where the author displays his gifts without knowing how to dispose of them to the best advantage . . . It needs no great sagacity to see that the writer is a novice at his task. The style is extremely uneven . . . He vacillates from one attitude to another. Indeed the whole fabric seems to rock a little insecurely . . . He has been . . . at great pains to destroy the conventional form of the novel . . . This defiance of the ordinary, these airs and graces . . . prepare the way for a new and an original sense of the human scene.[89]

Which was exactly what she achieved, both here and in the novels to come.

2

Into the Night

'Insanity is not a fit subject for fiction,' [Aunt Eleanor] announced positively.

'There's the well-known case of Hamlet,' Mr Hilbery interposed, in his leisurely, half-humorous tones.

'Ah, but poetry's different, Trevor,' said Aunt Eleanor, as if she had special authority from Shakespeare to say so. 'Different altogether. And I've never thought, for my part, that Hamlet was as mad as they make out. What is your opinion, Mr Peyton?' For, as there was a minister of literature present in the person of the editor of an esteemed review, she deferred to him.

Mr Peyton leant a little back in his chair, and, putting his head rather on one side, observed that that was a question that he had never been able to answer entirely to his satisfaction. There was much to be said on both sides, ... [p.296][1]

Virginia Woolf's second novel, *Night and Day*, published in 1919, often sounds like a drawing room comedy, a comedy of manners insulated against unwelcome eruptions or interruptions, and concentrating instead on character, and the delicate minuet of love. It ends, uniquely for Woolf, in marriage – a marriage that recalls some of the social tensions of her own. Katharine, the well-born heroine, is the scion of 'one of the most distinguished families in England'. Her ancestors include famous explorers, military leaders and poets, and her gene pool has been celebrated in *Hereditary Genius* (1869) by Sir Francis Galton, founding father of the sinister pseudo-science of eugenics.[2] Katharine falls in love with an outsider, a man of vision but, as yet, no achievement; a man whose grandfather had been a shopkeeper (Leonard's had been a tailor).[3] It is Thomas Hardy's fable of 'The Poor Man and the Lady', played out in a leisured Edwardian

Chapter XI

Dreams & Realities.   Chapter Twelve.   Oct. 6th 1916

She could not entirely forget Williams presence, because, in
spite of his efforts to control himself, his nervousness was
apparent. On such occasions his eyes protruded more
than ever, & his face had more than ever the appearance of
being covered with a thin crackling skin, which through
which his very flush of his volatile blood showed itself
so instantly. By this time he was very red.

"You may say you dont read books, he remarked, but
all the same you know about them — I've kept all
your criticisms — One day —— Besides, who wants you
to be learned? You've leave that to the poor devils
who've got nothing better."

"Well then, why dont you read me something before
I go?" said Katharine, looking at her watch —

"But you've only just come — Let me see now, what
have I got to read to you?"
He found his manuscript, & & after spreading it
smoothly upon his knee, he looked up suspiciously round at.
Katharine He caught her smiling.

"I believe you only ask me out of kindness" he

world of absurdity, irony and affection. *Night and Day* is at once the most accessible and the most neglected of Woolf's novels, the most conventionally narrated and organized, as if its structure reflected the carefully regulated circumstances of its composition, and its humour masked the personal and social traumas which its author had barely survived.

If *Night and Day* includes aspects of Leonard's courtship, these have been filtered through Leonard's own retelling of it in his second novel, *The Wise Virgins*. Begun on their honeymoon and published in 1914, its title gestured towards Virginia's name. *The Wise Virgins* also emphasizes its heroine's upper-class family, in contrast to that of its suburban Jewish hero, Harry Davis. Harry is intensely aware of being different from his English companions; if they ever manage to forget their anti-Semitism for a few minutes, he feels driven to remind them:

'You talk and you talk and you talk – no blood in you! You never *do* anything.'
  'Why do you think it's so important to do things?'
  'Why? Because I'm a Jew, I tell you – I'm a Jew!'[4]

At art school, Harry, a young painter, meets and falls in love with Camilla, herself a painter and one of two sisters – the other, Katharine, is a writer. Beautiful but sexually cold, Camilla fails to return his passion, but values his friendship. Back in the suburbs, Harry is pursued into bed by Gwen, the girl next door. Having 'compromised' her, he finds himself obliged to marry her, and thus abandoning all hope of future happiness. It is an angry, powerful book, influenced by H. G. Wells's satires on the contemporary social scene, but with a special bitterness of its own.

The Wise Virgins is also a *roman à clef*, providing harsh caricatures of everyone concerned – above all of Leonard himself, but also of Virginia, her brother Adrian, Clive Bell and even of Leonard's sisters and mother (who pleaded with him not to publish it); only Vanessa emerges unscathed. *Night and Day*, by contrast, reworks Leonard's painful triangle as a fable of reconciliation and integration. At its centre, Virginia sets Katharine, the Vanessa figure in Leonard's novel, adopting the name and its less usual Greek spelling for her heroine[5] (later, she would use 'Camilla' for herself as a child in *To the*

Lighthouse). In fact, while writing *Night and Day*, Virginia thought of it as a story about Vanessa. She dedicated the book to her, and recommended her friend Janet Case to 'try thinking of Katharine as Vanessa, not me'[6] – all ways of warding off too obvious an identification of herself with her heroine; she further distanced Katharine from herself by giving her an active dislike of books, poetry and fiction.[7]

But *Night and Day* baulks at the topics of race and sex, precisely those topics which Leonard had treated with exceptional frankness, for they had also been the main obstacles to their marriage. Her hero Ralph resembles Leonard's Harry Davis at several moments and in several respects, but he has lost the Jewish identity which conferred on him his outsider status; and while Ralph is intensely conscious of his inferior financial and social position, neither creates an insurmountable barrier to his marrying Katharine because as a 'good Cambridge man' he already belongs to an acknowledged intellectual elite. Sexuality is also avoided here, although Woolf's fiction before and after *Night and Day* explores such issues. Virginia found herself agreeing with Lytton Strachey on the matter. 'I take your point about the tupping and had meant to introduce a little in that line, but somehow it seemed out of the picture'.[8]

In *The Wise Virgins*, the barriers of race and class prove insuperable, whereas in *Night and Day*, as in the Woolfs' marriage, intellectual sympathies between two people of high intelligence overcame differences of class and background. When Virginia met Leonard, she had already rejected several proposals from young men of a similar background to her own: Lytton Strachey had asked her to marry him in February 1909, and then hastily withdrawn his offer, recognizing how impossible it would have been.[9] In May that year, Hilton Young had proposed in a punt on the Cam. Ostentatiously eligible, educated at Eton and Trinity, President of the Union, a barrister and, later, a poet and a politician, he apparently had everything to recommend him.[10] But not to Virginia. In 1911 she received proposals from Sydney Waterlow, who became a diplomat, and Walter Lamb, later appointed Secretary to the Royal Academy (and a possible model for Hugh Whitbread in *Mrs Dalloway*).[11]

She had 'shunned the wealthy curled darlings of our nation' in order to marry, in her own words, 'a penniless Jew' – the phrase she used of

Leonard when announcing her engagement to her old friends Violet
Dickinson and Janet Case.[12] Perhaps by putting it so starkly, she hoped
to allay their prejudice or disappointment, as if by saying the worst first,
she left them free to discover his virtues for themselves. Objectively
speaking, her description was true enough, but Leonard was already a
person of notable intellect and achievement: he had been the first Jew
to be elected to the exclusive Cambridge society known as the Apostles
(a distinction that Leslie Stephen and both his sons failed to attain); he
had survived seven years in the Colonial Service in Sri Lanka, under
conditions of great stress and personal isolation. Such experiences,
combined with an innate fatalism, a sense that 'in the last resort
nothing matters',[13] were to carry him through the earliest and most
testing years of his marriage.

Like Camilla in *The Wise Virgins*, Virginia could not reciprocate
Leonard's sexual passion, and, with characteristic honesty, she had
told him so before they were engaged. Yet she valued the love and
companionship he offered, and 'took him into her service' on her own
terms. One crucial factor for her was Leonard's emotional intelligence;
another was his total commitment, his absolute and unflinching certainty that he wanted to spend the rest of his life with her, a conviction
that nothing could shake. What altered and rebalanced their relationship was her need for protection and mothering, functions that Vanessa
and Violet Dickinson had previously fulfilled. It was this quasi-parental
role that Leonard took on even before they were married, and never
thereafter relinquished. He became her guardian, and in the process –
inevitably and unavoidably – her gaoler. His sustained care for her,
his interventions when she grew tired or overexcited, his supervision
of her social life have been seen both as heroic self-sacrifice on his part,
and as power-play, conscious or unconscious, a determination to curb
and control his more brilliant wife, using her ill-health as his pretext.
His most adverse critics have held Leonard partially, and sometimes
wholly responsible for his wife's major breakdown.[14] Certainly the
relationship, which had begun with Virginia in control as the less
emotionally involved, quickly reversed itself.

For whatever reason, during the first year of her marriage Virginia
slipped into her worst breakdown ever, extending from the summer
of 1913 to the autumn of 1915, and bringing her close to death and

permanent imprisonment in an institution. This was the real night or nightmare through which she struggled towards daylight, through which and after which she wrote the Mozartian comedy of *Night and Day*, its old-fashioned charm and poise salvaged from an inner maelstrom. The wonder was not its various suppressions and omissions, but rather its clarity, delicacy and lightness of touch. She survived to celebrate marriage as a happy ending, even though her own had begun so disastrously. It was the only time she was ever to do so in her work.

Night and Day questions social and literary convention, yet in the end it remains confined within them, as *The Voyage Out* had refused to be. It was provisionally entitled 'Dreams and Realities',[15] but its dreams were no longer eruptions from beyond consciousness, as they had been in *The Voyage Out*. Instead *Night and Day* focuses on day dreams, the willed or controlled fantasies in which both the hero and heroine indulge in order to hold the dissatisfactions of their daily lives at bay. Until they meet, Ralph and Katharine have kept their day dreams separate from their everyday lives, but once each recognizes the dreamer within the other, they are drawn together by the possibility that each might fulfil the other's most private desires. As they allow their private dreams to encroach on their actual lives, each begins to feel at once entranced, yet also uncomfortably threatened and exposed.

Her admirers, and even Woolf herself, came to regard *Night and Day* as a step backwards. Justifying its shortcomings to Ethel Smyth a decade later, she explained 'I was so tremblingly afraid of my own insanity that I wrote Night and Day mainly to prove to my own satisfaction that I could keep entirely off that dangerous ground. I wrote it, lying in bed, allowed to write only for one half hour a day.'[16] Leonard alone knew when she had begun it, and he reckoned it had taken her six years[17]: if his memory was accurate (which it wasn't always), she must have begun it in 1913, probably soon after completing *The Voyage Out*. She was certainly at work on an early version of it during a lucid interval, late in 1914 and early in 1915, but for much of those years, she was either too ill to write, or too exhausted to be allowed to write. If the completion of *The Voyage Out* through all its various drafts and difficulties had been an amazing achievement, a triumph against all the odds, the writing of *Night and Day*, a long, complex and carefully orchestrated comedy of love, was little short of a miracle.[18]

Even before they were married, Leonard had realized how fragile Virginia's health was: his first proposal to her in February 1912 had precipitated an attack of the mysterious but recurrent nervous illness from which she had suffered since childhood. Dr Savage, the family consultant, sent her for a fortnight to Jean Thomas's private nursing home in Twickenham, where she had spent six weeks, eighteen months earlier. As their marriage approached, Leonard, who was by then renting rooms in the same house as Virginia at 38 Brunswick Square, had begun to assume responsibility for her health, administering sleeping draughts when he thought she needed them. 'I've been rather headachy, and had a bad night, and Leonard made me into a comatose invalid,'[19] she complained to Violet Dickinson in June 1912, shortly before they married. Bad headaches were the usual prelude to these attacks, accompanied by sleeplessness and a reluctance to eat. According to Leonard, she would become either ominously quiet, or over-excited and compulsively talkative. In looking after her, he drew upon the self-reliance acquired during his years in Sri Lanka. That experience had changed him, and taught him a stoicism in the face of loneliness and unhappiness that distinguished him from his Cambridge contemporaries. He expected less, and had learned to survive under stress through a system of strict self-discipline and the careful maintenance of records and routines. By January 1913, Leonard had begun to note the daily changes in his wife's health and moods, her sleeping and eating patterns, in his diary. From August 1913, he recorded these in a private code of his own invention.

Within the Stephen family, Virginia had always been notorious for her flights of fantasy, and sudden violent rages. 'Goat's mad', her brothers and sisters would say, using her family nickname, perhaps as a joke, perhaps not. But the family as a whole, especially in the paternal line, was subject to various forms of psychic illness, ranging from schizophrenia to depression or melancholia. Her father, Leslie Stephen, had undergone some kind of breakdown while editing the *Dictionary of National Biography*, finding himself afflicted with insomnia, 'fits of the horrors', 'the fidgets' and 'hideous morbid fancies'.[20] Virginia liked to blame the DNB for the family neuroses: in some inexplicable way, it had crushed the energy out of her younger brother Adrian even before he was born. 'It gave me a twist of the head too,' she added; 'I shouldn't have been so clever, but I should have been more stable, without that contribution to the history of England.'[21]

Virginia had an older half-sister, Laura, the only child of Leslie Stephen's first marriage to 'Minny' Thackeray; from her twenties (and she outlived Virginia) she was confined to a mental institution. From early childhood, something had seemed wrong with Laura. She had been slow to learn, although she eventually did manage to read 'after a fashion',[22] and her behaviour was strange and unpredictable; to the younger children, she was 'her Ladyship of the Lake'.[23] More recent categories of dysfunction or autism might have resulted in different and, one would hope, kinder treatment. Laura's problems were attributed to her inheritance – her grandmother, Thackeray's wife, had been diagnosed as mad and confined to an asylum. Leslie Stephen's nephew, Jem (the poet, J. K.) Stephen, also went mad, pursuing and threatening Virginia's other half-sister Stella. His state was attributed to a blow on the head, but there was always an underlying anxiety that 'it ran in the family'.[24] Virginia must secretly have feared that she would suffer the same fate as Laura.

At the end of the nineteenth century, mental illness in women was usually classified either as hysteria or as neurasthenia.[25] Hysteria was characterized by overtly sexual behaviour ('erotomania' or 'moral insanity'), and was particularly associated with the lower classes, while 'neurasthenia' was thought of as a more modest and middle-class complaint (during the First World War, it would be attributed to officers, rather than common soldiers). George Savage, the Stephens' consultant on nervous illness, diagnosed Virginia as suffering from neurasthenia, having made the same diagnosis in the case of her father.[26] Under the influence of Galton's eugenic theories, he believed that families like the Stephens, which had produced outstanding intellects, even 'men of genius', were by the same token inclined to neurotic illness, melancholy and mental breakdown. Brilliance was of its nature unstable. Leonard shared this widely held view – he quoted Dryden's line, 'Great wits are sure to madness near allied', when discussing Virginia's illness.[27]

Although neurasthenia affected the mind, it was believed to have a physiological cause in the degeneration of the nervous system, being a disorder in which the nerves lost their normal and healthy elasticity. Treatments were intended to restore them through rest, and a general build-up of the body's strength. The standard cure was that of the American Silas Weir Mitchell, who believed that irregularities of the brain could be stabilized by overfeeding.[28] He set out to increase his patients' body weight through a fattening diet that included frequent glasses of milk, and the avoidance of all intellectual stimuli. For someone suffering from eating difficulties or anxiety about body image, for whom reading and writing were favourite activities, such a cure might actually bring on madness instead of relieving it (as Charlotte Perkins Gilman's story 'The Yellow Wallpaper' (1892) famously illustrated[29]).

Anorexia (identified as a distinct syndrome from the early 1870s) was one of Virginia's main symptoms, perhaps linked with a reluctance to accept adult sexuality. She had lost her mother not long before puberty, and watched her half-sister Stella die within months of marriage. As a child, Virginia constantly suffered from poor health. Her mother, Julia Stephen, had made sickroom nursing her special gift and study and recognized that little 'Ginia' was particularly prone to nervousness and illness. Perhaps it was her only way of claiming attention within that large and competitive family, for Julia was bringing up eight children – in addition to Virginia and her three siblings, there were the three Duckworths, half-brothers and sister from Julia's first marriage, as well as poor Laura Stephen. Looking back, Virginia wondered whether she had ever been alone with her mother for more than a few minutes: 'Someone was always interrupting.'[30] Virginia had been ill herself at the time her mother contracted rheumatic fever in 1895, and was ill again two years later, when her half-sister Stella was dying. Virginia's first breakdown had occurred in 1895, in the wake of her mother's death. As a child, and later as a young adult, she was sexually abused by both her half-brothers, first by Gerald Duckworth, when she was little (an episode examined more fully in Chapter 13), and much later by George, who would demand demonstrations of affection while she was studying, or worse still, come into the bedroom at night and 'fling himself on my bed, cuddling and kissing and otherwise embracing me in order . . . to comfort me for the fatal illness of my father – who was dying three or four storeys lower down of cancer'.[31]

Woolf's oddly impersonal account of George's misbehaviour occurs in 'Old Bloomsbury', a talk she gave, late in 1921 or 1922, to the Memoir Club – a group of her oldest, closest friends who agreed to amuse each other with gossipy, intimate revelations. The experience is thus treated as a kind of joke, perhaps the only way she could address it at all. In the same talk, she described her second major breakdown, following her father's death in 1904, as 'the illness which was not unnaturally the result of all these emotions and complications'.[32] During that breakdown, Virginia had stayed with Violet Dickinson in Welwyn, under the care of professional nurses. She heard horrible voices and felt tormented with guilt that she had not done enough for her father. She jumped from a window, but it was too low for her to be hurt. She recalled lying 'in bed at the Dickinsons' house at Welwyn thinking that the birds were singing Greek choruses and that King Edward was using the foulest possible language among Ozzie Dickinson's azaleas'.[33] Like her account of George's unwelcome embraces, the tone is detached and ironic, mingling incongruous details of the suburban garden with scholarship and a suggestion of public scandal.

In 'Old Bloomsbury' Woolf created comedy out of her darkest moments, yet old men mumbling obscenities, as King Edward had done, occur elsewhere in her accounts of inner horrors. She remembered from childhood lying awake one night, 'hearing, as I imagined, an obscene old man gasping and croaking and muttering senile indecencies – it was a cat, I was told afterwards'.[34] Describing her symptoms to Ethel Smyth, she wrote of her 'inexplicable susceptibility' to particular impressions, which brought her close to 'madness and that end of a drainpipe with a gibbering old man'.[35] Similar fears had haunted Rachel's nightmares in The Voyage Out, yet those are not the visions of madness – they occur in Rachel's dreams or in delirium, as, probably, had the hallucination set off by the yowling of a cat. Such experiences are common: a small rise in body temperature creates a large distortion in the field of perception, throwing up chunks of a dark inner world only otherwise encountered in sleep. All of us are subject to such invasions. Woolf often ran a temperature when suffering from her recurrent illness, and that may have made its own contribution to 'those horrible voices'.

But if Virginia was susceptible to voices and other nervous symptoms, she could also be strong, as she had shown when she nursed first Vanessa, and then Violet through serious illness in Greece in 1906, and later Vanessa and Thoby when she got home. She survived Thoby's death and Vanessa's marriage, set up house with Adrian and began her first novel. She was ill for a while in 1910, when Vanessa was pregnant with her second child, but in the following year, it was the turn of her siblings: by Christmas 1911, Adrian was in a nursing home,[36] while Vanessa, who normally cultivated an air of calm and tranquillity,[37] had a long-drawn-out breakdown after a miscarriage. Towards the end of 1912, the sisters' usual roles were reversed, with 'Nessa more or less broken down',[38] and Vanessa writing to Roger Fry, 'Virginia has been very nice to me. She saw that I was depressed yesterday & was very good – & cheered me up a great deal . . . I think she has in reality amazing courage & sanity about life.'[39]

Virginia's marriage relieved Vanessa of the burden of responsibility for her younger sister. Leonard now took on the role of carer, yet that created new and different tensions. After the Woolfs' long honeymoon, it was clear that conventional sexual intercourse was never going to be entirely easy, although they developed other ways of expressing physical affection, adopting their own private names and games – the love of mongoose for mandrill, the marmots' antics – through which to express them. Like many women, Virginia apparently loved being cuddled and caressed, but did not enjoy sexual penetration. She did, however, look forward to having children, but Leonard had begun to doubt whether she was sufficiently robust to cope with the physical and psychological stress involved. Early in 1913, he went in search of medical advice on the question.

Inevitably, he received a number of conflicting opinions: Jean Thomas, who ran the Twickenham nursing home where Virginia had already stayed several times, apparently advised against (though not altogether consistently), as did the nerve specialist Maurice Craig, when consulted. On the other hand, the Stephens' family doctor, Sir George Savage (as he now was), took a surprisingly sanguine view, assuring Leonard that it would 'do her a world of good' – no doubt he thought her health would improve if she concentrated on bringing up babies, instead of writing books.[40] Vanessa seems to have supported both sides, on the one hand sympathizing with Leonard's doubts, while on the other reassuring Virginia and dissociating herself from Leonard's opposition. Another nerve specialist, Theo Hyslop, advised the couple to wait and see. While his response did not, apparently, decide the outcome, his views on conception in relation to mental health reflected some of the nastier aspects of contemporary eugenic theories.

For Hyslop, mental illness was a symptom of 'degeneration', a Darwinian regression supposed to affect foreigners and the 'criminal classes', causing their children to suffer from actual or 'moral' insanity. In common with a growing body of opinion, Hyslop believed that so-called 'degenerates' should be prevented from having children by law, in order that the vigour of the race should be preserved. The concept of degeneration was race- and class-based, and while Hyslop was unlikely to have attributed it to the upper-class Mrs Woolf, nevertheless the taint of mental illness seemed to run in the family, and may have been a factor weighing on Leonard's mind. Virginia recognized the power of the medical profession to 'forbid childbirth', as can be seen from her portrait of the nerve specialist Sir William Bradshaw (in *Mrs Dalloway*): he exercises a repressive authority in the name of 'society'. Invoking the god 'Proportion', he 'made England prosper, secluded her lunatics, forbade childbirth, penalised despair, made it impossible for the unfit to propagate their views until they, too, shared his sense of proportion'.[41]

Leonard's motives were ostensibly protective, and, given his passionate devotion to her, he may even have feared the medical risk that giving birth then involved. His consultations as to whether Virginia should have children had not, however, included Virginia. While he sought to protect her from the dangers of motherhood, she was looking forward to it: 'next year I must have a child',[42] she told Violet Dickinson, a month before her marriage. Violet responded by sending her a cradle as a wedding present, and Virginia promised that her baby would sleep in it.[43] In April 1913, she told Violet, 'We aren't going to have a baby, but we want to have one, and 6 months in the country or so is said to be necessary first.'[44] She seems either not to have known, or not to have accepted, the outcome of Leonard's consultations over the previous months. In later years, she would bitterly envy Vanessa her children, and feel disappointed and sometimes deeply dejected that she had none of her own. Characteristically, she refused to pretend that anything else could compensate for the absence of children, and blamed both Leonard and herself for their loss: 'I'm always angry with myself for not having forced Leonard to take the risk in spite of doctors; he was afraid for me and wouldn't; but if I'd had rather more self-control no doubt it would have been all right.'[45] In her diary, she noted that 'a little more self control on my part, & we might have had a boy of 12, a girl of 10: This always rakes me wretched in the early hours.'[46]

Leonard's decision taken on her behalf may have contributed to his wife's breakdown in the summer of 1913, though in Jean Thomas's view, it was caused by her anxiety over *The Voyage Out*, which had been submitted to Gerald Duckworth's publishing house in March that year: 'It is the novel which has broken her up. She finished it and got the proof back for correction . . . couldn't sleep & thought everyone would jeer at her . . . the collapse came from the book – and as the doctors say, it might have come to such a delicate brilliant brain after such an effort *however* much care and wisdom had been shown.'[47] This explanation is confirmed by subsequent episodes: Virginia frequently experienced depression and sometimes despair on completing a major novel, whether because she feared hostile criticism, or because she couldn't bear to let it go, or because the sheer effort of finishing it to her satisfaction had exhausted her – or perhaps a combination of all three.

By July 1913, Virginia had begun to suffer from her usual symptoms of headaches and insomnia. Sir George Savage sent her to Jean Thomas's nursing home for a rest cure. Her letters home to Leonard were laden with guilt: 'You've been absolutely perfect to me. It's all my fault'; 'Dearest, I have been disgraceful – to you, I mean'.[48] She was suffering from 'vile imaginations'. After three weeks, Savage agreed that she could return to Asheham, the house on the South Downs that she and Vanessa rented for country weekends. After that, she and Leonard had planned to take a short holiday at the Plough, an English country pub at Holford in the Quantocks where they had spent the first night of their honeymoon the previous year. But she was still depressed and finding it difficult to sleep or eat, although she was just as terrified of having to go back to the nursing home for a further rest cure, and would not admit that she was ill. On 8 September Leonard took her back to London, where she had agreed to see a consultant recommended by Roger Fry: this was Dr Henry Head, a neuropsychologist of progressive views who had taken an early interest in Freud, and had conducted the famous 'regeneration' experiment on his own nerves, with W. H. R. Rivers.[49] Virginia promised to accept Head's judgement as to whether she was ill or not, and thus whether she needed further treatment.

Leonard also took her to see Dr Maurice Wright, a nerve specialist he had consulted about his hand tremor on his return from Sri Lanka. They saw Wright in the morning and Henry Head in the afternoon. Each of them explained to her that she was suffering from neurasthenia and needed treatment. She and Leonard then went back to 38 Brunswick Square for tea with Vanessa; after tea, the punctilious Leonard went to see Savage to apologize for approaching Head without his prior agreement. While he was out, Virginia found the sleeping drug veronal in Leonard's unlocked case. She took 100 grains, a potentially fatal dose. When her friend Ka Cox looked in later, she was unconscious. She could not face another 'cure'.

Her life was saved by Geoffrey Keynes, who was luckily staying in his brother Maynard's rooms at Brunswick Square. Keynes was training as a house surgeon at St Bartholomew's Hospital. He and Leonard drove headlong across London to fetch a stomach pump from the hospital with which to wash the drug out of her system. During the night she nearly died, but by next morning, though still comatose, she was out of danger.

She did not accept that she was ill, merely anxious, guilty and unhappy, and then tipped into despair by the treatments to which she was subjected – the sleeping draughts that failed to put her to sleep and only increased her headaches, and the absence of the only drugs she had come to trust, her reading and writing.[50] Years earlier, she had written to her friend Nellie Cecil, 'when my company seems an infliction to myself, . . . I can drug *it* (that is me) in a book, or an ink pot . . . it would be best to keep within reach of drugs for the present.'[51]

The written word or words to be written were her preferred therapy, and being deprived of them was itself a kind of torture. In her unfinished autobiography, she would explain how she had dealt with the meaningless shocks of life by translating them into 'a revelation of some order; . . . It is only by putting it into words that I make it whole; this wholeness means that it has lost its power to hurt me.'[52] The rest cures deprived her of this resort. Many of the treatments meted out to the disturbed or the distressed were (and still are) intended as aversion therapy, to speed the process of recovery by making the patient recognize, at some level, how undesirable it is to be ill. But their punitive elements can, and often do, drive a sensitive person to despair, transforming an unhappy state into an unbearable one: 'You can't think what a raging furnace it is still to me – madness and doctors and being forced',[53] she wrote, more than a decade later. Clarissa Dalloway would suspect Sir William Bradshaw 'of some indescribable outrage – forcing your soul, that was it'.[54] In such a situation, suicide might look like the only way out.

Yet to attempt suicide was to qualify as insane, by the standards of the day, and thus risk being confined to a lunatic asylum – gruesome institutions, usually appalling to anyone still conscious of their surroundings. To avoid this, Leonard accepted the alternative proposed by Virginia's half-brother, George Duckworth: with two nurses in attendance day and night, he and Virginia stayed at George's country house at East Grinstead from September until November, 1913. Virginia was now obviously anorexic – her weight had fallen to eight and a half stone, an all-time low, and for three months her periods stopped.[55] By January 1914, she had gained a stone, and was closer to her normal weight. She later came to believe that weight-loss itself brought with it illness and hallucinations[56] – certainly the two were apparently linked, though exactly how was less certain. By the spring, however, her health had improved, and she and Leonard moved to Asheham, taking two nurses with them. There, deep in the Sussex Downs, they spent much of the rest of 1914.

Early in August, Britain declared war on Germany. By October, Virginia seemed sufficiently recovered for the Woolfs to consider moving back to London. They compromised by taking rooms on the Green at Richmond, well away from the excitement of life in

Bloomsbury, but within easy visiting distance of the city. They started house-hunting, and in January 1915 Virginia began a diary, from which it is clear that she was already at work on her second novel: 'I do about 4 pages of poor Effie's story', she recorded on 2 January[57] (Effie would soon be renamed 'Katharine'). She noted her programme of reading, intended to supply background for her novel: 'I read about 1860 – the Kembles – Tennyson & so on; to get the spirit of that time, for the sake of The Third Generation'.[58] This early title suggests that she had originally conceived *Night and Day* as a family saga such as D. H. Lawrence was currently engaged upon in *The Rainbow* (1915) and *Women in Love* (1920); and such as she herself would write in *The Years* (1937). So much had already changed within her lifetime. Her sister Vanessa's marriage had turned out unimaginably different from that of her parents: Clive pursued his mistresses, while Vanessa, having embarked on a love affair with the art critic Roger Fry, was now in love with the painter Duncan Grant, eight years younger than herself and the former lover of their younger brother Adrian. A novel exploring how marriage and domestic life had altered between 1860 and 1911 looked full of possibilities, with many illustrations to hand.

In January 1915, Virginia seemed ready to resume her old life. She had reread the proofs of *The Voyage Out* late in the previous year, and, having satisfied herself that it wasn't 'pure gibberish',[59] had agreed to its publication (though privately she still thought it deserved 'to be condemned'[60]). At the end of January, Leonard showed her his own novel, *The Wise Virgins*, for the first time (it had been published the previous October). Given its portrait of Virginia as an ice-maiden, and the scandalous and unsuccessful outcome of Harry's courtship, Leonard had good reason to delay showing it to her, yet she seems to have enjoyed it: 'I was made very happy by reading this: I like the poetic side of L. & it gets a little smothered in Blue-books, & organisations'.[61] Above all, it inspired her to rebut his bleak view of love and marriage: its triangular struggle, even its details began to determine the structure of her own novel, as Effie became Katharine, and Ralph took on some of Harry's characteristics. On Virginia's thirty-third birthday, the Woolfs made three decisions: to take the lease of Hogarth House (an elegant and beautifully proportioned eighteenth-century house in

Richmond – 'a perfect house, if ever there was one'[62]); second, to acquire a printing press, and third, to buy a bulldog 'probably called John. I am very much excited at the idea of all three – particularly the press.'[63] They never bought the bulldog.

Her diary entries for January and February include a number of troubling notes: 'I begin to loathe my kind, principally from looking at their faces in the tube'; 'I do not like the Jewish voice; I do not like the Jewish laugh'; 'I dislike the sight of women shopping', and, most alarming of all, 'On the tow path we met & had to pass a long line of imbeciles ... It was perfectly horrible. They should certainly be killed'.[64] By mid-February, the diary entries give out altogether. Her headaches had returned, sleeping was growing difficult and she began to suffer from hallucinations. On 25 March 1915, the day before *The Voyage Out* was finally published, she was sent to a nursing home. Leonard pressed on doggedly with the move to Hogarth House, and Virginia was sent back there at the beginning of April, in the expensive full-time care of two day and two night nurses. According to Leonard's account, she was violent, talked incoherently and incessantly for days on end, and finally fell into a coma. He scarcely saw her for the next couple of months. Now her anger was no longer turned in on herself but directed against those around her. 'She won't see Leonard at all & has taken against all men', Vanessa told Roger Fry.[65] Leonard had become part of the conspiracy against her, in league with other resented figures of authority, such as her doctors.

What was wrong with Virginia? Henry Head, the most humane of her consultants, assured her that 'she was ill, ill like a person who had a cold or typhoid fever'.[66] But did the episodes of 1895, 1904 and 1913 all have the same origin? And if so, was it an identifiable illness, the effect of some genetic or chemical imbalance, or was each particular episode brought on by local stress? The subject has been discussed extensively, if inconclusively, for the very concept of mental health is itself dubious, the product of a particular cultural moment. The opinions expressed in Leonard Woolf's autobiography or Quentin Bell's biography of his aunt tell us more about their authors' generation, social milieu and the doctors they trusted than they do about what was actually wrong with her. Leonard left the fullest account of the course and nature of Virginia's illness, but that too was coloured by his own need to understand and come to terms with it. Confronted with a condition that was both unpredictable and inexplicable, and for which conventional medicine had no cure, he sought to identify some kind of rhythm or pattern among her varied symptoms and fugues. Leonard had read and admired Freud's writings from 1914,[67] and would later publish his works in translation, but he did not apparently draw on them for explanations of his wife's illness. In any case, psychotherapy had not, originally, been intended as a treatment for those suffering from severe psychotic disorders.

By the 1960s, when Leonard came to write his own autobiography, the old diagnosis of neurasthenia had long since fallen out of use. Instead, he described Virginia as suffering from manic depression (a condition identified by Emil Kraepelin early in the century). He saw her as passing from a depressive phase, in which she found it difficult to sleep or eat, to a manic and paranoid phase, in which she talked incessantly, felt furious with those looking after her and suspected them of conspiring against her.[68] Such a diagnosis, like that of neurasthenia, implies an innate disorder, rather than explaining her attacks in terms of the shocks she had undergone, although the series of sudden deaths in her family, sexual abuse and, later, her difficulties within their marriage and the seven-year task of completing *The Voyage Out* might be considered sufficiently traumatic in themselves to account for her suicide attempt and the long collapse that followed.

Today, manic depression is known as 'bipolar syndrome' and is thought to be genetically transmitted, so Sir George Savage's assumption that there was a significant family context to Virginia's breakdowns appears to be re-affirmed. Thomas Caramagno's account of her illness provides a family tree illustrating how many members suffered from one form of depression or another.[69] Yet the family tendency to depressive illness could also be cited as evidence of environmental influence, as an example of a 'Laingian' dysfunctional family in which one member bore the burden of chaos, doubt or anxiety on behalf of the others, so that Virginia became not merely 'Goat', but 'scapegoat' – a replacement for Laura, even. She certainly seemed to carry more than her fair share of the family's psychological baggage.

There is also the larger question of whether Virginia's illness reflected her exceptional sensitivity, not merely to the events of her own life, but to those of her society and her times. While *The Voyage Out* is not an overtly political novel, its heroine Rachel experiences terrors that reflect her social milieu – the threat of the outcast and the vulnerability of young women. The novel's early chapters expose British imperialist assumptions, while the warships sighted by the Dalloways act as a reminder of the arms race and the build-up of the fleet of Dreadnoughts – political conditions in which the shooting of an archduke in a Balkan town could trigger European war on an unprecedented scale. Woolf's headaches of 1910, 1912 and 1913 may be attributed to genetics or personal trauma, to biochemistry or family interaction, but her inner tensions parallel those of a darkening world beyond. As an artist Woolf was committed to telling the truth as she saw it, and the very practice of her art required her to adopt a position as a critic and outsider, even as 'mad', if the society she criticized defined its particular prejudices as 'sane'. The 'insane truth'[70] as seen by the shell-shocked soldier Septimus Warren Smith in *Mrs Dalloway* includes literal impossibilities – paranoid delusions of personal guilt and responsibility for the Great War – yet these are more than matched by the aggression and self-deception of the doctors who attempt to silence him and bury the guilt and terror that the war had left behind. In exploring 'all the horrors of the dark cupboard of illness',[71] in dismantling the tidy filing cabinets of the comfortable and familiar to confront chaos, Woolf suffered from madness, as conventionally defined, yet there was also something of poetic frenzy in it, and her art drew on what she found there.

Although her long breakdown left her terrified that her inner chaos might return and prove uncontrollable, that there would be no recrossing those dark waters for a second time, she managed to take a more detached, constructive and positive view of it than Leonard ever could. For the rest of her life, she would often retreat to bed on Leonard's orders, and while she sometimes resented this, she also saw it as a licensed self-indulgence, something to be enjoyed as well as endured. Her essay 'On Being Ill' celebrates the pleasure of withdrawing from everyday life and engaging in fantasy and free association: 'how astonishing, when the lights of health go down, the undiscovered countries that are then disclosed.'[72] While the sense of its horrors never entirely left her, she recognized that 'the dark underworld has its fascinations as well as its terrors';[73] there were revelations to be had there, as well as miseries to be endured. Despite, or perhaps because of, the intensity of her suffering, she evolved a philosophy in which even her illnesses carried within them the seeds of creativity: 'these curious intervals in life – I've had many – are the most fruitful artistically – one becomes fertilised – think of my madness at Hogarth [House] – & all the little illnesses.'[74]

Slowly she began to recover and by the autumn of 1915 she was well enough to go to Asheham with Leonard. Her weight had risen to over twelve stone as a result of the rest cure, 'three more than I've ever had,' she explained to Lytton Strachey, 'and the consequence is I can hardly toil uphill, but it's evidently good for the health. I am as happy as the day is long, and look forward to being rid of the nurse soon (she is at present dusting the room, and arranging the books).'[75] She had narrowly escaped death, and imprisonment in a mental institution. She had come through. Though she would be subject to unexplained fevers, pains and sudden dipping depressions for the rest of her life, sometimes lasting for weeks or even months, she would never again experience a breakdown as devastating or extended as she had undergone from the summer of 1913 to the autumn of 1915. She was now living under a strict regime of frequent and nourishing meals, limited social engagements and bed by 11 p.m. Under these conditions, she was at last permitted to resume her writing. At times, she despaired 'of finishing a book on this method', as she complained to Lytton Strachey: 'I write one sentence – the clock strikes – Leonard appears with a glass of milk.'[76] Yet finish it she did.

Returning to *Night and Day*, Virginia wrote her way back into the lost, secure world of her childhood – the world of her remarkable family, with their love of books, writers and literary gossip. At the heart of the novel stands the house in Cheyne Walk, shrine of the dead poet Richard Alardyce, presided over by his daughter and Katharine's mother, Mrs Hilbery. Scatty, spontaneous and delightful, she was inspired by Virginia's 'aunt', Anny Thackeray Ritchie, Leslie Stephen's sister-in-law by his first marriage and the elder daughter of the great Victorian novelist. Anny inherited something of her father's genius, and was the author of a series of biographical introductions to his work, as well as novels and memoirs of her own.[77] Cheyne Walk faces the river, beyond the Embankment, in literary Chelsea. Thomas Carlyle, a friend of Anny's and a mentor of Leslie Stephen, had lived round the corner at 24 Cheyne Row (Leslie had taken the young Virginia to see his house there in 1897, and she revisited it in 1898, and again in 1909 and 1931[78]). Henry James had spent his last London years at Carlyle Mansions, close by; lightly disguised as Mr Fortescue, he takes tea with the Hilberys in the novel's opening chapter.[79] The photographer Julia Margaret Cameron, Julia Stephen's aunt and a close friend of Anny Ritchie, is remembered in the novel as 'Queenie Colqhoun', while other Stephen aunts, among them the high-minded Caroline Stephen and the interfering Mary Fisher, also put in cameo appearances.[80] Just as Virginia preferred to represent Katharine as Vanessa rather than herself, Katharine's parents in the novel are ostensibly portraits of aunt Anny and her husband Richmond Ritchie, yet unlike Ritchie – and like Leslie Stephen – Mr Hilbery is a literary biographer by profession. He shares Leslie Stephen's enthusiasm for Scott (Katharine reads either *The Antiquary* or *The Bride of Lammermoor* to her father, to soothe him), while Mrs Hilbery shares Julia Stephen's delight in love and romance. The cosy world of Stephen jokes, anecdotes and feuds is displayed in Woolf's second novel for the first time (though by no means the last).

Yet if Virginia re-created something of the atmosphere of her childhood, it was only to discover how suffocating and entrapping that world had been, and to re-enact her rejection of its values and make good her symbolic escape. Like her heroine, 'sometimes she felt that it was necessary for her very existence that she should free herself from the past' [p.32]. Nor was the past necessarily free from dangerous corners merely because it was over and known: Mrs Hilbery's great task, in which Katharine is also involved, is the writing of her father's biography, but she cannot complete it, partly because she 'could not decide how far the public was to be told the truth about the poet's separation from his wife' [p.30]. Behind the breakdown of Richard Alardyce's marriage (which itself prompts awkward questions for Katharine) lies the buried truth of Thackeray's marriage: after six years and the birth of three daughters, his young wife had gone mad and been confined to an asylum; he had never spoken of her again.

For Virginia, the worlds of Victorian literature, romance and family life were deeply linked as sources of both nostalgia and claustrophobia. Her heroine, Katharine, is devoted to her parents, yet so desperate to find the privacy she needs for herself and her work that she is prepared to embark on a loveless marriage. The alternative, a relationship with Ralph, poses an even greater threat to her sense of self because it will draw her into a genuine intimacy, and with a man from a background entirely different from her own, a man who has had to make his own way, a man who belongs to the modern world of Ibsen and Samuel Butler that her parents find so barbarous. But Ralph, like Katharine (and like Leonard and Virginia), recognizes the importance of the world of work. The novel begins by satirizing the suffrage office where its 'New Woman', Mary Datchet, is working, but it ends up celebrating the inspirational power of her political commitment, as the light from her window shines out like a beacon across the street. The leisured world of the tea party, over which Julia Stephen had presided so gracefully, and which she bequeathed to her daughters Vanessa and Virginia, had come to seem the real prison. Later, Virginia would equate this 'Victorian game of manners' with what she took to be a limitation in her writing: she blamed her 'tea-table training' for 'my old *Common Reader* articles . . . for their suavity, their politeness, their sidelong approach'.[81] And when Vanessa eventually read *Night and Day*, it reminded her all too vividly of the old horrors of family life.[82]

For an experimental writer, the house in Cheyne Walk with all its literary associations was potentially threatening: Thomas Carlyle had been both sage and domestic tyrant, as Leslie Stephen could be.[83] Within the novel, the gentle, musical Mr Hilbery is transformed by fatherly possessiveness into 'the extravagant, inconsiderate, uncivilized male . . . gone bellowing to his lair with a roar.' [p.126] Henry James had made Virginia feel oppressed by identifying her as her father's daughter.[84] Katharine, its heroine, is in flight from poetry and novels because they are 'all about feelings'. She repeats to herself almost like a mantra a sentence from Dostoevsky ('[s]he liked getting hold of some book which neither her father or mother had read, and keeping it to herself . . . [p.106]): 'It's life that matters . . . the process of discovering, the everlasting and perpetual process, not the discovery itself at all.' [p.111][85]

Katharine repeats these words to herself as she walks down the

Strand, the spot from where *The Voyage Out* had begun. The final page of *Night and Day* gestures towards its own unfulfilled potential, as the lovers imagine their future: 'Together they groped in this difficult region, where the unfinished, the unfulfilled, the unwritten, the unreturned, came together in their ghostly way and wore the semblance of the complete and the satisfactory.' [pp.431–2] In the final paragraphs, Ralph and Katharine walk beside the river, about to embark on the deep waters of their relationship, the very waters in which Rachel had drowned. From the Thames, the 'dark tide of waters' flows out to all the oceans and rivers of the world, and the reference to Conrad's novella with which *The Voyage Out* had opened is here made explicit, as if Woolf was deliberately closing the circuit and leaving this first phase of fiction behind her: 'From the heart of his darkness he spoke his thanksgiving.' [p.432]

At first the writing of *Night and Day* had proceeded at a snail's pace, for Virginia was strictly rationed to an hour's work each day. Yet she moved forward steadily, and almost unfalteringly, judging from the only fragment of manuscript that survives, composed between October 1916 and February 1917. 'I don't suppose I've ever enjoyed any writing so much as I did the last half of N. & D.', she recorded, 'if one's own ease & interest promise anything good, I should have hopes that some people, at least, will find it a pleasure.'[86]

Late in March 1919 Virginia gave the completed typescript to Leonard to read – this time, she had showed it to no one during its composition. Much as he admired it, he admitted to her as they walked along the river at Richmond, that he found its philosophy 'very melancholy',[87] perhaps because her lovers were plagued with self-doubt. Virginia responded by setting down her own dissatisfactions with it later that evening. She was not disappointed with *Night and Day* in itself, but she recognized that she had failed to solve the riddle of how a modern novel should be written: 'as the current answers don't do, one has to grope for a new one; & the process of discarding the old, when one is by no means certain what to put in their place, is a sad one.'[88] A few days later, she reworked these self-criticisms into an article for the *Times Literary Supplement* on 'Modern Novels'. Revised as 'Modern Fiction', it became a manifesto for modernism as well as a programme for her own future as a writer.

NIGHT AND DAY: THE AFTERMATH

I see that Night and Day *will be out shortly. Gerald Duckworth lost the last chapter, so I daresay it will be November instead of October. I don't feel nervous; nobody cares a hang what one writes, and novels are such clumsy and half extinct monsters at the best; but, oh dear, what a bore it will be! All one's friends thinking they've got to say something . . .*[89]

Night and Day *was published by Duckworth on 20 October 1919 in an edition of 2000 copies, and sold for 9 shillings*[90] *(3 shillings more than* The Voyage Out *– it was significantly longer, and post-war inflation had set in). As this letter to her friend Ka Cox indicates, Virginia felt unusually confident about her second novel. She had enjoyed writing it and expected her pleasure to be shared by her readers. Her diary records in detail the reactions of friends and reviewers, and the elation or depression they induced in her: 'if I could treat myself professionally as a subject for analysis I could make an interesting story of the past few days, of my vicissitudes about N. & D.',*[91] *she wrote a month later, but in general her expectation 'that the people whose judgement I value will probably think well of it'*[92] *was largely fulfilled. The novel's later neglect could scarcely have been foreseen from its initial reception.*

Of her six author's copies, she sent off five to the people whose opinions she most valued after Leonard's – Vanessa, Clive Bell, Lytton Strachey, E. M. Forster and her old friend Violet Dickinson.[93] *All but Forster praised it, although it reminded Vanessa of their oppressed youth, and Clive later rescinded his admiration, and by 1924 judged it 'her most definite failure'.*[94] *Lytton's letter, now lost, rightly complimented her on the dialogue, one of the novel's outstanding features.*[95] *It was also admired beyond her immediate circle: when Sir George Savage, who had treated her during the early stages of her illness, pronounced it 'A great novel – particularly in its psychology'*[96] *she didn't know whether to be amused or embarrassed.*

In terms of sexual politics, this was a more conservative novel than The Voyage Out, *and her comic depiction of the suffrage office, with its absurd and self-important voluntary workers, seemed something of a betrayal to her feminist friends: when she ascended 'the immaculate & moral heights of Hampstead'[97] to visit her old Greek teacher, Janet Case, she learned that neither Janet nor Margaret Llewelyn Davies[98] had cared for it.* Margaret tried to explain tactfully to Virginia their view that her novel lacked the imaginative identification they had found in her essays – she mentioned an essay on rereading Charlotte Brontë, written three years earlier.[99] Virginia was always hurt by the accusation of narrow sympathies, and she turned it back on her accuser, writing to Margaret to suggest that they both had their blind spots: 'You'll never like my books, but then shall I ever understand your [Women's Co-operative] Guild? Probably not.'[100] She enclosed a review praising the warmth of her sympathies, and added that the Times Literary Supplement *reviewer had found her 'chiefly remarkable for common human wisdom'.[101] For Woolf there was a further irony in Margaret's criticism, since the character of Mary Datchet, the 'New Woman' in the novel, had originally been inspired by aspects of Margaret's own life – her history as the daughter of a clergyman who had abandoned family duties to dedicate herself to social change and improving women's lives; her affection for Leonard (Mary is in love with Ralph Denham, the Leonard figure); even the light from her window which shines out like a beacon in the novel's final chapter may have been inspired by a memory of seeing the light from Margaret's window in Barton Street, eight years earlier.[102]*

The reviewers were full of praise for Night and Day: The World *considered it 'without a doubt the best novel written in English during the last seven or eight years',[103] and comparisons were drawn with George Eliot (by Ford Madox Ford), Charlotte Brontë, George Meredith, the early Henry James, Dostoevsky, but most often, with Jane Austen[104] (whose presence in the novel was in any case suggested by the use of her sister's name, 'Cassandra'). Henry Massingham, editor of the* Nation, *complained that he couldn't see the point of the comparisons with Austen, that the heroine spent too much of the novel drinking tea, and described the lovers as 'Four Impassioned Snails'.[105] More judicial was Harold Child's (anonymous) review for the* Times Literary Supplement, *which observed that, though this novel was less superficially brilliant than* The Voyage Out, *there was more beneath, waiting to surface. Virginia re-interpreted this as having 'more depth than the other; with which I agree'.*[106] *Child also pointed out that the novel included some curious mistakes: in the penultimate chapter, Mrs Hilbery returns from Stratford, laden with branches from Shakespeare's tomb, whereas the tomb is actually inside Holy Trinity church, and no flowers grow from it.*

Another error, noticed not only by Child, had been introduced during the process of revision. In chapter XV, Mary Datchet's sister Elizabeth cuts long-stemmed roses at Christmas time in a Lincolnshire garden, a detail which also produced an enquiry from the painter Dora Carrington. Virginia assured her through Lytton that 'I went into the question of the roses with some care',[107] *but a month later she was consulting Violet Dickinson as to whether this constituted a mistake: 'At Kew there are certainly roses at Christmas – the long pink ones.'*[108] *She had, in fact, altered and simplified this scene in the process of rewriting it. In the holograph draft, Elizabeth and Mary were more plausibly cutting chrysanthemums, and Mary takes her father a Christmas rose (a hellebore) which, being short-sighted, he mistakes for an actual rose.*[109]

In general, she was amused when reviewers or correspondents niggled over trivial detail, while sometimes finding the demands of naturalism trying: 'the great battle, so [Middleton] Murry tells me, is between those who think it unreal and those who think it real,' she told Clive Bell; 'What do they mean?'[110] *The sharpest criticism had come from Murry's wife Katherine Mansfield, by now a difficult friend. From the moment Woolf heard that Mansfield was to review novels for the* Athenaeum *earlier that year, her first thought had been 'pray to God she don't do mine!'*[111] *Mansfield's review recognized the novel's attempt to reconcile 'the world of reality with what . . . we call the dream world';*[112] *like other reviewers, she could not 'refrain from comparing* Night and Day *with the novels of Miss Austen', but the weight of her criticism fell in her opening and closing paragraphs, where she discussed the direction that the post-war novel should take, and, by implication, condemned it for its pre-war serenity, for 'the absence of any scars'.*[113]

Virginia was upset by Mansfield's review, but wrote it off as spite, 'her wish for my failure'.[114] *She was consoled by the fact that two American publishers had made offers for the novel, along with* The

Voyage Out. *When she asked Lytton Strachey to list 'any special misprints, obscurities or vulgarities',*[115] *he drew her attention to a syntactic confusion in chapter III ('pointed out by Saxon [Sydney-Turner], I need hardly say' – Saxon was the most pedantic reader in their circle).*[116] *Preparing* Night and Day *for the American publisher George Doran, Virginia changed the ungrammatical sentence in chapter III, but she let other mistakes – the roses cut at Christmas, and the laurels from Shakespeare's tomb – stand. Someone had also pointed out to her an error in chapter V, where Ralph Denham takes up 'a small and very lovely edition of Sir Thomas Browne, containing the "Urn Burial", the "Hydriotaphia", the "Quincunx Confuted", and the "Garden of Cyrus" . . .' [p.59]. In fact 'Hydriotaphia' and 'Urn Burial' are two names for the same work, while 'The Quincunx Confuted' garbles the long subtitle of 'The Garden of Cyrus'. The American edition removes 'The Quincunx Confuted', but still includes both 'the "Urn Burial", [and] the "Hydriotaphia"'.*[117] *She also made a small but deliberate number of changes in wording, perhaps on the principle that she had set out to Lytton, 'the more alterations the better – because of copyright'.*[118]

'I like it less than the V. O.', Forster had written to her, on receiving his copy of Night and Day, *and 'this rubbed out all the pleasure of the rest'.*[119] *He was, after all, a fellow practitioner: 'he says the simple things that clever people don't say; I find him the best of critics for that reason'.*[120] *A week later, Forster dined with the Woolfs and when he had explained what he meant, Virginia felt she took his point, and could see that it was 'not a criticism to discourage'.*[121] *That evening, he had characterized the novel as 'a strictly formal & classical work', describing it in a later essay as 'a deliberate exercise in classicism'.*[122] *He had seen conscious intention in what was probably an effect of convalescence and recovery. Woolf welcomed his view, assimilating it into her own account of her growth as a writer. She accepted* The Voyage Out *as the more original, but represented* Night and Day *as a necessary phase in her education, not unlike the 'antique classes' that Vanessa had attended at art school. Apologizing for the novel's weaknesses to Ethel Smyth in 1930, she explained 'I made myself copy from plaster casts, partly to tranquillise, partly to learn anatomy. Bad as the book is, it composed my mind and I think taught me certain*

VIRGINIA WOOLF

Night and Day

NINE SHILLINGS NET

elements of composition which I should not have had the patience to learn had I been in full flush of health always.'[123]

In this letter, Woolf went on to claim that the real development of her art lay in the experimental short stories written at the same time, but she was wrong. Its seminal elements – the story as she had first conceived it, the story of 'The Third Generation',[124] in which the claustrophobic warmth of Victorian family life gives way to the isolation and confusion of a world where women must choose for themselves – remained central to her vision, to be dramatized seriously in To the Lighthouse, *light-heartedly in* Orlando, *and at length and in depth, as the story of three generations, in* The Years.

Her initial hopes for the success of Night and Day were disappointed. It sold slowly on both sides of the Atlantic. A second British impression of 1000 copies was issued in 1920, but nine years later, when Duckworth sold the copyright to the Hogarth Press, more than 500 copies and sheets remained unsold.[125] The novel was included in the uniform edition in 1930, but over the next fifty years, its sales averaged fewer than 400 a year, and it was not until 1969, when it first appeared in Penguin Modern Classics, that it began to sell in any numbers – the first paperback print run of 22,500 copies was more than the Hogarth Press had sold in total since 1930, and two years later it was reprinting again. Further paperback editions ran into substantial numbers, and by the 1990s, Penguin printed 16,000 copies of my own edition of the novel over three years, in the face of competition from other paperback versions.[126] With Woolf's popularity still growing, even a neglected novel now commands substantial sales.

3

'Our Press Arrived on Tuesday'[1]

'[I]f one were free and could set down what one chose,' Woolf wrote in 1919, 'there would be no plot, little probability, and a vague general confusion in which the clear-cut features of the tragic, the comic, the passionate, and the lyrical were dissolved beyond the possibility of separate recognition.'[2] In two experimental short stories, composed while working on *Night and Day*, she had already made a bid for such freedom. The agent of her liberation had been the hand printing press, installed by the Woolfs on the dining-room table at Hogarth House two years earlier. It required to be fed with writing – poetry or short stories – while imposing few constraints on what was printed – indeed the more unconventional the better. To justify the necessarily short print runs, the Woolfs consciously sought out work that might not otherwise get into print. Once they had acquired the press, Virginia had only her own standards, and Leonard's, to satisfy: 'It is tremendous fun, and it makes all the difference writing anything one likes, and not for an Editor.'[3] The short stories she began to write were not only radically experimental, they were also radically different from one another – an unfolding meditation on time and memory; a painterly vision of public gardens; fantasias that began with a woman before a fire or in a train, a chamber concert, glass lustres on a mantelpiece; a rhapsodic haunting, and some fables. In their variety, intensity and originality, these short stories anticipated the novels to come, helping to release her from the burden that had weighed on her first two books, that she ought to be writing like other novelists, that her books should read like other people's. She no longer felt obliged to stick to conventional limits in representing life in fiction. Most of these short stories were published in *Monday or Tuesday* in 1921, a collection of

HOGARTH   HOUSE
RICHMOND.

THE   HOGARTH   PRESS.

It is proposed to issue shortly a pamphlet **containing two**
short stories by Leonard Woolf and Virginia Woolf,(price,includ-
-ing postage 1/2).

If you desire a copy to be sent to you,please fill up   the
form below and send it with a P. O. to L. S. Woolf at the above address before June   .

A limited edition only will be issued.

———————————

Please send   copy of Publication No. 1 to

for which I enclose P. O. for   .

NAME

ADDRESS

'allsorts', unified by a delight in the colour and rhythm of language that brought several of them close to poetry.

The decision to buy a printing press had been taken on Virginia's thirty-third birthday, in January 1915, along with the decision to move into Hogarth House in Richmond and to buy a bulldog (which they never did). Leonard, looking for an occupation that would at once absorb and relax her, hit upon printing as appropriate, given Virginia's passion for books as physical objects, as well as reading matter. As a young girl she had learned bookbinding and, with Vanessa, had once done some silver-point printing (a process for reproducing drawings, not words),[4] but neither she nor Leonard had ever set type. Towards the end of 1916, they tried to sign up for classes at St Bride's School of Printing, only to find that these were intended for trade union apprentices, rather than genteel amateurs. The following spring, armed with an income-tax refund, they visited the Excelsior Printing Supply Company in Farringdon Street, where they bought a hand press, some boxes of type and various other essential tools of the trade, receiving with it an instruction manual which told them everything they needed to know in order to begin printing.[5]

'Our press arrived on Tuesday', she wrote to Vanessa on 26 April 1917. 'We unpacked it with enormous excitement, . . . the arrangement of the type is such a business that we shant be ready to start printing directly. One has great blocks of type, which have to be divided into their separate letters, and founts, and then put into the right partitions. The work of ages, especially when you mix the h's with the ns, as I did yesterday. We get so absorbed, we can't stop; I see that real printing will devour one's entire life.'[6] It took the Woolfs about a month to learn how to set up the type and lock it into forms, ready for printing. Their first production was an announcement that the Hogarth Press would publish two short stories by Leonard Woolf and Virginia Woolf in a limited edition, priced at one shilling and twopence, including postage (though in the event they charged one shilling and sixpence).[7] Virginia was half-way through her second novel, *Night and Day*, and hard at work on it as they began to typeset Leonard's story, 'Three Jews', which, with 'The Mark on the Wall', became their first publication.

'I shall never forget the day I wrote The Mark on the Wall – all in a flash, as if flying',[8] Woolf recalled, many years later. It was a visionary monologue on the nature of perception, just such a rhapsody as Clive Bell had admired in the early stages of *The Voyage Out*. It follows a train or flow of thought, yet the movement of thought and feeling is also its subject; like a railway train, it is always carrying the thinker away from a full engagement with passing sights or thoughts, so that knowledge and certainty are never achieved, and nothing can be defined. Sights (in the form of thoughts) flash past so fast that there is no distinguishing between trees and men and women, between camps and tombs, between a nail, a rose-leaf, and a crack in the wood. The thinker (clearly a woman) contrasts this flux of thought and memory with the external, regulated world of common assumptions and social expectations; the world that determines what kind of tablecloth one ought to have, imposing rigid systems of behaviour and represented in the story by the official guide to status, 'Whitaker's Table of Precedency'. The initial confusion of what is seen with what is imagined gives place to an acknowledgement of the power of social signifiers, but then reverts to a rich and generative outpouring that is consciously feminine, and consciously opposed to the 'masculine point of view which governs our lives'.[9] In its final moments, this meditation is violently disrupted by a male voice talking (significantly) about newspapers and war, a voice which reduces the mysterious mark from a nail on which anything or everything may hang, to a snail. The artist Dora Carrington, who provided woodcuts for it, emphasized the femininity of the narrator by depicting her as a woman, apparently naked, sitting in front of a fire with a dog.[10]

The business of setting type by hand would remain lastingly 'fascinating',[11] but it was also immensely time-consuming. It occupied both the Woolfs most afternoons, and though, exceptionally, the Hogarth Press made a profit from the outset owing to Leonard's careful accounting and strong business sense, he never included in that reckoning the time they spent on their new game; and, strictly speaking, handprinting could never have been an economic use of it. Each of them had other paid work as journalists: Leonard was writing for the *New Statesman* (in 1916 he had published *International Government*, which provided a blueprint for the future League of Nations, and in 1920, a critique of colonial exploitation, *Empire and Commerce in*

Africa). As well as helping Leonard with his work by taking notes and typing out drafts for him, Virginia had resumed her own reviewing, and by 1916 was once again writing regularly for the *Times Literary Supplement*, and by 1917 contributing essays every fortnight and sometimes more frequently.[12] Though their earnings were important to them, financially as well as psychologically, they would have found it difficult to survive had they not been able to draw on Virginia's inherited capital. The cost of her illness, including many months of full-time nursing, had been high, and they were, after all, maintaining handsome eighteenth-century houses at Richmond and Asheham, and employing a full-time 'general' (i.e. cook) and an 'hpm' (house parlour maid), as well as more casual help.[13]

Two Stories was published early in July 1917, and by the 21st, most of the print run of 150 copies had been sold (the price for the remaining copies then went up from one shilling and sixpence to two shillings).[14] Writing 'The Mark on the Wall' so quickly and easily had opened a door for Virginia, and in the wake of its publication, she was ready to walk through it. On the 24th, she wrote to thank Clive Bell for his commendation, recalling that he'd been the first person to admire her work, and adding, 'its high time we found some new shapes, don't you think so?'[15] '[I]ts easier to do a short thing, all in one flight than a novel', she confessed to the young novelist David Garnett, two days later. 'Novels are frightfully clumsy and overpowering ... I daresay one ought to invent a completely new form.'[16] New shapes, new forms, crucial to her own development, were also exactly what a small press needed, the kind of experimental work that commercial publishers or editors were unwilling to risk, the 'writing of merit which the ordinary publisher refuses'.[17] Their second publication was more than twice the length of the first: Katherine Mansfield, invited to write for the Press,[18] had offered them her long short story, 'Prelude'.

'Prelude' is a powerfully evocative account of childhood, passed in a remote and beautiful corner of New Zealand. Mansfield, the daughter of a small-time businessman, had later left her family to come to England and write. There, she fell in love with and married the critic John Middleton Murry. The couple became friends with Frieda and D. H. Lawrence, and through them met Ottoline Morrell and Lytton Strachey. Katherine and Virginia finally met early in 1917, an occasion that each had wished for and feared – Virginia already felt that Katherine had 'dogged' her steps for three years before she met her,[19] just as Katherine felt 'haunted' by Virginia and courted her good opinion.[20]

Virginia's first response, and one that recurred at intervals throughout their friendship, was distaste – she found Katherine hard, cheap, unscrupulous, too blatantly sexual, too manipulative, utterly inscrutable.[21] Katherine wooed Virginia with extravagant compliments, yet privately thought the Woolfs stuffy, even 'smelly'.[22] At the same time, there was an instant rapport between them: both wanted to use their experience as women to produce a new kind of writing, and their intuitive understanding of the pleasures and problems of their task drew them into an intimacy – they became 'a public of two'.[23] Conversations about 'our precious art'[24] became of great importance to both of them. For months during 1918 and 1919, Virginia travelled up to Hampstead one afternoon a week to visit Katherine, for despite mutual distrust and even dislike there was still everything to be said: 'You are the only woman with whom I long to talk work. There will never be another', Katherine told Virginia, in her final letter,[25] and Virginia had admitted as much to her diary: 'had 2 hours priceless talk – priceless in the sense that to no one else can I talk in the same disembodied way about writing; without altering my thought more than I alter it in writing here'.[26]

In August 1917, Virginia invited Katherine to spend a few days with them at Asheham. At the end of July, Katherine had been staying with Ottoline Morrell at Garsington; she evoked its enchanting garden in a letter to Virginia which has not survived. Virginia, writing to Ottoline on 15 August, enlarged upon her rapturous account: 'Katherine Mansfield describes your garden, the rose leaves drying in the sun, the pool, and long conversations between people wandering up and down in the moonlight. It calls out her romantic side.'[27] On the same day Katherine herself had written to Ottoline, wondering 'who is going to write about that flower garden ... There would be people walking in the garden – several pairs of people – their conversation their slow pacing – ... the pauses as the flowers "come in" as it were – ... A kind of, musically speaking – conversation set to flowers.'[28] The answer, surprisingly, turned out to be Virginia: Katherine's word-picture uncannily anticipates her short story 'Kew Gardens', which survives in a typescript dated 'Aug 7, 1917'[29] – a week before either of these letters was sent to Ottoline. Did Katherine's missing letter about Garsington provide the starting point for Virginia's story, with the moonlight transformed into sunlight and the privacy of Garsington changed to the public gardens at Kew – or had she composed it earlier and quite independently, the several similarities being just a curious coincidence?

Katherine took the text of 'Prelude' down to Asheham for the Woolfs, and while she was there, Virginia apparently showed her the typescript of 'Kew Gardens'. We do not know whether Katherine thought Virginia had borrowed from her, but in her thank-you letter, she assured Virginia, 'Yes, your Flower Bed is <u>very</u> good. Theres a still, quivering, changing light over it all and a sense of those couples dissolving in the bright air which fascinates me – '.[30] '[I]t is really very curious & thrilling', she had written in the previous paragraph, 'that we should both, quite apart from each other, be after so very nearly the same thing'.[31]

Mansfield's missing letter, or even a meeting between the two might have suggested to Virginia the flower bed and the conversations of passing couples, but the Kew setting also recalled Leonard's use of it in 'Three Jews', his contribution to *Two Stories* which Virginia had helped to typeset and print earlier in July. 'Three Jews' begins in Kew Gardens one Sunday in spring; its Jewish narrator has gone to Kew to escape from the city's asphalt and chimney pots. After his visit, he finds a nearby tea shop where he recognizes another Jew in what both feel to be a very English – and therefore alien – setting. The stranger then tells the narrator the story of the third Jew, an old man who kept the Jewish cemetery where the stranger's first wife was buried. With the cemetery keeper, he had discussed the old faith and its gradual erosion. Visiting his wife's grave at intervals, the stranger learns first that the keeper's wife has also died, and, on his last visit, that the keeper has disowned his son for secretly marrying their maidservant. The keeper's anger has less to do with his son marrying 'out' (as it might have done for a previous generation) than with her being the servant who washed his dishes. His story exposes the awkward mixture of pride and narrow-mindedness that Leonard saw as characteristic of his race.

The story creates a painful sense of how it feels to be identified as an outsider on the basis of appearance alone – Leonard himself had the long nose and Jewish features that the story defines as stereotypical, and he had many opportunities to see himself through the eyes of the anti-Semitic upper-class Englishmen whose cultural identity he had adopted at Cambridge. Virginia did not record what she thought of 'Three Jews', and judging by her silence on the race issue when she reworked material from *The Wise Virgins* into *Night and Day*, she was reluctant to address it directly. Yet Leonard's presentation of the outsider's consciousness, walking among 'quiet orderly English people' in 'the quiet orderly English spring'[32] anticipates the opening of *A Room of One's Own*, where the female narrator is shooed off the grass and shut out of the college library. Virginia's sense that being a woman in a patriarchal culture made her an outsider partly reflected and developed Leonard's sense of his exclusion as a Jew, and the oblique angle it gave him on Englishness – envied, adopted, admired and loved, yet for ever closed to him. Cambridge, the Apostles, and the whole system of English political and professional institutions were similarly coveted by and closed to Virginia – yet there were large differences. Leonard was at once further out, in being a highly visible member of a small minority, and further in, in that he was to devote most of his working life to English political institutions of one kind or another – he was by nature a team player.

'Three Jews' sets up a series of sharp demarcation lines: between the English and the Jews; between the middle-class Jews who meet in the tea room, and the lower-middle-class cemetery keeper, and then again between the keeper and the maidservant whom he cannot accept as his daughter-in-law. Gender is not overtly an issue (all the speakers are male), but a double standard is suggested by the cemetery keeper's half-boast that his elder son has 'an eye for the petticoats',[33] and his corresponding disgust when his son marries the (probably pregnant) serving girl behind his back. Similar binary oppositions of class and gender would provide the fourfold structure of 'Kew Gardens'.

The Royal Botanical Gardens at Kew were just visible from the back windows of Hogarth House, and they had quickly become a favourite walk for the Woolfs. Just as the Strand and the alleys leading to the river had been a generative site in her first two novels, so Kew also became a place where writing began, the garden of paradise where Katharine and Ralph would find each other in *Night and Day*.[34] But 'Kew Gardens' rejected both Leonard's tough naturalism and the interior monologue of 'The Mark on the Wall' in favour of a new technique that distanced and objectified: the conversations of four different couples are overheard as they pass the oval flower bed and merge into the dapple of light and shade, where people and flowers are no more than spots of colour in the shimmering air, observed with the passionate detachment of Seurat, in 'La Grande Jatte'. Alternating with the world of human dialogue is the narrative of the snail, progressing gradually through the mountains of stone and precipices of leaves in the flower bed. 'The Mark on the Wall' had exposed the purely verbal and imaginative nature of all writing, its simultaneous need and failure to impose meaning on the 'incessant shower of innumerable atoms'[35] that make up experience. 'Kew Gardens', on the other hand, appeals to the visual imagination, reaching for painterly analogies, set out within a formal structure such as Clive Bell, following Roger Fry, believed essential for a work of art.

In 'Kew Gardens' the flower bed becomes a sequence of primary colours – red, blue or yellow petals growing among heart-shaped or tongue-shaped leaves that seem on the point of throbbing or speaking, while the world of human conversation alternates with the vegetable world of the flower bed, as seen by the snail. Four human couples walk past the snail, distinguished by gender and class: the first and last are linked by romance, the other two couples concentrate on more topical issues – war widows, food shortages. While the first two couples belong to the upper middle class, the third and fourth belong to the lower middle class. The conversations begin with Simon and Eleanor, married and walking with their children (also a boy and a girl), remembering Kew as a place of love, the scene of a former proposal, a former kiss. They are followed by two men, the elder of whom is 'mad', and believes he can make contact with the dead. These are followed, in turn, by two working women whose conversation is rendered as a comic (and condescending) shorthand of gossip and complaints. The last couple, 'Trissie' and her young man, talk of nothing very much, clinging to the reality of here and now as the excitement of falling in love threatens to overwhelm them. The people in the garden fade into flower-like forms, and their shapes and voices are succeeded by the mechanical clangour of London's buses.

The couples, so many spots of colour, fade into a green-blue haze, as in an impressionist painting, and this suggestion is intensified when the roofs of the palm house shine 'as if a whole market full of shiny green umbrellas had opened in the sun',[36] a description that recalls Renoir's 'Les Parapluies', which Virginia had looked at in the National Gallery in July 1918, while revising 'Kew Gardens' for publication later that year.[37] She had also seen Berthe Morisot's '2 women in a boat' and 'a picture of still life on a mantelpiece by Vuillard', as she told Vanessa in a letter which also thanked her for her design for 'Kew Gardens': 'a most successful piece; and just in the mood I wanted'.[38] Vanessa's two woodcuts for the story mark the beginning of the sisters' artistic collaboration – she would later illustrate the short story collection *Monday or Tuesday*, and design dust-jackets for most of Virginia's books, from *Jacob's Room* onwards. The frontispiece for 'Kew Gardens' shows two women in conversation, their hats sprouting flowers that dissolve into further flowers above or behind them, while the tailpiece evokes the world of the flower bed, the miniature world of butterfly and caterpillar. The black-and-white woodcuts at once correspond to and contradict the glowing colours that the story evokes in words, in its printed, black-on-white text. And there is a further connection between form and content in that the story's fourfold structure echoes the folded page used by the Woolfs for their folio printing.[39]

Vanessa's woodcuts became the occasion of a rare quarrel between the sisters when the Woolfs published 'Kew Gardens' on 12 May 1919 – Vanessa thought that they hadn't been properly inked, and even 'went so far as to doubt the value of the Hogarth Press altogether. An ordinary printer would do better in her opinion. This both stung & chilled me',[40] Virginia recorded, indignant at this slight on their skills. But by the end of the month, a second printing was needed anyway. The Woolfs came back from Asheham to discover the hall of Hogarth House piled high with orders, after a rave review of 'Kew Gardens' in the *Times Literary Supplement*.[41] This time, the job was entrusted to Richard Madley, a professional printer who had set several hand-printed books for Roger Fry at his Omega Workshop (Virginia did not think the result any better than they had managed[42]). The Workshop, founded in 1913 with support from Vanessa and Duncan Grant, was Fry's attempt to revitalize British taste, and to promote and finance the work of young artists. Omega produced fabric designs and decorated furniture, sold hats, hand-thrown pottery, jointed wooden toys, carpets and fire screens. Its example had encouraged the Woolfs to think of starting their own business, and Virginia had asked Fry for Omega's list of clients for their first mail shot.[43] Omega also published slim volumes, illustrated with woodcuts, but the Hogarth Press publications were aimed at a less arty and more literary readership, being cheaper, more homespun and more focused on content than presentation.

'Kew Gardens' was the first of Virginia's raids upon her sister's art. The Press had provided an opportunity for them to work together, but the influence of Vanessa's art extended much further than her woodcuts. As one reviewer observed, Woolf's short stories were examples of 'the "unrepresentational" art which is creeping across from painting to see what it can make of words'.[44] Vanessa had long before abandoned surface realism to concentrate on the impact of form and structure in painting. Her approach, and the theories that underwrote it, helped Virginia to make her own art 'new' – and it was the more powerful for the cross-fertilization involved, the necessity of adapting visual and spatial ideals to her own medium of writing. The urgent controversies over painting and visual aesthetics that occupied Vanessa and her circle introduced Virginia to the concept of the avant-garde, and the idea that her own generation were somehow 'Orphans',[45] had suffered a radical loss of the past, and were now committed to new shapes and new forms; the old conventions, whether of painting or fiction, would no longer do, and could never be used unquestioningly again.

Virginia's relationship with her older sister had always been passionate and possessive[46]: she adored and imitated her. When Vanessa began to paint professionally, Virginia had taken to writing standing at a high desk, as if working at an easel. Imitating Vanessa was not only the sincerest flattery – it included a barely suppressed rivalry. While she wanted Vanessa to be happy, she also feared that Vanessa's life was more fulfilling, more successful, more exciting than her own. Those fears underlay her long-sustained flirtation with Clive, as well as her efforts to establish intimate friendships with Vanessa's later lovers, the art historian Roger Fry and the young painter Duncan Grant. Her desire to learn the language of painting and visual aesthetics had a personal as well as an intellectual dimension. The similarities and differences between painting and writing fascinated her: while the plastic arts created a more immediate impact, they also generated a sense of silence, a short-circuiting of language to which her fiction often aspired. Painting could cut through the novelist's task of recording time passing by making it stand still, making a single moment last for ever. Her own art was to reach out for that effect.

Dining with Roger Fry and Clive Bell late in 1917, Virginia found herself discussing the representational nature of art, the relationship between poetry and painting and 'the meaning of structure & texture in painting & in writing'. Roger had asked her whether she based her writing on structure or texture, and she had replied 'texture', thinking of structure as the painter's equivalent of the plot. To talk about art to Vanessa, Clive or Roger Fry was to recognize that a genuine revolution in visual sensibility was under way: 'the atmosphere puts ideas into one's head'.[47] Roger Fry's two post-impressionist exhibitions held at the Grafton Galleries in November 1910 and October 1912 had aroused the indignation of the press, and many of their visitors, yet Fry and Clive Bell continued to defend the vitality and sensuality of the paintings on show, and after the war, they succeeded in establishing the popularity of post-impressionism – Van Gogh's sunflowers, Monet's water lilies; in due course, they would become the most popular paintings of all time. Roger Fry had announced the 'revolution that Cézanne inaugurated and that Gauguin and Van Gogh continued',[48] while Clive Bell, observing the gulf between the nineteenth and twentieth centuries, described Cézanne as 'the Christopher Columbus of a new continent of form'.[49]

Each of them maintained that the representation of life should not be the primary concern of art, and Bell went further, arguing that representation itself threatened to distract the artist from the more urgent requirements of form: only too often, representation was 'a sign of weakness in an artist'.[50] Fry thought art should be 'the expression of the imaginative life', rather than of the outer world,[51] that, like contemporary science, it had 'turned its vision inwards'.[52] For both

Fry and Bell, art's first commitment was to express 'significant form', the aesthetic ideal characteristic of all great works of art, and which, in Clive's view, was universally recognizable, though difficult to define. It included design, structure, rhythm, and was linked to larger rhythms: for Fry, 'the greatest art seems to concern itself most with the universal aspects of natural form, to be the least pre-occupied with particulars'.[53]

These ideas, discussed with Virginia, were to influence her profoundly, not least because they articulated, complemented or reinforced existing convictions of her own. 'The Mark on the Wall' was a direct 'expression of the imaginative life', while the symmetries of 'Kew Gardens' aspired to 'significant form' and painterly effects. Reworking some of their ideas about aesthetics in the language of fiction, she felt a confidence that deserted her when she attempted to pass judgement on individual paintings. On the same visit to the National Gallery that she had described to Vanessa, she admitted to herself that she liked pictures 'as things that stir me to describe them', adding hastily, as if Clive might be reading over her shoulder, 'I insist (for the sake of my aesthetic soul) that I don't want to read stories or emotions or anything of the kind into them'.[54]

The dangers of reading stories and emotions into paintings became the subject of her critique of the 1919 Royal Academy Summer Exhibition, written for the *Athenaeum* (now under the editorship of Middleton Murry, Katherine Mansfield's husband). At the Academy, genre painting still reigned unchallenged, every picture told a story, and every story celebrated the grandeur, fine feelings and splendid traditions of the British upper classes, or otherwise paid tribute 'in a general way to the island race'.[55] Her review unpicked these assumptions, and exposed the narrative impulse which drew the viewer to identify with the scene. Looking at 'Cocaine', a melodramatic painting of a woman in evening dress, with a man collapsed in her arms, she wrote, 'the queer thing is that one wants to be her. For a moment one pretends that one sits alone, disillusioned, in pink satin.'[56] Her comments endorsed Clive Bell's argument, that to respond to created form as if it was imitated form is to misunderstand its purpose; to read into a work of art 'the ordinary emotions of life' is to miss what it has to offer, reducing its significance to that of feelings that have already been experienced, so that 'no new thing is added to their lives, only the old material is stirred'.[57] Once Woolf had recognized the force of such arguments in relation to painting, she could not fail to see their implications for her own art of fiction: stereotypical plots that prompted predictable reactions had nothing to do with art. Yet there was a deeper paradox involved, since stories and emotions were the natural currency of narrative, even though they were often burdened with cultural meanings – how was it possible for the writer to avoid them altogether?

As Woolf's review of the Summer Exhibition had revealed, her society's cultural narratives were steeped in unspoken class assumptions. The ideal of significant form, by freeing itself from particular contextualizing detail, held out the promise of a more democratic experience of art. Roger Fry had recognized this, and suggested that one reason for the hostility to post-impressionist painting was that it was more accessible than many other forms of art: it required less specialized knowledge than, for example, the appreciation of Chinese porcelain, or early Italian frescoes. Its sensuousness and immediacy meant that 'one's maid' might understand it better than one did oneself.[58] Time has proved him right, although when he wrote this in 1920, it was still mainly the educated wealthy who patronized avant-garde art and literature, who employed Vanessa and Duncan Grant to decorate their dining rooms, bought their carpets from Fry's Omega Workshop, and subscribed to the Hogarth Press.

Virginia had been discussing aesthetics with Clive since 1907, and with Roger Fry since 1911; her much quoted sentence 'on or about December 1910 human character changed'[59] registered, among other things, the impact of Fry's first post-impressionist exhibition which had opened that November, reinforced by a sense of the ending of the Edwardian era with the King's death the previous May. Yet her announcement implies more than a revolution in artistic sensibility: the new art was itself an expression of changes in society, and even in the individual. 'The human soul . . . orientates itself afresh every now and then. It is doing so now',[60] she told the aspiring writer, Gerald Brenan. She shared with her most forward-looking contemporaries the belief that fiction should record the life of the mind, the life of imagination and of vision that, according to Fry and Bell, was also the subject of modern painting. For a while, such art would necessarily be fragmentary, incomplete: 'No one can see it whole . . . The best of us catch a glimpse of a nose, a shoulder, something turning away, always in movement.'[61] Such glimpses were the antithesis of the novels and art of the previous age, which she described in terms that recalled the Royal Academy, as 'large oil paintings of fabulous fleshy monsters complete from top to toe'.[62] The modernists concentrated on the world lived inside the mind: the primacy and function of acts of mind, especially in the engendering of narrative fictions, are much in evidence in Woolf's experimental writing, and their presence operates as the mark or guarantee that her stories are representations. Such acts register their fictional nature and origin, rather as the visible swirls of paint brush or palette knife did in post-impressionist painting.

The search for new forms was by no means confined to painting; yet although Virginia had been reviewing contemporary fiction since 1905 and counted E. M. Forster among her close friends, it was the Hogarth Press, with its aim of producing 'writing of merit which the ordinary publisher refuses'[63] that was to bring her into contact with her fellow modernists. Stories by the Woolfs and Katherine Mansfield were followed in 1919 by T. S. Eliot's verses and, in 1920, by Hope Mirrlees' 'Paris', 'a very obscure, indecent, and brilliant poem',[64] full of allusions to politics, culture, race, sex, even to Freud. Its idiosyncratic layout and mélange of languages and discourses, inspired by Apollinaire and Cocteau, made great demands on its typesetter – who was, of course, Virginia (three years later, she would set Eliot's 'The Waste Land').[65] But while indecency in a difficult poem was one thing, it was a somewhat different matter in novels, which, being supposedly more 'realistic', were liable to public prosecution if they crossed certain unspoken lines. Knowing this, the Woolfs turned down the opportunity of publishing that masterpiece of modern fiction, James Joyce's *Ulysses*, while still at an embryonic stage. In April 1918 Harriet Weaver, editor of *The Egoist* and publisher of Joyce's earlier *Portrait of the Artist as a Young Man*, took tea with the Woolfs, leaving with them the early chapters of *Ulysses*. Virginia tartly contrasted Miss Weaver's shy manner and conventional appearance – neat mauve suit and grey gloves – with the uninhibited contents of the brown-paper parcel left behind her: 'Why does their filth seek exit from her mouth?'[66] Leonard consulted a couple of commercial printers who warned him that any

British publisher would be laying himself open to legal action. A month later, Virginia wrote to Miss Weaver explaining politely that their hand press was too small for them to take on a work of any length.[67]

'I've been reading Joyce's novel. Its interesting as an experiment; he leaves out the narrative, and tries to give the thoughts',[68] she wrote to Roger Fry, a week after Miss Weaver's visit. A year later, rereading the opening chapters of *Ulysses* as they appeared in the *Little Review*, she was still impressed by its 'attempt to get thinking into literature',[69] and her 1919 essay, 'Modern Novels', struggled to give Joyce his due, praising his attempt to 'come closer to life ... by discarding most of the conventions which are commonly observed by the novelists'.[70] She acknowledged his courage, and even found his writing 'spiritual' compared to the materialism of 'the Edwardians' – Bennett, Galsworthy and Wells. Yet despite having no patience with the laws of censorship then in force, Joyce's preoccupation with sexuality and other bodily sensations, what she termed his 'indecency', upset her in ways that she never really analysed. She struggled to rationalize her feelings in a series of preparatory notes for her 1919 essay: it was a mistake to suppose the body's functions 'more real than anything else – a dodge now because of the veil of reticence, but a cheap one'.[71] Recalling Freud's theories, she reflected that 'it may be true that the subconscious mind dwells on indecency'.[72] She wondered how far her objections would apply to old favourites such as *Tristram Shandy* (which 'has a warmer temperature than Ulysses') or Byron's poem, *Don Juan*? Yet, '[f]or all I know, every great book has been an act of revolution'.[73] Might her sense of shock simply register Joyce's originality?

Her knee-jerk reaction to its 'indecency' exposed the gap between prim Miss Stephen, full of inadmissible anxieties, and sophisticated Mrs Woolf, the Bloomsbury habituée. She was often irritated by middle-class prudery: '[i]f the British spoke openly about W.C's, & copulation, then they might be stirred by universal emotions'.[74] It was only the 'mum[m]ified humbug' of South Kensington which refused to mention such things; Bloomsbury, by contrast, was 'life crude & impertinent perhaps, but living';[75] Bloomsbury could and did talk about semen and buggers, might even write about shit, if it could be made amusing.[76] But Bloomsbury's self-confidence, like that of Joyce and Lawrence, was fundamentally masculine, and while she could share its jokes and assumptions in private, in public, women were still expected to display ignorance or fastidiousness concerning the body's feelings and functions. There were whole areas of experience that could not be discussed in print under a woman's name, just as there were areas of life that could not be explored in a skirt. As a writer, she could never join in the boys' games, and Joyce's celebration of bodily experience acted as a painful reminder of her exclusion.

Rereading *Ulysses* when it was published in 1922, she disliked it even more, linking its 'dirt' with class, and dismissing it in her snootiest tones: '[a]n illiterate, underbred book ... the book of a self taught working man, & we all know how distressing they are'. But her distaste was in part a reaction to T. S. Eliot's unreserved enthusiasm, since 'Tom, great Tom, thinks this on a par with War & Peace!'[77] Eliot's admiration for Joyce seemed an implicit criticism of her own fiction, an assertion of male difference, solidarity, even superiority. The Woolfs had first met T. S. Eliot in November 1918, when Roger Fry (who knew everyone) told Leonard that Eliot was looking for a publisher for some of his post-*Prufrock* poems.[78] The Press printed a selection of these as their fourth publication, issuing them in May 1919, at about the same time as 'Kew Gardens'. Eliot was then working in a bank, and acting as Harriet Weaver's assistant on *The Egoist*. Though six years older than him, Virginia found Eliot a formidable young man: 'very intellectual, intolerant, with strong views of his own, & a poetic creed.'[79] She was intrigued by his mixture of diffidence and assurance, and alarmed by his dogmatism. His three great enthusiasms – for Ezra Pound (whose work she never read, assuming she would dislike it), Wyndham Lewis (who quarrelled irredeemably with Roger Fry and Bloomsbury) and Joyce – she found entirely alien.[80] A wary friendship developed between them in which she was always liable to feel put down, despite admiring his poetry, and perhaps learning from it how to 'leave out' (as Clive Bell had put it) 'with the boldest of them'.[81]

Against the 'he-goat'[82] voices of Joyce and Eliot, with their invest-ment in classical tradition, new feminine voices were being raised, however. The most challenging was that of Dorothy Richardson, whose long sequence of novels, *Pilgrimage* (begun in 1915, but not completed until 1938), narrated the moment-to-moment sensations of living as experienced by its heroine Miriam Henderson – the term 'stream of consciousness' was adopted to describe it.[83] Virginia recognized the power of the mind 'plaiting incessantly the many-coloured and innumerable threads of life',[84] and the resulting sharpness of perception, and sense of greater truth to experience achieved; she recognized that the style conveyed a feminine absorption in the nature of living for its own sake, but she felt Richardson's approach was unselective and limited in its viewpoint. Like Katherine Mansfield, she hoped to find a way of writing as a woman, but both of them thought *Pilgrimage* too close to monologue – in their own work, they sought more, and more differentiated, voices.

Woolf's experiments in fiction had alerted her to those of others, yet her attitude to her major competitors (as she felt them to be) was at best uneasy. She could praise Richardson and Joyce for inventing new techniques of representation in fiction, and finding new forms to convey the nature of lived experience. She shared their concern to record the processes of thought, as well as the material conditions of existence, but she found their fiction self-centred, egotistical, narrow[85] and lacking in structure (though as both *Pilgrimage* and *Ulysses* were still in the process of being written, their structures were more difficult to discern). She considered the fourth novel in the 'Pilgrimage' sequence, *The Tunnel*, 'better in its failure than most books in their success'[86] and commended Richardson's creation of a woman's sentence and the way she represented a woman's feelings, but she could not dismiss the fear that '[i]f she's good then I'm not', a fear that also coloured her response to the work of Joyce and Mansfield.[87] She learned from all three of them, but her very recognition of their originality, and of qualities in their writing which she would never attain, also disheartened her, causing her to devalue her own distinctive abilities beside theirs. On hearing of Katherine's early death, she admitted 'I was jealous of her writing – the only writing I have ever been jealous of'[88] (though this was not strictly true).

Yet dissatisfaction with competitors was also a way of defining her own territory. If they seemed too narrow, her own work must be alive with proliferating possibilities:

As we face each other in omnibuses and underground railways we are looking into the mirror . . . And the novelists in future will realise more and more the importance of these reflections, for of course there is not one reflection but an almost infinite number; those are the depths they will explore, those the phantoms they will pursue, leaving the description of reality more and more out of their stories, taking a knowledge of it for granted . . .

she wrote in 'The Mark on the Wall'.[89] As if exemplifying this idea, the narrator of 'An Unwritten Novel' sits in a railway carriage, reflecting upon the middle-aged woman seated opposite her, observing her as she scratches her back, eats a hard-boiled egg and makes desultory conversation. She constructs an elaborate fantasy around the mysterious woman which will come crashing down in the final paragraphs. She pictures her as an unhappy spinster, 'Minny Marsh', tormented by a spot between her shoulders that dates from a guilt-laden incident of her childhood, living reluctantly in Eastbourne with a condescending sister-in-law and a sniggering nephew, in an oppressive atmosphere of 'crusts and cruets, frills and ferns'.[90] But when the train reaches Eastbourne, the woman's son is there to meet her, and the narrator's invention collapses, first to her alarm and then to her delight, as she gladly exchanges her dreary invention for a sense of the self-renewing possibilities of the world beyond, and its inexhaustible powers of suggestion.

Writing the short stories had shown Woolf how to exploit those 'flights of fancy' that would not easily fit into a novel: such flights were as 'real' as any external incidents, and sometimes more vivid. An intensely imagined experience, even when it had no factual basis, could eclipse or overshadow external events. As Katherine Mansfield's 'Prelude', indeed most of her writings, had illustrated, most human beings live largely in dream or fantasy worlds, constantly transforming or remaking their actual surroundings. 'An Unwritten Novel' does not deal in fantasies of the self (Woolf had explored those in *Night and Day*), but rather in the way we respond to other human beings – and the way our reading habits may colour our reconstruction of them. The game of attributing character on the basis of appearance, what Virginia sometimes thought of as 'the railway game',[91] was amusing to play, yet full of dangers for the serious artist – dangers exemplified by Conan Doyle's detective, Sherlock Holmes, whose deductions were always proved right, at the cost of any sense of the complex and evasive nature of reality. Virginia's 'Unwritten Novel' voices an implicit protest against fiction that simplifies and sums up human beings, regarding them as primarily the product of their circumstances. The explanation of the woman's itching back is 'Freudian' (another form of determinism that Woolf found unsatisfactory[92]); the evocation of suburban life parodies the popular novelist Arnold Bennett, who summed up for Woolf the failings of exact observation and realistic representation.

Woolf later reworked the initial situation of this story into a critical essay, 'Mr Bennett and Mrs Brown', in which the mystery of Mrs Brown, sitting in the corner of the railway carriage, becomes a measure of the inadequacy of the materialist novelist.[93] It was characteristic of her that her insights usually came in the form of fictions; only later did she extract their theoretical lessons and argue them out as polemics.[94] But her argument with Arnold Bennett and his style of fiction was itself unexpectedly rooted in Fry's first post-impressionist exhibition of 1910, and the controversies it had generated. In his column in *The New Age* Bennett had recognized, with real prescience, not only that the value of the best of the new school was already 'permanently and definitely settled', but also that the lessons to be learned from them might also be applied to fiction, including his own.[95] Such paintings made others look wearisome, like 'the tops of chocolate boxes or . . . "art" photographs'. He wondered whether a day might come when his own art would look similarly jejune to a new generation of writers, and thus oblige him and his contemporaries 'to admit that we had been concerning ourselves unduly with inessentials, that we had been worrying ourselves to achieve infantile realisms? Well,' he concluded, 'that day would be a great and disturbing day – for us.'[96] This article was reprinted in *Books and Persons*, which Virginia reviewed for the *Times Literary Supplement* early in July 1917, between finishing 'The Mark on the Wall' and starting 'Kew Gardens'. At the time, this passage impressed her as evidence of Bennett's artistic integrity;[97] later she would find herself acting as spokeswoman for that rising generation.

'An Unwritten Novel' and the other short stories written around 1920 were five-finger exercises, preliminary sketches for the full-scale experiments to come. The Hogarth Press played a key role in freeing Woolf from the need to satisfy a commerical publisher. Vanessa, Clive and Roger Fry had opened new perspectives on the nature of art itself, encouraging Virginia to reject surface realism and to trust in her inner vision, to think of narrative in spatial or textural terms, and to aim for a form or structure which would embody the meaning of the work as a whole. Her developing critique of her contemporaries helped her to define what she was after herself, and how her goals differed from theirs. In her preliminary notes for the 1919 essay 'Modern Novels' she began to outline her own direction:

reality, or life, or interest, has come for us to lie rather in the emotions of people. We believe that we can say more about people's mind and feelings. Well then it becomes less necessary to dwell upon their bodies (. . . Why not in fact leave out bodies?) All sorts of new situations become possible . . . New visions of beauty; demanding, of course, a new form. We see stories where people did not see them in the past . . . Things do seem, suddenly for the most part, to compose a whole –[98]

As Katherine Mansfield wrote of 'Kew Gardens', 'anything may happen; her world is on tiptoe'.[99] It was now the shortest of steps to her first modernist novel, *Jacob's Room*.

MONDAY OR TUESDAY: THE AFTERMATH

The first publication of the Hogarth Press, Two Stories *(Virginia's 'The Mark on the Wall' and Leonard's 'Three Jews'), was issued in mid-July 1917, with four woodcuts by Dora Carrington, in an edition of 150 copies, most of which sold in the first three months.[100] Virginia was in the middle of writing* Night and Day. *'Kew Gardens' was finished the following summer, and typesetting began just before Armistice Day, 11 November 1918 (and a fortnight before the completion of her novel).[101] On 12 May 1919* Kew Gardens *became the Press's fifth publication, with two woodcuts by Vanessa, in an edition of 150 sold at two shillings each.[102] By the end of the month, Harold Child, writing anonymously in the* Times Literary Supplement, *had pronounced it 'a work of art, made, "created", as we say, finished, four-square; a thing of original and therefore strange beauty, with its own "atmosphere", its own vital force' – he even seems to have picked up the allusion to Renoir's 'Les Parapluies'.[103] Orders poured in, including twelve copies for Mudie's lending library.[104] Richard Madley, the printer who worked for Roger Fry's Omega workshop, provided a second edition of 500 copies in June, and at the same time Francis Meynell's Pelican Press printed a second edition of* The Mark on the Wall.[105]

Written first, these two stories stood last in her collection Monday or Tuesday *(1921). The others were probably composed around 1920, though most cannot be dated with any certainty – the volume as a whole has a 'post-war' atmosphere, created by three references to the signing of the Versailles Peace Treaty in June 1919.[106] It opens with 'A Haunted House', a story 'which would be very sentimental were it not exquisitely strange' (Harold Child again) – Virginia had doubts about its inclusion.[107] It was inspired by the haunting of Asheham, which, according to Leonard, 'sounded as if two people were walking from room to room, opening and shutting doors, sighing, whispering'. He added, 'I can immediately see, hear, and smell the house when I read the opening words'.[108] In March 1919, the Woolfs learned that the owner intended to terminate their lease; that summer they found and bought Monk's House in Rodmell, where they settled for good. The story's nostalgic air may reflect Virginia's sense of its loss. The second story, 'A Society', is very different in mood, being a sharply critical feminist fable. While a couple of reviewers recognized its brilliance, it was more often the piece most disliked. Mary Agnes Hamilton, reviewing it for the feminist weekly,* Time and Tide, *while admiring the collection as a whole, dismissed it as 'quite a stupid story', though it is seminal for so much of Woolf's later writing.[109] 'An Unwritten Novel' was begun early in 1920, and published in the* London Mercury *in July, before appearing in* Monday or Tuesday. *Virginia was already planning 'A String Quartet' when she visited the house of the shipowner George Booth, on 7 March 1920, to hear a Schubert quintet.[110] By October she had decided on the title of the collection, but was afraid she had left herself too little time to write the title story.[111]*

Vanessa made a woodcut for the front board of Monday or Tuesday *in the form of a circle with curlicues (echoing Fry's 'Omega'), and provided four further woodcuts. A local Richmond printer, F. T. McDermott, who had helped Leonard out on earlier occasions, produced an edition of 1,000 copies. The result, according to Leonard, was 'one of the worst printed books ever published, certainly the worst ever published by the Hogarth Press'.[112] Even the enthusiastic Harold Child admitted to 'one slight complaint': 'Mrs Bell's delightful woodcuts . . . have left ghosts of themselves on the pages opposite; and also they show through the paper, so that the backs are difficult to read'.[113] Virginia was even more outspoken: it was 'an odious object, which leaves black stains wherever it touches'.[114] On its publication in the first week of April 1921, Woolf's mood rose and fell according to her reviews. She was, she felt, in competition, not only with Leonard's* three Stories of the East, *hand-printed at the Hogarth Press and published a week or so later, but far more threateningly, with Lytton's* Queen Victoria, *his follow-up to* Eminent Victorians *and a runaway success, with 5,000 copies sold in the first four hours.[115]*

Work on Jacob's Room *ground to a halt: 'I'm a failure as a writer. I'm out of fashion; old; shan't do any better; have no headpiece', she wrote on 8 April. There were three columns of praise devoted to Lytton in the* Times Literary Supplement, *whereas she had only received a short notice that was 'quite unintelligent', and entirely failed to register that she was 'after something interesting'.[116] In fact the reviewer was, once again, Harold Child, and though he questioned whether it was possible to achieve the effects of 'non-representational' art in language, he also found touches of beauty, humour and wit.[117] But she was in no mood to read between the lines, and was further disheartened when her American publisher, George Doran, turned the book down (this was on a Friday). By the Sunday she was ready to analyse her changing emotions as 'symptoms of the disease . . . The first day one's miserable: the second happy.' Her old friend Desmond MacCarthy had reviewed the book warmly for the* New Statesman, *making her 'feel important (& its that that one wants)'.[118] On Tuesday and Wednesday she noted 'more symptoms . . . I'd worn through the acute stage' and 'the latest symptom – complete absence of jealousy'. She would, she promised herself, feel 'instantly warm & pleased' if there was a long, appreciative review of Leonard's* Stories of the East *in the* Times Literary Supplement: *'I think this is perfectly true. Most people, though, would not have to write this down.'[119] By Friday, she was comparing Lytton's huge sales with her own insignificant ones, and wondering whether they gave any indication of what their relative reputations might be in the future.[120] On the following Sunday, her thoughts had turned outwards to the threatened General Strike and Leonard's plans for his next novel, while she doubted whether* Monday or Tuesday *would sell 500 copies, or even cover its expenses.[121] She was wrong, but not by very much: by April 1922, they had sold 503 copies, and when Leonard closed the account in 1924, the Press had only sold 643, making a small profit of just under twelve pounds.[122] On the other hand, the American publisher Donald Brace made an offer for it, thus embarking on a long and successful association with the Woolfs.*

Whether because of poor sales or for some other reason, Monday or Tuesday *was not included in the uniform edition of Virginia's work published by the Press in 1929. She continued to write short stories (she would later complete a substantial group set at Clarissa Dalloway's party), though many of them were left unpublished. The short story remained for Woolf a place for experiment and an occasion for learning – their value was primarily for her, rather than for her readers. One exception was 'Kew Gardens', which, because of its complex interplay between verbal and pictorial effects, was reprinted by the Hogarth Press in 1927 in a limited (third) edition with a new set of woodcuts by Vanessa. This time the illustrations surrounded and sometimes erupted into the printed text, making their interaction visually explicit. The new edition, 500 numbered copies in a larger format than the original, was probably planned as the first of a series of illustrated books to be published by the Press, but it was the only one to appear, a unique synthesis of the sisters' arts.[123]*

Two years after Virginia's death in 1941, Leonard published a new collection of her short stories, entitled A Haunted House. *The introduction explained that she had been planning a volume of short stories, to include most of* Monday or Tuesday, *'as well as some published subsequently in magazines and some unpublished'. He had tried to fulfil her intentions, knowing that she had decided to omit 'A Society', and probably the prose-poem 'Blue and Green' as well.[124] It*

MONDAY OR TUESDAY

VIRGINIA WOOLF

WOODCUTS BY
VANESSA BELL

was wartime, and there were eager readers everywhere: 6,000 copies were printed at the beginning of 1944, and a further 9,000 within the year. When the volume became a Penguin Modern Classic in 1973, 33,000 copies were printed in the first year – more than confirming her highest hopes for her posthumous reputation.[125] In 1985, the Canadian editor Susan Dick brought together Woolf's Complete Shorter Fiction, *including a number of early unpublished stories, as well as those from* Monday or Tuesday *and her later stories. With the publication of this volume, Woolf's readers could finally see for themselves the key role that her short stories – and the Press that prompted them – had played in her development as a novelist.*

4

In Search of Jacob

Like blocks of tin soldiers the army covers the cornfield, moves up the hillside, stops, reels slightly this way and that, and falls flat, save that, through field-glasses, it can be seen that one or two pieces still agitate up and down like fragments of broken match-stick. [p.136][1]

Woolf's third novel, *Jacob's Room*, is her protest against the First World War, and the shocking impersonality of its killing machine. She makes it by relating the life of one individual in human close-up, that of a young man whose life will prematurely come to an end. By the final page, Jacob's shoes, like his room, are empty, and his death must stand for that of a generation. 'The reason why it is easy to kill another person', she wrote, 'must be that one's imagination is too sluggish to conceive what his life means to him – the infinite possibilities of a succession of days which are furled in him, & have already been spent.'[2] The novel arouses our imagination on behalf of Jacob Flanders, whose surname announces his ultimate destiny. Scarborough, where he grows up, is a holiday resort on the east coast, notorious as the first British town to have suffered civilian casualties when it was shelled by German battleships in December 1914 (a famous recruiting poster had warned 'Remember Scarborough!').[3] Yet, as always, Woolf evokes the desolation of death through a corresponding intensity of life and feeling. The novel hardly mentions the war, yet we read it knowing that Jacob, like millions of other young men, is doomed merely by when and where he was born. That knowledge brightens and darkens its pages, leaving the reader to ask, 'Why did it happen?', 'How did it happen?'

Katherine Mansfield, reviewing *Night and Day*, for the *Athenaeum*

his hair as he ⊘ did so there remains over something which
can ⊘h never be conveyed to a second person save by Jacob
himself. Moreover, part of this is not Jacob but ~~Arthur~~ Richard
Bonamy; the room; the market carts; the hour; the very moment
of history. Thn consider the effect of ~~sex~~ us, how between man and
woman it hangs, wavy, tremulous, so that there's a valley,
here's a peak, when in truth^perhaps all's as flat as my hand. Even
the exact words get the wrong accent on them. ~~And~~ but something is ~~always~~ impelling one to hum^vibrating, like that hawk moth,
~~vibrating~~ at the mouth of the cavern of mystery, endowing
Jacob Flanders with all sorts of qualities he had not at all,
--for though ~~he~~ certainly/^he sat talking to Bonamy, half of what he
said was too dull to repeat; much unintelligible (about
a ~~square root~~ unknown people and Parliament) ; what remains is matter of
guess work. And ~~yet~~ over him we hang vibrating.

" Yes, said Captain Barfoot, knocking out his pipe on ~~the~~ Betty
Flanders hob, & ~~few~~ buttoning his coat, "it doubles the
work, but I dont mind that"
He was now town councillor. ~~what~~
~~he asked, rising to go~~ They looked at the night. which was
the same as the ~~night of~~ London night, only a good deal
more transparent. ~~A~~ Churches ~~bells~~ down in the town
~~before~~ were striking gently Eleven o'clock.   The wind
was off the ~~sea~~ And all the bedroom windows were
Dark, whereas in London at this hour
What news of Jacob? said Captain Barfoot.
And ~~Betty replied~~

he ...

in November 1919, had criticized it for its refusal to engage with the war:

We had thought that this [pre-war] world was vanished for ever, that it was impossible to find on the great ocean of literature a ship that was unaware of what has been happening. Yet here is *Night and Day* fresh, new, and exquisite, a novel in the tradition of the English novel. In the midst of our admiration it makes us feel old and chill: we had never thought to look upon its like again![4]

Privately and more explicitly, she wrote to Murry, 'it is a lie in the soul. The war never has been: that is what its message is. I don't want (G[od]. forbid!) mobilisation and the violation of Belgium, but the novel can't just leave the war out.'[5]

Mansfield did not know, and Woolf could not yet admit to herself, that in order to write *Night and Day* at all, she had withdrawn into the apparently stable, pre-war world where it seemed as if individuals could still decide for themselves what shape their lives might take – the war had interrupted all such expectations. With the coming of conscription in 1916, no one could call their lives their own, and the shadows of war were everywhere – as 'The Mark on the Wall' and 'Kew Gardens' had registered. 'The war [had] opened its chasm at the feet of all this innocence and ignorance',[6] polarizing political differences, cutting off the past from the present, the Victorians from the moderns, visions of romance and marriage from the muddle that was modern love.

Virginia was a little older than the generation of young men who joined up directly from school, university or first jobs. Her husband Leonard, her young brother Adrian and her closest male friends refused to fight and all survived the war, but the senseless death of a young man in the prime of life was only too actual to her, through the premature death of her brother Thoby from typhoid, ten years earlier. Leonard's younger brothers, Philip and Cecil, inseparable from childhood, joined the Royal Hussars together. At Cambrai, late in 1917, they were struck by the same shell, killing Cecil and wounding Philip. The Woolfs visited Philip in hospital at Fishmongers Hall, a grim illustration of 'the uselessness of it all, breaking these people & mending them again'.[7] When Philip recovered, he seemed aimless, only wanting to get back to France. The Woolfs helped him to collect Cecil's poems, write an introduction and typeset them, to occupy him in the meantime. These poems became the third publication of the Hogarth Press, sandwiched between Mansfield's 'Prelude' and Eliot's 'Poems'. 'The more one sees of the effects on young men who should be happy,' Woolf observed, 'the more one detests the whole thing.'[8]

Six months before Cecil's death, she had reviewed Siegfried Sassoon's collection of poems, *The Old Huntsman*. She admired his war poetry for the way it allowed a savage indignation to build up beneath 'jaunty matter-of-fact statements', using the power of realism to create a moral shock. 'It is realism of the right, of the poetic kind.'[9] Reviewing his second collection in the following year, she recognized that 'The vision of that "hell where youth and laughter go" has been branded upon him too deeply to allow him to tolerate consolation or explanation. He can only state a little of what he has seen'.[10] In stark contrast to Sassoon's denunciations were the patriotic sonnets of Rupert Brooke, written from the anticipation rather than the experience of fighting. The five-year-old Rupert had played with the ten-year-old Virginia on the sands at St Ives. Almost twenty years later, she had been drawn into his set at Cambridge, coining the term 'Neo-Pagans' to describe them. She went camping with them, and stayed with Rupert at the Old Vicarage at Grantchester in 1911, where they bathed naked together, though their friendship did not, apparently, survive her marriage to a Jew.

Brooke was to die of blood poisoning on Skyros, on his way to Gallipoli in 1915. After his death, his spectacular good looks, sexual glamour and impassioned poetry (which Virginia did not much like[11]) became legendary, and myths grew up around him that she thought distorting and distasteful. She agreed to review Edward Marsh's adulatory edition of Brooke's poems for the *Times Literary Supplement*, intending to correct the balance, but then found herself unable to do so, obliged instead to write 'as decorously as possible'.[12] Privately, she agreed with James Strachey, that Rupert had been 'jealous, moody, ill-balanced, all of which I knew, but can hardly say in writing'.[13] Instead, she presented his life as tragically, typically interrupted: 'One turns from the thought of him . . . to wonder and to question still: what would he have been, what would he have done?'[14]

Woolf had instinctively hated violence from childhood. She

remembered the exact moment when she had turned against fighting: she and Thoby had been 'pommelling each other with our fists' on the lawn at St Ives when suddenly she thought, 'why hurt another person? I dropped my hand instantly, and stood there, and let him beat me.' A sense of 'hopeless sadness' followed: 'I slunk off alone, feeling horribly depressed.'[15] It was a precocious reaction, yet unsurprising, given the humane, high-minded atmosphere in which she grew up. To her father, Leslie Stephen, 'all wars were hateful'. '[D]uring the South African War', she remembered, 'he lay awake thinking that he heard the guns on the battlefield'; his sons might follow any profession they chose, 'with the exception of the Army and Navy'.[16] Her aunt, Caroline Stephen, had been a Quaker convert and a committed pacifist.[17] Even the killing of animals for sport, which loomed so large in British upper-class life, lay outside the Stephen girls' experience. Vanessa wrote to Virginia from Scotland in 1908, horrified at her husband's indulgence in blood sports: 'Clive killed three rabbits. Oh Billy! poor little furry beasts. It surpasses my imagination entirely, this wish to kill – does it yours?'[18]

'We were all C[onscientious]. O[bjector].'s in the Great war',[19] Virginia wrote, looking back. Her friends were united in their condemnation of war and militarism, and, when conscription was introduced in January 1916, found themselves facing appeals tribunals, with powers to impose sentences of labour, imprisonment, and even to insist upon military service (rumours circulated that C.O.s were being sent to France, to be court-martialled and shot). Lytton Strachey made a famous appearance before the Hampstead tribunal, carefully seating himself on an air cushion for the proceedings.[20] Though his appeal failed, he later got off on medical grounds. Leonard (probably the least pacifist) was also exempted: a congenital tremor of the hands made him unfit for service, though he also included Virginia's ill health in his submission.[21] The best outcome for those in good health was to be granted exemption on condition that they carried out work 'of national importance', which might range from Maynard Keynes's work for the Treasury, to agricultural labour. Clive Bell, who had risked being disinherited by publishing an anti-war pamphlet in 1915, was working on Ottoline Morrell's farm at Garsington, and Duncan Grant and David Garnett also worked on the land, first in Suffolk, and then at

Charleston, under the Downs near Asheham, where Vanessa had moved with her two children in September 1916. So did Adrian Stephen, when he was not defending C.O.s at tribunal hearings. Bertrand Russell was arrested, fined and lost his Cambridge lectureship for his uncompromising attacks on the government. In 1918 he was imprisoned for an article written for the *Tribunal*, the organ of the 'No Conscription Fellowship' – Adrian was its secretary, Lytton was a member, and even the apolitical Vanessa took on part-time voluntary work for it.[22]

During the early years of the war, Virginia suffered from a profound sense of alienation, perhaps intensified by illness. In January 1915, she attended a concert at the Queens Hall where 'the patriotic sentiment was so revolting that I was nearly sick'.[23] She could feel overwhelmed by the 'violent and filthy passions'[24] on display. *The Times* (as the organ of government) was particularly to blame, publishing shameless anti-German propaganda. 'I become steadily more feminist', she wrote to Margaret Llewelyn Davies, 'owing to the Times, which I read at breakfast and wonder how this preposterous masculine fiction keeps going a day longer – without some vigorous young woman pulling us together and marching through it – Do you see any sense in it? I feel as if I were reading about some curious tribe in Central Africa –'.[25] The possible intervention of vigorous young women was not simply a private fantasy. Among women on the left, there had been proposals for a 'Peace Expeditionary Force' that would form a living barrier between the armies and so somehow bring the whole killing machine to a halt, on the supposition that soldiers would not fire on defenceless women.[26]

The Women's Movement had split over whether or not to support the fighting, and Woolf's sympathies were with the women working for peace. Unlike her mother and sister, she had been interested in the Movement from her youth. Janet Case, her Greek teacher, and Mary Sheepshanks, principal of Morley College (where Woolf gave adult education classes from 1905 to 1907), were among her earliest mentors, while other old friends like Pippa Strachey and Ray Strachey (Lytton's sister and sister-in-law) were active in the (non-militant) NUWSS (National Union for Women's Suffrage Societies); Ray later wrote the standard history of the movement (*The Cause*, 1928). Virginia's New

Year's resolution for 1910 was to make her own contribution. 'You impressed me so much the other night with the wrongness of the present state of affairs that I feel that action is necessary',[27] she wrote to Janet Case, who found her some voluntary work in a suffrage office, preparing for the coming election. 'I spend hours writing names like Cowgill on envelopes', she reported. 'The office . . . is just like a Wells novel.'[28] It later appeared in *Night and Day*, where Mary Datchet, the novel's 'New Woman', also works for a Society for Adult Suffrage.[29] Woolf made fun of the earnest, parochial views of Mary's co-workers, while admiring her single-minded commitment – such inconsistencies ran all the way through her political attitudes, contrasting sharply with Leonard's calm convictions. She liked to have room for manoeuvre, for doubts, detachment and sudden rushes of sympathy. Although she subscribed to an idealistic form of socialism – 'I'm one of those who are hampered by the psychological hindrance of owning capital'[30] – she could be thoughtlessly snobbish and intolerant. Despite being a committed feminist, she disliked the word and dissociated herself from those aspects of the Women's Movement that she found tedious, humourless and, during the war years, mindlessly patriotic.

On the evening of 4 August 1914, the day England declared war on Germany, the Woolfs were living quietly at Asheham, but in London an 'International Peace Meeting of Women' was scheduled to take place at Kingsway Hall. Its original aim had been to support 'Britain's stand for peace', but news of the ultimatum to Germany that morning had ended hopes of British neutrality. Even so, Millicent Fawcett, president of the NUWSS, decided to go ahead with it, addressing an audience of 2,000 women, while hundreds more had to be turned away. Two contradictory resolutions were adopted: that women should take up their duties as citizens within their local communities, and that the government should be urged to back initiatives for peace. The second resolution was taken round to Downing Street, where the Cabinet awaited the German response to their ultimatum, due by 11.00 p.m. that evening.[31] With the declaration of war, the NUWSS gave its support to the government, which in turn granted an amnesty to militant suffragettes who, like Christabel Pankhurst, had been imprisoned. Once released, they turned their energies to the war effort, recruiting men to the army, women to munitions factories, and denouncing shirkers, pacifists and Bolsheviks. Their newspaper, formerly *The Suffragette*, now became *Britannia*. But many other women opposed the war on moral grounds – women like Janet Case, Mary Sheepshanks and Margaret Llewelyn Davies, who felt isolated and betrayed. 'It was lonely in those days', wrote Helena Swanwick, 'I felt that men had dropped their end of the burden of living, and left the women to carry on, while they played this silly, bloody game of massacring the sons of women.'[32]

There was still a great deal of work for them to do: committed to peace and reconstruction after the deluge, women's groups sought to advance international understanding and co-operation through a 'League of Nations'. Feminist, pacifist and socialist, Margaret Llewelyn Davies, who had met Virginia in the years before the war, probably through Janet Case, now became a close friend of both the Woolfs, drawing them into her work for the Women's Co-operative Guild, an organized body of 32,000 working women of which she was secretary. In 1913, the Woolfs had attended the Annual Conference at Newcastle, where Virginia was impressed by the courage and commitment of the speakers, yet felt herself excluded, 'irretrievably cut off from the actors . . . an outcast from the flock.' Their demands for shorter working hours and better wages and living conditions were urgent and practical, unlike her own concerns, privileged as she was to 'fly free at the end of a short length of capital'.[33] But they had longer-term aims, too: in addition to the vote, they were demanding education, changes in the divorce law, peace, disarmament and the spread of co-operative principles.

Margaret Llewelyn Davies supported Leonard through the early years of the war, the years of Virginia's breakdown. She encouraged him to write about the value and example of the co-operative movement (as he would do in *Co-operation and the Future of Industry*, 1919), and to investigate how an international agency, regulating and, if necessary, arbitrating between nations might operate – his blueprint for the League of Nations, *International Government* (1916), was the result. She introduced him to Fabian socialism and its most influential exponents, Beatrice and Sydney Webb. In doing so, she played a key role in determining the direction of his future career.

Virginia felt at once proud of Leonard's success in this new political sphere, and uncomfortably overlooked. She found the Webbs cold, joyless, practical and prosaic. She could feel childishly jealous of their respect for Leonard's views and indifference to her own (Beatrice made her feel 'insignificant' and 'practically non-existent', giving her 'a sense of my own nothingness in her field of vision'[34]). On the other hand, she genuinely liked and admired Margaret Llewelyn Davies (Mary Datchet in *Night and Day* is, to some extent, a portrait of her), though she sometimes found Margaret's different scale of values annoying (as when she and Janet Case dismissed *Night and Day*[35]). Even so, she sympathized with Margaret's ideals, and in the autumn of 1916, agreed to host the monthly meetings of the Richmond branch of the Women's Co-operative Guild at Hogarth House, and organize speakers for them, duties she carried out conscientiously for the next four years. Ten years later, affection for Margaret prompted her to write an introduction to *Life As We Have Known It*, a collection of working-class women's accounts of their lives which Margaret had assembled.[36]

Support for the war effort won women the vote in January 1918, but a more general disillusion with the fighting had already set in as hostilities dragged on and the death toll continued to rise. Woolf later recognized what women had stood to gain from the war, seeing in retrospect that they had unconsciously encouraged men, 'unconsciously . . . desired our splendid war', because they were so desperate to exercise their pent-up energies, to escape from 'the education of the private house with its cruelty, its poverty, its hypocrisy, its immorality, its inanity'.[37] When the vote was granted, she was sceptical of its value, comparing it to the conferment of establishment honours (which she always refused). 'Its like a knighthood; might be useful to impress people one despises.'[38] Two months later, she and Leonard attended a rally at Kingsway Hall to celebrate the achievement of the vote, but after the initial thrill of seeing the size of the crowd, she grew bored and disappointed with the failure of the many women speakers to rise to the occasion. She noticed the bright spring sunshine outside – 'a difficult light for speakers to speak down'.[39]

The Armistice of November 1918 brought the killing to an end, and with it grew hopes for a better society, less riven by class and gender distinctions. But the scale of loss – almost a million British and Commonwealth soldiers killed – was hard to absorb. As Katherine

Mansfield had written to Murry, 'nothing can ever be the same . . . as artists, we are traitors if we feel otherwise: we have to take it into account and find new expressions, new moulds for our new thoughts and feelings'.[40] With *Night and Day* completed and published in November 1919, Woolf was ready to do just that, yet the scale of the war, its peculiar horrors, even its distance from non-combatants, made it difficult to confront. The only possible way of making sense of the catastrophe was to focus on the fate of an individual, and his loss for those who loved him. But to show such a tragedy truthfully, as it actually happened, the victim must have no inkling that his life was going to be interrupted and ended, nor should death confer an empty elegiac grandeur on life, when its effect had actually been to drain away meaning: in other words, her hero was not to be heroic. And there was a further difficulty: though Jacob is the victim of the darkness at the heart of patriarchal culture, only the narrator can know that. Jacob himself cannot see it. Instead, he shares in the illusions of his culture and enjoys its privileges. Woolf's response to the war as a pacifist, her compassion for its victims, was thus in tension with her sense as a feminist that men had made it happen.

Jacob Flanders is the unknown warrior, individual and representative, yet minus the distortions of sentiment or retrospective glory. There is nothing military about him, for this was a war fought largely by civilians in uniform. He is both unknown and unknowable, for the war had made irrelevant old certainties, traditional narratives in which young men sought out their destinies or their partners, moved towards self-knowledge, enlightenment, or even revelation. Woolf had put behind her the forms of nineteenth-century realist fiction which falsified, she thought, by assuming the novelist's omniscience. Instead, her novel admits to uncertainties at every turn. She set out to write a novel about not knowing, about the unknowability of Jacob, presenting him in a series of episodes only loosely strung together. The narrative searches for him, calls for him, as does his brother Archer on the second page, and his friend Bonamy on the last. 'It is no use trying to sum people up', she tells us. 'One must follow hints, not exactly what is said, nor yet entirely what is done.' [p.24] Jacob himself remains mysterious, opaque, as other people always are, as men are to women, as Thoby had seemed to his sister:

why are we yet surprised . . . by a sudden vision that the young man in the chair is . . . the most real, the most solid, the best known to us – why indeed? For the moment after we know nothing about him.

Such is the manner of our seeing. Such the conditions of our love. [p.60]

The nature and limitations of our perceptions are determined by who we are: 'Either we are men, or we are women. Either we are cold, or we are sentimental. Either we are young, or growing old.' [p.60] These are 'the conditions of our love' that we cannot choose or change, any more than we can change the time of our birth within the process that is history. Jacob's experiences and his responses to them alternate with other people's views of him – they are no more than 'hints and guesses' since each individual viewpoint is strictly limited. While Clara Durrant writes in her diary, 'I like Jacob Flanders . . . He is so unworldly' [p.59], Jacob himself is telling his friends a dirty joke. The novel seeks to hold together the multiplicity, inconsistency and variety that characterize our experience of living, that belongs to 'Monday or Tuesday', by providing pictures rather than explanations, questions rather than answers, the elusiveness of the short story rather than the solidity of the novel.

Writing the short stories had shown her how to write a different kind of novel, a novel that reflected the uncertainties of the post-war world. Its episodic structure was like nothing so much as a sequence of short stories, which is how she had originally envisaged it. In the second week of January 1920, still surrounded by reviews and congratulations on *Night and Day* (published the previous November), she began to write 'An Unwritten Novel', setting it on 11 January 1920, the day after the Treaty of Versailles had been formally ratified.[41] About a fortnight later (and the day after her thirty-eighth birthday) she suddenly realized that she had discovered how to write her next novel, even though she did not yet know what it would be about. 'Suppose one thing should open out of another – as in An Unwritten Novel – only not for 10 pages but 200 or so – doesn't that give the looseness & lightness I want: doesn't that get closer & yet keep form & speed, & enclose everything, everything? . . . conceive mark on the wall, K[ew]. G[ardens]. & unwritten novel taking hands & dancing in unity . . . I see immense possibilities in the form'.[42]

The differences between Woolf's short story 'An Unwritten Novel' and *Jacob's Room* are as significant as their similarities: 'An Unwritten Novel' is an extended fantasy, a fiction within a fiction, while *Jacob's Room* avoids inner narratives, yet the two are closely connected, and at the end of the short story, as the mysterious figures of mother and son walk away, they seem to walk straight into Woolf's as yet unwritten novel, becoming Betty Flanders and her son Jacob. As if to emphasize their links, Woolf rewrote the railway carriage scenario of 'An Unwritten Novel' as chapter III of *Jacob's Room*, but this time the middle-aged woman (Mrs Norman) is the subject, while a strange young man (Jacob, going up to Cambridge in 1906) becomes the object of her gaze in a reversal, perhaps even a deliberate reworking of the earlier story. Mrs Norman is initially alarmed ('it is a fact that men are dangerous'), then reassured ('after all he was just the same age as her own boy'). Their encounter rehearses the novel's puzzles over perception and knowledge: 'Nobody sees any one as he is, let alone an elderly lady sitting opposite a strange young man in a railway carriage. They see a whole – they see all sorts of things – they see themselves . . .' [pp.23–4]

'Let us suppose that the Room will hold it together', Woolf told herself, three months later, sitting down to begin 'a work of fiction to be called, perhaps, Jacob's Room'[43] (it was unusual for her to begin with a title). The 'opening out' principle devised for 'An Unwritten Novel' allowed her to invent as she went along, and use those inventions to carry the story forward, rather than having to follow some preconceived plan; but its freedom was to be kept in check by a counter-balancing principle of enclosure, 'the Room'. Rooms carry complex meanings as the spaces we occupy and shape around ourselves, metaphorically as well as literally, and, like physical appearance, they may be used to characterize their owner. In Woolf's first handwritten draft, the description of Jacob's room at Trinity College was followed by a parallel account of a room belonging to a woman undergraduate at Newnham, that of Angela Williams,[44] and these two student rooms, full of their hopes, ideas and aspirations, were then followed by a description of Mrs Pascoe's narrow cottage in Cornwall, crowded with a sense of the body and its needs: 'there would be no escaping the body. An earth closet out in the rain – sickness – a

woman's period – copulation upstairs in the double bed, – childbirth
– as the room filled with bodies, it would be impossible not to think
solely of these functions & desires'.[45] But Mrs Pascoe's cottage, like
the chapter on Angela Williams, would be omitted altogether from the
published text.

Rooms, like our bodies or our lives, express us yet are only partly
ours, carrying the marks of our predecessors as well as our own
histories. They had already fulfilled something of this diagnostic function in *Night and Day*, where Ralph Denham's room with its tame
rook, its shabbiness, muddle and college photos expresses something
of his character and history.[46] There is an echo of E. M. Forster's
The Longest Journey (Woolf had reviewed it for the *Times Literary
Supplement* in 1907[47]), where Ricky's room at Cambridge with its
photograph of Stockholm provides a key to who he really is. Woolf
offsets private rooms with public spaces, and the 'opening out' implied
by streets, theatres, restaurants, colleges. Such public spaces are filled
with people absorbed in their own concerns, who see and hear each
other without ever meeting, for first at Scarborough, and more insistently in London, walk-on parts proliferate in the novel, creating a
sense of a city swarming with individual lives. At Mudie's Corner
(where New Oxford Street crosses Museum Street), 'Mr Spalding
going to the city looked at Mr Charles Budgeon bound for Shepherd's
Bush', while little Johnnie Sturgeon swung down the staircase of an
omnibus and 'was soon out of sight – for ever' [pp.53–4]. Elsewhere,
in a café, 'Nelly Jenkinson, the typist, crumbled her cake indifferently
enough . . . The coal merchant read the *Telegraph* without stopping',
and Mrs Parsons brushed the crumbs from her furs.[48] They recall
Joyce's Dubliners or T. S. Eliot's city of flowing crowds, alleyways and
cheap tea rooms (though Woolf wasn't to hear *The Waste Land* until
June 1922, when the manuscript of *Jacob's Room* was already being
typed out[49]). As if to offset the sense of teeming strangeness, the
impossibility of knowing other people, Woolf familiarizes them by
naming them. As a device, it is sometimes suspect, and it can hold up
the action as well as move it forward, but it does allow for 'interlocking
wheels', the complex interaction of different social scenes and settings.

These multiplying characters, many of them glimpsed only momentarily, contrast with the purposeful and elaborately coincidental plot-

weaving of the traditional novel, which Woolf had avoided in *The Voyage Out*, found wearisome in *Night and Day*, and now rejected altogether in *Jacob's Room*. But she did retain the Victorian novel's fondness for generalizing reflections – on the tiers of the opera house as a figure for class difference, on the role of Japanese water flowers as a figure for the frail and deceptive nature of romance, and on the great dome of the British Museum Reading Room as a figure for patriarchal culture, perhaps even for the collective male brain.[50] Such set pieces, like the confident movement of the narrative from one scene to the next, from London traffic to a shepherd on a fell, from King's College Chapel to a boat off the Scilly Isles,[51] establish a sense of control and purpose. But one aspect of her subject remained a problem.

Though Virginia had never had a formal education, she had enjoyed something of the Cambridge experience at second hand – she had learned Greek, read Plato and the philosopher G. E. Moore, and had met Thoby's Cambridge friends and listened to them talking evening after evening at Gordon Square. Thus she had acquired the materials with which to re-create Jacob's intellectual life; but his physical life, the maleness that would condemn him to the killing fields, was another matter altogether. Much though she had loved Thoby, she had grown up knowing virtually nothing of male sexuality, except when it had intruded on her in hateful ways, ways that seemed to have no connection with the romance and love that had invested her parents' relationship, or her half-sister Stella's short-lived marriage. She was twenty-five when Jack Hills, Stella's widower, enlightened her as to 'the part played by sex in the life of the ordinary man. He shocked me a little, wholesomely. He told me that young men talked incessantly of women; and "had" them incessantly.'[52] If Jacob was to carry conviction, he must be given the body as well as the mind of a young man: he is seen sailing and riding to hounds – should he also be seen making love?

The novel's narrator identifies herself as ten years older than Jacob, and a woman – her sexual difference making Jacob a source of curiosity to her, even of excitement: 'the effect of sex . . . hangs wavy, tremulous' between men and women; the narrator hums vibrating over her subject 'like the hawk moth' [p.61] – a comparison suggesting the attracting power of pheromones, as well as the hawk hovering over its prey. When Lawrence and Joyce had written the body into their fiction,

Woolf had found their 'indecency' offensive, but at the same time she was conscious of having avoided the issue in *Night and Day*; one reviewer had ridiculed her quartet of lovers as 'four impassioned snails'.[53] If, as she constantly told herself, freedom was 'the main point',[54] the key to empowering herself as a writer, she had to tackle Jacob's sexual life as directly as his social and intellectual development – yet powerful constraints held her back, and not merely those of ignorance: in 1920, as well as legal limits on what could be published, there was still a great deal of hypocrisy as to what it was acceptable for a woman to know, even a married woman. Woolf recognized that for a woman to write knowingly about a young man's sexual life and feelings as a woman (that is, under her own writing name), threatened to shock her male readers and reviewers profoundly. As Virginia Woolf, she could not share whatever limited licence was enjoyed by James Joyce or D. H. Lawrence (both of whom would fall victim to current censorship laws). As it was, the *Daily News* would complain of this novel's 'lapses into indelicacy'.[55] Thus the freedom conferred by the Hogarth Press to write whatever she liked, however she liked, had already come up against its first and greatest obstacle. The experience of writing *Jacob's Room* introduced Woolf to the necessity for self-censorship. Even in her first novel written for her own Press, Woolf felt her wings clipped, and the fishing line that was her imagination snagged upon a rock.[56]

Once encountered, the subject of censorship could hardly be ignored, though it would be another ten years before she could speak openly of her own particular difficulties. Instead, she displaced some of her frustration onto Jacob, who in chapter V composes an essay on 'The Ethics of Indecency', an attack on one Professor Bulteel who has published a silently bowdlerized (or 'disembowelled') edition of the Restoration playwright William Wycherley. Indeed, Jacob is copying out this very essay when Florinda, his lover-to-be, sits down beside him at a café table. In the wake of their meeting, 'Jacob was restless' with a barely suppressed excitement that the narrator conveys by exploring contemporary double thinking on the subject of sexual desire. While society insists on the one hand that sex 'is a matter of no importance at all', behind drawn blinds and in darkened squares all over the city, couples embrace, and '[l]ittle else was talked of in theatres and popular novels'. In polite society, however, 'the fact is concealed, and . . . concealment by itself distracts the mind from the print and the sound.' [pp.66–7]

This concealment, practised by society and literary convention, is played out in the form of a mini-drama involving a letter from Mrs Flanders to Jacob, which Florinda brings up from the hall as she visits Jacob one evening. She and Jacob withdraw into the bedroom to make love, leaving the letter on the table outside. And there it lies, personified, silently pleading with Jacob not to 'go with bad women', voyeuristically listening, 'torn by the little creak, the sudden stir. Behind the door was the obscene thing, the alarming presence' [p.79]. Woolf's first attempts to convey the presence of sex were significantly more alarming, however: 'Behind the door knives cut human flesh from the bone, as death alights', she wrote, deleted and tried again. 'Surgeons were there with their knives. Something was visible that only austere men or women in white caps might see; & having seen would never speak of.' To have seen Jacob stretched out in bed with Florinda would have been unbearable to Mrs Flanders, yet 'if the marriage had been solemnised would she have felt anything of the kind?'[57] a further deleted sentence wonders. Woolf's manuscript gropes in different directions, unable to find the appropriate weighting for an action at once so commonplace and yet, at that time, so unspeakable. Finally, she abandoned the images of knives and surgery and redressed the balance by having Jacob come out in his dressing gown, looking 'beautifully healthy, like a baby after an airing' [p.79]. The action in the bedroom, overheard by Mrs Flanders' plump blue envelope, registers the gap between her motherly hopes for him and the young adult he has become. It also mocks the politeness of the world of polite letters that insists on the pulling of curtains and the closing of doors.

Mrs Flanders' letter is made the unwitting witness of what cannot be said in print, yet it also makes manifest 'the power of the mind to quit the body' [p.79], since letters carry our thoughts, wishes and desires away from us and from our own agency. Paradoxically, it is this power – the power of imagination – that invites us to follow the lovers into the bedroom, just as it is also the power that enables the writer to create the room, the lovers within it, and all the rest of the fiction. But the mind's freedom to travel, to 'open out', has no counterpart in the confining body, which cannot even enjoy its own satisfactions without recognizing itself as subject to the thoughts of the mind. For Jacob, sexual desire cannot cut itself loose, but seeks to idealize or romanticize, even to disguise its object. Confronted with Florinda's stupidity, Jacob's desire momentarily fails him. He is obliged to recognize that '[t]he body is harnessed to a brain . . . In spite of defending indecency, Jacob doubted whether he liked it in the raw.' [p.69] And when he visits the prostitute, Laurette, the split becomes alarming: 'Altogether a most reasonable conversation; a most respectable room; an intelligent girl. Only Madame herself seeing Jacob out . . . threatens to spill the whole bag of ordure, with difficulty held together, over the pavement. In short, something was wrong.' [p.90]

As Tristan, the hero of Wagner's opera and the epitome of uncontrollable passion, dies twice weekly at Covent Garden, Jacob struggles to harness love and sexual desire. There is clearly something wrong with a society in which Clara Durrant is too timid and well brought up to give Jacob any indication that she is as attracted to him as he is to her. Instead, her little social duties, so scrupulously observed, carry her steadily away from him. Jacob, in turn, carelessly exploits the women who sleep with him – Florinda, and Fanny Elmer, the artist's model. Here, and even when he falls in love with the older, colder and already married Sandra Wentworth-Williams, love is characterized by misconstruction and misunderstanding. Jacob and Sandra climb the Acropolis together in the dark. In Woolf's manuscript, the scene is written out at troubled length, as the couple hesitate, searching for a resolution: 'They wanted certainty; separate, they wanted that the thin shell dividing them should break. Once united, something even in the waste of chaos, survives.'[58] The published text is less confident. 'The columns and the Temple remain; the emotion of the living breaks fresh on them year after year; and of that what remains?' [p.141]

The novel's structure follows Jacob from early childhood into his twenties, but in an open and anecdotal way that allowed Woolf to draw on material from recent experience as well as from memory and imagination. When their new assistant at the Press, Ralph Partridge, talked about his visit to a brothel, 'how, after the event, he & the girl sat over the fire, discussing the coal strike',[59] he unknowingly helped her to visualize the scene with Laurette (though the second half of Partridge's experience – 'Girls paraded before him – that was what pleased him – the sense of power' – she omitted as an aspect of male sexuality she could not deal with). Other episodes were based on her own experiences: the drunken woman singing in Kingsway, in chapter V, she had noticed on her way home a couple of months previously,[60] and the sequence in chapter VI, where a young woman in a café makes a scene and marches out, humiliating her young man, was based on an incident she had watched the previous year, during an evening spent with Clive at the Café Royal.[61]

The early months of writing *Jacob's Room* (from April until mid-September 1920) were sheer pleasure: Virginia found herself making it up 'incessantly on my walks'.[62] Her new technique gave her the freedom she had hoped for, to unfold her narrative while bringing in her own impressions, speculations and experiences, but her progress was interrupted in September, when T. S. Eliot came to stay, and the conversation turned to Joyce's *Ulysses*: 'I reflected how what I'm doing is probably being better done by Mr Joyce. Then I began to wonder what it is that I am doing: to suspect . . . that I have not thought my plan out plainly enough.'[63] A period of headaches followed ('It was this, not Eliot I suppose, that broke off Jacob'[64]), but something else was worrying her, too, something that threatened her confidence quite as much as Joyce had done. That month, Arnold Bennett had published *Our Women*, a collection of essays in which he argued that men were cleverer and more creative than women – variations on the refrain that would haunt Lily Briscoe in *To the Lighthouse*, 'Women can't write, women can't paint.'[65]

Her old friend Desmond MacCarthy, reviewing Bennett's book for the *New Statesman* at the beginning of October, endorsed its view that women were men's intellectual inferiors, and what he considered to be the 'proof' of it – their desire to be dominated. Woolf felt compelled to respond in a letter to the editor, in which she defended women's achievements and intellect, pointing out how rapidly their contributions to literature had increased with their educational opportunities, and claiming that Sappho was pre-eminent as an early lyric poet. Desmond MacCarthy replied, questioning her examples and arguments, and Woolf wrote a further letter, reminding him of the

practical and biological difficulties women have always laboured
under, since they have 'brought forth the entire population of the
universe'.[66] Women lacked both education and liberty of experience,
yet there would always be a 'a nucleus of women who think, invent,
imagine, and create as freely as men do'.[67] The assumption of male
superiority merely increased the obstacles that confronted women, and
perpetuated existing inequalities.

In the course of her arguments, Woolf voiced an even more fundamental doubt concerning the male intellect: if it was so superior, where
was this superiority taking the human race? '[T]hough women have
every reason to hope that the intellect of the male sex is steadily
diminishing, it would be unwise, until they have more evidence than
the great war and the great peace supply, to announce it as a fact.'[68]
Late in September 1920, before MacCarthy's favourable review of
Bennett had appeared, but with the writing of *Jacob's Room* stalled,
she found herself 'making up a paper upon Women, as a counter blast
to Mr Bennett's adverse views reported in the papers'.[69] This was either
the seed of her letter to the *New Statesman*, or perhaps the beginnings
of her short story 'A Society', a fable that recognized with alarming
prescience just where the combination of technological advancement
and war might lead:

'Oh, Cassandra, for Heaven's sake let us devise a method by which men may
bear children! It is our only chance. For unless we provide them with some
innocent occupation we shall get neither good people nor good books; we
shall perish beneath the fruits of their unbridled activity; and not a human
being will survive to know that there once was Shakespeare!'[70]

This cry of despair is followed by the announcement that the Peace
Treaty has been signed. For those hoping to safeguard international
peace, its terms were far from reassuring: 'The rain was falling and
interfered no doubt with the proper explosion of the fireworks.'[71]

The 'Society' of the title consists of a group of idealistic young
women who gradually recognize that women have been deceived
into trusting men to do their thinking for them, while they devote
themselves to child-bearing and -rearing, with disastrous results: 'our
belief in man's intellect is the greatest fallacy of them all'.[72] The Society
explores and exposes the absurdities of military, legal and academic

institutions, literature and the arts, only to remember, as war is announced, that they had forgotten to send anyone to the House of Commons. Castalia later regrets that her daughter is learning to read, since she has already begun to ask awkward questions – whether the newspapers are ' "true": next she'll ask me whether Mr Lloyd George is a good man, then whether Mr Arnold Bennett is a good novelist, and finally whether I believe in God. How can I bring my daughter up to believe in nothing?'[73]

'A Society' upends the old idea that women's charms were spoilt by education by comically reversing the usual patronizing question: 'What could be more charming than a boy before he has begun to cultivate his intellect?'[74] Yet this reversal also makes a serious comment on the war machine: male beauty, its fragility and destruction, had become a frequent theme of war poetry. In this story, Polly has been condemned by her father's will to read all the way through the books in the London Library, from English Literature on the top floor to the bound volumes of *The Times* in the basement. But the Library is not merely the repository of what men have written – it also stands for the achievements of the male intellect, of patriarchal culture. In what may have been a late addition to *Jacob's Room* Woolf reworked this theme, changing the London Library (by subscription) to the more public British Museum Reading Room, whose dome is pictured as a vast male skull, an enormous mind. Julia Hedge, the feminist, with her untied shoelaces (a detail that recalls Polly in 'A Society'), reads the names of male writers inscribed in gold letters round the dome, and feels shut out as a woman, and irrationally angry with privileged young men like Jacob. Her sense of exclusion is echoed, later in the chapter, by a woman 'who has come home drunk and cries all night long, "Let me in! let me in!"' [p.94]

Woolf's revisions to her manuscript were designed to tighten up the framework, and so are particularly concentrated at the beginning and the end. The original opening chapter in which Jacob's panic on the beach filters into his dreams is developed into a clearer, and more anticipatory sequence that includes Mrs Flanders' tear-stained letter, a painter (for it is St Ives), a couple lying on the beach, the search for the missing and panic-stricken Jacob and, later that evening, a (symbolic) rising storm.[75] Woolf also added a penultimate chapter set in London on the afternoon and evening of 4 August 1914, in which she imagined what it must have felt like to be in London, at the centre of the impending crisis, that day. The main characters reappear: Jacob is talking to Bonamy on one side of Hyde Park, while on the other Clara Durrant walks her dog, and sees a riderless horse gallop past; Florinda, pregnant, waits for Nick Bramham at Verrey's (a café in Regent Street); Fanny, still hoping Jacob will come back to her, catches a bus to Piccadilly. The wires at the Admiralty hum, bringing news of the developing crisis from all over the world.[76] In Whitehall, the Prime Minister is speaking, his hollow-looking head representing 'all the heads in the building'. As for the Cabinet members, 'some were troubled with dyspepsia; one had at that very moment cracked the glass of his spectacles; another spoke in Glasgow tomorrow; altogether they looked too red, fat, pale or lean, to be dealing, as the marble heads [of former statesmen] had dealt, with the course of history.' [p.152][77] These only too human heads contrast with the 'enormous mind' of the British Museum Reading Room dome and, perhaps, look back to a diary entry of June 1920, in which Woolf blamed 'the bloody war' on the 'thick skulls at Westminster & Berlin', which, between them, had created a Golgotha of soldiers' skulls.[78]

A pro-war demonstration passes under the windows of Whitehall, waving banners and singing patriotic songs. 'Another procession, without banners, was blocking Long Acre', holding up the carriages and motor cars carrying ladies and gentlemen in evening dress to the opera. As they pass under the arch at Covent Garden, the narrator observes, 'one must follow; one must not block the way', as if recalling men marching obediently 'up the line to death', as in Wilfred Owen's line, 'None will break ranks, though nations trek from progress'.[79] This bannerless procession is that of the Women's Movement on its way to Kingsway Hall on the evening of 4 August 1914, and the meeting that failed to hold up history – but the reference would only mean something to those who recalled its significance. *Jacob's Room* employs the technique Woolf had envisaged in 'The Mark on the Wall', by which novelists would leave 'the description of reality more and more out of their stories, taking a knowledge of it for granted'.[80] From now on, Woolf's fiction would expect the reader to fill in the gaps, 'to make a whole'.[81] Human character was changing, and so must the nature of the reader.

JACOB'S ROOM: THE AFTERMATH

'I have found out how to begin (at 40) to say something in my own voice', Woolf announced on completing Jacob's Room. Late in July 1922 she had shown the final typescript to Leonard, who thought it her best work so far, amazingly well written, a work of genius.[82]

She had begun it on 16 April 1920, and completed the first draft, set out in three notebooks, on 4 November 1921.[83] At that stage, she reckoned it had taken her about a year of actual writing, given how much of 1920 had been spent on the stories for Monday or Tuesday, and that she had lost at least two months through illness during the summer of 1921, when she had suffered from 'wearisome headache, jumping pulse, aching back, frets, fidgets, lying awake, sleeping draughts, sedatives, digitalis, going for a little walk, & plunging back into bed again – all the horrors of the dark cupboard of illness'.[84] It took a further six months' work to pull the manuscript into shape ('I could have screwed Jacob up tighter if I had foreseen; but I had to make my path as I went'[85]); at this stage she apparently rewrote the opening, and added the scene in the British Museum Reading Room, as well as the penultimate chapter set in London on 4 August 1914.

Now (in June 1922) began a 'season of doubts & ups & downs'.[86] The manuscript was typed out; a copy was despatched across the Atlantic to Donald Brace, and another submitted to Leonard. By August, Vanessa, though suffering from mumps, was working on the dust-jacket.[87] By September, the first proofs had arrived. Virginia found them depressing, and feared that the book was 'thin & pointless', but felt consoled by the sense that she was 'about to write something good'[88] – Mrs Dalloway was already walking down Bond Street. Early in October, Donald Brace wrote to say what a distinguished and beautiful work he thought Jacob's Room was, and he would be delighted to publish it. Lytton and the artist who lived with him, Dora Carrington, had read advance copies and also wrote to congratulate her. Carrington recognized its painterly dimension – 'Your visions are so clear & well-designed' – and Lytton assured her that he found it 'more like poetry ... than anything else, and as such I prophecy immortal.'[89] Ten days before publication, Virginia drew up some *predictions as to Jacob's sales and success, reckoning they would initially sell 500 copies, rising to 800 by the following June, and that it would be praised for its beauty and criticized for its lack of human character. She was still drawing confidence from her current writing: 'nothing budges me from my determination to go on . . . so whatever happens, though the surface may be agitated, the centre is secure.'[90]*

The Woolfs had decided, soon after she began it, that they would publish her third novel themselves. That way she would avoid having to submit it to the inspection of her half-brother Gerald Duckworth, or his reader, Edward Garnett. It would also help the Press to grow up and become 'a proper publishing business'.[91] Thereafter, the rest of her books would be published from home, Gerald having agreed to surrender his option on her next novel. 'I daresay Duckworth is a little cross with me. I snuff my freedom,' she breathed – she didn't think he would have liked Jacob's Room anyway.[92] Professionalizing the Press meant finding an assistant, since both the Woolfs had heavy commitments elsewhere: in October 1920 they took on Ralph Partridge, soon to marry Dora Carrington. He was the first of a series of assistants who found Leonard's exacting standards difficult to meet.

Jacob's Room was the Press's first novel, and its first full-length production. As such, Leonard sent it out to 'one of the biggest and best of British printers', R. & R. Clark of Edinburgh, who continued to print Virginia's work (and much else for the Press) until the late 1950s.[93] It was published on 27 October 1922 in an edition of 1,200 copies, selling at seven shillings and sixpence in Vanessa's elegant dust-jacket: on a cream background cinnamon-coloured curtains framed the corner of a table with a bowl of flowers, the lettering in black.[94] As Leonard later observed, it was a very good jacket, but 'it did not represent a desirable female or even Jacob or his room, and it was what in 1923 many people would have called reproachfully post-impressionist. It was almost universally condemned by the booksellers, and several of the buyers laughed at it.'[95] Almost immediately, the Press ordered a further 1,000 copies, on the grounds that it was selling 'fairly briskly'. But this vote of confidence on Leonard's part made Virginia feel edgy: 'Publishing one's own books is very nervous work, and we don't know how this is going.'[96] By the end of the following year they had sold fewer than 1,500, yet they had made a

Jacob's Room

Virginia Woolf

small profit on it (Leonard noted that 'Virginia Woolf, the publisher, had to some extent swindled Virginia Woolf, the author').[97]

Her friends, this time including E. M. Forster, praised Jacob's Room *for its beauty and originality, though her replies to them suggest that she had already somehow outgrown it: 'its too much of an experiment'; there were 'grave doubts about the form', and, anyway, 'how far can one convey character without realism?'*[98] *The reviewers divided much as she had predicted they would: A. S. McDowall, in the* Times Literary Supplement, *located the novel within Woolf's wider development, as 'the opposite of* Night and Day' *and 'rather like the method of* Monday or Tuesday *applied to a continuous story'; he recognized what she was trying to achieve and admired her 'adventurousness'.*[99] *But the* Daily News *and the* Pall Mall Gazette *were offended by the same quality, finding it 'very pretentious and very cheap', with no story and 'no perceptible development of any kind'. The* New Age *was dismissive: 'little flurries of prose poetry do not make art of this rag-bag of impressions'.*[100] *For the first time, the impact of her fellow-modernists was apparent: her work was 'just a little like . . . Mr James Joyce', 'now and again . . . reminds us of Dorothy Richardson'. Other reviewers commented on the novel's affinities with the pictorial arts, or described it as 'impressionist'.*[101]

Absorbed in the excitement of a new novel, she scarcely noticed the reviews of the old one until March 1923, *when Arnold Bennett attacked* Jacob's Room *in an article provocatively entitled 'Is the Novel Decaying?' 'I have seldom read a cleverer book', he sneered. 'It is packed and bursting with originality, and it is exquisitely written. But the characters do not vitally survive in the mind . . . I regard this book as characteristic of the new novelists.'*[102] *Already irritated by Bennett's misogyny in* Our Women, *Woolf could not let this challenge go unanswered, and before the end of the year she had composed a reply – the first version of 'Mr Bennett and Mrs Brown'.*[103] *But, for the moment, '[p]eople – my friends I mean – seem agreed that [*Jacob's Room*] is <u>my</u> masterpiece, & the starting point for fresh adventures'.*[104]

5

A Woman Connects

'Somehow the connection between life & literature must be made by women,' Woolf wrote in her diary in July 1922, between finishing *Jacob's Room* and beginning *Mrs Dalloway*, '& they so seldom do it right'.[1] Her task as a writer, as she saw it, was to bring the woman's point of view, with its different values and concerns, to bear on the male-dominated traditions of literature. As always, fiction came first for her,[2] – as a novelist, she had already begun to voice the woman's viewpoint, but it was already well established and widely accepted in fiction. The world of journalism and belles-lettres, on the other hand, was still dominated by masculine voices and pronouns, though gender difference was often concealed beneath the convention of anonymous reviewing still retained by many periodicals. For Woolf, the processes of reading and writing were inextricably intertwined, and she had been tuned in to their gendered nature from childhood, when her father had been the solitary writer and scholar, her mother the family story-teller. In different ways, she had followed in both their footsteps. Women's position in society was rapidly changing – the result of their political and educational demands before the Great War, and their new roles, during and after the war – but British society was still fundamentally patriarchal in its operations. Now Woolf braced herself to confront them.

Reading, writing and story-telling had been favourite occupations in the Stephen household, indulged alone or in company. Both her parents were avid readers, as well as published writers: Leslie Stephen was the professional – an editor, and expert on literature and philosophy, later knighted for his contributions. His wife Julia published only her modest *Notes from Sick Rooms* in 1883, when Virginia was

THE INTELLECTUAL STATUS OF WOMEN

To the Editor of THE NEW STATESMAN.

SIR,—Like most women, I am unable to face the depression and the loss of self respect which Mr. Arnold Bennett's blame and Mr. Orlo Williams' praise—if it is not the other way about —would certainly cause me if I read their books in the bulk. I taste them, therefore, in sips at the hands of reviewers. But I cannot swallow the teaspoonful administered in your columns last week by Affable Hawk. The fact that women are inferior to men in intellectual power, he says, " stares him in the face." He goes on to agree with Mr. Bennett's conclusion that " no amount of education and liberty of action will sensibly alter it." How, then, does Affable Hawk account for the fact which stares me, and I should have thought any other impartial observer, in the face, that the seventeenth century produced more remarkable women than the sixteenth, the eighteenth than the seventeenth, and the nineteenth than all three put together ? When I compare the Duchess of Newcastle with Jane Austen, the matchless Orinda with Emily Brontë, Mrs. Heywood with George Eliot, Aphra Behn with Charlotte Brontë, Jane Grey with Jane Harrison, the advance in intellectual power seems to me not only sensible but immense ; the comparison with men not in the least one that inclines me to suicide ; and the effects of education and liberty scarcely to be overrated. In short, though pessimism about the other sex is always delightful and invigorating, it seems a little sanguine of Mr. Bennett and Affable Hawk to indulge in it with such certainty on the evidence before them. Thus, though women have every reason to hope that the intellect of the male sex is steadily diminishing, it would be unwise, until they have more evidence than the great war and the great peace supply, to announce it as a fact. In conclusion, if Affable Hawk sincerely wishes to discover a great poetess, why does he let himself be fobbed off with a possible authoress of the Odyssey ? Naturally, I cannot claim to know Greek as Mr. Bennett and Affable Hawk know it, but I have often been told that Sappho was a woman, and that Plato and Aristotle placed her with Homer and Archilocus among the greatest of their poets. That Mr. Bennett can name fifty of the male sex who are indisputably her superiors is therefore a welcome surprise, and if he will publish their names I will promise, as an act of that submission which is so dear to my sex, not only to buy their works but, so far as my faculties allow, to learn them by heart.—Yours, etc.,

VIRGINIA WOOLF.

a year old. But Julia made up stories for her children, stories of talking animals in which the children occasionally put in an appearance themselves: 'little Ginia . . . thought she would bury her shoes and socks in the sand'.[3] Though Julia had written out some of her stories with publication in mind, she never published them. Leslie drew animals, some of them as illustrations to his wife's stories, to amuse his 'ragamice', but he had a high regard for fact, and left the fiction to Julia and his sister-in-law (and Julia's close friend), Anny Thackeray Ritchie.

'I cannot remember a time when Virginia did not mean to be a writer and I a painter', Vanessa later recalled.[4] Virginia had told stories from early childhood – of Jim, Joe and Harry Hoe, 'three brothers who had herds of animals and adventures'; of Beccage and Hollywinks, evil spirits who lived on the rubbish heap at Talland House in St Ives, and later, of Clémont and the Dilkes, the family who actually lived next door to the Stephens at Hyde Park Gate, and who they imagined to have discovered a hoard of gold under their bedroom floor. When Virginia was nine, she started her own newspaper with Thoby:[5]

How excited I used to be when the 'Hyde Park Gate News' was laid on [Mother's] plate on Monday morning, and she liked something I had written! Never shall I forget my extremity of pleasure – it was like being a violin and being played upon – when I found that she had sent a story of mine to Madge Symonds; it was so imaginative, she said; it was about souls flying round and choosing bodies to be born into.[6]

Virginia was also a voracious reader, to the amusement of her father who gave her the run of his library, later supplementing it with books brought back from the London Library (of which he was President).[7] Books remained her delight, her solace and her refuge. As a young woman, she had read 'the whole of Meredith, the whole of Ibsen, and a little of Bernard Shaw' as well as Thomas Hardy, Conrad and Henry James; the classic novelists – George Eliot, Jane Austen, Thomas Love Peacock, Henry Fielding – and a variety of other things – the Book of Job, Hakluyt's Voyages, and 'a great deal of Webster, Browning, Shelley, Spenser, and Congreve'.[8] From early on, she had developed a taste for what she termed 'bad' books – memoirs and autobiographies, stories of 'lives', whose characters became 'actors in those private dramas with which we beguile our solitary walks and our sleepless hours'.[9] Reading and walking were activities that stimulated her to 'make up', generating new fictions. She was particularly fascinated by the 'obscure' and unrecorded lives of women, identifying with their marginal position in a society dominated by men. In London in 1903, she noted 'I read – then I lay down the book & say – what right have I, a woman to read all these things that men have done? They would laugh if they saw me', but packing up her books to take on holiday, she promised herself 'I am going to forget all that in the country'.[10]

Two years later, in 1905, at the suggestion of her friend Mary Sheepshanks, she began to give adult education classes to working men and women at Morley College. 'I am going to write history one of these days', she told Violet Dickinson. 'I always did love it; if I could find the bit I want. I have got a ticket for Dr Williams Library across the square, and describe myself as a "journalist who wants to read history" and so I do feel a professional Lady.'[11] While reading often led her back to writing, (historical) fact often led to fiction, and the neglected lives of women stimulated her imagination. In 1906, while staying with her brothers and sister at Blo' Norton, a Jacobean manor house in Norfolk, she wrote 'The Journal of Mistress Joan Martyn', a short story in two parts. In the first, Rosamund Merridew, an enlightened modern historian, recalls how she came across the journal of a fifteenth-century woman, Joan Martyn, in a remote corner of Norfolk. Miss Merridew's mission is to recover the silent history of women, 'the reality of mediaeval bodies, and . . . the reality of mediaeval brains',[12] and she rescues Joan's journal from oblivion, breathing life into the dry bones of scholarship. The second part consists of the journal itself, for Joan had been born with a novelist's instincts, but no opportunity to exercise them.

Another early short story, 'Memoirs of a Novelist' (1909), was written in the form of a review – that of an (imaginary) biography of a popular and sentimental Victorian novelist, thus sending up the conventions of Victorian biography, rather as Lytton Strachey would do ten years later. The reviewer reassesses the novelist's life, suggesting that she was a great deal tougher and more ruthless than her biographer had ever supposed, on the basis of a photograph: 'The sight of that large selfish face, with the capable forehead and the surly but intelligent eyes, discredits all the platitudes on the opposite page.'[13] The story was intended as the first of a series of lives of eccentric women, but Reginald Smith, editor of the *Cornhill*, turned it down, and the scheme was abandoned. Here, as in 'The Journal of Mistress Joan Martyn', an (imagined) experience of reading is reworked as writing, as one text generates another.

'Memoirs of a Novelist' was written from Woolf's experiences as a reviewer: her earliest published work had been essays and reviews. After her 1904 breakdown, her friend Violet Dickinson had introduced her to Margaret Lyttelton, editor of the women's pages of the *Guardian*, a weekly newspaper originally addressed to high Anglican clergymen.[14] In 1905, she began writing reviews for Bruce Richmond, editor of the *Times Literary Supplement*, and continued to do so until his retirement in 1938.[15] Her contributions to both journals were published anonymously, so her gender remained concealed behind an impersonal plural: 'we do not count Mr James's characters among the creatures of our brains, nor can we read his books easily and without conscious effort'.[16] This convention had enabled her to enter the world of literary journalism passing as a man, but she was well aware that it involved an element of deceit.

Were women unwelcome in the world of letters? Libraries, like the literary traditions they housed, usually consisted of men speaking to men: 'in all the libraries of the world the man is to be heard talking to himself and for the most part about himself'.[17] As a woman user, it was difficult not to feel out of place, as the feminist Julia Hedge had felt in the British Museum Reading Room in *Jacob's Room*; or even shut out altogether, as Woolf's narrator would be shut out of Trinity Library in the opening chapter of *A Room of One's Own*.[18] In September 1919, Woolf responded by inventing for herself her own ideal 'gentleman's library', complete with Jacobean panelling, and set in an English country house looking out towards the sea. It was the moment when the Woolfs had surrendered their retreat at Asheham, but had not yet acquired Monk's House, and Britain was in the throes of a railway strike (which they actively supported). The library she created houses the tradition of English literature, itself a reflection of the watery climate, and the surrounding countryside. For the reader seated at an open window, 'instead of being a book, it seemed as if what I read was laid upon the landscape not printed, bound, or sewn up, but somehow the product of trees and fields and the hot summer sky, like the air which swam, on fine mornings, round the outlines of things'.[19]

The contents of the library shelves anticipate *The Common Reader*, running from Chaucer to the Elizabethans, the Restoration, 'and so down to our time or very near it, Cowper, Burns, Scott, Wordsworth and the rest',[20] though they also include volumes by neglected seventeenth-century women – Lucy Hutchinson, Lady Fanshawe and the eccentric Lady Margaret Cavendish. The library's Jacobean carvings were inspired by those of Blo' Norton; its garden by that of Talland House at St Ives. The essay ends by celebrating the personal character of writing as represented in the work of Sir Thomas Browne. 'Somewhere, everywhere, now hidden, now apparent in whatever is written down is the form of a human being. If we seek to know him, are we idly occupied . . . ? Sir Thomas is the first English writer to rouse this particular confusion'.[21]

The English house, with its English library, was Woolf's private version of 'the great good place', a fantasy that would resurface in her last novel, *Between the Acts*. But the essay evoking it, entitled 'Reading', though long and eloquently written, was never published. It translates the activity of reading into an idyll, a world of leisured privilege that had traditionally been the prerogative of men, deliberately ignoring the gender and class divisions Woolf had identified in the practices of reading and writing. Its celebration of Englishness was also suspect, out of step with a post-war mood of internationalism, and a contempt for patriotism and national pride. Only a few months before, Woolf had mocked the Royal Academy Summer Exhibition for its self-indulgent celebration of all things English. Aligning herself with Roger Fry, her review had made fun of the many paintings of English village life, in which '[t]he yew hedges are irreproachable; the manor house a miracle of timeworn dignity; and as for the old man with a scythe, the girl at the well, the village donkey, . . . each is not only the saddest, sweetest, quaintest, most picturesque, tenderest, jolliest of its kind, but has a symbolical meaning much to the credit of England.'[22]

With the publication of *Night and Day* in 1919, and the critical acclaim for her experimental short stories, Woolf was gaining confidence, and gradually abandoning her shell of anonymity to publish under her own name in the *Athenaeum* (edited by John Middleton Murry, Katherine Mansfield's husband) and the *New Statesman* (where the literary editor was her old Bloomsbury friend Desmond MacCarthy). But the process of anonymous reviewing, of writing as a member of a community of writers and readers assumed to be male, had heightened her sensitivity to the position of women, and not merely in the world of literature. She had begun to consider, not only the nature of patriarchy, but also the silent antagonism between the sexes. 'To cast out and incorporate in a person of the opposite sex all that we miss in ourselves and desire in the universe and detest in humanity is a deep and universal instinct on the part both of men and of women.'[23]

In the summer of 1920, Ray Strachey, editor of the *Women's Leader* and a key figure in the Women's Movement, persuaded Woolf to write on a current topic of feminist concern – the Plumage Bill. This was a parliamentary proposal to outlaw the use of egrets' feathers (then an item of high fashion) because of the cruelty inflicted on the birds. The Bill had repeatedly failed to attract sufficient support to be put before Parliament. The journalist Henry Massingham had written an angry piece in the *Nation*, denouncing the cruelty, and demanding '"what do women care? Look at Regent Street this morning!"'[24] Woolf responded by pointing out that it was actually men who maltreated the birds, men who profited by the sale of their feathers and men who had failed to support the Bill through Parliament, yet 'what do men care?' Rewording his sentences and substituting 'men' for 'women', as a way of exposing his thoughtless misogyny, her rhetorical questions answered his: 'Can it be that it is a graver sin to be unjust to women than to torture birds?'[25]

Massingham replied, pointing out that if women had refused to wear egret plumes in the first place, the Bill would have been unnecessary. Woolf defended her position, stating that she was not 'writing as a bird, or even a champion of birds; but as a woman'. His casual denigration of women was 'disastrous not merely to women's relations with men but to her art and her conduct'.[26] His article reflected the prejudices that ran through the fabric of society, undermining the self-confidence of the woman artist. A few months later, Woolf's work on *Jacob's Room* was interrupted, first by Eliot's enthusiasm for Joyce, and shortly afterwards by Desmond MacCarthy's praise for Arnold Bennett's *Our Women*, inspiring her to send an angry letter to the *New Statesman*. MacCarthy had reported with approval that Bennett 'finds it difficult to say, yet say it he does, that women are inferior to men in intellectual power, especially in that kind of power which is described as creative. Certainly, that fact stares one in the face'.[27] Woolf's letters of protest to the *New Statesman* were a turning point for her: through them, she successfully converted depression and discouragement into social analysis, and a critique of patriarchal attitudes. She had set out her convictions, in the process crossing swords with a Bloomsbury friend and well-respected literary journalist. Such courage was itself an act of liberation.

Just before Christmas 1920, Ray Strachey and her husband Oliver dined with the Woolfs and discussed Roger Fry's recent book of essays, *Vision and Design*. Ray invited Virginia to review it for the *Women's Leader*,[28] which she did, rightly describing it as 'probably the most important art criticism of our time'. Though the discourse of art history was thin compared to that of literature, Woolf was enormously impressed by Fry's range of taste that could comprehend '[a] broken pot, a negro's carving, a child's drawing, a fresco by Giotto', as well as his democratic spirit – 'he makes it possible for the ignorant to communicate with the artist'.[29] She had been thinking about publishing a collection of her own best reviews and critical essays. Now she saw how such a collection might work to develop and extend its readers' sympathies, as Fry had developed and extended those of his viewers. At this stage, it was provisionally entitled 'Reading' (as the essay on her ideal library had been).

She did not actually start writing 'Reading' (later, *The Common Reader*) until March 1922, when *Jacob's Room* had safely reached the revision stage. She began with an opening chapter, provisionally entitled 'Byron and Mr Briggs'.[30] Byron was chosen because in his case, as in Sir Thomas Browne's, it was 'difficult to be certain whether we are looking at a man or his writing'.[31] From the start, Byron's personality had coloured his reception as a poet. He was evidently a great letter writer, and on the basis of his poem *Don Juan*, he was also a novelist manqué. Woolf chose him because in and around him, life and literature were so richly, so complexly connected. Moreover, he elicited very different responses from male and female readers, as Woolf later pointed out in an essay for *Vogue*, suggestively entitled 'Indiscretions'.[32]

If Byron is the poet, an imaginary Tom Briggs (1759–1859) is his reader, a maker of spectacles living in Cornhill (a street in the City of London). His profession suggests sight and its possible improvement, and so, by extension, debates between life and literature – Shakespeare, according to Dryden, 'needed not the spectacles of books to read nature'.[33] When Woolf famously declared that life was 'not a series of gig lamps symmetrically arranged', she may have been thinking not so much of lined-up carriage lamps, as of the spectacle of Mr Briggs's spectacles, neatly laid out in their trays – 'gig lamps' has been slang for glasses from the middle of the nineteenth century.[34]

'Byron and Mr Briggs' makes a series of attempts to define what happens when we read a book. Woolf compared it to the process of 'reading' people, and she illustrated what she meant from her favourite scene of such reading – the railway carriage scenario, already deployed in 'An Unwritten Novel' and the third chapter of *Jacob's Room* (it would later resurface in 'Mr Bennett and Mrs Brown'):

To make a whole ... Our reading is always urged on by the instinct to complete what we read, which is, for some reason, one of the most universal and profound of our instincts. You may see it at work any night among the passengers in a third class railway carriage. – Is he related to the woman opposite? No they work in the same office. In love then? No; she wears a wedding ring. Going home then to the same suburb? Ah, yes ... Everyone plays this familiar game. Everyone feels the desire to add to a single impression the others that go to complete it.[35]

'Byron and Mr Briggs' was too ambitious: overcrowded with all the things she wanted to say about the processes of reading and writing, it never got anywhere at all. Where the abandoned 'Reading' essay had been highly polished, 'Byron and Mr Briggs' was not only abandoned but unfinished; it exists only in transcriptions from a heavily corrected manuscript. Like *The Common Reader*, which it was intended to introduce, 'Byron and Mr Briggs' is fascinating for what it never quite manages to say. In it, Woolf had wondered what happens when a person reads, and what difference it makes if that person is a man or a woman, knowing from her own experience that the apparently genderless reviewer might well be a woman, with a woman's responses: "He," do we say? But it is obvious from the shape of each sentence, from the tilt & atmosphere & proportion of the whole that he is a woman . . . But', she continues, 'the writer's sex is not of interest; nor need we dwell upon the peculiarities of temperament which make one person's reading of Byron's letters different from another's. It is the quality that they have in common that is interesting.'[36] And so, for the time being, the woman reader gives place to the common reader, though the suspicion that the common reader may, even so, be a woman remained, to emerge as a significant undercurrent running through *The Common Reader*.

'Byron and Mr Briggs' had come to nothing, but Woolf still intended to collect the best of her *Times Literary Supplement* reviews and articles into a book, though she was uncertain how to organize them – merely assembling and arranging them seemed inadequate, 'an inartistic method'.[37] In August 1923 she wondered whether she might embed them 'in Otway conversation' – the Otways were a large and talkative family, cousins of Katharine Hilbery in *Night and Day*, with affinities to the Stracheys. Such an arrangement would reduce the dogmatism of her essays, 'mitigate the pomposity & sweep in all sorts of trifles', while involving the reader more closely.[38] She had been experimenting with recording conversations in her diary, and was writing a review of Conrad's fiction in the form of a conversation between Penelope Otway ('a small dark woman turned forty, her complexion a little roughened by country life') and her old friend David Lowe[39] – one way of making a woman connect life and literature. But the scheme for 'Otway conversation' didn't seem to work any better, and only the concept of 'making a whole' survived from 'Byron and Mr Briggs'. 'Reading' became *The Common Reader*, a phrase taken from Dr Johnson, whose definition supplied much of the single-page preface.[40]

While finishing *Jacob's Room*, Woolf had been rereading Homer and Aeschylus, and the Paston letters in preparation for her collection of essays.[41] In the autumn of 1922, her fourth novel, *Mrs Dalloway*, began to take shape, and she decided to write the two books side by side – 'certainly I enjoy my reading with a purpose'.[42] The slog of reading, analysing and revising old essays would, she thought, whet her appetite for writing fiction, while offering an alternative when inspiration fell to a low ebb, or particular episodes (such as Septimus's madness) grew too difficult. *The Common Reader* and *Mrs Dalloway* were published successively, in April and May of 1925, and thereafter Woolf tried to plan her writing life so that she was working on fiction and non-fiction simultaneously: at the end of the 1930s, she would compose her biography of Roger Fry back to back with her last novel, *Between the Acts.*

The Common Reader acted as a foil to *Mrs Dalloway* in other respects, too, for the novel was shamelessly 'highbrow'. Shaped by a modernist aesthetic whose key elements were form and the nature of subjectivity, it made few concessions to its readers. Even her concern to record 'an ordinary mind on an ordinary day' would, paradoxically, make the novel more difficult. Woolf could not decide what she thought about popularity, especially before she acquired it. She snobbishly dismissed the success of Katherine Mansfield's collection of short stories, *The Garden Party* (1922): 'The more she is praised, the more I am convinced she is bad . . . She touches the spot too universally for that spot to be of the bluest blood.'[43] Yet Woolf had grown up with the view that literature should be accessible – the great Victorians had all reached a large reading public: its extent had been one measure of their success. That ideal was reflected in the title and some of the aims of *The Common Reader*, while *Mrs Dalloway* was a post-impressionist text, turning its back on popularity to pursue a particular vision.

The Common Reader fell short of Woolf's highest hopes: it never managed to define the relation between reader and writer, or between literature and life, or to explain what happens in the process of reading a novel – unanswerable questions that she continued to turn over for the rest of her life.[44] Nor did it analyse women's relationship to literature – we have to wait for *A Room of One's Own* (1929) for that. But it did open up the canon of English literature, as Fry had enlarged the canon of visual taste in *Vision and Design*, for alongside Woolf's earlier writings on Jane Austen, the Brontës and George Eliot, there were essays on several long-forgotten women writers – Margaret Cavendish (mentioned in the essay on 'Reading'), Laetitia Pilkington,

Maria Edgeworth and Anne Taylor – the last primarily a writer for children, though Woolf concentrated on their lives rather than their work. Other essays in the volume expanded the definition of literature to take in such marginal genres as letters and diaries, genres that were somehow nearer to 'life' and so were often overlooked in more official histories. She included essays on Greek, French and recent Russian literature, and set out her own modernist agenda in 'Modern Fiction', a revised version of the 1919 essay 'Modern Novels', that had sprung from her dissatisfaction with *Night and Day*.

At Rodmell, in the summer of 1922, and then again in the summer of 1923, Woolf made fresh starts, amused by the enthusiasm she always felt at the beginning of a project: 'I shall write next that I have never enjoyed any writing more, or felt more certain of success'. She drew up a list of the essays she intended to reprint.[45] Since *Jacob's Room*, she had been reading, in preparation for writing two new and substantial essays that she intended to accompany her existing essays – one on Chaucer and the Paston Letters, and the other on Greek literature (the discussion of drama would link it with an existing essay on the Elizabethan dramatists). These two pieces, requiring much thought and reading, would establish her scholarly credentials at the outset. 'The Pastons and Chaucer' reads the English poet through the surviving letters of a fifteenth-century Norfolk family. Woolf brought their story to life by focusing on the matriarch, Margaret Paston, who wrote to her husband and son 'asking advice, giving news, rendering accounts'.[46] Her eldest son, Sir John, spent time and money on poetry books, and found a world he recognized in Chaucer's poetry, yet somehow 'rounded and complete'.[47] For Woolf, Chaucer was a great story-teller, with a novelist's eye for telling detail, but oddly, given her own powers of irony, she failed to notice his, finding moral simplicity and certainty where more recent critics have found parody and self-mockery. It was not Chaucer's high art but the very plainness of the Paston letters that stimulated Woolf to re-create the world they inhabited. Letters, diaries, the lives of the obscure by their very frag-mentariness invite rewriting, invite the imagination to 'add to a single impression the others that go to complete it', 'making up a whole'.[48]

The second essay, 'On Not Knowing Greek', is also haunted by what is missing, as its title indicates. It registers the feminist undercurrent running through *The Common Reader*, while apparently making different points. Woolf did not need to explain to contemporary middle-class readers that a knowledge of classical Greek was what distinguished the public-school educated male (who had it beaten into him) from his sister, educated at home. When Ethel May in Charlotte M. Yonge's popular novel *The Daisy Chain* (1856) told her elder sister Margaret how much she longed to study Greek, Margaret had answered, 'And for that would you give up being a useful, steady daughter and sister at home?' To such an appeal, there was, of course, no reply.[49] Like Ethel May, and many other Victorian sisters, Virginia had longed to learn Greek to keep up with her brother Thoby. Greek stood for the easy intellectual exchanges that Thoby (like Jacob) had enjoyed at Cambridge, and his sister at home had pined for. Although she belonged to a later generation than Ethel May, Virginia was still unusual in having learned Greek – her father had paid for her lessons, first with Dr Warr and Clara Pater (the writer Walter Pater's sister), and later with Janet Case, who became a lifelong friend as well as a strong feminist influence. Greek was a skill Woolf was justly proud of; displayed in the course of this essay, it laid claim to intellectual equality.[50]

Woolf never refers to her silent subtext – the divisive nature of Greek as a subject for study. Instead, she points out that Greek scholars delude themselves in assuming they know the language, since they cannot agree how it should be pronounced, let alone how to recognize Greek jokes, nor do they know what the words would have meant to their original readers. Knowledge of the past must always be reconstructed, and in the process it is inevitably mediated and distorted. Knowing the literal meaning of the words does not confer an understanding of the discourse from which they derive, nor of the context which gives them their full meaning. While Woolf acknowledged the power and appeal of Greek literature, of the great dramatists and Plato, she was also suspicious of the romantic feelings they induced; her own sense of understanding Greek might be also an illusion; was she, too, 'reading into Greek poetry not what they have but what we lack?'[51]

The essay on Greek literature is followed by one on Elizabethan literature, also specially written for the volume, and focusing on one of Woolf's adolescent passions, Hakluyt's *Voyages, Travels and Discoveries* (one of the books her father had lugged back from the London Library for her). The Victorians read the *Voyages* as anticipating their own imperial ambitions (also reflected in Millais's painting 'The Boyhood of Raleigh', and Newbolt's poem 'Drake's Drum'). As a girl, Virginia had been fascinated by its adventures set in snowbound Muscovy, South American rainforests or upon the high seas – imaginative responses that crept into her first two novels, and return in *Orlando*. Yet she also recognized the material greed that drove the voyages – 'Hakluyt is not so much a book as a great bundle of commodities'. She paused uneasily over its more disturbing episodes, such as when a native American man and woman are abducted, and penned up on board ship, to see how they will respond sexually to one another (they blush deeply, and conduct themselves chastely).[52] This essay, 'The Elizabethan Lumber Room', is followed by one on the Elizabethan dramatists. She avoided discussing Shakespeare, either then or later; his work remained a significant silence at the core of her literary canon.

The Common Reader balances the tastes and enthusiasms of her parents' generation against those belonging to her own, such as Elizabethan drama. She included an essay on the Russian novelists whose work bridged the gap between Victorian realism and the moderns. She and Leonard (like many of their contemporaries) had been overwhelmed by Dostoevsky's novels as they appeared in the translations of Constance Garnett, during the first decades of the century. In 1921 they actually set out to learn Russian themselves from 'Kot' – Samuel Koteliansky, a Jewish Ukrainian intellectual, and close friend of Katherine Mansfield.[53] They never mastered it, but used what they had learned to help Kot with his translations by rewriting his English. The Hogarth Press published a number of his translations from Gorky, Tolstoy and Dostoevsky (including the suppressed chapter of *The Possessed* in which Stavrogin confesses to the rape of a ten-year-old child[54]).

Woolf's essay, 'The Russian Point of View', reopened 'the question of our own fitness as readers', the question that crucially linked *The Common Reader* with the difficult text of *Mrs Dalloway*. Chekhov's short stories, Woolf argues, will seem inconclusive, until we learn to read them properly, and 'we need a very daring and alert sense of literature to make us hear the tune'.[55] But great art has always made demands on its readers: 'it will not suffer itself to be read passively, but takes us and reads us; flouts our preconceptions; questions principles which we had got into the habit of taking for granted, and, in fact, splits us into two parts as we read, making us, even as we enjoy, yield our ground or stick to our guns.'[56] Readers of modern texts must be prepared to let their old habits go, and learn to read in a new way. Woolf recognized the need to change her readers' approach if they were to cope with *Mrs Dalloway*, and modernist texts more generally. *Vision and Design* was relevant here, too, since in it, Fry had been concerned not so much with defining the nature of artistic vision as with clearing the obstacles to its reception.

The problem for the moderns (Woolf refers to them as the 'Georgians') was that they had created a cultural rupture, a smashing and crashing, by abandoning the methods and conventions of their predecessors, 'the Edwardians': 'Orphans is what I say we are – we Georgians –',[57] she told Janet Case in May 1922, since the Edwardians – 'Shaw, Wells, Galsworthy, the Webbs, Arnold Bennett' – had failed her generation. She developed this argument in the opening paragraph of her essay 'On Re-reading Novels', written a couple of months later, and took it a step further in a letter of commiseration to the aspiring writer Gerald Brenan, written on Christmas Day, 1922. Between her generation and the previous one, there had been more than the usual 'smash and splinters'; if writing was to be easier for the next generation, her own must first 'break its neck'.[58]

Her list of culpable Edwardians was to alter a little – Leonard persuaded her that Shaw had had a positive influence, but Bennett remained a source of annoyance, both on grounds of style and sexual politics. In March 1923, he had reviewed *Jacob's Room*, asserting that 'The foundation of good fiction is character creating, and nothing else', while mere cleverness was 'perhaps the lowest of all artistic qualities'. He had 'seldom read a cleverer book than . . . *Jacob's Room* . . . But the characters do not vitally survive in the mind because the author has been obsessed by details of originality and cleverness.' Finally, contemplating the future of the English novel, Bennett announced that he could not yet identify 'any coming big novelists'.[59]

His condemnation followed close on a comparable warning from Middleton Murry in the *Nation and Athenaeum*: 'the novel has reached a kind of *impasse*. The artists have, to a very large extent, outrun their audience.'[60] Murry's previous paragraph had identified Woolf by name, along with Lawrence and Mansfield. Unknowingly, he had voiced her own anxieties about the difficulty of *Mrs Dalloway*, and eighteen months later she still felt threatened by his criticism.[61]

While her diary worries over Murry's remark, Bennett's review of *Jacob's Room* provoked her to a public showdown in the form of a signed article for the *Nation and Athenaeum*, the earliest version of 'Mr Bennett and Mrs Brown'. Here she set out the argument between the Georgians and Edwardians as to how novels ought to be written. While she agreed with Bennett about the importance of character creation, she disagreed about how it was to be achieved, pointing out that the Russians had revealed the inadequacy of Victorian methods. She emphasized the break between one generation and the next, yet 'it is from the ruins and splinters of this tumbled mansion that the Georgian writer must somehow reconstruct a habitable dwelling-place; it is from the gleams and flashes of this flying spirit that he must create solid, living, flesh-and-blood Mrs Brown.' She ended by revising Bennett's gloomy prophecy, redefining the Georgians as 'at once the least successful, and the most interesting generation . . . for a hundred years . . . [T]he next chapter . . . will be one of the most important, the most illustrious, the most epoch-making of them all.'[62]

Woolf's essay occasioned several sympathetic responses in the *Nation and Athenaeum*, though no reaction from Arnold Bennett. Meeting him at a party a few months later, she found him 'a lovable sea lion, with chocolate eyes, drooping lids, & a protruding tusk'. She felt comfortably superior, for his accent was odd, his manner provincial, and his conversation decidedly defensive: ' "I don't understand women – . . . No woman is as sensitive as I am – no woman could be." I suspect he minds things, even my pinpricks', she added, with more satisfaction than sympathy.[63]

But Woolf was not finished with Arnold Bennett. He had identified himself with all that she, as a woman and a modernist, opposed in the literary establishment. Invited to speak to the Cambridge Heretics Society in May 1924, she read an expanded version of 'Mr Bennett and Mrs Brown', in which Bennett's failure to do justice to Mrs Brown is explained in terms of his inappropriate methods (too heavily materialist) and his inadequate reading skills. Now the imaginary Mrs Brown takes centre stage, seated in her railway carriage and engaged in a mysterious and inconclusive conversation, for life happens anywhere, often among places and people that art has not yet recognized. With 'Byron and Mr Briggs', Woolf had abandoned her thoughts on 'reading' people, a skill typically practised in a railway carriage – now they returned, revised, to find their proper place.

'Character in Fiction' (as this lecture was entitled) further develops the concept of social and cultural rupture, famously tying it down to a single historical moment: 'on or about December 1910 human character changed'.[64] The end of the essay perceives a growing gap, not merely between Edwardians and Georgians, but between the Georgians and their reading public, a gap that had provoked the Georgians to go too far, encouraging them to undermine 'the very foundations and rules of literary society'. Now it was up to their readers, not only to accept 'a season of failures and fragments', but to demand that Mrs Brown be properly 'read' and truthfully represented, for '[i]t is this division between reader and writer, this humility on your part, these professional airs and graces on ours, that corrupt and emasculate the books which should be the healthy offspring of a close and equal alliance between us.' This was the division that *The Common Reader* had failed to confront, and Woolf's image for resolving these differences, both here and later in *A Room of One's Own*, was marriage.[65]

The connection between life and literature, like the connection between *The Common Reader* and *Mrs Dalloway*, must be made by the woman as artist, a role that had unexpected affinities with more traditional female tasks. Woolf gestured towards these in the holograph draft of *Mrs Dalloway*, where Clarissa, stung by Peter Walsh's sneer that she is 'the perfect hostess', attempts to justify herself: 'Life meant bringing together. An artist did the same sort of thing presumably', but the wording was wrong. Woolf struck it out, and took a second shot at it: 'And she did it because it was an offering. Just as somebody writes a book after all.'[66] Neither formulation seemed quite right, and neither survived into the published text. Instead, the analogy between writer and hostess slipped into her essay 'Character in Fiction': '[b]oth in life and in literature it is necessary to have some means of bridging the gulf between the hostess and her unknown guest on the one hand, the writer and his unknown reader on the other.'[67]

Woolf had taken on her father's mantle as a public intellectual, engaging in public debate, yet at the same time she had adopted a decidedly anti-patriarchal stance, repudiating male assumptions about traditional roles, and arguing that women had a significant contribution to make to literary culture, despite or even because of their difference (unlike Desmond MacCarthy, she did not consider men and women to be alike[68]). In entering the predominantly male arena of literary journalism, she had rejected her mother's ideal of womanhood – that of the wife who lived for her husband and family, enlarging men's view of themselves – in order to expose masculine prejudice. No wonder she now reached for the conciliating images of hostess and guests, or of the equality of marriage. She had analysed the 'smash and splinters' that separated the pre-war from the post-war generation. She had dismissed the view that 'Women can't paint, women can't write'. She was now ready to reconsider the roles performed by her mother and father, as well as that of the independent woman artist she had become, and set them out in relation to one another. Once *The Common Reader* and *Mrs Dalloway* had been completed, she would be ready to begin *To the Lighthouse*.

THE COMMON READER: THE AFTERMATH

'Character in Fiction', Virginia's lecture to the Cambridge Heretics Society, was published in T. S. Eliot's quarterly, the Criterion, *in July 1924, and at the end of October was reprinted as a pamphlet under its earlier title, 'Mr Bennett and Mrs Brown', as the first of a series of 'Hogarth Essays'.[69] Thereafter it was variously reviewed. Frank Swinnerton picked up her comments on modern servants, 'in and out of the living room', to point out that it wasn't only modern cooks who were human beings: 'servants were quite alive in the Elizabethan era': Woolf ought to look at the character of Hannah in* Little Women.

Vivien Eliot, writing under a pseudonym in the Criterion, *suggested that one source of Mrs Brown's interest for her author was 'the romance of the humble to the humble's betters'. As Robin Majumdar and Alan McLaurin point out, this essay was to become 'a key document, not only in the assessment of Virginia Woolf's work, but in relation to twentieth-century fiction generally'.[70] In late August, it was published in the* New York Herald Tribune *in two instalments, under the title 'Mr Bennett and Mrs Brown'.[71]*

Did Woolf regard her American readers as different from the British? Though she never discussed the question, she published significantly different versions of her work in the United States. The American edition of The Common Reader, *for example, includes an extra story, 'Miss Ormerod', in the section 'Lives of the Obscure'. This may have been simply because it had first been published in New York, in* The Dial *(a highbrow literary journal edited by Eliot's friend Scofield Thayer), but she may also have expected her American readers to be more responsive to its idiosyncratic blend of biography and fiction. Miss Ormerod had been a distinguished Victorian entomologist, who only figured in the* Dictionary of National Biography *within an entry for her (less distinguished) father. Using Miss Ormerod's memoirs as her point of departure, Woolf created a series of vivid little scenes, from highchair to deathbed, as a sort of novel in miniature. 'Miss Ormerod' was written in 1919, as part of a projected series of 'Eccentrics' intended for the* Athenaeum, *under Middleton Murry's editorship.[72]*

The Common Reader *was published on 23 April 1925, three weeks or so before* Mrs Dalloway, *in an edition of 1,250.[73] In the days that followed, her diary records the usual see-saw of emotions she experienced as her books came out: 'so far I have not heard a word about it, private or public . . . And I am perfectly content, & care less than I have ever cared' (27 April); 'a little fidgety . . . But this is quite recognisably superficial' (29 April); 'a dull chill depressing reception; & complete failure' (1 May).[74] Ten days later, it was clear that the book was widely admired – by Cambridge, in the person of Goldsworthy Lowes Dickinson, as 'the best criticism in English'; by the literary establishment in the person of Thomas Hardy, '[a]nd I get treated at great length & solemnity by old gentlemen'.[75] The climax came in the*

The common reader

Virginia Woolf

form of an encomium from Lytton, by now an influential critic himself.
He thought it 'divine, a classic', preferring it to Mrs Dalloway. *After*
that, the scales tipped the other way, and The Common Reader *became*
'a book too highly praised now'.[76] *Other friends, including Janet Case,*
considered it the more material achievement – for Case, Mrs Dalloway
was 'all dressing', whereas The Common Reader *had 'substance'. As*
Leonard observed, 'many of the people who cannot understand or
dislike or ridicule her novels agree that in The Common Reader *and*
her other books of essays she showed herself to be a very remarkable
literary critic.'[77]

Although The Common Reader *was nowhere explicitly feminist, as*
A Room of One's Own *would be, it was written as Woolf began to*
announce her concern for equality of education, opportunities and
acceptance for women. Her Bloomsbury friends were often puzzled
by her attitude, finding the clear-cut political goals of Ray and Pippa
Strachey easier to understand and accept. Woolf's critique of patri-
archy was subtler and further reaching, less narrowly political, and
thus, ultimately, more threatening. First Forster, and later her biogra-
pher Quentin Bell and her editor Nigel Nicolson, were to find them-
selves alienated by aspects of her feminism (a word she disliked),
though as they wrote, the Women's Movement had begun to echo her
demands, and her outlook suddenly seemed extraordinarily topical.[78]

6

'What a Lark! What a Plunge!'[1]

Near the beginning of Stephen Daldry's film *The Hours*, a preoccupied Virginia (famously played by Nicole Kidman) announces, 'Leonard, I believe I may have a first sentence', retreats upstairs, lights a cigarette and takes up a pen, murmuring, ' "Mrs Dalloway said she would buy the flowers herself." '[2] While this is an effective device for introducing the novel that holds the three narrative strands of the film together, it is most unlikely to have happened this way. For one thing, the first sentence of *Mrs Dalloway* actually reworks the first sentence of Woolf's short story, 'Mrs Dalloway in Bond Street' ('Mrs Dalloway said she would buy the gloves herself').[3] For another, novels usually begin long before their opening words. The central idea for *Mrs Dalloway* had occurred to Woolf twenty years earlier, as a plan for a play she had thought of writing: 'Im going to have a man and a woman – show them growing up – never meeting – not knowing each other – but all the time you'll feel them come nearer and nearer. This will be the real exciting part.'[4]

Mrs Dalloway is the story of a day in the lives of a man and woman who never meet – a society hostess who gives a party, and a shell-shocked soldier who commits suicide. What they have in common or why their stories are told in parallel, the reader must decide, for this is a modernist text, an open text, with no neat climax or final explanation, and what happens seems to shift as we read and reread. Woolf intended her experiment to bring the reader closer to everyday life, in all its confusion, mystery and uncertainty, rejecting the artificial structures and categories of Victorian fiction – its comedy, tragedy, love interest,[5] its concern with secrets, marriage and death. For Woolf, fiction's traditional focus on highly charged moments threatened to

The Hours

Chapter One.

Mrs. Dalloway said she would buy the flowers herself.

For Lucy had her work cut out for her.
The doors would be taken off their hinges; Rumpelmayers
men were coming. And then, thought Clarissa,
what a day! fresh

What a morning! what a plunge! For so it had
always seemed to her, when, with a little squeak of the
hinges, which she could hear now, she had burst open
the French windows as a blessed cut, out on to the
terrace at Bourton, & plunged, at Bourton, out the
terrace into the open air. How fresh, how calm, stiller
than this of course, the air was in the early morning; like
the flap of a wave; the chill of a wave; yet wonderful
out Peter Walsh would say, like the flap of a
wave; like the kiss of a wave; fresh & chill & sharp & yet,
for a girl of eighteen as she was then, how a
little solemn. Peter Walsh would say —
whatever Peter Walsh did say when he found her
"Musing among the vegetables?"
was out that it? "Eliza who didn't know a rose from
a cauliflower." "preferred men to cabbages." She
"I prefer men to cabbages." He must have said it
at breakfast, for her to be thinking out in the terrace.

devalue daily experience. In *Mrs Dalloway*, she set out to restore 'the life of Monday or Tuesday'[6] to its proper, central place in fiction. At the same time, avoiding familiar narrative sequences made greater demands on her readers, requiring them to take a more active role in the process of interpretation.

'Examine for a moment an ordinary mind on an ordinary day',[7] she had urged, in her essay on 'Modern Fiction', and, though the ordinary day turns out to be an extraordinary one, this is just what she does in *Mrs Dalloway*. Using the technique of interior monologue (as in 'The Mark on the Wall'), her fourth novel records the 'myriad impressions'[8] received by the hostess, Clarissa Dalloway, and the soldier, Septimus Warren Smith, and those around them. Seeing their experiences from within gives the reader a more fluid and changeable sense of who they are – more like the confused and fluctuating sense we have of ourselves, compared to the more sharply defined pictures we have of other people. Some readers found this technique unsettling, and complained, as Arnold Bennett had complained of *Jacob's Room*, that she could not create character, but for Woolf it was the traditional way of representing character that was inadequate. Events occurred only insofar as they were registered in and through the mind of an individual. All experience was subjective, as post-impressionist art had recognized, and that subjectivity was part of a wider vision. Working on *Jacob's Room*, she had told Katherine Mansfield, 'I think what I'm at is to change the consciousness, and so to break up the awful stodge'.[9]

She was by no means the only novelist of her generation in flight from inherited conventions: 'This generation must break its neck in order that the next may have smooth going', she had warned Gerald Brenan.[10] E. M. Forster and D. H. Lawrence had rejected the old forms, while Katherine Mansfield, Dorothy Richardson and James Joyce had, in their various ways, all attempted 'to come closer to life', as Woolf had defined it in 'Modern Fiction', aiming to 'record the atoms as they fall upon the mind . . . [to] trace the pattern . . . which each sight or incident scores upon the consciousness'.[11] Mansfield had remained primarily an author of short stories (thus posing less of a threat), but the fiction of Dorothy Richardson and James Joyce, Woolf thought, was ruined by 'the damned egotistical self'. Could this be avoided? '[I]s one pliant & rich enough to provide a wall for the book from oneself?'[12] she wondered. Joyce was most nearly after the same thing as she was. Reluctantly she acknowledged the 'brilliancy' of his writing, while disliking his 'sordidity', his masculine approach to the physical and sexual aspects of life.[13] Nevertheless, she adopted from *Ulysses* the idea of describing a June day in the life of a city, substituting London for Dublin; and the separate paths of Stephen Daedalus and Leopold Bloom (who only meet at night in the later chapters) may also have contributed to the construction of her novel.

Clarissa Dalloway and Septimus Warren Smith, hostess and ex-soldier, are at once linked and antithetical, for Clarissa is the insider, living at the heart of the English establishment – at Westminster, the seat of government. Septimus is the outcast; the victim of shell shock, he embodies the troubled unconscious of a society that has buried its dead and turned back to the business of living. The term 'shell shock' itself only became familiar in the autumn of 1922 (as Woolf began her writing) with the publication of a government report on its 'deferred effects'. The doctors, society's psychic policemen, try to bully Septimus into conformity, urging him to behave normally, and threatening to shut him away if he cannot do so. Clarissa belongs to the society that would silence him, though as a woman, she takes no part in the workings of power. Instead, her role is to entertain, to encourage her husband and his friends to relax after the burdens of decision-making. She leads a frivolous and snobbish life, yet beneath that there is something genuinely creative in her delight in London and her pleasure in giving parties that offsets her social irresponsibility. Woolf was uniquely placed to create these two contrasting characters. As her friend E. M. Forster observed, this was a novel 'written from personal experience'.[14]

Suicide and a party provide the climaxes of Woolf's novel. They correspond to an artistic problem, addressed here, and later, in *To the Lighthouse* and *The Waves*: how to negotiate between individual consciousness, conveyed through interior monologue (sometimes called 'stream of consciousness'), and the consciousness of the group.[15] Writing *Jacob's Room* had alerted her to a problem created by interior monologue – that it risked producing a series of self-absorbed, non-interactive characters. *Mrs Dalloway* is centrally concerned with the relationship between the individual and the group, and in it, Woolf

solved this problem triumphantly, so that, though individual characters affect one another in powerful (and sometimes powerfully oppressive) ways, all respond to shared experiences – an explosion in Bond
Street as a car backfires, an aeroplane sky-writing,[16] an old woman
singing in Regent's Park, the striking of clocks, the heat of the day, the
excitement of the London season, and, most nebulous of all yet also
most significant, the mood of post-war disillusion, the mood of a
society that has resumed its former way of life, as if the millions of
young men had not died, as if the war had been no more than a test of
British stoicism in the face of adversity.

Relating events through the consciousness of individuals provides
fewer opportunities for the traditional voice of the narrator to pass
judgement, and gives the reader greater freedom to judge, as in a play.
Indeed, at an early stage Woolf had thought of creating 'the impression
of a play; only in narrative',[17] but that had led to further problems.
She had begun to experiment with combinations of interior monologue
and shifting viewpoint in *Jacob's Room*, where street or café scenes
had often involved various characters who appeared only once. There
she had adopted a narrative persona from which to record her response
to Jacob's masculinity, to the English class system, and other topics.
In *Mrs Dalloway*, however, the role of the narrator is significantly
reduced, and most of what happens is seen through the eyes of a
particular individual, and sometimes more than one. Clarissa's party
itself posed the greatest problem. It fascinated Woolf so much that
after the book was finished, she composed a further series of episodes
from it.[18]

The suicide and the party correspond to individual versus group
consciousness, and also to solitude versus company. During the early
1920s, Woolf was sharply conscious of moving, sometimes abruptly,
from one to the other. Writing is a notoriously solitary occupation,
but when Woolf was absorbed in it (and *Mrs Dalloway* was written in
parallel with *The Common Reader*), she would spend hours rehearsing
an argument or acting out a scene in her head: 'I am ashamed, or
perhaps proud, to say how much of my time is spent in thinking,
thinking, thinking about literature',[19] she told one correspondent. 'I'm
much interested; can't stop making it up,'[20] she wrote in her diary, and
'how entirely I live in my imagination; how completely depend upon

spurts of thought, coming as I walk, as I sit; things churning up in my mind & so making a perpetual pageant, which is to me my happiness'.[21] At such times she wanted only to be alone, even to the extent of wishing she lived by herself,[22] despite her pleasure in Leonard's quiet comradeship. At the same time, she delighted in laughter, congenial company and partying, and was increasingly attracted by London and London society, unlike Leonard, who found it irksome. She was becoming 'a small Lioness', her growing reputation bringing invitations from society hostesses such as Sybil Colefax and Emerald Cunard.[23]

If the contrast between isolation and involvement was an aspect of personal experience, it also corresponded to one of the major political debates of the post-war years. During the First World War, pacifists and socialists had pinned their hopes for the future on improving international relations through the establishment of a League of Nations, providing mutual protection. After the war, England might have drawn closer to Europe, both politically and culturally (Europe was already central to the modernist aesthetic of Fry and Bell). But as *Mrs Dalloway* reveals, the English governing classes traditionally distrusted Europe and preferred their insularity, concentrating instead on the special relationship with the Empire (crumbling though it now was, as Ireland achieved independence and India demanded it). The insularity of English 'society' (in the limited sense of its ruling elite, as opposed to the community as a whole)[24] also contributed to unrest at home. The war had ploughed up the social system, taking out a whole generation of young men, giving women work and votes and establishing the Labour Party as a political force, yet the old class structure had scarcely changed. Rail and coal strikes registered working-class resentment.

Virginia and Leonard were Labour Party members (Leonard stood for Parliament in 1920, but failed to get elected, to their mutual relief) and supported the strikers,[25] but their own position, like that of many of their contemporaries, was one of compromise. By this stage, the Woolfs had homes at Richmond and Rodmell, and two live-in servants, Lottie Hope and Nelly Boxall. Virginia had a distinctly uneasy relationship with them. She could not bring herself either to patronize them confidently (as her mother would have done, and as Clarissa does in the novel) nor concede them equal status, lest they became demanding and intruded upon her work. In theory, she could celebrate the Georgian cook as 'a creature of sunshine and fresh air; in and out of the drawing room, now to borrow the *Daily Herald*, now to ask advice about a hat';[26] in practice, she resented such interruptions. Her unease over the 'servant problem' echoed the unease she felt over her unearned capital – they provided the freedom to write, while making her feel guilty, as a member of the ruling class rather than the ruled.[27] Now she found herself welcomed by exactly those 'South Kensington' circles that she and Vanessa had rebelled against in their youth – and not merely welcomed, but embraced as one of their own.

Ambivalent feelings about her own social status leaked into the new novel and became a part of its texture. Clarissa, like her author, lives a woman's life, with a woman's changing consciousness. We see the world as Clarissa sees it, shopping, coming into the house on a hot day ('the hall . . . was cool as a vault' [p.31]), mending her dress, lying down after lunch – the life of an English lady. Women readers have often identified with her, yet to do so unquestioningly is to overlook her harsh judgements and narrow sympathies. Clarissa hates the bitter feminist Miss Kilman, with her dreary clothes, her religious fanaticism and her barely suppressed anger; she does not want to invite Ellie Henderson to her party because she dislikes 'frumps'; she is too snobbish to visit her old friend Sally Seton in Manchester. And in a notorious passage, as Richard goes back to sit on a committee on the Armenian question, she 'cared much more for her roses than for the Armenians. Hunted out of existence, maimed, frozen, the victims of cruelty and injustice (she had heard Richard say so over and over again) – no, she could feel nothing for the Albanians, or was it the Armenians?' [p.132] Clarissa's uncertainty exposes both her ignorance and her lack of sympathy, yet perhaps Woolf was less critical of her reaction than we are. When, soon after the war, her friend Janet Case was depressed by the Turkish massacres of Armenians (often cited as the first deliberate genocide of the twentieth century), Woolf was surprisingly dismissive: 'I laughed to myself over the quantities of Armenians. How can one mind whether they number 4,000 or 4,000,000? The feat is beyond me.'[28]

For Clarissa, the Russians, Germans and Armenians do not count;

like the poor mothers of Pimlico with their babies, they are beyond her purview. She, and her friends, have turned their back on the lower levels of society, as they have on Europe and the war dead, represented in the novel by Septimus and his Italian wife, Rezia.[29] When Septimus refuses to be silenced, he is driven to his death in what amounts to a ritual re-enactment of the sacrifice of his generation, impaled on the spikes of the area railings rather than on the barbed wire of No Man's Land. When Clarissa learns of his death, she is momentarily shaken into identifying with him, yet what does her identification amount to? Woolf worried, as we do, about the value of sympathetic feelings that have no practical outcome: thinking about the War Reparations Conference and the civil war in Ireland in 1921, she wondered whether it was 'a proof of civilisation to envisage suffering at a distance'.[30] Clarissa turns back from confronting Septimus's death to rejoin the party (and Woolf would continue to rewrite the feelings with which she did so[31]).

Clarissa is humanly inconsistent: at once cold and self-absorbed ('some distaste for her persisted', Woolf recalled, but 'one must dislike people in art without its mattering'[32]); yet also warm, quick and full of sympathy. Peter Walsh had once sneered at her as 'the perfect hostess', an accusation that had made her cry,[33] yet there is also something creative about her party-giving. Clarissa herself sees the party as an 'offering', an 'offering for the sake of offering' (Septimus's suicide is also described as an offering in Woolf's manuscript version).[34] Clarissa does what women do best, do supremely – she has 'that extraordinary gift, that woman's gift, of making a world of her own wherever she happened to be.' [p.83][35] At such points Clarissa seems close to Woolf's party-loving side, 'a piece of jewellery I inherit from my mother'.[36] She stands at the centre of the novel, its starting point and ending, with a generative power of presence that she shares with Julia Stephen and Mrs Ramsay in To the Lighthouse – 'For there she was.'[37]

On Good Friday 1922, with Jacob's Room effectively finished, Virginia replied to an invitation from 'Tom' (T. S.) Eliot to write something for the Criterion, explaining that she would not send him the short story she was working on, but might write something else for him, and enquiring 'When are we to see your poem?'[38] His poem was *The Waste Land*; her short story was 'Mrs Dalloway in Bond Street'. In it, she brought the Dalloways, the couple who had first appeared in *The Voyage Out*, to London. Several characters from earlier books turn up again in *Mrs Dalloway*: Mr Bowley from *Jacob's Room* looks up at the aeroplane sky-writing, at the beginning, and Mrs Hilbery from *Night and Day* attends Clarissa's party at the end.[39] In *The Voyage Out*, the Dalloways had boarded the *Euphrosyne* at Lisbon, and left soon afterwards, staying just long enough to be mocked for their chauvinism. When the Mediterranean fleet appears, 'two sinister grey vessels . . . with the look of eyeless beasts seeking their prey', Clarissa squeezes Rachel's hand, and asks her, 'Aren't you glad to be English?'[40]

In 'Mrs Dalloway in Bond Street', Clarissa is older but not noticeably wiser. High Tory complacency is still in evidence as she approaches Buckingham Palace, reflecting on what the monarchy means 'to the poor, . . . and to the soldiers . . . There it stood four-square, in the broad sunshine, uncompromising, plain. But it was character, she thought; something inborn in the race; what Indians respected.'[41] Yet there is one crucial difference from *The Voyage Out*: the story's events are now seen through Clarissa's eyes. And creating her consciousness from within also involved giving her a body, and a woman's distinctive awareness of her body. Woolf may have had in mind how frankly Joyce had represented men's experience of their bodies in *Ulysses* – she had been rereading *Ulysses* in August 1922, while working on 'Mrs Dalloway in Bond Street'.[42]

In the short story, Clarissa walks from Westminster to Bond Street to buy a pair of gloves. Looking at the tired shop girl, she wonders whether it was 'perhaps the one day in the month . . . when it's an agony to stand' (Woolf's own periods were notoriously painful, especially on the first day, when she often took to her bed).[43] Earlier, Clarissa had chatted to Hugh Whitbread about his wife, whom he described as 'out of sorts', though both silently recognize that she is undergoing the menopause. Their polite skirting around the subject reminds Clarissa of how, when she was a girl, 'one would rather die than speak to one's brother' about menstruation, when 'perhaps one of them (drat the thing!) couldn't ride. How then could women sit in Parliament? How could they do things with men? For there is this extraordinarily deep instinct, something inside one; you can't get over it; it's no use trying.'[44] For Clarissa, women's 'disabilities' effectively exclude them from participating in the male sphere of politics. The novel, by contrast, does not address the question of women's bodily processes explicitly, or their connection with male power, yet Clarissa's life at the heart of Westminster and her exclusion from any of its workings reflects her assumption that women could not 'do things with men'. Woolf's short story registers her impatience with conventions that prevented women writers from writing openly about their own bodies, while imposing fewer such restrictions on men.[45]

'Mrs Dalloway in Bond Street' includes many elements that reappear in the novel – Clarissa growing up in an English country house, her pleasure in the greenness of the London park, the restrained opulence of Bond Street, the fullness of life in June at the height of the season, and, by contrast, death – the deaths of Jackie Stewart, of Clarissa's sister Sylvia, of Lady Bexborough's favourite Roden, but above all, the war dead: 'Thousands of young men had died that things might go on.'[46] Yet what goes on is merely a continuation of the old pre-war existence: Clarissa is still buying gloves for her party, even though 'Gloves have never been quite so reliable since the war'.[47] She consoles herself with words from Shakespeare and Shelley: the dead have escaped life's miseries – the 'heart grown cold', the disappointments and doubts of middle age.[48]

By 4 October 1922, the story was finished. Two days later, Woolf set out her 'Thoughts upon beginning a book to be called, perhaps, At Home: or The Party'. It would consist of 'six or seven chapters, each complete separately, yet there must be some sort of fusion'.[49] She listed eight chapter headings, starting with 'Mrs Dalloway in Bond Street' and 'The Prime Minister', which she intended to begin writing that morning.[50] This second 'chapter' opens with the off-stage explosion that had ended 'Mrs Dalloway in Bond Street', and concerns the members of a lunch club who meet in Leicester Square to discuss politics, perhaps inspired by Leonard's 1917 Club in Gerrard Street, Soho.[51] One of them, Septimus Smith, is the victim of paranoiac delusions. He believes he is Christ and plans to kill himself and the Prime Minister: 'My name will be on all the placards, he thought. He could do anything, for he was now beyond law.'[52]

'The Prime Minister' articulates several of the novel's political strands, though it was never published, and all but the character of Septimus Smith was discarded. Her aim here, as in the novel, was 'to criticise the social system, & to show it at work, at its most intense – '.[53] 'The Prime Minister' examines some of the political implications of the peace, treating them rather more explicitly than the ensuing novel would do, where sympathy for the Russians and Austrians is confined to the odious Miss Kilman.[54] Among the luncheon club members, H. Z. is conscious of 'the overwhelming injustice which at that very moment, . . . weighed upon Russians, Germans, Austrians', as well as 'the injustice which Turks inflict upon Armenians'.[55] Mrs Lewis is delighted to read in the newspaper that 'the coalition candidate had been hopelessly beaten by labour' (the first ever Labour government would come to power two years later, in January 1924).[56] The Prime Minister is denounced for having 'brought this country to depths of degradation "unparalleled" said H. Z. Prentice "in my experience!" '[57] Woolf explores the mystique that surrounds the Prime Minister, but in a vein of scepticism that recalls chapter XIII of *Jacob's Room*, where the Cabinet, meeting on the eve of war, had been dwarfed by the busts of great eighteenth-century statesmen.

'Authority issued; and government; power; order', when the Prime Minister's car reaches Downing Street.[58] In *Mrs Dalloway*, Woolf caricatured the English ruling classes – politicians, courtiers, aristocrats, heads of professions – and the way they dress up for their various roles. The Prime Minister himself sets the tone for the whole establishment; the grandeur of his costume diminishing, rather than enhancing, his stature: 'You might have stood him behind a counter and bought biscuits – poor chap, all rigged up in gold lace.' [p.188][59] The English class system produces an exaggerated respect for authority. The ruling classes expect and receive obedience. They set the tone, just as the clocks set the time, with Big Ben regulating and presiding over them all, like the Prime Minister himself.[60]

The day after Woolf began to write 'The Prime Minister', Saturday 7 October, was interrupted 'so strangely – by Kitty Maxse's death; . . . I read it in the paper.'[61] Kitty Maxse was the point of origin for the character of Clarissa Dalloway. As Kitty Lushington, she had been a protégée of Virginia's mother, an intimate of her half-sister Stella and, for a while, of Vanessa. Like Minta in *To the Lighthouse*, she got engaged under the clematis in the 'love corner' at Talland House, St Ives, the Stephens' holiday home.[62] Kitty's fiancé, Leo Maxse, later became the editor of the right-wing, imperialist periodical the *National Review*. After their mother's death, Kitty had encouraged the Stephen girls to enter 'society', but her 'South Kensington' outlook seemed to them increasingly absurd – Virginia remembered 'How she used to implore Nessa and me not to know people like Leonard!' She caricatured her, first in a private fantasy (where she utters such banalities as 'The great thing in life, I'm sure (& so is Leo) . . . is never to lose your interest in things . . .'),[63] and later (and more sharply) in *The Voyage Out*, as well as in a diary entry, after bumping into her in Knightsbridge in December 1917. Now she recalled with affection 'her white hair – pink cheeks – . . . her earrings, her gaiety, yet melancholy; . . . very charming – very humorous'.[64] Kitty had inexplicably fallen over the banisters. Dying, she apparently told the doctor, 'I shall never forgive myself for my carelessness'. Virginia could not understand how it had happened, and could not believe it was an accident. Could it have been suicide?[65]

When Woolf described how she came to write *Mrs Dalloway*, six years later, she represented it as an organic process, 'as the oyster starts or the snail to secrete a house for itself. And this it did without any conscious direction, . . . it was necessary to write the book first and to invent a theory afterwards.'[66] She seems to have done just that, explaining 'that in the first version Septimus, who later is intended to be her double, had no existence; and that Mrs Dalloway was originally to kill herself, or perhaps merely to die at the end of the party.'[67] Yet there is no independent evidence of any such 'first version', and she later commented that 'the character of Septimus in Mrs Dalloway was invented to complete the character of Mrs Dalloway' (which looks nearer the mark). There is certainly no suggestion of Clarissa's death in 'Mrs Dalloway in Bond Street', where it is the young men who die, and are survived by mourning older women.[68]

Woolf's memories of composing do not always correspond to how it seemed to her at the time: while Kitty Maxse's sudden death could easily have suggested Clarissa's, it seems instead to have brought Septimus into the story. The following Saturday, 14 October, Woolf was still wondering how Kitty had died – 'Some one presumably knows,' – but the same diary entry notes that 'Mrs Dalloway has branched into a book; & I adumbrate here a study of insanity & suicide: the world seen by the sane & the insane side by side – something like that. Septimus Smith? – is that a good name?'[69] It seems that Kitty Maxse's death focused her thoughts about suicide as a motif in the new novel, yet at the same time she recognized the need to displace it onto a character more obviously distanced from herself in terms of gender, age and experience than Clarissa was. Septimus, the victim of paranoiac delusions in 'The Prime Minister', and of shell shock in the novel, stood for an aspect of herself that Woolf was now determined to set behind her. The previous summer of 1921 had been interrupted by two months of her old illness. Recovering, she had resolved that 'this shall never, never, happen again'.[70] The following year, she set about exorcizing her experience through the creation of Septimus.

Once Septimus had split off from Clarissa, he introduced an alternative rhythm: 'The pace is to be given by the gradual increase of S's insanity on the one side; by the approach of the party on the other',[71] Woolf noted. Clarissa and Septimus come together only when Clarissa learns of Septimus's death: 'Oh! thought Clarissa, in the middle of my party, here's death, she thought' [p.201] – a sentiment as old as the Prayer Book's 'In the midst of life we are in death',[72] and as new as Joyce's masterpiece, 'The Dead', the last story in *Dubliners*. During November, she wondered whether to bring the two stories to a simultaneous climax: 'All must bear finally upon the party at the end; which expresses life in every variety & full of conviction: while S. dies.'[73] At the height of a June season two years earlier, there had been a party at 50 Gordon Square, where the guests sat and chatted on the roof, among chairs and fairy lights. One young man had stepped off and fallen thirty feet to his death. Only Virginia's brother Adrian had seen it happen. He summoned help and climbed over the wall to give first aid, but the boy had died in the ambulance. Just as Clarissa would imagine what Septimus's death must have felt like – 'Always her body went through it first, when she was told, suddenly, of an accident' [p.201] – so did Virginia: 'It was odd how, sitting high up, one began to get a sense of falling.' Though there was no apparent connection, the same diary entry observed 'Our generation is daily scourged by the bloody war.'[74]

Through the winter of 1922, Woolf continued to work on the early sections of *Mrs Dalloway* and to plan the novel as a whole. *Jacob's Room* had been published in late October, and the admiration of her close friends brought her great satisfaction. In November, she felt very busy and very happy, wanting to say (like Mrs Ramsay) ' "Time stand still here", which is not a thing that many women in Richmond could say I think.' And in December, she was singing to herself 'People & books . . . to the tune of Woman & Wine', from *The Beggar's Opera*.[75] But early in the new year came the news of Katherine Mansfield's death of a lung haemorrhage. Woolf's reaction, as she recorded, was initially cool: 'A shock of relief? – a rival the less? Then confusion at feeling so little – then, gradually, blankness & disappointment; then a depression.'[76] Mansfield's death continued to haunt her during the writing of *Mrs Dalloway*, and in October 1924, as she wrote the final words and glimpsed her next novel, her thoughts returned to Katherine, 'the strange ghost' whom she had now so far outdistanced.[77] Her next novel would be strangely coloured by Mansfield's vision of a childhood beside the sea – 'Prelude', typeset and printed by the Woolfs in 1917.

For the first six months of 1923, Woolf sketched out scenes and ideas, wondering whether she could use nameless bystanders as choric figures, and whether to break up her text into chapters or divide it into scenes, like the acts of a play. By 7 May, she realized that she needed another character, 'some old buck' to share Clarissa's past, and by the 18th, he had become the passionate and unreliable Peter Walsh, whom Clarissa had rejected in favour of the steadier Richard Dalloway.[78] Walsh would return unexpectedly from India. Like Clarissa, this new character was rooted in Woolf's early life, being inspired, in part at least, by her older cousin Harry Stephen, who had retired from the Indian Civil Service near the end of the war. He was '[a]n undoubted failure . . . He still takes out an enormous pocket knife, & slowly half opens the blade, & shuts it.'[79] By June 1923, she had drafted the early scenes of Clarissa buying flowers, the explosion and the sky-writing. She reckoned the 'real beginning' of her novel from August that year, though the first surviving manuscript notebook, tentatively entitled

'The Hours?', is dated 27 June, and begins at section 4, with Peter Walsh's walk through Westminster, after leaving Clarissa's house (in the event, the novel was not divided into chapters but into twelve unnumbered sections).[80]

'Dalloway Day' is an unidentified Wednesday in June 1923, perhaps the 13th, when, according to Woolf's diary, 'Nessa is back & the London season of course in full swing'. The previous day, she had attended the first performance of Edith Sitwell's *Façade* at the Aeolian Hall, where the poet read her verses through a megaphone to the music of William Walton.[81] Virginia had felt a sense of inexplicable elation: 'Often now I have to control my excitement – as if I were pushing through a screen; or as if something beat fiercely close to me.'[82] But what was all this about? A week later, she arrived at a major decision: 'we must leave Richmond & set up in London . . . Leonard remains to be converted'.[83] After ten years of marriage, their relationship had settled into a close and dependent companionship, with deep affection on both sides. But persuading him turned out to be more difficult than she had expected, and she found herself 'baffled & depressed' at his reluctance.[84] His chief objection was the old one, that it would be bad for her health – always a difficult issue between them. While she enjoyed parties and socializing, he attempted to protect her from the consequences of over-excitement and over-stimulation. She did not like to 'venture against his will', yet resented his nannying, finding him 'too much of a Puritan, of a disciplinarian'. 'But then, Lord! . . . what I owe to him! What he gives me!' Though her diary could be harsh about others, she was careful what she said about Leonard – he was, after all, its likeliest reader, both then and later.[85]

By July, Leonard had relented sufficiently to agree that a move might be possible, though not until autumn or the new year.[86] By October, she had begun actively house-hunting, while the novel slowly edged forward with Septimus as its new focus: 'I am now in the thick of the mad scene in Regents Park. I find I write it by clinging as tight to fact as I can, & write perhaps 50 words a morning.'[87] Woolf's manuscript notebooks are full of deletions and insertions; she rewrote whole paragraphs and sequences, end on end, sometimes several times, but this is particularly true of the scenes with Septimus, which gave her real difficulty.[88] Much of what she wrote found its way into the finished text, but only after careful cutting and polishing: the terrors and visions of Septimus, and his painful relationship with his doctors, Holmes and Bradshaw, were especially heavily revised. Yet though she was writing slowly, she was deeply absorbed: the design was the most original and demanding she had ever worked on, and she was evolving a technique for narrating the past as memories, almost like cinematic flashbacks – 'what I call my tunnelling process, by which I tell the past by instalments, as I have need of it.' Though writing about Septimus upset her, she was more worried about the character of Clarissa, which 'may be too stiff, too glittering & tinsel[l]y'.[89]

Although she looked at houses in Chelsea, Maida Vale and Battersea, her house-hunting focused chiefly on Bloomsbury, where her family and many of her friends still lived. She finally found what she was looking for at 52 Tavistock Square, and on 9 January 1924, she took out a ten-year lease on that tall, eighteenth-century house – so tall, indeed, that the Woolfs shared it with Dollman and Pritchard, a firm of solicitors who occupied the ground and first floors.[90] The Hogarth Press was relegated to the basement, while the Woolfs lived upstairs, 'over the shop'. At last the whole of London was within her grasp, bringing her 'music, talk, friendship, city views, books, publishing, something central & inexplicable'.[91] But Leonard was still reluctant, and she was not always confident that her enthusiasm would carry them through the inconvenience, mess and expense of it all. Signing the lease, she looked back over her years at Hogarth House, recalling that she had moved there in the middle of her worst breakdown, 'when I was creeping about, like a rat struck on the head'. Yet she had also experienced strange ecstasies there, 'lying in bed, mad, & seeing the sunlight quivering like gold water, on the wall. I've heard the voices of the dead here. And felt, through it all, exquisitely happy.' Septimus too would have his moments of rapture, moments when 'Beauty was everywhere.'[92]

The move to London finally took place in mid-March. Leonard lapsed into gloom – 'Not a stroke of work done he says, since we came to London'[93] – but Virginia was in high spirits, so excited by the beauty of the city that she was afraid it might interrupt her diary for good. The house was 'perfect', her studio, 'the best study I've ever had', and now the novel began to flow. By early April, she had finished the scene of Septimus's consultation with Sir William Bradshaw; four months later, she had reached his suicide.[94] By September 1924, she was on her 'last lap', Clarissa's party, and she completed the first draft by mid-October with a sense of being 'rather more fully relieved of my meaning than usual'. Now she was ready to revise, though she had yet to reread the early chapters, and confessed to 'dreading the madness rather'.[95]

Rewriting madness had involved partly reliving it: 'the mad part tries me so much, makes my mind squint so badly that I can hardly face spending the next weeks at it', she confided to her diary. In lines later deleted from the manuscript, Septimus 'squinted too . . . It was his eyes that were terrible. He wished to die.'[96] Creating Septimus had been an act of exorcism, in which she summoned up her own experiences in order to write them out of her system and into his, and ultimately into the imagination of her readers. While shell shock (or war trauma) was distinctly different from her own breakdown, the symptoms were comparable, and so was the treatment. As Elaine Showalter has pointed out, the treatment of shell-shocked soldiers was influenced by that of pre-war women patients, and for both, class distinctions often determined the nature of their treatment. As an officer, Septimus Warren Smith would be forced to undergo a rest cure, as Virginia had been, and 'neurasthenics' were. Had he been a private, he might have been subjected to the electric shocks and cigarette burns administered to the lower ranks, when they suffered breakdowns.[97]

'Septimus Smith? – is that a good name?'[98] she asked herself, without explaining why she had named him 'the seventh'. Could it refer, consciously or unconsciously, to the seven trips into her own inner darkness, in 1895, 1904, 1910, 1912, 1913, 1915 and, most recently, in the summer of 1921? Or had she seen herself as 'Septima', the seventh of the eight children in the Duckworth–Stephen family? Septimus's experiences are virtually the only record we have of what Woolf's illness felt like from the inside, and as such, they echo moments from her earlier fictions. Like the delirious Rachel in *The Voyage Out*, Septimus imagines himself drowned or exposed upon a high mountain ledge;[99] like the old man in Woolf's short story 'Kew Gardens', he identifies Thessaly as the country of the dead, fearing their return;[100] like Virginia in 1904, he hears the birds singing in Greek, not as a moment of grotesque comedy (as in the paper she read to the Memoir Club), but as a revelation of beauty; like Virginia in 1915, he is appalled by the sight of 'a maimed file of lunatics'.[101] Woolf both articulates and analyses the stages of his madness. When his beloved friend Evans was killed, Septimus could feel nothing (Woolf remembered her own embarrassed giggles at her mother's death). This failure, as he sees it, is succeeded by guilt, persecution, delusions of grandeur – 'the most exalted of mankind; the criminal . . .; the victim . . .; the fugitive; the drowned sailor; the poet . . .; the Lord' – and finally despair.[102]

Between them, his two doctors, Holmes and Bradshaw, epitomize the many consultants that Virginia had endured. Holmes (whose name recalls both the Victorian sleuth and that of a contemporary army neurologist[103]) is stupid and insensitive, while Bradshaw is smooth and at the top of his profession. Both insist upon the importance of maintaining weight by eating porridge and drinking milk, the need for calm and sleep (if necessary, induced by bromide or veronal), and 'rest, rest, rest'.[104] In their different ways, each is repulsive, and not merely to Septimus. Clarissa, who had once accompanied a friend to a consultation with Dr Bradshaw, suspects him of some unspeakable act of coercion – 'some indescribable outrage – forcing your soul, that was it' [p.202].

Septimus's interview with Sir William Bradshaw was particularly difficult to write. In her first attempt, Woolf described it from Septimus's point of view: 'Most human beings betray each other . . . They cant help finally. Then what remains.'[105] When Bradshaw takes Rezia into the next room, Septimus believes he is about to seduce her, and says so, to Bradshaw's embarrassment. 'Sir William came back with Rezia, who had been crying – naturally. She had been seduced . . . Rezia had fallen clearly into the power of this man . . . They had [indecently] plotted some conspiracy against him.'[106] Septimus's fantasies, as described in the holograph, recall the terrible moments when Virginia had imagined Leonard and Vanessa in league against her, in the depths of her illness: 'Loneliness is a condition of human life' (thinks Septimus):

Marriage even leaves room for treachery.

Get two human beings together & they will always plot against a third.

    You can't really hurt me, Septimus said.

    We don't wish to hurt you, Sir William replied.[107]

At a later stage, Woolf would shift the point of view from Septimus to Bradshaw, thus reducing the element of distortion while increasing the reader's sense of Bradshaw's intolerable egotism, his need to assert himself at the expense of his patients, and his failure to understand or pity them.

Septimus's fear that he has been sexually betrayed is part of a wider preoccupation with sexuality, which he finds reflected in the plays of Shakespeare ('The business of copulation was filth to him before the end' [p.97]), as well as among the people at his office. While Rezia longs for a child, Septimus believes that mankind is vile, and must not be allowed to reproduce. He draws obscene pictures of his fellow-clerks, believes that he has seduced Rezia, and 'outraged' Miss Isabel Pole. At times he is simultaneously conscious of delusion and reality, as when he listens to motor-horns in Regent's Park and hears them as a primeval anthem, bouncing off the rocks and becoming visible columns, or when an old man playing on a penny whistle becomes a shepherd boy piping an elegy. Yet such double visions, though delusional, also affect other characters in the novel. Septimus's state of mind is oddly volatile; moments of terrible despair alternate with moments of intense happiness, and even of calm. Tragically, when he and Rezia finally find a point of serenity, Holmes interrupts and destroys it. Although Septimus had earlier contemplated suicide, he had felt deterred by the practical difficulties. But as Holmes comes up the stairs, he feels cornered, and can find no way out but to fling himself from the window, even though '[h]e did not want to die. Life was good.' [p.164] Like his author in 1913, Septimus turns to suicide from a sense of being trapped – if he falls into Holmes's hands, he will be sent for a rest cure. His suicide is contingent, rather than inevitable; perhaps it always is.

Septimus's voices and visions distinguish him from the other characters in the novel who are better adjusted to the world around them, yet his experiences and theirs seem surprisingly similar, perhaps because so much of the narrative is set out as interior monologue. Their rapidly changing moods seem to echo his, or vice versa, so that the distinction drawn at the outset, between the sane and insane truth, is gradually broken down. E. M. Forster praised this aspect of the novel, considering Woolf 'civilized and sane on the subject of madness . . . she tied it down to being a malady, and robbed it of the evil magic it has acquired through timid or careless thinking'.[108] Peter Walsh, dozing in Regent's Park, also experiences a vision, and he fantasizes about (and follows) a woman he passes in the street, while Clarissa shifts, quite as rapidly as Septimus does, from intense happiness to misery, and back again. She shares something of his sense of profound and unassuageable loneliness, and like him, feels herself a part of everything around her – of people, and even of trees – '[o]dd affinities she had with people she had never spoken to' [p.167]. Like that of Septimus, her marriage is close and loving, yet passionless.

Clarissa's isolation is both personal and political (or rather, apolitical). Living at Westminster, at the hub of governmental decision-making, close to those circles of power that reach out to the far-flung empire and the leaden circles of sound that radiate from Big Ben, she keeps a different time, a different tune, like the little bells of St Margaret's. As a woman she is at once out of place, since political power is a masculine prerogative, yet central, the hostess round whom the party will revolve. Images of circles and margins recur, as characters walk towards or away from the Dalloways' house near Dean's Yard, at the heart of the kingdom, circles that extend but also exclude. Beyond the little enclave of Westminster, on the streets or in the parks live 'the poor mothers of Pimlico' and Westminster with their crawling babies, and the flower-sellers, costermongers, prostitutes and 'female vagrants' whose lives scarcely impinge on Clarissa's. Yet they are not totally invisible: Richard Dalloway, reincarnated as a conscientious conservative (on the model of Woolf's old friend Sir Robert Cecil, perhaps), has taken up their cause, and is fighting on committees for the downtrodden, people whom the police move on, rather as he has taken up the (hopeless) cause of the Armenians. Clarissa herself sometimes feels an affinity with 'the veriest frumps, the most dejected of miseries sitting on doorsteps' because she imagines 'they love life' [p.4].

Close to the physical centre of the novel, where Peter's path crosses that of Septimus and Rezia, Woolf has set the most mysterious of the novel's several old women and female vagrants. Blind and outcast, a beggar woman sings opposite Regent's Park underground station of timeless love with a present passion – a visionary, almost Wordsworthian figure, a survivor from beyond recorded time, she retains the choric status Woolf had sought earlier. A similar figure had appeared in chapter V of *Jacob's Room*, sitting on a camp-stool, and clutching a brown mongrel. Woolf remembered seeing a blind singer in London in 1905, and again in Kingsway, in June 1920: 'There was a recklessness about her; much in the spirit of London. Defiant – almost gay, clasping her dog as if for warmth. How many Junes has she sat there, in the heart of London? . . . gay, & yet terrible & fearfully vivid. Nowadays,' Woolf added, 'I'm often overcome by London; even think of the dead who have walked in the city.'[109] The beggar woman in the novel belongs to an impossibly distant past, to the present and to an equally distant future (she 'would still be there in ten million years'). Her song consists of a series of meaningless syllables – 'ee um fah um so/ foo swee too eem oo –', noises that mean nothing to her listeners (or readers), yet they are also, and antithetically, given a specific point of reference, for as Hillis Miller has pointed out, they are a rough translation of a German poem *Allerseelen* ('All Souls' Day'), by Herbert von Gilm. It was set to music by Richard Strauss, and also by a Belgian composer, Eduard Lassen (1830–1940).

Concerned with the past, lost love and the return of the dead, his melancholy version was popular in its day (1894), and was apparently part of Leonard's repertoire (he was impressively well versed in German poetry and music). In January 1931, Woolf reported to her nephew Quentin that Leonard had sung it at a family party (though whether seriously or as a joke is unclear).[110] The English version (written by Mrs Malcolm Lawson) runs thus:

> Lay by my side your bunch of purple heather,
> The last red asters of an autumn day,
> And let us sit and talk of love together,
> As once in May, as once in May.

Give me your hand, that I may press it gently,
And if the others see, what matter they?
Look in mine eyes with your sweet eyes intently,
As once in May, as once in May.

The third stanza recalls the flowers laid upon graves on All Souls' Day, the day of the year dedicated to the dead.[111] From this point onwards, a sense of past lives linked to the present moment through love and death begins to recur in Woolf's fiction – some continuity of which we are all a part, yet which lies beyond us.[112] While planning Septimus's interview with Sir William Bradshaw, Woolf had groped to define what she meant: 'There must be a reality which is not in human beings at all. What about death for instance? But what is death? Strange if that were the reality – but in what sense could this be so?'[113] The old woman's song, at once incomprehensible, yet heavy with a sense of love and loss, links these mysteries together.

All Souls' is the day when the spirits of the dead traditionally return, rather as Peter Walsh and Sally Seton, once loved by Clarissa, return to her from the past. And, as in the song, there is a sense that, for Clarissa and her friends, passion is confined to the past – it can only be voiced by someone free of social inhibitions. The radical sympathies and strong passions of their youth have gone. Peter still mourns the fact that Clarissa turned him down all those years ago, while she feels torn between relief and regret at her decision. Though she thinks he is absurd to be in love at his age, she also envies him the experience. But later, just before he hears the old woman's song, Peter realizes that he was not actually in love with Daisy – '*she* was in love with *him* . . . Every one if they were honest would say the same; one doesn't want people after fifty' [p.87]. As Peter had boarded the boat for England, he had felt relief at being alone. His imagination is most intensely aroused by the woman he follows across Trafalgar Square, a fantasy creature he can invent and control; unconscious of him, she makes no demands.

Desire in the novel is thus confined to the distant past, or to the possible future of Clarissa's daughter Elizabeth, though even she attracts it rather than experiencing it: she draws not only the desire of young men at the party but also of her tutor, Miss Kilman, who covets her with the same hunger that she feels for a pink cake. Even love cannot redeem poor Miss Kilman, yet women's desire for women is presented very differently in the early pages of the book, where Clarissa remembers the moment on the terrace at Bourton, when Sally Seton kissed her on the lips. It was 'the most exquisite moment of her whole life . . . The whole world might have turned upside down! . . . And she felt that she had been given a present, wrapped up, and told just to keep it, not to look at it.' [p.38] If she had unwrapped it, what would she have found?

The novel is delicately alive to the power of same-sex love, the theme at the heart of Daldry's film of *The Hours* – it is another of the strands that tie Clarissa to Septimus, for his problems had apparently begun with the death of Evans, the commanding officer who became his friend: 'They had to be together, share with each other, fight with each other, quarrel with each other.' [p.94] Woolf does not need to say more; the homoerotic nature of many wartime friendships was familiar from the poetry of Sassoon, Owen, Graves and others.[114] Late in 1919, Woolf had read the memoirs of Ethel Smyth, the composer and lover of women (and later of Woolf herself), noting that 'friendships with women interest me'.[115] Clarissa's passion for Sally echoes Virginia's early crush on Madge Symonds, who was to marry her first cousin Will Vaughan. Like Sally Seton, Madge had grown dull and 'ordinary' with motherhood. After a dire evening in June 1921, when Madge had bored Leonard and Roger Fry to desperation, Virginia remembered her old passion for Madge; she saw herself 'standing in the night nursery at Hyde Park Gate, washing my hands, & saying to myself "At this moment she is actually under this roof." '[116] Madge, like Kitty Maxse and Harry Stephen, were *revenants* from the past, summoned back for the party she had imagined for them.

Though Clarissa's passion for Sally is buried in the past, she retains a sense of not being sexually at home in marriage, and still enjoys a special intimacy with women. When they confide 'some scrape, some folly' to her, she feels 'what men felt'. Woolf describes the experience with an intense – and an intensely sexual – immediacy, in what appears to have been a late addition to her narrative:

It was a sudden revelation, a tinge like a blush which one tried to check and then, as it spread, one yielded to its expansion, and rushed to the farthest verge and there quivered and felt the world come closer, swollen with some astonishing significance, some pressure of rapture, which split its thin skin and gushed and poured with an extraordinary alleviation over the cracks and sores! Then, for that moment, she had seen an illumination; a match burning in a crocus; an inner meaning almost expressed. But the close withdrew; the hard softened. It was over – the moment. [pp.34–5]

Two years earlier, in December 1922, as Woolf was drafting the opening scenes of the novel, Clive Bell had introduced her to a great admirer, the Honourable Vita Sackville-West. Vita recorded her first impression of Virginia for her husband, Harold Nicolson: 'You would fall quite flat before her charm and personality, . . . she dresses quite atrociously. At first you think she is plain; then a sort of spiritual beauty imposes itself on you, and you find a fascination in watching her . . . She is both detached and human, silent till she wants to say something, and then says it supremely well . . . I have quite lost my heart.'[117]

Their friendship began slowly, and with some hesitation on Virginia's part, but twenty months later, as the novel neared its end, Vita spent a night at Monk's House, and Virginia found herself 'peering across Vita at my blessed Mrs Dalloway; & can't stop, of a night, thinking of the next scene & how I'm to wind up. Vita, to attempt a return, is like an over ripe grape in features, moustached, pouting, will be a little heavy; meanwhile she strides on fine legs, in a well cut skirt, & though embarrassing at breakfast, has a manly good sense & simplicity about her . . . Oh yes, I like her; could tack her on to my equipage for all time; & suppose if life allowed, this might be a friendship of a sort.'[118] As she made the final revisions in November 1924, Woolf had tea with Clive Bell's mistress, Mary Hutchinson. Their wary intimacy prompted her to think again about the possibilities of friendship with women: 'what a pleasure – the relationship so secret & private compared with relations with men. Why not write about it? truthfully?'[119]

MRS DALLOWAY: THE AFTERMATH

Woolf completed the first draft of Mrs Dalloway *on 9 October 1924 with a sense of satisfaction: by her own reckoning, it had taken her no more than a year to write, and from the end of March (and the move to Tavistock Square), she had worked away at it with scarcely a break.[120] Eleven days later she began the process of revision, retyping it entirely from the beginning, as she had done with* The Voyage Out *– 'a good method', she thought, 'as thus one works with a wet brush over the whole, & joins parts separately composed & gone dry.'[121] Just before Christmas, she put on 'a spurt' to finish it so that Leonard could read it while they were at Monk's House, over the holiday. 'L. thinks it my best', she noted, '– but then has he not <u>got</u> to think so? Still I agree.'[122] Early in January 1925, the typescript was despatched to R. & R. Clark, the Press's Edinburgh printers, who sent her three sets of proofs, one to be returned for the first British edition, one to cross the Atlantic for simultaneous publication in America, and one to keep for herself. The last two sets have survived, with Woolf's corrections written in.*

She did not keep her own set. During the summer of 1922 she had begun writing to an old friend from the Cambridge group around Rupert Brooke, the 'Neo-Pagans', as she had called them: Jacques Raverat was an English-educated French painter, dark, saturnine and self-confident, whom Virginia had always found attractive.[123] He had been in love first with Ka Cox, and later with Gwen Darwin (who, as Gwen Raverat, is known as a distinguished woodcut artist, and the author of A Period Piece). *The couple had married in 1911 and settled in the artists' colony at Vence, in the south of France. Eleven years later, Raverat wrote to Virginia to tell her how much he had enjoyed* Monday or Tuesday *– but also that he had been struck down with multiple sclerosis, and was forced to give up painting for reading. She was delighted by his praise, and an oddly intimate correspondence ensued, a mixture of reminiscence about old friends and indiscretions about new ones (she confided in him her preference for her own sex, as well as her desire to incite her 'violently Sapphic' friend Vita 'to elope with me next'[124]). In February 1925, as Raverat lay dying,*

Virginia wanted to send him Mrs Dalloway, *but it wasn't due out till May (*The Common Reader, *written alongside* Mrs Dalloway, *would be published in April). She decided to send him her own set of proofs: 'For no other human being in the world would I do this.'*[125] *She would send them uncorrected, so that he might even 'do a little writing on my behalf', she suggested, but then changed her mind.*[126] *There are no alterations to the early pages, but after page 91 she made more than fifty emendations, and at one point pinned in a page of typescript, to be substituted for the printed text. She sewed the pages together and sent them off to 'Jacques/ with love/ from Virginia/ 6th Feb. 1925'.*[127] *Gwen read them out to him, and he dictated a final letter to Virginia: 'Almost it's enough to make me want to live a little longer, to continue to receive such letters and such books . . . I am flattered, . . . proud & pleased . . .'*[128] *He died on 7 March 1925.*

Mrs Dalloway *was the first of Woolf's novels to be published simultaneously in Britain and the United States. She had corrected all three sets of proofs at Rodmell early in February, but had not done so consistently. While she sometimes copied changes from one set to another, she also made independent corrections, so that the version published in America by Harcourt, Brace differs significantly at several points from the British first edition, and the proofs sent to Raverat are different again – in other words, she continued to revise her text right up to the point of publication. The scenes that received most attention were, predictably, those of Septimus's suicide (both surviving sets of proofs have typescripts pinned in here), and Clarissa's response to his suicide. In the typescript additions (and ultimately in the published texts), Septimus considers other ways of killing himself – the bread knife, the gas fire, his razors – while an old man, originally in the house opposite (and thus corresponding to the old woman in the house opposite Clarissa), becomes an old man descending a staircase.*[129] *In the party scene where Clarissa withdraws to think about Septimus's death, something about it 'made her feel the beauty; made her feel the fun' – a phrase that appears in the corrected American proofs, and in the American but not the British first edition, while the Raverat proofs add to that 'immeasurable delight' at surviving, 'that insolence that levity'.*[130] *One critic has objected that these changes are out of character with how Clarissa is portrayed elsewhere in the novel,*[131] *but both passages reflect Woolf's fluid sense of her, even at this late stage of composition.*

In describing Clarissa's reaction in terms of insolence and levity, or a sense of beauty and fun, Woolf may have intended to emphasize courage in the face of death, whether that of Kitty Maxse, Jacques Raverat, or even her own (in 1922 she had undergone a series of medical scares as various specialists diagnosed her as suffering from one serious illness or another).[132] On the other hand, these phrases may act as a criticism of Clarissa as she dismisses Septimus's death – and, by extension, the countless war deaths. Lytton Strachey, exceptional among Woolf's friends in disliking the novel, had a particular problem with the presentation of Clarissa, as Virginia recorded: 'he thinks she is disagreeable & limited, but that I alternately laugh at her, & cover her, very remarkably, with myself.'[133] She saw his point, remembering that she too had found Clarissa 'in some way tinselly' until she had invented her memories – 'I think some distaste for her persisted. Yet, again, that was true to my feeling for Kitty.'[134] For her creator, Clarissa retained a living, inconclusive quality which contributes to the extraordinary power of the book. Later criticism has split along comparable lines, with Marxist (or at any rate, Scrutiny's) attacks on Clarissa as 'a portrait of a privileged woman written by a privileged woman', and feminist defences of her as the 'life force that endures and creates'.[135] One aspect of the problem of Clarissa as a character is the (Victorian or Edwardian) assumption that the novelist – and perhaps her reader – must identify with the 'heroine'.

Mrs Dalloway was published on 14 May 1925, in Vanessa's dust-jacket of black on yellow – a powerful, almost abstract design of a bridge, reflected in water, with a fan and a bunch of roses below, and curtains looped about.[136] At the moment of publication, Virginia found herself surprisingly calm. This was partly due to the critical acclaim for The Common Reader, published in the previous month, but partly from a sense that 'writing is the profound pleasure & being read the superficial'.[137] She was working on a series of short stories set at Clarissa's party, and was already excited by the prospect of To the Lighthouse.[138]

'"This time you have done it – you have caught life & put it in a book"', wrote an unknown man from Earl's Court (according to her diary[139]), consoling her for the reviewers who found Mrs Dalloway

puzzling, or lacking in story or character. Most of Bloomsbury – the faithful Clive Bell, Roger Fry, Raymond Mortimer and E. M. Forster – was enthusiastic,[140] and beyond, though there was some indignation, there was also praise: the Times Literary Supplement *was impressed by the novel's experimentalism, and its power to 'enhance the consciousness and zest of living' (but she was always disappointed by its reviews);[141] the* Saturday Review *singled out 'the sensation of seeing and feeling the very stream of life' in the book, and '[t]he fact that the life of the mind is more significant than the life of the body'; the* New Statesman, *though carping, noticed the cinematic quality of its narrative.[142] Later came warm appreciations from Forster and a young poet, Edwin Muir,[143] but perhaps the most perceptive review of all was that of the future novelist Richard Hughes, writing in the* New York Saturday Review of Literature: *he admired Woolf's re-creation of the visible world, and compared her to Cézanne on the basis of her sense of form in writing (which he carefully distinguished from form in painting). He was particularly struck by the subjective or relative character of the world she had created, noticing that she 'touches all the time the verge of the problem of reality'.[144]*

Woolf's concern with the subjective nature of reality, the separateness of individuals, yet their longing to come together to share experience, extended into the short stories that were the overspill of the novel, yet which might form 'a corridor leading from Mrs Dalloway to a new book'. These stories might 'fill half the book; & then the other thing would loom up; & we should step into quite a different place & people? but what?'[145] In the event, they led nowhere, practically speaking, and only the first of them, 'The New Dress', was published during her lifetime. But they belong with Mrs Dalloway *insofar as they explore the dichotomy at the heart of the novel, the space between the individual and the group: 'people have any number of states of consciousness', she noted. 'I should like to investigate the party consciousness, the frock consciousness &c.'[146]*

Mrs Dalloway *sold slowly at first – just over 2,000 in the first year in Britain. But sixty-seven years later, in January 1992, Penguin printed 12,000 copies, and by the following January had reprinted 14,000 more.[147] Since the success of Daldry's film,* The Hours, *it has become the most popular of Woolf's novels. It is certainly the one that gripped other creative imaginations at the end of the twentieth century. In 1994, it inspired an opera by Libby Larsen, with a libretto by Bonnie Grice, which, while boiling down the plot, made full use of music's power to express feeling in its reworking of Woolf's most contrapuntal narrative.[148] In 1997 it became a film, starring Vanessa Redgrave as Clarissa, Rupert Graves as Septimus and Michael Kitchen as Peter Walsh, scripted by Eileen Atkins and directed by Marlene Gorris.[149] Beautiful to look at, the film introduced much that Woolf's novel had carefully avoided: by making the flashbacks to Bourton central to the unfolding narrative, and turning Clarissa's party into a dance,[150] it effectively recast the novel's action into romance mode. The novel, by contrast, is wary of, and perhaps uneasy with, heterosexual relationships, an aspect picked up in two recent novels that, without exactly being sequels, take* Mrs Dalloway *as their point of departure. In Robin Lippincott's* Mr Dalloway,[151] *Richard celebrates his thirtieth wedding anniversary by taking Clarissa and a party of friends to see the eclipse of 1927 (as Virginia and Vita would do), meanwhile confiding in a sympathetic Clarissa the story of his ten-year love affair with a young man, Robbie Davies.*

Michael Cunningham's prize-winning novel The Hours[152] *weaves together the narratives of a present-day Clarissa, living with Sally in New York, Mrs Brown, a Los Angeles housewife of 1949, and Mrs Woolf herself on a day in 1923, when she is writing* Mrs Dalloway, *negotiating with Leonard and Nelly, entertaining Vanessa and her children, fending off her 'voices', and desperate to escape from Richmond to London. By the end of the day, she has realized that Clarissa will not commit suicide, as she had planned, but that someone else – 'a deranged poet, a visionary, will be the one to die' – and Septimus's death is re-enacted by Richard, a writer dying of AIDS, in the present-day sequence.[153] Cunningham's novel was movingly filmed by Stephen Daldry from a script by David Hare, starring Meryl Streep as the modern Clarissa, Julianne Moore as Mrs Brown in Los Angeles and Nicole Kidman as Woolf herself.* The Hours *is a fascinating novel and makes a remarkable film; yet to turn back from it to* Mrs Dalloway *is to recognize how easy and uncontrived, but at the same time how inward, experimental and still startlingly modern is this novel, written more than three-quarters of a century ago.*

MRS
DALLOWAY
VIRGINIA WOOLF

7

Writing Itself

'With a curious physical sensation, as if she were urged forward and at the same time must hold herself back, she made her first quick decisive stroke' [p.172]¹ – so Lily Briscoe sets paint brush to canvas, and so her author set pen to paper. When she looked back on the process of writing *To the Lighthouse*, it seemed to have flowed from her 'in a great, apparently involuntary, rush', like '[b]lowing bubbles out of a pipe'. But what, she wondered, 'blew the bubbles? Why then?'² At first she saw it as an exorcism: 'I used to think of [father] & mother daily; but writing [it], laid them in my mind . . . I was obsessed by them both, unhealthily; & writing of them was a necessary act.'³ Ten years further on, she felt she had done for herself 'what psycho-analysts do for their patients. I expressed some very long felt and deeply felt emotion. And in expressing it I explained it and then laid it to rest. But,' she could not resist adding, 'what is the meaning of "explained" it?'⁴

To the Lighthouse is usually regarded as Woolf's masterpiece – that was the word chosen by its first reader, Leonard, to describe it,⁵ and by many others since. It stands at the centre of her career, the fifth of nine novels, and the most directly autobiographical, although personal memories are controlled within an aesthetic form so demanding that it surfaces in the text as Lily Briscoe's meditations on her painting. According to Woolf's plan for it, the novel would begin in Eden, with 'father & mother & child in the garden', but that happy garden state is interrupted by the mother's death. It will end with 'the sail to the lighthouse'.⁶ The garden Woolf envisaged was that of Talland House, near St Ives, with its view across the bay to the Godrevy lighthouse (the same seaside setting that had opened *Jacob's Room*). The Stephen

Aug. 6th 1925

The plan of this book is roughly that it shall consist of three parts:
one; Mr & Mrs Ramsay (?) sitting at the window: while Mr R. walks up &
down in the dark. the idea being that there shall be curves of
conversation or reflection or description or in fact anything, modulated
by his appearance or disappearance at the window. Gradually it
shall grow later; the child shall go to bed: the engaged couple shall
appear: But this is able to be filled up as richly and variously as
possible. My aim is being to find a unit for the sentence which
shall be less emphatic & intense than that in Mrs. D: an everyday
sentence for carrying on the narrative easily. The theme of this 1st
part shall really contribute to Mr R's character; at least
Mrs R's character shall be displayed, but finally with in
conjunction with his, so that one gets an impression of their relationship
To precipitate feeling, there should be a sense of waiting, of expectation:
the child waiting to go to the Light house: the woman awaiting the
return of the couple.

2) The passing of time. I am not sure how this is to be given: an
interesting experiment, giving the sense of 10 years passing

3) this is the voyage to the Lighthouse.

Various characters can be brought in: the young atheist: the old
gentleman: the lovers: episodes can be written on less known by their
beauty; on truth: but there should be a greater
unison in Mrs. W: making a more harmonious whole.
There need be no specification of date.
Whether this will be long or short I do not know. the dominating impression
is to be of Mr R's character.

family had spent each summer there from Virginia's birth in 1882 until 1895, the year of her mother's sudden death. There the children could run wild, fight, tell stories, play cricket, hunt for moths, walk on the sands and swim in the sea. The terrace beyond the French windows, the stone urns with their tumbling geraniums, the beds of fuchsia and red-hot pokers, the scent of the escallonia hedges, the rubber-shod pony pulling the mower were among Virginia's best-loved memories. Favourite sounds, too, haunted her inner ear – the beat of the waves upon the shore; the sigh as the acorn of the blind was tugged across the nursery floor by a light draught.[7] That corner of Cornwall was to remain for her 'the loveliest place in the world'.[8]

After his wife's death, Leslie Stephen gave up the lease of Talland House, feeling it unbearable to go back to a place where they had once been so happy, but in 1905, the year after his death, his four grown-up children, Vanessa, Thoby, Virginia and Adrian, returned to nearby Carbis Bay for a long, nostalgic summer holiday. In the twilight, they visited their old home, peering at it through a gap in the hedge, but 'The lights were not our lights; the voices were the voices of strangers. We hung there like ghosts in the shade of the hedge, & at the sound of footsteps we turned away.' The house, once so reassuringly famil-iar, now made them feel 'like ghosts'. And yet, it was 'all, so far as we could see . . . as though we had but left it in the morning'.[9] That sense of a decade having slipped by as if it were no more than a few hours would be incorporated into her novel, and their Wordsworthian revisiting contributed importantly to her sense of the lost house and garden. Late in 1925, as she prepared to write the novel, she reread her account of that holiday twenty years earlier.[10]

St Ives and Cornwall continued to draw Virginia back in her early years. With Clive, Vanessa and their new baby, she returned in the spring of 1908, and in November that year, stayed at the Lizard with Adrian and Lytton Strachey. She spent the following Christmas at Lelant, close to St Ives, going back again with the Bells in the spring of 1910, and taking a Cornish walking holiday that summer. After her marriage to Leonard, the couple visited St Ives in spring 1914, and again in September 1916 and May 1917. Returning once more in March 1921, she recognized it as the foundation of her imaginative life: 'Why am I so incredibly & incurably romantic about Cornwall?

One's past, I suppose: I see children running in the garden. A spring day. Life so new. People so enchanting. The sound of the sea at night ... & almost 40 years of life, all built on that, permeated by that: how much so I could never explain.'[11] This was the vision that inspired *To the Lighthouse*.

Her first glimpse of the novel came in October 1924, as she was finishing the first draft of *Mrs Dalloway*: 'I see already The Old Man',[12] she wrote (the capitals indicating that she meant her father). Six months later she was wondering whether the cluster of short stories she had composed in the wake of *Mrs Dalloway* and set at Clarissa's party might not act as 'a corridor leading from Mrs. Dalloway to a new book'. It did. 'What I expect to happen is that some two figures will detach themselves from the party & go off independently into another volume.'[13] They didn't. Instead, she found herself with that 'quick decisive stroke' writing the words 'To the Lighthouse' at the top of a fresh page of her notebook, and following it with a diagram rather like a letter 'H' – the 'two blocks joined by a corridor', which would make up the structure of the novel – the longer 'Window' and 'Lighthouse' sequences joined by 'Time Passes'.[14] The linking of two contrasting aspects of experience would become a central theme, reflected in Lily Briscoe's struggle 'to connect this mass on the right hand with that on the left' [p.60], her search for 'the light of a butterfly's wing lying upon the arches of a cathedral' [p.54], 'that razor edge of balance between two opposite forces; Mr Ramsay and the picture' [p.209].

For among the opposing forces of the book were Mr and Mrs Ramsay, portraits of Virginia's parents, each of whom claimed her attention. In May 1925, the novel was to focus on 'father's character, sitting in a boat, reciting We perished, each alone, while he crushes a dying mackerel';[15] by August, 'The dominating impression is to be of Mrs R.'s character'.[16] Meanwhile, Virginia was deliberately holding herself back: 'I must write a few little stories first, & let the Lighthouse simmer, adding to it between tea & dinner till it is complete for writing out.'[17] The short stories (eventually eight of them) came quickly, but then so did *Lighthouse* ('thought out, perhaps too clearly'[18]). She put off the actual writing until she and Leonard had retreated to Rodmell for the summer, where she planned to surrender herself to the summers of her childhood.

The short stories that make up *Mrs Dalloway's Party*[19] explore the space between the individual and the group, reworking material left over from *Mrs Dalloway* – loneliness and the subjective nature of experience conflict with the desire to communicate and share. At the same time, their portrayal of the divisions between and within individuals anticipates *To the Lighthouse*, where she would try to 'split up emotions more completely'.[20] '[N]othing is so strange as human intercourse', thinks Ruth Anning in 'Together and Apart', 'because of its changes, its extraordinary irrationality, . . . how obscure the mind was, with its very few words for all these astonishing perceptions, these alternations of pain and pleasure.'[21] Such alternations look forward to 'the terrific high waves and the infernal deep gulfs'[22] that characterize *To the Lighthouse*, and echo her diary entries ('How many phases one goes through between the soup & the sweet!'[23]) She wanted to re-create the constant changes of feeling that pass through human beings as rapidly as clouds or notes of music, changes ironed out in most conventional fiction.

The short stories consist largely of the interior monologues of various party guests, isolated in their self-absorption, self-consciousness or social discomfort, annoying or momentarily delighting each other. Mabel Waring is chagrined by her cheap, unsuitable dress (echoing Virginia's own frequent 'frock' anxieties[24]); Stuart Elton desperately clings to a conviction of his own happiness and inner calm; Mrs Vallance has retreated to the safety of childhood memories; Lily Everitt's elation is dashed by the condescension of Bob Brinsly; Mr Serle and Miss Anning reach a moment of intimacy, only to lose it again; Prickett Ellis and Miss O'Keefe loathe each other,[25] while Mr Carslake observes them all, pitying their 'silences and unhappinesses', and wondering whether they are very similar to one another, but somehow lack the ability to recognize it, or else very dissimilar: 'People pressed upon each other; rubbed each other's bloom off; or, for it told both ways, stimulated and called out an astonishing animation, made each other glow.'[26] In the last story, 'A Summing Up', Sasha Latham is torn between opposing visions – an enchanting golden evening, and a sordid 'bucket or perhaps a boot . . . Then she asked herself, which view is the true one? She could see the bucket and the house half lit up, half unlit.'[27] Woolf was fascinated by her own rapidly changing impulses towards and away from other people, as well as by the artistic problem of how to convey an individual's experience of a shared event. She solved it triumphantly in the dinner party scene that ends the first half of *To the Lighthouse*, and later, with the dinner at Hampton Court in *The Waves*, the party at the end of *The Years* and the audience's reactions in *Between the Acts*.

On 5 August 1925, the Woolfs left London for Rodmell, and the following day Virginia set down her plan for the novel that was so rapidly taking shape. It would begin with Mrs Ramsay sitting in the window, while her husband walked up and down on the terrace outside. Her son (later, James) wants to go the lighthouse the next day, but Mr Ramsay insists that the weather is changing, and they won't be able to go. Mrs Ramsay awaits the return of 'the engaged couple' (later, Paul and Minta). The second section would deal with the passing of time ('I am not sure how'), and the voyage itself would provide the final section.[28] Already Charles Tansley ('the little atheist') and Augustus Carmichael ('the old gentleman') have been envisaged. Only the key figure of the artist, Lily Briscoe, has not yet appeared.

The Ramsays have eight children, as (between them) had Leslie and Julia Stephen. As the second youngest, Virginia's position in the family corresponds to that of Cam. She had written indirectly about her family before – for example as the Hilberys in *Night and Day* – but now she wrote of them uninhibitedly, accepting that they would be recognized,[29] and with an intense nostalgia, changing little other than their names and the location of Talland House. The example of Katherine Mansfield's 'Prelude',[30] which celebrated scenes from her childhood while exposing the grown-up tensions that lay beneath, was a liberating one. Both here and in the sequel 'At the Bay' (in *The Garden-Party*, 1922), Mansfield had drawn her parents with an adult insight into their sexual interaction, as well as the effect of contemporary ideals of masculinity and femininity upon them. Woolf could not follow Mansfield in every respect – the narrator of *To the Lighthouse* knows scarcely more than the seven-year-old Cam how the Ramsays came to engender eight children – yet Woolf's novel does show how the Ramsays respond, consciously and unconsciously, to Victorian ideals of masculine and feminine behaviour. Like Mansfield, she could see how her parents must have appeared to other adults; like Mansfield, she re-created 'the raptures and miseries of childhood',[31] the fears, anger and pain, so tightly threaded through its joys.

Woolf had just begun work on her new novel when she visited Charleston, the farmhouse under the South Downs, where Vanessa and her three children lived. At her nephew Quentin's fifteenth birthday party (on 19 August 1925), she quite suddenly had a fainting fit. A long period of ill health followed, characterized by 'that odd amphibious life of headache' – 'amphibious', because she was 'in bed & out of it'.[32] Yet despite this, by 5 September she had managed to make 'a very quick & flourishing attack on To the Lighthouse, . . . 22 pages straight off in less than a fortnight.'[33] Within these pages she had introduced the plump and middle-aged painter, Miss Sophie Briscoe, 'a kindly, rosy lady' with a taste for 'hedgerows, cottages (especially the thatched cottage of the south)',[34] only to reconstruct her on the next page as Lily Briscoe, '33 & would never marry'. No longer that of a sentimental Sunday painter, Lily's work is serious, modern; she will stand for the artist within the novel and bind its arguments together.

But by the end of 1925, Woolf had completed fewer than forty pages. Back in London that autumn, almost any effort brought on further headache, and she was condemned to her old regime of milk-drinking and woolwork, bed at 5.00 p.m. and visitors rationed to one a day. At the same time, she knew that enforced leisure brought its own creative opportunities, as her essay 'On Being Ill' records. Written in response to Eliot's request for a contribution to the *New Criterion*, and published in January 1926, this essay begins by invoking Proust and De Quincey (the former a crucial new discovery, the latter a favourite of both her parents, and an appropriate mentor for a fantasia on the theme of the body), to introduce the dramas, or possibly wars, that disease or disorder can impose. To convey such sensations, we need 'not only a new language . . . primitive, subtle, sensual, obscene, but a new hierarchy of the passions'.[35] She opens up the changing perspectives that being ill can bring, finding in them sources of self-renewal. In this state of suspended animation, the novel continued to grow in her mind, while she noticed that '[t]he best of these illnesses is that they loosen the earth about the roots. They make changes. People express their affection.'[36]

One person to express affection was Vita Sackville-West, who wrote and visited whenever she could. They had first met in December 1922, and curiously, the diary entry of their first meeting finds Virginia experiencing 'shocks from my childhood . . . I keep thinking of sounds I heard as a child – at St Ives mostly.'[37] Their friendship had developed slowly. While Vita paid homage to Virginia's intellect and beauty, Virginia held back, finding in Vita 'all the supple ease of the aristocracy, but not the wit of the artist'. Yet, '[s]nob as I am, I trace her passions 500 years back, & they become romantic to me'.[38] Vita was descended from the Sackvilles, sometime Earls of Dorset, and had grown up at Knole, their great country house near Sevenoaks. As the 'Honourable' daughter of the third Baron Sackville, Vita was 'in Society', as well as being a successful writer. At a lunch party at Knole in July 1924, Virginia felt overwhelmed by its size and antiquity, though a twinge of socialism reminded her that Vita's ageing father was living all alone in this huge pile 'capable of housing all the desperate poor of Judd Street'.[39] Her feelings about the aristocracy were ambivalent.

A few months earlier, Virginia had invited Vita to write a book for the Hogarth Press. Vita had immediately accepted, composing *Seducers in Ecuador* in just under a fortnight while on a walking holiday in the Dolomites. The resulting fable explores the role of fantasy in relationships, and was dedicated to Virginia herself. Its title may indicate Vita's further intentions: a letter to Virginia, written that summer, urged her to go to Spain with Vita, to Santiago, since 'I shan't be really satisfied till I have enticed you away.'[40] Virginia remained guarded, while admitting that 'if life allowed, this might be a friendship'.[41]

Another year elapsed before the progress of *To the Lighthouse* and Virginia's growing intimacy with Vita would form a delicate counterpoint. Then Vita became her other beacon, a source of life, of light: that autumn, she seemed to Virginia 'like a lighthouse, fitful, sudden, remote', and as the novel drew to an end, she was 'very distant and beautiful and calm. A lighthouse in clean waters.'[42] During the autumn of 1925, although her writing was interrupted by bouts of headache and spells in bed, it was nourished by a new-found confidence that enabled Virginia to confront the loss of her mother at the same time as she embarked on what promised to be an entirely new type of relationship. Vita's reputation for what Virginia termed 'Sapphistry'

– her love of her own sex – was well known. The painter Ethel Sands had already warned Virginia of Vita's interest: 'She . . . may . . . have an eye on me, old though I am.'[43] Now Virginia's thoughts began to venture along similar lines: 'If one could be friendly with women, what a pleasure',[44] she observed, late in 1924, and early in 1925 she confided to Jacques Raverat, 'My aristocrat . . . is violently Sapphic . . . To tell you a secret, I want to incite my lady to elope with me next.'[45]

Yet by October 1925, neither the novel nor the affair had got off the ground. Finally, fate intervened, posting Vita's diplomat husband, Harold Nicolson, to Persia, to Teheran – a long and difficult journey before air travel became commonplace. Vita agreed to join him there in the following spring, leaving in January and returning in May. Taking her own emotional pulse in late November, Virginia 'minded the thought so much . . . that I conclude I am genuinely fond of her.'[46] Vita invited Virginia to stay with her at Long Barn after Harold's departure, but by 7 December, Virginia had heard nothing more: 'No letter. No visit. No invitation', she mourned, knowing instinctively that 'if I do not see her now, I shall not – ever: for the moment for intimacy will be gone, next summer.'[47] At this critical juncture, it was Leonard who prevailed upon Virginia, in the face of her own 'fears and refrainings', to send a note of acceptance, and next day Vita renewed her invitation. On 17 December, Virginia caught a train to Sevenoaks, and in the three days that followed, they became lovers. Back home, with the delicious complacency of the loved one, Virginia wrote to Vita, 'I am dashing off to buy, a pair of gloves. I am sitting up in bed; I am very very charming.'[48]

'These Sapphists *love* women; friendship is never untinged with amorosity', Virginia wrote, as she tried to define the candle-lit radiance that emanated from Vita in a grocer's shop in Sevenoaks, 'pink glowing, grape clustered, pearl hung'. She spelled out their differences – '[i]n brain & insight she is not as highly organised as I am', yet, despite Vita's androgyny and love of women, she was, nevertheless, 'a real woman. Then there is some voluptuousness about her; the grapes are ripe; & not reflective.'[49] The two women met for tea the day after Virginia's return from Long Barn, and again on Boxing Day, when Vita joined the Bells for a family lunch at Charleston. Quentin Bell recalled the conversation after Vita had left: ' "How beautiful she is," said Clive to Virginia . . . "An aristocrat of ancient race," said Virginia to Clive. Leonard turned to Julian. "What snobs they are," he said.'[50]

By early January, both women were ill, Virginia suffering from 'flu and Vita from a reaction to the various inoculations necessary for her travels, but they recovered sufficiently to dine at the Ivy with Clive and Leonard on 18 January, and on the 19th Vita came to Tavistock Square to say goodbye, sitting as usual on the floor of the studio while Virginia ruffled her hair and knotted her pearls. As Vita set out into the raw air of the winter evening, Virginia followed her, listlessly drifting towards Marchmont Street where a barrel organ was playing.[51] Vita was a source of energy, a source of life, yet so too was the novel pressing to be written. Having picked up her manuscript a few days earlier, she realized that '[t]he idea has grown in the interval since I wrote the beginning.'[52] Now she foresaw that the first part would include a scene in 'Mrs Rs. bedroom, with children choosing jewels while the birds rise & fall outside;' 'a great dinner scene', and would end with the couple alone together. It would be 'important to bring out the sense of life in opposition to fate – i.e. waves, lighthouse',[53] a sense of the continuity of the natural world that lay, impervious, beyond death and loss.

On the morning of the 18th, the day of Clive's dinner at the Ivy, Virginia began to compose the scene between Lily and Mr Bankes in the garden (section 4 of the final text), anticipating the need for an absorbing occupation once Vita had left. Vita's presence may be fleetingly suggested, perhaps, by the singing of 'Luriana Lurilee' at the dinner party, since a letter from Virginia to Vita that Christmas alludes to the poem, as if assuming Vita would recognize the reference (it was first published in full in an anthology edited by Vita and her husband in 1945).[54] Vita's absence is hinted at when Mrs Ramsay reads Shakespeare's 98th sonnet, 'From you have I been absent in the spring' (though so was that of Julia Stephen, who had died in May 1895).

'I wish you could live in my brain for a week,' Virginia wrote to Vita. 'It is washed with the most violent waves of emotion. What about? I dont know.'[55] Inexplicable fluxes of emotion, reflected in *To the Lighthouse*, make it difficult to assess her feelings for Vita. Her diary, in this matter as in so many others, affords incomplete evidence, since it was written in the knowledge that Leonard sometimes read it, and was expected to be its ultimate editor.[56] In fact, Leonard seems to have been entirely supportive throughout their love affair – he liked Vita more than anyone else in Virginia's circle did, apart from Clive, sharing her love of dogs and gardening. Virginia herself had already confided in Vita 'how I should hate Leonard to be in Persia! But then, in all London, you and I alone like being married.'[57] Even so, the passions of one's nearest and dearest can be irritating, and the occasional quarrels between the Woolfs in the spring and summer of 1926 may reflect new tensions in their relationship.[58] Virginia's diary echoed what her letters to Vita assert, how much she missed her, while adding 'not very intimately. Nevertheless, I do . . . & wish it were May 10th; & then I don't wish it; for I have such a razor edge to my palette that seeing people often disgusts me of seeing them.'[59]

Vita, in her turn, had hastened to reassure her husband that she was not going to fall in love with either Virginia or Leonard,[60] though her protestations suggest a lack of self-awareness that Virginia had already observed. She regularly accused Vita's letters of being 'dumb'[61] – certainly they were less intimate (though more demonstrative) than her own, and they did not employ the same range of private reference and allusion (a range that would later characterize *Orlando* and such essays as 'The Sun and the Fish'). Vita responded by assuming the role of 'Your faithful Towser',[62] though this was also part of a larger doggy discourse between them, in which Virginia compared herself to a spaniel, or to her mongrel fox-terrier Grizzle as she missed Vita or welcomed her back, or else demanded who Vita liked best out of her elk-hound Canute, Canute's wife or Virginia.[63] These games continued the following summer, when Vita gave Virginia the spaniel pup Pinker or Pinka,[64] a gift eventually requited with the writing of *Flush* (1933), the biography of a spaniel, which also reworks the love story of two great writers, the nineteenth century's most famous true-life romance. Virginia's own pet games, first acted out with Violet Dickinson and then with Leonard, also resurfaced as she imagined herself a squirrel, nestling inside the top button of Vita's jersey, above that ample feminine bosom.[65]

Once Vita had actually set out for Persia, the words flowed 'fast & freely . . . more so – 20 times more so – than any novel yet.'[66] Virginia was now deeply absorbed, and resented interruptions. 'I am back again in the thick of my novel,' she told Vita, early in February, 'and things are crowding into my head: millions of things . . . which I make up walking the streets, gazing into the gas fire. Then I struggle with them, from 10 to 1: then lie on the sofa, and watch the sun behind the chimneys: and think of more things: then set up a page of poetry in the basement, and so up to tea and Morgan [E. M.] Forster. I've shirked two parties, and another Frenchman, and buying a hat, and going to tea with Hilda Trevelyan: for I really can't combine all this with keeping my imaginary people going.'[67]

Sometimes, the events of her daily life seemed to creep into her fiction: on 3 March, her diary recorded 'how I lost my little mother of pearl brooch', and the next day, in her manuscript, 'Minta discovered how she had lost her grandmother's brooch . . . a pearl brooch . . . Tears streamed from her eyes' (though this note of her own loss may simply reflect her preoccupation with Minta's).[68] At other times, the novel's concerns seeped into her social life. In early April, the Woolfs visited an old friend, Walter Leaf, and his family, an exuberantly healthy, wealthy upper-middle-class family living at Regent's Park. Their warm display of physical affection for one another convinced Virginia that she was 'exiled from this profound natural happiness . . . geniality & family love & being on the rails of human life'. She analysed her sense of loss at some length in her diary, and in letters to Vita and Vanessa, and found herself quarrelling with Leonard, who thought she was being sentimental (a word that also expressed her fears for To the Lighthouse).[69] But the real exile was from her own lost childhood, and the contrast she set up between exile and natural happiness was the contrast between 'The Lighthouse' and 'The Window', between the present and the past, intensified through the idealizing perspective that loss creates. With the rational part of her mind, she knew the sacrifices that the Victorian ideology of love, marriage and 'family values' had demanded from women, but she mourned its loss in Mrs Ramsay, even while she enjoyed the exile's freedom with Lily Briscoe.

Yet though To the Lighthouse celebrates what Woolf termed 'natural happiness' – children playing in the garden or on the beach on a perfect summer's day, and the special beauty of Mrs Ramsay (as much an aspect of character as of appearance), the narrative never conceals the serpents lurking in Eden – the way that Mr Ramsay's needs engender resentment, while Mrs Ramsay's generosity arouses competition, fuelling the Oedipal jealousy between father and son with which the book begins; Mrs Ramsay's efforts to console James provoke her husband so much that he swears at her. The couple walk down the garden in the evening, between clumps of red-hot pokers and silver-green spear-like plants, carefully re-establishing communication, for 'both felt uncomfortable, as if they did not know whether to go on or go back.' [p.75][70]

Lily Briscoe, like her author, rejects Mrs Ramsay's gospel of love and marriage, yet at the same time she could recognize its appeal, could 'feel violently two opposite things at the same time; . . . It is so beautiful, so exciting, this love . . . also it is the stupidest, the most barbaric of human passions.' [p.111] Her troubled response to Minta and Paul replays the discomfort of the Ramsay children, Andrew and Nancy, when faced with adult desire.[71] While the couple bring with them the seductive hum of sexual excitement, Paul seems brutalized by its selfishness, its 'unscrupulosity'. For Lily, Mrs Ramsay's ideal of marriage is outdated, absurd. A later age dealt with these things differently, but not necessarily worse: adultery was no longer seriously condemned (thus destroying the rationale for the plot of *Anna Karenina*, so Virginia argued[72]). It might even save a marriage, as it would save Paul and Minta's (and had saved Clive and Vanessa's?) In a manuscript passage that did not reach the final text, Lily thinks that 'pictures are more important than people', and that 'all this little trivial baseness . . . about which we made so incessant a to do of marrying & giving in marriage, pales beside it', perhaps unconsciously echoing Mrs Moore's impatience in *A Passage to India*. 'Why all this marriage, marriage? . . . And all this rubbish about love, love in a church, love in a cave, as if there is the least difference'[73] (Woolf had read, or perhaps reread, Forster's novel in December 1925[74]). But life and art cannot be separated, and Lily recognizes that art feeds upon life while life, in turn, may be 'susceptible, like a picture, to arrangement & order'.[75]

If love's heat is experienced as an unbearable scorching, its absence is equally unendurable. The sense of 'nothing, . . . nothing, nothing', the rifts and discontinuities of love gape wide as the family assembles for dinner. Looking at her husband at the end of the table, Mrs Ramsay 'could not understand how she had ever felt any emotion or any affection for him', and with love's withdrawal, beauty and community also vanish, so that 'all sat separate' [p.91]. In this desolate moment, Lily takes refuge in her painting 'as if she had found a treasure' [p.92], deciding to move the tree closer to the centre. In the waste of Charles Tansley's anger and Mr Bankes's disillusion, she is sustained by the thought of it. Mr Ramsay loses his temper because Augustus Carmichael asks for a second plate of soup. As the children threaten to collapse into giggles, Mrs Ramsay sets them to light the candles. At once the atmosphere changes, and a 'sudden exhilaration' stirs, as the maid brings in the dish of Boeuf en Daube and, simultaneously, Paul and Minta arrive in a golden glow. The second half of the dinner becomes something of a sacred rite, as the guests form a community; Mrs Ramsay, presiding like a priestess over this last supper, serves morsels of eternity and Mr Ramsay brings the evening to an end by chanting the mysterious words of 'Luriana Lurilee', as if in the agnostic world of the Ramsays, the joys of family life have come to replace more traditional ceremonies. 'Of such moments, she thought, the thing is made that remains for ever after.' [p.114]

> And all the lives we ever lived and all the lives to be
> Are full of trees and changing leaves

The words of Charles Elton's unpublished poem, 'Luriana Lurilee', suggest the joyful repetitions that characterize marriage and family life – 'a sense . . . of one thing falling where another had fallen, and so setting up an echo which chimed in the air and made it full of vibrations' [p.215],[76] as Lily defines it when thinking of the Ramsays' marriage. These words also suggest the communion of the living and the dead, as the old woman's song at the centre of *Mrs Dalloway* had done, and so offset the shadows that creep up on Mrs Ramsay as the first part of the novel draws to a close, for death also lurks in this Arcadian world. For Mrs Ramsay, '[t]here was no treachery too base for the world to commit; she knew that.' [p.71] She labours to shelter her husband and children from its blows, 'boasting of her capacity to surround and protect' [p.44], yet her vigilance against time and fate, figured as the waves and 'the pitiless, the remorseless' beam of the lighthouse, gradually wear her down. 'Never did anybody look so sad.' [p.33]

Mrs Ramsay's sense of imminent tragedy, of some implacable cruelty in the world, what her husband calls her 'pessimism', simultaneously glances back to Julia Stephen's early widowhood in her first marriage, and forward to her sudden death in her late forties. The tragedy she anticipates is her own, and the final pages of 'The Window' are heavy with premonitions of it, as she glides 'like a ghost' through her memories of Carrie Manning's drawing-room, twenty years earlier; as she leaves the dining-room, glancing back over her shoulder at what has already become 'the past', and as she hurries to protect her children from the threat of death symbolized by that classic reminder of it, the skull. Nailed to the nursery wall, the pig's skull is keeping the children awake. In a moment of inspiration, she wraps her green shawl around it, transforming it into a source of imaginative life: 'how the fairies would love it; it was like a bird's nest' [p.124].

Downstairs again, Mrs Ramsay waves off the older children on their way to the beach 'like a girl of twenty, full of gaiety', and rejoins her husband, who is reading (and weeping over) the episode of Steenie's drowning in Scott's *The Antiquary*. The words of 'Luriana Lurilee' are still running through her head, and, in the manuscript version of this scene, the leaves of the book she opens mingle with the poem's 'changing leaves', and she climbs through its lines as if through a tree.[77] In the manuscript version, her tranquillity is still clouded by a sense of foreboding: 'if anything happened, it was always the tragic . . . always death, somehow, dark somehow; ruin coming.'[78] Mrs Ramsay has struggled to make 'Time stand still', to create pools of tranquillity in the midst of flux, and for this she will be remembered by her children, by Lily in her painting and by the novel itself, for the art of holding back time's swift foot, the recurrent theme of Shakespeare's sonnets, belongs as much to Mrs Ramsay as it does to the artist Lily Briscoe – or the novelist Virginia Woolf.

She finished the first draft of 'The Window' section on 29 April 1926, and now confronted 'the most difficult abstract piece of writing – I have to give an empty house, no people's characters, the passage of time, all eyeless & featureless with nothing to cling to: well,' she added with amusement, 'I rush at it'.[79] 'Time Passes' is the brush stroke through the centre that will join the novel's two halves, the Victorian world of her parents and her own times. It must express all that the skull had threatened: the alien universe, 'not oneself but something in the universe that one's left with'; 'fate – i.e. waves, lighthouse'; the family deaths, the Great War, and whatever deep social and cultural ruptures had affected society, so that 'On or about December 1910 human character changed'.[80] In her own version of abstract painting, Woolf employed a technique derived from 'Kew Gardens', dramatizing a natural world emptied of human agents and observers.

'One by one the lamps were all extinguished.' The familiar domestic ritual also anticipates the deaths of Mrs Ramsay, Prue and Andrew and the advent of war. As at the close of *Jacob's Room*, it recalls the words of Lord Grey, 'The lamps are going out all over Europe; we shall not see them lit again in our lifetime.'[81] 'Time Passes' is a rhapsody upon time, death and endings – the kind of free flight that Clive Bell had so much admired in the earliest versions of *The Voyage Out*.[82] It comprehends a range of different modes of time – public and private, personal and historical. The regulated hours of family life, broken up by meals, give way to sequences of natural – diurnal or seasonal – change. Woolf employs a quasi-Shakespearean 'double time scheme', compacting the passage of ten years into that of a single night, sandwiched between two daytime episodes, so that in one sense, James does go to the lighthouse the next morning, but that morning takes place ten years on.

The flood of darkness that now descends on the house, engulfing 'the little island of home and garden',[83] carries away reason and civilization, and releases the unconscious, whose private dreams of chaos and violence generate the communal madness of war. The events of 'Time Passes' are figured as dreams, played out in the decaying house as if in a brain drifting steadily further from consciousness and the body's waking life. Consciousness registers existence in time, whereas sleep, like death, eliminates time and individuality. The slowly delapidating house, the overgrown garden, the bodiless airs and spirits that walk, or rather float along the shore, the engulfing storms and floods all belong to the common language of our dreams of change and loss (which themselves structure our sense of the passage of time). Though the deaths of Mrs Ramsay, of Andrew, and Prue are isolated within brackets, 'Time Passes' also registers their loss symbolically, just as it registers the Great War as nights 'full of wind and destruction', and as the ghastly, unforgotten ashen-coloured ship, the Dreadnought, 'come, gone; there was a purplish stain upon the bland surface of the sea, as if something had boiled and bled, invisibly, beneath.' [p.146][84]

The troubled seas are part of a meditation on cultural change, as the war brings to an end romantic and Victorian perceptions of nature as a benevolent force, a nurturing mother: 'That dream, then, of sharing, completing, finding in solitude on the beach an answer, was but a reflection in a mirror, . . . contemplation was unendurable; the mirror was broken.' [p.146] It is succeeded by a sense of nature as impervious to human suffering, blind and silent, a sadly familiar theme in twentieth-century literature. 'Time Passes' is a sustained meditation on the workings of time, reaching beyond the human and personal to a world 'on the mystical side of this solitude; . . . not oneself but something in the universe'.[85]

'I was doubtful about Time Passes', Virginia later told Vita. 'It was written in the gloom of the Strike.'[86] She began it on 30 April 1926. By 1 May, the miners had walked out, and by the 2nd, a General Strike had been declared. All public services broke down. Virginia saw '5 or 6 armoured cars slowly going along Oxford Street; on each two soldiers sat in tin helmets, & one stood with his hand at the gun'. Their house was suddenly filled with visitors, interrupting, arguing, urging Leonard to use his printing press to attack the Government, but none of this was 'nearly as exciting as writing To the Lighthouse'.[87] Leonard passionately supported the Strike and thought the miners' demands fully justified. His enthusiasm irritated her and they quarrelled briefly over it. Vivid accounts in her diary and a letter to Vanessa describe 'what it felt like', but give no sense of her personal response to this violent display of class hatred, although the theme of 'divisions between people . . . [as] The source of all evil' had been one of the novel's starting points.[88] In the end, class hatred, linked with misogyny, is concentrated in the character of Charles Tansley (who does not appear in 'Time Passes'). Instead, the Ramsays' decaying house (Europe? Civilization?) is rescued and restored by two working-class women, Mrs McNab and Mrs Bast, suggesting, perhaps, that patient female drudgery maintains the fabric of life through the (often male-inflicted) traumas that beset it. Yet however idealistic the impulse that created them, the actual portraits of Mrs McNab and Mrs Bast remain stereotyped, even 'sentimental' (an adjective that can be applied to them with some justice).[89] Woolf had, within earshot, two suitable models in the shape of Nelly Boxall and Lottie Hope, her own live-in servants, but she found their intimacy disturbing, and tried her best to censor them out of her consciousness.

The Strike ended on 12 May, although the miners' claims were far from settled. A few days later, Vita arrived back from Persia, and they met for lunch on 21 May. 'I like her presence & her beauty. Am I in love with her?' Virginia asked herself, characteristically adding, '[b]ut what is love?' Seeing Vita again, she felt shy, 'disillusioned by the actual body', yet rightly foresaw that '[t]his may well be more lasting than the first rhapsody.'[90] The closest and happiest phase of their relationship now began. Meanwhile, the first, somewhat sketchy draft of 'Time Passes' was completed a day or two later. So far her first draft had been looser and freer than on any previous occasion, yet always purposeful. Woolf was averaging two pages a day without difficulty, though every few pages she would backtrack and rewrite several paragraphs from the previous day. Style, she told Vita, was simply a matter of rhythm, and should flow like a wave, 'as it breaks and tumbles in the mind, it makes words to fit it'.[91]

But the last part was more difficult. 'The problem is how to bring Lily and Mr R. together & make a combination of interest at the end.'[92] Here, the draft is much less close to the printed text, and several pages at a time are abandoned altogether or boiled down into a single, succinct sentence. She resumed work on it at the end of May, but was interrupted, first by flu, and then by writing an essay on De Quincey entitled 'Impassioned Prose', an essay full of echoes of the dream-like world of 'Time Passes', and the 'serene and lovely light [which] lies over the whole of that distant prospect of ... childhood'.[93] De Quincey's power lies not so much in his depiction of events as of their 'reverberations', memories of events that run through the third part of *To the Lighthouse*, to be recaptured through Lily's painting. Woolf turned back to her novel in the third week of June, but, feeling oppressed by numerous social 'odds and ends', she set it aside, to be finished on their summer visit to Rodmell. Now it had become 'that python, my book', its difficult completion 'like some prolonged rather painful & yet exciting process of nature, which one desires inexpressibly to have over.'[94]

The problem was still one of balance, as Virginia had foreseen when she first drew the figure 'H' in her notebook, the problem of connecting 'this mass on the right hand with that on the left' [p.60], but now the two forces were Mr Ramsay, trying to reach the lighthouse in Macalister's boat, and Lily trying to finish her painting of Mrs Ramsay. Woolf's tendency to define her problems in terms of form or mass reveals the painterly nature of her aesthetic, so that, inevitably, the richness now lay with 'Lily on the lawn'.[95] She solved her problem through the kind of spatial thinking characteristic of modernism, with its concern for expressive form. The thirteen numbered sections that make up 'The Lighthouse' alternate between Mr Ramsay and Lily, beginning and ending with Lily, but the structure of the whole book – that is, of two parts around a central third (the 'line there, in the centre') – is now repeated on a smaller scale, so that in the climactic central section (numbered 7), Lily summons Mrs Ramsay, and feels 'a sense of some one there, of Mrs Ramsay' [p.196].[96] The placing of this section is emphasized by the 'brown spot', later identified as Macalister's boat 'half way across' or 'in the middle of the bay'. The third part constantly plays back scenes and encounters from the first part, reworking them in different keys.

Lily's experiences as a modernist artist struggling to express her vision recapitulate Woolf's efforts to complete her novel. She linked herself verbally with Lily when she wrote of 'brisking, after my lethargy' (Lily was Mrs Ramsay's 'little Brisk').[97] Lily, like her author, makes up scenes while she is working, and, like her author, she is 'tunnelling her way into her picture, into the past'. The poet Augustus Carmichael, asleep on the lawn, further links Lily with words as, in some mystic fashion, he seems to 'hear the things she could not say.' He is gathered up in her conclusion that 'nothing stays; all changes; but not words, not paint.'[98]

If Woolf is Lily, an adult self, struck by the tragedy of 'children coerced, their spirits subdued', she is also Cam, who must endure it. She found it difficult to decide how much to include of the dark years with her father after her mother's death. Here, the manuscript is more expansive than the published text, but at proof stage, Woolf included a scene in which James remembers Mr Ramsay lecturing, in 'those long twilight months which seemed interminable' [p.163] – only to take it out again before publication.[99] Cam escapes from her pact with James to resist their father's tyranny when she feels a passionate impulse of love for her father, and later, a fountain of spontaneous joy, partly prompted by the excitement of her own future. James, too, recognizes that his father is prey to overriding psychological needs, but also that he is not identical with those needs, and he begins to forgive him. Mr Ramsay himself finds a momentary self-renewal as he 'sprang, lightly like a young man' onto the lighthouse rock. His children's changes of feeling towards him parallel the changes of mood that Lily undergoes as she passes from pain and anger at Mrs Ramsay's absence to admiration and forgiveness. 'The Lighthouse' replays the process of mourning which the book allowed Woolf to complete. No wonder she considered calling it an 'Elegy'.[100]

The first draft, as so often for Woolf, ended in a depression that had been threatening for some months, a conviction of failure entirely at odds with her certainty that this was 'easily the best of my books'.[101] She finished it in mid-September, and began revising in late October, typing out six pages a day and adding new material wherever the first draft was too sketchy. At this stage she wrote in the words of a number of other texts – the Grimms' fairy tale that Mrs Ramsay reads to James became 'The Flounder', with its dissatisfied wife and symbolic storms; lines from William Browne's 'Sirens' Song', and from Shakespeare's 98th sonnet appeared, and the last lines, '[i]t was done; it was finished' echoed the last words of Christ. *Anna Karenina* replaced *War and Peace*, since it was more relevant to the novel's marriage questions.[102] If using an echo-chamber of quotations is a feature of modernism, then the novel was growing more modernist. By mid-January, with the revisions completed, Virginia paid a farewell visit to snow-bound Knole, before Vita set out once more to rejoin Harold in Persia. On her return, Leonard gave his verdict on her typescript.[103]

Never had she put so much of herself so directly into her fiction. Not only had she re-created her parents and family life at Talland House, but in Lily Briscoe she drew her fullest portrait of the artist, a self-portrait that revealed how intensely and exclusively she lived out her writing. That Lily is a painter rather than a writer reflects her lifelong competition with Vanessa, as well as the intellectual impact of Roger Fry and Clive Bell which had led her to construct for herself an aesthetic based on visual, rather than literary values. But Lily is not merely a self-portrait: she is a portrait of the artist as woman, anticipating the portrait of the woman writer who would demand *A Room of One's Own*, two years later. As a woman artist, she participates in Woolf's self-doubt, finding 'this passage from conception to work as dreadful as any down a dark passage for a child' [p.23] (a simile that re-unites Lily with the nervous Cam). Like Woolf, Lily is disheartened by the easy misogyny of 'Women can't paint, women can't write', but the manuscript includes two or three pages in which she defines her response more precisely; one heavily cancelled passage tells us that 'she had no militancy in her, & could not bear to [be] called, as she might have been called had she come out with her views a feminist, for it was safer, easier, less agitating to accept things'.[104] Lily murmurs Tansley's phrase, 'Can't paint, can't write' [p.173], as if warding off evil spells, the moment before she begins painting.

For 'it would never be seen, never be hung, even' [p.54]. Lily represents one ideal of the woman as artist: her self-effacing commitment to her work is free from (male?) egotism; she practises her art for its own sake, without regard for fame, reputation or self-perpetuation: 'the whole secret of art' (she thinks, in the manuscript) is '[t]o care for the thing: not for oneself'.[105] Her art is at once agony and ecstasy, a rich inner resource and a refuge from social discomfort. She finds the act of painting all-absorbing, and the need to be true to her vision overrides any concern for its future survival – she accepts that her canvases will be 'hung in the servants' bedrooms . . . [or] rolled up and stuffed under a sofa.' [p.173] Her indifference to praise or recognition contrasts with Mr Ramsay's anxiety as to whether his work will last. Virginia's attitude was closer to her father's – she liked to be reassured of her work's merits, and worried whether it would last. Lily's outlook is closer to that of Mr Bankes, who enjoys work for its own sake rather than for the status it confers; it is even closer to that of the painters' painter, Cézanne, as described by Clive Bell: 'He had no use for his own pictures . . . He tossed them into bushes, or left them in the open fields'.[106]

The early pages of the novel locate Lily firmly outside the more traditional schools of painting, in particular the high Victorians (painters who made their own colours, according to Mrs Ramsay), and the English impressionists typified by Mr Paunceforte, who worked in 'green and grey, with lemon-coloured sailing boats, and pink women on the beach.' [p.17][107] Painters had begun to arrive at St Ives in the 1880s, soon after the Stephens themselves, working in the open air, as did the Pont-Aven artists. The dandified Mr Paunceforte (he wears yellow boots!) may be an allusion to James Whistler, who visited St Ives in 1883–4 (too early for Virginia to have remembered him). His predilection for silver-grey tones was said to have influenced later painters working there, such as Louis Grier and Adrian Stokes, but the lemon and pink colours that Mrs Ramsay describes suggest a later generation of Cornish painters, more in the style of Laura Knight. It was another St Ives painter, Thomas Millie Dow, who took over Talland House from the Stephens in 1895.[108]

Lily, unlike Mr Paunceforte, is a post-impressionist, concerned with 'the shape', with form rather than with surface effect or realistic detail, as she explains to William Bankes: 'she had made no attempt at likeness', being absorbed instead in 'the relations of masses, of light and shadows' [p.59]. She closely echoes Roger Fry in her artistic ideals and her concern for underlying form and inner truth, and with composition and the problems of balance. Mass and light are among the five qualities listed in Fry's 'Essay in Aesthetics', the others being rhythm, space and colour. When Lily completes her picture by drawing 'a line there, in the centre', she gives it the unity that Fry considered the chief aspect of order in a work of art. 'In a picture this unity is due to a balancing of the attractions of the eye about the central line of the picture.'[109] When Roger Fry congratulated Woolf on her achievement, adding that 'the Lighthouse has a symbolic meaning which escapes me', she disclaimed any such intention, reasserting what they held in common as artistic goals: 'I meant <u>nothing</u> by The Lighthouse. One has to have a central line down the middle of the book to hold the design together.' She also told him that she had wanted to dedicate her novel to him, and 'Now I wish I had'.[110]

Yet as a symbol, the lighthouse is rich in significance. Associated with isolation and, by extension, the inner life, as well as with the saving power of light that opposes the flood of darkness in 'Time

Passes', its three beams correspond to the structure of the novel – two long beams, one of them Mrs Ramsay's, and a short beam. Placed at the centre of the novel (like Big Ben in *Mrs Dalloway*), its beams measure time in terms of light, for, if light is in some sense the painter's medium, time is the novelist's, and the two correspond, since time is one way of describing the cycles of sun and moon which we experience as light. Time is the element that makes novels differ fundamentally from paintings, giving them what Fry termed 'a successive unity'. Time brings change, and though the mind can move backwards and forwards across it ('with an extraordinary enrichment of each moment of consciousness', as Fry told her[111]), resisting time's action and the body's involuntary ageing, what has been lost can only be restored by the imagination and its arts. Yet, though *To the Lighthouse* brings tragedy and loss, exceptionally among Woolf's novels, it also brings positive growth, as James and Cam reconsider their father and find their own freedom, and Lily summons Mrs Ramsay back in order to finish her painting.

The question of whether light defined or created form had been hotly debated in painting circles: the impressionists had concentrated on recording the fall of light on their subjects, while the post-impressionists had aimed at presenting the form within, or beneath. For Woolf, one equivalent to the painter's revelation of inner form lay in those spots of time that imagination revisited and was nourished by – moments such as those created by Mrs Ramsay – in which something might be held back from its inexorable current: 'In the midst of chaos there was shape; this eternal passing and flowing (she looked at the clouds going and the leaves shaking) was struck into stability.' [p.176] Nature's mysterious combination of permanence and flux, of light changing and time passing, and how best to record them would be central to *The Waves*.

TO THE LIGHTHOUSE: THE AFTERMATH

When Vita returned from her second trip to Persia in May 1927, she found a copy of To the Lighthouse *waiting for her, inscribed 'Vita from Virginia (In my opinion the best novel I have ever written.)' Opening it, Vita was amused to find all its pages blank – Virginia had sent her the publisher's dummy.[112] It was not entirely a joke: Woolf's first reaction to the proofs was one of disappointment, but three weeks later, she was struck by 'how lovely some parts of The Lighthouse are! Soft & pliable, & I think deep, & never a word wrong for a page at a time. This I feel about the dinner party, & the children in the boat; but not of Lily on the lawn. That I do not much like. But I like the end.'[113]*

To the Lighthouse *was published on Thursday, 5 May 1927 – her mother's death day, thirty-two years before. As usual, the* Times Literary Supplement *review depressed her, partly, as she admitted, because of her 'bad habit of making up the review I should like before reading the review I get'. Yet the reviewer had praised her for being 'so adventurous and intellectually imaginative', and had recognized how central to the novel was the theme of time passing, and 'this question of the meaning of things'.[114] Inevitably, the experimental 'Time Passes' sequence attracted the greatest criticism (for Arnold Bennett, it did not succeed, though otherwise he thought the novel her best work) and the greatest praise. According to Edwin Muir, it was 'the best of the lot ... For imagination and beauty of writing it is probably not surpassed in contemporary prose', while another Scottish poet, Rachel Taylor, heard resemblances to 'the prose litanies of Mallarmé'.[115] Prose poetry has always been more easily accepted in France than in England, and Charles Mauron's translation of 'Le temps passe' came out in Paris late in 1926, the first of her work to be translated (it was soon followed by extracts from 'La Chambre de Jacob' and 'Jardins de Kew', published between December 1926 and August 1927).[116] From the outset, certain French critics seemed to recognize exactly what she was doing. In an interview, the painter and writer Jacques-Émile Blanche teased Woolf about her painterly affinities: 'But you would purse your lips, Madame, if I described you as* Impressionist. *One is more up-to-date than that in Bloomsbury.'* *Jean-Jacques Mayoux's review of* To the Lighthouse *in 1928 was sharply incisive, perceiving at once the dominant paradigm of painting, as well as Woolf's 'feminine vision', the novel's rhythms and structure (he described 'Time Passes' as being 'perpendicular' to the other two parts, as if seeing Woolf's figure H on its side), and the significance of death and distance in the novel. His final comparison shifted from Vermeer to Cézanne.*[117]

Woolf was also making her name in North America, where Louis Kronenburger, writing for the New York Times, *shared in the general admiration for 'Time Passes' ('here is poetry'), and called attention to the courage of her development, how an author must 'always break down the perfection he has achieved in an earlier stage of his writing in order to reach new objectives'. Conrad Aiken, in* The Dial, *though less enthusiastic, noticed the way that Woolf replaced the naturalism of Chekhov and Katherine Mansfield with 'the frame of the picture, and the fact that the picture was a picture'.*[118] *Harcourt, Brace published* To the Lighthouse *in a first edition of 4,000 copies (a thousand more than the more cautious Leonard had issued) and reprinted a further 3,600 in June and August that year. Again, the US text differed significantly from the Hogarth Press edition, and the differences occur at key points – the ending of the first part, 'The Window', for example, or the parenthesis which records Mr Ramsay's reaction to his wife's death. As with* Mrs Dalloway, *Woolf corrected the two sets of proofs separately. Judging from the surviving set of proofs, it seems that rather more revisions were made for the British printers, R. & R. Clark, but the proofs marked up for Harcourt, Brace also record many (and many different) changes.*[119]

The Hogarth Press edition came out with Vanessa's wonderfully phallic lighthouse on the dust-jacket, in blue and black on cream, perfectly capturing the 'fountain of joy' experienced by Cam and Mrs Ramsay in the novel.[120] *This time, Vanessa (whom Virginia sometimes accused of not reading her work with due attention) was awestruck:*

you have given a portrait of mother which is more like her to me than anything I could ever have conceived possible. It is almost painful to have her so raised from the dead . . . It was like meeting her again with oneself grown up and on equal terms and it seems to me the most astonishing feat of creation to have

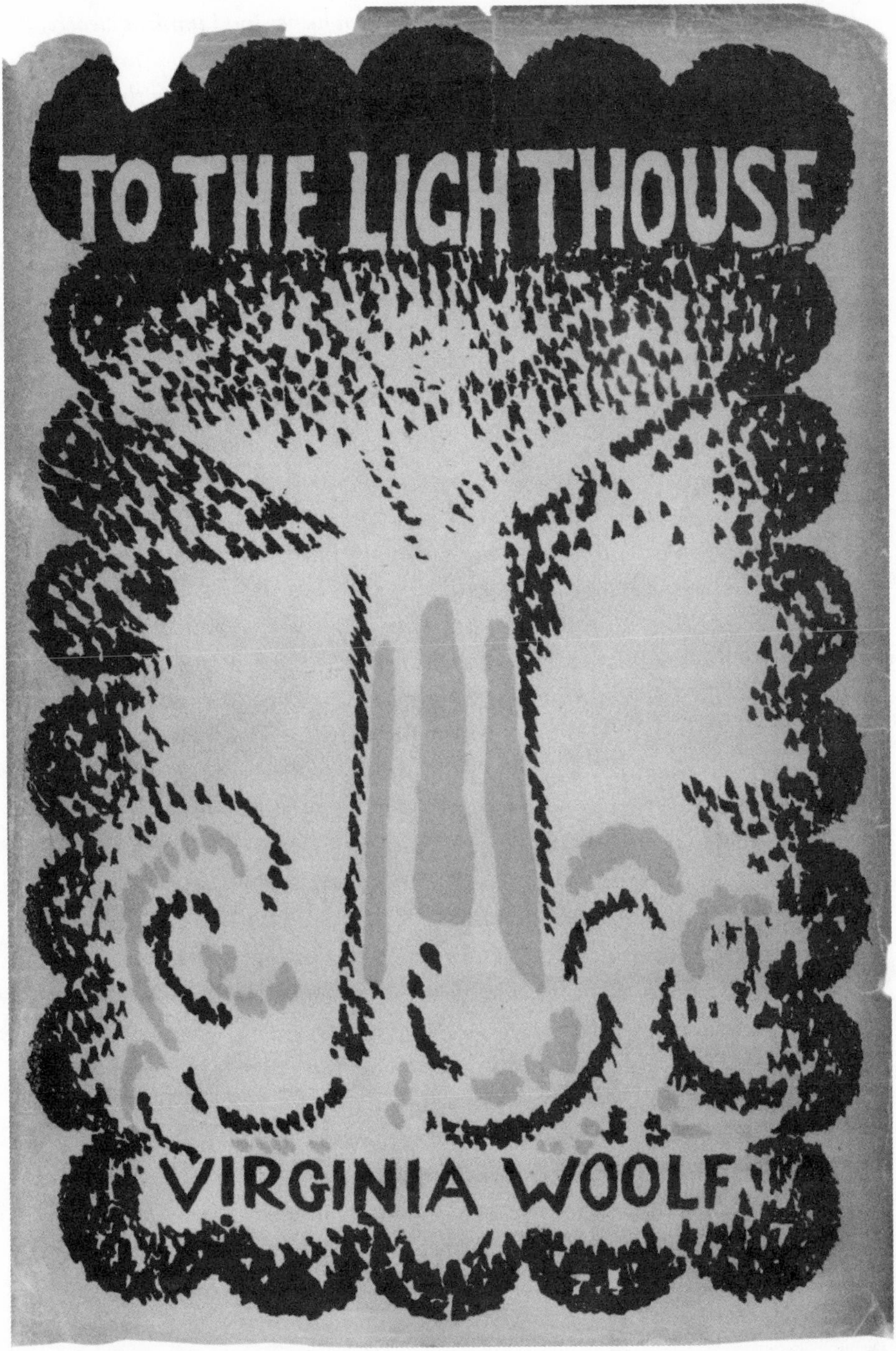
TO THE LIGHTHOUSE
VIRGINIA WOOLF

*been able to see her in such a way. You have given father too I think as clearly,
. . . as far as portrait painting goes, you seem to me to be a supreme artist and
it is so shattering to find oneself face to face with those two again that I can
hardly consider anything else.*

As Vanessa recognized, she was uniquely placed to judge her sister's
achievement.[121] Roger Fry and E. M. Forster, whose views also mattered very much to Virginia, had both declared it her best book so far,
as had Clive, and she basked in their enthusiasm: 'positive praise, . . .
gives one such a start on, that instead of feeling dried up, one feels, on
the contrary, flooded with ideas'.[122]

To the Lighthouse *sold well from the outset, and the initial print
run of 3,000 was quickly followed by a further thousand in June 1927,
and another 1,500 in May of the following year, 'much more nearly a
success, in the usual sense of the word, than any other book of mine.'
Almost forty years on, in 1965, Leonard made the same point to
Queenie Leavis, repudiating her claim (in* Fiction and the Reading
Public, 1932) *that it was 'not a popular novel' – by then, it had sold
253,000 copies in Britain and America. Four years later, he observed
that sales had been running at over 50,000 copies per year for the
previous three years.*[123] *When the Penguin edition came out in January
1992, the first print run was 15,000, and as many again had been
reprinted by September – and this was in open competition with the
several other paperback editions that appeared as Woolf's work came
out of copyright (temporarily, as it turned out). The cheapest paperback edition, published by Wordsworth, printed a run of 64,000 copies
in February 1994 and more than 31,000 in the following year – but
by then,* To the Lighthouse *had long been established as a text for
study, as well as a bestseller.*[124] *Perhaps because of the perfect match
of content to form, it has been adapted or reworked less often than*
Mrs Dalloway, *though Colin Gregg filmed it for the BBC in 1983,
with a young Kenneth Branagh playing Charles Tansley.*[125]

*Meanwhile, back in the summer of 1927, Virginia was celebrating
the tangible result of her success: a second-hand Singer, 'a nice light
little shut up car in which we can travel thousands of miles. It is very
dark blue, with a paler line round it. The world gave me this for writing
The Lighthouse, I reflect'.*[126] *She was learning to drive.*

8

'The Secret of Life is . . .'[1]

[O]ne lizard is mounted immobile on the back of another, with only the twinkle of a gold eye-lid or the suction of a green flank to show that they are living flesh, and not made of bronze. All human passion seems furtive and feverish beside this still rapture. Time seems to have stopped and we are in the presence of immortality.

In this essay, 'The Sun and the Fish', Woolf records the visions of the inner eye on a 'dark winter's morning, when the real world has faded'.[2] Published early in 1928, it is in part a coded message from Virginia to Vita, who had shared the experiences it describes, and who would inspire her next novel *Orlando*, itself a series of variations on the themes of rapture and stillness, sex, time and immortality.

'The Sun and the Fish' brings together two experiences from the previous summer: the total eclipse of the sun, which Virginia watched from Bardon Fell in Yorkshire, early on the morning of 29 June 1927 (it was the first to be visible in England for two hundred years, and would not be repeated till 1999), and a visit to the London Zoo, with its new aquarium, on 12 July, less than a fortnight later.[3] What linked the events and lent them both rapture was Vita's presence – the Nicolsons and the Woolfs travelled up to Yorkshire together by train to see the eclipse, along with Virginia's nephew Quentin, Vita's cousin Eddy and Saxon Sydney-Turner. Eclipses had aroused excitement since Arthur Eddington had used that of 29 March 1919 (only visible from the Tropics) to prove Einstein's General Theory of Relativity, and introduce his work to the British public. Alone together, Vita and Virginia had visited the Zoo. 'I can't tell you how much I like "The Sun and the Fish",' Vita wrote to Virginia, '(all the more because it is

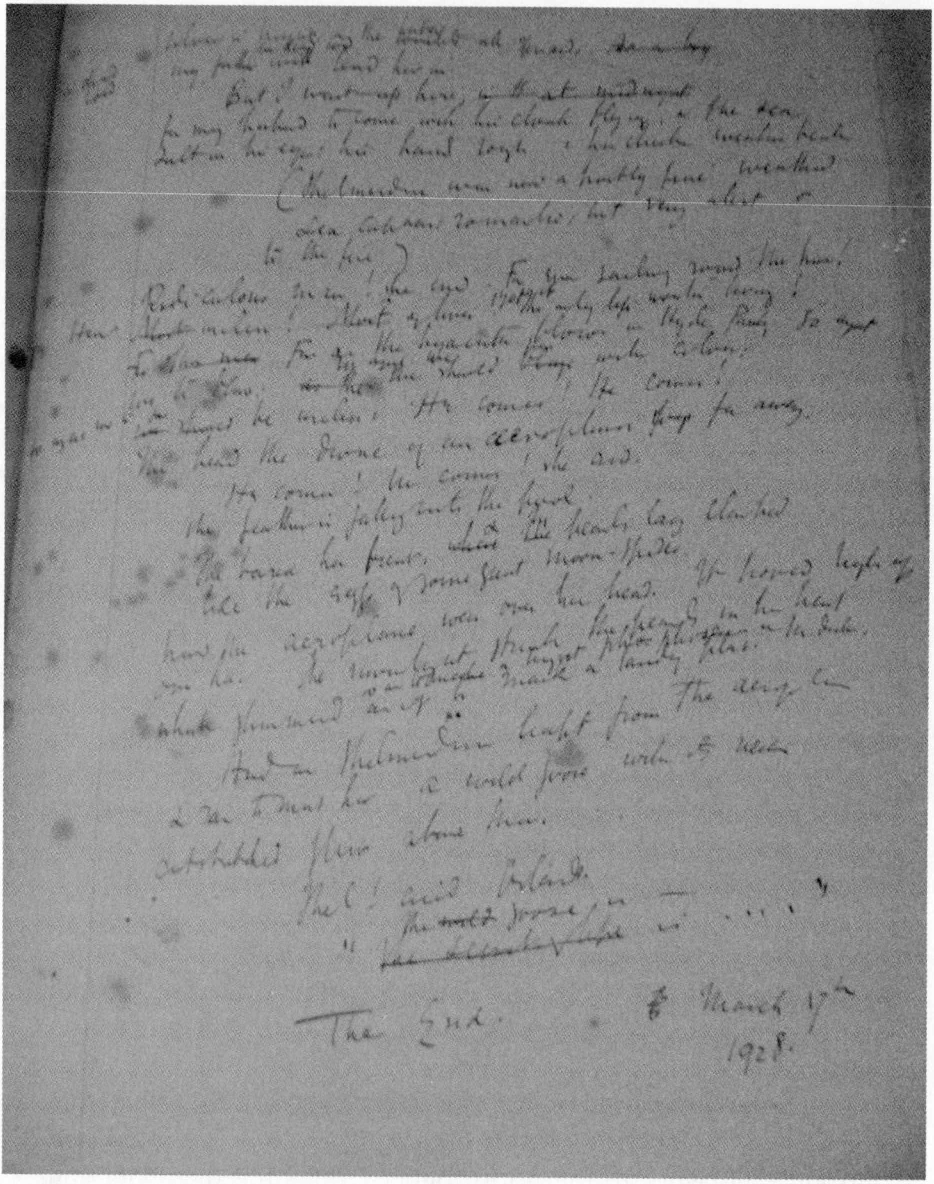
But I wait up here, without ...
for my husband to come with his cloak flying ...

He comes! He comes!
He comes! he comes! she cried.
... the eggs of some giant moon-spider.
... aeroplane was over her head.
And as Shelmerdine leapt from the ...
Ah! cried Orlando.
"The wild goose is ..."

The End.

March 17th
1928.

all about things we did together,) and I am ordering a copy of Time and Tide'[4] (the feminist weekly where it was published, so called from its motto, 'Time and Tide Wait for No Man').

Vita had changed Virginia's awareness of her own desires, encouraging her to think differently about gender, its nature and meaning, and, in particular, its fluidity, for Vita believed that 'as centuries go on . . . the sexes become more nearly merged'.[5] While several of Virginia's friends, as well as Vanessa, lived sexually (as well as artistically and intellectually) unconventional lives, it was Vita's sexual ambivalence that caught Virginia's imagination. She had first seen Vita as 'a grenadier; hard; handsome, manly', but as she came to know her better, a tender and motherly side had unfolded.[6] Yet that first impression was not wrong: Vita loved wearing trousers, and was thrilled to pose and pass as a man in public, at a time when love affairs between women were often constructed in terms of the masculine and feminine roles of heterosexual romance.

So far Virginia had not drawn upon the insights Vita had brought her (although they may have intensified the relationship between Lily and Mrs Ramsay in To the Lighthouse), and her earliest intimations of the next novel pointed in quite a different direction. As she finished the first draft of To the Lighthouse in the early autumn of 1926, she had had a vision of waves crashing, of 'a fin passing far out', an experience of otherness ('not oneself but something in the universe that one's left with') which she recognized as 'the impulse behind another book',[7] but it was growing slowly and elusively, reluctant to come into focus. She was also toying with a critical study of fiction, urged on by Leonard and 'Dadie' Rylands (properly, George, a young man who had briefly worked for the Hogarth Press, and was now Fellow of King's College, Cambridge).

Woolf's vision of crashing waves had been accompanied by several severe bouts of depression, a reaction that often followed the completion of a draft.[8] Wanting Vita was one element, yet during the summer and autumn of 1926, the two women had grown steadily closer. Virginia sought opportunities to be alone with Vita, and Vita responded eagerly, on one occasion enclosing a love-letter inside a letter intended for Leonard to read.[9] Each protested her need of the other: 'I do want to see you, I do – I do'. 'Now never say again that I don't love you. I want dreadfully to see you. That is all there is to it.'[10] Vita's letters, as she set out on her second visit to Teheran in January 1927, were full of yearning: 'It's time I either lived with Virginia or went back to Asia, and as I can't do the former I must do the latter'; 'I don't know how I shall get on without you – in fact I don't feel I can – you have become so essential to me.'[11] This time, Vita travelled through Moscow in winter, visiting Lenin's lying in state in the Kremlin, and describing for Virginia 'all the traffic passing to and fro over the frozen river as though it were a road'.[12]

'I lie in bed making up stories about you', Virginia wrote to Vita early in March 1927.[13] A week later, she suddenly envisaged a complete novel, 'a whole fantasy to be called "The Jessamy Brides"':

Two women, poor, solitary at the top of a house. One can see anything (for this is all fantasy) the Tower Bridge, clouds, aeroplanes . . . It is to be written as I write letters at the top of my speed: on the ladies of Llangollen; . . . Sapphism is to be suggested. Satire is to be the main note – satire & wildness. The Ladies are to have Constantinople in view. Dreams of golden domes. My own lyric vein is to be satirised. Everything mocked. And it is to end with three dots . . . so. For the truth is I feel the need of an escapade after these serious poetic experimental books whose form is always so closely considered . . . it will rest my head before starting the very serious, mystical poetical work which I want to come next.

Later, she added in the margin, 'Orlando leading to The Waves.'[14]

'Jessamy Brides' was a phrase Woolf coined for lesbian lovers: 'Jessamy' (an old-fashioned name for jasmine) was eighteenth-century slang for an effeminate man – 'a Jemmy Jessamy' – the references to 'Sapphism' and the notorious 'ladies of Llangollen'[15] make her meaning clear. This alternative vision of lesbian love would challenge and mock the marital and family values of Mrs Ramsay far more explicitly than Lily Briscoe's art had done, and would give her a standpoint from which to make fun of patriarchy. The extensive view that took in both Tower Bridge and Constantinople foreshortened space, and would ultimately foreshorten time. As she had foreseen in her 1926 essay on 'Cinema', 'The past could be unrolled, distances could be annihilated'[16] in celebrating the transcendent powers of love and the imagination.

'But you dont see, donkey West, that you'll be tired of me one of

these days (I'm so much older) and so I have to take my little pre-
cautions', Virginia had warned Vita, while admitting that 'donkey
West knows she has broken down more ramparts than anyone'.[17]
As usual, Virginia saw further than Vita. On her second return from
Persia in May 1927, the pleasure of being together gave way to a new
restlessness on Vita's part. She was impatient for an intensity that
Virginia's marriage, writing and physical frailty ruled out. By the end
of May, Virginia was in bed again, with a headache. She was reading
Challenge, Vita's novel about her passionate love affair with Violet
Trefusis. In it, Vita had cast herself as Julian, a young revolutionary,
and Violet as Eve, the eternal woman.[18] Playing Julian had been one
of the greatest sources of excitement in their love affair; she and Violet
had walked out, danced together, even rented a room in respectable
Orpington as a married couple. As well as Julian, Vita was 'Mitya',
while Violet became 'Lushka', his Russian princess.[19]

Remembering her mad escapades with Violet, Vita fantasized about
driving down surreptitiously, late one evening, to spend the night with
Virginia at Rodmell – 'But, you being you, I can't; more's the pity'.
Virginia wired back 'Come then', but she recognized the subtext: 'I
was reading Challenge and I thought your letter was a challenge "if
only you weren't so elderly and valetudinarian" was what you said in
effect'.[20] Not long after that, Vita resorted to a different kind of teasing,
letting Virginia know that she had spent a night with Clive's mistress,
Mary Hutchinson,[21] and in September, she began an altogether more
serious affair with another Mary, wife of the poet Roy Campbell, to
whom she was renting a cottage in the grounds of Long Barn. At first
Virginia teased her back – she was seeing the beautiful Dadie Rylands,
Philip Morrell had proposed to her[22] – but she minded more than she
admitted, and as the summer of 1927 drew to a close, she sensed a
change in the emotional climate.

At the beginning of September, the Woolfs visited Tilton, the
Keynes' farmhouse near Charleston. After dinner, guests and hosts
performed some amateur theatricals – the kind of cross-dressing and
camping it up that Lytton loved, though on this occasion he was absent,
and Virginia sent him an account of the proceedings.[23] At Tilton that
night, one of the guests had brought a newspaper cutting with 'the
photograph of a pretty young woman who had become a man'.

Virginia (according to her nephew Quentin) could talk of nothing else.[24]

She was now reviewing for the *New York Herald Tribune*, discussing the work of Ernest Hemingway, E. M. Forster, the poet Shelley, as well as *Some People*, the latest book by Vita's husband, Harold Nicolson. Amusing and original, it consisted of a series of autobiographical anecdotes, written in a comically self-deprecating English style. Her review praised Nicolson for having 'devised a method of writing about people and about himself as though they were at once real and imaginary', and for his success in combining the 'granite' of truth with the 'rainbow' of personality, 'his mixture of biography and autobiography, of fact and fiction, of Lord Curzon's trousers and Miss Plimsoll's nose'.[25] His method opened a path before her: in a diary entry for September 1927, while working on the review, she decided to write 'the memoirs of one's own times . . . Vita should be Orlando, a young nobleman . . . & it should be truthful; but fantastic.' A fortnight later, she finished her review ('The New Biography'), and started upon 'a biography beginning in the year 1500 & continuing to the present day, called Orlando: Vita; only with a change about from one sex to another'. Back in London that autumn, she could scarcely put it down. She was launched 'somewhat furtively but with all the more passion' on a small book to be finished by Christmas.[26]

But first, Vita's permission was required. She immediately saw where Virginia's proposal was leading – indeed, she could hardly have failed to do so, for the request was laced with reproaches: 'listen; suppose . . . its all about you and the lusts of your flesh and the lure of your mind (heart you have none, who go gallivanting down the lanes with [Mary] Campbell) . . . Shall you mind? Say yes, or No.'[27] 'What fun for you; what fun for me', Vita replied. 'You see, any vengeance that you ever want to take will lie ready to your hand.' She cheerfully accepted her role as the dirty puppy that had made a mess, and deserved to be rapped on the nose, insisting only that Virginia should 'dedicate it to your victim' (as she had dedicated *Challenge* to Violet).[28] The writing of *Orlando* was to be a revenge for infidelities, and an act of disengagement. It allowed Virginia to write out her sense of betrayal, while legitimating further demands for information, pictures, photographs (since *Orlando* must look like a 'real' biography).[29] It provided new ways of flattering and intriguing Vita ('a heroine to everyone including her own darling self', according to her husband[30]), while restoring to Virginia her dignity and a degree of control: 'If you've given yourself to Campbell, I'll have no more to do with you, and so it shall be written, plainly, for all the world to read in Orlando.'[31] She had found a way of using her art not merely to exorcize past relationships, but also present ones.

'Making people up' had always been her favourite occupation; 'if you'll make me up, I'll make you', Virginia had promised Vita.[32] The writing of biography was a Stephen family tradition that had become a Stephen family joke. Virginia's grandfather, Sir James, had been the author of two volumes of *Essays in Ecclesiastical Biography* (1849); her father, Sir Leslie, had been editor of the *Dictionary of National Biography*, sixty-eight volumes in all – Virginia sometimes blamed it for her instability, but more often she giggled over all those lives of great men.[33] Several of her own earliest writings had used biographical frameworks – sometimes seriously, as in the life of Vanessa written for the newborn Julian in 1907, but more often comically, as in the (lost) lives of her aunts Caroline Stephen and Mary Fisher, and those of her 'aunt' Anny Ritchie as Mrs Hilbery in *Night and Day* and of her great-aunt Julia Margaret Cameron in her comic play *Freshwater*, and her introduction to a selection of Cameron's photographs.[34] She also wrote an imaginary life of her first love, Violet Dickinson ('Friendship's Gallery', 1907), in which Violet (who was remarkably tall) becomes a benevolent giantess, and rescues the city of Tokyo from an invasion of sea monsters with the tip of her umbrella. Like *Orlando*, this was a love-gift, copied out especially, in violet ink. Other early pieces such as 'Memoirs of a Novelist' make fun of the creaking narrative techniques of Victorian biography – the arbitrary chapter divisions, the coy yet self-effacing appeals to the reader.[35] In an entirely different mode, *To the Lighthouse* had created within a fictional framework an idiosyncratic blend of biography and autobiography that was not quite either. *Orlando* would parody both the stiff conventions of biography and the extravagance of her own 'lyric vein'.

If biography was one shaping force, Orlando's name was itself another. It was arrived at on day one quite as definitely as the title of *To the Lighthouse* had been, perhaps because of its hesitations between 'or' and 'and' (as in 'male and/or female', or 'married and/or lesbian'), or even because it echoed the title of Vita's long poem, *The Land*, published at the end of September 1926, and awarded the Hawthornden Prize the following summer.[36] It was a name familiar from contemporary politics, being that of a recent Italian prime minister (one of the 'big four' at the Paris Peace conference), but it had older and closer connections: Orlando is the lover of the cross-dressed heroine Rosalind in Shakespeare's *As You Like It* (1598), while his name, in turn, derives from Ariosto's *Orlando Furioso* (1532), whose hero anticipates Shakespeare's in his concern with names carved on trees. Orlando ('Roland' in French) was a Knight of Charlemagne, famous for his battles against the Saracens. He goes mad ('furioso') when he discovers from an inscription in a cave that his beloved Angelica has given herself to Medoro. This literary pedigree was written into Woolf's first draft, where the library of Orlando's house at Blackfriars included 'many of the Italian & French romances; Petrarch; Boccaccio; Ariosto'.[37] But does Orlando in his fury reflect Vita's desperate passion for Violet Trefusis or does it refer covertly to Virginia herself – not merely jealous, but famous in her own right for bouts of madness? (Harold had asked Vita of their first encounter, 'Did she look very mad?'[38])

The novel opens by recalling Orlando's crusading ancestors – the unselfconscious racism of this scene is disturbing for the reader: 'He – for there could be no doubt of his sex, though the fashion of the time did something to disguise it – was in the act of slicing at the head of a Moor which swung from the rafters.' [p.113][39] Caught in the act, both Orlando's undoubted masculinity and the disguise of clothing will soon be open to doubt. This first chapter was written in three weeks, so fast that Woolf had no time to type it out before lunch. It felt 'extraordinarily unwilled . . . as if it shoved everything aside to come into existence'. It was entirely absorbing: 'this is our happiest autumn. So much work; & success now; & life on easy terms'.[40] *Orlando* was to be an imaginary life of Vita, incorporating details of her 'real' life, her ancestors' lives, and of Knole itself, as Virginia had seen it in deep snow at the beginning of the year, when 'All the centuries seemed lit up, the past expressive, articulate; not dumb & forgotten; but a crowd of people stood behind, not dead at all; not remarkable; . . . & so we reach the days of Elizabeth quite easily.'[41] Orlando's longevity would represent the continuity of English aristocratic life, and of English literary history. To mark her visit (on 17 January 1927), Vita had given Virginia a copy of her family history, *Knole and the Sackvilles*.[42]

Now Virginia was reading it closely, borrowing from it names for household servants and catalogues of household furnishings, noting the friends, titles and habits of Vita's ancestors, as well as details of the great house itself – the split tree trunks that made up the floor of the Cartoon Gallery, the swaying tapestries in the Venetian Ambassador's room.[43] But, like a cabinet with secret drawers, this imaginary biography of Vita included just as many elements of autobiography, fragments from Woolf's own life as a reader and writer: 'It was the Elizabethan prose writers I loved first & most wildly . . . I used to read [Hakluyt] & dream of those obscure adventurers, & no doubt practised their style in my copy books.'[44] Accordingly, *Orlando* opens in the Elizabethan age, with sea dogs drinking at riverside taverns, a glimpse of the greatest of them all – the globe-eyed playwright in his dirty ruff – and the state visit of the ageing Queen, who presents Orlando's father with the great monastic house (never named in the novel), taking his son into her service.

Vita's visit to Moscow, with its traffic on the ice, had prompted memories of another favourite Elizabethan work – Dekker's pamphlet 'The Great Frost/Cold Doings in London, except it be at the Lottery'. Virginia had come across it in her father's library, in the first volume of Edward Arber's prose anthology, *An English Garner*[45] (which even today is still the easiest place to find it). Dekker gives an unforgettable account of the legendary winter of 1607–8 when the Thames froze over, creating a playground where citizens could disport themselves and buy food and drink, as they walked, miraculously, upon the frozen waters. In *Orlando*, time itself seems frozen, creating a 'Midwinter spring . . . Suspended in time . . . In windless cold that is the heart's heat',[46] a stillness in the midst of flux, in which Orlando consummates his love for the Russian princess. As Sasha skates towards him in her velvet tunic and trousers, Orlando initially mistakes her for a boy, in the first of the novel's sexual mistakings – that September, at Long Barn, Virginia had watched as Vita dressed her son Nigel in a long Russian tunic. ' "Dont. It makes me look like a little girl" ' he complained.[47]

Orlando's love affair is archetypal – all-consuming and brief, compounded of poetic images and unanswered questions. Whereas Orlando tells Sasha about his family and his feelings, she remains entirely enigmatic, revealing nothing of who or what she is, or what she wants. Their love is acted out in the Great Frost as if inside a crystal sphere. Their graceful sweeps across the ice echo those of the gulls overhead, making the rest of the court look clumsy. When the ice ruptures and time is unbound, their love is swept away in the thaw that follows, along with a bizarre medley of animals, objects and human beings trapped on the ice floes and hurtling towards destruction.

Reckless, doomed passion, and a love so intense that it cannot survive the everyday world – these were the keynotes of Vita's novel, *Challenge*. Virginia's rewriting of that romance recaptures Vita's sense of herself and Violet as rebels, adventurers defying the world.[48] Yet although Vita believed that Violet had betrayed her by marrying Denys Trefusis, their affair had actually ended with Vita in flight from Violet's demands, taking refuge in home, husband and children. And it was Vita, not Violet, whose beauty was so androgynous, 'an olive tree, an emerald, and a fox' ('I want to see you in the lamplight, in your emeralds', Virginia told Vita, days after she had begun writing; Vita, too, was 'a crafty fox').[49] Jealousy, the grit in the oyster of love, generates the first chapter, as the old Queen collapses on catching sight of Orlando kissing a girl in a window-seat, and Orlando collapses on catching a glimpse of Sasha on a Russian sailor's knee – abandonment is at once the ultimate terror, and the inevitable outcome. As Woolf revised the first chapter, she further emphasized the theme of jealousy by altering the entertainment on the ice from a court masque for King James to a performance of *Othello*, pointedly quoting the hero's words after he has murdered Desdemona:

> Methinks it should be now a huge eclipse
> Of sun and moon, and that the affrighted globe
> Should yawn [at alteration].[50]

Orlando retreats from his flood of grief into a preternatural sleep that continues for seven days (perhaps recalling Virginia's own two-day coma at the height of her 1915 breakdown; her early life, like his, had been marked by a sense of rupture and abandonment, in her case occasioned by her mother's death). Orlando's biographer is left wondering whether he had 'died for a week, and then come to life again? And if so, of what nature is death and of what nature life?' [p.49][51] When Orlando awakens, he has changed from an Elizabethan man of action to a Jacobean melancholic, much possessed by death, frequenting the crypt, playing with the bones of his ancestors and poring over the funerary meditations of Sir Thomas Browne (his Jacobean morbidity may reflect the prolonged mourning imposed on the Stephen children).[52]

From too much reading Orlando turns to writing, and after glancing through a heap of his own cast-aside juvenilia, he settles down to compose 'The Oak Tree', the novel's equivalent of Vita's poem, *The Land* (and perhaps of Lily Briscoe's painting, taking him not ten, but more than three hundred years to complete). As he pauses in thought, the narrative is arbitrarily interrupted by a meditation on memory and its arbitrariness, its habit of assembling 'a perfect rag-bag of odds and ends . . . – a piece of a policeman's trousers lying cheek by jowl with Queen Alexandra's wedding veil' [p.55]. Saucily suggestive in itself, this passage echoes Nicolson's sentence, 'on the linoleum of the gangway Lord Curzon's armorial dressing-case lay cheek by jowl with the fibre of Miss Petticue's portmanteau'.[53] It sets the tone for the switchback rhythms of the narrative, as it chops and changes from one voice or mood to another, from frivolity to profundity in the space of a few pages, or a few paragraphs.

Each time Orlando begins to write, his biographer begins to fret over the paradoxes inherent in the writing process, wringing metaphorical hands over the difficulties of narrating a writer's life when its central activity – sitting still and thinking – is no activity at all: even 'killing a wasp . . . is a fitter subject for novelist or biographer than this mere wool-gathering; this thinking; this sitting in a chair day in day out, with a cigarette and a sheet of paper and a pen and an inkpot. If only subjects . . . had more consideration for their biographers!' [p.187] For 'Life' (with a glance at Vita, whose name means 'life' in Latin) 'is the only fit subject for novelist or biographer', whereas 'thought and imagination . . . are of no importance whatsoever'. According to this view, the biography of a writer becomes impossible to write (as it had proved to be in *Night and Day*, where Mrs Hilbery had failed to write the life of her father, Richard Alardyce), since writing and thinking are such invisible, such interior (and anterior) experiences.

If the action is suspended while Orlando writes, what is there left for his biographer to do?

[P]robably the reader can imagine the passage which should follow . . . how things remain much as they are for two or three hundred years or so, except for a little dust and a few cobwebs which one old woman can sweep up in half an hour; a conclusion which . . . might have been reached more quickly by the simple statement that 'Time passed' (here the exact amount could be indicated in brackets). [pp.67–8]

This explicit self-parody is part of a more extensive mockery of *To the Lighthouse*, with its insistent brooding upon the nature of death, time, loss and change, its concern with memory, survival and art's ability to outface time. Orlando's literary ambitions, his thoughts of 'Fame', will be explicitly aligned with 'that beam from a lighthouse', while Nick Greene, the universal man of letters, is preoccupied with '*La Gloire*', in a distant echo of Mr Ramsay's aspirations. Greene's dismissal of Shakespeare, Marlowe, Jonson and Donne ('No, he concluded, the great age of literature is past' [p.62]) reflects the difficulties of judging one's contemporaries without jealousy, a weakness common to artists and lovers (just as Greene's betrayal of Orlando replays Sasha's, in a comic vein). Orlando, however, follows Lily Briscoe in embracing obscurity and anonymity as the conditions most conducive to creativity: 'Shakespeare must have written like that, and the church builders built like that, anonymously, needing no thanking and no naming' [p.72].

Orlando's narrator slips from mocking 'Time Passes' into a rhapsody on the relative nature of time, and the 'extraordinary discrepancy between time on the clock and time in the mind' [p.68]. The novel revalues subjective consciousness at the expense of the world of action, while suggesting Einstein's theories of relativity.[54] Vita, having reached Teheran the previous February, had complained to Virginia that she could scarcely write to her because 'everything is so confused, so Einsteinian', and Virginia had responded by asking her about her expedition to the Bakhtiari, while recognizing that '[w]hat I pretend to be past is all in the future. Yet to you, reading this, its over. All very confusing . . .' Vita, too, was troubled, when writing to Harold or Virginia, by the sense that her letters travelled so slowly that they made nonsense of the immediacy of her experiences, that when the writer's 'present moment' reached the recipient, three weeks later, 'I am no longer coasting Baluchistan; I am driving in a cab in Bagdad, or reading in a train, or asleep, or dead; the present tense has become meaningless.'[55] 'Time travels in divers paces with divers persons', as Rosalind explained to Orlando in *As You Like It*, but the effect was greatly magnified when travel and the post created long delays. Einstein's Special Theory of Relativity had demonstrated that, in the world of physics, time was not a constant, but flowed at different rates for objects travelling at different speeds. And there was a further implication: if it were possible to travel fast enough, the body might age more slowly, an idea that may underpin Orlando's speed on the ice, her rattling from lamp-post to lamp-post across London in a coach, or driving fast from London to Sevenoaks.[56]

'Brevity and diuturnity' are 'the two forces which alternately, and . . . at the same moment, dominate our unfortunate numbskulls' ('numbing our skulls' in the process?) The sense of time as both transitory and eternal, like Woolf's sense of life as both 'very solid' and 'very shifting'[57] continued to haunt her, finding its fullest expression in *The Waves*. But from *Jacob's Room* onwards, time became a key element in the construction of Woolf's novels, the essential medium in which the novelist worked; in *Mrs Dalloway* and *To the Lighthouse* the movements of time and memory determine the form. *Orlando*'s time structure is at once more and less conventional: its action proceeds chronologically from the sixteenth to the twentieth century (with different 'ages' constituting what plot there is[58]), yet its hero/ine reaches thirty at the beginning of the eighteenth century, and then ages a further six years over the next two centuries. The relative nature of time and space, so inconspicuously borrowed from the new physics, also extends to gender and the life of the body.

'The true length of a person's life, whatever the *Dictionary of National Biography* may say, is always a matter of dispute. For it is a difficult business – this time-keeping.' [p.211] *Orlando* treats time rather as it treats sex – as if both were convenient fictions. It

energetically resists the 'facts of life' – birth, death and our subjection
to the bodies we have been given, and their desires. Instead, it focuses
upon what the imagination seizes as truth, giving that priority over
more probable circumstance. Vita often resented her allotted gender
role, and never more than when it debarred her from becoming the
fourth Baron Sackville and inheriting Knole in her own right. But
Orlando celebrates Knole as her rightful and permanent home, just as
it celebrates – and even explains and justifies – her sexual ambivalence.
Like Orlando himself, the great house, and even its servants, seem
exempt from the passage of time, or perhaps some power over time
has been built into it, for it is constructed upon the numbers of time,
having seven courts, fifty-two staircases and 365 bedrooms.[59] Perhaps
the house resists death, too – in the final pages, the dead Queen returns,
and steps from her chariot: ' "The house is at your service, Ma'am,"
[Orlando] cried, curtseying deeply. "Nothing has been changed. The
dead Lord, my father, shall lead you in." ' [p.227] By the time Woolf
wrote this scene, Vita's father was indeed dead, and Knole, descending
exclusively through the male line, had gone to her uncle Charles; it
could only be restored to her in the pages of *Orlando*.[60]

As the seventeenth century draws to a close, Orlando abandons his
lives as lover and poet and takes on public office as British Ambassador
to the Turks in Constantinople – Vita had begun her married life there
as an Embassy wife, and the Sackvilles had often fulfilled such tasks,
though seldom so far afield. But Constantinople, with its 'dreams of
golden domes' had been 'in view' from the beginning, a fantasy city
on the threshold of Asia, outside European history and tradition, a
city looking in two directions at once, a city of dualities.[61] Woolf had
travelled there with Adrian and Vanessa in 1906, and seen the dome
of Santa Sofia, 'like a treble globe of bubbles frozen solid, floating out
to meet us.'[62] Evanescent, yet also very solid, it corresponded to her
sense of the nature of life in time. That extraordinary combination
of delicacy and strength had also characterized Lily Briscoe's artistic
ideal, and a view of Constantinople had opened up unexpectedly
before Nancy Ramsay, as she walked to the beach with Minta in the
first part of *To the Lighthouse*.[63] Nancy's vision was also the view
from Vita's first home after her marriage, looking down over Santa
Sofia and the Golden Gate in 1913, and it would become Orlando's:

his day begins with a vision of domes floating like bubbles upon the morning mist.[64]

In Constantinople, Orlando is dubbed Knight of the Bath (as various Sackvilles and Leslie Stephen had been). Raised to the highest possible standing, as an English duke, he clandestinely marries the gipsy Rosina Pepita (Vita's grandmother)[65] and falls into another seven-day sleep as a palace revolution breaks out. Violent change in the body politic is reflected in the private body, as Orlando wakes to find himself transformed into a woman (his patriarchal honours preceding, and perhaps even precipitating, this event). The change is heralded by a masque that erupts quite as suddenly into the narrative as the Turkish uprising had done. The unconcealed artifice of the court masque is as far removed as possible from the genre of biography, with its attention to documented fact. Possibly for that very reason, masques had already appeared in the first draft, as part of King James's entertainment on the ice (later, to be altered to a performance of *Othello*), and, in the manuscript, Milton's *Comus* is performed as part of the Embassy celebrations for Orlando's new honours.[66]

Woolf heralds Orlando's sex change with a Jonsonian masque, a form in which the antimasque of vices is dismissed and a sacred figure invoked. In Woolf's version, Truth banishes the antimasque, consisting of the Ladies of Purity, Chastity and Modesty, and summons in their place the naked and now female Orlando. The dismissal of these false goddesses to the hen roost and the 'still unravished heights of Surrey' is part of the novel's attack on prudery and sexual concealment (a concealment which it also practises). In an earlier episode (ultimately omitted) Nick Greene had given Orlando 'Shakespeare's own account of his relations with Mr W. H. & the dark Lady written by him with great fulness & spirit in a letter Greene happened to have on him & gave to Orlando as a pleasant curiosity & keepsake'. But his prudish biographer feels obliged to consign this document to the fire, on the ground that 'when Truth & Modesty conflict [as they so often do], who can doubt which should prevail?'[67]

Both psychically and structurally, Orlando's unexplained sex change is the novel's central event, providing a parallel with the change in *Lighthouse* from patriarchal Victorian family life ('The Window') to a modern world of independence ('The Lighthouse'); the Masque of

Truth, with its radical change of discourse, corresponds to 'Time Passes'. Yet Orlando's progression from male to female does not follow Vita's biography so much as provide her with a rationale for dressing up and playing the man. In fact, though Vita had always loved women, she had been married and had children before she became Violet's Julian. In making her a man who becomes a woman, Woolf may have recalled her own initial sense of Vita's masculinity, yet there is a further sense in which all women begin their imaginative lives, if not as men, then at least as unconscious of their gender, and have to learn to think of themselves as women. If they are also readers, they will have participated in a world of adventure where to be masculine means to be free. In any case, as Woolf later observed (mistakenly), 'nothing is known about women before the eighteenth century'.[68]

At first Orlando is protected from the full implications of her womanhood by her Turkish costume, 'coats and trousers which can be worn indifferently by either sex' [p.98], and more generally by life among the gipsies, a society free from distinctions of gender or class, and from Western notions of 'beauty', a society outside history (their blend of kindness and suspicion towards Orlando recalling *Gulliver's Travels*.) A vision of Knole in the snow (Woolf's own vision from her stay in January 1927) turns Orlando homewards. Once on board the *Enamoured Lady*, however, she experiences the rare pleasures and frequent frustrations of her new sex. She remembers how, as a man, 'she had insisted that women must be obedient, chaste, scented, and exquisitely apparelled', and sees that ' "Now I shall have to pay in my own person for those desires" ' [p.110]. And when she remembers her former (male) vanity and ostentation, she begins to change her opinion of masculinity: ' "to deny a woman teaching lest she may laugh at you; to be the slave of the frailest chit in petticoats, and yet to go about as if you were the Lords of creation – Heavens!" she thought, "what fools they make of us – what fools we are!" ' As the narrator points out, here 'it would seem . . . that she was censuring both sexes equally, as if she belonged to neither' [p.113].

On shipboard, Orlando's womanhood casts her as one of a dangerous yet protected species. Her new experiences expose the artificial nature of gender construction: 'it is clothes that wear us and not we them' [p.132], the narrator declares, reversing the more usual assumption that clothes are superficial, while the body beneath is essential. But is there anything fixed or constant in human nature that time and culture cannot alter? The rest of Woolf's fiction was to return compulsively to this question: '"D'you think people change? Their clothes, of course . . . But I meant ourselves . . . – do we change?"'[69] And since the sexes treat one another differently in different societies (as *Orlando* had already shown), what is the significance of biological difference? Vita had thought of the sexes as gradually merging. Now Virginia echoed her conviction: 'Different though the sexes are, they intermix . . . often it is only clothes that keep the male or female likeness, while underneath the sex is the very opposite of what it is above.' [pp.132–3]

After her initial excitement, Orlando grows impatient with eighteenth-century society, with its coffee-houses and salons where men congratulate themselves on their wit, and women listen admiringly and pour the tea. Feeling imprisoned by social expectations and the limits on her freedom, and irritated by the misogyny of Addison, Pope and Lord Chesterfield, Orlando reverts to male clothing and seeks out the company of women of the streets. The anecdotes of Nell and her friends amuse her far more than those of the reputed wits, but at this point, Woolf's mockery of polite concealment goes into reverse, and the reader is excluded from their intimacies: 'when women get together – but hist – they are always careful to see that the doors are shut and that not a word of it gets into print. All they desire is – but hist again – is that not a man's step on the stair?' Yet 'Women have no desires, says this gentleman, coming into Nell's parlour . . . Without desires (she has served him and he is gone) their conversation cannot be of the slightest interest to anyone.' [p.152] The brutality of this parenthesis, and the indifference to women's desires so manifest in the economic exchange of prostitution, is the more shocking for being so quietly voiced. Woolf's writing had been troubled by prostitution from the beginning, but Nell's casual self-surrender, in a novel whose very wellspring is women's desire, sits in the text like an unexploded mine. Woolf's anticipation of this passage in her diary – 'O. meets a girl (Nell) in the Park & goes with her to a neat room in Gerrard Street . . . This will bring in O.'s night life; & her clients (thats the word)' – further underlines its significance for her.[70]

Women's weapon against such brutality is secrecy, that 'secret and private' freemansonry of women's friendship that Woolf found so appealing.[71] If men assume that women have no desires, and take no pleasure in their own company, let them continue in their ignorance. Women's meetings behind closed doors may be sexually, and even politically subversive (as coffee-house meetings could be), but women guard their secrets as carefully as Woolf guards them from the reader.[72] This tone of textual (and sexual) teasing, which slips easily from discomfort to comedy, characterizes the novel more generally. *Orlando* is exceptional among Woolf's fiction in its evident delight in *double entendres*: 'the Queen . . . knew a man when she saw one, though not, it is said, in the usual way'; Shel, asked where he is bound for, replies ' "For the Horn," . . . and blushed'; the pyramid of Victorian sacred cows in front of Buckingham Palace becomes 'that vast erection', which suddenly shrinks to nothing, leaving 'not a stain, not a puddle even'. Such teasing was also a feature of Virginia's letters to Vita:

Should you say, if I rang you up to ask, that you were fond of me?
If I saw you would you kiss me? If I were in bed would you –
I'm rather excited about Orlando tonight: have been lying by the fire and making up the last chapter.

This was written as Orlando was returning from Constantinople. From the beginning, Woolf had intended the last chapter to end in three silent yet suggestive dots, thus . . .[73]

According to the first draft, none of the Augustan wits 'took her fancy corporeally'[74] – Nell and her friends seemed far more exciting. No longer a man yet disguised as one, Orlando has come full circle.[75] '[T]hough she herself was a woman', she still loved women, 'through the culpable laggardry of the human frame to adapt itself to convention' [p.115]. Since male company leaves so much to be desired, she closes the doors and enjoys 'the love of both sexes equally'. In a covert reference to Vita's flight with Violet, it is even rumoured that she had 'fled with a certain lady to the Low Countries where the lady's husband followed them' [p.153]. Yet although the topic of lesbian love is often indicated, it is never referred to explicitly; *Orlando* cannot, after all, retell the story of *The Jessamy Brides*. Whether because of such self-imposed restrictions or for some other reason, as Orlando tires of eighteenth-century society, so her author began to tire of her. Virginia retreated to bed with a headache, followed by an attack of 'flu ('[n]ever was anyone so tossed up & down by the body as I am'). Vita's father was dying, and Virginia wrote her anxious, affectionate letters. But the excitement that had sustained her through the first three months of writing was giving way to self-doubt – *Orlando* was 'empty', was 'freakish'; she preferred 'woolgathering' about 'Women & Fiction' (later, *A Room of One's Own*).[76] By mid-February, she was definitely bored, 'hacking rather listlessly' at it. A week later, full of premenstrual tension, writing came to a complete standstill: 'It is the oddest feeling: as if a finger stopped the flow of the ideas in the brain: it is unsealed, & the blood rushes all over the place.' At the same moment, the ink began to flow unbidden from Orlando's pen in sentimental verse effusions – 'all about death too, & the widows heart; & going home to rest'.[77]

The Victorian age had arrived; its rising damp penetrates everything, from the woodwork to the inkpot. The climate has changed; 'the constitution of England was altered'; ivy and babies proliferate, and 'the British Empire came into existence' [pp.157–8]. Orlando is increasingly alienated by the sudden reverence for marriage, while finding it difficult to resist the spirit of the age. Sentimental gush flows uncontrollably from her pen, and her finger tingles until she puts on a wedding ring. During a romantic walk across the moors, she meets and falls in love with the sea captain Marmaduke Bonthrop Shelmerdine, whose sexuality is as doubtful as her own (' "You're a woman, Shel!" ' ' "You're a man, Orlando!" ' [pp.174–5]). They are married in the chapel in a rising storm, and it seems that Orlando has indeed capitulated to the spirit of the age, yet amidst the thunder, 'no one heard the word Obey spoken' [p.181].[78]

The final chapter opens and closes with marriage – an institution unquestioningly accepted by Vita and Virginia in their daily lives, yet a potential threat to women's autonomy, as well as a source of perplexity: 'If one liked [one's husband], was it marriage? If one liked other people, was it marriage? And finally, if one still wished, more than anything in the whole world, to write poetry, was it marriage? [Orlando] had her doubts.' [p.182] She puts these to the test by writing four lines of poetry: taken from Vita's poem *The Land*, they describe a field of fritillaries as 'Scarfed in dull purple, like Egyptian girls', thus revealing a deeper disturbance than marriage: 'girls? Are girls necessary?' Orlando's marriage and her (very British) love of nature allow her to slip this line past the spirit of the age, as a traveller under the eye of the customs officer conceals 'something highly contraband for which she would have had to pay the full fine' [pp.183–4].[79] And that is as far as the text is prepared to go. If Orlando has evaded the spirit of the age, so has her author. This line from Vita's poem turns out to be the novel's most explicit expression of lesbian desire. For all its critique of prudery and false modesty, *Orlando* conceals its own point of origin. Yet Woolf's caution was shortly to be justified: while she worked on *Orlando*, the Home Secretary, William Joynson-Hicks, started proceedings against Radclyffe Hall's frank (though sexually inexplicit) lesbian novel, *The Well of Loneliness*.

As the reader approaches the present moment (identified as 11 October 1928, the book's designated date of publication), Orlando's fantasy attributes give place to Vita's more familiar roles as wife, mother and prize-winning poet; she shops at the West End department store of Marshall and Snelgrove, drives down to Sevenoaks in her Austin Twenty, welcomes her husband who arrives by private aeroplane.[80] But Vita's twentieth century was substantially different from Virginia's, as the last chapter – and Vita's reaction to it – reveal. Woolf continues to endow Orlando with her own experiences: the housekeeper Mrs Bartholomew worked for the Woolfs at Rodmell; the revelation of the toy boat on the Serpentine recalls her childhood at Hyde Park Gate, and though she had visited Kew with Vita, it held a particular importance for her, since her short story 'Kew Gardens' had marked her emergence into modernism. Indeed, the Hogarth Press published a wonderful new edition of it in November 1927, as Woolf wrote the third chapter of *Orlando*. At Orlando's age of thirty-six, Woolf had met Katherine Mansfield and T. S. Eliot, read James Joyce and written 'Kew Gardens' for the newly born Hogarth Press.[81] Modernism as a literary style dominates the final chapter, just as the vigour of Elizabethan and the eloquence of Jacobean prose had coloured the first two, eighteenth-century memoirs the fourth, and the romanticism of De Quincey, the Brontës, and Tennyson pervades chapter V. But modernism was entirely alien to Vita: when Edith Sitwell sneered at her poem *The Land*, Virginia had consoled her, 'I dont think you probably realise how hard it is for the natural innovator as she is, to be fair to the natural traditionalist as you are.'[82]

Kew had a further role to play in Orlando's history: it would 'do' to conceal the mystery of her pregnancy, which cannot be mentioned openly and so is set about with distractions (such as the kingfisher), and Miltonic exclamations ('Hail! natural desire!'). It is heavily veiled, not merely because such physical processes were seldom referred to in polite print or society, but also because there is a genuine mystery about it. Orlando's pregnancy, which began with 'bulbs, hairy and red, thrust into the earth in October', ends six months later as she is delivered of a child, on 20 March, when Woolf completed the first draft of the novel.[83] Woolf's occasional history of English prose thus culminates in the birth of the novel itself, with a glance at Joyce's 'Oxen of the Sun' chapter in *Ulysses*.

Orlando's giving birth to a book may be related to Woolf's own gradual acceptance of childlessness. That December (1927), at a party for her niece Angelica, she noticed, 'I scarcely want children of my own now. This insatiable desire to write something before I die . . . makes me cling . . . to my one anchor. I don't like the physicalness of having children of one's own.' Six months later, she repeated, 'I don't want [children] any more, since my ideas so possess me'.[84] *Orlando* has been rightly admired for its evocation of sense experience, for having 'at the centre of its discourse the body', yet at the same time, it is also Woolf's farewell to the flesh. The natural body, subject to time, sickness and death, is here replaced by an imaginary body, impossibly freed from all those burdens – 'the only exciting life is the imaginary one'.[85]

As Orlando drives down the Old Kent Road, her vision becomes fragmented:

Nothing could be seen whole or read from start to finish. What was seen begun . . . was never seen ended. After twenty minutes the body and mind were like scraps of torn paper tumbling from a sack and, indeed, the process of motoring fast out of London so much resembles the chopping up small of identity which precedes unconsciousness and perhaps death itself that it is an open question in what sense Orlando can be said to have existed at the present moment. [p.212]

The speed of modern travel demands new forms of expression, and technological change alters our artistic and cultural perceptions. The very process of driving (as in Woolf's essay 'Evening over Sussex: Reflections in a Motor Car') releases the mind into a self-conscious reverie where it is free to identify the 'seventy-six different times all ticking in the mind at once', and even the 'two thousand and fifty-two' different selves (traditional biography had been satisfied with a mere six or seven). Orlando calls upon another self, but that particular self ('the most profound and secret side of [her] character') eludes her.[86]

While this proliferation of selves, like the fragmenting of experience, supersedes older and simpler views of character, it was also peculiarly appropriate to the contradictions and complexities of Vita's personality.[87] Orlando ranges through her corridors and flowerbeds, remembering the past in the present, and calling upon her soul within the house. Her search for herself mingles the modernist sense that individuals are unknowable, mysterious (the theme of *Jacob's Room*), with the romantic and Victorian sense of the lover's pursuit of the loved one. The search for Vita pervades the final chapter, concealed beneath the search for the meaning of life itself: 'Life, life, what art thou? What's life, we ask . . . Life, Life, Life! cries the bird' [p.188].[88] It climaxes in the flight of the wild goose: if the wild goose chase is proverbially pointless or unfulfilled, its sudden flight also promises imminent revelation. The end of the first draft brought the two together:

Shel! cried Orlando.
The wild goose is –
'The secret of life is . . .'[89]

The first draft was completed by the third week of March 1928, just in time for Leonard and Virginia to take a spring holiday in Cassis, in the south of France. On their return, in mid-April, Woolf set about revising at top speed, adding, deleting and tightening. She cut out some comic episodes involving Tennyson and Carlyle and their overprotective wives (literary jokes or allusions were often sacrificed at the revision stage), and added Nell Gwyn's regret at Orlando's posting to Constantinople ('''Twas a thousand pities, that amorous lady sighed, that such a pair of legs should leave the country'), and much else besides.[90] The typescript was ready for Leonard to read by the end of May, and publication was scheduled for October. But who had won the battle between the Victorians and the moderns? The outcome seems doubtful, for though the novel has been described as 'the longest and most charming love-letter in literature',[91] Orlando/Vita is finally restored not to her lover or to freedom but to her husband; she is confined to marriage, that most patriarchal of institutions. No wonder Vita was disappointed with the ending, while Leonard unexpectedly thought it 'better than The Lighthouse; about more interesting things, & with more attachment to life, & larger ... He says it is very original.'[92]

'Did you feel a sort of tug, as if your neck was being broken on Saturday last at 5 minutes to one?' Virginia demanded, as she brought *Orlando* to an end. 'The question now is, will my feelings for you be changed? ... what are you really like? Do you exist? Have I made you up?'[93] Either the process of time or the process of writing did affect her feelings for Vita (as perhaps she hoped it would). Visiting Long Barn in the summer of 1928, she noticed 'the gnawing down of strata in friendship; how one ... takes things easier; ... scarcely feel[s] it an exciting atmosphere', and in that 'gnawing down', regret was mingled with relief ('saner, perhaps deeper').[94] Their friendship had grown safer, come to accept its limitations, yet as it ceased to beat against circumstance, the magic of the unpredictable inevitably faded from it. The summer before, a dissatisfied Vita had attempted in different ways to wind things up more tightly between them. Virginia could not afford to let her do so for the sake of her writing – and it was her writing that she had used to prevent her from doing so.

In September, shortly before *Orlando*'s publication, the two women set out on their long-promised and deferred 'elopement', a week's visit to Burgundy during the grape harvest. In prospect, Virginia found it 'alarming': she was afraid that she and Vita would 'find each other out', afraid that Leonard would miss her, afraid that she would miss Leonard, afraid that she might be simply too afraid to go.[95] In the event, her departure was spoiled by 'a small and sudden row' with Leonard, and she spent much of the holiday worrying about him, buying him a jacket, sending him letters (and, later, a telegram), as if being with Vita only emphasized how much she missed and needed him. Afterwards, both Vita and Virginia protested how much they had enjoyed their time together, but they came home a day earlier than they had originally planned.[96]

Orlando's roots lay in deep anxieties about infidelity and abandonment, age and death, yet it transforms these into comedy, celebrating the power of the imagination to surmount time and chance. In freeing Orlando from the ticking of time's clock, Virginia also released herself, the self that felt old beside Vita, the self that travelled so much more slowly. In the wake of *Orlando* and whatever sexual passion Vita had aroused in her, Virginia felt 'as if the sun were sinking . . . my physical state being colder now'; she hated 'the slow heaviness of physical life, & [I] almost dislike peoples bodies, I think, as I grow older'.[97] She longed to follow Orlando into the realm of imagination, to retreat into the weightlessness of words and thoughts. Yet the novel itself is a triumph of synthesis: in inventing Vita's 'biography', Virginia had re-created the beloved in her own image; in painting her portrait, she had included much of herself. *Orlando* ends in marriage, but it is a mystic marriage of opposites that would be consummated in darkness in the final chapter of her next book, a marriage Shakespearean in its optimism, its unions of irreconcilables – not just the marriage of Orlando and Shel, of male and female, but of homo- and hetero-sexual love, of biography and autobiography, of literary history and quantum physics, of the body and the universe, of eternity and time – 'that queer amalgamation of dream and reality, that perpetual marriage of granite and rainbow.'[98]

ORLANDO: THE AFTERMATH

Orlando *was published on 11 October 1928 as 'a Biography'. It was soberly dedicated 'To V. Sackville-West', prefaced by warm acknowledgements to all Woolf's friends and relations, and rounded off with an eccentric index. It included eight photographs, three of them of Vita (in her pearls, by Vanessa and Duncan, by the professional photographer Lenare, and the last, probably, by Leonard). The others are reproductions of portraits (mainly from Knole) and a touched-up photograph of Virginia's niece Angelica as the Russian princess. To*

maintain the joke, the black and white dust-jacket reproduced a paint-
ing of a bearded Elizabethan nobleman, brandishing a sword and a
shield – a portrait of Thomas Sackville, the founding father of the
dynasty, discovered at the Worthing Museum and Art Gallery.[99] *A*
copy specially bound in black leather with gold lettering on the spine
was delivered to Vita, who had been teased with progress reports but
had not, as yet, seen any of it (this copy is now at Sissinghurst Castle).
Two months later, Virginia also sent Vita a bound copy of the first
handwritten draft (usually on view at Knole).[100]

Vita was, of course, 'completely dazzled, bewitched, enchanted,
under a spell. It seems to me the loveliest, wisest, richest book that I
have ever read, – excelling even your own Lighthouse.' She added,
'you have invented a new form of Narcissism, – I confess, – I am in
love with Orlando – this is a complication I had not foreseen.'[101] *But*
writing to Harold next day, though still enthusiastic, she admitted
reservations she could not acknowledge to Virginia. She was vaguely
resentful that, despite the insistent mockery of marriage, Orlando had
somehow been handed back to Shel: 'she has slightly confused the
issues in making Orlando (1) marry, (2) have a child', she told Harold.
'Shelmerdine does not really contribute anything either to Orlando's
character or to the problems of the story'. She was predictably puzzled
by the ending. 'The more I think about it, the weaker I think the end
is. I simply cannot make out what was in her mind. What does
the wild goose stand for? ... The symbolism doesn't come off.'[102]
Nevertheless, she was and remained entranced with her extraordinary
present, justifiably proud of having inspired it. Versified lines from it
appeared in an anthology she published with Harold during the war,
and she quoted passages from the manuscript in a broadcast made in
1955.[103] *Ideas from* Orlando *crept into later editions of her book*
Knole and the Sackvilles, *and in a guidebook to Knole written for the*
National Trust in 1948, she described the tapestries in the Venetian
Ambassador's bedroom (previously supposed to show medieval or
classical themes) as depicting scenes from Orlando Furioso *– thus*
fiction infiltrated fact.[104]

In the run-up to publication, 'the news of Orlando [was] black'.
Apparently booksellers were chary: 'No one wants biography. But it
is a novel, says Miss Ritchie [the Press's traveller]. But it is called a

biography on the title page, they say. It will have to go to the Biography shelf, . . . And', adds Virginia, 'I was so sure it was going to be the one popular book!'[105] Her instincts were sound. Leonard, in his own autobiography, described it as 'the turning-point in [her] career as a successful novelist . . . In the first six months the Hogarth Press sold 8,104 copies, over twice as many as To the Lighthouse *had sold in its first 12 months, and Harcourt, Brace sold 13,031 copies in the first six months.'[106] Orlando was easier to read than her earlier novels ('Orlando taught me how to write a direct sentence'), more of a romp; besides, there was the added excitement of the inner story, its act of homage to a well-known poet, novelist and aristocrat. Although Woolf herself turned down an invitation to publish it with Penguin ('I was asked . . . and in my hoity toity way refused'), it became the first of her novels to go into paperback, as a Penguin in 1942, in a huge edition of 75, 000 copies, priced at ninepence (its original price had been nine shillings – twelve times as much). A note on the cover identified the author as 'the daughter of Sir Leslie Stephen, K. C. B., and the wife of Leonard Woolf'.[107]*

From the moment of publication, it was a succès fou *– almost embarrassingly so: when Rebecca West proclaimed it 'a poetic masterpiece of the first rank', Virginia felt 'a little sheepish & silly'.[108] More often, it was judged 'a high-spirited lark' or a 'jeu d'esprit', but even its critics recognized its sense of history ('Mrs Woolf seems also to have the story of English literature and the English people in mind'). Her old antagonist Arnold Bennett began his review with a sneer at how fashionable it had become. 'You cannot keep your end up at a London dinner-party in these weeks unless you have read Mrs Virginia Woolf's* Orlando.'[109] *For once, Virginia seemed untouched by the few adverse reviews (Vita was more annoyed by them than she was), and amused to find herself 'two inches & a half higher in the public view . . . I am now among the well known writers.'[110] It was also well received in America, where Helen MacAfee thought it so characteristic that it 'might in a sense have been called an autobiography'. The ending that had so disappointed Vita was particularly praised, both by Conrad Aiken in* The Dial *and by the* New York Times *reviewer, who also noted its 'application to writing of the Einstein theory of relativity.'[111] Like* Mrs Dalloway *and* To the Lighthouse, *the American* *first edition differed in numerous small but significant respects from the British first edition.[112]*

Orlando *retained its popularity, and Penguin continued to reprint it both in England and the US, where at the end of the war it appeared in an edition of more than 200,000, priced at 25 cents. In 1960 it became a Signet Classic, priced at 50 cents. Another distinguished novelist, Elizabeth Bowen, contributed an afterword, which established a new approach by locating the novel in its particular cultural context. For Bowen's generation, Woolf had been the high priestess of aesthetic seriousness, so its publication was 'a setback'; its playfulness, allusiveness and personal element were marks against it, and its warm reception was proof, if proof was needed, that Woolf had betrayed her ideals. Bowen then, of course, proceeded to revise and reverse her earlier judgement.[113] In the later years of the twentieth century, responses to and versions of* Orlando *were largely determined by that 'spirit of the age' that its heroine had struggled to resist. In 1973 Carolyn Heilbrun published* Towards a Recognition of Androgyny, *a plea for freedom from 'sexual polarisation and the prison of gender', and thereafter both Vita's relationship with Virginia and its reflection in* Orlando *were caught up in the movement to extend sexual tolerance in most directions. The novel's very disguising of lesbian desire has, paradoxically, enhanced its appeal for gay, bisexual and transvestite readers, who trace their own narratives in its indirections.* Orlando *never actually employs the term 'androgyne' (although Woolf wrote on a blank page of her manuscript, the words 'androgyne' and 'gynandros'). However, its centrality as a concept for her is apparent from* A Room of One's Own, *published the following year.[114]*

The biography of the Biography, the story of Vita and Virginia, was the subject of Edna O' Brien's play Virginia (1981), *in which Maggie Smith took the title role, as it was of Eileen Atkins's dramatization of their love letters,* Vita and Virginia (1992), *performed by Atkins herself as Virginia, with Harriet Walter in the UK, and Vanessa Redgrave in the US – Atkins had earlier played Woolf in a programme of readings from* A Room of One's Own, *and would go on to write the film script for* Mrs Dalloway.[115] *Robert Wilson created an avant-garde adaptation of the novel for a single actress, which was performed by Jutta Lampe in Berlin in November 1989, and subsequently by Isabelle Huppert in*

ORLANDO

A BIOGRAPHY

VIRGINIA WOOLF

THE HOGARTH PRESS, 52 TAVISTOCK SQUARE, W.C.1

Paris and Miranda Richardson at Edinburgh. Robin Brooks' play Orlando *(1992) ingeniously cast Virginia and Vita, Harold and Violet Trefusis as characters who act out the novel in the form of a play within a play – both of these are among the several versions discussed by Brenda Silver in* Virginia Woolf Icon. *She also contrasts Ulrike Ottinger's highly subversive and disturbing film of 1981,* Freak Orlando *('freak' was a word Woolf herself used of the novel), with Sally Potter's more mainstream treatment, in which Tilda Swinton played the hero/ine and Quentin Crisp the ageing Queen. Potter brilliantly re-created several of the book's great set-pieces in visual terms, though, as Jane Marcus complained, 'the film rewrites all the words'.*[116]

Woolf herself anticipated a musical version, telling Clive Bell that 'Lydia [Lopokova/Keynes] proposes to set a scene in Orlando to music and to dance to it behind a microphone at Savoy Hill [the BBC] – Will I therefore rearrange the words to suit music to be written by Constant Lambert?'[117] *Angela Carter in later life described it as 'a slobbering valentine to an aristocrat' (perhaps countering Nicolson's much-quoted description of it as the 'most charming love letter in literature'), although in her youth she had composed an unfinished opera libretto entitled* Orlando: or, The Enigma of the Sexes. *For Jeanette Winterson, Woolf has always been an exhilarating influence, and the open fictionality of* Orlando *a source of inspiration. The novel's flights, its idiosyncratic version of 'magic realism' have proved particularly freeing and enabling for other women writers, and at some level, Woolf may have hoped this would be so, though such a purpose only becomes explicit in* A Room of One's Own.[118]

9

To the Women of the Future

'& here we are again', wrote Woolf in May 1929, 'after one of these little journeys which seem to have last[ed] 600 years. Everything looks a little strange & symbolical when one comes back [to London]. I was in a queer mood, thinking myself very old: but now I am a woman again – as I always am when I write.'[1] *To the Lighthouse*, *Orlando* and *A Room of One's Own* are inextricably linked; they form a triptych. Each was written at high speed, as if from some great inner pressure, and the writing of all three was completed in less than four years, from the summer of 1925 to that of 1929. Fastest of all, *A Room* was drafted in a single month (March 1929), and then heavily revised: 'It made itself up & forced itself upon me . . . as I lay in bed after Berlin . . . at such a rate that when I got pen & paper I was like a water bottle turned upside down. The writing was as quick as my hand could write.'[2] The speed of their composition reflected the urgency of their subject matter for Woolf. *To the Lighthouse* explores the problems confronted by the woman artist in a patriarchal society; *Orlando* sets them in their historical perspective; *A Room of One's Own* analyses their source and nature. Like *To the Lighthouse*, *A Room* uses the symbolism of frames – windows and doors – of being shut in or shut out, to explore representation and its relation to cultural myth. It too concludes with a glimpse of some ultimate reality that 'fixes and makes permanent' whatever it touches.[3]

How far, all three books demand, do women's arts differ from those of men? Why is it harder for a woman to become an artist than for a man, and in what ways does gender hold her back? How far do patriarchal assumptions and institutions (among them, Oxford and Cambridge) discourage the woman artist? *Orlando* opens up a further

A Room of ones Own.

But, you may say, we asked you to speak about
women & fiction: What has that got to do with
a room of ones own? I will explain. When you asked
me to speak about women & fiction it seemed simple
enough. A few . . . . .

But these on thinking over, the subject, but at second
sight the words seem not so simple.
I sat down on the banks of a river & began to think
what the words meant. They might mean simply . .

And when I began to consider them in this last way I
saw at once that [they would] never of I considered women &
fiction in that way I should never come to any
conclusion Except a few
saw that I should never come to any conclusion.
I should only come Express an opinion... that one must
that she must have 500 a year
have money & a room of one's own: And [a room with a]
But why did I come to hold that opinion? [ ] the to.
That's what I propose to tell you, & that
I am only giving you an opinion, & not a conclusion,
I am going to let you see for yourselves how I came by it.
I am going to develop in your presence as fully ~
freely as I can the train of thought which led me to
think this. The only way when a subject is as
controversial & as complicated as this one appears is not

*which seemed
the most
interesting*

*And that is
not what you
asked me
only an
opinion by any
means or a material
to a . . . my own. This
which . . .
when*

series of questions about the absence of history of women and women's writing before the eighteenth century, and both *Orlando* and *To the Lighthouse* question whether marriage is compatible with creativity for the woman artist (though neither does so explicitly). Then there was the satire that Woolf had envisaged from the point of view of 'two women', her 'Jessamy Brides' scenario, a satire that arose from the laughter of women behind closed doors.[4] Could such secret thoughts and conversations be published in a book for readers of both sexes?

The subversive laughter of women alone together appealed strongly to Woolf – the laughter that Orlando had enjoyed with Nell and her friends in eighteenth-century London, and that Jane and Castalia had shared in her earlier short story 'A Society'. Denied the giggles (and tears) of a girls' school, she was intrigued by the possibilities of female friendship that the newly founded women's colleges at Oxford and Cambridge seemed to offer (she had dramatized them in the abandoned 'Angela Williams' episode of *Jacob's Room*[5]). So Woolf was pleased when, early in 1928, she was invited by the Newnham Arts Society to address just such an audience of Cambridge women undergraduates. As *Orlando* flagged, she found herself 'woolgathering away about Women & Fiction, which I am to read at Newnham in May. The mind is the most capricious of insects —'.[6]

In the event, her talk was postponed until October, and delivered nine days after *Orlando*'s publication. She drove down to Cambridge with Leonard, Angelica and Vanessa (Julian was then a second-year undergraduate at King's College). With Leonard, she arrived late for dinner at Newnham, where she sat down to a disappointing meal of soup, beef and sprouts, prunes and custard. She spoke immediately after dinner, arguing that women needed a room and an income of their own in order to write, and advised her listeners (according to a contemporary report) not to 'try to adapt themselves to the prevailing literary standards, which are likely to be masculine, but make others of their own; they should remake the language'.[7] Next day, the Woolfs lunched at King's, where 'Dadie' Rylands was now a Fellow, in the college rooms that the artist Dora Carrington had recently decorated for him.[8] Woolf would later use the contrast between the dreary dinner at Newnham and the delicious lunch at King's to expose inequalities that the extension of women's higher education had disguised. While the young women of Newnham revelled in their new-found freedom, Woolf's sharper eye detected many differences between their conditions and those enjoyed in the men's colleges, and she pondered their implications.

The following week, this time accompanied by Vita, Woolf spoke to a similar group of young women at Cambridge's other women's college, Girton. She was dismayed by its institutional architecture: long corridors, 'like vaults in some horrid high church cathedral – on & on they go, cold & shiny – with a light burning'. The young women impressed her as 'Starved but valiant ... Intelligent eager, poor; & destined to become schoolmistresses in shoals. I blandly told them to drink wine & have a room of their own. Why should all the splendour, all the luxury be lavished on the Julians & the Francises, & none on the Phares & the Thomases?' (Elsie Phare and Margaret Thomas were the two students who had invited her to speak.)[9] 'I cannot think what to "write next"', she confesses, in her next diary entry, and wonders about reworking the 'Orlando' vein of fun, fantasy and caricature: 'I want to write a history, say of Newnham, or the womans movement, in the same vein. The vein is deep in me – at least sparkling, urgent.'[10] A critique of patriarchy was brewing.

Meanwhile, she was plodding on with 'Phases of Fiction' – a book commissioned by Leonard and Dadie Rylands for a series of 'Hogarth Lectures on Literature', it never grew beyond a long article, and had become 'a book I hate', 'that cursed book', and (with darker undertones), 'that stone that plunges me deeper & deeper in the water'. By contrast, her next novel – ultimately The Waves – continued to beckon, even though 'I am going to hold myself from writing till I have it impending in me: grown heavy in my mind like a ripe pear'.[11] In January 1929, she and Leonard enjoyed a 'rackety' week in Berlin, where Harold Nicolson had recently been appointed Counsellor at the British Embassy. Harold and Vita were joined by Vanessa, Quentin and Duncan Grant, who were touring European art galleries. Virginia came home exhausted and ill, and spent the next three weeks in bed brooding. The result was 'one of my excited outbursts of composition – writing what I made up in bed, a final version of Women & Fiction'.[12]

By now, she was well aware of the close connections between illness and creativity: To the Lighthouse had been incubated during a long illness, and when the writing of *Orlando* slowed down, early in 1928, she had retreated to bed. She was increasingly interested in how her work came into being, observing and recording in her diary 'these premonitions of a book – states of soul in creating'.[13] Illness, she recognized, could function as a form of 'lying in', a process that brought the work to birth: 'these curious intervals in life – I've had many – are the most fruitful artistically – one becomes fertilised', she wrote in September 1929. 'Six weeks in bed now would make a masterpiece of Moths.'[14] The process of being ill itself anticipated several of the central themes of *A Room of One's Own*, though they are there played out in a different key. Her illnesses put Leonard in charge, giving him the only excuse he ever used to control her activities. When ill, she was confined to a room of her own yet, paradoxically, she was 'not allowed to write books or even see the human race – except for a moment'.[15] There, as if in silent defiance of such orders, a process of conception took place, a process dramatized in the final chapter of *A Room* (with a touch of irony?) as a mystic marriage, as the curtains are drawn, and the artist lies back, letting her 'mind celebrate its nuptials in darkness' [p.94].

Being ill was thus a process of self-surrender. There should be no 'irritable reaching after fact'; the artist 'must not look or question what is being done', but yield to the current as it sweeps her 'into that tremendous stream' [p.94]. Whatever was floating on the surface of her mind would then be caught up in the flow and carried into her writing. Among her recent thoughts were 'the egotism of men' (occasioned by an unwanted Saturday afternoon visit from Desmond MacCarthy),[16] the restrictions imposed by poverty (banished, for the Woolfs, by *Orlando*'s unexpected success), and last but by no means least, the vindictive prosecution of that 'meritorious dull book', *The Well of Loneliness* ('so pure, so sweet, so sentimental, that none of us can read it').[17] Forty expert witnesses had been called to speak in its defence, and Woolf had agreed to be one of them. She duly turned up at Bow Street Magistrates Court on the morning of 9 November 1928 only to find herself dismissed with all the rest, when the Chief Magistrate, Sir Chartres Biron, ruled that he would decide for himself whether the book was obscene. A week later, he found that it was, and all copies were condemned to be collected and burnt.[18] The love of women for women could not be represented in print, or, as Woolf wryly put it, 'Beauty shines on two dogs doing what two women must not do'.[19]

The texts of the lecture (or lectures) that Woolf gave to the young women of Newnham and Girton have not survived, but they provided the basis for an article on 'Women and Fiction', which Woolf published in the American periodical *Forum* in March 1929, the same month that she began drafting *A Room*. It describes the adverse conditions in which women have struggled to write, concluding that they will write better and more variously when they have 'what has so long been denied them – leisure, and money, and a room to themselves.'[20] Its arguments anticipate those of *A Room*, and lie beneath it like a skeleton, fleshless yet supportive.

A Room was drafted at great speed and with great carelessness. In an effort to get everything down, phrases and whole paragraphs were repeated or reworked. At this stage, Woolf made little or no attempt to produce a readable or coherent text, although the scrambled, and sometimes almost illegible, draft is often surprisingly close to the published text. Many amusing and characteristic details were added in revision, while others were abandoned. The losses include an imaginary tribe of Amazons whose women have 'written a play better than Lear, . . . made a discovery of greater importance than Einstein's' (their chief poetess is 'Maya Hina'); and the poignant figure of a primeval woman, sitting in a tree and denying 'that this civilisation was any of her doing'.[21]

The view that men had determined the course of human history through their aggression and their love of war and cruelty was widely and understandably held by many feminists in the wake of the First World War, lending their writings a tragic note. That note can be heard sounding intermittently through Woolf's book, but it never becomes the dominant key (not until its sequel, *Three Guineas*). Indeed, *A Room of One's Own* remains the most amusing, imaginative and optimistic of the feminist polemics of its day, and though others often addressed the same or closely related issues, Woolf treated them as fresh and personal discoveries. Today, only *A Room* has survived, and it is usually read in isolation, as one of the founding documents of the women's movement (often with Mary Wollstonecraft's *Vindication of the Rights of Women*, written a century earlier).

As Jane Marcus has pointed out, it can be read as 'the last in a long series of women's suffrage pamphlets, despite the fact that it survives as "literature" and the others do not',[22] (women over thirty had been granted the vote in 1918, but women over twenty-one had to wait until 1928, when 'the Flapper vote' was granted).

By the mid-1920s, the Women's Movement, so often divided over one question or another, was split between 'new' and 'old' feminisms.[23] The 'old' feminists represented an aspiring and predominantly middle-class group, campaigning for equal treatment for women in education and the professions. The 'new' feminists, on the other hand, believed that the key reforms had already been achieved, and instead focused their efforts on 'women's issues' – contraception, state support for widows and unmarried mothers, and a 'family allowance'. 'New' feminists prioritized the problems of poverty and oppression facing working-class women, whereas 'old' feminists had feared that any concentration on the problems peculiar to women would undermine their arguments for equality, and would emphasize differences by reinforcing traditional stereotypes of women as mothers and wives. Debates between the two factions were a regular feature of the feminist weekly, *Time and Tide*. 'New' feminism was represented by Dora Russell's *Hypatia or Women and Knowledge* (1925), with its celebration of female archetypes; 'old' feminism by Elizabeth Robins's *Ancilla's Share* (published anonymously in 1924), a powerfully argued critique of militarism, patriarchy and misogyny, ending with a passionate plea for peace. Woolf's exploration of equality and difference in *A Room* is thus rooted in contemporary debate. Her emphasis on women's education and the need for independence, money and 'a room of one's own' reflects her sympathy with 'old' feminism, while her focus on women's poverty and the burden of child-bearing points towards 'new' feminism. But her overriding concern with the woman artist and the conditions necessary for her art led Woolf to analyse women's history, cultural politics and gender representation, and in so doing, to reach beyond the concerns of her particular moment and speak to later generations.

Despite the seriousness of the issues involved, *A Room* is also a very playful text: it plays upon difference at every level, opening with the difference between speaking and writing, since it represents itself as a lecture given to an audience of young women, while actually being a book addressed to the common reader, regardless of gender. This difference is evident from the very first sentence, which breaks an old rule of written English by beginning with 'But': 'But, you may say, we asked you to speak about women and fiction – what has that got to do with a room of one's own?' [p.3][24] – it's a sentence that seems to belong in the middle, or even at the end of an argument, as if the lecture was already almost over, and the speaker was expecting questions at the end. Yet this grammatical irregularity sets the tone for what follows, since 'But' is a conjunction indicating contradiction, exclusion or interruption – in other words, the main strategies of Woolf's text; strategies that precisely define women's relation to the dominant culture.[25] The opening sentence thus anticipates the advice she will give to women later in the book, to break the sentence, and break the sequence in order to make it their own.[26] This opening contrast between spoken and written English prepares us for further binary oppositions: truth and fiction, mind and body, male and female, public space and private space, freedom and confinement, King's and Newnham, partridges and prunes, etc. Yet the argument consistently refuses to set up one term as good, and the other as bad. Instead it examines the uses and abuses that each is prone to and weighs them up critically, gradually reaching out towards an ideal of equality that is an important aspect of its optimism.

   A Room begins as it will end, with a series of unexpected reversals. Warning that she will 'never be able to come to a conclusion', Woolf almost immediately supplies one: 'a woman must have money and a room of her own if she is to write fiction'. She informs her audience that she does not intend to carry out 'the first duty of the lecturer', that is to pass on 'a nugget of pure truth'. Instead, she will exploit 'all the liberties and licence of a novelist'. 'Lies will flow from my lips', she promises, 'but there may perhaps be some truth mixed up with them; it is for you to seek out this truth and to decide whether any part of it is worth keeping'; here and later she continues to remind her listeners/ readers that they must think for themselves. She defends the value of fiction by arguing that 'when a subject is highly controversial . . . Fiction . . . is likely to contain more truth than fact.' [pp.3, 4] Not only will fiction enable her to fill in the great gaps in women's history, but it allows her to adapt or invent scenes that dramatize women's exclusion from the groves of Academe, and the dominant culture more generally, scenes such as being shooed off the grass, or shut out of the library.

In a book dedicated to women's creativity, Woolf begins by relating the genesis of her own text in the form of her Cambridge visits, while continually adjusting the actual circumstances for the maximum effect – thus lunch at King's is followed by dinner at Newnham, rather than the other way round, as they actually happened. The biblical story of Genesis, in which Eve breaks an irrational taboo and is turned out of paradise, is suggested when the Beadle turns her off the grass, while the librarian who turns her out of Trinity Library recalls the angel with the flaming sword, who prevented Eve from (re)entering.[27] In the library, the narrator had intended to follow up other examples of textual genesis in the shape of the manuscripts of Milton's poem *Lycidas*, and Thackeray's novel *Esmond* (ironically, the latter had been given to Trinity Library by Woolf's father, Leslie Stephen). *Lycidas*, a favourite poem of hers, concerns the temptations for artists to give up their vocation, though Milton himself went on to fulfil his own by rewriting the story of Genesis as *Paradise Lost* (from a masculine point of view, of course). Elsewhere in *A Room*, Milton's patriarchal attitudes identify him with a male literary tradition to be resisted.[28]

The encounter with the Beadle (he is given his Oxford title, just as the Cambridge courts become 'quadrangles') is both excluding and interrupting. Male interruption becomes a recurrent device in *A Room*, beginning, innocently enough, when an undergraduate 'oars' his boat through the river's (and the female narrator's) reflections. Such male interruption of female creativity had been a theme in Woolf's fiction from Terence's interruptions of Rachel in *The Voyage Out*, and the ending of 'The Mark on the Wall', to Mr Ramsay's interruption of Lily Briscoe, or the imaginary customs officer who threatens to break in on Orlando's lesbian writing at the beginning of chapter VI.

The narrator's exclusion from college lawns, library and chapel is reversed when she is invited to join the charmed (and masculine) circle sharing a delicious lunch of white wine, sole and partridges 'many and various' (a meal apparently being enjoyed by young men all over the college, as 'Men with trays on their heads went busily from staircase to staircase') [p.9][29] Restored to the community of the blessed, the narrator feels 'We are all going to heaven and Vandyck is of the company.' [p.10][30] Once again her flow of thought is interrupted, this time by the sight of a cat without a tail 'padding softly across the quadrangle'. But what is its significance? The cat embodies a riddle – 'Was he really born so, or had he lost his tail in an accident?' [p.12] Manx cats (from the aptly named 'Isle of Man') are born without tails, but perhaps this one has had its tail chopped off? Seeing the cat alerts the narrator to the sense of some absence or lack. In the first version of this passage, Woolf attributed her response to 'some fluke of the subconscious soul which I leave to Freud to explain', yet for Freud, masculinity normally signified presence, and specifically the presence of the penis, which women supposedly lack and envy. The connection between the Manx cat and something lacking in men (whether sexual, social or creative) had been made by Blanche Warre-Cornish, mother of Woolf's friend Molly MacCarthy, when she exclaimed over one, 'No tails! no tails! like men! how symbolical everything is'. Aldous Huxley had quoted her words in his novel *Limbo*, and Woolf had requoted them in her review of his book.[31]

But what exactly *is* the lack signified by the absence of a tail? Woolf defines it as a 'humming', that hum of erotic anticipation to be heard in the love songs of Tennyson and Christina Rossetti, heard at 'luncheon parties before the war', the 'hum' of romance that Paul and Minta had brought to the dinner table in *To the Lighthouse*.[32] Did Woolf, then, actually believe that human character (and with it, human sexuality) had fundamentally changed in 1910, as she had once asserted (and this passage seems to endorse), or was that sense of change merely the result of growing older herself? In her first draft, the narrator wonders 'what sort of future will men & women produce when they have ceased to find each other romantic? . . . Fewer children were born in England last year than have ever been born before.' Was the Women's Movement responsible for the death of romance? A draft of the last chapter admits that 'No age can have been so stridently sex-conscious as ours . . . the Suffrage Campaign was the cause of it'. The First World War had also played its part, though the narrator recognizes that, in that old Victorian world of romance, it had often been difficult to decide 'which was truth and which was illusion'.[33]

Did the Manx cat have a further significance for Woolf in terms of the Cambridge ethos of homosexuality from which she had always felt painfully excluded (since it excluded heterosexual romance)? Lytton Strachey and Maynard Keynes had been among the guests at Rylands' lunch, so the atmosphere might well have occasioned such feelings.[34] Or does it indicate some lack of generosity, or of creative thought among the richly endowed male colleges, by contrast with the mood of excitement and aspiration Woolf encountered in the women's colleges? The chapter concludes that however 'unpleasant it is to be locked out . . . it is worse perhaps to be locked in'. Yet as long as 'there is no gate, no lock, no bolt that you can set upon the freedom of my mind', a room with 'a lock on the door' can also stand for 'the power to think for oneself'. The tension between outsider and insider status is no easier to resolve than that between homo- and hetero-sexuality.

Education need not be a prison – it can be a garden in spring, and as Woolf turns towards 'Fernham', the October flowerbeds magically fill with blowing lilac and the silver of unfurling leaves. She is still a trespasser (getting in 'by the wrong door' in the first draft, and through a door 'left open' in the published text[35]), yet in another sense this garden of women had always been hers, making its first appearance in her imaginary life of Violet Dickinson ('Friendship's Gallery', 1907). Fernham's particular Eden is a vision of freedom and blossoming disorder, daffodils and bluebells flowering among the long grass, and young women 'swinging in a hammock, . . . racing across the grass; . . . banging on a piano'.[36] The great classical scholar, Jane Ellen Harrison, who had reinterpreted ancient Greece as irrational, Dionysian and matriarchal, steps out for a breath of air; she is 'venerable – & perhaps lovable would be the better word'.[37] Woolf met Jane Harrison after she had left Newnham in 1922, having been finally defeated in the battle for women to be allowed to take degrees at Cambridge (they could not do so until 1948). Woolf had visited her in Paris in April 1923, and more recently in London. Harrison had died in the spring of 1928, and Woolf remembered her on her deathbed as she had seen her a month or two earlier, 'raised on her pillows, . . . exalted, satisfied, exhausted'.[38] Now resurrected, she steps onto the terrace to unleash the numinous, with '[t]he flash of some terrible reality leaping out of the spring'.[39]

In order to answer the questions posed in the opening chapter, the narrator – or Mary Beton – sets out to investigate the intellectual, historical and literary causes of misogyny, beginning in the great (and for Woolf, distinctively male) space of the British Museum Reading Room, with its dome like a 'huge bald forehead ... so splendidly encircled by a band of famous [male] names' [p.24]. Her search exposes inequalities: while women have little or nothing to say about men, men have written extensively about women, although they disagree: 'Goethe honoured them; Mussolini despises them. Wherever one looked, men thought about women and thought differently.' [p.27] Observing her own rising anger against a particular 'Professor von X' (author of *The Mental, Moral and Physical Inferiority of the Female Sex*), she wonders why men are so angry with women, given their superior power. In a reworking of Hegel's master–slave theory, she perceives that for all their appearance of power, men depend on women, and their 'delicious power of reflecting the figure of man at twice its natural size'.[40] Indeed, all those activities for which Mrs Ramsay so revered the opposite sex and took them under her protection, require women's active support, if they are to get done at all, for 'How is [man] to go on giving judgement, civilizing natives, making laws, writing books, dressing up and speechifying at banquets, unless he can see himself at breakfast and at dinner at least twice the size he really is?' [p.33][41] Yet while women's construction of men is enabling, men's construction of women is disabling. At some level, Mrs Ramsay's role within her marriage and Lily's artistic celibacy are profoundly connected.

The excess of texts by men about women produces mental indigestion, for nourishment is as symbolic as it is material, as much a spiritual as a physical necessity. 'Now what food do we feed women as artists upon? I asked.' The rich diets of the men's colleges reflect their material wealth, and their wealth of history and learning, whereas 'Fernham's' meagre fare corresponds not only to the comparative poverty of its endowment but also to the poverty of women's history and cultural opportunities more generally. The narrator retreats to have lunch at a small restaurant nearby, where an abandoned evening newspaper reveals to the 'most transient visitor to this planet ... that England is under the rule of a patriarchy' [p.30].[42]

Women are absent from history yet overwhelmingly present in the literature written by men – a paradox analysed in the central chapters of the book. Woolf's search for women in history had begun with her short story 'The Journal of Mistress Joan Martyn' (1906), continued through her reviews of women's memoirs, and animated *Orlando*, where the Elizabethan Orlando was necessarily male because 'nothing is known about women before the eighteenth century'.[43] Woolf deplores this fact, urging her audience of young women to fill the missing gaps, and, since 1929, they have been doing so, revealing the existence of Elizabethan women writers – poets, playwrights and polemicists – and rewriting the history of women. Winifred Holtby, in the first full-length study of Woolf's work, recognized the close links between *Orlando* and *A Room*. 'Different as they are ... the two books are complementary. *Orlando* dramatises the theories stated more plainly in the essay. The essay makes clear the meaning of the allegory.'[44] There are even structural parallels: each book has six chapters, the fourth of which celebrates women's emergence from oblivion in the eighteenth century, while the sixth focuses on marriage as a metaphor for creativity (and both make fun of contemporary fiction – or, more specifically, of D. H. Lawrence – for his obsession with 'slipping off one's petticoat and – But we all know what love is').[45]

Orlando, who embodies the essential androgyny of the writer, is himself haunted by the memory of the man with globed eyes and a dirty ruff who had 'sat at Twitchett's table'. It was Shakespeare who, in the first draft of *To the Lighthouse*, had linked Charles Tansley's misogyny with the woman artist's sense of exclusion and insignificance, in a passage from the dinner party scene that was later discarded:

Why, then, did one mind what [Charles Tansley] said, Lily Briscoe wondered, insignificant as he was! O it's Shakespeare, she corrected herself – as a forgetful person entering Regents Park, & seeing the Park keeper was coming towards her menacingly; might exclaim, Oh [of course], I remember dogs must be on a lead! So Lily Briscoe remembered that every man has Shakespeare [behind him] & women have not. What then could she say, inferior as she was; & was it not much easier to be inferior after all? – That is the whole secret of art, she thought to herself. To care for the thing [not for oneself]: what does it matter whether I succeed or not?[46]

Three years later this sequence fermented into the arguments of *A Room*, where an unidentified bishop warns that 'Cats do not go to heaven. Women cannot write the plays of Shakespeare' [p.42], yet Shakespeare nevertheless becomes the paradigm of the impersonal artist, who cares 'for the thing' rather than for his reputation.

Though Shakespeare was regularly enlisted to reinforce male claims to superiority, he is also the supreme example of the androgynous author, the only author whose 'poetry flows from him free and unimpeded. If ever a human being got his work expressed completely, it was Shakespeare.' [p.52] As both poet and androgyne, Shakespeare figures as Orlando's silent double, his artistic completeness mirroring that of Orlando/Vita as man-woman or woman-man. And since Orlando had been male in Elizabethan England, his unwritten history as a woman becomes the story of Shakespeare's lost sister Judith, who first appears in the middle of chapter III of *A Room*, at a point closely corresponding to the moment of Orlando's sex-change in Woolf's novel.[47] When Judith Shakespeare had first appeared in the manuscript, Woolf had also identified her with Vita/Orlando: 'Once she went gallivanting off in the woods dressed like a man', just as Vita had done (indeed, Virginia had accused Vita of 'gallivanting down the lanes with [Mary] Campbell').[48] But this sentence was later cut out, since Judith Shakespeare was intended to illustrate the adversity experienced by the woman artist, whereas Vita's cross-dressing reflected her comparative freedom.[49]

Even so, women's love for women remained one of the energies behind *A Room*, just as it had been in *Orlando*, and just as in *Orlando*, it is largely kept out of sight. When it appears, it is within the optimistic framework of a new dispensation for women and their writing. Chapter IV provides a roll-call of women writers, whose achievements (with the exception of Jane Austen and Emily Brontë) have been undermined by the struggles they had endured. Arriving at the present, Woolf ignored the work of women contemporaries, and instead imagined a first novel that broke the mould of both sentence and sequence, that 'lighted on small things and showed that perhaps they were not small after all. It brought buried things to light and made one wonder what need there had been to bury them.' [p.84][50] One of those 'buried things' it has brought to light is women's friendship – or is it women's erotic friendship? – so that it appears 'perhaps for the first time in literature'. The degree and nature of their liking remain conveniently unspecific, yet 'Chloe liked Olivia'. Chloe's name may be taken from that of a character in Vita Sackville-West's unfinished novel, 'Reddin', a woman who 'resented love's slavery, but felt lost without it'.[51] Olivia's name is probably taken from *Twelfth Night*, where she is the young heiress who falls in love with a girl dressed as a boy.

To describe their mutual liking will be to 'light a torch in that vast chamber where nobody has yet been'; but Woolf initially wrote 'that vast dark cave', suggesting at once the power and maternal longing present in such feelings (human life having supposedly begun in caves or up trees), and perhaps more specifically, the lesbian venue 'the Cave of Harmony', whose name may underlie Radclyffe Hall's title, 'The Well of Loneliness'.[52] Their liking also ignites major disruptions in the text. In Woolf's first draft, the words 'Chloe liked Olivia; they shared a . . .' appeared (so we are told) at the bottom of the page, and the ensuing pages are stuck together. As the narrator fumbles to open them, 'there flashed into my mind the inevitable policeman; the summons;' the trial, the condemnation for obscenity and the book-burning that ensues. 'Here the pages came apart. Heaven be praised! It was only a laboratory.'[53] Although the published text is less explicit, it too alludes to the recent trial of *The Well of Loneliness* as the narrator enjoys a moment of intimacy with her all-female audience: 'Are there no men present? Do you promise me that behind that red curtain over there the figure of Sir Chartres Biron is not concealed? We are all women you assure me? Then I may tell you that the very next words I read were these –' [p.74]. Sir Chartres Biron, the presiding magistrate at the trial, like the Home Secretary, Sir William Joynson-Hicks and Sir Archibald Bodkin, the Director of Public Prosecutions, are now little more than footnotes to Woolf's most widely read text[54] (and thus 'The whirligig of time brings in its revenges'). Woolf uses Chloe's non-specific liking for Olivia to link the woman's novel, the novel of lesbian love and the novel of the future, while Olivia, with her work and her two children, and her (Shakespearean) status as a great heiress, glances once more towards Vita.

Yet *A Room* ultimately adopts the strategy that Woolf had used in *Orlando*, when she neutralized the threat of Vita/Orlando's love of women by re-integrating her into marriage – a move that Vita herself had resented, even though it reflected a central aspect of her actual life. Any threat of militant feminism or lesbian separatism is similarly banished from *A Room* with a gesture of reconciliation that redefines the nature of androgyny, shifting its meaning from a woman with masculine traits (such as Orlando/Vita) to its more traditional sense of a being in whom the sexes meet (such as Shakespeare might have been). The narrator confesses to 'a profound, if irrational, instinct in favour of the theory that the union of man and woman makes for the greatest satisfaction, the most complete happiness.' [p.88] Such reconciliation has already been enacted at another level – that of narrative technique – by the way in which *A Room* continually unites 'the two great powers of fact & fiction'.[55]

Amidst the hum of traffic, the London street plays out its little dramas. A taxi driver stops to pick up a pretty young woman in patent leather shoes ('she was pretty, & he was a man'), sweeping her off into the current of the traffic. Then, after three pages of deleting and rewriting, 'the sight of the girl greeting the young man at the corner' works to relax the tension created by the separation of the sexes. On the next page, 'the sight of a couple meeting by appointment at a street corner has the power to . . . make my mind easy'.[56] In the published version, the young man has acquired a maroon coat, and he and the girl and the taxi-cab all come together 'beneath my window', as if by mutual agreement. They get in 'and then the cab glided off as if it were swept on by the current elsewhere', while the narrator admits that 'thinking . . . of one sex as distinct from the other is an effort.' [p.87] The 'severances and oppositions' of the mind, its separation or splitting off, are now felt to be uncomfortable, a potential threat to the integrity or impersonality of the artist. Instead, the writer must allow the male and female elements to come together, 'must lie back and let his mind celebrate its nuptials in darkness' [p.94]. As the masculine possessive adjective indicates, the text has moved on from the particular situation of the woman writer to what she has in common with male writers. The art (or perhaps act)[57] of creation is represented as a wise passivity, a flowing with the current of the river through the Cambridge Backs, or with the current of the traffic through the London streets, the self-surrender of sexual consummation. With this moment of quiet ecstasy comes the first of the book's several endings, marked by a change of narrator as 'Mary Beton ceases to speak', and there follows a search for a new voice and a new direction which will knit together the various threads left hanging, and find the right note on which to close a discourse that has consistently refused to be pinned down to a single position.[58]

Which is one source of its enduring appeal: *A Room of One's Own* is not merely controversial in content, it is in continual debate with itself. It assumes different voices and adopts inconsistent positions, and in the process of writing out its own indignation, arrives, for better or worse, at exactly those compromises with the world of men as most women act out on a daily basis, while scarcely noticing that they are doing so. Its prevailing mood of optimism corresponds not only to women's dreams of a more creative future but to their sense of realities, as the possible is elbowed out by the probable.

A Room acknowledges the evils that Woolf had first listed in 'A Society' – that 'instinct for possession, the rage for acquisition which drives [men] to desire other people's fields and goods perpetually; to make frontiers and flags; battleships and poison gas; to offer up their own lives and their children's lives' [p.35].[59] Yet despite that, and despite the dark history of women's oppression – 'liable to be locked up, beaten and flung about the room'[60] – this is a utopian text in several respects, and not merely for its vision of a freer and more powerful future for women as artists, and perhaps even as lovers. Its recurrent naming of Shakespeare evokes not only his richly androgynous world of cross-dressed women, all too briefly accepted as equals in a man's world, but also another feat his plays perform – that of admitting without dismissing their own fictional nature, so that, while they remain only fictions, their enactment brings hoped-for change a little clearer, a little nearer.

The final paragraph is more than utopian – it is positively messianic. In the most subversive of its many parodies, this book, which began with a woman breaking patriarchal taboos in an Edenic garden, ends with the promise of the second coming of Shakespeare's sister Judith, for which women must patiently wait. 'As for her coming without that preparation, without that effort on our part, without that determination that when she is born again she shall find it possible to live and write her poetry, that we cannot expect.' [p.103] The suffering heroine, despised and rejected of men, now stands in place of the saviour of the scriptures, and is promised a better and a more productive future.[61]

Woolf began writing the first draft of *A Room of One's Own* in the last week of February 1929, after nearly a month in bed. It had been a terribly hard winter, and all the pipes had frozen: 'Our water-closet is our glory – the plug still pulls', she told Vita. 'No bath, though. Whats happened is that nature, having read a certain description of a frost (see O–o) was so taken by it that she determined to do it better.'[62] The first date to appear on the manuscript is 6 March 1929, at the beginning of chapter II, by which point she had already written thirty-odd pages of what later became chapter I. At the end of her draft, she wrote '2nd April / 1929'.[63] She then revised it through May and June, and by August, she was correcting proofs, and wondering whether it was 'watery & flimsy & pitched in too high a voice'.[64] At the same time, she was hatching plans to build a literal room of her own, in the form of an extension to Monk's House that would provide a study looking out on the garden, with a bedroom above. An entry for 28 March, the day she first mentions the book in her diary, also notes 'I am summoning Philcox [a local builder] next week to plan a room – I have money to build it, money to furnish it.'[65] She wrote to Vanessa about her plans and the furnishings she would need, listing things she wanted and arguing with her when Vanessa was reluctant to send in the bill. In the third week of April, she and Leonard went down to Rodmell 'to see Philcox, who will build two rooms for £320, & take only two months.'[66] But the optimism of builders exceeded that of her essay – *A Room of One's Own* was published in November, while Philcox's extension wasn't completed until the end of the year. Once built, the ground floor room became her bedroom, and the room above was used as a second sitting room, where Leonard and Virginia listened to the gramophone. By the following spring, she could lie in bed, and watch the moon rising through the apple tree.[67]

A ROOM OF ONE'S OWN:
THE AFTERMATH

The day before A Room of One's Own *was published (on 24 October 1929), Woolf was uneasy, fearing that it had 'a shrill feminine tone in it which my intimate friends will dislike. I forecast, then, that I shall get no criticism, except of the evasive jocular kind, from Lytton [Strachey], Roger [Fry] & Morgan [E. M. Forster]; that the press will be kind & talk of its charm, & spright[l]iness; also I shall be attacked for a feminist & hinted at for a sapphist; . . . I shall get a good many letters from young women.'[68] She was not far wrong. The* Times Literary Supplement *thought that it glanced 'in a spirited and good-tempered way over conflicts old and new', while always being 'bent on more intrinsic matters . . . a love of life, a love of freedom and of letters'. Arnold Bennett, in the* Evening Standard, *grumbled good-humouredly about Woolf's grammar, and the fact that she had not decided whether it was a lecture or a book. Vita, in a broadcast, thought 'Mrs Woolf . . . too sensible to be a thorough-going feminist', and returned her compliments by claiming that she combined masculine and feminine qualities of mind.[69] Rebecca West disagreed with everyone else, finding the book 'an uncompromising piece of feminist propaganda: I think the ablest yet written'. West (whose praise for* Orlando *had embarrassed Woolf the previous year) admired Woolf's good temper in the midst of controversy, recognized her as 'the talent of this generation which is most certain of survival', and found 'Her argument . . . all the more courageous because anti-feminism is so strikingly the correct fashion of the day among the intellectuals.'[70] The sharp-eyed critic, William Empson, fell upon the paradox that 'when you have said, as Mrs Woolf does say, that every complete author must be spiritually hermaphrodite, you seem to have quelled this aspect of the sex war as vehemently as you called it into being', while adding 'But her best work is certainly illuminated by this notion'.[71]*

Vanessa's design for the dust-jacket was at once simple, yet powerful: printed in blue on a pale pink background, it depicted a dark arch (apparently that of an overmantel mirror), with a clock on a stand in front of it, the hands at ten past ten, making a 'V', which Virginia read as a reference to Vita: 'I forgot to say that I thought your cover most attractive – but what a stir you'll cause by the hands of the clock at that precise hour! People will say – but there's no room.'[72] This was Vanessa's first opportunity to make a visual reference to her sister's friendship, since she had not designed the jacket for Orlando, *though it was, of course, true that all three women shared the same initial. Virginia felt she had at last found a (sexual) space where her sister had not preceded her. She enjoyed teasing Vanessa about it, and wrote to Vita, 'I told Nessa the story of our passion in a chemists shop the other day. But do you really like going to bed with women she said – taking her change. "And how d'you do it?" and so she bought her pills to take abroad, talking as loud as a parrot.'[73]*

From the outset, A Room *sold more rapidly than anything else Woolf had written. The first English edition of 3,040 was followed by a 'second impression' of 3,030 just over a fortnight later. Extracts appeared in* Time and Tide *during November, and in December there were further print runs of 6,080. By the following March, the Hogarth Press had issued 14,650 copies, and thereafter it went into the Press's 'Uniform Edition' of Woolf's work, where it continued to do well. The first Penguin edition was published in 1945 for ninepence, in a startling run of 100,000 copies. It sold steadily but much more slowly in America: Harcourt, Brace printing 22,640 copies between its first publication and February 1953.[74] Unlike* To the Lighthouse *and* Orlando, *there are minimal differences between the British and American first editions, though one is intriguing: the mystic nuptials in which the (British) 'art of creation can be accomplished' becomes 'act of creation' (though whether one of these was an error, or whether Woolf deliberately altered the US proofs is uncertain).[75] She made one very striking change in the second British impression (published on 9 November), in a passage near the end about why she liked women: the passage had originally read 'I like their unconventionality. I like their subtlety. I like their anonymity'. This passage, which occurs three pages from the end, and on the top line of the left-hand page, had been printed with two word-breaks, reading in the British first edition 'tionality. I like their subtlety. I like their anony-', as if visibly fragmenting women's attributes. Its typographical oddity may have caught her printer's eye. At any rate, she changed the (subversive) middle term, 'subtlety' to the (comprehensive) 'completeness', tightening the line and counteracting the two broken words.[76] Perhaps it was yet another re-balancing of the book's swerve from feminist separatism to marriage, since 'completeness' is the characteristic of the androgyne, the characteristic of Shakespeare.*

With the second wave of feminism, A Room of One's Own *found its moment. Though many of the legal battles had long been won, women still felt held back, and* A Room *explained to them why, reaching to the roots of their unexamined feelings of inferiority. In the US, particularly, Woolf inspired modes of self-discovery and self-empowerment that would have surprised her, while the personal voice of* A Room *and its injunction to 'think back through our mothers' contributed substantially to a revolution in reading, thinking and teaching among women academics and their students. The American Marxist feminist Jane Marcus showed the way, and* A Room of One's Own *became the key text for new courses in women's studies, as well as for feminist revisions of older literary and historical programmes, previously dominated by 'dead white male' writers, and more traditional methods of structuring knowledge.[77]*

In particular, that swerve from chapter V to chapter VI, from separatism to reconciliation, attracted intense critical debate: Nancy Topping Bazin saw androgyny as Woolf's way of harmonizing conflicting impulses within herself, while Carolyn Heilbrun (in Towards Androgyny, *1973) read it as a wider social solution, offering a way of escape from the old order. For Elaine Showalter (*A Literature of Their Own, *1977) it was sterile, a retreat from, or even a betrayal of, Woolf's justified and necessary anger.[78] Toril Moi, in turn, questioned the value of a feminist criticism that rejected Woolf – 'not only a novelist of considerable genius but a declared feminist and dedicated reader of other women's writings' – rereading Woolf in the light of contemporary French feminist theory, particularly that of Julia Kristeva. Poststructuralist readings of Woolf, notably those of Makiko Minow-Pinkney and Rachel Bowlby, have emphasized Woolf's playfulness, her open-ended arguments and shifting genres, so much in evidence in* A Room of One's Own.[79] *Woolf's first feminist polemic employs the imaginative fluidity of fiction, serenely allowing her readers' dissent, because it sets intellectual freedom above the force of its own arguments.*

a room
of one's own

virginia woolf

10

'Into Deep Waters'[1]

I . . . shall gently surge across the lawn (I move as if I carried a basket of eggs on my head) light a cigarette, take my writing board on my knee; and let myself down, like a diver, very cautiously into the last sentence I wrote yesterday. Then perhaps after 20 minutes, or it may be more, I shall see a light in the depths of the sea, and stealthily approach – for one's sentences are only an approximation, a net one flings over some sea pearl which may vanish; and if one brings it up it wont be anything like what it was when I saw it, under the sea. Now these are the great excitements of life.[2]

So Woolf pictured herself at Rodmell in the autumn of 1930, half-way through writing *The Waves*. Despite an energetic and enjoyable social round, she always felt that the life of the mind was the only 'real life': its 'great events & revolutions' were always, for her, the most affecting, the most absorbing, even though 'people talk of war & politics'.[3] This is reflected in all of her fiction, but most of all in *The Waves*, where she turned her back on the outer world, producing an effect like that of a photographic negative, in which what is 'said' by the characters is actually what they think or feel, while their actual speech remains out of earshot. Thus she reordered the traditional hierarchy of inner and outer experience, and wrote the novel about silence ('the things people don't say') that Terence had planned in *The Voyage Out*,[4] the culmination of an old and enduring ambition.

She had been pressing against the limits of conventional fiction for more than a decade, and *The Waves* emerged as the most experimental novel in a uniquely original and experimental oeuvre. Writing it required a long and dedicated expedition into the interior. The first summons reached her late in September 1926, as she was finishing *To*

The interludes consist of :—

1   Dawn.

21.   The sun rose. (before B. goes to school)

61   The sun rose — further (between school & college)

95   The sun even erect. (after college: before
     Bernard arrives in London.

133   Percival in Jone.
     The sun had risen to its full height...

149   after Percival's death. when Rhoda flings
     violets. Complete maturity. but with doom
     added.

165   afternoon beginning.
     aunt Judy. The shadow of a moth.
     goes on, And time lets fall its drop.

199 (?) after his climb: "have drawn a French door."

196   The final night fall —

the Lighthouse, amidst an intense depression that felt like a series of waves, rising and crashing down upon her. All confidence in her 'brilliancy, genius, charm, beauty' evaporated, to be replaced by a sense of herself as 'an elderly dowdy fussy ugly incompetent woman vain, chattering & futile'.[5] She envied Vanessa and quarrelled with Leonard. But she had learned to practise a psychological economy in which adversity – illness or despair – could have its uses. That experience was to be seminal: looking back a year later, she wrote that she had 'never forgotten it, or my vision of a fin rising on a wide blank sea. No biographer could possibly guess this important fact about my life in the late summer of 1926: yet biographers pretend they know people.'[6] The transforming moments of life were inward – solitary and invisible – like the silent 'events & revolutions' of thought.

One outcome of this depression, according to her later reconstruction of the event, was a financial arrangement that allowed her to bank and spend her own earnings after she had paid an agreed contribution to household costs (though Leonard thought that they had been operating such an arrangement since the beginning of their marriage).[7] Thus, as *Orlando*'s sales rose, so did her spending power. More significant was the vision her dejection had brought her, of 'a fin passing far out', accompanied by a childhood memory of not being able to step across a puddle for thinking how strange life was.[8] These feelings were, she guessed, 'the impulse behind another book', a book which would investigate feelings of desolation and abjection, a sense of alienation, 'not oneself but something in the universe', and a sense of emptiness, 'Where there is nothing', that had seized her in the depths of her depression. Yet even as she described the experience in her diary, she could not find the image she wanted to convey what she meant, and for once, her writing did not seem to 'reach anything'.[9] That experience of emptiness, loss of self and the failure of language would, paradoxically, provide the climax of her book.

She envisaged it as a 'very serious, mystical, poetical work', without having 'any notion what it is to be like'.[10] By February 1927, she was wondering whether she might write 'a new kind of play . . . prose yet poetry; a novel & a play', and she enlarged upon this scheme in a lecture read to the Oxford University English Club on 18 May, and later published as 'Poetry, Fiction and the Future'.[11] This essay is a manifesto for the book she did not know how to begin. The modern writer feels 'baffled, frustrated' when trying to record modern con- sciousness – 'some dissatisfaction, some difficulty, is lying in our way.' But a new form will emerge, with 'something of the exaltation of poetry, but much of the ordinariness of prose. It will be dramatic, and yet not a play . . . it will stand further back from life. It will give, as poetry does, the outline rather than the detail . . . it will give the relation of the mind to general ideas and its soliloquy in solitude.' But (she warned herself) the author of such a work 'will have need of all [her] courage'.[12]

May 1927 was a month of excitements: *To the Lighthouse* was published on the 5th, and a few days later Vita returned from four months abroad, and travelled with Virginia to Oxford for her lecture. Meanwhile, Virginia had received a letter from Vanessa, who was staying in Cassis with Duncan Grant and Angelica. It described the moths that were invading their villa. A huge one had tapped at the window, and her 'maternal instinct' had obliged her to catch and kill it (the children would have been disappointed had she failed to do so). 'Then I remember – didn't Fabre try experiments with this same creature and attract all the males in the neighbourhood by shutting up one female in a room? Just what we have done. So probably soon the house will be full of them'. She wished that Virginia would 'write a book about the maternal instinct . . . which is one of the worst of the passions, animal and remorseless.'[13] Her letter focused on two primal urges that link human behaviour to the world of nature – the sexual instinct and the maternal instinct. In *Social Life in the Insect World* (1913), the French entomologist, Jean Henri Fabre, had famously described how the male Emperor moth was drawn by the pheromones emitted by the female; though he did not identify the chemical, he recorded its effects with concentration and precision.

'[Y]our story of the Moth so fascinates me that I am going to write a story about it. I could think of nothing else but you and the moths for hours after reading your letter', Woolf replied. Moths brought back their shared childhood and moth-hunts with Thoby at St Ives,[14] while the insects' physical metamorphoses suggested the changing phases of human lives, or even the self-transformations of the artist (Woolf described her mind as becoming 'chrysalis', when she was ill).

Fabre's experiments made a link between moths and the hum of sexual attraction described in *A Room of One's Own* (and the female narrator of *Jacob's Room* had hung vibrating 'like the hawk moth' over Jacob).[15] A month later, Woolf saw how she might make up 'the story of the Moths' (now plural) so as to include 'the play-poem idea; the idea of some continuous stream, not solely of human thought, but of the ship, the night &c, all flowing together: intersected by the arrival of the bright moths', all to be written 'very quickly'.[16]

Over the next two years, the Moths continued to haunt her, 'coming, as they always do, unbidden, between tea & dinner, while L[eonard]. plays the gramophone.' She was anxious to begin the new novel, yet felt 'up against some difficulties'.[17] Finally, at the end of May 1929, when she had finished drafting *A Room*, she began to picture it in terms of '[a] mind thinking', evidently a female mind, and so, perhaps, a vision of herself trying to write it? Certainly the difficulties of the writing process came to be reflected in the text in various ways. The physical world might be represented by a lamp and a flower-pot upon a table, a still life. There would be 'two different currents – the moths flying along; the flower upright in the centre',[18] the animal and vegetable worlds existing on contrasting planes. She knew that it must begin at dawn, on the beach, with scenes of childhood – 'not <u>my</u> childhood', and yet 'Autobiography it might be called'. Most of the experiences she now described were actually her own earliest memories (later to be identified as such in 'A Sketch of the Past').[19] On the second page of her earliest draft appeared a 'moody fitful little girl' called 'Jinny' (her own pet name as a child), among a group of children who were 'not related'. Around them would be 'the unreal world . . . the phantom waves . . . Could one not get the waves to be heard all through?'[20] Listening to the sound of the waves breaking at St Ives was not just the earliest, but also 'the most important of all my memories . . . the purest ecstasy I can conceive',[21] its haunting rhythm a distant echo of the mother's heartbeat, and the forgotten moments that stretched back to conception itself.

On 2 July she wrote at the top of a new notebook the title, 'The Moths? or the life of anybody'. The story began with '[a]n enormous moth', whose markings 'made a mysterious hieroglyph, always dissolving'.[22] This unreadable sign reflected the difficulties of composition, her sense of the book's importance, yet her uncertainty as to where it was going. In a room, an unidentified (and this time, genderless) 'lonely mind' contemplates scenes from childhood, glimpsed in the folds of a napkin.[23] The writing comments on itself, torn between 'meaning; or . . . no meaning', disintegrating into chaos ('without being able to finish any sentence . . . without attempting to make a coherent story'), yet 'attempting to make a whole', complete and comprehensive: 'I am telling myself the story of the world from the beginning. I am not concerned with the single life, but with lives together.'[24]

'[T]his is the beginning of the story. The white fresh page has this on it.'[25] With this partly deleted announcement, the text launches into two, or perhaps three narratives of origin. The first is biological and general, while the others are psychological, specific and literary. The first, the 'story of the world from the beginning', is a surreal vision of '[m]any mothers, & before them many mothers, & again many mothers', groaning and giving birth, '[l]ike one wave succeeding another . . . And all these waves have been the prostrate forms of mothers, in their flowing nightgowns, with the tumbled sheets about them holding up, with a groan, as they sink back into the sea, innumerable children'.[26] It is a vision of life emerging from the sea, of individual lives endlessly begetting others, like waves, and of the endlessly repeated throes of childbirth, through which each self must enter the world – a vision of maternal genesis challenging the patriarchal narrative of scripture.

The second narrative immediately succeeds the first. It is characterized by childish 'jealousy & hatred', and is much closer to the biblical Genesis since it concerns a couple in flight from that 'first' Edenic garden. At this stage, there are also links between 'death' and an 'apple-tree' (the published text, however, begins with the indistinguishable sea and sky being separated to make the first day).[27] In the garden, Jinny alights on Louis and kisses him. Susan, seeing them, runs from the garden in torment. In the beech wood, Bernard catches up with her, and tries to console her with words and phrases ('The point of the story is the phrasemaking').[28] In the second phase of the story, Bernard takes Susan exploring, and they come upon 'the white house lying among the trees'. Climbing the garden wall, they see the lady who 'sits between the two long windows, writing. The gardeners sweep the lawn with giant brooms.' [pp.10–11][29] When one of the gardeners catches sight of them, they run for the shelter of the wood. The lady writing will be remembered at key moments throughout the novel – an image of the novelist writing the book (amidst the splendours and antiquities of the House of Fiction? The real author never lived anywhere so grand). Her written words correspond to Bernard's spoken phrases, while the long lawns are another version of Eden, from which the fallen couple are banished, not by an angel with a sword, but a gardener with a broom.

For all its hallucinatory power and symbolic significance, Woolf never managed to integrate that first scene of maternal engendering into her novel. Perhaps the endless births reminded her of the infinite (and so defeating) possibilities of fiction. By contrast, the second story survives through the various drafts with only minimal variations (initially Bernard was called 'John', and peacocks strayed on the lawn of the great house[30]). Its retention as a point of origin suggests its importance as a founding myth for Woolf: it is a memory of the primal scene, displaced and reworked to include her jealousy of her older sister (a still powerful but more admissible scenario). Had she come upon Vanessa kissing Thoby, and felt herself abandoned to 'the brown water where dead leaves have rotted' [p.9], as Susan does? And did she then find comfort in 'phrasemaking', her defence against a hostile world from an early stage? If so, in writing the scene she disguised her identity by reversing her relationship with Vanessa, so that it is 'Jinny' who gives the kiss and Susan, the character closest to Vanessa, who becomes the onlooker, while Bernard (later to become the narrator and central consciousness) plays the part of the 'phrasemaker' and comforter. The story traces intimate connections between jealousy and the creative impulse (as *Orlando* had done). Vanessa aroused Woolf's most passionate feelings, whether as envied rival (Woolf began her first novel during Vanessa's first pregnancy) or inspiring muse (Susan is only one of several heroines inspired by Vanessa).

Yet it is only by reading the kiss as a memory of the primal scene (Daniel Ferrer has pointed out that Virginia's night nursery and her parents' bedroom were adjacent to one another at St Ives[31]) that the parallels between the first and second part of this narrative become fully apparent; for each represents a moment of conception, of absorp-

tion in a creative act that necessarily excludes and ignores the accidental (or illegitimate) observer. The moment at which the child witnesses
the act that brought her into being is itself replayed as the two children
witness, unforgettably, the lady writing – that is, in the act of creating
the very characters who are watching her. The expulsion from paradise
(from both gardens) punishes Adam and Eve for prying into the secrets
of God's creation; a sense of guilt, exile and exclusion is the price to
be paid for witnessing forbidden acts.

The second part of the story, the vision of the woman at the writing-
table between the windows of the great house, remains mysterious,
its mystery intensified by the house's specificity: it is named Elvedon
from the earliest draft, in a novel that seldom identifies local habi-
tations and names. Perhaps it was chosen for its combination of elements ('Elv – edon'). Aurally, it is identical with 'Elveden', the name
of a large and handsome country house set among woods and surrounded by long lawns and walls, not far from Thetford in Suffolk. In
1906, immediately before the holiday in Greece during which Thoby
fatally contracted typhoid, the Stephen sisters spent August in an
Elizabethan house at Blo' Norton, close by (that area is identified in
the first draft of the novel as Susan's home ground, 'where Suffolk and
Norfolk meet'). Did Virginia visit Elveden with Thoby? He and Adrian
were there only for two days, and Virginia's journal only records her
walking with Thoby – to reach Elveden, they would have needed to
cycle.[32] But that house is also part of a more sinister history of the
British in India, which may also be inscribed in *The Waves*, for in the
mid-nineteenth century it was presented by the British government to
the Maharajah Duleep Singh as compensation for the annexation of
the Punjab.[33]

The Waves was written in an atmosphere of growing tension over
British rule in India. 'Dominion' status had been promised since before
the First World War, but had been postponed, first in 1919 and then
again by the Simon Commission in June 1930, amid mounting anger
and campaigns of passive resistance led by Gandhi and Nehru; in
October 1930, it was conceded.[34] That turbulence has been read into
the imagery of the interludes[35] as well as into Percival's death, prefigur-
ing the end of empire. At one level, the novel consciously ignores
political events: 'An army marches across Europe' [p.189]; 'What is to

be done about India, Ireland or Morocco?' [p.196] – sentences almost as parenthetical as those recording the deaths of Mrs Ramsay, Andrew and Prue in *Lighthouse*'s 'Time Passes'. Rare glimpses of contemporary politics break in upon the text, momentarily shifting consciousness onto another plane, as when the peaceful evening at Hampton Court is darkened for Louis by 'the shadows of dungeons and the tortures and infamies practised by man upon man' [p.168], or when Neville announces (with an echo of *Orlando*), 'it is the present moment; I am become a subject of King George' [p.175].[36] In *The Waves*, Woolf peeled away the present moment to reveal the enduring 'moments of being' that lay beneath.

As early as 'The Mark on the Wall', she had suggested that future novelists would leave 'the description of reality more and more out of their stories, taking a knowledge of it for granted'.[37] *The Waves* dives into interiority, setting its monologues in the context of permanent natural cycles, day to night, spring to autumn. Yet consciousness is always the product of history. In her diary for December 1930, Woolf recorded newspaper headlines about the new Viceroy, the India conference and Gandhi; in August 1931, as she corrected the proofs of *The Waves*, she wondered whether she wasn't 'fiddling' while the international economy crashed. 'Sometimes I feel the world desperate; then walk among the downs.'[38]

In the late summer of 1929, she found herself 'circling around' rather than 'forging ahead', uncertain as to what she was aiming for. She had long been interested in the genesis of her own fiction, but the rapidity and fluency with which she had composed her most recent books had genuinely surprised her, and since the depression that had provided the novel's first seed, she had been determined to 'watch & see how the idea at first occurs. I want to trace my own process.'[39] The originating experience had been one of 'a plunge into deep waters', a descent into herself, and now, as she worked at it, she watched herself in the process of self-exploration, of going 'down step by step into the well' of her imagination, of longing 'to swim about in the dark green depths'.[40] Her diary charted her progress, and the more baffling and frustrating it became, the more her diary entries dwelt upon it, and puzzled over it.

'One thinks one has learnt to write quickly; & one hasn't.' She worked on in a cloud of unknowing, sometimes impatiently, at other times with contentment. 'Now & again I feel my mind take shape, like a cloud with the sun on it, as some idea, plan, or image wells up, but they travel on, over the horizon, like clouds, & I wait peacefully for another to form, or nothing.'[41] Her diary entries alternate between the repeated admission 'I don't know', and the firm conviction that 'there is something there'.[42] Chaos and flux left their mark not only on what she wrote, but on how she wrote it, as the frequent repetitions, deletions and marginal annotations of the manuscript reveal:

I write two pages of arrant nonsense, after straining; I write variations of every sentence; compromises; bad shots; possibilities; till my writing book is like a lunatic's dream. Then I trust to some inspiration on re-reading; & pencil them into some sense. Still I am not satisfied. I think there is something lacking. I sacrifice nothing to seemliness. I press to my centre. I dont care if it is all scratched out. And there is something there.[43]

That mixture of doubt and inexplicable faith reflected the nature of her subject matter. The originating experience had been one of 'the mystical side of this solitude'. Writing it out required her to 'come to terms with these mystical feelings',[44] to acknowledge, if not a universal consciousness, then at least a wider design and meaning to which art aspired. Though Woolf shared her father's impatience with conventional religion, her novel took up the challenge thrown down in the concluding sentences of Fry's *Vision and Design*, where the attempt to explain aesthetic emotion threatened to land its author 'in the depths of mysticism. On the edge of that gulf I stop.'[45] *The Waves* went down into those deep waters, aiming to re-create the 'moments of being' which imply 'a revelation of some order . . . a token of some real thing behind appearances'. Her philosophy, as set out in her unfinished autobiography, recognized a pattern concealed behind the 'cotton wool' of daily life, and 'that we – I mean all human beings – are connected with this; that the whole world is a work of art; that we are parts of the work of art'.[46] Such patterns and harmonics made up 'the singing of the real world',[47] the deeper order that *The Waves* sought to apprehend. That rocking from uncertainty to conviction registered in her diary could be interpreted as varieties of religious experience, while the novel's sense of the limits of language also reflects its mystic and spiritual aspects.

In the earliest drafts, some kind of wider consciousness was written into the novel in the form of a mind who thinks it – an old, sleepy, obscure and sometimes hooded figure who never emerges from the shadows.[48] As the work progressed, that scarcely defined presence was replaced by the 'interludes' – word-pictures of the natural world – of waves in sunlight, birds singing in the garden or sunbeams illuminating the furniture of the room. These alternated with the unspoken soliloquies, recalling the structure of 'Kew Gardens', where the world of snails and grasshoppers in the flowerbed had alternated with the conversations of the visitors (in 1927, the Hogarth Press had reissued it with extra woodcuts by Vanessa). Meanwhile, crucial technical problems remained to be solved: 'Who thinks it? And am I outside the thinker?'[49]

On 4 September 1929, Woolf made a new start, this time with a list of 'Dramatis Personae' that identified six children and their teachers. Someone 'whose sex could not be distinguished' was trying 'to find in the folds of the past such fragments as time, who has broken the perfect vessel, keeps safe'. A few pages later, the text peters out, with a plan dividing life into 'seasons' ('Childhood/Maturity/Middle Age/ Death').[50] On 22 September, she made yet another start. This time, the light of dawn reveals 'the table with its crumpled cloth; a flower pot, perhaps a book, or the plate & knife of last night's dinner.' She knew now that it would not be called 'The Moths'.[51] Though female sexual attraction and the maternal instinct were primal forces, uniting human and animal life, they were limited to that life, whereas the older, colder voice of the waves, the monthly and daily rise and fall of the tides were part of the great oceans of liquid that make up much of the planet's surface, and most of the human body. They contributed to the deep and deeply female rhythm of life.

Woolf turned back once more to her vision of mothers as waves giving birth, and this led her to an even stranger scene of a seashore crawling with babies: 'the beach was black with them'.[52] Their seething, undifferentiated mass emphasized the varied circumstances of their birth, according to different social positions, for 'The life of anybody' would have to include 'Albert whose father was a cowman', as well as 'Roger whose father was a civil servant', Florrie the kitchen maid as well as Susan, daughter of a gentleman farmer. But writing class difference created insoluble linguistic problems for Woolf: 'No single person could follow two lives so opposite; could speak two languages so different.'[53] She abandoned the impulse to comprehensiveness, and the novel thereafter confined itself to the consciousness of its six middle-class children.

These 'Six Characters in Search of an Author' (though their fictional nature is never acknowledged in so many words)[54] grow up and become individuals, and though their speech patterns are scarcely differentiated, each expresses a distinctive outlook through the use of particular image clusters. The origins of Susan and Jinny seem to lie in the narrative of 'The Moths' that Woolf was now ready to discard. Susan embodies the 'maternal instinct' that Vanessa had wanted Virginia to write about, while her pale eyes and possessiveness recall aspects of Vanessa. As a child, Susan hates school, tearing the meaningless days off the calendar until she returns to her home, her father and her pets. She will marry a farmer and find fulfilment in 'natural happiness',[55] in bearing and rearing children. From the moment of their meeting in the beech wood at Elvedon, she had been linked with Bernard.[56] A born storyteller, and naturally gregarious, Bernard displays a novelist's curiosity about other people which licenses him to imagine their feelings, and finally to act as the book's central consciousness. Like Susan, he marries and raises a family, resisting the inroads of time through the futurity of children or words. Jinny and Neville, on the other hand, live for new experiences, new loves, constant in their inconstancy. Jinny is the female moth at the heart of Fabre's experiment; her raised arm, bidding 'Come, come,' cannot be resisted. She delights in the pleasures of the body, in clothes and her powers of sexual attraction. She loves London and the tenderness of the night. Neville is cool, fastidious and self-conscious. His passion is always directed towards a single companion, though that companion is continually changing.

While, in their several ways, the others are firmly attached to life, Louis and Rhoda think of themselves as social misfits, 'the youngest, the most naked', for whom life is a continual struggle. For Bernard, they are '[t]he authentics [who] exist most completely in solitude.' [p.87][57] More spiritual than the other characters, their spirituality nevertheless takes distinctive forms. Louis from childhood feels himself part of a historical continuum, of eternal cycles of recurrence, or even reincarnation. He has lived other lives at other times, in ancient Egypt or eighteenth-century France, though quite how is never defined,[58] like Tiresias in Eliot's *The Waste Land*, perhaps, or 'Luriana, Lurilee', the poem chanted at the end of the *Lighthouse* dinner party. Louis finds it hard to reconcile his present state with the dignity and distinction of his former selves. Rhoda, on the other hand, is tormented by a sense of the transitory and disjunctive nature of life, by absence and loss, including self-loss. Hers is the 'negative way' of mysticism, 'Where there is nothing'.[59] Her vision of herself gathering flowers, and yet not knowing 'To whom' she must give them suggests the search for an absent God. Clutching them, she is Persephone, doomed to descend to the underworld.[60] Louis and Rhoda recall Woolf's distinction between her sense of life, as either 'very solid or very shifting', though ultimately the two are reconciled, since 'though we change; one flying after another, so quick so quick, yet we are somehow successive, & continuous – we human beings; & show the light through'. And then, in a characteristic afterthought, 'But what is the light?'[61]

No suggestion of moral superiority attaches to Louis's and Rhoda's deeper spirituality; nor are the other characters correspondingly diminished by their focus on worldly pleasures and desires (though traditionally idealist or transcendent philosophies might condemn them). And it may be that their search for love or sexual ecstasy, maternity or friendship somehow leads them back to the spiritual world. Towards the end of the novel, Bernard, Susan and Jinny turn against their chosen ways of life, but this does not necessarily devalue their choices. As always, Woolf allows her characters to speak for themselves, silhouetting them against the sky, the waves, the world beyond themselves.[62]

Woolf gave Rhoda her own childhood experience of existential horror as she tried to cross a puddle,[63] and Rhoda embodies her author's self-doubt and social anxieties as a young woman, as well as her recurrent failures of confidence, her nervousness and impulse towards death. Louis, it has often been observed, resembles T. S. Eliot (born in St Louis) in several respects, and shares his sense of alienation (an Australian, rather than an American accent), his pleasure in the order of office life, his nostalgia for 'loose slates, . . . slinking cats and attic windows', and for 'ABCs' (a popular chain of cheap eating places).[64] But the imagery of Eliot's angst-ridden poems pervades the novel as a whole: Rhoda's fear of 'shocks, sudden as the springs of a tiger' recalls 'Gerontion' ('The tiger springs in the new year. Us he devours'); Jinny identifies with the nightingale's 'Jug jug', echoing Philomel in *The Waste Land*, while 'envy, jealousy, hatred and spite scuttle like crabs' on the sea bed (recalling Prufrock's sense that he 'should have been a pair of ragged claws / Scuttling across the floors of silent seas').[65] In the second draft, Bernard pictures Percival in India, reading (appropriately) Johnson's poem on 'The Vanity of Human Wishes' 'with his legs over the arm of a camp chair', soon after Eliot had sent the Woolfs his edition of that poem.[66]

Above and beyond his impact on any particular character or imagery, T. S. Eliot's faith in the dynamic possibilities of modern art had contributed to the making of Woolf's novel. His ruthless certainties, often at odds with her more cautious approach, were liberating for her. When Eliot had first stayed with them at Rodmell, Virginia had accused him of 'wilfully concealing his transitions'. 'He said that explanation is unnecessary. If you put it in, you dilute the facts. You should feel these without explanation.'[67] In 1924 the Hogarth Press had published Eliot's *Homage to John Dryden*, which included his famous essay on 'The Metaphysical Poets', with its definition of poetry as amalgamating disparate experiences: falling in love, reading Spinoza, the sound of the typewriter and the smell of cooking might combine to form 'new wholes'. Eliot's sense of the saturated moment was close to Woolf's own concept of 'moments of being', not merely as determining character, but as giving a glimpse of a different order of being – 'Quick now, here, now, always – '.[68] While still contemplating how to begin 'The Moths' in November 1928, Woolf had advised herself 'to give the moment whole; whatever it includes. Say that the moment is a combination of thought; sensation; the voice of the sea.' The time had come, she had decided, to abandon 'this appalling narrative business of the realist: . . . Why admit any thing to literature that is not poetry – by which I mean saturated?'[69] Some weeks before, she had heard Eliot read an early draft of *Ash Wednesday*, his most explicitly spiritual (and Christian) poem yet. It probably prompted her to read Dante, which she began to do while working on the second draft of *The Waves*.[70]

Through October and November 1929 Woolf continued her search for a way of setting her people 'against time and the sea'. She had not yet solved her technical problem. At this stage, the text shifted from descriptions of the natural world to accounts of the characters' thoughts, in a manner reminiscent of *Jacob's Room*; Bernard's arrival in London was accompanied by a clutch of named but insignificant minor characters such as she had invented for the earlier novel.[71] These echoes may have been connected with the advent of the seventh character, who is linked with Jacob through memories of her brother Thoby, and the 'anguish' she felt after he died, 'alone: fighting something alone'.[72] 'The handsome Percival' first materializes in the chapel of the boys' public school. Worshipped by 'the little boys', he is 'all that was heroic & desirable'.[73] Like Jacob, he stands at the centre of the design, an absent presence, igniting the emotions and memories of the other six, while possessing no voice, no subjectivity of his own; but he is less substantial than Jacob, existing only through the consciousness of his friends (as, a quarter of a century on, Thoby existed for his brother and sisters, for Clive, Lytton and Leonard).

'Percival, a ridiculous name', says Bernard[74] – but evidently a significant one. It belongs to the knight in medieval literature whose quest for the Holy Grail Woolf would have known through Wagner's opera *Parsifal*. There, he is the holy fool who has lost his mother, who does not know who he is or where he comes from, yet ultimately heals the wounded king, the myth also central to Eliot's *Waste Land*, which the Woolfs had hand-set and printed. In 1909, Virginia had visited Bayreuth with her brother Adrian and Saxon Sydney-Turner, and seen *Parsifal* performed twice within a week. She described it as a supremely satisfying work of art, Shakespearean in its inspiration, 'poured out in a smooth stream at white heat, its shape . . . solid and entire'.[75] At the same time, as she recognized, it is a deeply religious, even religiose work, with the administration of the Eucharist at the end of Act I at its heart. *The Waves* recalls that structure through the farewell party for Percival, a secular act of communion, signified by its three choric sequences, and recapitulated in the Hampton Court reunion, much as the Last Supper itself is recalled in the foot-washing of Act III of *Parsifal*. The imagery of communion and the Last Supper was to run through Woolf's book.[76] The final scene of *Parsifal*, with the descent of the dove, associated with Whitsun (or Pentecost), is distantly echoed in Bernard's visit to St Paul's, where the boy's voice ascending the dome reminds him of a dove, as he feels himself 'fluttering, descending' ('*Et O ces voix d'enfants, chantant dans la coupole!*').[77] Yet *Parsifal* is the story of a patriarchal society, an exclusively male order of knights, reinforced by ties of religion and militarism, and threatened by distracting or even contaminating women. Percival inherits these values, yet stands at the centre of a book whose title promises flux and female rhythms. The novel gradually came to embrace its own antitheses.

All seven characters meet to say goodbye to Percival as he embarks for India. And, as Woolf worked on this scene early in January 1930, she finally hit upon a solution to her technical problem. She had long been fascinated by the question of how to represent the interaction between group experience and individual consciousness (she had dramatized it in the stories of 'Mrs Dalloway's Party' and Mrs Ramsay's last supper). This time, she saw how she might take her experiments in a new direction by creating a 'Phantom party', at which her six characters would speak their thoughts in a 'phantom Conversation'[78] that would be the unspoken equivalent of their actual, unheard conversation. From this point on, her characters silently 'said' their interior monologues, rather than 'said to themselves'; and though the narrator did not disappear altogether, the novel took a decisive step towards the kind of 'play-poem' she had earlier envisaged. With the discovery of how to achieve the effect she wanted came a sense of release: suddenly she could 'hardly stop making up The Waves', foreseeing that she would 'rush on, . . . & finish', though she still did not know exactly how.[79]

'[H]e sat there in the centre. Now I go to that spot no longer. The place is empty' [p.116] says Bernard, after Percival's death. Yet, in another sense, that place had always been empty. Percival is not only silent, he is also the point where the novel's different value systems clash and converge. He is a figure on a mythic or epic scale, 'some medieval commander', endowed with monumental or military imagery – 'perched on a great horse', or leading 'his faithful servants, to be shot like sheep' [p.26]. Woolf had a lifelong hatred of war, and while she was writing the novel, the conventions of epic, and the Carlylean ideal of 'the natural leader' were being actively adopted by Oswald Mosley for the politics of the far right. Yet Percival's courage is also endorsed, dramatizing the human need to 'fight, fight',[80] to resist an invisible enemy, even if that enemy is time itself. There are similar contradictions in his role as empire-builder, at a stage when empire was all too evidently breaking down. Bernard pictures Percival righting the lurching bullock cart that is India '[b]y applying the standards of the West, by using the violent language that is natural to him', so that '[t]he Oriental problem is solved' [p.102]; but the cartoon-like simplicity of that picture only underlines its absurdity, leaving Percival's pointless death to make its own comment on Bernard's fantasy. Percival's loss is felt in terms of the justice he would have administered, the tyranny he would have resisted.[81] If Jacob enjoyed and fell victim to the patriarchal system, Percival thoughtlessly perpetuates its values.

Percival's death is at once inevitable and of central significance, yet at the same time curiously incidental. He is the sun hero or year hero who falls back to earth when the sun is at its zenith. Woolf's use of insistently biblical phrases for him (such as 'the light[s] of the world') and her evocation of the Last Supper lend him supernatural power, though it's possible that she employed these terms simply because they were the most familiar versions of the archetypal feast at which (according to Jane Harrison) the tribal group celebrated its identity with the 'eniautos-daimon' or year hero. Certainly Woolf intended Percival to figure as Jane Harrison's 'daimon-functionary [who] represents the permanent life of the group'.[82] The Waves draws on nature myths as one of the ways in which human beings picture and act out their engagement with the world of nature, beyond themselves.

At another level, Percival's fall is an example of accident, and its puzzling nature. That Woolf herself saw his death thus (and so as an echo of Thoby's) can be shown from the second draft, where Neville first speaks of 'a molehill' as its cause (in the first draft, it is referred to merely as 'an accident'): 'Why a molehill – why a [small?] accident – how can that destroy [–] all that?'[83] Molehills, proverbially contrasted with mountains, are usually seen as trivial, yet their impact as historical stumbling blocks was part of the story of Hampton Court, which had already appeared in the first draft as the setting for the second reunion dinner. Hampton Court had been rebuilt by Sir Christopher Wren for William III, the Dutch Protestant king, who also laid out its gardens, and subsequently died there when his horse stumbled on a molehill. His Jacobite enemies toasted 'the gentleman in black' (the mole) for its part in the king's downfall. William III is remembered at the Hampton Court dinner, where Bernard pictures him as tiny and absurd: 'how strange it seems to set against the whirling abysses of infinite space a little figure with a golden teapot on his head', while Neville visualizes him in a more human perspective, as he 'mounts his horse wearing a wig', moments before his fatal ride [p.174].

Percival's death invokes the language of spiritual struggle. His fall is experienced as meaningless, an example of 'Crass Casualty' quite as inexplicable as Rachel's death in *The Voyage Out*.[84] Bernard's tightly furious denunciation of mindless, 'eyeless' destiny is an expression of human impotence, shaking its fist in the face of death: '"Is this the utmost you can do?" Then we have triumphed' [p.116]. The struggle against time's ravages increasingly dominates the second half of the book, culminating in Bernard's final soliloquy, an attempt to salvage and reconstruct what has gone before. In December 1930, Woolf copied into her diary the passage from Dante's *Inferno* where Ulysses rejects the various claims upon him in order to set out on a final voyage of exploration, the passage that inspired Tennyson's 'Ulysses', 'To strive, to seek, to find, and not to yield' (and later, Eliot's 'Old men ought to be explorers'). Woolf had written of Thoby, 'I think of death sometimes as the end of an excursion which I went on when he died. As if I should come in & say well, here you are.'[85]

Into that season of memories, doubts and uncertainties, intensified as usual by headaches and a temperature, marched a person of enormous definiteness and determination: she (for there could be some doubt of her sex, and the fashion of the time did something to disguise it) was Dame Ethel Smyth, composer and feminist. '"Let me look at you"', she demanded of Virginia as she climbed the staircase at Tavistock Square in her tailored suit and three-cornered hat. This 'bluff military old woman' had come to say how much she admired *A Room of One's Own*, and she stayed.[86] Virginia already knew of her through having read several volumes of her autobiography, and at first she was flattered by her attention – indeed, had experienced nothing like it since the heyday of her friendship with Vita. '[T]wo letters daily', she gloated. 'I daresay the old fires of Sapphism are blazing for the last time.' Yet if Virginia had felt too old for Vita, she was too young for Ethel, and was certainly not 'in love', though, touched by Ethel's energy, style and passion for life, she responded with a series of comic and high-spirited accounts of her own past life and present opinions. But Ethel's certainties, so reassuring in themselves, were the counterpart of a total lack of self-criticism. She never knew when to stop (Leonard found her twenty-minute monologues unendurable), and at times her demands well overstepped the mark.[87]

Ethel was 'the old crag that has been beaten on by the waves: the humane battered face that makes one respect human nature: or rather feel that it is indomitable & persistent.'[88] Part of her appeal was her refusal to 'be her age'. 'An old woman of seventy one has fallen in love with me', Virginia told Quentin, 'at once hideous and horrid and melancholy-sad'; yet she signed off this letter 'your old doddering devoted Aunt', as if recognizing how old she too must appear to the eyes of her nineteen-year-old nephew.[89] The sense of ageing came on her, as it does, in fits and starts. The previous summer her oculist had upset Virginia by observing, ' "Perhaps you're not as young as you were" ', making her feel quite suddenly that she was 'an elderly woman . . . wrinkled & aged for an hour'.[90] The strange and intermittent process of growing older would also affect the characters in her book, who saw themselves as 'middle-aged', or worse. 'Before, . . . we could have been anything. We have chosen now, or sometimes it seems the choice was made for us.' [p.164] In the first draft, Bernard becomes 'a bald & elderly man who does not take up a great deal of room', though 'to myself I was for many years a real person.'[91] Woolf finished that draft at the end of April 1930, with Bernard's soliloquy recapitulating the various strands: 'I have never written a book so full of holes & patches; that will need re-building, yes, not only re-modelling.'[92] She was still in doubt about the structure, but the main narrative elements were now falling into place.

Two days later, to her own surprise, she was itching to get on with it: 'Unlike all my other books in every way, it is unlike them in this, that I begin to re-write it, & conceive it again with ardour, directly I have done. I begin to see what I had in my mind; & want to begin cutting out masses of irrelevance, & clearing, sharpening & making the good phrases shine. One wave after another'[93] – even the process of writing had begun to echo the primal rhythm of the waves. Rhythm now governed the writing process, as it governed the cycles of nature, linking them with the stages of human life. She explained to Ethel, 'I am writing to a rhythm and not to a plot ... And thus though the rhythmical is more natural to me than the narrative, it is completely opposed to the tradition of fiction and I am casting about all the time for some rope to throw the reader.'[94] In June 1930, she began redrafting her novel from the beginning, now planning it as nine chapters or sections (although at this point she envisaged these in a different order from the final version; the episode recording Rhoda's death – at that stage, the 'death' chapter – fell between the Hampton Court reunion and Bernard's final soliloquy).[95] By August, she was rewriting the farewell dinner party.

The book had resolved itself 'into a series of dramatic soliloquies. The thing is to keep them running homogeneously in & out, in the rhythm of the waves.'[96] Yet even regarded as soliloquies, these are distinctly odd. Instead of the more usual 'stream of consciousness' method, they register sensations. 'Look, listen', the characters insist, describing their feelings in the simple present tense (for example, 'the light becomes richer ... and bloom and ripeness lie everywhere'), a tense more often found in poetry – the more usual form being the present continuous ('is becoming ...', 'are lying ...').[97] Yet even though their monologues are silent, the characters seem to reach each other through them, at times speaking in chorus, as they do at the farewell party, and again at their final reunion, while Bernard often describes the feelings of the others, and identifies with them. And the place or time they speak from can no more be identified than can that of the speaker of the interludes.[98] Woolf's rejection of conventional narrative viewpoints, voices and tenses reflects her search for a new way of redefining the compound, complex nature of consciousness itself.

Now the writing moved forward more easily, though late in the summer of 1930, Virginia had a curious 'brush with death'. Walking down the garden at Rodmell with Lydia Keynes, she suddenly fainted, and as she came to, she imagined herself dead and in the presence of God, 'with fists clenched & fury on my lips: "I don't want to come here at all!" '[99] That 'one new picture in my mind: my defiance of death in the garden' fed into the drama of the human struggle against time and death, the sense that 'the theme effort, effort dominates: not the waves: & personality: & defiance'. She had somehow decided to 'merge' the nature interludes into Bernard's final soliloquy, '& end with the words O solitude'.[100] She finished the second draft early in February 1931, in an extraordinary state of exhilaration, 'having reeled across the last ten pages with some moments of such intensity & intoxication that I seemed only to stumble after my own voice, or almost, after some sort of speaker (as when I was mad). I was almost afraid, remembering the voices that used to fly ahead. Anyhow it is done'. She thought immediately of Thoby, wondering whether she could put his name on the first page, and recorded with satisfaction that she had finally 'netted that fin in the waste of waters which appeared to me'.[101]

With a little tidying, Woolf might have published the second draft as it was, but she did not do so. Instead she rewrote the whole book a third time, so that although the finished novel corresponds closely to the second draft in structure and sequence, the actual words themselves are substantially different. This third revision was not written out in longhand but typed, and it has not apparently survived (few of her typescripts have). The changes she made at this stage can be inferred from the extensive differences between the second draft and the published text. J. W. Graham, who edited and transcribed the manuscripts, suggested that Woolf kept her handwritten drafts in preference to typescripts, because she 'associated the primary act of artistic creation with writing in longhand rather than with subsequent typing'.[102] In fact, the first two drafts had already generated their own typescript versions, since it was Woolf's practice to write in longhand in the morning and type up her work later in the afternoon. In the case of *The Waves*, it was written 'at such high pressure that . . . I can only write it for about one hour, from 10 to 11.30. And the typing is almost the hardest part of the work.'[103] When she had typed out the third version herself, she had it retyped professionally, and made a further series of corrections to the fourth (and final) typescript.

She embarked on the third revision early in May 1931, setting herself the task of completing it by mid-June. 'This requires some resolution; but I can see no other way to make all the corrections, & keep the lilt,

& join up, & expand & do all the other final processes. It is like sweeping over an entire canvas with a wet brush.'[104] Like Lily Briscoe's final brushstroke, this revision brought the different elements into a new relation with each other. At this stage, Woolf concentrated on tightening the form (as she had done in the late revisions of *Lighthouse*), while maintaining the rhythm. She rewrote her draft so that the novel's structure followed both the circuit of the sun across the sky and the pyramidal movement of a wave, rising to its crest as the sun reaches its zenith, with the climax of the farewell party. It then falls back to the evening scene of the Hampton Court reunion. The novel was divided into nine unnumbered chapters or sections, and Woolf reworked these so that they would correspond more closely with one another – one and eight, two and seven, etc. through to four and five – forming the wave-like or pyramidal shape that she had envisaged (there are also further links between four and eight, the shared suppers). In the ninth section, the wave breaks upon the shore, as Bernard sums up.

More explicitly now than before, the individual monologues provide a history of the growth of consciousness, from the first '[b]right arrows of sensation', as Mrs Constable squeezes the sponge over the children's bodies. The second section, with its alternation of school and holidays, reflects their growing awareness of time – the present moment in which Bernard sets off for school, the future moment when Susan will go home (she has 'torn off the whole of May and June, . . . and twenty days of July' from the calendar), and the passage from the first school day to the last. That awareness finds its counterpart in section seven, with its focus on the loss of youth and the fall of 'time's drop'.[105] The third section brings self-awareness – 'I am not one and simple, but complex and many' – closely linked with language, from which the sense of self is structured. Bernard, Neville and Louis read poetry, searching for words through which to create themselves. Susan wonders 'Who am I . . . ?' Jinny feels her body springing to life, but Rhoda feels endangered. Its counterpart, section six, begins, appropriately, with Louis signing his name over and over again.[106] The fourth section, the party, binds the individuals into a group, so that they hold 'for one moment . . . this globe whose walls are made of Percival', feeling 'We are creators. We too have made something that will join the innumerable congregations of past time.' [p.110] The space between the fourth and fifth sections, the novel's fulcrum or point of change, is marked by Percival's fall.

'But for pain words are lacking.' Inevitably, it was 'the death chapter' (now, the fifth) that held her up. 'I . . . have rewritten it twice. I shall go at it again & finish it, I hope, this afternoon . . . the most concentrated work I have ever done – . . . also the most interesting.' Its evocation of raw grief was difficult to handle. At the end of that section in the second draft, she wrote on the left-hand page, 'The author would be glad if the following pages were read not as a novel',[107] but what had she meant by that? Bernard and Rhoda look for consolation through art. Recalling Percival's mastery 'of the art of living', Bernard visits the Italian rooms at the National Gallery, where 'Lines and colours almost persuade me that I too can be heroic' [p.118], while Rhoda visits the Wigmore Hall, where she hears a string quartet – perhaps one of the late Beethoven quartets that Leonard used to play on his gramophone in the early evening. The music assumes geometric shapes, becoming oblongs and squares that 'make a perfect dwelling-place . . . our triumph; . . . our consolation.' [p.123] The revelation of art gives access to the artist's vision, recovering order and meaning, while the novel finds its own way of resisting time and loss, even while it explores the human need to do so.

'"Now to sum up," said Bernard. "Now to explain to you the meaning of my life."' In the ninth and final section, Bernard delivers to his listener (and the reader) the outcome of that long gestation, his sermon in the form of a rereading of what has happened so far, offering himself to us in words that recall those of the Last Supper: '"Take it. This is my life."' [p.183][108] Assembling and reviewing the key experiences of the book, he sweeps them into his own consciousness, renewing the suggestion that 'we are not single, we are one' [p.50], that the characters are merely characteristics of a single mind, different ways of perceiving: 'We saw for a moment laid out among us the body of the complete human being whom we have failed to be, but at the same time, cannot forget.' [p.213] It is quite plausible that the six should be aspects of a single person, given the notion articulated in *Orlando*, that we consist of multiple selves. In the third section, Bernard had wondered 'which of these people am I? . . . When I say

to myself, "Bernard", who comes?', and by the ninth section he wonders 'Am I all of them? Am I one and distinct? I do not know.'[109]
Woolf's letters and diary register the variety of selves that she regularly called upon: she was married, lesbian; anxious, confident; spiritual, worldly; loved London, loved the South Downs, etc., etc. At
the strictest narrative level, some of these options rule out others
(you cannot simultaneously be a mother and childless, although
you can live simultaneously in London and Rodmell). Woolf was
convinced that 'one's life is not confined to one's body and what one
says and does', and she explained to a friend, 'I did mean that in some
vague way we are the same person, and not separate people. The six
characters were supposed to be one.'[110]

'For this is not one life; nor do I always know if I am man or
woman.' [p.216] The boundaries that separate the six speakers from
the group, and Bernard from the others (and possibly even Bernard
from his author), dissolve, inviting us to see them as aspects of a
single engendering consciousness, possibly even as the outcome of
the androgynous marriage envisaged at the end of A Room of One's
Own.[111] This helps to explain the otherwise surprisingly conventional
divisions of the characters along gender lines, so that the male characters are the writers, potential poets or novelists, whereas Susan exemp-
lifies traditionally female forms of creativity such as child-bearing and
cooking.[112] Reading the characters as aspects of a single being, or the
monologues as part of a woman's consciousness (as the earliest scheme
had envisaged) reduces this difficulty. The dissolving of boundaries in
the final section also carries away with it the stories and sequences that
prop up masculine constructions and divisions of the world and the
self, the scaffolding of patriarchy: 'I distrust neat designs of life . . . I
begin to long for some little language, such as lovers use'. Fragments
of poems and nursery rhymes flow through the episode, creating a
rhythmic babbling such as precedes sleep, reaching back to early
childhood, before separation from the mother (a language later used
by such female characters as Sara in The Years or Isa in Between
the Acts).[113] Bernard, like his author, rejects the coercive aspects of
language, its 'designs' upon the listener, denouncing 'this extreme
precision, this orderly and military progress' as 'a convenience, a
lie' [p.196]. His 'summing up' thus 'unwrites' itself, exposing the

impossibility of recording the meaning of life in stories, or the fullness of consciousness in words. It is too manifold and various – it includes the certainty of death and the knowledge of human insignificance, as well as that 'cloud of unknowing' in which the novel had been conceived and written. Experience more closely resembles the chaos and flux of storm clouds – 'something sulphurous and sinister, bowled up, helter-skelter; towering, trailing, broken off, lost' [p.184]. As the storyteller, Woolf had reached the limits of her art: '[l]ife is not susceptible perhaps to the treatment we give it when we try to tell it.' [p.205]

This dissolution of familiar narratives culminates, as it must, in the loss of selfhood. Leaning on a gate, Bernard experiences that sense of the absence of meaning that had provided the book's point of origin, seeing the familiar world of lives and illusions crumble into 'the dust dance', in an experience of spiritual death. 'How describe or say anything in articulate words again?' Meaning gradually returns, conferring shape and form on the physical world as the sun returns after the eclipse.[114] Without a self, Bernard becomes one with the others, becomes all of us, becomes his own body, an animal greedily consuming 'the bodies of dead birds'. Finally he leaves the table (our shared existence? the altar of the quotidian?) for the solitude of the street; here, the wave rises like a horse beneath him, carrying him on a final ride against imminent dissolution. The theme of heroic struggle ends the novel, as imagination triumphs over the irresistible advance of time and physical decay, in a gesture at once exultant and absurd.[115]

And even then, The Waves was not finished. Late in June 1931, Woolf set to work 'to correct the re-re-typing' of the fourth typescript (provided by her typist, Mabel): 'I am doing the interludes'.[116] She rewrote these (later italicized) episodes so that nine of the ten open with the progression of the sun across the sky, thus tightening the parallels between the lives of the speakers and the rhythms of the natural world. Not only did she have in mind Shakespeare's sonnet 60,

> Like as the waves make towards the pebbled shore,
> So do our minutes hasten to their end

but also 73, 'That time of year thou mayst in me behold', which identifies old age with winter and evening twilight, paralleling the passing of the day and the year with the passage of human life.[117] This late concern with the sun's progress emphasized its generative role in stirring natural life, awakening birds and plants and giving form and shape to solid objects. In its eclipse, light, colour and depth are drained from the world, as meaning drains away when the light of selfhood goes out. The development of consciousness seems to follow the trajectory of the rising sun, the rising wave, turning to resistance in the tragic phase as the light declines and the wave falls back. For the sun is not only the source of all earthly energy, it is also the great regulating clock that drives forward the 'unfeeling universe',[118] perhaps the source of our own arbitrary beginnings and endings, and linked with whatever lies beyond our control or choice.

'We have arranged it so that each interlude and each section is to begin a new page', Leonard explained to the managing director of the Edinburgh printers, R. & R. Clark, 'and . . . the interludes are to be printed in italics.'[119] With this letter, *The Waves* assumed its final form. By then, Leonard had, of course, read it and declared not only that it was a masterpiece, but 'the best of your books'. At the same time, he warned Virginia of what she already knew, that 'the first 100 pages [were] extremely difficult, & [he] is doubtful how far any common reader will follow.'[120] To write it, Woolf had plunged deeply into her own earliest memories, had patiently sought for the right style and structure, and had finally explored the meaning of that 'fin in the waste of waters',[121] the experience of despair that had threatened to overwhelm her almost five years earlier. In the process she had made greater demands than ever before, not only on herself but also on her readers. Yet the novel itself suggests how we might read it, while telling us how it had been written. Neville, taking a book off the shelf, muses:

Certainly, one cannot read this poem without effort . . . To read this poem one . . . must be sceptical, but throw caution to the winds and when the door opens accept absolutely. Also sometimes weep, also cut away ruthlessly with a slice of the blade soot, bark, hard accretions of all sorts. And so . . . let down one's net deeper and deeper and gently draw in and bring to the surface what he said and she said and make poetry. [p.152]

THE WAVES: THE AFTERMATH

On a pearly-grey evening at the end of September 1931, Woolf walked across the grass to her garden room at Rodmell in order to sort out the piled-up drafts that had accumulated there during the summer. The Waves was due out the following week, and its reception was on her mind: 'I am slightly less naked than usual, as I've had 3 outside opinions', she reminded herself. These were from the novelist Hugh Walpole, who had depressed her by failing to like or understand it; from the latest apprentice at the Hogarth Press, John Lehmann, who 'loved it, truly loved it'; and from Winifred Holtby, who was preparing the first full-length critical account of Virginia's work, and found it – as so many readers would do – 'a poem, more completely than any of your other books'.[122] The following week, Woolf had a telephone call from Harold Nicolson, who had left the diplomatic service and was currently editing Action *(the journal of Oswald Mosley's British Union of Fascists). He thought it a masterpiece. 'Ah hah', she gloated, 'so it wasn't all wasted then. I mean this vision I had here has some force upon other minds', as if up to that point she could not have felt sure. Nicolson's review of it in* Action *showed how well he had grasped what she was trying to do, as he related it to wider developments in modern art. 'Her whole intention is to depict the fluidity of human experience, the insistent interest of the inconsequent, the half-realised, the half-articulate, the unfinished and the unfinishable . . . Her aim is to convey the half-lights of human experience and the fluid edges of personal identity.'[123]*

In the event The Waves *was published to wide acclaim, and its success astonished her: 'this unintelligible book is being better "received" than any of them . . . And it sells – how unexpected, how odd that people can read that difficult grinding stuff!' It came out on 8 October in Vanessa's dust-jacket of olive green and dark brown on cream, with waves framing shapes that suggested human beings, and a dark rose in the middle (perhaps the least successful of her designs for her sister's books). The first print-run was over 7,000, and before the week was out, it had 'beaten all my books: sold close on 5,000; we are reprinting . . . The reviews I think the warmest yet'. It was also* well received in the US, where Donald Brace, in a vote of confidence, had printed a first edition of 10,000 copies.[124] By the end of December 1931, British sales had passed the 9,000 mark, and by the end of February 1932, it had reached 10,000.[125]

Vita, unlike her husband Harold (but like poor Hugh Walpole), found herself out of her depth, as Virginia had anticipated. On the other hand, the less literary Vanessa was 'so overcome by the beauty ... For it's quite as real an experience as having a baby or anything else, being moved as you have succeeded in moving me.' Others shared her feelings. The Cambridge don, Goldsworthy Lowes Dickinson, wrote to tell Virginia, 'Your book is a poem, and as I think a great poem. Nothing that I know of has ever been written like it ... The beauty of it is almost incredible. Such prose has never been written and it also belongs to here and now though it is dealing also with a theme that is perpetual and universal.'[126]

For most reviewers, it was 'more like a poem than a novel', 'something very like a poem', a 'prose poem', 'a kind of symphonic poem' and even 'imagist poetry of the first order'. The distinction of its style, and the vision and beauty of its writing were readily acknowledged, though not invariably regarded as strengths. The best reviews admired its form and 'essential' qualities: writing in the Times Literary Supplement, A. S. McDowell observed that '[i]ts substance is not to be divided from its form; the form has been evoked by the essence'. The novelist Storm Jameson, after wrestling with her class prejudices against Woolf, announced that '[o]nce in a long while a writer appears whose interest is less in the appearance than in the essence ... In this book she is striving ... to convey a whole vision, the essence of life, not a story-full of scattered and fragmentary forms.' For the poet Edwin Muir, The Waves was the culmination of Woolf's achievement, a meditation on time and consciousness comparable in its impact to Rilke's prose. Woolf was now dealing with 'immediate and essential truths of experience'. Like Nicolson, he considered it 'an authentic and unique masterpiece, ... bound to have an influence on the mind of this generation.'[127]

In Bloomsbury, E. M. Forster shared in the general admiration, writing to explain that he found it difficult to express himself '"about a work which one feels to be so very important but I've the sort of *excitement over it which comes from believing that one's encountered a classic"'. Woolf was, of course, delighted by all these compliments, and observed ironically that she was 'in danger, indeed, of becoming our leading novelist, & not with the highbrows only.'[128] At the same time, her imagination was reaching towards just those aspects of life that* The Waves *has sometimes been criticized for ignoring. She had not, after all, entirely lost sight of 'The Life of Anybody'. Fortified by Forster's praise, she noted that 'in the city today I was thinking of another book – about shopkeepers, & publicans, with low life scenes ... between 50 and 60, I think I shall write out some very singular books, if I live ... What a long toil to reach this beginning – if The Waves is my first work in my own style!' At the same time, she was conscious that she was avoiding Roger Fry and Lytton Strachey 'whom I suspect do not like The Waves'. But Roger had influenza, and Lytton was more seriously ill.[129]*

Eighteen months after its publication, at a new year's party for Angelica's birthday in 1933, Woolf chatted to the painter Wogan Phillips and his wife, the novelist Rosamond Lehmann: 'Wogan drifted up. We talked. I was very polite, because of John [Lehmann, his brother-in-law, then working for the Press]. He was very polite. Rosamond I thought a little chill – no, shy I daresay. Wogan said The Waves sh[oul]d. be filmed: I in my vague way, said V[irginia]. Isham wants to do it – but she meant to broadcast, & oddly enough, when I came home I found a letter from her saying so.'[130] Virginia Isham was an actress and a distant cousin of Woolf's. Although she did not carry her proposal through, The Waves *clearly lent itself to radio adaptation, and a version by the poet Louis MacNeice was broadcast on 7 October 1976, with Peggy Ashcroft as the 'Choral Voice'. Since then, there have been musical settings by Bruce Saylor in 1985, and by David Bucknam and Lisa Peterson at the New York Theater Workshop, in April 1990.[131] But no one has yet made a film of it, though it seems rather a brilliant idea – a film in which the tumbling clouds, the turning heavens and the changing landscape would play a central part.*

In Woolf's will, she had asked that Vita be given one of her manuscripts, and in the months immediately after her death, Leonard wrote to ask Vita which one she would like, suggesting Flush *(the novel inspired by the spaniel, Pinka, that Vita had given the Woolfs), or else*

the Waves
Virginia Woolf

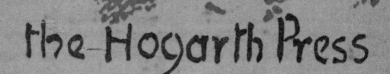

the Hogarth Press

The Years. *Instead, and surprisingly, given her initial reaction, Vita asked for* The Waves. *Leonard refused her request, and eventually sent her the manuscript of* Mrs Dalloway, *explaining that he might one day 'write something about Virginia's actual method of writing. I should like to compare her first draft with the final draft and also with what she says in her diaries at the moment about writing them. It happens that the last part of* The Waves *is extraordinarily interesting from this point of view as she gives a description in her diary of the actual writing of it.'[132] Woolf's careful self-documentation ('I want to trace my own process') unfolds a story of the artist's extraordinary faith in her own vision long before she could see where it might take her – the somnambulist picking her way along the tightrope of words. Near the end of his life, arguing with the novelist Dan Jacobson about Bloomsbury's achievements, Leonard told him that he thought* The Waves *'a very considerable work of art. I do not think that any of my wife's other books come near it.'[133]*

11

The Years of *The Years*

One Wednesday evening in January 1931, the feminist journalist Vera Brittain found herself thinking how much the mood of the Women's Movement had changed since the Great War. She was sitting beside her friend Winifred Holtby, among an audience of two hundred well-dressed young women, all shrieking with laughter. Both the platform speakers had spoken clearly and pointedly about the difficulties they had encountered as women artists, yet both had been, in Brittain's words, 'hilariously serious'.[1] Dame Ethel Smyth, square and heavy in a blue silk kimono, had explained how she had accepted her D.B.E. with alacrity, ' "especially as it was all due to an absurd row in the Woking Golf Club" '.[2] The second speaker, Virginia Woolf, tall and angular in a camel coat, told them how she had hurled her ink bottle at the spirit of the 'Angel in the House', how hard she found it, as a novelist, to accommodate herself to male prudery, and how difficult it was for men to share the workplace with women. She ended by predicting that the next phase – the step on the stair, the tap on the door – would result in 'the most interesting, exciting, and important conversation that has ever been heard'.[3] It was all a very long way from the earnest calls to action of the old days.

Vera Brittain was attending a meeting of the National Society for Women's Service, directly descended from the first women's suffrage committee. Its Secretary, Pippa Strachey, was Lytton's older sister and an old friend of the Woolfs. Virginia's speech had focused on the problems that confront the woman artist, the theme that had preoccupied her since Lily Briscoe in *To the Lighthouse*. Indeed, her speech reworked in a comic mode the conflict between the Victorian 'Angel in the House' – the internalized voice of her mother, or of Mrs Ramsay

and began to cut a piece of stuff into long strips.
Elvira lay back on the sofa now and again looking
into a book which she opened and shut.

"But Maggie look here" she said after a time:
"We may be Englishwomen; perhaps we cant help it.
Passports you know. "Magdalena Pargiter, Bi
British subject--wha about that?"
Oh I daresay said Maggie, on passports. But what
about Eton and Harrow, Oxford and Cambridge--
that sort of thing? " She pinned the hem of the
long strip of silver stuff that lay on her knee.
Tats true" said Elvira. Thats a blessed and un
denibale fact, Maggie. Thats what I shall say to
Rose next time Rose comes to lunch. I shall say,
Look here Rose. Two women who are completely withou
education, who have never dr eaten drunk or
smoked or whored--excuse the word I shall say--
for she blushes-- at the public cost;
cant be Ebglish; therefore--

"I should simply say to Rose" said Maggie.
If you dont take a bribe you neednt be an ass."
"What Maggie says is, Elvira repeated,
is, If you dont take the bribe you neednt be an
ass. Like Papa she added.

– and that of Lily Briscoe, or herself as artist.[4] She was refining and complicating her analysis of cultural change to show how the Victorian idealization of motherhood had also been a source of restraint and oppression, and, in particular, of sexual repression. She talked about the creative process, describing it as one of apparent inertia, of 'mooning', in which the artist as fisherwoman lets herself 'down into the depths of her consciousness', surrendering herself to 'the mysterious nosings about, feelings round, darts and dashes and sudden discoveries of that very shy and illusive fish the imagination'. But the process is interrupted from time to time as the line slackens, and the diving imagination floats 'limply and dully and lifelessly' to the surface, frustrated because it lacks sufficient experience, or because it is not allowed to say what it wants about women, their bodies and their passions, lest '[m]en . . . be shocked'. It will be another fifty years before 'men have become so civilised that they are not shocked when a woman speaks the truth about her body.'[5]

Woolf then encouraged her listeners to extend their sympathy to men as they lost their exclusive privileges – she pictured the male householder coming home to his library to find

the kitchen maid curled up in the arm chair reading Plato. He goes into the kitchen and there is the cook engaged in writing a Mass in B flat. He goes into the billiard room and finds the parlourmaid knocking up a fine break . . . He goes into the bed room and there is the housemaid working out a mathematical problem. What is he to do? . . . He had thought that nature had meant women to be wives, mothers, housemaids, parlourmaids and cooks.

Instead, it seems that they were intended to be anything from doctors to aero-engineers – and a host of other professions, from the commonplace to the bizarre.[6]

The previous morning (20 January 1931), while taking a bath, Virginia had suddenly 'conceived an entire new book – a sequel to a Room of Ones Own – about the sexual life of women: to be called Professions for Women perhaps – Lord how exciting!' On Friday 23rd, having given the lecture, she was still too excited to settle back into *The Waves*, where she had reached the last lap: 'One goes on making up The Open Door, or whatever it is to be called. The didactive demonstrative style conflicts with the dramatic: I find it hard to get back inside Bernard again.'[7] 'The Open Door' (this title was to change many times) seemed to open both ways: since Ibsen's *Doll's House*, women had thought of opening the door as walking out, a bid for freedom and a farewell to domestic servitude, yet, as Woolf's words to the Society had indicated, she had been thinking of someone coming in – the step on the stair, the knock on the door of a younger generation, with different needs and desires from their elders – perhaps even an emancipated man.[8] The themes of her speech to the Society – the enormous differences in attitude and experience between herself, her audience and the Victorians, the complex interaction of class and gender, and women's need for freedom to speak more openly of their bodies and their sexuality – became central elements in her thinking over the next decade, and contributed substantially to her final works of fiction.

Was it serendipity that made Virginia pick up Elizabeth Barrett Browning's long poem *Aurora Leigh* the following month? She had not apparently read it before, though she knew Tennyson's *The Princess*, that other long Victorian poem on 'the Woman Question' (she had, indeed, referred to it in *Night and Day*).[9] In its own distinctive style, *Aurora Leigh* is quite as preoccupied as Woolf herself was with exactly those issues that had inspired her speech to the Society: the role of the woman as artist, the effects of class on how women were expected to behave, and the need to speak more openly of their bodily experiences.

She saw at once that she wanted to write about *Aurora Leigh*, and asked *The Yale Review* if they would be interested in an article (they were). The resulting essay provides an engaging and sympathetic account of the poem without ever quite identifying the parallels between her own thinking and Browning's on the problems of the woman as artist – parallels that now seem obvious, but were perhaps so much at the forefront of her mind as to have been almost invisible to her. While noting that the Brownings' love story attracted more attention than their poetry (much as her own life would one day do), she praised the poem's energy and originality, yet felt bound to admit its shortcomings – its inconsistencies, its stiff and archaic language. Yet despite them, this long poem 'still lives and breathes and has its being'. Moreover, it had no successors: the poets of George V had not attempted a narrative of modern life in verse.[10]

'I was so tired after The Waves, that I lay in the garden and read the Browning love letters, and the figure of their dog made me laugh so I couldn't resist making him a Life', Woolf later explained to Ottoline Morrell. The Brownings' story was the most popular of all 'true-life' romances, and Elizabeth Barrett's escape from her London sickbed to love, sunshine and freedom in Florence with Robert Browning had recently been dramatized for the London stage by Rudolf Besier in *The Barretts of Wimpole Street*. Woolf had found the play disappointing, while being amused by 'the astonishing story – which is not an exaggeration'.[11] Could she, perhaps, do better? Meanwhile, on 19 July 1931, Leonard had declared *The Waves* 'a masterpiece', the signal she needed to dispatch it to the printer. On the 20th she began a new notebook with the words 'Notes for The Knock on the Door'; on the 21st she began a different notebook with the words 'The Life, Character & Opinions of Flush, the Spaniel'.[12]

Progress on *Flush* was soon interrupted by the arrival of proofs of *The Waves*. Even so, she noted, it was 'a good idea . . . to write biographies; to make them use my powers of representation reality accuracy; & to use my novels simply to express the general, the poetic'.[13] Writing *The Waves* had turned her inwards, in search of a metaphysical or quintessential humanity; it had been 'an adventure which I go on alone', 'along this very lonely path';[14] *Flush*, by contrast, was a social and sociable text, in several senses. While it told the story of Flush's developing relationships with Elizabeth Barrett and Robert Browning (as well as their relationship with one another, of course), it indirectly celebrated two of her own close friendships: like *Orlando*, it was designed to appeal to Vita, the dog-lover, and her portrait of Flush was partly inspired by Pinka (or Pinker), the cocker spaniel that Vita had given her in 1926. In September, she wrote to Vita asking for a photograph of her spaniel Henry, as if licensed to renew the demands she had made while writing *Orlando*, three years earlier.

But it was primarily intended for Lytton, or so she later told her friends.[15] Though she now saw less and less of him, she had conceived *Flush* as a skit on his best-selling biography, *Queen Victoria* (1921). Though he had dedicated it to her, she had never greatly cared for it, indeed had resented its success. In part a parody of Lytton's style, *Flush* would be a joke to share with him, and in mid-December, after a season of headaches, she wrote to tell him that she had dreamed they were sharing a joke: 'I was at a play, in the pit and suddenly you, who were sitting across a gangway in a row in front, turned and looked at me, and we both went into fits of laughter.'[16] But Lytton was already desperately ill with cancer. On Christmas Eve, she and Leonard sobbed at the thought of his imminent death. Vanessa and Clive, spending Christmas in Wiltshire with Clive's family, visited Ham Spray, where they found 'the lounge at the Bear filled with Stracheys reading detective novels in despair' – Lytton was one of ten brothers and sisters, and they had all assembled – 'all grey, all woollen, all red nosed, swollen eyed, logical, quiet, exact, doing cross word puzzles; thinking of Lytton.' Three weeks later, on a beautiful January day, with larks 'singing over the petrol pumps . . . on the Great West Road', the Woolfs motored over to Ham Spray where Pippa Strachey sobbed on Virginia's shoulder.[17] It was only their second visit to the house.

Lytton was too ill to see them, but apparently 'liked our coming'. A week later, days before Virginia's fiftieth birthday, he died. A telegram arrived in the middle of Angelica's birthday party. Virginia, Vanessa and Duncan retreated to the studio to weep: as Vanessa said, he was 'the first of the people one has known since one was grown up to die'.[18] In the weeks that followed, his friends and relatives mourned in helpless, isolated groups, but there was no funeral. His body was cremated in the presence of his brother James, and the faithful Saxon Sydney-Turner. Meanwhile there was general anxiety about Dora Carrington, who had adored Lytton and did not wish to survive him. On another sunny day in early March, the Woolfs drove back to Ham Spray to see her. She made them lunch and tea, and talked about Lytton, his illness and the plans he had been making for the future. As they left, Virginia reminded her ' "Then you will come & see us next week – or not – just as you like?" "Yes, I will come, or not" she said. And kissed me again, & said Goodbye. Then she went in.' Early next morning, she shot herself with a borrowed rifle. The Coroner's Inquest reported her death as accidental, a fiction that she maintained as she lay dying.[19]

'Shall I ever "write" again? And what is writing?' Virginia asked herself, replying, 'The perpetual converse I keep up . . . Why take to it again?' She had ended 1931 in poor health, but with various projects on the go: 'there's Flush: theres the Knock on the door; there's the appalling novel; theres Common Reader . . . there's my little letter to a Poet' (the 'appalling novel' remains a mystery).[20] She was writing essays on John Donne, Sidney and the Elizabethans to front a new Common Reader, and at the same time composing an open letter to John Lehmann as a representative 'young poet', her contribution to a new Hogarth Press series. In February 1932, she worked away dutifully at her essay on John Donne, but woke in the night with 'the sense of being in an empty hall: Lytton dead . . . What is the point of it'.[21] *Flush*, too, seemed pointless, without Lytton to giggle over it.

Despite her inner heaviness, the book she had thought of in the bath continued to knock on the door. It would illustrate some of the great changes in the position of women that had taken place during Woolf's lifetime, changes that revealed how partial and prejudiced Victorian views of the nature of women had been, and how far they had been determined by the reigning patriarchy. Montaigne, Woolf noticed, had conceived of women as naturally sexually voracious, thus completely reversing the notion of innate chastity with which she had grown up. Now she came across a dismissive account of women's achievements over the previous ten years, the work of H. G. Wells. 'Hitherto the role of women has been decorative and ancillary. And today it seems to be still decorative and ancillary', he had written. 'Her recent gains in freedom have widened her choice of what she shall adorn or serve, but they have released no new initiative in human affairs.' Woolf found herself 'quivering & itching to write my – whats it to be called? "Men are like that?" – no thats too patently feminist: the sequel then [to *A Room of One's Own*], for which I have collected enough powder to blow up St Pauls.'[22]

Between finishing *The Waves* in June 1931 and starting *The Years* in October 1932, Woolf worked on *The Common Reader: Second Series* and *Flush*. Neither wholly satisfied the extraordinarily high demands she made of herself; each is considerably more entertaining than she makes it sound. The summer of 1932 was tense, overcast by Maynard Keynes's gloom about the current economic crisis in Europe: ' "Never been so bad. We may go over the edge – but as its never been like this, nobody knows. One would say we must." ' In the relative peace of Rodmell, Virginia bought herself a little desk, and Leonard

acquired a beehive. With the help of their gardener, Percy Bartholomew, he collected a swarm of bees clinging to a tombstone in the
graveyard at the back of Monk's House. The insects released some
deep-seated excitement in Virginia: 'Bees shoot whizz, like arrows of
desire: fierce, sexual; weave cats cradles in the air; each whizzing from
a string; the whole air full of vibration: of beauty, of this burning
arrowy desire; & speed: I still think the quivering shifting bee bag the
most sexual & sensual symbol.'[23]

The essays for the *Second Common Reader* could hardly compete
with the vibrant, 'quivering' bee bag; but that and her work on *Flush*
were, in part, acts of self-discipline, as she patiently waited for the day
when 'all of a rush, fiction will burst in',[24] bringing freedom from the
claims of fact and the need to subordinate her invention to research.
The Common Reader: Second Series allowed her to rescue the best of
her literary essays from oblivion, setting them in a sequence of studies
from 'The Strange Elizabethans' to 'Thomas Hardy', while taking in
Donne, De Quincey and the question of class in fiction in 'The Niece
of an Earl'. On 11 July, she finally 'slipped a green rubber band round
the Common Reader, second series . . . no sense of glory; only of
drudgery done . . . I doubt that I shall write another like it all the
same'.[25] It was unusual among her books in re-using an earlier formula.
Like its predecessor, it focused mainly on neglected figures, memoirists,
'the lives of the obscure' and of Victorian women writers, gathering
up essays on Jane Carlyle and her friend Geraldine Jewsbury, Elizabeth
Barrett Browning and Christina Rossetti.

With *The Common Reader* completed, Woolf turned back to *Flush*
for the first time since the previous summer, hoping, perhaps, that it
would give her that 'fling . . . into fiction & freedom'[26] she had been
searching for. She wrote the first draft at Rodmell that summer. Her
task was to re-create the spaniel's world from the inside, to find words
for a mode of existence unhampered by words, subject instead to the
urges of the body, as alive to smell as to touch and sight. Flush, hearing
'the hunting horn of Venus' [p.11][27] is free from moral censure, as only
an animal could be. His biography begins in a space of freedom and
primal delight, a pastoral idyll from which he is too soon transported
to Elizabeth Barrett's narrow and oppressive sickroom, where his
sentimental education properly begins. But his new mistress feels quite

as imprisoned as he does, stretched on her plush sofa, amidst the sickly odour of eau-de-cologne. She too hears and heeds the call of freedom and passion, and eventually throws off the chains of patriarchal Wimpole Street for Robert Browning and Italy, a second paradise, free of hypocrisy and class-consciousness (or so it appeared to Woolf's contemporaries E. M. Forster and D. H. Lawrence).

Like Orlando, Flush is a profoundly ambiguous hero: while his masculinity may act as a literary liberation for his author, his fine-tuned social sensibilities and lack of social agency suggest the feminine. Strong and independent as he is among his own kind, he is only a spaniel, unable to understand or participate in human conversation or decision-making, to share his mistress's or his author's knowledge of a world beyond his senses. Woolf wrote into his 'biography' her own reading of the fissure at the heart of Victorian society, its peculiar dialectic between fear and freedom – its gap between idealism and squalor, upstairs and downstairs, inside and outside, respectable and criminal. The violence, filth and moral darkness that she (like others before her) had imagined at the heart of the Victorian city are made manifest in the novel's central episode (chapter IV), in which Flush is stolen and carried off to the nightmare world of Whitechapel.[28]

Whitechapel, the city as dreadful night, recalls Rachel's dreams of sinister old men and women squatting in dank tunnels, or beneath dripping arches, nursing the simmering resentment of the underdog, in *The Voyage Out*.[29] In Woolf's first novel, these threatening, marginalized figures, who could hardly be thought about, much less talked of, are mysteriously connected with the strict rules as to where young women may walk in London, rules which Rachel finds frustrating and unjust. For Woolf, the constraints on her freedom to walk where she wanted would be linked with the constraints on writing as she wanted – one of the themes of her speech to the National Society for Women's Service; both sets of limitations were imposed by 'what men thought'. The restrictions and taboos of Victorian life, as observed in *A Room of One's Own*, *Orlando* and *Flush*, were nowhere more visible than upon the London streets.

Yet she adored London with a passion that inspired her six 'London Scenes', written for the magazine *Good Housekeeping* in the early 1930s.[30] They describe in memorable detail the docks, with their great ships and variegated merchandise, and 'the tide of Oxford Street', all glittering shop windows and humming traffic. She paused to notice how the lack of running water in the Carlyles' house in Cheyne Row had enslaved the great man's wife and servant. Her pleasure in walking the London streets sprang in part from the city's vitality, but also from a sense of newly enjoyed freedom as she remembered the old days, and how she had yearned to walk thus. She loved to walk alone, with only her dog for company, writing in her head, whether over the Sussex Downs or through the London streets. Her 1927 essay 'Street Haunting'[31] tacitly admits the parallels between walking and writing when a winter evening ramble ends in the purchase of a pencil, since the pencil signifies the beginning of writing just as surely as (in its different way) walking did. Woolf, like so many writers, carried out much of her creative thinking, planning and 'scene-making' as she walked.[32] Her next book, 'on the sexual life of women', would begin with her memories of the threat of the streets as a figure for the numerous restrictions laid upon women's freedom of thought and action during the nineteenth century – rather as her dismissal from the lawns and libraries of Cambridge had stood for women's exclusion from higher education.

Meanwhile, she was growing uneasy, though reluctant to admit to herself the source of her unease lest doing so might lend it force. Since *The Waves*, she had been running in low gear, preparing essays for *The Second Common Reader* and writing *Flush*, no doubt because 'the strain of The Waves weakened my concentration for months'. Tucked away inside a long list of ongoing worries, she asked herself, 'shall I write another novel?[33] For a moment, she felt she had 'invented the skeleton of another novel: but it must wait . . .', or that she had been 'sleeping over a promising novel'.[34] She was collecting her energies to spring. Back from the summer at Rodmell, and with *The Second Common Reader* about to appear, she determined to be 'withdrawn; & concentrated' in preparation for the morning when she wrote 'An Essay based upon a paper read to the London/National Society for Women's Service' – the morning of 11 October 1932. Yet as soon as she began writing 'When your Secretary asked me to come here tonight . . .', her planned sequel to *A Room* turned into fiction before her eyes, and the essay turned into a 'Novel-Essay'.[35] At once she felt herself flooded with new ideas: 'I have been in such a haze & dream & intoxication, declaiming phrases, seeing scenes, as I walk up South-ampton Row that I can hardly say I have been alive at all, since the 10th Oct. Everything is running of its own accord into the stream'.[36]

The opening of the first draft emphasized its continuity with *A Room* by addressing an imaginary audience of young women (as *A Room* had done), explaining that, to understand their present situation, they needed to understand the past, and therefore must 'become the people that we were two or three generations ago. Let us be our great grand-mothers.' In her role as novelist, she offered to effect that transforma-tion for them by reading from a novel that 'tries to give a faithful and detailed account of a family called Pargiter', and at once we are having tea in the drawing room at Abercorn Terrace in 1880.[37] The Pargiter daughters, Delia and Milly, feel entrapped, as their mother slowly dies upstairs (perhaps as the young Stephens had felt trapped at Hyde Park Gate with their dying father). Delia wants to study music in Germany (one of several details deriving from the life of Ethel Smyth[38]), but there is no money for her to do so, and the girls peer out of the window with envy or desire at a young man making a visit further down the street. The pretty but impractical tea kettle that refuses to boil reflects their impatience.

Spelling out a distinction that *A Room* had never quite reached, Woolf began by alternating fictional episodes with essays offering wider historical explanations for the plight of the Pargiter girls, quoting from Victorian authors (Walter Bagehot and Mary Kingsley), but the 'essays' themselves also tend to slide towards fiction: it is in the second 'essay' that we meet Delia's violin-teacher, Signor Morelli, in his house at Maida Vale, and the girls' small dressmaker, Miss Edwards.[39] Woolf concentrates on the themes of money and love, showing how money was spent on boys' education rather than on girls'. She reveals the growing desires of young women, and the constraints imposed on them: 'For any of them to walk in the West End even by day was out of the question . . . unless they went with a brother or their mother'. And their sense of being at risk gave them 'curious sensations, unpleasant dreams'.[40]

Woolf defines that threat as 'street or common love', a term that seems oddly inappropriate until we remember that she was obliged to invent for herself a discourse of social and cultural analysis that had not yet come into being. 'Street love' is shown in action, when Rose, the youngest, breaks all the rules by slipping out to a nearby toyshop alone in the growing dark. As she returns, she encounters a sinister man who 'gibbered some nonsense at her, sucking his lips in & out; and began to undo his clothes . . .' Terrified, she rushes home, but cannot sleep for fear that the man has got into the house (her nightmares again recall those of Rachel in *The Voyage Out*, or of Woolf herself as a child).[41] At the same time, she cannot speak of what she has seen because of some obscure sense of shame: 'she was terrified, not only terrified: somehow, it was horrid, nasty, what she had seen: she could not tell any one: not even Eleanor. He had undressed.' In the essay that follows, Woolf explores Victorian inhibitions about sexuality, indicating their survival and impact on her own writing. There is 'a convention, supported by law, which forbids . . . any plain description of the sight that Rose, in common with many other little girls, saw under the lamp post by the pillar box'.[42] In discussing 'indecent exposure', the dangers she exposed were real enough, yet, as she recognized, they gained in terror in proportion to the ignorance of the victim. Rose is not merely frightened; her curiosity is aroused: 'Rose, next day, of course, began to observe Bobby [her older brother, later Martin] more closely. She began to hunt about . . . for some of [her father's] old books about the treatment of Tropical Diseases, because they had certain pictures.' Woolf contrasts Rose's guilt and anxiety with the way Bobby acquires a knowledge of sex – not only does he learn in an atmosphere of male camaraderie, but what he learns confirms, rather than undermines, his self-confidence.[43]

The second half of this section (the whole section would later become '1880') moves to Oxford, to introduce the Pargiters' cousin, Kitty Malone, whose problems are almost the opposite of theirs: she is an only child, and, as the daughter of the Master of St Katharine's College, she has more male admirers than she can handle, yet she feels equally imprisoned, for her deepest desire is to escape from Oxford tea-tables and dinner-tables to farm in Yorkshire. For a moment, windows seem to open for her when she has tea with the Hughes or Brook family (later, the Robsons). Sam Brook is a proto-feminist, a man who recognizes that he has reached Oxford through his mother's self-sacrifice, who admires his wife and hopes that his daughter Nell will pass her exams and become a doctor. As Kitty notes with satisfaction, he treats her not as a young woman but as a human being.[44]

Woolf discovered this exemplary figure in the biography of Joseph Wright by his wife Elizabeth. Oxford scholar and author of the *English Dialect Dictionary*, Wright had been the classic 'outsider'. Coming from a very poor Yorkshire family, his studies had been paid for by his mother's work as a cleaner. When he proposed to Elizabeth, he told her that his greatest ambition was that she should '*live*, not merely exist; and live too in a way that not many women have lived before'; he had promised to make that possible. Woolf contrasts Joseph Wright, who 'had received no schooling', with 'men like Mark Pattison, Walter Pater, Oscar Browning, and Walter Bagehot,'[45] who had enjoyed all the supposed advantages of a public school and university education and, as a result, could not recognize women as fellow human beings. In Wright's *Dialect Dictionary*, Woolf would have found the word 'pargeter', meaning 'a plasterer; a whitewasher', suggesting the Victorian penchant for concealment, in particular of sexual matters. That penchant became even more explicit in March 1933, when she described Colonel Pargiter's visit to his mistress, Mira, which she then decided to use as the opening scene.[46]

Woolf drafted the first sequence of her 'novel-essay' very fast, completing it in ten weeks, on 19 December 1932. By then, she had already written 60,320 words. She felt intensely excited. The new book was to 'take in everything, sex, education, life &c; & come, with the most powerful & agile leaps, like a chamois across precipices from 1880 to here & now'. She already felt sure it was going to be 'important', not 'a novel of vision, but a novel of fact' – 'I find myself infinitely delighting in facts for a change, & in possession of quantities beyond counting: ... This is the true line, I am sure, after The Waves.'[47] She recognized her own pendulum swing from *The Waves*, a novel of vision *par excellence*, to this new 'novel of fact'; a comparable swing had carried her from *Lighthouse*, (through *Orlando*) to *A Room of One's Own*. By contrast, *Flush* had now become the tedious task, the nestling pushed out by the cuckoo, as she forced herself to rewrite the Whitechapel scene for the third time. Yet, '[w]hat a joy – what a sense as of a Rolls Royce engine once more purring its 70 miles an hour in my brain . . . I am on the flood of creativeness in The Pargiters – what a liberation that gives one – as if everything added to that torrent – '[48] As always, there were moments of self-doubt, yet 'what fun that book is to me!' She had the highest ambitions for it: it was 'to give the whole of the present society – nothing less: facts, as well as the vision . . . The Waves going on simultaneously with Night & Day . . . And there are to be millions of ideas but no preaching – history, politics, feminism, art, literature – in short a summing up of all I know, feel, laugh at, despise, like, admire hate & so on'.[49]

As she started out on her 'novel of fact', she was also engaged in composing an attack on the 'Middlebrow' as represented by J. B. Priestley – it took the form of a letter to the *New Statesman*, though on Leonard's advice it remained unsent.[50] She was more conscious of a younger generation of women writers 'knocking at the door' than she liked to admit, writers such as Storm Jameson, Winifred Holtby or Phyllis Bentley who had very different conceptions of what fiction ought to be, who wrote of the 'everyday' world as they saw it. In the late summer of 1933, she read Vita's 'The E[dwardian]s all in a gulp with pleasure in bed; . . . also [E. Arnot-Robertson's] Ordinary Families . . . very good: I thought.' She then consumed 'with extreme greed' Vera Brittain's memoir, *The Testament of Youth* (Brittain had, of course, been among the audience when Woolf lectured on 'Professions for Women'). She suspected she would dislike Brittain 'in real life', but was fascinated by her memoir, finding it 'very good . . . of its sort. The new sort, the hard anguished sort, that the young write; that I could never write. Nor has anyone written that kind of book before.'[51]

Novels of this kind, based on first-hand experience or engaged with contemporary social life, 'the novel of fact', were typical of the 1930s. Woolf had already written such a novel in *Night and Day*, a book that had more in common with *The Years* than its author may have remembered, for it had begun as an account of the contrasting lives of different generations since the mid-nineteenth century – its earliest title had been 'The Third Generation'. In January 1915, Woolf had made plans to prepare for it by reading some Victorian memoirs, though as she wrote, the previous generations (Mrs Hilbery and her father, the poet Richard Alardyce) gave place to the story of Katharine in 1912.[52] Starting out upon this new novel-essay, Woolf was surprised and delighted to discover the 'torrent of fact' that she had been 'observing & collecting these 20 years'. To supplement her own memory, her reading and a wealth of family legend, she returned to Victorian memoirs and consulted the old bound volumes of *The Times*, then (as now) in the basement of the London Library. There was not a statement that could not be verified,[53] she announced, and in this respect (as perhaps in others), *The Years* anticipates the carefully researched fiction-writing of our own time.

But the 'novel of fact' brought its own difficulties. Her objections to Arnold Bennett's novels had focused on their amassing of facts as a substitute for deeper insights, and she had criticized the 'Edwardian' novelists for their social programmes, for writing novels that demanded that their readers do something – 'join a society, or, . . . write a cheque.'[54] In setting out her own feminist agenda, Woolf laid herself open to the same criticism, as she now began to realize. The opening episodes, 1880 and 1891, concentrate upon features of social life either already discussed in *A Room*, or to be discussed in *Three Guineas* – the constraints of all kinds imposed on young women, the uneasy combination of contempt and idealism in which women were held, and the resistance they encountered on entering such traditional male enclaves as clubs, universities, hospitals and law courts.

Woolf's generation had despised the teaching and preaching so characteristic of Victorian literature, suspecting any writing that had manifest designs upon its readers: Leonard, she noted, thought that 'politics ought to be separate from art'.[55] Roger Fry had argued that art should be made and judged according to aesthetic principles, and Woolf herself had always encouraged her readers to come to their own conclusions. And these theoretical problems underlined more practical ones: though Woolf's earlier novels had drawn on and been energized by moral and political thinking, they had never before been so directly inspired by them. A novel thus based risked psychological thinness; its presentation of arguments risked diminishing the complexity of experience.[56] By February 1933, she had decided to abandon the mixture of fiction and discussion, and set about revising the 1880 section 'leaving out the interchapters – compacting them in the text'. It was to be the first of many revisions. But already by December 1932, Woolf had invented two new characters, Magdalena and Elvira, intended to counter the conventional worlds of Abercorn Terrace and the Master's Lodge. Although intensely excited by them, she did not allow herself to begin writing their scenes till March.[57]

'An outsider – and it is part of a writer's profession to be an outsider – can see aspects of things that are not visible from the inside',[58] Woolf had noted in her opening essay. Now she imagined two young women who, unlike the Pargiter daughters or Kitty Malone, lived outside the loop of Oxford or 'Kensington' tea parties, and so felt free to criticize current social assumptions. Magdalena and Elvira (who have affinities with Vanessa and Virginia), daughters of the sensual and exotic Eugenie, would voice their author's rejection of 'the system'. 'It is an utterly corrupt society I have just remarked, speaking in the person of Elvira Pargiter, & I will take nothing that it can give me &c &c', wrote Woolf, as she turned down the offer of an honorary degree from Manchester University in 1933; 'I hardly know which I am, or where: Virginia or Elvira: in the Pargiters or outside.' From the moment of her invention, Woolf identified strongly with Elvira. She looked up her old diaries, and found an account of a dance in Queen's Gate written in 1903.[59] Out of this, she created the heart of the 1907 episode, in which Elvira (later renamed Sara, and reduced in other ways, too) lies awake on a hot summer's night at the height of 'the season', reading *Antigone*, listening to dance music and watching couples flow in and out of the back garden below, as she feels the excitement of her future before her. Woolf loved this scene, perhaps for the opportunity it gave her to revisit her own youth, and she would revise it many times. Elvira was not merely an outsider, however; she was also a cripple, a hunchback, and in the first draft, Maggie calls her 'Hunch'. Her status as a physical cripple (and a wise fool) indirectly exposes other characters as emotionally or psychically damaged.[60]

By April Woolf was launched on 'Elvira in bed – the scene I've had in my mind ever so many months . . . Its the turn of the book. It needs a great shove to swing it round on its hinges.'[61] Elvira represents the book's 'turn' because she voices not only Woolf's politically subversive feelings, but also something of her inner vision. The novel of fact could not ultimately exclude the demands of the spirit. Thereafter, the interactions of Maggie and Elvira/Sara with their cousins Rose, Martin and Eleanor would come to constitute the novel's emotional core. The

Pargiter brothers Edward and Morris, their sisters Delia and Milly, and their other cousin Kitty remain on the periphery; they are lay figures, by comparison.

The long Edwardian summer reflected in the novel's 1907 episode gives place to winds of change (1908), and by the summer of 1933, Woolf had reached 1910, a year she had once identified as a turning point in human history. Here, Maggie, Elvira and Rose Pargiter explore (at enormous length, in the fourth MS notebook) the great feminist issues – contraception, chastity, rape, patriarchy ('every patriarch has his prostitute'), the future ('time past is but a roseleaf on Cleopatra's needle')[62] and the nature of patriotism, a theme she would return to in the 1911 episode (which she worked on in August and September) and that of 1917 (begun in January 1934).

Meanwhile within her novel, in the bitter January of 1913, the house at Abercorn Terrace is finally packed up in the wake of Colonel Pargiter's death. The faithful family retainer, Crosby, and 'the rather smelly, wheezy and unattractive' family dog [p.159][63] are 'put out to grass' at Richmond (Woolf's own place of exile in the years after her breakdown). Finishing *Flush* at the same time as she began *The Years*, she had added a lengthy footnote on Elizabeth Barrett Browning's maid, Lily Wilson, suggesting that Lily's biography also deserved to be written and acknowledging parallels between the positions of servants and dogs: 'Since [Wilson] spoke almost as seldom as Flush, the outlines of her character are little known; and since Miss Barrett never wrote a poem about her, her appearance is far less familiar than his.' [p.94] Woolf was well aware of her own difficulties when it came to writing about the lower classes: beginning *The Waves*, she had imagined working-class counterparts to her main characters, but she could not visualize the inner life of Albert the cowman's son, or Florrie the kitchen maid, and so abandoned them. The children of the poor, she knew, worked from an early age; they were obliged to support the needs and addictions of adults, to endure sickness, hunger and cold, when other children ('ordinary' children, from her point of view) 'were still dabbling in seaside pools and spelling out fairy tales beside the nursery fire'.[64]

In spring 1930, Woolf wrote a preface for a collection of testaments from working-class women gathered by her friend Margaret Llewelyn

Davies. She admitted that while she too had attended meetings of the Women's Co-operative Guild, she could not identify with their problems – nor would their solutions 'touch one hair of my comfortable capitalistic head', for, unlike the working women, her life had been cushioned by her private income, so that 'however much we had sympathised our sympathy was largely fictitious.'[65] She could not cross the gap between working women's experiences and her own, and that limitation also affected her fiction. Though Crosby's departure is a moment of general social significance, exemplifying those enormous changes in social relations that Woolf had located 'on or about December 1910', the actual portrait of Crosby lacks inner life. Martin's claim that he is 'Crosby's God' is the more disturbing since Crosby's only emotion is her worship of the family. She lacks the inner life that Woolf had demanded for Mrs Brown, seated in her railway carriage.[66]

'Why is there always this relationship between master & servant? . . . Always deceit & distrust . . .' If Woolf found the outlook of servants hard to handle in fiction, it was scarcely easier to cope with in real life. The early 1930s were years of crisis over 'the Nelly question', as Woolf's problems with her live-in cook Nelly Boxall came to a head[67] (the housemaid, Lottie Hope, had long since gone to work for Adrian Stephen). She found Nelly's voice and presence irritating and their forced intimacy oppressive, particularly so in the close quarters of Monk's House. At Tavistock Square, she could retreat to the printing shop in the basement, and thus be well out of earshot. She disliked the journey to Rodmell by car with Nelly in the back, and was irrationally annoyed with Nelly's innocent remark on the eve of the 1929 election, ' "We are winning" . . . I was shocked to think that we both desire the Labour party to win.'[68] Woolf's 1924 essay 'Mr Bennett and Mrs Brown' had recorded with amusement the transformation of the Victorian cook, who had 'lived like a leviathan in the lower depths, formidable, silent, obscure, inscrutable', into the Georgian cook, 'a creature of sunshine and fresh air; in and out of the drawing-room, now to borrow the *Daily Herald*, now to ask advice about a hat';[69] but when it happened at Monk's House or Tavistock Square, she was rather less amused. Woolf's relations with Nelly were the more difficult because, while she recognized Nelly's dependence on her, she concealed from herself her own dependence on Nelly, whose poorly paid labour made her writing possible. At the same time, she recognized Nelly's fictional potential, as a key character in the unfolding drama of her life: 'If I were reading this diary . . . I should seize with greed upon the portrait of Nelly, & make a story – perhaps make the whole story revolve round that'.[70]

The tension between them broke out in scenes of mutual reproach, in which mistress and cook gave each other notice, scenes in which Woolf felt torn between shame and a longing to be rid of Nelly and the uncomfortable feelings she provoked – guilt and anger at Nelly's 'malice and spite', as well as anger with herself for her cowardice and failure of sympathy. At other times, she could recognize and acknowledge Nelly's loyalty and trust (she was also an excellent cook). Soon after Woolf finished her introduction to Margaret Llewelyn Davies's testimonies, Nelly, who had been unwell for some time, went into hospital for a kidney operation. Woolf seized the opportunity to place an advertisement in *Time and Tide* for 'A woman of intelligence and initiative', but failed to find a satisfactory substitute, and by 1931, Nelly was once more 'installed for life', as it seemed.[71] Then in February 1934 (as Woolf was drafting the 1917 episode), Nelly made a scene 'about the workmen & her day out'. Leonard and Virginia cooked eggs for lunch and went out for their evening meal, but the atmosphere was so bad that Virginia determined this row should be the last. Braced by previous confrontations, she finally and irrevocably gave Nelly notice, and after 'the most disagreeable six weeks of my life', found herself free of her, after eighteen years of service.[72]

'We dine in the basement,' [Maggie] continued, turning to Eleanor, 'because we've no servants.' She led the way down the steep little stairs . . .
'Isn't it much nicer,' said Eleanor, taking her plate, 'not having servants . . .'
'We have a woman to do the washing up,' said Maggie. [pp.206–7]

If the First World War affected any single social structure, it was the position of servants. The alternatives that the war opened up, in particular the munitions factories, dangerous and disagreeable though they were, offered higher pay, more opportunities to make friends and greater equality, even respect. Maggie and Renny, though they don't mention her, also employ a 'Nurse', to look after the children; she eats the same food as they do (and during the dinner party Maggie takes her a plate of food). Servants had formerly been invisible presences, taken for granted but scarcely discussed in polite society. The 1917 dinner party reflects changes not only in discourse but in habits of living.

Eleanor, like her author, saw the departure of servants as a blessed relief, yet with that even-handedness that characterizes the novel as a whole, she also felt the appeal of the long Edwardian summer: the 1911 episode, in particular, seems to constitute a farewell to an England that was fast disappearing. It celebrates the power and appeal of 'Englishness', creating a vision of a traditional way of life, with its village fete, and the social space between the 'big house' and its lesser neighbours, all set in an idyllic pastoral landscape, where the owl swoops low over the garden hedge, and Eleanor notices the peculiar beauty of the English language: 'This is England, Eleanor thought to herself' [p.152], anticipating Woolf's words the following spring, when she and Leonard drove through Warwickshire, through Shakespeare's county, on their return from Ireland: 'I saw a stallion being led, under the may and the beeches, along a grass ride; and I thought that is England.'[73] Yet such moments of unqualified patriotism are always linked to a sense of external threat. In the 1911 episode, the dinner conversation turns to the situation in the Balkans. ' "There's going to be trouble there in the near future," Sir William was saying.' [p.147] *The Years* was written through years of growing political crisis – Hitler's seizure of power in Germany, Japan's invasion of China, Mussolini's invasion of Abyssinia. The imperialist dictators were gaining ground and England was once again under threat, a threat that made 'Englishness' feel all the more precious. Woolf evoked what she saw as the permanent features of English life – the old house, the village, the green countryside, the beauties of the English language and its literature – and that vision, complexly qualified, would return in her final novel, a story of England on the brink of war. Later, when she found it difficult to keep *The Years* in any clear perspective, she still liked the 1911 episode, thinking it 'about the best, in that line, I ever wrote'.[74]

Woolf completed the first draft of her novel on 30 September 1934, 'quite calmly too.' It now occupied most of eight large bound notebooks, and stood at 900 pages long: 'L says 200,000 words. Lord God what an amount of re-writing that means! . . . Anyhow the design is there. And it has taken a little less than 2 years . . . written at a greater gallop than any of my books.' Indeed, much of it had been written in a state of 'intoxicating exhilaration', in which Woolf felt 'free to define my attitude with a vigour & certainty I have never known before.'[75] During the summers of 1933 and 1934, she had found herself 'in full flood with The P[argiter].s' – 'An exciting book to write.' At such times, she resented visitors, feeling that they took her too far from 'the other world; I only want walking & perfectly spontaneous childish life with L. & the accustomed when I'm writing at full tilt'. Walking, linked as it was to creation, was a delight: 'the trance like, swimming, flying through the air; the current of sensations & ideas; & the slow, but fresh change of down, of road, of colour'.[76] The book flowed steadily forward, filling her with self-confidence, joy and a sense of liberation. As usual, various day-to-day experiences – staying with her cousin Herbert Fisher in the Master's Lodge at New College, reading a biography of Parnell or the poems of Andrew Marvell, visiting Ireland, catching sight of political graffiti – fed steadily into her work.[77] At Rodmell in August 1934, she was preoccupied with the problems posed by the 'Present Day' section, which, she saw, must counterbalance the long 1880 section in depth and complexity.[78]

The process of inventing a new type of novel was utterly absorbing: she was 'making up all the time', thrilled that she could 'break every mould & find a fresh form of being, that is of expression, for everything I feel & think . . . the sense of being fully energised'. Until 9 September, her anxieties had focused upon the technical problems posed by her last scene.[79] Late that afternoon, as she and Clive walked on the terrace at Monk's House, Vanessa came out with the news that Roger Fry had died. He had been looking older recently, Woolf had noticed, and a few days earlier had gone into hospital after a bad fall, but no one had expected him to die. Without Roger, '[t]he substance [has] gone out of everything'; energy, colour and richness seemed drained from the world. 'Such a blank wall. Such a silence. Such a poverty. How he reverberated!' It was far worse for Vanessa, his former lover and close friend for twenty years. A month or two later, Roger's younger partner, Helen Anrep, and his sister Margery enquired whether Virginia would consider writing his life.[80]

Almost as soon as the first draft was completed, she began to revise her 'nameless' novel – its title had changed from 'The Pargiters' to 'Here & Now', but she had also considered other titles such as 'Music, or Dawn'; later, she would try out 'Sons & Daughters' (or else 'Daughters & Sons'), 'Ordinary People', 'The Caravan' and 'Other People's Houses' before settling upon 'The Years' in September 1935 ('fixed; dropped like a billiard ball into a pocket').[81] Like *The Waves*, *The Years* was rewritten at least four times, though only the first holograph draft has survived. The second revision took her a further year, and its results are recorded in a set of galley proofs. As 1935 began, the revision process was clarified when her original impulse (to write a sequel to *A Room*) crystallized into a scheme for a separate book, initially entitled 'On Being Despised', and later, *Three Guineas*. She had been steadily accumulating ammunition for this feminist polemic since 1931, though she did not actually begin drafting it until late in 1936.[82] Planning it helped her to let go of some of the more didactic sequences in the first draft – discussions of patriotism or contraception or the condition of women could now be deferred to the new polemic, where they might be more fully explored. For the present, she advised herself against starting 'On Being Despised . . . until the P[argiter].s is done with'. An attempt made one morning in April 1935 seemed to prove that 'one cant propagate at the same time as write fiction. And as this fiction is dangerously near propaganda, I must keep my hands clean'.[83]

The process of revision was inevitably less exhilarating than the first full flow of inspiration. Woolf blamed her sense of emptiness on Roger's death, and Vita's defection: when she and Leonard had visited Vita at Sissinghurst in the spring of 1935, Vita casually told her that she would not be coming to London before she travelled abroad, and her thoughtlessness made Virginia feel that their friendship was over – 'Not with a quarrel, not with a bang, but as ripe fruit falls.'[84] But she was still deeply and consolingly absorbed in the problems presented by her novel: her diary puzzles over the handling of particular scenes, urging herself not to be hurried: 'I'm going to let every scene shape fully & easily in my hands, before sending it to be typed, even if it has to wait another year'. As with *The Waves*, writing had become a learning process, a process in which she had 'to stop: go upstairs . . .

come back; find a little flow of words'.[85] Patience and perseverance had paid off then; she was still confident they would do so again.

She had begun to see her narrative as deliberately interweaving 'different levels in writing', on the surface and in depth. Part of Shakespeare's power lay in his surface realism, she thought: 'one c[oul]d work out a theory of fiction &c on these lines: how many levels attempted. whether kept to or not'. In her novel, she planned to set 'upper air scenes' beside episodes carrying 'a great pressure of meaning' (indeed, the novel's action is often markedly symbolic); 'My idea is to . . . contrast the scenes; very intense, less so: then drama; then narrative. Keeping a kind of swing & rhythm through them all.'[86]

From the outset, the scheme of the novel had allowed for a variety of treatments, and for expansion or contraction: individual episodes might be short or long, set nearer or further in time from one another, for memory and time were subjective and relative, not merely in the obvious, experiential sense, but also according to modern physics, which envisaged the whole system of the universe in movement, a movement in which the different elements subtly affected one another. Woolf makes this relativity explicit at the second 'turn' of the book, the 1914 episode. It begins in spring, with all the clocks of the city 'gathering their forces together; they seemed to be whirring a preliminary warning.' [p.166][87] It ends as Kitty slips away from her evening party and travels northwards. Her journey from the formal evening party to the 'silence and solitude' of her country house stands for the transition of the war years, that gaping chasm and abyss of difference which Woolf had fantasized in 'Time Passes'. As Kitty's train rushes through the night, the nature and relationship of time and space are explored in terms of new conceptions of time's workings, so that the journey subtly and obliquely suggests Einstein's theory of relativity, or Heisenberg's 'Uncertainty Principle' (according to which, time and position cannot be defined simultaneously). On her arrival, Kitty steps out into a landscape renewed by the spring, into the permanent world of nature that far outlasts brief human lives: 'A deep murmur sang in her ears – the land itself, singing to itself, a chorus, alone . . . Time had ceased.' [p.203][88]

What relativity contradicted were the old, simple schemes of cause and effect and, by extension, traditional narrative structures, such as

Bernard had so decisively rejected in the final section of *The Waves*. His vision of experience as chaotic and unpredictable, falsified or distorted by neatly contrived patterns that came down, plump, 'with all their feet on the ground' now began to exert its influence on *The Years*. Conversation (as opposed to constructed 'dialogue') became a haphazard business, often interrupted or tailing off into silence. The novel's sequences of argument were gradually rejected and rewritten, while Elvira's articulate social indignation gave way to Sara's fragments of nursery verse and rhyme, themselves a version of that 'little language' that Bernard had called for.[89] But as the novel opened itself further to chaos and uncertainty, to disruption and interruption, a firm framework was needed to clamp the different elements together. From an early stage, Woolf had structured her text around principles of change and repetition: 'I want to keep the individual & the sense of things coming over & over again & yet changing. Thats whats so difficult: to combine the two.'[90]

As the novel winds to its close, Eleanor has a sense of '*déjà vu*' as Nicholas says exactly what she had thought he was going to say, and she wonders 'Does everything then come over again a little differently? . . . If so, is there a pattern; a theme, recurring, like music; half remembered, half foreseen? . . . a gigantic pattern, momentarily perceptible? . . . But who makes it? Who thinks it?' [p.270] The nature of the pattern, the 'figure in the carpet', remains elusive, but the alternation and repetition of different kinds of movement do suggest the existence of some larger pattern or texture. The novel's forms of repetition are numerous and varied. Family faces reappear, and particular gestures – Eugenié's way of throwing out her hands, for example – seem to be unconsciously echoed by other people.[91] Particular objects – Eugenié's gilt-clawed chairs and her spotted mirror, or Martin's brush-backed walrus – turn up in different scenes,[92] while newspapers, newsboys or news placards appear in virtually every episode, often conveying some significant item of news – the reconsecration of Cologne Cathedral and the British election in 1880, Parnell's death in 1891, Edward VII's death in May 1910, or the picture of Mussolini which Eleanor tears up in the final episode.[93] Newspapers stand for the world of politics and external reality, of historical events as they determine individual lives. They became a significant feature of modernist writing, on display in the work of Eliot and Joyce.

In addition to the world of newspapers, there is a further world of phrases, echoes and literary allusions or quotations which interact with and comment upon the novel's action, offering yet another map of thought and feeling. In the 'Present Day' section, North opens a volume of 'The Complete Works of Shakespeare' near the beginning, and reads Sara a stage direction that seems to express her isolation: ' "The scene is a rocky island in the middle of the sea" ' [p.253] (Woolf would finally come to see the novel itself as just such 'an inaccessible Rocky Island which I cant explore, cant even think of'). Peggy, at the final party, takes a book off the shelf only to find lines that exactly express her own disgust with life.[94] Woolf made use of buried allusions and references at every stage of her work – it is part of her sense (and ours) of its depth. Elements of her meaning are always located offstage. A characteristic example occurs in the novel's closing lines, where, as dawn breaks, Eleanor watches a young couple get out of a taxi and go into a house on the opposite side of the square. As they open, and then shut, the door behind them, she finds in their action a sense of completion, the whole dance of life starting all over again. But their action completes a pattern that is largely outside the novel: the significance of 'opening the door' had inspired her speech to the National Society for Women's Service in January 1931; earlier still, in the last chapter of A Room (to which The Years was originally intended as a sequel), the narrator had watched a young couple getting into a taxi together. Finally, it seemed, they had arrived.[95]

The Years ends with a large party, celebrated with a shared meal that recalls comparable climaxes in Mrs Dalloway, To the Lighthouse and The Waves. Such scenes allowed Woolf to counterpoint the experience of the individual with that of the group, and to bring out the ceremonial, even sacramental nature of the occasion. Here, it is enhanced by a sense of the family as an epitome of society itself – within it, individuals take up positions as insiders or outsiders, exploiting, accepting or criticizing its workings. But the pleasure of community, especially dear to an older generation of 'insiders', is rejected, and a sense of bitterness and exclusion is felt by a younger generation of 'outsiders', particularly by Peggy and her brother North. Eleanor's conviction that life has changed for the better, that 'We're happier – we're freer' [p.283], gives place to Peggy's recognition that 'On every placard at every street corner, was Death; or worse – tyranny; brutality; torture; the fall of civilization; the end of freedom.' [p.284] Both Eleanor and Peggy recognize the need for 'another life', the chance to 'live differently'. That yearning becomes the burden of an unspoken chorus, as the future, in all its mystery, is signified by the coming of dawn, and a rather different 'chorus': the caretaker's children sing, producing a series of rhythmic sounds that have no meaning for their listeners. The noise they make is at once 'hideous', yet at the same time,

'Beautiful?' [Eleanor] said, with a note of interrogation, turning to Maggie.

'Extraordinarily,' said Maggie.

But Eleanor was not sure they were thinking of the same thing. [p.315][96]

The Years had begun with an impulse to explain to a younger generation how women's lives had changed during Woolf's lifetime. Eleanor, entranced by the world of modern 'conveniences' and rapid travel, is delighted and exhilarated by her release from the heart of the family into new-found freedoms. But her author knew that, although women had made great strides in terms of their professions, opportunities and personal freedom, no simple narrative of steady advance or progress could be written. If there had been gains, there had been as many losses. Peggy, the young doctor, who has apparently benefited from these social changes, is exhausted and embittered by her work, and both she and Eleanor recognize that their freedoms are threatened by the alarming economic and political developments of the 1930s. The 1917 episode anticipates this complex dialectic of gain and loss: set at the height of the war, during an air-raid, it opens a new and, in some respects, more optimistic movement in the book, as Eleanor and Nicholas become friends. Nicholas, Sara explains, 'ought to be in prison . . . Because he loves . . . the other sex'. He is identified not only as a foreigner, but also as a sexual outsider. Sara's close friendship with Nicholas, that of a woman with a gay man, recalls Virginia's love for Lytton Strachey, or perhaps Vanessa's for Duncan Grant. At the end of the evening, Nicholas proposes a toast 'to the New World', but Renny refuses to join in, feeling that he has ' "spent the evening sitting in a coal cellar while other people try to kill each other above my head"' [p.216].

Even Eleanor's pleasure in the post-war world is qualified in the 1921 episode, which Woolf later cut from her final text. Here an evening spent dining alone in London becomes steadily more disappointing and disillusioning, while the world of the young, which till then had appealed to Eleanor so much, suddenly depresses her. At the restaurant table, 'Things seemed to lose their meanings. That's an odd assembly of objects, she thought, dully observing the shapes and positions of the things on the table; though they were knife, fork and flower, they had for a moment lost their identity. Black marks on a white ground they seemed to be for a moment' – and with that definition, Woolf empties of meaning the very letters we are reading on the page, and yet almost immediately reverses the process, for they form 'a pattern: something fixed'. And Eleanor wonders, 'If there were a pattern . . . what would it be?', and 'How would it be . . . if this fork, this knife, this flower and my hand . . . were thought together by another mind, so that what seemed accidental . . . were in fact all one?' [p.397] At such a moment, the author almost emerges from behind her own text. Eleanor's evening ends in indignation at the oppressive heterosexuality of a couple kissing on a cinema poster, and an uncharacteristic loss of nerve, when she decides against walking home alone through the Park. An upsurge of irrational fear deprives her of that hard-won and highly symbolic freedom. In a moment of almost Yeatsian vision, Eleanor felt that 'there was no order, no purpose in the world, but all was tumbling to ruin beneath a perfectly indifferent polished moon.' [p.401][97]

From the earliest drafts, The Years had been defeatingly long, far too long for Woolf to hold it all in her head with her usual ease. She had recognized at every stage that it needed cutting, yet she had been so fascinated with it that she had made as many additions as deletions. Until late in 1935, she continued to feel reasonably confident of its value. But by March 1936, all such confidence deserted her, leaving her on a see-saw of uncertainty: 'acute despair on re-reading . . . complete failure', yet 'it may be my best book'; 'Book again very good; very bad yesterday'.[98] How far were her reactions justified? The Years is undoubtedly less consistent than earlier novels, in proportion to its greater length. But Woolf was now in her early fifties and these violent mood swings may have been an effect of the menopause: diary entries later that year (1936) describe the unpleasant sensations resulting from the 'T[ime] of L[ife]'.[99] For whatever reason, after more than three years' work, she had failed to bring her novel to a satisfactory conclusion. She realized that she could not go on revising piecemeal indefinitely. In bafflement and the beginning of despair, she did something she had never done before: with Leonard's agreement, and at considerable expense, she arranged for the printers R. & R. Clark to set up continuous 'galley' proofs, instead of the page proofs they normally set from her typescripts. She would carry out the final stage of revision on the galleys themselves.[100]

'[T]hese are disgusting, racking at the same time enervated days': for almost a month, from 10 March to 8 April 1936, she concentrated exclusively on revising and dispatching huge packages of typescript to the printers: 'Never again, never again.'[101] She had driven herself to the edge of a breakdown. Leonard took her down to Monk's House, where she lay in bed exhausted, suffering from headache, insomnia and weight loss – alarming and all too familiar signs. In May, her doctor agreed that she might take a holiday in the West Country (Leonard hoped that her beloved Cornwall would restore her spirits), but she was not much better on their return to London. Leonard took her back to Rodmell once more.[102]

But ill though she was – too ill to keep her diary or to see friends – she would not give up on her book. Quoting Flaubert, whose letters she was reading, she invoked art, patience and courage. 'Yet I see it now, as a whole: I think I can bring it off, . . . take each scene quietly: compose'. Looking back on the nightmare summer of 1936, she remembered 'every morning a headache, & forcing myself into that room in my nightgown; & lying down after a page: & always with the certainty of failure.' Looking back, a year later, it still seemed an 'agony . . . when I used to stumble out & cut up those proofs & write 3 lines, & then go back & lie on my bed – the worst summer in my life, but', she added, with a characteristic turn, 'the most illuminating.'[103] In despair, she was still determined to wrestle her monstrous text into submission. At some level, she knew that her problems with it were technical, rather than emotional. She had noticed earlier that '[t]he difficulty is always at the beginning of chapters or sections where a whole new mood has to be caught plumb in the centre.' To counteract these abrupt scene-shifts, she now added the 'interludes', the evocative scene-setting passages that open different sections, or effect transitions between different scenes.[104] She had made use of such openings before: they occur in *Night and Day*, and much more freely and fantastically in *Jacob's Room*, *Orlando* and, most recently, *The Waves*. As well as smoothing out the jumps and jerks of the narrative, such passages provided a link between the author's discourse and the narrative, or between symbolic and realistic modes (much as they had done in the hands of Dickens or George Eliot).

Woolf had pegged away at her proofs through the summer, seeing practically no one, lying quietly or sleeping, occasionally writing to Vanessa or to the fiercely devoted Ethel Smyth. It was the end of October 1936 before she felt strong enough to take up her diary again. Now, on Tuesday 3 November, she recorded how, in a state of 'stony but convinced despair', she had decided to 'carry the proofs, like a dead cat, to L. & tell him to burn them unread.' And so she did. She felt 'very tired. Very old. But at [the] same time content to go on these 100 years with Leonard.' Over lunch, she told him that she would pay back the cost of the proof-setting, and ask Bruce Richmond (the editor of the *Times Literary Supplement*) for some books to review. She felt defeated, 'no longer Virginia, the genius', yet at the same time relieved by her decision. Leonard (who was privately in a state of extreme anxiety about her) suggested that she might be wrong about the book. That Tuesday evening he began to read it, reaching the 1908 section, and finding it 'extraordinarily good – as good as any of them'. The following evening, he reached the end of the 1914 section, again pronouncing it 'extraordinarily good: very strange; very interesting; very sad'. At midnight on Thursday night, he finished it in silence and tears: it was 'a most remarkable book – he <u>likes</u> it better than The Waves & has not a spark of doubt that it must be published.'[105]

'Remarkable' was – and is – the right word: if it is not her greatest masterpiece, it is nevertheless a dense, intense novel, full of passion and, at times, compelling beauty. Contrasting his praise with her own despair, she feared that Leonard had exaggerated its merits, and wondered whether they ought to 'appeal to Morgan [E. M. Forster]'.

When she could accept it, Leonard's conviction seemed to her 'a miracle',[106] and she felt that she had never experienced such a startling reversal of feeling. But the real miracle had been her own perseverance in the face of illness and despair. Even now there were further revisions to be made: Leonard, with his publisher's eye, thought it was too long and sagged in the middle, so she cut from the proofs 'two enormous chunks' – a sequence from the end of the 1914 section that occurs in the early days of the war, with uniformed soldiers everywhere; Crosby takes two children for a walk, and Eleanor goes to the theatre. And she cut the longer and more significant 1921 episode, in which the now-widowed Kitty walks with Edward in Richmond Park. Kitty then returns to tea with Eleanor, and Eleanor herself spends an increasingly miserable evening dining in a bad restaurant in town (described above). These cuts spoilt the novel's proportions, both psychological and structural, as Woolf later explained to Stephen Spender. The scene of Eleanor's miserable evening qualifies her optimism in the 'Present Day' section, and both scenes help to balance the second half of the novel against the first. According to Woolf's original conception, there should have been twelve sections (as in *Mrs Dalloway*), with the eighth (1914), divided into May and September. With the omission of 1921, there were only eleven.[107]

Yet despite being pruned to the expectations of contemporary readers, *The Years* remains a remarkable achievement, and by the end of November, Virginia too felt she could quietly congratulate 'that terribly depressed woman, myself, whose head ached so often: who was so entirely convinced a failure; for in spite of everything I think she brought it off . . . How she did it, with her head like an old cloth I dont know.' The proofs, 'a sort of stinging nettle', were returned to Clarks in Edinburgh for the last time at the end of 1936, and Woolf scarcely gave them another thought, till two months later she crept past the Press table, averting her eyes from the piles of review copies waiting to be sent out.[108]

THE SECOND COMMON READER,
FLUSH, AND THE YEARS:
THE AFTERMATH

On 13 October 1932, two days after Woolf began The Years, The
Common Reader: Second Series *was published, but she was too deeply
absorbed in her 'Essay' (as it was then) to worry about its reception,
though she was pleased when Vita devoted much of a radio review of
new books to it: 'you said what I most wanted – not that I'm an
enchanting gossip, but that my standard is high.'*[109] *If its publication
scarcely caused her 'a single tremor', she had already felt several on
learning that Winifred Holtby's book about her had as its frontispiece
a snapshot taken by Leonard which she did not like, instead of a more
flattering studio portrait by the professional photographer Lenare: 'I
am revealed to the world (1,000 at most) as a plain dowdy old woman.'
Holtby's was the second account of Woolf's work published in 1932.
When the first,* Floris Delattre's Le roman psychologique de Virginia
Woolf, *had come out in March, she had warned herself, '[t]his is a
danger signal. I must not settle into a figure'.*[110] The Common Reader:
Second Series *cost ten shillings and sixpence, and sold a little over
3,300 copies in England in its first six months, and a little under that
amount in the US for the same period, according to Leonard's sums.
Its sales remained comparatively low until 1944, when it was published
in paperback by Penguin, at ninepence a copy, in a print-run of
50,000.*[111]

Flush, *by contrast, was a runaway success from the outset. Published
a year later, its dust-jacket followed the pattern of* Orlando, *and
contemporary expectations of biography, by providing a portrait of
its subject – in this case, a photograph of a cocker spaniel (probably
Pinka, given to Virginia by Vita in 1926). As publication day
approached, Woolf foresaw that this time she was going to be
depressed not so much by the book's failure as by its success. 'They'll
say its "charming" delicate, ladylike. And it will be popular ... And I
shall very much dislike the popular success of Flush.'*[112] *But what else
could she expect of a nation of dog-lovers? It appealed to precisely
those 'Middlebrow' readers that Woolf had least time for (as she had*

explained in an unpublished letter to the New Statesman *written the previous year). The* Daily Mail *reassured its readers that those 'who dread Mrs Woolf's "difficulties" need not alarm themselves' over her latest book.* Flush *sold over 18,000 copies in its first six months in the UK alone, and over 14,000 in the US. It was the Book Society's choice for October ('my opinion of the Book Society has sunk 10 degrees', she told Hugh Walpole), became the selection of the American Book-of-the-Month Club, and was serialized in the* Atlantic Monthly *from July to October. Alison Light has pointed out the irony that 'what began life as a coterie publication, a private joke, became her most accessible work, perhaps the only one to reach the common reader.'*[113]

'The problem will now be how to guide oneself through popularity: a curious reversal of my old problem; but I daresay the same.' Inevitably, there were brickbats among the bouquets: Rebecca West, in an embarrassed circumlocution, thought that Flush *was 'not one of the works over which Mrs Woolf's most devoted admirers will feel their greatest enthusiasm', while Geoffrey Grigson simply considered it her 'most tiresome book . . . yet'. On the other hand, David Garnett found it 'quite fresh' and 'as well proportioned as its subject was himself.' The important thing, Woolf told herself, was not to be petrified into fame or greatness, but to 'go on adventuring, changing, opening my mind & my eyes, refusing to be stamped & stereotyped.'*[114]

Yet despite its initial popularity (there was even talk of a film!), Flush, *perhaps with* Night and Day, *has become Woolf's most neglected fiction, and her own insistence that it was intended as a joke seems to have put off more readers than it has attracted.*[115] *While* Flush *looks back, on the one hand, to Kipling's sentimental yet brilliantly ventriloquized* Thy Servant a Dog *(1930), on the other hand, it looks forward to modern or even post-modern historicisms, as it relates the almost mythological love story of the Brownings, viewed, quite literally, from 'below'. Like* Orlando, Flush *made fun of eminent, and less eminent Victorians, and in this respect, at least, it can be read as a light-hearted overture to* The Years.

'Its going to be pretty bad, I'm certain . . . the point is that I myself know why its a failure, & that its failure is deliberate', Woolf told

herself, four days before The Years *was published, on 11 March 1937, reaching for a stratagem to defuse possible criticism. She had lost confidence in her ability to judge the book's value objectively during the prolonged revision process, and that confidence had never really returned: 'Honestly I do not know what to think of this book: is it good or bad? Honestly I am floored'.[116] The earliest reviews, in the* Times Literary Supplement *and* Time and Tide, *were encouraging, reassuring her that 'its <u>not</u> nonsense; it does make an effect. Yet of course not in the least the effect I meant'. The weekend brought a thoughtful review in the* Observer, *making her feel that at least one critic had tuned in to her wavelength. She began to consider whether she might not 'recast the rejected section of The Years for the Uniform Edition? Why do I bother? Only I rather suspect its needed for the whole argument impression.'[117]*

Though she no longer had Lytton's opinion or Roger Fry's to face, there were still dissentient voices amongst 'the praise chorus' 'almost universally' insisting (to her great surprise) that The Years *was 'a masterpiece'. The perceptive Scottish poet Edwin Muir, a great admirer, thought it a failure, and so did R. A. Scott James, reviewing it for Desmond MacCarthy's* Life and Letters. *The All Souls lawyer John Sparrow dismissed it as 'an ordinary book' in* The Spectator *but then cravenly wrote to ask her not to read his review. On the other hand, David Garnett and Howard Spring admired its poetic sensibility, while Maynard Keynes thought it her best book ever.[118] She had (she told Stephen Spender) 'wanted to catch the general readers attention', and she had succeeded, better than she dared to hope: 'it sells – best of all my novels'. The Press printed more than 23,000 copies, and in America it became a best-seller, with nearly 38,000 copies sold in the first six months. In 1945, a special Armed Services Edition was sold at a price of one cent each, with a print run of 156,700 copies.[119] Its success was partly due to its naturalistic mode, its representation of 'real' life, 'real' people, and a familiar middle-class world – and those features also partly explained her pleasure in writing it, during the first three years. She had at last composed a novel that was not merely a* succès d'estime, *but one that could be read and enjoyed by anyone.*

Oddly, the initial popularity of The Years *seems later to have undermined its critical standing, a phenomenon discussed by Leonard in his* Autobiography. *An extraordinarily, and sometimes painfully, truthful man, he had 'praised the book more than I should have done if she had been well', but privately thought it 'the worst book she ever wrote'. Its damaging effect on her health may have contributed to his dislike, but he also linked it to a wider theory about the nature of her art and the relative value of her writings. Commenting on the comparative neglect of* Orlando *and* The Years *by the early 1960s, he read from that 'the exact opposite of Gresham's law by which bad money drives out good' – i.e. Woolf's good novels were now driving out the weaker ones. For Leonard,* The Waves *was at once 'the most difficult and the best of all her books'. He believed that Virginia had written* The Years *as a response to the frequent criticism that she could not 'create real characters or the reality of life', and thought that her determination to produce a 'novel of fact' had driven her to write 'against the grain, to resist her own genius'.[120] Yet those closest to Woolf have sometimes held narrower views of her 'natural' bent than her varied achievements in a range of genres actually suggest. Leonard's sense of her as essentially a visionary writer (a view he shared with Clive Bell) was not wrong, but it was not an exclusive truth: it suggests that even Leonard sometimes subscribed to those myths of femininity as charming, intuitive and irrational that Virginia herself repudiated and anatomized in her two 'fact-bound' analyses of recent history,* The Years *and* Three Guineas. *When the feminist re-assessment of Woolf began in the 1970s, these two books were revalued, and their close relationship to one another and to feminism were regarded as a source of strength, especially after Mitchell Leaska published the 1880 holograph draft as* The Pargiters *in 1977.*

As if apologizing to or for herself, Woolf's diary several times suggested that the apparent simplicity of The Years *(and in consequence, its wide appeal) concealed some deeper purpose. It was 'a deliberate failure', it had not had the effect she intended, and 'no one has yet seen the point – <u>my</u> point'. Two letters to the young Stephen Spender promise to explain 'what I meant', yet fail to throw light on any intentions but the obvious ones – to give 'a picture of society as a whole', of the way the old fabric slowly gives place to the new, of 'a recurrence of some pattern'.[121] If there was indeed such a hidden*

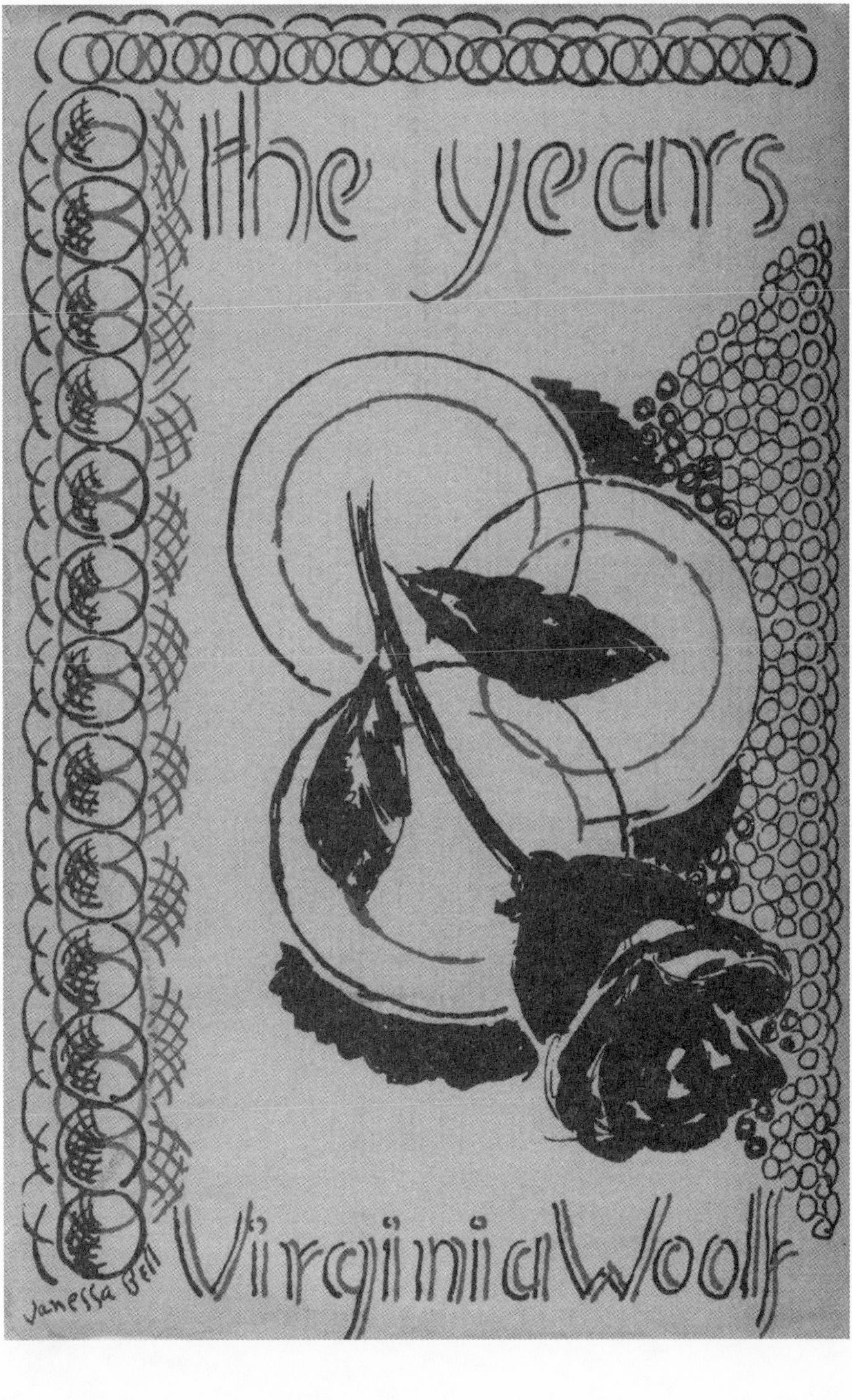
the years
Virginia Woolf
Vanessa Bell

'point' or pattern, it was surely the unseen but pervasive operation of patriarchy within English society – in other words, precisely the case she would argue with cool objectivity in Three Guineas.

12

Attacking Hitler in England[1]

Was Virginia Woolf anti-Semitic? And if so, can her anti-Semitism be distinguished from that of the society she belonged to, in which a degree of 'genteel anti-Semitism'[2] was so widespread as to be scarcely visible? Although it is a recurrent theme in her diaries, it was not until 1937–38 that she published work with an explicitly anti-Semitic content – at exactly the same moment as she was attacking fascist activity in Germany and Italy. The 'Present Day' episode of *The Years* includes a much-discussed scene between Sara, the hunchback, and her nephew North.[3] While they are having dinner together in her cheap lodgings, and North is reciting Marvell's poem 'The Garden' ('Society is all but rude/To this delicious solitude . . .'), they are interrupted by the sound of footsteps and bath water running. It's ' "[t]he Jew having a bath," she said . . . "And tomorrow there'll be a line of grease round the bath" '. She has to 'share a bath' with a fellow-lodger, a Jew called Abrahamson, who works in the tallow trade.

Sara is so disgusted by his proximity that she has seriously contemplated taking a job in order to escape from it, and indeed has got as far as visiting a newspaper office, with a letter of introduction, as she relates. North follows her narrative with some difficulty, but supposes she 'meant that she was poor, that she must earn her living'. The manuscript version of this scene makes it clear that working in a newspaper office would have resulted in another, and more damaging form of contamination, not of the body but of the brain: Sara would have had to sell her writing, and thus to 'prostitute' herself intellectually, to commit 'adultery' of the brain, and that she cannot bring herself to do.[4] Sara's singsong repetition, 'the Jew's in my bath', and North's exclamation, 'Pah!' ('other people's hairs made him feel

INDEX

physically sick') produce a nausea that the narrative does little to diminish – in fact it emphasizes the noise, dirt and sordidness of the lodging house, its locale, and even of the Thames flowing nearby.[5] Sara's dilemma – having to choose between the purity of the body or of the mind – is so appealingly neat that Woolf might simply have overlooked the myth of Jewish contamination on which it depends.

In the absence of any clear narrative directive, Woolf's defenders argue that this episode was intended to expose rather than endorse the myth of Jewish contamination here displayed.[6] It would be easier to agree if Sara did not so often embody the independent and morally desirable attitudes of the outsider: in her earlier incarnation as 'Elvira', Woolf had consciously identified with her. It is Sara, after all, who accepts and loves the foreigner and homosexual (and possibly even Jewish) Nicholas. But if the significance of this episode is impossible to decide, that of Woolf's short story 'The Duchess and the Jeweller', written in 1932 but revised and published in spring 1938, is only too explicit. Woolf could scarcely have failed to see its implications, especially as they were pointed out to her by the New York literary agent Jacques Chambrun, who had asked her for a story. Chambrun initially accepted her synopsis, but then rejected it on the grounds that his client would find this 'psychological study of a Jew' racist, and therefore unacceptable.[7] Inevitably, it was Leonard who intervened to effect a compromise, persuading Virginia to cut the more explicit references to the Jeweller's Jewishness, and Chambrun to accept her changes.

Woolf was revising 'The Duchess and the Jeweller' in August 1937, in the intervals of writing *Three Guineas*, in which she was to point out parallels between the persecution of women and the persecution of Jews:

Now you are being shut out, you are being shut up, because you are Jews, because you are democrats, because of race, because of religion . . . The whole iniquity of dictatorship, whether in Oxford or Cambridge, in Whitehall or Downing Street, against Jews or against women, in England, or in Germany, in Italy or in Spain is now apparent to you. [p.228][8]

So what was she thinking of when she published this story? How could she fail to connect her caricature of a Jew with the anti-Semitic propaganda of the Nazis? Had the racist myths on which her story depended become invisible to her? And to Leonard?

Woolf had originally written 'The Duchess and the Jeweller' in the curious state of exhaustion and uncertainty that followed *The Waves*. Like 'The Shooting Party', another satire on the upper classes, it was intended for a book of 'Caricatures' or 'Scenes from English Life'. The Duchess of Lambourne cheats the Jeweller, while bribing him with an invitation to her weekend house party, knowing that he has fallen in love with her daughter. He buys ten pearls from her for twenty thousand pounds (a very large sum, in those days), suspecting that they are fakes, yet being willingly deceived. The pearls themselves, 'like the eggs of some heavenly bird', recall Vita Sackville-West, who always wore pearls that Virginia loved to play with, knotting them 'into heaps of great lustrous eggs'. And the Duchess herself suggests Vita's cantankerous mother: in April 1928, Lady Sackville-West had accused Vita of selling the pearls she had given her and replacing them with false ones. She had then forced Vita to cut up her pearl necklace and hand over the twelve largest.[9]

Although the Duchess in the story cheats the Jew, thus 'winning' the unspoken contest between them, the Jeweller combines two threatening racial stereotypes: that of the Jew at the bottom of society, breeding in the East End slums (he had begun his career selling stolen dogs in Whitechapel, recalling the fourth chapter of *Flush*), and that of the Jew as banker and political conspirator, masterminding international finance (he is 'the richest jeweller in England'). Even after Woolf's revisions and excisions, his racial identity is never in doubt:

his nose, which was long and flexible, like an elephant's trunk, seemed to say by its curious quiver at the nostrils (but it seemed as if the whole nose quivered, not only the nostrils) that he was not satisfied yet; still smelt something under the ground a little further off. Imagine a giant hog in a pasture rich with truffles.[10]

As if to underline this comparison with an animal that Jews consider unclean, his name is 'Oliver Bacon'.

Different kinds of apology may be offered for this story: the Duchess's success in deceiving the Jeweller may be intended to expose the English upper classes as even more ruthless than the financiers who sustain them; and in any case, this is hardly Woolf's best or most serious writing. Yet a tendency to stereotype Jews was visible in her work as early as 1909, as a recently discovered notebook reveals. In it, Virginia Stephen described a certain Mrs Loeb, a society hostess and the widow of a German-Jewish businessman, as a 'fat Jewess' who wished to ingratiate herself with her company, but whose food 'swam in oil and was nasty', and whose social aims – men and marriage – 'seemed very elementary, very little disguised, and very unpleasant'.[11] In 1912, she had warned two close friends, Violet Dickinson and Janet Case, that she was about to marry 'a penniless Jew', no doubt insuring against their possible disappointment that the clever and beautiful daughter of Sir Leslie Stephen hadn't made a more successful match from a worldly point of view. Twenty years later, she told Ethel Smyth (from a similar social background as herself) in a much-quoted letter how she had 'hated marrying a Jew – how I hated their nasal voices, and their oriental jewellery, and their noses and their wattles', while adding, 'what a snob I was: for they have immense vitality, and I think I like that quality best of all'. Yet their very vitality had its sinister aspect. 'They cant die – they exist on a handful of rice and a thimble of water – their flesh dries on their bones but still they pullulate, copulate, and amass . . . millions of money.' In terms of race and class, at least, she was very much the insider – and that was no small source of her attraction for Leonard.[12]

Leonard, like so many German and some British Jews, was in love with the host culture. He had assimilated to it, becoming a member of the British Colonial Service, and subsequently dedicating his life to socialist politics in Britain with an unhesitating patriotic fervour. As the first Jewish member of the Cambridge 'Apostles' group, his friends were typically upper-middle-class Englishmen, whose anti-Semitic views he absorbed and exposed in his early fiction. It was Leonard's description of the Jewish nose in his short story 'Three Jews', Leonard's assertion of Jewish energy in his novel *The Wise Virgins*[13] that Virginia echoed, perhaps feeling (if she thought about it at all) that if Leonard wrote thus about his own race, there could be 'no offence, no offence in the world' in following his example. She found it difficult to like his family, as repeated diary entries reveal. No doubt they represented in exaggerated form those elements that she found most alien in Leonard himself (as in-laws so often do). The name of the Jew in Sara's bath – Abrahamson – is not only a generic name for the sons of Abraham; it was also that of Leonard's first cousin, Sir Martin Abrahamson.[14] Woolf's anti-Semitism is characteristic of her class and her moment – casual, unsystematic, and apparently thoughtless. It was as invisible to her as sexism was to the rest of Bloomsbury.

Woolf's feminism offended her friends, who liked to think that they treated women as equals. E. M. Forster, a novelist genuinely sympathetic to women, criticized her 'spots of feminism' in his commemorative Rede lecture, regarding them as a throwback to women's struggle for political recognition before the First World War, and thus inappropriate to the 1930s.[15] But for Woolf, male chauvinism looked more dangerous than ever in the 1930s, and she was determined to take the arguments of A Room of One's Own a stage further. The result was Three Guineas, a wide-ranging critique of patriarchy and its outcomes in domestic oppression, separate spheres, militarism and imperialism – a book that would take another thirty years or more before it was fully understood or appreciated. Then, its utopian vision of an outsiders' society, and its analysis of the links between constructions of masculinity and war, would speak with urgency to a new generation of readers attempting to prevent new wars.[16] Today Three Guineas is generally recognized as a founding document in the history of gender studies.

Its critique of patriarchy sprang from Woolf's youth, going back at least to 1902, when she had taken Greek lessons with Janet Case, and they had first studied Sophocles' Antigone together – a play that seemed to accumulate meaning for her as she grew older (it was central to The Years, where Sara reads a translation of it in bed in the 1907 episode). Its heroine stands out against the political might of the dictator Creon, determined to give her brother proper burial.[17] Janet Case was herself a strong and independent thinker, and as a young girl, Virginia had harboured a crush on her teacher: 'how I loved her . . . & how I went hot & cold going to Windmill Hill: & how great a visionary part she has played in my life'. They had remained friends ever since, and it was Janet who had first encouraged Virginia to undertake voluntary work on behalf of the suffrage movement in 1910. As Woolf drafted

Three Guineas, in the early months of 1937, Janet lay dying. Woolf paid her a last visit, and later wrote an affectionate obituary of her for *The Times*.[18] Janet's inspiring feminism, the haphazard nature of education for girls, and the heroism of Antigone would all be woven into the fabric of her polemic.

Three Guineas crystallized a number of ideas that had figured in Woolf's fiction from the early days. Her short story 'The Mark on the Wall' had mocked the hierarchies of *Whitaker's Almanack* as symbolic of the establishment and its patriarchal attitudes ('Everybody follows somebody, such is the philosophy of Whitaker'). Another early story, 'A Society', concerns a group of young women who set out to study British institutions, including the universities and the professions (thus anticipating the Society of Outsiders in *Three Guineas*). As they denounce their various shortcomings, the First World War breaks out, making their critique of how men misuse knowledge, and how badly they run things, even more painfully pointed: ' "Oh, Cassandra . . . let us devise a method by which men may bear children! It is our only chance." '[19]

The penultimate chapter of *Jacob's Room* had represented society as a procession, which could not be opposed or held back ('one must follow, one must not block the way'), and the image of that procession haunts both *The Years* (at one stage, Woolf considered calling it 'The Caravan') and *Three Guineas*.[20] *Mrs Dalloway* had analysed the centre and the margins of political power, locating Clarissa herself within them, while *To the Lighthouse* had explored the pleasures and frustrations of the patriarchal family, and the ideology that underpinned its workings. The struggle between Mrs Ramsay and Lily Briscoe, between nineteenth- and twentieth-century outlooks, would be played out again in *Orlando* and *A Room of One's Own*; even *The Waves* had begun as an exploration of feminine consciousness. Indeed, Woolf had been enquiring as to 'What is really the woman's angle?' from the outset of her career, but always, as with *The Years*, 'the fiction came first'.[21] Now she was ready to marshal some of her conclusions.

It was not till the beginning of January 1935, when she had been working on *The Years* for two years and more, that she finally decided 'now I want to write On being despised', while recognizing that she could not begin work on it until the novel was finished. Ultimately, she would regard *The Years* and *Three Guineas* as 'one book – as indeed they are'. In the meantime, Princess Elizabeth Bibesco (daughter of the former Prime Minister, Asquith) had invited her to join a committee organizing an anti-fascist exhibition. When Woolf asked what provision there would be to represent women under fascism, the Princess had replied, somewhat high-handedly, 'I am afraid it had not occurred to me that in matters of ultimate importance even feminists could wish to segregate and label the sexes'. Woolf replied, 'What about Hitler?', meaning hadn't Hitler done just that? Their argument became a turning point in her thinking, and the following month, she felt 'plagued by the sudden wish to write an Anti fascist Pamphlet'. She talked it over with Leonard.[22]

At the same time, she was steadily collecting ammunition for her feminist polemic – 'enough powder to blow up St Pauls', as she put it. More was supplied when she bumped into E. M. Forster in the London Library, and he introduced the subject of women on the Library Committee. Suspecting that they intended to ask her to join as a token woman (Leslie Stephen had been President of the Library from 1892), she recalled Mrs Green having sat on the Committee. At this point, the Assistant Librarian chimed in: ' "Yes yes – there was Mrs Green. And Sir Leslie Stephen said, never again. She was so troublesome. And I said, haven't ladies improved? But they were all quite determined. No no no, ladies are quite impossible. They wouldnt hear of it." ' Furious at having her nose rubbed 'in that pail of offal' (her father's sexism?), Woolf immediately began making up her feminist pamphlet, but stopped a few days later when it seemed to be interfering with her novel. That spring her diary seems to consider a feminist pamphlet and an anti-fascist pamphlet as two separate projects; but they were growing steadily closer.[23]

She was about to encounter fascism at first hand: in May 1935 she and Leonard planned to drive through Germany, en route from Holland to Austria, on their way to Rome, 'concealing Leonard's nose', as she put it. Apparently the Foreign Office was advising Jews not to travel in Germany, so Leonard consulted Ralph Wigram, a Sussex neighbour who worked in the Foreign Office. Wigram said privately it was 'nonsense', but advised them not to get mixed up in

Nazi party demonstrations. At the same time, he admitted that he had found Hitler himself very frightening. Woolf was struck by his reaction: 'having seen this mad dog, the thin rigid Englishmen are really afraid. And if we have only nice public schoolboys like W[igram]. to guide us, there is some reason I suppose to expect that Oxford Street will be flooded with poison gas one of these days.'[24]

In the event, any difficulties Leonard might have encountered in Hitler's Germany were unexpectedly dissolved by the charm of Mitz the marmoset. Leonard, a great animal-lover, had rescued her from Victor Rothschild. In return, Mitz adored him, and liked to sit on his shoulder whenever possible. Everywhere the Woolfs drove, they were greeted by a sentimental outcry at the 'kleine apzi', and no one, apparently, looked too closely at Leonard. Quite by accident, they did exactly what Ralph Wigram had warned them not to do: driving along the Rhine, they found themselves in the middle of a public reception for Göring, and surrounded by lines of uniformed Nazis and school-children waving flags. The marmoset received the Nazi salute. So it was with some justification that T. S. Eliot later asked for 'the mar-mozets view of Germany'. But in Germany, the Woolfs had seen the writing on the wall, quite literally – banners and placards announcing 'The Jew is our enemy' and 'Jews are not wanted in . . .' On her return, Woolf told Victoria Ocampo, who was planning to translate *A Room of One's Own* into Spanish, that she wanted 'to write a sequel to it, denouncing Fascism: but must finish my novel first'.[25]

The second chapter of *A Room* had already identified a link between war and women's admiration of men: women served as looking-glasses, 'reflecting the figure of man at twice its natural size'. Such inflation was 'essential to all violent and heroic action. That is why Napoleon and Mussolini both insist so emphatically upon the inferi-ority of women, for if they were not inferior, they would cease to enlarge.' *Three Guineas* would also take up what was for Woolf an even more fundamental question: what was the cause of misogyny – the male anger with and hatred of women? *A Room* had light-heartedly speculated as to whether the misogynistic Professor von X might have 'been laughed at, to adopt the Freudian theory, in his cradle by a pretty girl?' She already recognized that its origins must lie beneath conscious thought. *Three Guineas* offers a more searching account of it, deriving it from an 'infantile fixation', though that term is never really explained or explored. Woolf's final novel would return to this question, and address it in greater depth, but for the present (despite misgivings), her chosen weapon was polemic.[26]

History had not stood still since Woolf first conceived her book 'about the sexual life of women: to be called Professions for Women perhaps', back in January 1931.[27] Even then, the Depression and unemployment were beginning to bite; Mussolini had been established in Italy since 1922. In the 1930s, Japan invaded China; Hitler became Chancellor of Germany in 1933, and a year later disposed of his rivals; Italy invaded Abyssinia late in 1935, and the following summer, Franco besieged the elected Republican government in Madrid. All over the world, the imperialist dictators were flexing their muscles for action. England had its own fascist party, led by Oswald Mosley, but it had met with a growing distrust of nationalism among an increasingly politicized middle class.

Instead, a longing for peace seemed to grip the country; pacifism had gained ground in the early 1930s, especially on the left. Despite Hitler's programme of remilitarization, the British government, tightly pressed for money, put off rearming. While young people were joining the Communist Party, committing themselves to an international cause, their parents, who had survived the Great War, felt that 'it must never happen again', and regarded the pre-war arms build-up as a contributory cause. Pamphlets exposing the interests of arms manufacturers (such as *The Secret International* and its sequel, *Patriotism Ltd*) were widely read and discussed: did arms manufacturers foment or even cause wars? Certainly they were its only beneficiaries. In February 1933, the Oxford Union voted against fighting for King and Country. In 1934, Dick Sheppard founded the Peace Pledge Union, whose members promised not to fight or support another war. Within Woolf's immediate circle, Aldous Huxley and Bertrand Russell were actively campaigning for peace.[28] Leonard Woolf had hoped that the League of Nations would provide collective security (he had been one of its founders); but Hitler had taken Germany out of the League, and by 1935 it had failed to prevent Mussolini's invasion of Abyssinia – indeed, it was looking increasingly toothless. Closely involved in the formation of the Labour Party's foreign policy, Leonard now recognized that Britain would have to rearm, if her views were to carry any weight in the wider world.

The earliest refugees from Germany had been horrified at what was happening there: the great conductor Bruno Walter spoke to Virginia of 'this awful reign of intolerance' that was transforming his beloved country. The rest of the world should unite to condemn it: 'We must say that they are uncivilised ... we must make them feel themselves outcasts – not by fighting them; by ignoring them' – the Nazis must be treated like so many naughty children showing off (something of this response would be echoed in *Three Guineas* where the Outsiders pledge themselves to indifference, in the face of military activity). However, another refugee, the playwright Ernst Toller, thought that the allies should declare war on Hitler without further delay.[29]

Rearmament and support for the League of Nations were key issues at the 1935 Labour Party Conference. With Leonard, Virginia attended on 1 October and saw the party leader, George Lansbury, resign after declaring his commitment to Christian pacifism (two days later, Mussolini finally invaded Abyssinia). Woolf felt her 'sympathies were with [Dr Alfred] Salter who preached non-resistance. He's quite right'. But Leonard thought otherwise: he was impatient with the Party for refusing to recognize the necessity of rearming against Hitler. By mid-October the 'pamphlet' she was planning had become 'The Next War', and was causing her 'wild excitement': 'the result of the L[abour]. P[arty]. at Brighton was the breaking of that dam between me & the new book, so that I couldn't resist dashing off a chapter'. The pressure to get on with it was so intense, it felt 'like being harnessed to a shark'.[30]

The link between feminism and pacifism was not a new one for Woolf, nor for other feminists of her generation. The First World War had split the Women's Movement between patriots and pacifists, a split almost more painful than the earlier question as to whether to fight for the vote inside or outside the law. Mrs Pankhurst's own family divided when her younger daughter Sylvia declared herself a pacifist. Woolf (like her friends Janet Case and Margaret Llewelyn Davies) was a committed pacifist, and despised the jingoism displayed by ex-suffragettes when they urged young men to join up – and handed them white feathers if they did not. The penultimate chapter of *Jacob's Room* had referred obliquely to the difficult women's meeting on

4 August 1914, at which women's duties in wartime had been debated, and the issue comes up again in the 'Present Day' section of *The Years*. Kitty asserts 'Force is always wrong', but then remembers she may be upsetting her cousin Rose, who had been imprisoned as a suffragette, and had afterwards actively supported the war effort, as so many of them had. '"She smashed his window," [Rose's brother] Martin jeered at her, "and then she helped him to smash other people's windows. Where's your decoration, Rose?"' Woolf understood, while regretting, the pent-up frustration that caused women to throw themselves into recruiting or nursing. Now patriotism, militarism and imperialism were on the upsurge once again, and all her instincts were against them. Preventing 'the Next War' was the urgent task.[31]

And not for her alone. A symposium published in 1932, *Man, Proud Man*, including essays by Rebecca West, Sylvia Townsend Warner, G. B. Stern and others, had examined different aspects of male militarism, and the backlash against women's emancipation under fascist regimes, in the years following the Great War. Other writings of the period, such as Winifred Holtby's 'Black Words for Women Only', had argued the centrality of gender politics to fascist ideology, while her play, *Take Back Your Freedom*, links war to gender construction. Holtby also contributed 'An Apology for Armourers' to Storm Jameson's collection of peace essays, *The Challenge to Death* (1934). Women novelists foresaw dark futures under totalitarianism in Naomi Mitchison's *We Have Been Warned* (1935), Storm Jameson's *In the Second Year* (1936), and Katherine Burdekin's sequence, *Proud Man* (1934), *The End of this Day's Business* (written 1935, published 1989) and *Swastika Night* (1937). A more realistic novelist, Phyllis Bottome, portrayed daily life in contemporary Germany in *This Mortal Storm* (1937), the story of a German-Jewish family in Munich between 1932 and 1934. It is difficult to tell whether Woolf had read all or any of these, since she could well have reached the same conclusions independently. '[W]hy do I always fight shy of my contemporaries?' she asked herself, and 'Why does so much of this seem to me in the air?'[32]

By the end of the year, she suddenly saw 'how to make my war book – to pretend its all the articles editors have asked me to write during the past few years – on all sorts of subjects. Sh[oul]d. women smoke.

Short skirts. War – &c. This w[oul]d give me the right to wander: also put me in the position of the one asked. And excuse the method: while giving continuity.' Four days later, the project was renamed 'Answers to Correspondents', and for much of 1936, she warned herself not to 'stop & make it up', 'to read as few weekly papers . . . as possible'. But it continued to unwind in her head, and by March had become a single 'Letter to an Englishman . . . because after all separate letters break continuity so'. By April, it was 'Two Guineas', and by November, 'Three'.[33]

Today, 'Three Guineas' is Woolf's most puzzling title. A guinea was the name for a gold coin worth one pound and one shilling, but the coin itself had not been in circulation since 1813. Even so, certain professional fees, in particular those of lawyers and doctors, as well as horse-racing prizes and subscriptions to societies were still charged in guineas. Three guineas, in particular, seems to have been a standard medical consultation fee: in a long and largely abandoned scene in *The Years* manuscript between Rose Pargiter, Maggie and Elvira (later, the 1910 episode), Rose counters Elvira's arguments for contraception by pointing out that the women on the street below were too poor to be able to afford it: 'But I don't see that woman down there going to Harley Street? With three guineas?'[34]

When the crisis of *The Years* was finally resolved in November 1936, Woolf felt free at last to make a tentative start on *Three Guineas*. A week earlier, an old friend, the Conservative politician and peace-worker Lord Robert Cecil, had come to tea. In the course of their conversation, he had dismissed Bertrand Russell's extreme pacifism as 'Complete insanity! To tell us we are to submit to Hitler!' He was more 'convinced by Winston [Churchill]', who was urging rearmament, but Winston, he thought, did not command wide respect: 'He changes his mind & policy'. For Woolf, Cecil was the '[b]est type of Eng[lish] Governing class . . . the flower of 19th Century civilisation',[35] yet that was also part of the problem – the government of England was still in the hands of conscientious gentlemen who could no more deal with ruthless political opportunists than fly.

Woolf began *Three Guineas* in earnest on 28 January 1937, and took a little over a year to complete it. It came quickly, and she did not experience any of the difficulties that had held up the writing of

The Waves or *The Years*, for example. Within three weeks, she had written thirty-eight pages, and forecast that 'once I get into the canter ... I shall see only the flash of the white rails & pound along to my goal.' Recording her progress in her diary, Woolf often lapsed into racing metaphors, taking a little canter or a gallop at it, unless she felt 'jaded', or was 'dismal[ly] hacking'.[36] Composing *The Years*, she had often felt herself 'in flood', as if she were a river or pool, suddenly filled up, or herself filling up the dry waste of pages. The riding metaphors, by contrast, imply a more deliberate exertion of control, and that difference is felt in the text itself: *Three Guineas* is further from fiction than most of her work, yet at the same time more consciously contrived. Its strenuous prose is a strength paid for with a certain loss of lightness and spontaneity.

Beginning *The Years* in its novel-essay form, Woolf had declared that though history was easier to write, 'I prefer, where truth is important, to write fiction'. Although *The Years* had employed fictional methods, it had remained determinedly committed to facts: 'I am not making an empty boast if I say that there is not a statement in it that cannot be verified'.[37] Facts, in the form of quotations and examples, carefully filed or pasted newspaper cuttings and the extracts from biography and autobiography that she had collected and copied out from the beginning of the decade, now provided the building blocks from which to construct the argument of *Three Guineas*.

She had been keeping 'cock a doodle dum' scrapbooks into which she pasted 'history in the raw' – photos, newspaper articles or passages typed out from her reading, illustrating the absurdities or injustices of patriarchy, fascism and domestic tyranny, at home and abroad. Like the outsider in *Three Guineas*, she evidently took three daily and three weekly newspapers in order to 'know the facts'.[38] These scrapbooks of cuttings became the seedlings from which *Three Guineas* would grow: not only did they provide the starting point for many of its lines of argument, but also the illustrations on which those arguments depended; and, more important still, they suggested a structural method, since Woolf had arranged her cuttings so that they commented on one another, multiplying each other's meanings. Thus the scrapbook sets the arrest of Frau Pommer for her denunciation of 'the thorn of hatred' next to a speech in which Hitler announces that Germany is 'A nation of men' (both cuttings from *The Times*, 12 August 1935), and beside them both she set a photo of Count Ciano (Mussolini's son-in-law), looking very handsome and gallant in flying gear. A photo of four trumpeters 'proclaiming the coronation of King Edward in London' is set opposite a picture of four women in elaborate hats at the races (both from the *Daily Telegraph*, 30 May 1936), while a photo of the Pope seated in state 'on his throne in St Peter's Rome' takes the comparison a step further.[39]

Three Guineas makes use of the scrapbooks' method of juxtaposing pictures to create a hierarchy of representations, in which the various 'letters to correspondents', the pictures and photos described and contrasted in the text, the endnotes, and the five glossy photographs that accompany the text, are all structured and enfolded, one round another. Thus Woolf's 'anti-fascist pamphlet' ultimately came to frame and subordinate the narrower issues of sexism in Britain, although her argument identified fundamental connections between the two. Close to the physical centre of her enquiry she set the crucial question, 'Should we not help [woman] to crush [the patriarchal oppressor] in our own country before we ask her to help us to crush him abroad?' [p.176]

Woolf's 'Answers to Correspondents' structure allowed her to frame her discussion as a response to a letter inviting her to support a society for the prevention of war (a note comments on the numerous 'manifestos and questionnaires issued broadcast during the years 1936–7'[40]). Beneath this overriding issue, she sets her two leading yet necessarily subsidiary concerns about the position of middle-class women, or as she terms them throughout, 'the daughters of educated men' – concerns with women's higher education, and their subsequent entry into the professions. These are set out in the form of begging letters she has received, the first asking for a contribution to Newnham College, Cambridge from its Principal (Pernel Strachey), and the second inviting a contribution from her sister, the Secretary of the National Society of Women's Service, committed to advancing women in the professions (Pippa Strachey, Pernel's actual sister). There was a certain symmetry in this scheme, since *A Room* had originated in a lecture Woolf gave to the Arts Society of Newnham in October 1928, while *Three Guineas* (and *The Years*) had begun as a lecture given to

319

Pippa's Society on 21 January 1931, when Woolf had shared the platform with her friend Ethel Smyth. Her carefully defined objections to donating a guinea to each of these three causes, also set out largely in the form of letters, make up much of her argument. Answering the various letters (there are twelve in all) provides the necessary element of fiction: in doing so, she adopted a neutral and impersonal voice, quite distinct from her own.[41]

The first chapter of *Three Guineas* focuses, as does the opening (1880) section of *The Years*, on the oppression of women in the home, by family life, and their consequent need to escape. Beginning with Mary Kingsley's claim that 'being allowed to learn German was *all* the paid-for education I ever had' [p.118] (also quoted in the 'Second Essay' of *The Pargiters*), Woolf develops the case earlier made in *The Pargiters*, that women contributed to the high costs of their brothers' education: for some 'daughters of educated men', the pleasures and privileges of attending Oxford or Cambridge must have appeared as so many deprivations – so many 'petticoats with holes in them, cold legs of mutton, and the boat train starting for abroad while the guard slams the door in their faces.' [p.119][42] Woolf recounts men's opposition to women's higher education, both in the past (Walter Bagehot's disobliging response to Emily Davies, again referred to in the 'Second Essay' of *The Pargiters*, appears here in full) and in the present (Cambridge did not award women degrees until 1948). And since Oxbridge education appears to promote, rather than diminish, male aggression, perhaps women should take 'Rags, petrol, matches', and burn the colleges down instead, while the daughters of educated men dance round the bonfire.[43]

This chapter confronts the issue of gender difference, showing how differently war appears to men than it does to women, who are seldom tempted to join in. Investigating women's relations with (male) political power, Woolf examines the nature of feminine influence, showing how it had changed since 1919, when women were first permitted to enter the professions. A further example of gender difference lies in attitudes to dress: Mr Justice MacCardie had commented patronizingly that ' "Dress, after all, is one of the chief methods of women's self-expression . . . In matters of dress women often remain children to the end." . . . The Judge who thus dictated', Woolf informs us, 'was wearing a scarlet robe, an ermine cape, and a vast wig of artificial curls.' Male ceremonial dress (on display in the accompanying photographs) exposes links between war, male rivalry and ceremonial display.[44]

Woolf had reacted to the First World War by becoming a pacifist, but her analysis of domestic oppression shows why so many other women had been so eager to embrace the new opportunities provided by the war. It had given them a popular cause to support, and the chance to take on paid work, with all the benefits of fresh company and financial independence that paid work conferred – advantages that men had traditionally been reluctant to share. The first chapter concludes that while 'consciously [women] desired "our splendid Empire"; unconsciously [they] desired our splendid war' [p.161] in order to escape domestic oppression. If higher education does nothing more than release women from ignorance and the tyranny of the family, that is justification enough – and so she writes a cheque for the first guinea.

The second chapter focuses upon women's entry into the professions, and the linked question, still relevant today, of why they are so often underpaid and under-promoted. *Whitaker's Almanack*, which listed civil servants and their salaries, is called in evidence of prejudice against women at work, though women at home, then as now, are paid nothing at all, and so depend on their husbands for maintenance. She argued that women whose profession was marriage and motherhood should be supported by the state.[45] As in the first chapter, the disadvantages of professional life (seen as 'joining the procession') are weighed against its advantages, but Woolf argues women's unpaid-for education has taught them to think independently, so they may be able to join the male professional world while avoiding its more damaging consequences. Thus equipped with minds of their own and disinterested influence, they might indeed be able to help prevent war – and so the second guinea is also sent off.

The third chapter reverts to the opening request for help in preventing war. If women are to defend their newly gained freedoms, it must not be with men's weapons. If culture and intellectual liberty are to be achieved, women must not commit 'adultery of the brain' or 'prostitute their minds' for money. They must think for themselves, use what they have learned from their own history, and resist being drawn into the male 'procession'. Instead, they must constitute a Society of Outsiders, free of all 'unreal loyalties', including patriotism. The history of women's exclusion and oppression should warn men of the comparable dangers threatened by the fascist state. Finally Woolf returns to the problem that runs all the way through her text, that of separate spheres, in which men occupy the public and women the private realms – a separation actively reinforced by fascism. She demonstrates conclusively 'that the public and the private worlds are inseparably connected; that the tyrannies and servilities of the one are the tyrannies and servilities of the other.' [p.270]

But outlining the main arguments of *Three Guineas* gives little idea of the vitality, resonance and play of the text itself. Writing *The Years* had shown Woolf the value of repetition as a structural device, but its use in *Three Guineas* demonstrates a larger, and more alarming historical truth. 'Things repeat themselves it seems. Pictures and voices are the same to-day as they were 2,000 years ago.' Frau Pommer is a latter-day Antigone who also stands up to be counted. If 'there were no progress in the human race, but only repetition', then 'war is imminent', and 'again its 1914'. And perhaps the new war arises from the same old causes as the last one: the refrain. 'Three hundred millions spent upon war' is repeated seven times in the course of the text.[46] Woolf streamlines her argument by using a series of metonymic images: 'the procession' stands for work within the traditional patriarchal professions, while the narrator is poised on the threshold or bridge between the old world and the new, between private and public worlds, between the capitalism of the city and the government of the state. The 'mulberry tree' (echoing the nursery rhyme's 'bush') stands for 'the sacred tree' of wealth and property, though on its final appearance it has become 'the poison tree of intellectual harlotry' (recalling William Blake). At the lowest level, the repetition of three dots . . . (a convention which had always amused Woolf), becomes the visual code indicating imposed silence or interruption, doubt or hesitation.[47]

Of the many images employed in *Three Guineas*, the photographs of the Spanish Civil War are the most emotive, standing for the atrocities of war, and its legacy of dead children and ruined houses. But they take their place within a larger system of comparisons, in which the reader (like Hamlet's mother) must 'Look here upon this picture, and on this'. The several pictures are, of course, evoked in words. Some of these are simply 'pictures of other people's lives and minds', that is to say, quotations from biographies, histories or newspapers, while others are 'pictures of actual facts; photographs'. '[L]ooking at the picture of the lives of others' is intended to show how difference, and in particular gender difference, can alter one's point of view, so that 'though we look at the same things, we see them differently' [p.119]. While different viewpoints are used to develop the argument, the provision of pictures (whether in the form of quotations, or photographs) encourages an element of independent judgement, as if, with the evidence before us, we might be free to reach different conclusions. Woolf was always uneasy with the coercive nature of rhetoric, and here the different layers of illustrations within the text and the endnotes help her readers to follow her arguments, and widen the basis of the discussion.

The actual photographs of the Spanish Civil War that Woolf describes have not been finally identified, though they were probably a set of photographs of children killed during a German air raid on Getafe, near Madrid on 30 October 1936 (the fascist forces were besieging the republican government in Madrid). Woolf received 'a packet of photographs from Spain all of dead children, killed by bombs' on 14 November, nine days before she began writing. The fact that the photographs are described but not shown, that they are represented yet absent from the text ('the photographs . . . are all this time piling up on the table – photographs of more dead bodies, of more ruined houses') at once shields the reader from their full horror, yet at the same time lends them an imaginative force.[48]

The use of word-pictures as a structural device can be seen from the way that the essay is framed by two contrasting portraits of men (Hamlet's 'Hyperion to a satyr'?), in another version of 'Men Are Like That'. Woolf begins by imagining the correspondent who had written to ask 'How in your opinion are we to prevent war?' She pictured him as an Englishman, a middle-aged barrister, 'a little grey on the temples', with 'wife, children, house' and 'a few acres in Norfolk . . . you began your education at one of the great public schools and finished it at the university.' [pp.117–18] It is a vision of her lost brother Thoby, as he might have been, had he lived to become Mr Justice Stephen (and as she would later imagine him in 'A Sketch of the Past').[49]

The last portrait is his antithesis, 'Man himself, the quintessence of virility', with his eyes glazed, his body 'tightly cased in a uniform ... His hand is upon a sword' [p.270]. This is the picture that Leonard in *Quack, Quack!* (1935) had juxtaposed with totem images, the picture that Eleanor had torn up at the end of *The Years*[50] – 'called in German and Italian Führer or Duce; in our own language Tyrant or Dictator'. Yet it is also one of us: 'we cannot dissociate ourselves from that figure but are ourselves that figure.' [pp.270–1] The dictator is not outside us but within us, present in our own fear and anger. We must begin by crushing fascism within ourselves before we attempt to crush it in our society, and we must first crush it in our society before we attempt to crush it abroad.

Woolf's long and substantial endnotes provide a further layer of 'pictures' through which to read the text, and she also added five actual photographs. Though never explicitly referred to, these comment on the text, and not merely as illustrations of men's (unadmitted) love of dressing up. The abstract captions – 'A General', 'A University Procession', 'A Judge' etc. – widen their scope, while at the same time releasing them from their particular historical moment, since at least four of them were of well-known public figures of the day, instantly recognizable from newspapers or newsreels. And, in contrast with the (absent and tragic) photographs of war atrocities, these actual photographs have a strong comic dimension. They depict leading British patriarchs from different walks of life – the army, education and government, the law, the church – in full regalia; and since the main thrust of the polemic is against war and militarism, they begin with 'A General' – a figure who doubles as a representative of 'our splendid Empire', since this is the ageing Lord Robert Baden-Powell, famous for his heroics in the Boer War, ardent supporter of the British Empire and founder of the British Boy Scout and Girl Guide movements (whose pseudo-military structure had provided a model for the *Hitlerjugend*).[51]

The photograph of 'A University Procession' also brings together two key images for Woolf: two processions occur at the end of *Jacob's Room*, while her story, 'The Prime Minister', had been one of the starting points for *Mrs Dalloway*. At the centre of this procession walks Stanley Baldwin as Chancellor of the University of Cambridge. Baldwin was the Prime Minister who had appeared in *Mrs Dalloway*: 'One couldn't laugh at him. He looked so ordinary.' Despite, or even because of his very 'ordinariness', Baldwin was again Prime Minister when Woolf began writing *Three Guineas* – he resigned in May 1937 to accept an earldom. Baldwin, the politician most frequently blamed for Britain's failure to rearm during the 1930s, also appears in the text, commending the women of the civil service, and regretting that he had missed the pageant of apple blossom in Worcestershire (whereas his wife is relegated to an endnote, advocating anaesthesia in childbirth).[52]

'A Judge' turns out to be Gordon Hewart, Lord Chief Justice since 1922, and head of the British judiciary. He also provides one of the earliest voices in the text, announcing that 'Englishmen are proud of England', where 'Liberty has made her abode'. In fact, Leonard and Virginia had watched Hewart in action in the Court of Appeal in March 1932, where Leonard had thought him prejudiced, impatient and self-righteous.[53] The final picture of 'an Archbishop in full canonicals' shows Cosmo Gordon Lang, Archbishop of Canterbury and head of the Anglican Church since 1928. Lang, though not unsympathetic to disarmament, had failed to advance the cause of women in the ministry, as the third chapter makes plain.[54] There is also a picture of four trumpeters wearing the '[t]abards embroidered with lions and unicorns' described in the text a few pages earlier. Identified as 'heralds', they announce the one figure notably missing from this pantheon of patriarchs – the King, as constitutional head of the state. In the last days of 1936, as Woolf began writing *Three Guineas*, the King had indeed gone missing: after several weeks of rumours, Edward VIII abdicated in order to marry an American divorcee, Wallis Simpson, an episode that Woolf describes in gossipy detail in her diary (while an endnote compares him to D. H. Lawrence in his need to have 'a woman behind me').[55] Edward's shy younger brother Bertie – George VI – was crowned in May 1937. But powerful though these photographs are, it is the absent photographs from Spain that drive the argument forward.

In the third chapter of *Three Guineas* (the recurring threes are not accidental), the main correspondent had asked the narrator how war could be prevented, while at the same time urging her to sign a manifesto 'to protect culture and intellectual liberty'; yet how could these things be protected without rearmament? Woolf herself, Clive Bell, Vanessa and Duncan Grant, like many intellectuals of their generation, were committed pacifists, feeling, as Clive wrote in 1938, that 'a Nazi Europe would be . . . heaven on earth compared with Europe at war . . . War is the worst of all evils.'[56] The younger generation, with less experience and more idealism, saw matters rather differently. In March 1937, Vanessa's elder son Julian returned from China, where he had been teaching English, quietly determined that he must fight fascism in Europe by joining the International Brigade and going to Spain. Vanessa, convinced that he would be killed, could hardly bear the idea, so friends and family set about trying to persuade him to fight fascism at home – as Three Guineas would urge. After much discussion, he reluctantly gave up his first plan, and agreed instead to drive an ambulance for Spanish Medical Aid; the casualty rates among drivers were said to be low. Julian adored his mother, but he was fighting for his right to self-determination.[57]

Virginia felt completely baffled: 'I go on asking myself, without finding an answer, . . . What made him do it? I suppose it's a fever in the blood of the younger generation which we can't possibly understand. I have never known anyone of my generation have that feeling about a war. We were all C[onscientious]. O[bjector].'s in the Great war.' Though the writing of Three Guineas went forward, Julian's departure for Spain in the first week of June cast a cloud over the summer of 1937, particularly as Virginia privately shared Vanessa's conviction that he would be killed. News arrived on 20 July that he had been hit by a fragment of shell while driving his ambulance near the Escorial, and had died within a few hours.[58]

Vanessa was prostrate with grief, and for some weeks Virginia abandoned her own work and social engagements to sit with her in her despair – '[a]n atmosphere of deep grey waters; & I flopping like a dilapidated fish on top. Very hard work.' Even writing, her usual consolation, collapsed, and the last chapter of Three Guineas turned 'stiff & cold'. Four months later, she was still spending as much time as she could with Vanessa: 'dont I dread it? But I make myself all the same stay on when she's alone.' The pain of their early losses returned as she watched the convalescent Vanessa asking Quentin to help her, and remembered 'father taking Thoby's arm', after their mother's death. 'How can she ever right herself though?' she wondered. 'Julian had some queer power over her – the lover as well as the son. He told her he could never love another woman as he loved her.'[59]

Away from Vanessa, Virginia could hardly bear to think of her suffering; everything seemed drained of substance, and 'the only life this summer is in the brain. I get excited writing. 3 hours pass like 10 minutes'. She wondered how far work would sustain her 'if Leonard died, if Nessa died?' By 12 October, the first draft of *Three Guineas* was completed, and she felt that she had earned her 'gallop'. But Julian's death still made no sense to her: 'I cant make it fit in anywhere . . . I can do nothing with the experience yet. It seems still emptiness: the sight of Nessa bleeding: how we watch: nothing to be done. But whats odd is I cant notice or describe. Of course I have forced myself to drive ahead with the book. But the future without Julian is cut off. lopped: deformed.'[60]

'I often argue with him on my walks; abuse his selfishness in going'. Julian should have fought fascism at home, not abroad. But if Julian's death made the arguments for pacifism all the more urgent – the loss of mothers' sons, the appalling waste of a young life – it also complicated them. He had given his life to save the Spanish government and freedom and democracy in Europe, and the value of that freedom rose in proportion to the high price he had paid. It could be argued that '[i]f we [the British] allowed arms thro[ugh] we sh[oul]d save thousands of lives.'[61] Officially, the great powers had signed a pact not to intervene in Spain, but in practice, it had been completely ignored by Germany and Italy, who sent troops and arms in support of Franco, and by Russia, who was supplying arms to the International Brigade and the Spanish government. By contrast, the British government had observed the pact to the letter, hoping, it was said, that Franco would win as soon as possible. 'So we shant let arms through: we shall sit on the fence: & the fighting will go on', Woolf lamented, floundering between irreconcilable moral positions, for an absolute pacifism was hard to sustain.[62] The moral convictions of her generation, the sense that war was the ultimate evil, had not only shaped her views; they had been a key factor in the British government's confused and incoherent policy on Europe and rearmament during the 1930s.

The desolation of Julian's death, like the developing political crisis, cast its shadow over *Three Guineas*. Woolf recognized only too well that 'Art is the first luxury to be discarded in times of stress'. As the 1930s wore on, she hurled herself more and more single-mindedly into her writing, while increasingly feeling its pointlessness. In spring 1936, as Hitler marched into the demilitarized Rhineland, she felt she could already see and hear the roar of the guns, 'even though I go on, like a doomed mouse, nibbling at my daily page.'[63] A sense of frustration and helplessness, a recognition that some problems might have no solutions, is never far beneath the surface of *Three Guineas*, contributing to the complex twists and turns of the arguments, the occasional moments of defeat, the reluctance to give the guineas, and the non-involvement of the members of the Outsiders' Society – their role as observers rather than agents.

The narrator begins with an apology for a three-year delay in answering – a delay that measures the shift from a feminist to an anti-fascist polemic, a delay in which photos, events, dead bodies and ruined houses had been piling up – yet she is determined to attempt an answer, 'even if it is doomed to failure.' After enumerating the nullity, immorality, hypocrisy and servility of the private house, and the possessiveness, jealousy, pugnacity and greed of the public world, the narrator, faced with 'a choice of evils', feels at a loss: 'Had we not better plunge off the bridge into the river; give up the game; declare that the whole of human life is a mistake and so end it?' [p.199] The pacifist cannot fight either partriarchy at home or fascism abroad with its own weapons; new responses must be found. The third chapter thus carries a sense of defeat, alongside its hope of social reconstruction through the Outsiders' Society. But the lack of a solution (there could be no solution, given Hitler's aims and ambitions) does not invalidate the clarity of Woolf's analysis of fascist ideology, nor does it weaken her fundamental argument that the doctrine of separate spheres for men and women encourages male violence.

The Outsiders' Society rejects group solidarity in favour of the individual conscience, sharing with pacifism a certain awkward insistence on keeping its hands clean, on not joining a procession that was rapidly becoming a stampede to the cliff edge. Woolf herself refused state honours, and censured those writers who committed 'adultery of the brain', who in one way or another sold out to the system, in one of the book's less convincing passages. She prided herself on her own intellectual integrity. When the New York agent Ann Watkins urged her to lecture in America or sell her stories there, she felt literally sick: 'my gorge rises. No I will not write for the larger paying magazines: in fact, couldn't. In this way I put 3 Guineas daily into practice.'[64] But she could afford to adopt the moral high ground when it came to accepting or refusing commissions, could choose what she would write, and had been able to do so from the start because she had a small private income. When she sneered at Storm Jameson for being an 'old Prostitute' – that is, writing for money – she forgot that her unearned income gave her a safety net that Jameson lacked. *Three Guineas* implies that Mrs Oliphant compromised her writing because she had to earn her living and educate her children, but financial necessity, and even blatant commercialism are not necessarily enemies of great art – witness Shakespeare, Dickens or even Scott. Woolf's sense of her own integrity derived from accidental privileges, as she sometimes remembered; her occasional displays of moral fastidiousness could annoy the less privileged.[65]

Though Woolf classified herself as an outsider by virtue of being a woman, in terms of race and class she was an insider. Near the end, *Three Guineas* compares the oppression of women with that of the Jews:

You are feeling in your own persons what your mothers felt when they were shut out, when they were shut up, because they were women. Now you are being shut out, you are being shut up, because you are Jews, because you are democrats, because of race, because of religion. It is not a photograph that you look upon any longer; there you go, trapesing along in the procession yourselves. [p.228]

Yet her argument as a whole largely avoids issues of race and class by focusing on gender. In doing so, she was reversing the pattern of Nazi policy, which distracted attention from problems of class difference and gender oppression by focusing on the issue of race instead, by scapegoating Jews and gypsies (as well as communists, homosexuals and other minorities). As Woolf pointed out, patriarchal oppression was common both to Britain and Germany in the 1930s, but then so was anti-Semitism. Leonard's book of 1935, *Quack! Quack!*, an attack on the dictators (its use of telling photographs anticipates her own), had included an appendix 'on Anti-Semitism', pointing out that three thousand years earlier, the Jews had been civilized enough to sacrifice a scapegoat, rather than a human being, and contrasting the Jews, committed to 'their own civilization and the civilizations from which they had learnt', with those Europeans who were now 'struggling back to savagery'.[66] Fortunately Oswald Mosley's attempts to activate race hatred against British Jews in the East End of London had made only a limited political impact, though how limited could not have been guessed in advance. When Woolf insisted 'You cannot take away [woman's] right to earn a living' [p.226], she had temporarily forgotten that this was indeed one of the rights that Hitler had taken away from German women, and that the process of women's emancipation could be – had indeed been – reversed by state intervention in both Germany and Italy.[67]

In inventing an Outsiders' Society, and constructing herself as an Outsider, Woolf was both courageous and somewhat unrealistic: to do so, she had to blind herself to her own privileged status, rather as she blinded herself to her own anti-Semitism, and as many of her friends would blind themselves to the scale of gender discrimination in Britain that *Three Guineas* exposed. Yet if she could not always achieve the perfect disinterest she aimed for, her life was full of moral and artistic leaps over old prejudice and outmoded patterns of thought, and her marriage to Leonard was one of the greatest of those leaps, and one of the most successful. In October 1937, Vanessa visited Paris in an effort to pick up the threads of life broken off when Julian died. Virginia felt she should join her for the weekend, but Leonard did not want her to go. 'Then I was overcome with happiness. Then we walked round the square love making – after 25 years cant bear to be separate . . . it is an enormous pleasure, being wanted: a wife. And our marriage so complete.' The beginning of 1938 was darkened by Leonard falling ill with a kidney infection, at first suspected of being prostate cancer. 'How am I to describe "anxiety"? I've battened it down under this incessant writing, thinking, about 3 Gs – as I did in the summer after Julian's death.'[68]

From October through to January 1938, Woolf revised and restructured *Three Guineas*. Though she had known, more or less, what she wanted to say from the outset, it had taken six months of work before she suddenly 'saw it as 3 Chapters ... But theres a terrible lot of reasoning (for me) & fitting in of the right quotations.'[69] Several substantial sequences of manuscript and typescript drafts survive but these are exceptionally difficult to set in order because they have so few dates on them. And while they correspond closely to the published text in terms of content, the material is often differently arranged, so that illustrations to particular arguments that appear as text in the manuscript or typescript are later relegated to the endnotes (for example Bagehot's disobliging letter to Emily Davies, or Frau Pommer's denunciation of the 'thorn of hatred').[70] Woolf's endnotes are written in a more relaxed, comic, ironic voice than the main text; they offer an amusing commentary on it, and perhaps a parody of heavy-handed (male?) scholarship.

By mid-January 1938, the last pages of the text had been sent to the typist, and early in February she showed it to Leonard, who 'gravely approves ... Thinks it an extremely clear analysis' (in fact he did not sympathize with her pacifism, and only partially with her feminist critique of society). But at this stage the notes still remained to be written up. On 10 March she found herself working '5 hours a day to finish off those notes, those proofs'. If they were not despatched within the week, Leonard sternly warned her, its publication would have to be postponed till the autumn. As with *The Years* (though not for the same reason), Clarks sent galley proofs from Edinburgh, and she used these to cut out passages for its serialization in the *Atlantic Monthly*, under the title 'Women Must Weep, or Unite Against War'.[71]

Meanwhile, though the 'vulgarity', the insistency of the endnotes seemed to her somehow dubious, she was deeply absorbed in them. The main text was elaborately structured, each section carefully assembled and inserted, but with the endnotes she could relax into her own voice. Moreover, new illustrations of her points kept appearing in the newspapers – the American edition included several last-minute additions. And she could see possibilities for extending their scope – 'ideas for a new society at Newnham', 'an illustrated sheet to be called the Outsider'.[72] On 12 March, Hitler invaded Austria, 'which combines with the Russian trials, like drops of dirty water mixing, put its thorn into my morning: a pernickety one spent over notes.' Though *Three Guineas* was 'the thing I wished to say', saying anything now looked futile. 'When the tiger ... has digested his dinner he will pounce again.'[73]

The last of the page proofs were returned on 28 April, and she felt suddenly free, not only of *Three Guineas* itself, but also of public opinion: '[h]ave committed myself. am afraid of nothing. Can do anything I like.' She knew that it voiced views that would be unpopular in her circle – she had warned Vanessa that once it came out, 'I shan't ... have a friend left' – yet her courage in publishing it renewed her self-confidence, rather as her critique of Desmond MacCarthy's sexism had done in October 1920, so many years before (see Chapter 5). Writing *Three Guineas*, she not only did her 'bit for that cause': she had made a principled, serious and conscientious objection to sexism and militarism, as she saw them, in British society.[74] As such, it might even be of 'more practical value' than her fiction, even though Leonard rated it less highly. 'But I wanted – how violently – how persistently, pressingly compulsorily I cant say – to write this book; & have a quiet composed feeling; as if I had said my say: take it or leave it; I'm quit of that; free for fresh adventures – at the age of 56. Last night I began making up again: Summers night.'[75] The novel that began thus romantically would explore, more deeply and imaginatively even than *Three Guineas* had done, the intimate connections between the tyrannies and servilities of the public and private worlds.

THREE GUINEAS: THE AFTERMATH

According to his wife Lydia, Maynard Keynes was 'very critical' of Three Guineas. *When the Woolfs visited them at Tilton in August 1938, in the middle of the Munich crisis, 'Maynard never said a word. Some were unsaid. As for instance, Lydia: we all put up with you Virginia, said significantly, kissing me at parting.' Keynes had recently been seriously ill, and was doubtless preoccupied with the international crisis ('Hitler has his hounds only very lightly held. A single step ... & again its 1914,' Woolf noted).[76] Yet he had loved* The Years, *thought*

*it the best of her books, and had compared the scene where Eleanor
sends Crosby away (1913) favourably with Chekhov's* Cherry Orchard
*(perhaps recalling the scene of old Firs, left behind at the end). What,
then, was the book he had read? The history of women's changing
position in English society that* The Years *related culminated naturally
and inevitably in the arguments of* Three Guineas – *indeed, Woolf
herself had considered them 'one book'.*[77] *Keynes was immensely
intelligent; but gender can have peculiarly blinding effects.*

*Even before their visit to Tilton, Woolf had dreaded Keynes's 'heck-
ling', what he might say in his role as 'dear old Hitler'. His reaction
typified that of Bloomsbury: published on 3 June 1938,* Three Guineas
*was widely admired, but '[n]ot a word [was] said of it by any of my
family or intimates', 'my own friends have sent me to Coventry over
it.'*[78] *Woolf had expected that its reception would 'beat to the time
of sneer enthusiasm, enthusiasm sneer', and was pleasantly surprised
when* The Listener *said she was 'scrupulously fair' and the* Times
Literary Supplement *called her 'the most brilliant pamphleteer in
England'. She was glad to be 'taken seriously, not dismissed as a
charming prattler', but this time she felt comparatively unthreatened
by reviews since she had 'said what I wanted', at whatever cost, and
had paid what she saw as her 'debt to civilisation'. It was 'the end of
six years floundering, striving, much agony, some ecstasy: lumping the
Years & 3 Gs together as one book – as indeed they are'.*[79]

Publicly voiced hostility ranged from headlines in the Sunday
Referee, *screaming* WOMAN STARTS NEW SEX-WAR/SAYS MEN'S
CLOTHES ARE 'BARBAROUS', *to Queenie Leavis's long and troubling
attack in* Scrutiny *(which Woolf did not read to the end). Mrs Leavis
had seized, not without justification, on Woolf's critique of writers
as prostitutes ('alternative source of income for professional women
writers not inheriting five hundred a year and rooms of their own not
indicated'); but in the course of her argument, Mrs Leavis also observed
that as students, women were, by and large, intellectually inferior
to men – the kind of lazy, sexist assumption that Woolf had been
challenging for almost twenty years.*[80]

*If there were dissenting voices, there was also passionate enthusiasm:
Margaret Rhondda (editor of the feminist journal* Time and Tide*),
Pippa Strachey, Ray Strachey, Ethel Smyth, Roger Fry's sister Ruth,*

Shena Simon, Violet Dickinson, Helena Swanwick, Nellie Cecil (wife of Lord Robert), the novelist Naomi Mitchison, Margaret Llewelyn Davies and Emmeline Pethick-Lawrence, an old champion of the Women's Movement, all wrote to thank and congratulate her, while complete strangers wrote to praise the book's 'magnificent idealism', to assure her that she had 'put fresh courage into our dulled hearts and stimulate[d] us to take action'; her feminist polemics were 'the best help women have ever had towards their fight for justice'.[81]

Taking stock in September 1938, Woolf noted that her polemic had sold over 7,000 copies and that she had collected 'my own, now numerous, semi-official 3 Gs letters'. More than eighty of those letters survive and have been edited and published by Anna Snaith. Not all of them agreed with Woolf, of course: even a sympathizer like Shena Simon could see that, in the summer of 1938, thoroughgoing pacifism might mean becoming 'a supporter of N. Chamberlain & his policy of letting the dictators do what they like – in Spain, to the Jews & the socialists', but her letter started a correspondence that turned into a friendship. Woolf seems to have answered all her letters, and not only those from middle-class readers: she responded thoughtfully to a Birkenhead bus conductor, Ernest Huxley, and to a poor, unemployed weaver, Agnes Smith – their correspondence would continue till Woolf's death.[82] Late in 1938, she tried once again to take stock: Three Guineas *had sold 8,000 copies, and its reception had been 'interesting, unexpected – only I'm not sure what I expected . . . Not one of my friends has mentioned it. My wide circle has widened – but I'm altogether in the dark as to the true merits of the book. Is it . . . ? No, I wont even formulate qualities; for its true, no one has yet summed it up.'[83]*

Though Woolf had said what she wanted to, the issues that Three Guineas *had addressed became, if anything, more pressing with the Munich crisis of September 1938, Hitler's invasion first of Czechoslovakia and then of Poland, and the declaration of War on 3 September 1939. Woolf continued to cut out from newspapers and copy out from books evidence of misogyny and patriarchal assumptions. In November 1939, she received an invitation from New York to write about 'women & peace', though it was not until her experiences during the Battle of Britain, the following summer, that she wrote 'Thoughts on Peace in an Air Raid'.[84]*

As much, or possibly more than A Room of One's Own, Three Guineas *had been addressed to the younger generation. Soon after its publication, Woolf noted that there had been 'No thanks: no enthusiasm from the young for whom I toiled. But thats as I expected, & as it should be' – perhaps in response to an 'amusingly tepid' (indeed, thoroughly uncomprehending) letter from her niece Judith Stephen, then an undergraduate at Newnham. But a few months later, a young Rodmell neighbour, Diana Gardner, assured her that the young were reading it, and 'it is a revelation . . . It seemed to explain to us what we're doing'; she lent Woolf a copy of Thomas Mann's lecture, 'The Coming Victory of Democracy'.[85] And* Three Guineas *would speak forcefully to later feminist readers confronting war, from the 1970s until now. At the same time, the initial hostility of Woolf's circle was also handed on to a second generation: Vita had upset Virginia by complaining of its 'misleading arguments', and more than sixty years on, her younger son Nigel Nicolson was still criticizing its stridency and anger, quoting approvingly from Queenie Leavis's attack, 'this book is not merely silly and ill-informed, but contains self-indulgent sex-hostility' (a sentence that tells us more about its author than its subject). Quentin Bell, too, notoriously disliked its sentiments, describing it in his biography as 'the product of a very odd mind, . . . of a very odd state of mind', though later he backed down to the extent of admitting that 'it suffered from the deterioration of the political climate'. Both Bell and Nicolson pointed out inconsistencies in Woolf's position, inconsistencies resulting from the moral complexity of the situation, and perhaps inevitable when an instinctive hatred of force and violence had to confront the Spanish Civil War (and Julian's death in it), as well as the 'Jews persecuted, only just over the Channel'. Other women pacifists, among them Storm Jameson and Rose Macaulay, were gradually abandoning their pacifism, recognizing that some evils were even greater than those of war.[86]*

Is there still a vestigial reluctance to tolerate women's voices in the sphere of politics? Leonard disagreed profoundly with his wife's pacifism, famously describing her as 'the least political animal that has lived since Aristotle invented the definition', yet he went on to place her political pamphlets in 'a long line stretching back to Vindication of the Rights of Women *by Mary Wollstonecraft', and to acknowledge*

her practical contributions to the Labour Party and the Women's Co-operative Guild. Within their marriage, it was Leonard who was actively engaged in political debate and policy-formation on a day-to-day basis – Virginia sometimes felt that he did 'enough for both of us' in that area. But she also recognized that, for her, political resistance primarily took the form of writing – 'Thinking is my fighting'.[87] Today, our sense of Woolf as a serious political thinker derives from a wider sense of what politics might include, a sense that there is a politics of the hearth and of the heart, as well as of the state. And paradoxically, our own redefinition of politics, to include gender quite as much as race and class, events at home as well as away, is due in no small part to the arguments advanced in Three Guineas.

13

Life Writing

In the spring of 1936, when Virginia was overcome with the weight of *The Years*, Leonard took her down to the West Country, thinking that if anything could soothe her it would be St Ives, with its memories of childhood happiness. The two of them 'crept into the garden of Talland House', Leonard recalled, 'and in the dusk Virginia peered through the ground-floor windows to see the ghosts of her childhood'. For Leonard, that moment brought back Schubert's setting of Heine's poem 'Der Doppelgänger', where the poet returns to the house of the lost loved one and watches his own double, wringing his hands, as if in mockery of his former agony. For Virginia, it must have brought back memories of a visit made more than thirty years earlier with her brothers and sister, while Thoby was still alive. Even then, she had noted the uncanny feeling of return, as they walked up the drive, and stood beneath the familiar windows, 'like ghosts'.[1] Looking into the past, in conversation with the dead, we meet and re-meet our former selves.

The deaths of Lytton Strachey in January 1932 and of Roger Fry in September 1934 had torn holes in Woolf's inner circle. She had seen less of Lytton in recent years, but she had remained deeply fond of him: funny, sharp, erudite, unconventional and deeply affectionate, Lytton had proposed to her in 1909, and although he retracted almost immediately, he remained her 'dear old serpent'.[2] Her friendship with Roger Fry did not go back so far nor was it so intimate, and it was complicated by his passion for Vanessa, yet she had found his range of opinions, ideas and enthusiasms compelling. Life seemed to hum in his presence. His aesthetic ideals, his commitment to 'vision and design' had shaped her own writing practice. He was already recognized as a

19th July 1939. I was forced to break off again, & rather suspect that these breaks will be the end of my memoir writing. I was thinking about Stella, as I crossed the channel in June. I have not given her a thought since. But the past only comes back of an evening mostly, or when the present runs so smoothly that it is like the sliding surface of a deep river. And one sees through the surface to the depths. In those moments, which I find one of my greatest satisfactions, not that I am thinking of the past; but that I am living I think most fully in the present; for the present when backed by the past is a thousand times deeper than the present that is merely the present — the sliding, fussed surface. The film that jerks over the camera only reaches the eye. I like to feel depth upon depth beneath it. But for this peace is needed. It is necessary that the present should be smooth & habitual. Hence the extreme distress caused me by any break — like that caused an of house moving; like that of meeting complete strangers — it seems to smash, to end, to confuse. I write this indeed, partly in order to recover my sense of the present, to rescue a real moment from this unreal chaos. (I am stale with Roger again — words stale going, getting in — all that seems to me needed to make a continuous narrative of his past — an

AS.

key figure in the history of twentieth-century taste: 'someone will be certain to write about Roger – so it had better be by us'.[3] Lytton, too, had changed cultural perceptions in the field of life writing. When friends suggested that Virginia should undertake their biographies, she was excited at the thought of re-creating, for herself and friends, something of what had been lost when they died; but their lives posed problems, some more obvious than others.

In certain respects, Woolf's talents were better suited to Lytton's biography, but it was impossible to publish at a time when homosexuality, outside Cambridge and Bloomsbury, was still the love that 'dared not speak its name', punishable by law. Lytton's younger brother James had canvassed the possibility of putting together a life and letters, with an introduction by Virginia, but it had to be abandoned.[4] Fry's life looked altogether more possible. His favourite sister Margery (who had travelled to Greece with Roger and the Woolfs in 1932 and was Principal of Somerville College, Oxford), and Roger's former partner, Helen Anrep, both encouraged Virginia to take on the task. From 1935, Margery Fry began to supply her with the necessary raw materials: 'cardboard boxes stuffed with bills and love letters' began to arrive. Between then and 1938, 'reading Roger' became an occupation Woolf turned to when she was too tired to write. In her usual methodical way, she copied out extracts that she might use, and by 1936, there were already '3 stout volumes' of these.[5] The death of Julian in the summer of 1937 lent urgency to her task since she had conceived the biography partly as a present for Vanessa, a framed portrait of Roger in words to summon him back.

Roger's death felt 'worse than Lytton's . . . Such a blank wall. Such a silence. Such a poverty. How he reverberated! And I feel it through Nessa.' When Helen Anrep had 'tentatively' asked her 'to write Roger's Life', she had agreed, on condition that she 'could be free'. Margery, Roger's executor, came to tea and assured Virginia that she, too, wanted her to be free, but warned that 'family' sensibilities – in particular, those of Roger's other five sisters – would need to be respected.[6] And Woolf herself may have underestimated the constraints involved: it was not merely homosexuality that could not be discussed openly in the 1930s – the discussion of any form of sexuality was potentially difficult. Although Fry had discussed his erotic life quite candidly, his biographer would have to tread more carefully. In the end, the suppressions required became burdensome, and there was no escape into fantasy or alternative fictions. Instead Woolf turned to relate another life with all the frankness denied her in writing Roger's – her own.

Life writing was an impulse that ran through her work from the beginning to the end. 'The Journal of Mistress Joan Martyn' (1906) was an early story in which a young woman historian discovered a fifteenth-century diary in a remote country house.[7] Woolf also liked to invent, or enlarge upon, scenes from the lives of real people, and in particular those of neglected, unconventional women – Lady Stanhope, or Miss Ormerod, Miss Mitford, Laetitia Pilkington, Dorothy Osborne and many others.[8] Yet while nothing was stronger in her than this 'scene-making' impulse, the life that she related most continuously and consistently was her own – sporadically, in her letters, more formally in contributions to Bloomsbury's Memoir Club,[9] but above all in the diary which she kept for most of her adult life, and which ranges in mood from exhilaration to despair, reports on her reading and writing, on domestic conversations and political events, portrays people, places and passions, descends to trivial annoyance and rises to pure poetry. It grew with her in scope and complexity and, for some readers, it represents the summit of her achievements.

Woolf's diary was written primarily for her own rereading, the young Virginia writing to her future self. Sometimes she questioned who she was writing for, recognizing that Leonard would be its likeliest reader (and regulating her words accordingly). Sometimes she pondered whether she should report on the wider world, or the doings of her own circle or on her own thoughts and feelings, but increasingly it became a record of what mattered most to her – what she was writing or planning to write, a record of the unfolding creative process itself, which she observed with detachment, and found at once fascinating and mysterious: 'How I interest myself!'[10]

Her diary is the main source of our knowledge of Woolf's life, on a daily basis (and the main source for the present account of it), but its value lies quite as much in its subjectivity as in the information it provides. It gives us Woolf's viewpoint at the time she set it down. The particularity of that moment seemed to her a necessary condition of writing, and she was to adopt it as a structural principle when writing her memoir of her own life, 'A Sketch of the Past'. The particularity of viewpoint provided a solution to the question of how to write her biography of Roger Fry: she would tell it from his point of view, as far as the evidence (and his family) would allow.[11] During her last three years, Woolf was engaged in three distinct forms of life writing, which subtly enriched one another: she continued to keep her diary, and from spring 1938 (after *Three Guineas* had been despatched to the printers) to spring 1940, she worked on Fry's biography. She was also setting down material towards her own memoirs or autobiography, entitled 'A Sketch of the Past', during the spring and early summer of 1939, and again from June 1940 through till November. At the same time as she began writing *Roger Fry*, in spring 1938, she also began a novel, provisionally called 'Pointz Hall' (ultimately, *Between the Acts*), finishing it late in 1940 or early 1941 (its history is related in Chapter 14).

Biography, she noted, 'is made with the help of friends, of facts',[12] and during the 1930s Woolf concentrated on more factual and 'sociable' forms of writing. Though the biography of Fry was intended as both a memorial and a love-gift for his friends, it was perhaps a surprising task for her to have taken on since, while she delighted in all forms of life writing, she found many of the conventions of traditional biography comic or absurd. 'Memoirs of a Novelist' and *Night and Day* had exposed their limits, and she continued to make fun of them in *Orlando* and *Flush*. Now she was excited by their possibilities: 'If I could be free, then here's the chance of trying biography: a splendid, difficult chance – better than trying to find a subject – that is, if I am free.'[13]

'My God, how does one write a Biography? . . . And what is a life?'[14] Lytton Strachey in *Eminent Victorians* (1918), and Harold Nicolson in *Some People* (1927) had evolved new modes of biography, as she herself had done in *Orlando*. Now, perhaps, she might do so again. Fry was a particularly appropriate subject, since he had always encouraged her to experiment. His interest in modernist art and aesthetics had influenced both her critical thinking and her literary practice. His concern with form and proportion, with '[d]esign, rhythm and texture' are reflected in all her fiction from 'Kew Gardens' (1919) and *Jacob's*

Room (1922) onwards. At the same time, she was amused at how undeveloped art criticism was as a discourse, in comparison with literary criticism (a view shared by Fry himself).[15] She had adapted his theories of the visual arts to her own medium in preference to borrowing from contemporary literary discussions. On a personal level, he had been a stimulating friend and trusted critic. On reading 'The Mark on the Wall', Fry had assured her that she was 'the only one ... who uses language as a medium of art, who makes the very texture of the words have a meaning and quality really almost apart from what you are talking about.' He had particularly admired *Orlando*: 'There's no doubt this is in the great company – it's what I've dreamed of your doing since *The Mark on the Wall* – to let your spirit free ... you happen to have genius, my dear Virginia. It might have happened to any of us but it didn't.' In her turn, she told him that he had kept her 'on the right path, so far as writing goes, more than anyone –'.[16]

A darker thread ran through their relationship: what she and Roger had in common was their enduring passion for Vanessa. Virginia's relations with her sister's lovers were always uneasy, though whether from jealousy of Vanessa or of her lovers, or both, is uncertain. From early childhood, Virginia had tried to engage her brother Thoby in an exchange that would exclude Vanessa, and that pattern had been painfully repeated in her extended flirtation with Clive Bell in the early years of Vanessa's marriage. Virginia shared opinions and ideas with Roger in a way that she could not do with the more instinctive artist, Duncan Grant, who (perhaps for that reason, among others) succeeded Roger as the focus of Vanessa's emotional life.

Woolf never attempted to analyse her lifelong complex of feelings for Vanessa, nor what might be at stake in her literary re-creation of 'that iridescent man', Vanessa's most fascinating lover, through the writing of his life. But by the end of 1935, she noted in her diary that her friendship with Roger was already 'in some ways more intimate than any I had in life'.[17] In the midst of writing about him, she told Vanessa that he was 'so magnificent, I'm so in love with him; and see dimly such a masterpiece that cant be painted, that on I go. Also, reading his books one after another I realise that he's the only great critic that ever lived.' And as her biography awaited publication in

1940, she admitted to feeling 'intimately connected with him; as if we together had given birth to this vision of him: a child born of us', while at the same time recognizing that 'he had no power to alter it.' Her intense involvement may have fuelled Leonard's dislike of it, a response that puzzled her: she suspected some factor she could not pin down.[18]

While there were aspects of her motivation that she may have hidden from herself, the writing of *Roger Fry* also raised more straightforward issues of suppression and censorship. Woolf rejoiced in the freedom to write as she liked, conferred by joint ownership of the Hogarth Press, but it did not free her from the obligation to practise a degree of self-censorship – although she had laughed at it in *Orlando*, and attacked it in the expanded typescript of 'Professions for Women'.[19] The need to police her own text became apparent almost at once, as she prepared this private life for public consumption.

Roger had lived many lives, and though he was 'a man of the world', his intimate life, and the loves and loyalties it had generated, had been of central importance to him (many of his Cambridge contemporaries had felt the same). There was, inevitably, a gap between Bloomsbury conversations and what the public could be told. In addition, Woolf's knowledge of Fry's childhood depended largely on his own account of it, written for the Memoir Club. Not only did it reveal a sense of alienation from his family (which upset his sisters); it also exposed the sadistic activities of his prep-school headmaster, a man who enjoyed administering vicious beatings. Fry himself had been too well behaved to earn such punishments, but as head-boy, he was required to lead the victims to their 'executions', to be present while they took place and take them away afterwards. As well as his disgust at the pain and cruelty inflicted, he was disturbed by his own physical reaction: the 'connection with sex was suddenly revealed to me one day when I went back to my room after assisting at an execution by my having an erection . . . the first I had ever had. It was a great surprise to me. I had not even then the faintest idea of the function of the organ whose behaviour so surprised me.'[20]

Fry's retrospective analysis of his feelings reflected a current interest in child development, but when Woolf consulted Maynard Keynes, he advised her to cut the passage since '[s]uch revelations have to be in key with their time', and the word 'erection' was not yet acceptable in print with that sense. Uncertain whether he was 'right, or only public school',[21] Woolf adopted his advice, while continuing to ponder the psychic significance of early memories, and the need to record those shaping experiences that would otherwise remain unknown or un-examined.

Writing the life of Roger turned out to be an 'appalling grind', 'donkey work ... sober drudgery', 'so much fact seeking'. 'How can one cut loose from facts, when there they are, contradicting my theories?' she wondered (without specifying what her theories were). Too many facts risked producing a 'R[oyal]. A[cademy]. portrait'[22] – peculiarly inappropriate for Fry who had despised the Academy, and introduced the English to the visions of the Post-Impressionists (he had even coined their name!) At first, Woolf planned to 'go on doggedly till I meet [Roger] myself – ... & then attempt something more fictitious.' She felt the need to 'make the break in the book. A change of method', yet the requirement to provide a reliable account worked against any such change of key. In the meantime, turning to 'the airy world of Poyntz Hall' helped to lighten the 'stodge'.[23]

Settled at Monk's House for the summer of 1938, she drew up a plan for her biography, burying herself in Roger's old articles as a welcome distraction from the darkening world beyond. In Rodmell, the local Rural District Council was threatening to build a sewage pumping station in the field next to Monk's House.[24] In Europe, 'War seemed round the corner again': Hitler was massing his armies along the Czechoslovakian border, in preparation for an invasion. Kingsley Martin, the editor of the *New Statesman* (and no favourite with Virginia), lunched with the Woolfs, and they discussed whether Hitler was bluffing and whether the British and French would 'rat' on their commitment to support Czechoslovakia against attack. Martin said 'If there's a war, "my own solution is suicidal"', a view that many shared and some would put into practice in the years to come.[25]

As the political crisis unfolded, Woolf felt both its terror and its unreality; it was 'not so real as Roger in 1910 at Gordon Square' (where she had first met him). '[H]ow I bless Roger, & wish I could tell him so, for giving me himself to think of – what a help he remains – in this welter of unreality.'[26] Now the very tediousness of the task became a virtue – she could keep at it, and even found it soothing, as political tensions built up. On 12 September, Hitler demanded that the Germans in the Sudetenland (an area within Czechoslovakia) be allowed self-determination, and war looked inevitable. On the 15th, the Prime Minister Neville Chamberlain flew to Germany to talk to Hitler. At Rodmell, Virginia dreamed of encounters with the dead, arguing with Julian against his going to Spain, praising Cézanne to Roger. By the end of the month, the Woolfs had been issued with gas masks and had laid in extra supplies of candles and coal. Hitler had agreed to a four-power meeting, and Chamberlain returned from Munich announcing 'Peace for our time'.[27] Had British diplomacy saved the day? The Rodmell postman was sceptical. 'These dictators & their lust for power – they cant stop.' Later that day (1 October 1938), the Woolfs were driven indoors from their evening game of bowls by a sudden, violent storm. Virginia wondered if it was 'symbolical', a bad omen.[28]

In London, later that month, she acted on an impulse she immediately regretted. Helen Anrep was struggling with money worries and Virginia offered to pay off her overdraft. But when she discovered how large it was, she began to worry about the hole it would make in her own finances. She decided to make up the £150 by taking time out to refurbish an old story of twenty years earlier ('Lappin and Lapinova'), and to write a new article on 'The Art of Biography' (in which she concluded that the biographer is 'a craftsman, not an artist').[29] As if to compensate him, she made Lytton its focus, asserting his importance in the history of biography, and assessing why, in her view, his *Queen Victoria* had been a success and *Elizabeth and Essex* a failure. The answer, she suggested, lay in the abundance of facts available about Victoria and their shortage in the case of Elizabeth, while conceding that the facts of biography change over time, and even that 'the accent on sex has changed within living memory'. Above all, the subject matter of biography was changing: in future, it might include the failures as well as the successes, the humble as well as the illustrious.[30]

While she readily admitted 'I owed Roger £150', she continued to murmur resentfully about 'lending money; earning money in order to lend money; writing books in order to please Nessa & Ha [Margery Fry] & Helen', and one particularly dark day, felt she was 'for ever climbing the endless stair, forced; unhelped; unthanked'. Nineteen thirty-eight ended in a bitter winter. Snow fell on 19 December, coming through her skylight at Tavistock Square, and the Woolfs drove down to Rodmell next day in a blizzard. At Monk's House, the pipes were frozen, and the electricity failed. On Christmas Day, she got up to find that Mitz, Leonard's marmoset, had died of cold in the night: 'Leonard had taken her to sleep in his room, and she climbed onto his foot last thing', she told Vita, 'But enough – dont die – Please.'[31] Several close friends had died earlier that year: Ottoline Morrell, suddenly in April, and Ka Arnold-Forster, who had helped to nurse Virginia through her worst breakdown. The Woolfs had stayed with the Arnold-Forsters at their house, Eagle's Nest, high above St Ives, when they visited Talland House in the spring of 1936.[32] At the end of the year came news of the death of Jack Hills, long ago married to Virginia's half-sister Stella, and on 28 January 1939 the poet W. B. Yeats died in France, disappearing

> in the dead of winter: . . .
> The mercury sank in the mouth of the dying day.
> What instruments we have agree
> The day of his death was a dark cold day.

On the same day, the Woolfs visited Sigmund Freud, now living in Maresfield Gardens, Hampstead, with his daughter Anna – with difficulty, he had escaped from Nazi-occupied Austria the previous summer. 'Dr Freud gave me a narcissus', she reported. Now in his eighties, he was slowly and painfully dying of cancer, and seemed '[a] screwed up shrunk very old man . . . inarticulate: but alert', still alert enough to ask them as they left, 'What are you going to do? The English – war.'[33]

Six weeks later, she completed the first draft of Fry's biography: 'the facts [were] more or less extracted' and there was even 'a flick of life in it', yet there was also a 'terrible grind to come: & innumerable doubts, of myself as biographer: of the possibility of doing it at all.' There were also awkward changes of voice to be negotiated as Woolf moved from Roger's memoir of his childhood or his letters, or other people's letters, to her own words. And '[l]ove. How to say that he now was in love?' remained a problem such as Mrs Hilbery had confronted in writing her father's biography, in Night and Day. Roger's first wife Helen had suffered from paranoid schizophrenia, and had been confined to an asylum.[34] His love affair with Vanessa could not be discussed, since she was officially married to Clive, and nor could affairs with Ottoline Morrell (also married) or the gifted Nina Hamnett, while his liaison with a French woman, Josette Coatmellec, had ended with Josette's suicide. Finally, Roger had lived with, but could not marry, Helen Anrep, since she was still married to Boris Anrep, the Russian mosaic artist, by whom she had two children.

But perhaps the greatest challenge of all was how to represent that aspect of life that Woolf shared with Fry – the life of the practising artist. Fry had longed above all things to be a painter, but his own paintings, and their lukewarm reception, had usually disappointed him. Although Woolf could imagine the life of a painter (as her portrait of Lily Briscoe shows), she made little attempt to explore his development as an artist, perhaps because she felt unsure of her judgement or of the appropriate discourse, but mainly because she was influenced by his own self-doubts, and by the opinion held by Vanessa and Duncan that his painting did not 'count'. Woolf accepted their view, and invited them to contribute 'a technical appreciation' at the end of the book (though, as Diane Gillespie observes, it was neither very technical nor very appreciative).[35] Today, Fry's paintings are being revalued, both in relation to his critical writings (as in the Courtauld exhibition of 1999–2000), but also independently, for his achievements as a portraitist and a landscape-painter, in works that combine experiment with a formal beauty and tranquillity.[36]

Leonard criticized his wife's biography for its '[a]ustere repression . . . All those dead quotations', seizing on what is at once its strength and its weakness. In her determination to let Fry speak for himself, to 'see through Roger's eyes', Woolf had not only hurried past Fry's aesthetic theories, but had also 'repressed' her own personality, achieving an exceptional degree of self-effacement. She did, however, allow herself a few highly evocative scenes, re-created from memory: meeting Roger for the first time in Gordon Square; finding him looking after the sick Vanessa at Broussa in creative chaos; seeing him at Angelica's birthday party dressed as the White Knight from *Alice Through the Looking Glass* (a disguise that revealed an unexpected 'spiritual likeness . . . to Don Quixote'), and on the last occasion, as he turned from judging whether a painting was a fake to talking to guests, responding to 'the whole vibration – the still life and the laughter, the murmur of the traffic in the distance and the voices close at hand.' Woolf's biography conveys the force of Fry's personality, his energy, his diversity of interests in life and thought, and his centredness, his Quaker 'gravity and stillness'. Though new detail has been added, her outline has not been substantially altered. And though her biography failed to break the mould of traditional form that she had so often broken before, she deserved (as she claimed) to feel 'rather proud of my tenacity & conscience in that book'.[37]

By spring 1939, as she worked at the second draft, any hope of peace had evaporated. General Franco had taken Barcelona, won the Spanish Civil War, and by the end of February had been recognized by the British government – 'And Julian killed for this'.

By mid-March Hitler had invaded Prague ('not in the spirit of the Munich meeting', Chamberlain admitted), and in April Mussolini invaded Albania. Finally, the British and French pledged their support to Poland, Hitler's next military objective. Depressed after 'flu, Woolf felt everything become 'meaningless: cant plan: . . . all England thinking the same thing – this horror of war – at the same moment.'[38] She turned away from the threat of war and the 'drudgery' of revising her biography to look inward, searching for the self from which the writer had evolved. She turned back to a memory untouched by fear, loss or grief, a favourite memory of 'lying half asleep, half awake, in bed in the nursery at St Ives . . . of hearing the waves breaking . . . of hearing the blind draw its little acorn across the floor as the wind blew the blind out . . . of feeling the purest ecstasy I can conceive.'

The first thing she could remember, beyond the red and purple flowers on her mother's dress, was the nursery at St Ives, bathed in morning light, and, 'If life has a base that it stands upon, if it is a bowl that one fills and fills and fills', then this was it. The Stephen family's long summer holidays at St Ives (a fishing village on the toe of Cornwall) were the key to her imaginative life. In setting down her memories of them, she hoped to supply future biographers with that key – as Roger had perhaps done in his account of his childhood, and as Vanessa had warned her to do before she was 'too old . . . and should have forgotten'.[39] Yet the process of exposing the sources of her deepest feelings to the light of day was not without its risks. St Ives was at once inspiration and imaginative refuge. She returned to it as to an unfailing spring, a guiding light, like the Godrevy lighthouse beam that warned shipping off the rocks. It had provided the setting for the first chapter of *Jacob's Room* and the whole of *To the Lighthouse*; it pervaded the first chapter of *The Waves* – Woolf may even have derived 'Elvedon' from 'Fairyland, as we called that solitary wood, with a broad wall circling it. We . . . looked down into a forest of oak trees, and great ferns, higher than our heads. It smelt of oak apples; it was dark, damp, silent, mysterious.'[40] Setting out those early, generative memories risked demystifying them, making it more difficult to draw on them for future occasions; risked using them up.

Woolf began to write out her own beginnings at a moment when her personal and public futures were in doubt, yet she might have found them difficult to relate at all under more normal circumstances. In the space between the uncertainty of the present and the fixity of the past, she found the freedom to write about her childhood, the freedom of a moment of suspended being, a moment when meaning itself seemed to hang in the balance. The coming of war would bring a loss of identity, a sense that 'the writing "I", has vanished. No audience. No echo. Thats part of one's death.'[41] The question of who she was writing for, of whether anyone was listening, was both anxious-making and curiously releasing.

Of course, this was not the first time Woolf had related scenes from her own life. The Memoir Club, a group of thirteen 'old Bloomsbury' friends, met at intervals, and members read out amusing, carefully polished narratives of their lives. Three of Woolf's contributions have survived, and two of these recall her life as a young adult;[42] but it was not until she began 'A Sketch of the Past' that she described her early childhood directly. She avoided writing about some of the things that mattered to her most: though she often discussed Elizabethan literature, examining works by Sidney, Spenser, Donne and Hakluyt in detail, she never wrote about Shakespeare, not because he didn't matter to her but because (as her diary indicates) he mattered so much. Until she embarked on this memoir, her formative memories of St Ives had only been reworked as fiction.

At the outset of 'A Sketch', Woolf identified two problems: first, 'the enormous number of things I can remember', and 'second, the number of different ways in which memoirs can be written' – as an avid reader of the genre, she was familiar with most of them. She chose an approach that lay to hand, a voice and a method close to that of her diary, perhaps with some thought of integrating material from it at a later stage. The previous summer, she declared that she had 'half a mind one of these days to explain what my intention is in writing these continual diaries. Not publication. Revision? a memoir of my own life? Perhaps.'[43] As well as adopting the diary's informal voice, Woolf used dates as a way of defining who or where she was: 'Two days ago – Sunday 16th April 1939 to be precise – Nessa said . . .' is how she began. By the second entry, on 2 May, she had found 'a possible form for these notes': remembering that the past is 'much affected by the present moment', she intended to use 'the present [indicated by the date] to serve as platform to stand upon', since 'What I write today I should not write in a year's time'. The relation between the immediate present and the remembered past, the pressure that the one exerted upon the other, the divided nature of consciousness itself also lay at the heart of the novel she was working on. She was amused at the resulting juxtaposition of those 'two people, I now, I then' – Cam Ramsay meeting Lily Briscoe.[44]

The conditions under which she was writing were scarcely conducive to the making of 'an orderly and expressed work of art'. She promised herself that, 'one day, relieved from making works of art, I will try to compose this', but she was using the memoir to explore the raw material, the ingredients of her art, and perhaps the two activities pulled in different directions. There was a gain in immediacy: now her words seemed to fly unhesitating from the page, as she had once pictured them flying from 'the greatest book in the world . . . made entirely solely & with integrity of one's thoughts. Suppose one could catch them before they became "works of art"? Catch them hot & sudden as they rise in the mind'. That insight and frustration had been echoed by Lily Briscoe: 'Beautiful pictures. Beautiful phrases. But what she wished to get hold of was that very jar on the nerves, the thing itself before it has been made anything.'[45] 'A Sketch' achieves just that.

The family holidays at St Ives that Woolf now recalled had been major expeditions, requiring elaborate organization as the large family of Stephens, their servants and friends, had set out for Cornwall on the Great Western train from Paddington. The family included her parents, her older siblings Vanessa and Thoby and her younger brother Adrian, and their four half-siblings, Julia's three children by her first marriage: George, Stella and Gerald Duckworth, and Leslie's backward daughter Laura by his first mariage. With them went their cook, Sophie Farrell, and various maids and nurses, while family friends – the Lushingtons, the Stillmans, Arthur Llewelyn Davies, Leo Maxse, George Meredith, Henry James and others – would visit, staying either with the Stephens at Talland House or else at a nearby hotel.

Remembered moments, 'in the nursery, on the road to the beach', now seemed 'more real than the present moment'. Sometimes, she felt 'as if I were there', as if what she had felt was 'in fact still in existence' somewhere; she pondered whether the reality of the past might not have 'an existence independent of our minds'. But while she saw life at St Ives as a seaside idyll, heightened by moments of 'ecstasy' or 'rapture', its tensions and dissatisfactions – not all of them superficial – also returned.[46] Some of her earliest anxieties had been connected with gender and sexuality: Woolf recalled a compulsion to look at herself in the hall mirror, yet a sense of shame in doing so, and later 'a horrible face . . . the other face in the glass'. While she and Vanessa were 'tomboys; that is we played cricket, scrambled over rocks, climbed trees, were said not to care for clothes', their destinies as women were before them, embodied in their mother and half-sister, both much painted and photographed, and famous for their beauty. A darker aspect of sexuality threatened when Gerald Duckworth lifted the small Virginia onto a marble slab in the hall and 'began to explore my body. I can remember the feel of his hand going under my clothes; going firmly and steadily lower and lower . . . His hand explored my private parts'.[47] Where, as a person, had she come from that she should feel such shame? What, as a woman, must she become?

Recalling her early sensations without understanding what caused them, Woolf was struck by how little we know of ourselves, let alone of others: 'In spite of all this, people write what they call "lives" of other people; that is, they collect a number of events, and leave the person to whom it happened unknown.' Woolf had always believed that external events were insignificant in themselves: ultimately, the only 'real' events were those of the mind – exactly those that the biographer could scarcely hope to recover. But then neither could the autobiographer. Though she set down 'some of my first memories', she was sufficiently familiar with Freudian theory to know that 'the things one does not remember are as important; perhaps they are more important.'[48]

The process of remembering was itself strangely arbitrary. Woolf could recall 'the hum of bees in the garden going down to the beach', but not running on the sands or 'being thrown naked by father into the sea' (though the rather older Helena Swanwick had witnessed this and recounted it in her own autobiography). This led Woolf to distinguish between being and non-being – moments of intense sensation, and everyday existence which is only remembered if recorded – and, as if resisting such forgetfulness, Woolf recalled her walk of the previous afternoon, over the Downs and along the river, where the April willows were 'all plumy and soft green and purple against the blue' – another version of 'the platform of the present'.[49] She recounted the unforgotten shocks of childhood – despair after fighting Thoby on the lawn; a vision of wholeness as she gazed at a plant growing from the earth; a feeling of horror prompted by hearing of a suicide – and concluded that 'the shock-receiving capacity is what makes me a writer', since a shock was 'followed by the desire to explain it.' The shock signified 'some real thing behind appearances' which could only be discovered by being put into words. Only then did it become meaningful, 'a revelation of some order . . . It is only by putting it into words that I make it whole'.[50]

The need to 'make it whole' had long haunted Woolf's thinking (the wholeness of a plant in a flowerbed at Talland House had been one of her earliest memories). The idea had echoed through the abandoned introduction to *The Common Reader*, and a fragment of it survived into the published preface, where Woolf redefined the common reader as possessing 'an instinct to create for himself . . . some kind of whole'. For both reader and writer, 'making it whole' meant completing the experience by adding everything that belonged to it – 'making a scene come right; making a character come together' – and so making it complete.[51] But in her 'Sketch', we can now recognize its theraputic aspect: 'making it whole' implies healing a trauma, bringing split selves together, so that a shock loses its capacity to damage or wound:

'behind the cotton wool [of daily life] is hidden a pattern', an ultimate work of art to which all human beings are connected. The individual artist is insignificant, but 'we are the words; we are the music; we are the thing itself.' This philosophy, which Woolf calls an intuition ('so instinctive that it seems given to me, not made') convinced her that 'one's life is not confined to one's body and what one says and does'. She believed that there existed some kind of communal spirit, which she was exploring in 'Pointz Hall', and which might figure in a pro-jected book on literature, to begin with a chapter on 'Anon'. As an artist, her task was to discover the 'pattern hid behind the cotton wool' through her writing. Even though 'All artists I suppose feel something like this', it got left out of 'almost all biographies and autobiographies.' By writing, Woolf felt she was 'doing what is far more necessary than anything else.'[52]

Early in 'A Sketch', Woolf had noticed how often memoirs 'leave out the person to whom things happened', since events are easier to describe than the person they happen to. Childhood itself is, in any case, a state of constant growth and change. A child's view of other people is typically simplified, no more than a series of caricatures, though Woolf never saw her mother like that: Julia Stephen remained one of the 'invisible presences', the unseen forces that determine behaviour, though seldom acknowledged – yet without some account of them, 'how futile life-writing becomes. I see myself as a fish in a stream; deflected; held in place; but cannot describe the stream.'[53]

Child–parent relationships were, of course, fundamental to Freudian theory (though Melanie Klein, whom Woolf met and admired in March 1939, a month before beginning her memoir, had already challenged Freud's emphasis on the centrality of the father). Woolf was familiar with elements of Freudian thought from conversations with her brother Adrian and sister-in-law Karin, among the first prac-tising analysts in Britain, as well as with James and Alix Strachey, who from 1924 had been translating Freud's work for the Hogarth Press. Her initial reaction had been to dismiss it as another over-simplified system claiming to redefine the complexities of human nature (whereas Fry complained that it over-simplified the creative process).[54] But as war approached once more, she increasingly sought for an explanation of masculine aggression and violence, and by the end of 1939, she had begun to read Freud, and was soon 'gulping [him] up'. She did not share his predominantly patriarchal assumptions, and would probably have found Klein more sympathetic; but she accepted the formative nature of early experience, and in 'A Sketch' explored her own, drawing on psychoanalytical theory to describe her relationship to her parents. Woolf's obsession (her own word) with her mother was exorcized by writing *To the Lighthouse*: 'I did for myself what psychoanalysts do for their patients.' Thereafter, 'my vision of her and my feeling for her bec[a]me so much dimmer and weaker'.[55] This also bore out her personal theory as to the value of the shock-receiving capacity: when she finally put the shock of her mother's loss into words, remaking it as art, she overcame her obsession, and made herself whole once more.

The account of her mother given in 'A Sketch of the Past' is not so much a portrait as a series of snapshots and sound effects, as of a lost love: we see her in a dressing-gown on the balcony at Talland House, beside 'the passion flower', and hear her laughter, and the tinkle of her bracelets, and see her rings. She was '[v]ery quick; very definite; very upright'. And though she was always busy, and seldom gave the children her undivided attention, she created an atmosphere of cheerful bustle around herself: 'She was the whole thing; Talland House was full of her; Hyde Park Gate was full of her.'[56]

Vanessa, in her own Memoir Club contribution, recalled Virginia asking her one evening at bath-time, 'which I liked best, my father or mother'. After a moment of hesitation (for the question seemed scandalous), Vanessa replied 'Mother', while Virginia 'went on to explain why she, on the whole, preferred father.'[57] Both girls adored their mother, but they compensated for her early loss in contrasting ways. Vanessa adopted her as a role model, becoming an 'earth mother': her relationship with Duncan Grant resembled that of a mother with a spoilt but much-loved son. Virginia, on the other hand, followed her father's example in several respects, seeking out relationships in which she was the one who received mothering – from Violet Dickinson, from Vita, and above all, from Leonard, who also gave her the focused attention her mother had rarely found time for.

In addition to her own memories, Woolf re-created her mother's life in a series of episodes: as Julia Jackson, among the Pre-Raphaelites and poets at Little Holland House, painted by Watts, Holman Hunt and Burne-Jones, and photographed by her aunt, Julia Margaret Cameron. She had fallen in love with and married Herbert Duckworth, a mythically 'perfect type of public school boy and English gentleman'. She bore him two children, and was expecting a third when he died suddenly and tragically, of a burst abscess. She was devastated, 'as unhappy as it is possible for a human being to be'. In true Victorian fashion, she threw herself full-length on his grave, lost her belief in God and found comfort only in caring for others. In 1875, she moved to Hyde Park Gate, and a few months later, the newly widowed Leslie Stephen moved into the house next door with his backward child, Laura. His wife Minny, the younger daughter of the Victorian novelist Thackeray, had also died without warning. The bereaved couple became friends, and in 1878, Julia married her 'gaunt, bearded' neighbour, fifteen years older than she was. Vanessa was born in 1879, Thoby in 1880, Virginia in 1882 and Julia's favourite, Adrian, in 1883. At that time, Leslie was editor of the *Cornhill Magazine*, and soon to become editor of the *Dictionary of National Biography*. It was he who first discovered St Ives and Talland House, on a walking tour in Cornwall. He took out a lease, and the family stayed there for several months each summer from 1882, the year Virginia was born (so it naturally figured largely among her earliest memories). When Julia died suddenly in May 1895, the lease of Talland House was sold, and 'the crowded merry world which spun so gaily in the centre of my childhood' disappeared for ever. Her mother had been 'the centre; it was herself', and 'after that day there was nothing left of it . . . everything had come to an end.'[58]

Woolf set out her memories of her mother in May 1939. Sequences dated the 2nd and the 15th of the month both end with her death, but Woolf was reluctant to embark on the dark days that followed, although the 'unreality' of those events – 'those three or four days before the funeral . . . so melodramatic, histrionic and unreal' – now found an echo in the very different 'unreality' of the accelerating political crisis in Europe. For the thirteen-year-old Virginia, on the brink of puberty, there had been a few moments when grief gave a meaningful intensity to the experience of her mother's death: at Paddington, to meet Thoby who had been sent home from school, she was overcome with its 'great glass dome ... blazing with light. It was glowing yellow and red and the iron girders made a pattern across it.' That vision of colour and strength would become Lily Briscoe's, when she 'saw the colour burning on a framework of steel'. Reading a poem in Kensington Gardens, Virginia Stephen had felt not only that she suddenly understood what it said, but that somehow it was also 'coming true'. Back at Hyde Park Gate, their father's demands, the roles they were expected to play, the noisy sobs of one of the nurses who had scarcely known her mother, all seemed artificial. It was not grief that she found unbearable, but the requirement 'to act parts that we did not feel; to fumble for words that we did not know.'[59] As a novelist, Woolf would reject the contrivances of soap opera and melodrama in favour of her own conception of reality – a celebration of daily life – the place where many people live, much of the time. The 'Time Passes' section of *To the Lighthouse* had isolated its shocking and tragic events inside square brackets.

By July 1939, she was asking Leonard, '"What's there real about this? Shall we ever live a real life again?"' The prevailing sense of 'unreality' was intensified by the fact that they were on the point of leaving 52 Tavistock Square, their home for the previous fifteen years. The lease was running out, and the noise and the mess of other houses being pulled down around them had become intolerable. In May they had found a quieter house at 37 Mecklenburgh Square, several blocks to the east. The Hogarth Press would move with them (Virginia had sold her share in it to John Lehmann in April 1938), and so would their lawyer tenants, the Pritchards. The move was scheduled for August, during their summer retreat to Monk's House, where, Leonard had assured her, they would take up 'real' life again. Woolf intended to sum up her 'reflections on leaving Tavistock Square', but she never did. As she foresaw, 'these breaks will be the end of this memoir.' Almost a year passed before she took it up again.[60]

War grew steadily closer. Virginia took up a cigarette, some knitting, even her diary ('I have composed myself, momentarily, by reading through this years diary. Thats a use for it then. It composes'). She was still struggling to include Fry's love affairs in her biography without describing them, 'to deal with love so that we're not all blushing'. Germany, meanwhile, had signed a non-aggression pact with Russia ('a disagreeable & unforeseen surprise'), and was now poised to invade Poland.[61] But the atmosphere in London was very different from that of the Munich crisis, the year before: 'No crowd in the train . . . No stir in the streets . . . No enthusiasm. Patient bewilderment. I suspect some desire to "get on with it" . . . Unreal. Whiffs of despair. Difficult to work . . . And all mixed with the mess at 37 [Mecklenburgh Square].' Radio news bulletins now dominated everyone's lives. On the morning of 3 September, the Prime Minister broadcast to the nation that Hitler had ignored the British ultimatum to withdraw from Poland, and Britain was finally at war with Germany. In the tension of the moment, the Woolfs quarrelled over whether there was any point in winning; Virginia was doubtful.[62]

Her first response was total despair: 'this is the worst of all my life's experiences.' Everything seemed empty and meaningless, 'all creative power is cut off', and 'if one cant write, as Duncan said yesterday, one may as well kill oneself.' Although ships were being torpedoed, and air-raid sirens wailed, the next six months were those of the 'Phoney War', with nothing to do but wait. Instead of returning to London in October, the Woolfs stayed on at Monk's House. Things at Mecklenburgh Square were still in chaos, and at this stage, the blackout was 'far more murderous than the war'. There was no escaping the war in London, but at Rodmell, life grew calmer, and Woolf's impulse to write gradually returned: she began some articles, and continued to work on 'Roger', and her novel. From time to time, she thought about her memoir, and she may have typed some of it out, but she did not add to it.[63]

The winter of 1939/40 was even colder than the previous one: Leonard skated, and they returned from visiting London to frozen pipes. Virginia thanked God that she was 'not on the North Sea, nor taking off to raid Heligoland', and pressed on with her biography, completing the final draft in mid-February 1940. In March, after a bad bout of 'flu, she sent off typescripts to Vanessa and Margery Fry. Vanessa wrote back, 'Since Julian died I haven't been able to think of Roger – now you have brought him back to me. Although I cannot help crying, I can't thank you enough.' Margery also expressed 'unbounded admiration' – 'It's him', while making numerous small corrections that had to be written into the proofs. Only Leonard was disappointed, but she felt sufficiently detached to be more interested in the reason for his reaction than upset by it.[64]

Leonard thought she had chosen the wrong method, and said so: she wrote down his comment as 'Its merely anal, not history.' Transcribing extracts from her diary for publication, Leonard would expand 'anal' to 'analysis', but judging from the rest of that entry, what she intended to write was 'annal', which she wasn't sure how to spell. Annals are lists of events, as opposed to the overview that is 'history', and it was that larger conception that Leonard complained was lacking. But through writing her memoirs, Woolf had grown increasingly interested in the potential of the 'annal' as a place of creativity, the dated record of the present that might open, like a balcony or doorway, on to the vistas of the past.[65]

Roger Fry was scheduled for publication on 25 July 1940, and in the meantime there were more corrections to be inserted, proofs to be checked and an index drawn up. '[L]ife here alone, no London no visitors seem[s] a long trance of pleasure – or might be', yet 'the break in our lives from London to country is a far more complete one than any change of house', and 'I havent got the hang of it altogether' – it was 'an egg shell life'. Early in May came the 'tiresome' family news that her beloved niece Angelica was having an affair with the middle-aged David Garnett, the former lover of her father, Duncan Grant. Virginia could only hope it would not last.[66] And then came the first defeat of the war, as Germany invaded Norway and British troops were pulled out. On 10 May 1940, Winston Churchill, Chamberlain's most forceful critic, replaced him as Prime Minister. That day, Hitler attacked the Netherlands and Belgium, while German armoured divisions marched into France through the Ardennes, where no one had expected an invasion. French troops and the British Expeditionary Force were now trapped behind the German advance, and retreated to the beaches of Dunkirk, where, in a desperate rescue effort, a flotilla of boats of all kinds ferried as many as possible back across the Channel. By 10 June, the Germans had reached Paris, and the invasion of Britain was expected to follow. Churchill promised no surrender, but Czechoslovakia, Poland, Norway, Denmark, Belgium and the Netherlands had all surrendered, and France was on the point of doing so.[67]

'The battle is at its crisis; every night the Germans fly over England'. 'A Sketch of the Past' had admitted at the outset to being an escape from 'the pressure of writing about Roger', but it was not till the summer of 1940, that the war – the Battle of Britain – became the frame for her private memories, as if the one had called up the other. She found the memoir again while throwing out old drafts of her Fry biography, though her diary shows that she had thought about it at intervals during the intervening year. As she restarted it on 8 June 1940, she speculated about the future: 'If we are beaten then – however we solve that problem, and one solution is apparently suicide . . . – book writing becomes doubtful. But I wish to go on.'[68] She and Leonard had discussed the option of suicide a month earlier, in response to the threat of invasion. Leonard was keeping enough petrol for them to kill themselves in the garage by carbon monoxide poisoning. Suicide was now a subject 'seriously debated' with friends, and with news of the defeat of the French, Woolf considered what capitulation might mean: 'all Jews to be given up. Concentration camps. So to our garage.' This was by no means an over-reaction: both the Woolfs were on the Gestapo's black list for arrest after the German invasion. She consoled herself with the thought of 'my morphia in pocket' (her brother Adrian had promised them a prescription). At the same time she resented the idea, and didn't 'want the garage to see the end of me. I've a wish for 10 years more, & to write my book [*Between the Acts*]'. She was full of dark premonitions: on 21 June, she thought '[t]his . . . may be my last walk', and a week later, 'I cant conceive that there will be a 27th June 1941.'[69]

'The past only comes back when the present runs so smoothly that it is like the sliding surface of a deep river . . . For this reason – that it destroys the fullness of life – any break – like that of house moving – causes me extreme distress', she observed. While the activities of remembering and writing seem to depend on established routines and a degree of inner calm, Woolf began and continued her memoirs at a time when her life was more disrupted than ever before. Rethinking the relation between the 'platform of the present' and the past, she noted that it could also work the other way round, that 'living most fully in the present' required that present to be 'backed by the past'. Part of her purpose in writing the memoir, therefore, was 'to recover my sense of the present by getting the past to shadow this broken surface'. While the workings of memory required peace to function most effectively, the past and its certainties also offered a refuge from the disruption of the present. 'Let me then, like a child advancing with bare feet into a cold river, descend again into that stream.'[70]

She took up her memoir where she had left off, at the death of her mother – the earliest and most fundamental of those gaps between 'then' and 'now' that characterized her perspective. The previous summer, she had described her half-sister Stella, overshadowed by her mother, yet quietly herself. 'Very gentle, very honest, and in some way individual', Stella had protected her younger sisters after their mother's death. Two years later, following in her mother's footsteps, she had married an English gentleman and old Etonian, Jack Hills, but had fallen ill a few weeks later. Within four months (July 1897) she was dead, whether of appendicitis, an ectopic pregnancy or some other cause, no one knew. 'A Sketch' was becoming a gallery of family portraits, and that of Jack Hills came next: to the young Virginia, 'nothing in the whole world [was] so lyrical, so musical' as their engagement.[71]

Later that June, as 'the dictators dictate their terms to France', she began to describe her father, and how she and Vanessa had struggled with him in the years between Stella's death and his own, in 1904. Thinking about the 'platform of time', she had earlier noted in her diary '[h]ow I see father from the 2 angles. As a child condemning; as a woman of 58 understanding – I sh[oul]d say tolerating. Both views true?' But her double view of him was not simply a matter of past and present selves: 'rage alternated with love', and to explain that, she borrowed a term from Freud, for whom father–daughter relations were central. He had described that 'violently disturbing conflict' as 'a common feeling . . . called ambivalence.' Writing in Mecklenburgh Square in late July, she portrayed her father as a man of 'great charm for women' and yet a domestic tyrant, a flea-bitten old lion, penned up with his children in the cage of Hyde Park Gate. Then she described the house, with its green baize door behind which the servants lived; the drawing-room, with its tea-table – the social centre of Victorian family life; the first-floor bedroom, with its double bed – the sexual centre. Upstairs was her father's study – the intellectual centre, and her own nursery, divided between sleeping and living quarters, much as she felt her young self divided, a butterfly or moth struggling from its chrysalis, 'its wings still creased; its eyes dazzled, incapable of flight.'[72]

By July 1940, the Battle of Britain had begun in earnest: German planes were bombing British airfields in preparation for an invasion, and Rodmell was on their flight path from occupied Northern France. Now, as well as frequent air-raid warnings, they heard the 'hum, saw and buzz' of low-flying planes, the noise of bombs exploding, glass tinkling, the rattle of machine-guns and anti-aircraft fire. One hot evening in August (it was one of the hottest summers on record), a German plane flew low over Monk's House. Virginia and Leonard, trapped in the garden, lay face down under a tree, their hands over their ears, expecting to die at any moment. 'It is a queer experience, lying in the dark and listening to the zoom of a hornet, which may at any moment sting you to death.' She worked that particular shock into 'Thoughts on Peace in an Air Raid', an epilogue to *Three Guineas* written for US readers, in which she argued the need 'to drag up into consciousness the subconscious Hitlerism that holds us down . . . We must compensate the man for the loss of his gun . . . we must give him access to the creative feeling.'[73]

By September, the Germans had begun heavy air-raids on London itself. Returning on 10 September ('perhaps our strangest visit'), the Woolfs found Mecklenburgh Square cordoned off: one bomb had exploded, and another was ticking away. It went off a few days later, taking out their windows, bringing down ceilings and shattering china and glass. They hadn't lived there for more than a few days. 'Why did we ever leave Tavistock [Square]?' Woolf lamented,[74] but the following month, their old home in Tavistock Square suffered a direct hit. Venturing back, Woolf could see the remains of the panels Vanessa and Duncan had painted for them, hanging above an empty space. Otherwise, there was only 'rubble where I wrote so many books. Open air where we sat so many nights, gave so many parties.' With so much of the past literally blown away, she walked on to Mecklenburgh Square, to find the carpets 'inches deep' in broken glass and fallen plaster, and began to search for her old diaries. She salvaged twenty-four of them, 'a great mass for my memoirs', and took them back to

Rodmell in the car, along with her fur coat, the silver and 'Duncan's glasses, Nessa's plates'.[75]

Now more than ever, memory staved off the encroaching chaos. She had begun an account of Thoby, but in September set it aside to 'soothe [her]self to sleep' by returning to St Ives – the steep old fishing town, with its boats and nets, its Regatta and, above all, Talland House, and the sights and smells of the garden. Her imagination resisted bringing Thoby back to London: 'I do not want to go into my room at Hyde Park Gate. I shrink from the years 1897–1904, the seven unhappy years . . . I do not wish to bring Thoby out of the boat into my room.' Writing about him, she emphasized their intellectual compatibility, in particular their pleasure in Shakespeare, for '[w]e were, of course, naturally attracted to each other.' Vanessa, on the other hand, felt that she and Thoby 'had had an intimate friendship before [Virginia] came on the scene, doing everything together, and later, though life was more interesting and exciting, it was also less easy.'[76]

Woolf characterized her memories of events (as well as what she created in her fiction) as 'scene making', seeing herself as a sealed vessel afloat on 'reality', with the seal occasionally cracking to allow reality to flood in. Among the scenes she now recalled was one with Vanessa when she had fallen in love with Jack Hills, scandalizing the more conventional members of the family (since marrying your deceased wife's sister fell within the 'forbidden degrees'). A rather different kind of 'scene' took place between Vanessa and her father once a week, when she took him the household accounts; if she had spent more than £11, he 'went through an extraordinary dramatisation of self-pity, horror, anger.' Looking back, Woolf saw the gap between the Victorian conventions they had grown up with – tea-table manners, and 'dressing' (putting on evening dress) every night for dinner – and their sense, as young people, that their father was not merely terrifying, he was also ridiculous. Even more ridiculous was George Duckworth, their over-demonstrative half-brother, a social climber who insisted on his beautiful sisters accompanying him to parties and dances, as the ultimate accessories. Woolf recalled the misery and humiliation of these occasions, her hatred of dancing and lack of 'small talk' – 'There were so many different worlds'.[77]

Her memoir ends there. Elsewhere, Woolf had been more explicit about why she did not care to think about her room at Hyde Park Gate: while her father was dying of cancer, George not only took her on a round of parties, but also invaded her bedroom late at night to fondle and kiss her, though she never stated, in so many words, exactly what took place. A few months after her father's death in February 1904, she had her second major breakdown (the first had followed Stella's death in 1897), which she explained as 'the result of all these emotions and complications'.[78] She had heard voices, and made a suicide attempt. She had been nursed first by professionals, and later by Violet Dickinson, while Vanessa was moving Thoby, Adrian and herself out of Hyde Park Gate to 46 Gordon Square. George, meanwhile, had married, and Gerald had moved into a flat of his own. The young Stephens started a new life, largely centred on Thoby's friends from Cambridge, particularly Clive Bell, Lytton Strachey and Saxon Sydney-Turner. At last, Virginia began to find her adult self, writing reviews and giving adult education classes at Morley College. But life at Gordon Square, too, came to an abrupt end in November 1906, when Thoby died of typhoid; soon afterwards Vanessa married Clive.

Her memoir, she knew, was unstructured, 'too circuitous & unrelated', but that was inevitable, since '[a] real life has no crisis . . . It must lack centre. It must amble on.' She felt confident that she could 'weave a very thick pattern, one of these days, out of that pattern of detail.' Death was the only experience she would never be able to describe, though often, that autumn, it had come close, as bombs rained down around them. She told Leonard that she didn't 'want to die yet', but then allowed herself to imagine being killed by a bomb: 'the scrunching & scrambling, the crushing of my bone . . . Then a swoon; a drum; two or three gulps attempting consciousness – & then, dot dot dot'. In the third week of November, she finished 'Pointz Hall' (retitled *Between the Acts* three months later). To offset the depression that attended the end of writing (and she had consistently enjoyed writing it), she planned a book of criticism, provisionally called 'Reading at Random', and pondered writing a short story about a mountain that could not be climbed, appropriately called 'The Symbol'.[79]

As the days darkened and grew colder, and food shortages worsened, whether it was the effect of stress, of poor diet, or of completing her novel, she began to be ill. One characteristic symptom was a wave of irrational anger and disgust with those around her. Rodmell, till then a source of interest and even amusement, was now transformed into a village of vampires and leeches, all actively preying off her. Paranoia was succeeded by depression – 'so cold often. And so much work'; there was no sugar and little fat to cook with; petrol was in short supply (the Woolfs cycled); they were 'marooned here by the bombs in London.'[80] Adopting Leonard's remedies in adversity, she tried to practise '[m]easure, order, precision', but they did not come naturally. Yet the countryside beyond had never looked so beautiful. 'So lovely an evening that the flat & the downs looked as if seen for the last time', she had written in September, conscious of how easily a bomb could obliterate the view or the viewer. On Christmas Eve 1940, she saw '[a]n incredible loveliness', and was sustained, as many people were in wartime, by a vision. 'How England consoles & warms one, in these deep hollows, where the past stands almost stagnant. And the little spire across the fields . . . I can live in the moment'.[81]

ROGER FRY AND '*A SKETCH OF THE PAST*': THE AFTERMATH

Woolf's biography of Roger Fry was published on 25 July 1940: 'I'm not very nervous at the moment: indeed at worst its only a skin deep nervousness', she assured herself. The book was published in a cream dust-jacket, with a conventional layout quite unlike Vanessa's usual designs, although it reproduced her sketch of Fry. The book sold for 12/6, and the initial print run was just over three thousand copies. Like any portraitist, Woolf was anxious to know whether she had achieved a likeness – how it would strike Roger's friends – so that the response (or lack of it) from friends and family seemed the more sinister. She guessed that the reviews would swing between 'fascinating; dull; life like; dead', but in fact it was her own feelings that see-sawed thus. She travelled from a sense of pride and 'immunity' (a feeling she especially valued in these years), occasioned by warm reviews in the Times Literary Supplement *and* The Times, *to disappointment at her family's apparent silence.[82] Towards the end of the following week, she decided it was 'a dud to my friends', and joked,*

'"One of our books did not return"'; but by the weekend, Desmond MacCarthy's review for the Sunday Times said 'all I wanted said ... And it gave me a very calm rewarded feeling – not the old triumph, as over a novel; but the feeling I've done what was asked of me, given my friends what they wanted.' Clive wrote to say that it was the best biography for many years, and her sense of 'immunity' returned, only to be dampened by E. M. Forster's review, which though generous, didn't somehow say what she wanted. A second edition of just over a thousand copies was ordered a fortnight later, and within the week, Leonard was ordering a third edition: '"Its booming"', he announced. Another week later, 'Book flopped. Sales down to 15 a day'.[83]

In general, the reviews were more complimentary than Leonard had been, and even Fry's old antagonist Herbert Read thought she had made an excellent job of it. E. M. Forster found it 'a noble and convincing defence of civilization'; certainly a concept of 'civilization', of the importance of preserving moral and aesthetic standards in the face of imminent chaos, ran through the book, and overflowed into 'A Sketch of the Past', where Woolf quoted Fry's definition of it in the course of discussing her father: 'Roger Fry said that civilisation means awareness; [father] was uncivilised in his extreme unawareness.'[84] Not everyone agreed, however: amidst congratulatory letters from Fry's old friends, his sister Ruth and (unexpectedly) Ethel Smyth, Woolf found herself defending him and what he stood for against the harsh criticisms of Ben Nicolson, Vita's elder son, now an anti-aircraft gunner and seething with fury at his parents' generation. He complained that Fry and his friends had been living in a 'fool's paradise ... He shut himself out from all disagreeable actualities and allowed the spirit of Nazism to grow without taking any steps to check it'. Woolf wrote back carefully and at length, recognizing that his attack was symptomatic of a wider cultural reaction, an impatience with Bloomsbury's 'élitism'.[85] Endorsed by the Cambridge don F. R. Leavis, and his friends and disciples, that view would undermine Woolf's own reputation for twenty years or more after her death.

Fry's reputation was closely linked with the history of formalism as an aesthetic, at first enthusiastically embraced by Western art historians, and then as heartily rejected, along with modernism. As Fry lost his status as the champion of forgotten cultural wars, Woolf's biography of him was neglected, and it failed to make a comeback when the rest of her work did, in the 1970s; it was too atypical, too self-suppressing and lacking in her usual concern for the woman's angle – though paradoxically, as Diane Gillespie has pointed out, it performs 'a curious reversal of traditional gender roles' as Woolf had described them in A Room of One's Own, where, though men wrote at enormous length about women, 'Women do not write books about men.' When Woolf's work came out of copyright temporarily in 1992, neither Penguin nor World's Classics reprinted Roger Fry. By then, it had been succeeded, though not replaced, by Frances Spalding's very different biography, which is more open about Fry's love life, gives due weight to his aesthetic theories and reconsiders his paintings. Diane Gillespie edited Woolf's life superbly for the Shakespeare Head Press – this is the outstanding volume of the series (sadly, only 650 copies were printed).[86]

At the time of Woolf's death, 'A Sketch of the Past' remained unfinished – indeed, its roughness and immediacy are one source of its power. It survives in the form of a series of handwritten and typed drafts, most of them among the Monk's House papers at the University of Sussex. In 1976, Jeanne Schulkind transcribed and published a version of it, based on a corrected typescript (A.5.a) and a manuscript for the later section (A.5.d, composed in 1940) in her collection, Moments of Being: Unpublished Autobiographical Writings, which also included Woolf's unfinished life of Vanessa, written for Julian in 1907–8 ('Reminiscences'), and Woolf's three contributions to the Memoir Club, '22 Hyde Park Gate', 'Old Bloomsbury' and 'Am I a Snob?' Though all are of great interest, 'A Sketch of the Past' is indispensable for an understanding of Woolf's early development, as she surely intended it to be. In 1980, Leonard's companion, Trekkie Parsons, found a typescript continuation of seventy-seven pages, which transcribed and revised the manuscript A.5.d, and added twenty-seven pages of new material including a substantial portrait of Leslie Stephen (the typescript is now in the British Library, at BL 61973).[87]

In 1985, Moments of Being was reprinted, using the newly discovered typescript as the source for the second half of 'A Sketch', adding eighteen new pages, and in general smoothing out snags in the writing. The earlier version often has greater immediacy, while being

ROGER FRY

By
VIRGINIA WOOLF

less gracefully expressed (I have normally preferred the later text, but have reverted to the earlier version occasionally, where it seemed simpler, and more effective for being so). 'A Sketch of the Past' has been extensively used by Woolf scholars since its first appearance, but the process of revision and addition, the typing up of the manuscript, and the corrections to the typescript (though some of these are Leonard's) are uniquely interesting, since here Woolf was writing and rewriting the narrative of her own life. The 1940 sections (A.5.d and BL 61973), in particular, were written after she had read Freud, and may involve a conscious element of self-analysis. Certainly the sequence as a whole investigates the nature of consciousness, split between 'the platform of the present' and the depths of memory.[88] We now need a fuller, more informative and more flexible edition of these texts than has yet appeared – one that will reveal the several paths Woolf followed in this, her frankest exploration of memory, her boldest journey into the interior.

14

The Last of England

' "[A]s a woman, I have no country. As a woman I want no country. As a woman my country is the whole world" ', Woolf had written in *Three Guineas*, re-applying Engels' claim (from the Communist Manifesto), that 'The working people have no country'. Yet she immediately qualified her assertion by adding that 'some obstinate emotion remains, some love of England dropped into a child's ears by the cawing of rooks in an elm tree, by the splash of waves on a beach, or by English voices murmuring nursery rhymes'. Landscape and language here blend with the sound of the sea that was one of her earliest memories of the nursery at St Ives, a memory that brought 'the purest ecstasy I can conceive'.[1]

As war crept steadily nearer, Virginia Woolf, like many others, grew increasingly suspicious of patriotism, picturing herself as an outsider, exempt from the 'unreal loyalties' promoted by schools, universities and other British institutions. Yet her feelings on this score were profoundly ambivalent: she recognized and loathed the threat of nationalism, yet loved England – the St Ives of her childhood (Eden before the fall), London (her only patriotism, she told Ethel Smyth), and the South Downs, the valley of the winding Ouse and the jutting outline of Caburn, in front of her as she looked out from her writing room, in the garden of Monk's House. She loved the medium she worked in, the language and its literature, for literature, she insisted, was 'no one's private ground; [it] is common ground. It is not cut up into nations; there are no wars there'. England might have few outstanding composers, and fewer painters, but it did have a great and continuous literary tradition stretching unbroken from Chaucer to the present[2] – a tradition in which she hoped to find her own niche in due

P.H. (Dec 1938)

The dispersal.
The common mind broken up.
What each thought. perhaps.
I say had forgotten the hubbing.
Love half forgotten still the
   plant or the horse tail.
The man under the market . Rozzle.
without illusions.
Giles collision of emotions.
   Concussion. pain stops
   sees the snake eat the Toad.
Lucy is absolved from the
                     future.
   disinterested — Can make
Connections.
— Mrs La Trobe.
   the creators part.
   dissatisfied.
The play itself.
               Then the Barn.
               & the scenes.

course. Today, literature and landscape look less innocent: both can be taken over and exploited for political purposes.

The problems of patriotism, and in particular the attitude of the state towards its women, weighed on Woolf. Before setting them out incisively in the third chapter of *Three Guineas*, she discussed them at length in the (extensively rewritten and largely abandoned) 1910 section of *The Years*. In the manuscript notebook, Elvira, speaking for her author, observes at one point, 'Well suppose we had votes, then we should be Englishwomen. Do we want to be Englishwomen? I don't.' In the following (1911) section, Eleanor visits her brother Morris, who is staying at his mother-in-law's country house in Dorset, in an England she finds 'disappointing . . . it was small, it was petty'. On the journey from the station to the house, Eleanor drives past villagers returning from the fête held up at the big house, an event that had included a play, 'got up' by a Miss Green, the proceeds to go to the local church. After dinner that evening, Eleanor still finds England 'small; . . . smug; . . . petty'. Yet as she watches an owl flitting from hedge to hedge in the stillness of the summer's night, and listens to her sister-in-law's soft, West Country accent, she also thinks, 'What a lovely language.' When her brother Morris says, 'It's going to be a fine day tomorrow', she thinks to herself, 'This is England.'[3] Eleanor's vision of peace and continuity on the threshold of disruption would provide the seed for Woolf's final novel.

'Last night I began making up again: Summers night: a complete whole; that's my idea.' With the footnotes, index and galley proofs of *Three Guineas* finally despatched, she started work on her biography of Roger Fry, on 1 April 1938. The following day, she began writing 'Pointz Hall', 'to relieve myself of Roger' – the playground of fiction she needed, after the schoolroom of fact. From the first, she had a clear vision of what she wanted to write:

Let it be random & tentative; something I can blow of a morning . . . why not Poyntzet Hall; a centre: all lit[erature]. discussed in connection with real little incongruous living humour; & anything that comes into my head; but 'I' rejected: 'We' substituted: to whom at the end there shall be an invocation? 'We' . . . composed of many different things . . . we all life, all art, all waifs & strays – a rambling capricious but somehow unified whole – the present state of my mind? And English country; & a scenic old house – & a terrace where nursemaids walk? & people passing – & a perpetual variety & change from intensity to prose. & facts –:[4]

And so Poyntz[et] Hall it was, 'a scenic old house' in the heart of England, whose owners, the Olivers, are comparative newcomers, having lived there for only a century or so (genuine locals like the fishmonger's boy have their family names recorded in the 1086 Domesday Book). Bart Oliver, retired from the Colonial Service, is the patriarch, a modern version of the village squire, living with his widowed sister Lucy, his son Giles (who works in the City), daughter-in-law Isa and their two small children, and the servants – cook, butler, maids and nursemaids. The action is set in and around Pointz Hall, and contained within twenty-four hours, as tightly knit as Shakespeare's *Tempest*, another work with a pageant at its heart. Almost as soon as she began, Woolf discovered 'the difficulty . . . that I get so absorbed in this fantastic Pointz Hall I cant attend to Roger.' And by May, she knew that it, too, was 'to become in the end a play' – a form that several earlier novels had aspired to.[5]

'Summer Night.

1 . . . The Lamp.
Oh beautiful and bounteous light on the table; oil lamp; ancient and out-of-date oil lamp' are the first words Woolf typed out on the morning of 2 April 1938. Her invocation to the lamp celebrates the day's end, with labour temporarily over and the mind unbound. The lamp traditionally stands for illumination – the rising sun in the opening interlude of *The Waves* had sent out bars of light, 'as if the arm of a woman couched beneath the horizon had raised a lamp' – yet this novel seeks for the darkness that lies beyond and beneath light and reason: lust, jealousy, contempt, the eruptions of anger and desire that are part of the night world. In April 1937, Woolf had written to Stephen Spender: 'I think action generally unreal. Its the thing we do in the dark that is more real; the thing we do because peoples eyes are on us seems to me histrionic, small boyish.'[6]

Both the sketch in Woolf's diary and the invocation to the lamp introduce notions of unity and community that would be central to the book, for the lamp 'unifies the discordant'. Set against it is the idea of separateness, which occurs a few pages on, as 'the rocket that breaks and disperses . . . That feeling slipped between the space that separates one word from another; like a blue flower between two stones.' Woolf later used the prefixes 'un' and 'dis' (both of which can signify opposition) to figure the contrast between unity and dispersal, between women and men, between love and hate, between family ties and resentments, between the binding of an audience and their later separation. In earlier novels, she had explored the experience of an individual in relation to a group, and the movement towards and away from a centre ('What we need is a centre. Something to bring us all together . . .').[7] In 'Pointz Hall', these contrasting impulses are at once more conspicuous, yet also more closely linked.

Bart Oliver belongs to the 'separatists', whereas his sister, Lucy Swithin, is a unifier; their different attitudes are reflected in their actions. As hostess or artist, a woman may harmonize society and heal its divisions. Lucy and her niece-by-marriage, Isa Oliver, are both kind to the sexual outsider, William Dodge. Isa rejects her husband's unspoken intolerance, as she guesses 'the word that Giles had not spoken. Well, was it wrong if he was that word? Why judge each other?' [p.39], while the earlier typescript wonders, 'Can you condemn people for / their sexuality? / the way they feel?'[8] In a comparable moment in Woolf's first draft, Lucy Swithin tries to retrieve 'from sharks above and sharks below a foothold for new people, other people, the red-skinned or if you like the black, to settle on' (as the dragon-fly settles on the water-lily leaf). Yet her religion allows her to accept individual suffering as part of a wished-for and all-inclusive vision: '*all* is harmony, could we hear it. And we shall.' Alone, we are 'waifs and strays', 'Scraps, orts and fragments! Surely, we should unite?'[9]

Yet unity itself is not without its dangers, disastrously evident in totalitarianism, where mass demonstrations deter individuals from thinking morally for themselves, and encourage crowds to set upon outsiders. In his polemic of 1939, *Barbarians at the Gate*, Leonard had reported that 'Herr Hitler made it quite clear that what he was aiming at was the "unity" of a people drilled to obedience in every sphere of life; . . . so that the leaders would have in the "united" people an instrument of power which they could use for implementing any decision which they might make.' Towards the end of 1939, Woolf took up Freud's *Group Psychology and the Analysis of the Ego* (1921) in search of an explanation for this painful paradox. The conflicting or ambivalent nature of such feelings characterizes the novel: 'Nothing is any longer one thing.'[10]

At first, 'Pointz Hall' unfolded with speed and certainty, slipping from her as *To the Lighthouse* and *Orlando* had done, with minimal effort. By 11 May 1938 she had written thirty-one typescript pages, but then, what with the demands of *Roger Fry*, and the looming threat of war, it grew more difficult. During the Munich crisis in September, she found it easier to work on Fry's life; it was 'Pointz Hall' that brought on a headache: 'fiction is far more a strain than biography – thats the excitement', she noted, and '[l]ike the Waves, I enjoy it intensely.' By mid-December, she had written 120 pages:

I think of making it a 220 page book. A medley. I rush to it for relief after a long pressure of Fry facts. But I think I see a whole somewhere – it was simply seized one day, about April, as a dangling thread: no notion what page came next. And then they came. To be written for pleasure.

She pressed on intermittently with it until the summer of 1939, and then set it aside for almost a year, resuming work on it at the end of May 1940, when she found it, once again, exciting to write, yet 'so much more of a strain than Roger.'[11]

In the process of composing 'Pointz Hall', Woolf's method of working seems to have changed. Instead of writing the first draft out in longhand (and retyping it later that day), she left three typewritten drafts of 'Pointz Hall', and a series of short handwritten passages. Their editor, Mitchell Leaska, has divided these drafts into earlier and later typescripts (the later typescript was apparently written very quickly, between October and November 1940), followed by the 'final' version, from which the proofs were set. Each version has thirty-seven scenes (though these scenes are not identical in the two versions), and the earlier and later typescripts exist in sequences of drafts, written and extensively rewritten, often with comparatively minor changes. And her reason for typing rather than writing is not entirely clear: she had begun to use the typewriter more than before – several long letters to Vanessa, Quentin and others, written during the summer of 1938, were typed (she complained of a 'palsied hand' to Ethel Smyth), and again, during the bitterly cold winter of 1940, she apologized to friends for typing, explaining that her hand was frozen or shaking. But perhaps it was simply easier – more in accord with the 'random & tentative' mode aimed for – to knock out a few pages on the typewriter: better suited to the disturbance and interruptions of the times – experiences that would be written into the structure of the novel itself.[12]

The early sections of the earlier typescript were redrafted most substantially and extensively (as with *The Waves*). As if searching for a different way of setting out her narrative, Woolf began by composing a series of short titled sections or chapters – 'The Lamp', 'The Garden', 'Prayer to the Night Bird', 'At the Table', 'The Step on the Stair', 'The relationship between the people in the room', etc.[13] Once she had established the presence of guests in the garden of Pointz Hall, she reverted to the question of Englishness, employing a particular author to focus the themes of 'all lit.' and 'English country'. Mr Haines, the 'gentleman farmer', turns to old Bart Oliver, who has been reading Byron, to ask him if he has ever heard ' "of a chap . . . of a poet . . . called . . . Thomas?" ' When Bart repeats ' "Thomas?" ' Haines explains that it is ' "A surname" ', and Isa contributes a title

'Old Man's Beard!' . . .

Haines turned in his chair. And there was another collision. 'Hm,' he said, meaning, so you've read that . . .

'I Like the Cuckoo is it? and the deaf man who hears a voice . . .' They quoted; remembered; forgot; stumbled.

'I wish,' she said, shifting in her chair as they came to an end of what they remembered, 'I'd known him – Did you, Mr Haines?' He shook his head.

The romantically handsome Edward Thomas (1878–1917), killed in the First World War, and the legendary figure of Byron, who died fighting for Greek freedom at Missolonghi, momentarily come together to create a further 'collision', a *frisson* of sexual recognition and excitement between Isa and Rupert Haines ('the same nerve; in the thigh it was in her case; and tingling still in connection with his'). The narrative voice wonders whether Thomas's poetry might hold the same magic for them that Byron's had done for Bart's generation, for 'there was nothing but smoke to them in his recitation; and a decided prick in their own'. Was the memory of it 'so stringent, so pungent' for them?[14]

Edward Thomas had harboured 'a passion for English country and a passion for English literature', evident in prose works such as *The Heart of England* (1906), *The South Country* (1909) and *A Literary Pilgrim in England* (1917). Woolf had reviewed the last of these enthusiastically for the *Times Literary Supplement*, when it first came out. But he also had a poet's eye, and an acute ear for the English language and its rhythms. Encouraged by the American poet Robert Frost, and supported by his regular pay as an enlisted soldier, Thomas had devoted the last three years of his life to writing poems of a rare immediacy. They were admired by a comparatively small readership as 'Georgian' – the kind of poetry that Rupert Haines might have found in 'the shop in the High Street', and would have recognized and understood, yet there is far more to them, as the 'Pointz Hall' conversation indicates.[15]

Thomas's modernism has only recently been fully acknowledged: his poetry frequently focuses on what evades or eludes consciousness. By making it the object of further misrememberings, Woolf caught and emphasized that aspect of it. 'Old Man' is a poem about memory and loss, the remembering and forgetting of childhood, as the speaker imagines his own child pulling and smelling the bitter-scented leaves of the herb called by country people 'Old Man' or 'Lad's Love' (more commonly, southernwood, or *Artemisia abrotanum*). Thinking of the future, the poet mourns the loss of the past:

> I have mislaid the key. I sniff the spray
> And think of nothing; I see and I hear nothing.

Isa misremembers the poem's title (and the name of the plant, too), not as 'Old Man', but as 'Old Man's Beard', a country name more often used for a quite different plant – wild clematis, or 'Traveller's Joy'.[16] She then asks Rupert Haines whether he remembers another Thomas poem, 'I Like the Cuckoo' (in fact, simply 'The Cuckoo'), in which the deaf speaker cannot hear the bird, but can hear (in imagination) the voice of his dead shepherd,

> And I think that even if I could lose my deafness,
> The cuckoo's note would be drowned by the voice of my dead.

Her misquotation highlights the gaps and uncertainties in Thomas's poetry. His self-awareness differentiates him from other Georgian poets, and his sense of the loss of the past, and the fragmented nature of consciousness, is especially relevant to a novel that confronts disruption and discontinuity by gathering in 'all waifs & strays'.[17]

Woolf's use of Thomas in the first draft of *Between the Acts* is a reminder of how little we actually know of her thoughts and reading, despite the numerous surviving records she left, for there is no other evidence that she had read Thomas's poetry, let alone identified in its fugitive nature correspondences with her own concerns (her *Times Literary Supplement* review had been of his last prose work). Thomas had celebrated the appeal of the English countryside at a moment when it was threatened by war. He had explored the nature of his own patriotism, accepting that it was shaped by that threat, and by his conviction that he would die in battle.

Thomas and his poetry of the fugitive, of 'passing', act as a kind of shorthand (as Woolf's allusions usually do), introducing the sense of England under threat, yet the later typescript will cut him out of the conversation altogether. Bart Oliver still quotes Byron, but there is no mention of Thomas, although echoes of 'Old Man' recur in the published novel, when Isa takes William Dodge to the greenhouse, making up her own poetry as she goes:

"Alone I linger, I pluck the bitter herb by the ruined wall, the churchyard wall, and press its sour, its sweet, its sour, long grey leaf, so, twixt thumb and finger . . ."

She threw away the shred of Old Man's Beard that she had picked in passing. [p.69]

And later, after the pageant is over, 'In passing she stripped the bitter leaf that grew, as it happened, outside the nursery window. Old Man's Beard. Shrivelling the shreds in lieu of words, for no words grow there, nor roses either, she swept past her conspirator [William Dodge]' [p.123].[18] Once Thomas's presence in the text is recognized, other images and references recall his poems, but *Between the Acts* finds alternative ways of representing 'Englishness' under threat, excising this apparently foundational episode without any evident loss.

Woolf's ambivalent feelings about Englishness preceded the First World War, yet were coloured by it. Nostalgia inspires a long, unpublished essay of 1919 entitled 'Reading': here an English country house, its library, gardens and setting melt together, so that, reading beside an open window, the book and the world beyond it become indistinguishable: 'it seemed as if what I read was laid upon the landscape not printed, bound, or sewn up, but somehow the product of trees and fields and the hot summer sky, . . . circumstances, perhaps, to turn one's mind to the past'. 'Reading' also includes the plucking and sniffing of leaves of southernwood, thus evoking the past (as it had done in Thomas's poem 'Old Man', which may also lie behind this essay).[19] When, in the first draft of 'Pointz Hall', Woolf came to write about the library – 'the heart of the house' – its shelves reflected the continuities of English literature as they had done in her 'Reading' essay (or in *The Common Reader* which succeeded it). They include Chaucer, the Paston letters and Marlowe as well as *The Faerie Queene*, George Borrow, Shelley, Keats, Yeats, Donne and Browning.[20]

But the history of literature signified by the library (like the novel's other histories) is interrupted by the reading matter of the present moment – the abandoned 'shilling shockers' bought for a railway journey, or the newspaper that has replaced the book for Isa's generation. Isa, tormented by desire for Rupert Haines, 'wanted a sudden strong whiff' of poetry to allay her pain, but the old books no longer answer her needs, and instead she picks up *The Times*, where she reads of the rape of a fourteen-year-old girl by guardsmen at the Whitehall barracks.[21] Violent intrusions and unexpected entries characterize the early scenes of 'Pointz Hall': the opening conversation is interrupted by Isa appearing in her dressing-gown, and family lunch next day is interrupted by the arrival of the uninvited Mrs Manresa, with William Dodge 'in tow'.

More dramatic clashes or 'collisions' occur when a train of thought or imagination is suddenly broken up by the 'real' (external) world (as at the end of Woolf's early story, 'The Mark on the Wall'), temporarily confusing and re-arranging the usual relation of mind and body experience. Four such moments closely succeed one another: Lucy Swithin, absorbed in her 'Outline of History', takes 'five seconds in actual time, in mind time ever so much longer' to separate Grace, bringing the morning tea, from a 'leather-covered grunting monster' trundling through the primeval forest. As his small grandson surrenders himself to a vision of mystic wholeness – 'the grass, the flower and the tree were entire . . . he held the flower complete' – Bart breaks in with an ill-timed joke, concealing his face in a cone of newspaper. Thereafter, he retreats to the library, where his memories of action in India are disrupted when Isa opens the library door. Soon afterwards, as Isa reads of the barrack-room rape, her picture of it is interrupted, 'when the door (for in fact it was a door) opened and in came Mrs Swithin carrying a hammer.' The most deliberately anti-climactic of all these entrances occurs near the end, as Isa surrenders, once again, to her divided feelings for her husband:

Love and hate – how they tore her asunder! Surely it was time someone invented a new plot, or that the author came out from the bushes . . .
    Here Candish [the butler] came in. He brought the second post on a silver salver. There were letters; bills; and the morning paper – the paper that obliterated the day before. [pp.127–8][22]

In each of these 'collisions', one person impacts violently on another's active thoughts, but Woolf also evokes the impact of the living on the silence, stillness and emptiness that precedes human life – the house's own rapt communing with its past. She had an almost painful sense of the poignancy of things when they are emptied of us – our shoes, clothes, rooms, houses – emptinesses that she found at once melancholy and liberating for the alteration of scale and meaning they brought, the sense of slowed time and vast upheaval as a fold of material swung loose, or a light beam traversed an empty room.[23] As lunch approaches, Pointz Hall, and the dining room at its centre, become a shell, emptied of all former life, yet mystically transformed into a musical instrument singing to itself, its hollow spaces making a music as rare and inaudible as the music of the spheres: 'Empty, empty, empty; silent, silent, silent. The room was a shell, singing of what was before time was' [p.24]. Woolf's enduring fascination with 'the thing that exists when we aren't there', 'the world seen without a self'[24] goes back, on the one hand, to the scepticism of the empiricist philosopher Bishop Berkeley, as to whether an object exists when it is not being looked at – an old metaphysical chestnut that had exercised Mr Ramsay (as well as Leslie Stephen in his study, *English Thought in the Eighteenth Century*). On the other hand, it looks forward to the problems of quantum physics, where the conditions of observation always affect what is being observed: 'It's odd that science, so they tell me, is making things (so to speak) more spiritual . . . The very latest notion, so I'm told, is, nothing's solid . . .'[25]

As Woolf originally drafted this moment in the empty dining room, the moment before anyone came in, the narrator had sought for a name, an identity for whatever presence inhabits empty rooms, whatever presence

perceives pictures, knife and fork, also men and women; and describes them; and not only perceives but partakes of them, and has access to the mind in its darkness. And further goes from mind to mind and surface to surface, and from body to body creating what is not mind or body, not surface or depths, but a common element in which the perishable is preserved, and the separate become one. Does it not by this means create immortality?

This presence, 'this greatest of all preservers and creators', inhabits all life, conferring immortality upon it, yet it has 'no name but novelist, or poet, or sculptor, or musician'. Unseen, unnamed, memorializing and unifying, this presence seems to anticipate Woolf's account of her philosophy in 'A Sketch of the Past' (composed a year or so later), where she wrote, 'there is no Shakespeare, there is no Beethoven; certainly and emphatically there is no God; we are the words; we are the music; we are the thing itself.'[26] At one level, that presence is the artistic imagination, celebrating its freedom to wander through empty houses and rooms, to comprehend personal and communal narratives, both fictive and factual, and to envisage, beyond and behind these, a pre-history, before stories or story-tellers existed.

In the later typescript of 'Pointz Hall', this moment of mystic affirmation has been cut out, transformed into a song which is also a funeral lament:

Empty, empty, empty; silent, silent, silent. A shell singing of what was before time was; a vase stood in the very heart of the house, alabaster, smooth, cold, holding the still, distilled essence of emptiness, silence.

The alabaster vase is at once a symbol of artistic creation, a poetic monument such as Keats's Grecian Urn, or Eliot's Chinese jar,[27] but it is also a cenotaph, a funeral urn, perfectly wrought, yet memorializing a life that has ended, a past that has gone. Silence, emptiness and absence are central themes of Woolf's fiction, from Hewet's unwritten 'novel about silence' in *The Voyage Out*, to the emptiness of the 'Time Passes' section, and the absence that dominates the final section of *To the Lighthouse*. The alabaster vase, in its empty beauty and singing stillness, suggests both the power and the limitations of traditional forms of art. The empty dining room rivals the library as the 'heart of the house', itself set 'in the very heart of England', 'in the heart of the country', but the dining room is not the only space in Pointz Hall that stands empty and silent: Lucy Swithin will later show William Dodge the empty bedroom where she had been born, and the nursery, with its empty cot – 'the cradle of our race, she seemed to say'. The barn, formerly the storehouse for the village's communal food, now also stands empty (though alive with insects, birds and small mammals), and so, from time to time, does the stage of Miss La Trobe's pageant.[28]

Countering the emptiness and barren perfection of the alabaster vase is the lily pond, with its 'deep centre' or 'black heart'. As in Woolf's short story 'The Fascination of the Pool', the pond has accumulated a rich sediment of human life, so that words, narratives and events float down like petals or grains to be stored in its depths. Like the mind, the pool is haunted by romantic visions, yet dredging only throws up incongruities (the thigh-bone of a sheep). Its mud resembles the accumulating layers of memory, and like the primal sludge, the rich alluvium of the Nile, new life will rise from it. After the pageant is over, Miss La Trobe, like the pool's great carp, wanted 'darkness in the mud; a whisky and soda at the pub; and coarse words descending like maggots through the waters.' [p.120] There, glass in hand, she 'listened. Words of one syllable sank down into the mud. She drowsed; she nodded. The mud became fertile.' [p.125][29]

Woolf's vision of a world singing to itself before the arrival of people, her idea of an ancient and primitive music, often included a singer, and an incomprehensible but moving language. Mrs Manresa, the uninvited guest, plump, vulgar and middle-aged, with her painted nails, her powder-puff and her performance as 'a wild child of nature' may, ironically, be just that, for she is endowed with a lovely voice in which she yodels 'among the hollyhocks "Hoity te doity te ray do . . ."', in a version of the old woman's song at the Regent's Park underground station, in *Mrs Dalloway*.[30]

Nonsense (like Bernard's 'little language' such as lovers or children speak in *The Waves*), and 'English voices murmuring nursery rhymes' haunt *Between the Acts*. Where *Three Guineas* had played variations on 'Here we go round the mulberry bush', 'Pointz Hall' strikes up 'Sing a song of sixpence' and 'Hark, hark, the dogs do bark'. Lucy Swithin seeks to console William Dodge with 'an old child's nursery rhyme to help a child' [p.45].[31] Out of nonsense, nursery rhymes and their rhythms, and familiar phrases, Woolf created 'What I call P[ointz] H[all] poetry. Is it good?' she wondered; 'I suppose not, very.' From these elements, she wove what she termed 'a mellay', or medley, for the English language is as haunted as the English landscape. Ancestors, whether of the body or the mind (Lucy Swithin distinguishes between the two, as she leads William Dodge up the staircase), have left their imprint on it, and these are as deeply incised as 'the scars made by the Britons; by the Romans; by the Elizabethan manor house; and by the plough'.[32] Woolf surrendered herself to the rhythm and rhyme of language, telling herself that the poetry she was making might be one way of siphoning off 'the prose lyric vein, which, as I agree with Roger [Fry], I overdo.' In the last stages of writing, she felt that 'The rhythm of PH. (the last chapter) became so obsessive that I heard it, perhaps used it, in every sentence I spoke.' Above all, it colours Isa's consciousness, for like Elvira / Sara in *The Years*, Isa constantly talks to herself in verse (recording her best efforts in an account book, so that her husband won't find them).[33]

Rhythm and rhyme are part of a larger pattern of repetition, of sequences and traditions that, for better or worse, determine who we are and what we do: 'So one thing led to another; and the conglomeration of things pressed you flat, held you fast, like a fish in water.' [p.31][34] The central expression of these determining forces and pressures is the pageant itself, a rapid, comic dash through English literature which replaces earlier evocations of Englishness, such as the poet Edward Thomas and the library shelves. But like both of these, it reveals disruption quite as much as continuity. The pageant includes familiar 'history' and forgotten lives, and temporarily unites the big house with the village, since it is played by the villagers for 'the gentry', who act as audience. Like the barn, the pageant is itself (supposedly) part of an old English tradition – in this case, that of the old mummers' plays – yet it is also part of the modern reinvention of tradition, a nostalgic re-creation. Its performance is now well established: 'Every summer, for seven summers now ... [t]he same chime followed the same chime, only this year beneath the chime [Isa] heard: "The girl screamed and hit him about the face with a hammer"' [p.16] – violence, in the image of the guardsmen's rape, breaks in on that continuity.[35]

For Woolf, the pageant was simultaneously old and new: its roots were in 'the old play that the peasants acted when spring came', but the historical pageant had been reinvented in the early twentieth century by Louis Napoleon Parker, and had since become hugely popular as a local activity. During the 1930s, many small towns and villages acted out their own supposed pasts in secular pageants, often performed on Empire Day (24 May), though they could reflect a range of political attitudes: in 1936, the Communist Party performed their 'March of History' pageants in London, evoking a past of radical resistance, while Edith Craig (daughter of Ellen Terry and one model for Miss La Trobe) staged suffragette pageants.[36] Woolf's friend E. M. Forster wrote two pageants about 'Englishness' – The Abinger Pageant of July 1934, with folk-song settings by Ralph Vaughan Williams, performed in the garden of the old rectory at Abinger, and a second, England's Pleasant Land, was performed at Milton Court, near Dorking, in July 1938 (its title refers to Blake's poem 'Jerusalem', a key text for the concept of 'Englishness').[37]

Village pageants were equally popular in fiction – E. F. Benson's comic heroine, Lucia, drew up elaborate plans for a village fête whose climax would be Queen Elizabeth's visit to Drake's galleon, the Golden Hind. Woolf's portrait of life in upper-middle-class England responds to the vogue for accounts of well-heeled English domestic life such as E. M. Delafield's Diary of a Provincial Lady or Jan Struther's Mrs Miniver (which she could have read in Time and Tide from 1929 to 1930, and The Times from 1937, respectively). By the spring of 1940, Woolf herself had become an active member of the Rodmell Women's

Institute, and, as she told Margaret Llewelyn Davies, they had 'just asked me to write a play for the villagers to act. And to produce it myself. I should like to if I could.' In the event, she didn't, but it was a curious example of life imitating art, for Miss La Trobe and her pageant had already been written into her final novel. Miss La Trobe, whose name suggests 'invention' or 'finding' (Woolf had originally called her 'Tracy'), is an outsider, both by birth and sexual orientation: her masculine appearance and bossy manner suggest the composer Ethel Smyth, an archetype of the artist very different from Woolf herself.[38]

The pageant expresses the need to forge a relationship with the past and its narratives, yet the impossibility of doing so at a moment of national crisis, when the familiar is giving way to the unknown. Now, the loved landscape and language begin to look different: in the heat of the day, the beautiful view becomes a series of fields, glaring 'green yellow, blue yellow, red yellow, then blue again. The repetition was senseless, hideous, stupefying.' [p.42] Language, too, sounds worn out and second-hand, and, according to her holograph drafts, 'there's no voice that speaks fresh & strong, single & articulate, unspotted with damp, & free from the echoes & vibrations of the old voices in the great caverns'.[39] Living in an old country, writing in an old language, Woolf found its ancestral voices both seductive and inhibiting.

Orlando had laughed at such voices, but the Pointz Hall pageant is poised between laughter and the lament of Woolf's unfinished history, 'Reading at Random', begun as the end of her novel drew near, in the autumn of 1940. Its surviving chapters trace a version of English literature that begins with a shared song, a moment of social unity before the coming of the printing press, or the naming of authors. Thereafter, it descends through the shared experience of theatre to the emergence of the individual reader, the solitary writer in the eighteenth century. The brief recovery of that lost unity is suggested at the end of the first act of the novel's pageant as the audience, caught up by the verse rhythms, begin unconsciously to speak in verse: their shared language might break down the barriers of class and gender.[40]

The pageant seeks to unite its audience through the spell of language, but its narrative (like that of 'Reading at Random') tells of the progressive loss of community and the growth of the state that culminates in the rule of Budge the policeman. And the pageant itself is made up of disjointed fragments, pastiches of Elizabethan and Restoration drama and the Victorian novel, their plots revealing family disruption – orphans, long-lost heirs, found wills. The audience struggles to make sense of what it sees: some (like William Dodge) are touched by its beauty; others are puzzled or bemused. Its power of illusion ebbs and flows. At its height, one beholder responds to the action as if it were reality, but on the two occasions it fails, Miss La Trobe is panic-struck: '"This is death," she murmured, "death."' As if on cue, the natural world comes to her rescue as the cows' bellowing covers the awkward gap, their 'primeval voice sounding loud in the ear of the present moment.' On the second occasion, a sudden shower falls, suggesting 'all people's tears weeping for all people.'[41]

Most difficult of all is how to depict the present moment. Whereas the past is 'known', and can be called up in a series of caricatures, the present – June 1939 – is a moment of transition, almost the last moment of peace before England's declaration of war, a few months later. Like Woolf in *Three Guineas*, Miss La Trobe endeavours to make her audience confront themselves by holding in front of them a wilderness of mirrors and reflective surfaces which throw back disconnected images of themselves: 'Here a nose . . . there a skirt . . . Then trousers only . . . Now perhaps a face . . . Ourselves?' [p.109] Afterwards someone wonders, 'The looking-glasses now – did they mean the reflection is the dream'? [p.118] The wording recalls Lewis Carroll's *Through the Looking-Glass*, which ends as Alice wonders whose dream it was – 'Which dreamed it?'[42] The title Woolf finally gave her novel transfers attention from the pageant to what happens 'Between the Acts', suggesting that the 'real' performance takes place off-stage. The novel's imagery of performance and role-playing, of dressing up in different costumes to take on different roles, further encourages a view of the world as stage, and casts the reader as the pageant audience. Particular off-stage events seem themselves to constitute 'acts' of a somewhat different kind: Giles escapes from his enforced passivity as audience by stamping on a snake he finds choking on a toad it is attempting to swallow (in the first interval), and by taking Mrs Manresa out to the greenhouse (in the second). The violence and sexual aggression of his 'acts' link them to the two world wars (so that the novel performs the uneasy years between), which, in turn, recall Woolf's own rejection of force and violence as 'unreal' in the face of the daily (or nightly) life. It was in June 1939 that she had asked Leonard, 'What's there real about this? Shall we ever live a real life again?'[43]

If Giles enacts male violence, he is also intensely aware of the injustices and the arms build-up going on 'just over there, across the gulf in the flat land which divided them from the continent'. Returning from London, he can barely suppress his anger with the 'old fogies', and their complacent assumption that life will continue unchanged, and the beautiful view will be '"there . . . when we're not."' His private awareness is echoed by anonymous voices in the audience, wondering '"And what about the Jews? The refugees . . . the Jews . . . People like ourselves, beginning life again . . ."', or observing

'It all looks very black.'
'No one wants it – save those damned Germans.' . . .
'The glass is falling,' said a voice.[44]

And darkest of all, as the pageant ends, '"I agree – things look worse than ever on the continent. And what's the channel, come to think of it, if they mean to invade us? The aeroplanes, I didn't like to say it, made one think . . ."' Breaking the rhythm and abandoning the rhyme, the voice of the megaphone warns (as *Three Guineas* had done) against England's hidden Hitlerism; '"Consider the gun slayers, bomb droppers here or there. They do openly what we do slyly"', while the vicar's plea for unity is drowned out by the zoom and drone of twelve aeroplanes flying in formation overhead.[45]

Between the Acts destabilizes the relation between what is represented and what is 'real', what passes (within the novel) for actual life. Like a nest of Chinese boxes, play scenes are performed within the pageant, which is performed within the novel, yet the title directs attention away from the 'acts' to the interval that falls between them. And the final scenes suggest an even more complex and mysterious relationship between life, art and the artist. After the pageant, in Woolf's earlier typescript, Miss La Trobe retreats to the pub, and in its warm darkness, 'Words copulated, seethed, surged. Phrases began shouldering up from the mist . . . [She] was after something.' But Woolf herself did not know what that 'something' was until she reached the later typescript. For Miss La Trobe, as for her author, 'another play always lay behind the play she had just written' – the next invention reaches out for whatever the last one has failed to say. So, behind 'our island story', with its pastiche of different styles, behind the wall of civilization built to hold the wilderness at bay, lies the unrecorded space of prehistory, glimpsed from time to time through Mrs Swithin's readings in her 'Outline of History'.[46] Yet, as contemporary events were illustrating only too clearly, 'what is primitive' had never really been left behind. As Freud had pointed out, it was 'commonly preserved alongside of the transformed version which has arisen from it'.[47] Culture, perhaps even consciousness itself, had been built over 'the dark backward and abysm of time', a bridge over dark foundations.

What Miss La Trobe sees, in the later typescript, is the curtain rising upon a man and woman at midnight. 'A great rock. Then they speak . . .' Her vision anticipates the drama that will be played out between Giles and Isa, in the final moments of the novel: 'It was the night before roads were made, or houses. It was the night that dwellers in caves had watched from some high place among rocks.

'At last, the curtain rose. They spoke . . .'[48]

It remains an open question whether Miss La Trobe mysteriously foresees this ending or, in some inexplicable way, actually writes it. And these last words also suggest further questions about the novel, which suddenly appears as an interlude within the (unspoken) dialogue of Giles and Isa's marriage. Woolf felt her power as an author diminished by the lack of audience during the war years (Miss La Trobe's anxieties about her audience reflect her author's[49]), yet within the boundaries of the work itself, the artist enjoys total control. As the novel comes to rest in silence, something else begins, but what play does it belong to? Earlier, a voice from the audience had wondered aloud, 'He said she meant we all act. Yes, but whose play? Ah, that's the question!' while Isa thinks, 'Surely it was time . . . that the author came out from the bushes . . .' If there are patterns, there must be a pattern-maker, but who is it? Eleanor in *The Years* had also felt 'that there was a pattern. But who makes it? Who thinks it?'[50] A sense of design apparent in human life is contrasted with the distance and alienation of the natural world, conveyed in a description of drifting clouds. Beyond them lies 'blue, pure blue, black blue; blue that had never filtered down; that had escaped registration. It never fell as sun, shadow, or rain upon the world, but disregarded the little coloured ball of earth entirely.' [p.16]

Within the novel, Giles and Isa exchange no words, not because (as with Septimus and Clarissa in *Mrs Dalloway*) they do not meet, but because they know and read each other only too intimately: Isa knows the word that Giles does not use of William Dodge, while Giles guesses that Isa's contempt for him in the barn is connected with her interest in someone else. He operates a double standard. 'She could hear in the dusk in their bedroom the usual explanation. It made no difference; his infidelity – but hers did.' [p.68] Their relationship grows steadily worse as Woolf moves from the earlier typescript to the later one. As the Manresas' car drives off in the earlier draft, Isa actually speaks to Giles: ' "So we're alone at last," she said, slipping her arm inside her husband's.' At supper, 'Giles offered a banana to his wife. Isa took it.' And when Lucy Swithin mentions their children, they feel a sense of shared parenthood. 'Unfaithful all day, as they had been, the children, even the thought of the children, sleeping with paper garlands thrown over their beds, renewed their marriage; in spite of Manresa; in spite of the other man.'[51]

Such moments of temporary truce have been erased from the later typescript: there, when Giles offers his wife the banana, 'she took it: but laid it down', and according to a later cancelled sentence, 'She had rejected the banana; then he had stubbed his match.' It is only in the later typescript that Giles, as if responding to the play title, 'Where there's a will, there's a way', invites Mrs Manresa to see the greenhouse, and Isa watches them come out again, afterwards.[52] As night falls, the couple's atavism emerges:

Alone, enmity was bared; also love. Before they slept, they must fight; after they had fought, they would embrace. From that embrace another life might be born. But first they must fight, as the dog fox fights with the vixen, in the heart of darkness, in the fields of night. [p.129][53]

And it was only in her final draft that Woolf added the phrase 'heart of darkness', even though Joseph Conrad's story of that title was relevant from several angles. For Woolf (as for T. S. Eliot), it had always been a key text: the expedition up the South American river 'into the heart of the night' in *The Voyage Out* looks back to it, and as 'the heart of his darkness' it appears near the end of *Night and Day*, and twice in the final 'Present Day' section of *The Years* (the first time in the phrase 'in the heart of darkness, in the depths of night').[54] Conrad's *Heart of Darkness* begins on the Thames, where Marlow observes that England too had once 'been one of the dark places of the earth', and the rest of the tale explores the darkness at the heart of modern so-called civilization, with the cultivated, degenerate Mr Kurtz displaying a brutality that anticipates Hitler and the Third Reich. For Conrad, it is the European 'pilgrims' who are the true 'savages', a word that recurs in *Between the Acts*, as part of its search of the past for some explanation for the coming war: ' "Take the idiot. Did she mean, so to speak, something hidden, the unconscious as they call it? But why always drag in sex . . . It's true, there's a sense in which we all, I admit, are savages still. Those women with red nails. And dressing up – what's that? The old savage, I suppose . . ." ' [p.118][55]

According to her diary, Woolf finished the later typescript of 'Pointz Hall' on 23 November 1940, feeling 'a little triumphant about the book. I think its an interesting attempt in a new method. I think its more quintessential than the others . . . I've enjoyed writing almost every page.' Between then and February 1941, she reported 'copying P. H.', though the copying involved some rewriting, as her addition of the phrase 'in the heart of darkness' indicates. She finished the final version on 26 February, retitled it *Between the Acts*, and gave it to Leonard to read.[56] He was surprised, having 'expected from what she had said . . . a loss of vigour . . . but it seemed to me the opposite, to be more vigorous and pulled to gether than most of her other books, to have more depth and to be very moving. I also thought that the strange symbolism gave it an almost terifying profundity and beauty.' He thought it 'extraordinarily good; in fact, in some ways . . . better . . . than anything she [had] written.'[57]

On 14 March, the Woolfs went up to London to see John Lehmann, Leonard's new partner at the Hogarth Press, and agreed to send him the typescript, but by the time she sent it, a week later, Virginia had lost confidence in it: 'I've just read my so called novel over; and I really dont think it does. Its much too slight and sketchy. Leonard doesnt agree. So we've decided to ask you if you'd mind reading it and give your casting vote? Meanwhile dont take any steps.' She had been struggling with depression for a month or more, and had largely abandoned her diary, though she was still writing outwardly cheerful letters. Lehmann read it, and wrote back to say how much he admired it, but Virginia's mind was now made up:

I'd decided, before your letter came, that I cant publish that novel as it stands – its too silly and trivial.

What I will do is to revise it, and see if I can pull it together and so publish it in the autumn . . . The fact is it was written in the intervals of doing Roger with my brain half asleep. And I didnt realise how bad it was till I read it over.

Please forgive me, and believe I'm only doing what is best.

Her letter arrived enclosed in a note from Leonard explaining that she was 'on the verge of a complete nervous breakdown and is seriously ill. The war, food &c have been telling on her and I have seen it coming on for some time. It is out of the question for her to touch the book now and so we must put it off indefinitely. Send it back to me and don't answer this letter.'[58]

Woolf's failure of confidence was misplaced: *Between the Acts*, written in the intervals of her biography of Roger Fry, and under threat of invasion, has all the vigour Leonard claimed for it, and, as she recognized herself, it finds a new method, compacting English history and literature into a social comedy that accepts and embraces the incongruities of life, and the interruptions of thought and the existing social order by anger, desire and the coming of war. More than ever before, *Between the Acts* accepts the power of sexuality, both within marriage and outside it; accepts the creativity of the sexual outsider, and Mrs Manresa's power to lift and liberate the spirits, 'for everybody felt, directly she spoke, "She's said it, she's done it, not I" and could take advantage of the breach of decorum, of the fresh air that blew in, to follow like leaping dolphins in the wake of an ice-breaking vessel.' [p.27] The novel reflects Woolf's love for and doubts about England, and explores her conception of creativity, located somewhere between the perfection of the alabaster vase and the fecund mud of the lily pool. It celebrates and decries tradition, opening towards a future that included the certainty of war, but not its outcome. The last words signify a new beginning, and from Giles and Isa's embrace, 'another life might be born' [p.129]. It ends, as does Woolf's unfinished chapter for her next book, 'in a world where nothing is concluded'.[59]

BETWEEN THE ACTS: THE AFTERMATH

Between the Acts *was published posthumously on 17 July 1941, in Vanessa's black and white dust-jacket – ruched or folded curtains, framed by garlands of roses, though their fabric is made up of a series of pen strokes that look like writing. The first print run was over 6,300 copies. The war made it difficult to estimate how many copies to print, but reading was actually on the increase, providing a welcome distraction from boredom, and long hours of waiting. A second impression of 4,500 copies was issued that month, and a third, of a further 2,000, in November. The first paperback print-run, in 1953, would be 35,000 copies. In a prefatory note, Leonard explained that 'the manuscript had been completed, but had not been finally revised for the printer'. He believed that Woolf 'would not . . . have made any large or material alterations in it, though she would probably have made a good many small corrections and revisions'. Inevitably, his note begged more questions than it answered, and several reviewers were tempted into variations on the theme 'perhaps had she lived to revise the book . . .'[60]*

Woolf's reputation had already become a matter of controversy: in Cambridge, F. R. Leavis, blinded by class prejudice, proclaimed 'but for the name on the cover, and the mannerisms associated with that name, no one could have supposed it to be by an author of distinction and achievement', dismissing it as a work of 'extraordinary pointlessness and vacancy'; in New York, Louis Kronenberger saw it as a 'retreat from life, . . . the very immersion of self in a pool of pictures and phrases', considering it 'by all odds her weakest . . . another step in her steady creative decline.' Yet other critics thought, with Leonard, that it surpassed all her other novels, in some respects, and was 'perhaps the most complete expression of her world of imagination.' Woolf herself would have been both annoyed and unsurprised by the grudging praise of the Times Literary Supplement, which could not rank it with

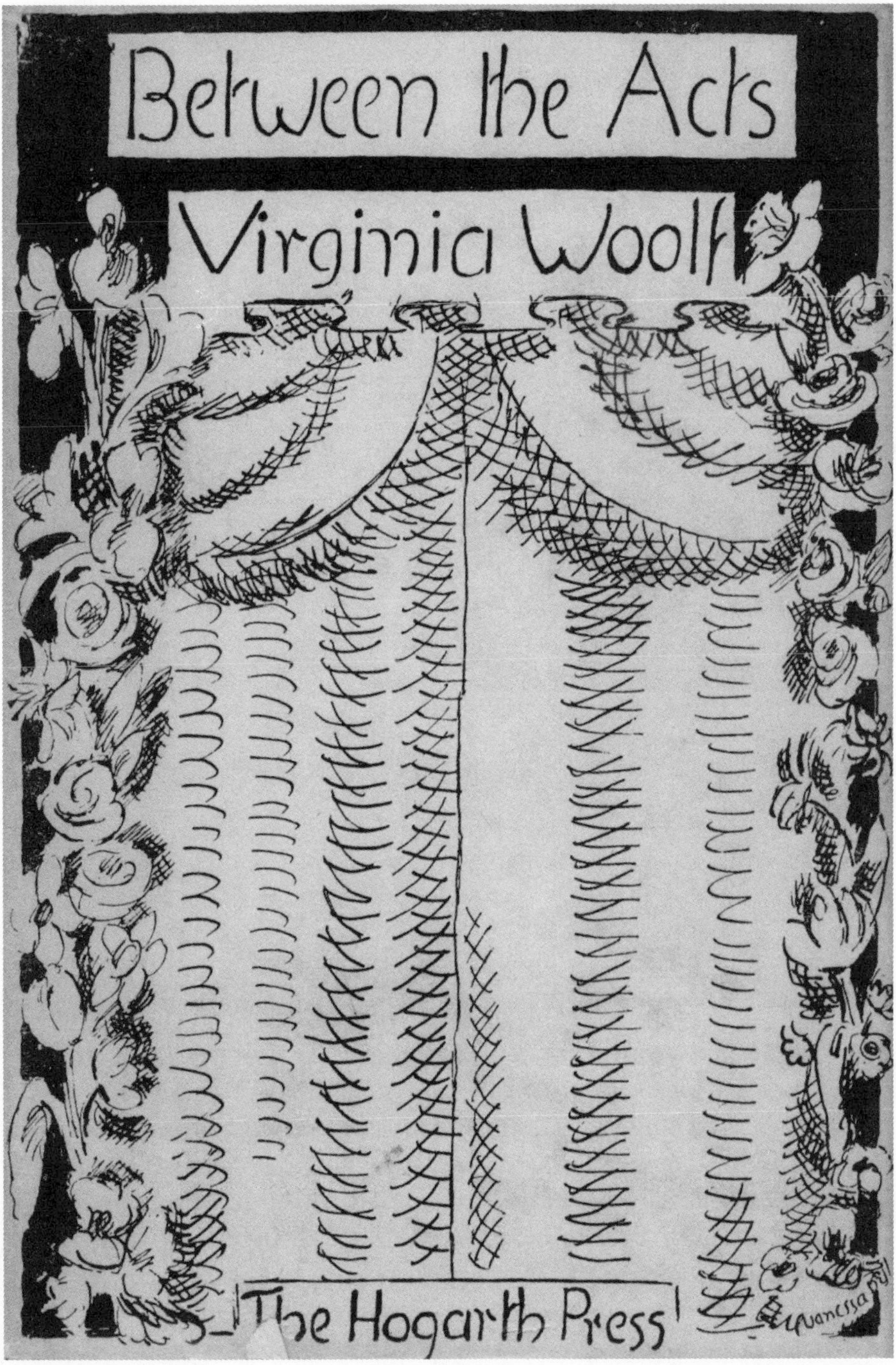
Between the Acts
Virginia Woolf
The Hogarth Press
Vanessa

her best work, yet found 'spells of loveliness and flashes of poetry that in style are hers alone.' This reviewer saw The Waves *as the pinnacle of her achievement, as it was of her experimental trajectory, glimpsing in* Between the Acts *'[s]omething left over from the high, pure song and poignant harmonies' of the earlier novel. Others compared it with* The Waves. *David Cecil thought both novels focused upon the question, 'How can we feel such ecstasy of the spirit if there is no spiritual significance in the universe?' For the poet Edwin Muir, Woolf had 'never written better prose than the prose in this last book, with its flashing, almost imperious curtness, its exact colouring, and its rapid, unhesitating movement.'*[61]

As critics began to discern a pattern in the shape of Woolf's career, teleological readings of Between the Acts *emerged, focusing on the novel's sly references to her own earlier fiction, and characterizing it as a summing up, even a farewell to her art. Shakespeare's* Tempest, *assumed to be his last play, with the author/magician at its centre, its repeated motif of interrupted action, and its pageant, offered tempting analogies.*

But a fellow novelist, Elizabeth Bowen, firmly rejected such readings: 'Because Between the Acts *is Virginia Woolf's last book, the reader may search it for some touch of finality. Of this I find, as I expected to find, none. The form and the combination of elements are, as always, new; she never used any combination or form twice . . .* Between the Acts *is incapable of being completed. One envisages or desires completion only upon a level upon which she neither wrote nor lived.'*[62]

A fuller account of the novel's complexities and contradictions, its mixture of genres, its parody and pastiche, its several levels of action, arrived with the concept of 'postmodernism' – a style characterized by self-consciousness, scepticism and mimicry, a style that questions the nature of representation itself by exploring the relationship between artist and audience, a style that dismantles the 'grand narratives' of culture and its institutions, a style that is '[o]pen, discontinuous, improvisational, indeterminate, or aleatory'.[63] *Thus defined, postmodernism can illuminate Woolf's practice in her last novel, which demonstrates, as all her writing does, her capacity to find, at every stage of her career, another and a newer way of expressing her vision.*

Epilogue

Woolf's life, like that of Sylvia Plath, is too often read in terms of her death, as if that was the most interesting or significant thing that happened to her. But like Septimus Warren Smith in *Mrs Dalloway*, her death was the outcome of a series of particular circumstances. Events seemed to conspire against her – there was, in Plath's memorable phrase, 'Such collusion of mulish elements'.[1]

Though Leonard was always protective, Woolf's life-threatening breakdown had occurred more than a quarter of a century earlier, and though she often suffered from debilitating illness, and, like most people, could feel angry, paranoiac or depressed, she was for much of the time, cheerful, lively and creative – at once intensely private and absorbed in her imaginary worlds, and warmly sociable, amusing and amused.

At the end of 1940, the odds began to stack up against her: she had just completed a major novel, and was in the trough of the wave that always followed the exhilaration and absorption of writing. To avoid that experience, she had for many years set up further projects that would carry her through that phase. This time, she began work on a book about literature, to be called 'Reading at Random' or 'Turning the Page' – a third Common Reader, or perhaps the book about reading that she had so often begun and abandoned.[2] But after Christmas, she increasingly felt that she could not write, that there was no 'echo': 'shall I ever write again one of those sentences that gives me intense pleasure? There is no echo in Rodmell – only waste air.'[3] She had been working on a short story, appropriately entitled 'The Symbol', about a mountain that cannot be climbed – it defeats all attempts – and about death in the snow. She typed it out at the beginning of March. Monk's

House was desperately cold (there were fuel shortages), and either cold, or tension, made writing physically, as well as psychically difficult: she apologized to friends for typing her letters – 'such a frozen claw'.[4] If body chemistry was implicated in her depressions, the severe rationing may have brought on a dietary deficiency. Octavia Wilberforce, a distant cousin and new friend at this time, a young doctor living in Brighton, thought both the Woolfs looked 'thin and half-starved', and began to send them milk and cream regularly, from a local farm.[5]

Virginia felt trapped at Rodmell. 'For almost the first time in my life I've not a bed in London.' She desperately missed her friends and the pre-war social buzz of city life; the mild curiosity of the locals was scarcely a substitute. She had lost her freedom to wander through city streets, 'street haunting', to buy a pencil when and as she wanted ('I am economising. I am to spend nothing'). She missed the small, pleasurable daily choices enjoyed by the middle-class Western world, while recognizing that '[t]hese are inconveniences rather than hard-ships'.[6] Worse still, the London that she loved so passionately that it was her 'only patriotism', was being bombed to bits. Former homes at Mecklenburgh and Tavistock squares had been damaged or destroyed. In January 1941, reading about the Great Fire of London of 1666, she realized that once more 'London was burning. 8 of my city churches destroyed, & the Guildhall.' Returning, later that month, Woolf took the underground to the Temple, to walk through her favourite streets between the Strand and the river – the streets where *The Voyage Out*, in all its versions, had begun, her own literary voyage out. There, she 'wandered in the desolate ruins of my old squares: gashed; dismantled; the old red bricks all white powder, something like a builders yard. Grey dirt & broken windows; . . . all that completeness ravished & demolished.'[7]

Haunted by visions of 'Oxford Street & Piccadilly', she gazed out at the snow-covered Downs towards Caburn and Asheham, quoting to herself, 'Look your last on all things lovely'.[8] Nineteen forty-one had begun inauspiciously with the death of her greatest rival, James Joyce – 'about a fortnight younger than I am'. They had never met, though he had been 'about the place', and she recalled Harriet Weaver 'in wool gloves, . . . spinsterly, buttoned up' visiting them at Richmond in April 1918 with the thoroughly unbuttoned typescript of *Ulysses*.

Woolf had put it away in a drawer, but then took it out to show Katherine Mansfield. Katherine 'began to read, ridiculing: then suddenly said, But theres some thing in this: a scene that should figure I suppose in the history of literature.' One after another, the age's great writers 'became [their] admirers'.[9]

'But . . . days will lengthen . . . Its the cold hour, this, before the lights go up', she wrote (thinking, perhaps, of life as theatre, as in *Between the Acts*). 'Yes, I was thinking: we live without a future . . . with our noses pressed to a closed door.'[10] Hitler's Third Reich was at the height of its power: Hungary, Slovakia and Romania had joined the Tripartite pact of the Axis powers, and soon Bulgaria and Yugoslavia would follow suit. It was 'the worst stage of the war . . . we have no future'. England was still expecting an invasion: 'I cant help wishing [it] would come. Its this standing about in a dentist's waiting room that I hate', she told Nellie Cecil, a week before her death.[11] That threat had turned several of her friends' thoughts towards suicide the previous summer, when she and Leonard had made preparations for it, though at the time she had resented the idea of retreating to the garage: 'I don't want to go to bed at midday'.[12] Three months later, in June 1941, Hitler would launch his fatal invasion of Russia, and by December, the Japanese bombing of Pearl Harbor would bring the Americans into the war at last.

As the winter of 1941 drew to an end, Woolf was working on 'The Reader', the second chapter of 'Reading at Random'. Behind a page of Robert Burton's *Anatomy of Melancholy*, the reader glimpses the author 'sitting alone in the centre of the labyrinth of words . . . thinking of suicide.' In a desperate effort to escape from herself, Woolf suggested to Octavia Wilberforce that she write a portrait of her: Octavia was a professional woman, a doctor, like Woolf's cousin Janet Vaughan. These young women's lives were so different from her own that she wanted to understand them from the inside. Octavia spent an afternoon at Rodmell, talking about herself, and Woolf began sketching out her life as 'English Youth'.[13] Although Octavia knew little of Woolf's previous history at this stage, she quickly recognized that she was terrified of a recurrence of her old illness, fearing '[t]hat the past will recur – that she won't be able to work again and so on'. On 27 March, Leonard was so worried about Virginia that he took her to see Octavia in Brighton. At first Virginia was reluctant to admit anything was wrong, but then when Octavia wanted to examine her, said, 'Will you promise if I do this not to order me a rest cure?'[14]

Although her worst breakdown had begun a year before the First World War, for Woolf it had always been linked with the war, and it may be that, in some mysterious way, mass murder, hatred and cruelty create a palpable psychic atmosphere that presses upon the sensitive, driving them towards those darker aspects of outer or inner life that we normally resist or dismiss. As the guardians and interpreters of culture, artists are or become peculiarly receptive, or vulnerable to their times. Though Woolf did not believe in a personal God, 'A Sketch of the Past' shows that she did believe in some kind of 'world soul' embodied in beauty, form and meaning, and transmitted by great artists: 'all human beings – are connected with this; . . . the whole world is a work of art; . . . we are parts of the work of art . . . we are the words; we are the music; we are the thing itself.'[15] But if we are the words and the music, we must also participate in evil creations – in bombs, concentration camps and gas chambers.

'Yet if one cant write, as Duncan said yesterday, one may as well kill oneself. Such despair comes over me', Woolf had written in September 1939. A few months earlier, in June, another friend and painter, Mark Gertler, had done just that, gassing himself in his studio at Grove Terrace, Highgate. As Virginia had recorded in 'A Sketch of the Past', he had dined with them in May, and discussed his earlier suicide attempt: then, he had claimed to be 'completely recovered . . . So why did he turn on the gas . . . ?' Woolf wondered. 'We know no more.'[16] Like other artists at that time, Gertler seems to have been overwhelmed by a combination of personal problems, a crisis in his own creativity and horror at the coming war. The old suffragist and pacifist Helena Swanwick (who remembered Virginia as a toddler, running naked on the sands at St Ives) also committed suicide in 1939, apparently unable to bear the thought of another European war. The older sister of the painter Walter Sickert, she had been born in Bavaria.

A number of German writers, persecuted and exiled, cut off from their roots or threatened with death at the hands of the Gestapo, also took their own lives: in 1935, the satirist Kurt Tucholsky committed suicide in Sweden. In 1939 in New York, the playwright Ernst Toller, whom Woolf had met in 1935, and who had written in 1938 (as Woolf, perhaps, knew), 'My home is the earth and the world is my fatherland', killed himself, and in Paris, in the wake of his death, the Austrian novelist Joseph Roth followed his example.[17] In 1940, the dramatist and poet Walter Hasenclever, and the cultural critic Walter Benjamin both committed suicide, in flight from the German invasion of France, and in 1942, the Austrian novelist and poet Stefan Zweig, who had escaped to Brazil, would commit suicide there.[18] And in Ashford, Kent in 1943, the young French philosopher Simone Weil died of self-neglect. For those who had set out to study or change society or culture, to think or to write, whatever they had believed in, worked for and celebrated seemed to have vanished: human ideals had been emptied, and abandoned.

Woolf's three suicide notes speak of her terror of going mad again, yet the evidence suggests that she was severely depressed, or in despair, rather than 'mad' (or mentally disturbed). She consoled Leonard with the cliché 'I don't think two people could have been happier than we have been', as if echoing Terence's grief for Rachel in *The Voyage Out*.[19] Even in her distress, she was conscious of the burden of guilt that suicide imposes on the survivors – her note to Vanessa insists that 'Leonard has been so astonishingly good, every day, always; I cant imagine that anyone could have done more for me than he has . . . Will you assure him of this?' In the light of her two notes to Leonard, it seems likely that she had already made an unsuccessful attempt a few days earlier, when Leonard recalled meeting her as she returned from a walk in the river meadows in pouring rain, 'soaking wet, looking ill and shaken. She said that she had slipped and fallen into one of the dykes'.[20]

On the morning of 28 March 1941, their housekeeper, Louie Everest, remembered seeing Woolf

come downstairs from the sitting-room and go out to her room in the garden. In a few minutes she returned to the house, put on her coat, took her walking-stick and went quickly up the garden to the top gate. She must have . . . rushed off like that so that we would not see her.

When I rang the bell at 1 o'clock to tell Mr Woolf that lunch was ready, he said he was going upstairs to hear the news on the radio and would only be a

Tuesday.

Dearest,

I feel certain that I am going
mad again. I feel we cant go
through another of those terrible times.
And I shant recover this time. I begin
to hear voices, & cant concentrate.
So I am doing what seems the best
thing to do. You have given me
the greatest possible happiness. You
have been in every way all that anyone
could be. I dont think two
people could have been happier till
this terrible disease came. I cant
fight it any longer, I know that I am
spoiling your life, that without me you
could work. And you will I know.
You see I cant even write this properly. I
cant read. What I want to say is that
I owe all the happiness of my life to you.
You have been entirely patient with me &
incredibly good. I want to say that —
everybody knows it. If anybody could

have saved me it would have been you.
Everything has gone from me but the
certainty of your goodness. I
cant go on spoiling your life any
longer. I dont think two people
could have been happier than we
have been.
V.

This is the letter left for me on the table in the sitting
room which I found at 1 on March 28

LW 11/5/41

few minutes. The next moment he came running down the stairs to the kitchen calling me. 'Louie!' he said, 'I think something has happened to Mrs Woolf! I think she might have tried to kill herself! Which way did she go – did you see her leave the house?' 'She went through the top gate a little while ago,' I said. It was suddenly a terrible nightmare.[21]

At 11.30, Virginia had walked down to the tidal river Ouse, now running swiftly between its grassy banks, put a large stone in her pocket and waded in, in a final bid for peace:

At last all the guns have stopped firing. All the searchlights have been extinguished. The natural darkness of a summer's night returns. The innocent sounds of the country are heard again. An apple thuds to the ground. An owl hoots, winging its way from tree to tree. And some half-forgotten words of an old English writer come to mind: 'The huntsmen are up in America . . .'[22]

Notes

List of Abbreviations

D – *The Diary of Virginia Woolf*, eds. Anne Olivier Bell and Andrew McNeillie (London: Hogarth Press, 1977–84), 5 volumes.

L – *The Letters of Virginia Woolf*, eds. Nigel Nicolson and Joanne Trautmann (London: Hogarth Press, 1975–80), 6 volumes.

Essays – *The Essays of Virginia Woolf*, ed. Andrew McNeillie (London: Hogarth Press, 1987), 4 volumes (6 projected).

CSF – *The Complete Shorter Fiction of Virginia Woolf*, ed. Susan Dick (London: Hogarth Press, 1985, rev. edn. 1989).

MoB – *Moments of Being*, ed. Jeanne Schulkind (1976 London: Chatto and Windus/Sussex University Press; London: Hogarth Press, 1985). Except where specifically stated, the 1985 edition is used.

Biography – Quentin Bell, *Virginia Woolf: A Biography* (London: Hogarth Press, 1972), 2 volumes.

An Autobiography – Leonard Woolf, *An Autobiography* (1964, 1967, 1969; Oxford: Oxford University Press, 1980), 2 volumes.

Critical Heritage – Robin Majumdar and Allen McLaurin, eds., *Virginia Woolf: The Critical Heritage* (London: Routledge and Kegan Paul, 1975).

A Bibliography – B. J. Kirkpatrick and Stuart N. Clarke, *A Bibliography of Virginia Woolf*, 4th ed. (Soho Bibliographies IX, Oxford: Clarendon Press, 1997).

Preface

1. *Orlando*, intro. Sandra Gilbert, ed. Brenda Lyons (1928; London: Penguin, 1993), pp. 145–6.
2. Ibid., p. 187.
3. The surviving manuscript fragment of *Night and Day*, running from the middle of chapter XI to the middle of chapter XVI, and entitled 'Dreams and Realities', is among the Woolf papers in the Henry W. and Albert. A. Berg Collection of the New York Public Library.
4. *CSF*, p. 89.
5. See, for example, 'Sympathy' (and its outline version, 'A Death in the Newspaper') and 'An Unwritten Novel', *CSF*, pp. 108–11, 315, 112–21.
6. Erich Auerbach, *Mimesis* (1946), trans. Willard Trask (Princeton: Princeton University Press, 1953), p. 488.
7. D1, 27 Aug. 1918, p. 186.
8. George Eliot, 'The Natural History of German Life', reprinted in A. S. Byatt and Nicholas Warren, eds., *George Eliot, Selected Essays, Poems and Other Writings* (Harmondsworth: Penguin, 1990), p. 110. An earlier sentence from the same essay, 'The greatest benefit we owe to the artist, whether painter, poet, or novelist, is the extension of our sympathies', opens David Bradshaw's essay, 'The Socio-political Vision of the Novels', in Sue Roe and Susan Sellers, eds., *The Cambridge Companion to Virginia Woolf* (Cambridge: Cambridge University Press, 2000), p. 191.

Chapter 1

1. Clive Bell to Virginia Stephen, ? Oct. 1908, cited in *Biography*, vol. 1, appendix D, p. 208.
2. *The Voyage Out*, ed. Jane Wheare (1915; London: Penguin, 1992). Page numbers appearing in square brackets after quotes refer to this edition of the book.
3. Louise A. DeSalvo, ed., *Melymbrosia: An Early Version of "The Voyage Out"* (New York: New York Public Library, 1982), appendix B, pp. 262–4. Rhoda, in *The Waves*, would also imagine the West End garlanded with vine leaves: 'I covered the whole street, Oxford Street, Piccadilly Circus, with the blaze and ripple of my mind, with vine leaves and rose leaves' – *The Waves*, ed. Kate Flint (1931; London: Penguin, 1992), p. 157.
4. Richard Jefferies, *After London; or, Wild England* (London: Cassell, 1885).

The surviving copy in Woolf's library is a 1939 Everyman edition (see Holleyman and Treacher, *Catalogue of Books from the Library of Leonard and Virginia Woolf* (Brighton: Holleyman and Treacher, 1975), section VII, page 2), but like most well-read Victorians, Woolf was familiar with Jefferies' work, as her essay on 'Thoreau', for example, indicates: *Essays*, vol. 2, p. 138.

5. David Bradshaw's essay, 'The Skeleton Beneath', in Sue Roe and Susan Sellers, eds., *The Cambridge Companion to Virginia Woolf* (Cambridge: Cambridge University Press, 2000) makes a number of these points in a different context – see esp. pp. 192–7.

6. *VO*, pp. 16, 20.

7. *An Autobiography*, vol. 2, p. 55.

8. D2, 3 Sept. 1922, p. 197.

9. L1, to Clive Bell, ? 7 Feb. 1909, p. 383.

10. Characters from *Night and Day* and *Jacob's Room* turn up in Bond Street or at the party in *Mrs Dalloway* – see Ch. 6, p. 138.

11. L2, to Lytton Strachey, 28 Feb. 1916, p. 82.

12. *Melymbrosia*, p. 21.

13. CB to VS, ? 5 Feb. 1909, reprinted in *Biography*, vol. 1, p. 210.

14. *Melymbrosia*, p. 201 and compare *VO*, p. 270. A sense of the jungle as alien and threatening is also present in Leonard Woolf's first novel, *The Village in the Jungle*: 'Once more evil had come out of the jungle' (London: Edward Arnold, 1913; reprinted New Phoenix Library, 1951), p. 122.

15. See *VO*, p. 16 – like Tennyson's Kraken.

16. This rhapsodic account of a 'voyage out' occurs at the end of Woolf's second novel, *Night and Day*, when Mrs Hilbery is consoling her daughter. *Night and Day*, ed. Julia Briggs (1919; London: Penguin, 1992), p. 411.

17. See Celia Marshik, 'Publication and "Public Women": Prostitution and Censorship in Three Novels by Virginia Woolf', *Modern Fiction Studies*, 45, 4 (1999), pp. 853–86.

18. See *VO*, p. 372, fn. 7. Elizabeth Heine quotes Sal's story in 'Virginia Woolf's Revision of *The Voyage Out*', *The Voyage Out*, Definitive Collected Edition (London: Hogarth Press, 1990), pp. 436–7.

19. *Melymbrosia*, pp. 150–1 (compare *VO*, p. 142, though there is no precise equivalent).

20. Compare *Melymbrosia*, p. 199.

21. In Woolf's second novel, *Night and Day*, Lady Otway warns the heroine, Katharine, 'I really don't advise a woman who wants to have things her own way to get married' (*ND*, p. 177).

22. E. M. Forster's review of the novel for the *Daily News* is quoted in *Critical Heritage*, p. 54.

23. *VO*, pp. 281–2 (and compare p. 308); 322.

24. Virginia Woolf, 'A Sketch of the Past', *MoB*, p. 137 (I quote the earlier, 1976 version of this text at this point).

25. *VO*, pp. 337, 339, 342, 346.

26. L1, to Violet Dickinson, 22 Dec. 1906, p. 269.

27. L1, to Madge Vaughan, 15 Feb. 1907, p. 283.

28. L1, to VD, 3 Jan. 1907, p. 276.

29. L1, to VD, 31 Dec. 1906, p. 274.

30. L1, to VD, ? Feb. 1907, p. 280.

31. *Biography*, vol. 1, p. 15 – Bell cites Woolf's then unpublished MS, 'The Cook', now edited by Susan Dick, *Woolf Studies Annual*, vol. 3 (New York: Pace University Press, 1997), p. 139.

32. L1, to VD, 3 May 1907, p. 293; see also L1, to VD, ? May 1907, p. 295.

33. L1, to VD, 18 Dec. 1906, p. 267.

34. L1, to VD, 7 July 1907, p. 299.

35. L1, to VD, 25 Aug. 1907, p. 307.

36. L1, to VD, 22 Sept. 1907, p. 311.

37. L1, to Vanessa Bell, ? Oct. 1907, p. 316.

38. L1, to VD, ? 30 Dec. 1906, p. 273.

39. L1, to VD, 3 June 1907, p. 297.

40. CB to VS, 11 Aug. 1907 (Clive Bell's letters to Virginia Stephen are among the Monk's House Papers at the University of Sussex Library); L1, to CB, 18 Aug. 1907, p. 304, and compare p. 310.

41. See Mitchell A. Leaska, ed., Virginia Woolf, *A Passionate Apprentice: The Early Journals 1897–1909* (London: Hogarth Press, 1990).

42. Clive Bell's diary is in the collection of Anne Olivier Bell. I am grateful to James Beechey for drawing my attention to it.

43. As in *Melymbrosia*, appendix B, p. 263; for the significance of 'Euphrosyne', see *VO*, p. 355, fn. 7.

44. L1, to CB, Summer 1908?, p. 336.

45. Clive Bell, *Civilization* (1928; London: Phoenix Library, 1932), pp. v, vi.

46. L1, to CB, 15 Apr. 1908, p. 325.

47. L1, to VD, 13 May 1908, p. 331.

48. 'A Dialogue on a Hill', *CSF*, appendix C, p. 326.

49. CB to VS, 3 May 1908; L1, to CB, 6 May 1908, p. 329; CB to VS, 7 May 1908 (compare CB to VS, 9 Apr. 1909).

50. *Virginia Woolf's Jacob's Room: The Holograph Draft*, ed. Edward L. Bishop (New York: Pace University Press, 1998), pp. 266–7 (I read 'chasms', not 'charms', and omit Woolf's numerous deletions).

51. L3, to Jacques Raverat, 5 Feb. 1925, p. 163; L4, to Ethel Smyth, 15 Aug. 1930, p. 200.

52. D2, 12 Mar. 1922, p. 171.

53. L1, to CB, 15 Apr. 1908, p. 325.

54. 'Friendship's Gallery', ed. Ellen Hawkes, *Twentieth Century Literature*, 25, 3/4 (Fall/Winter, 1979), pp. 270–302.

55. Woolf refers to the novel as 'Melymbrosia' from May 1908 (see L1, to CB, p. 334; CB to VS, 7 Aug. 1908); CB to VS, ? Oct. 1908, in *Biography*, vol. 1, appendix D, pp. 207–8; CB to VS, 23 Aug. 1908.

56. CB to VS, 4 Oct. 1908; CB to VS, early April 1908? (This letter appears to respond to VW's letter to CB, in L1, p. 336, tentatively dated 'Summer 1908?')

57. L1, to CB, ? 7 Feb. 1909, p. 383 (see also *An Autobiography*, vol. 2, pp. 17–18).

58. CB to VS, ? 5 Feb. 1909, reprinted in *Biography*, vol. 1, p. 209.

59. L1, to CB, ? 7 Feb. 1909, p. 383.

60. Ibid.

61. CB to VS, 27 Oct. 1909.

62. D1, 7 Dec. 1917, p. 86.

63. Cited by Michael Holroyd, *Lytton Strachey* (London: Chatto and Windus, 1994), p. 201.

64. L1, to VB, ? 8 June 1911, p. 466.

65. L2, to Molly MacCarthy, 28 Sept. 1912, p. 9; L2, to Ka Cox, 4 Sept. 1912, p. 6.

66. Leonard Woolf, *The Wise Virgins* (1914; New York: Harcourt, Brace, 1979), p. 231.

67. *A Bibliography*, p. 3.

68. The *Saturday Review* (19 June 1915, p. iv of supplement) and the *Glasgow Herald* are quoted from 'Some Press Opinions', which make up the last fourteen pages of the first edition of *Jacob's Room* (London: Hogarth Press, 1922), pp. 2, 3 (separately numbered sequence). The Woolfs included quotations from (comically) bad as well as good reviews of her first two novels.

69. Quotations from the *Spectator*, the *Nation*, the *Observer*, the *Morning Post*, the *Athenaeum* (all unsigned) are reprinted in *Critical Heritage*, pp. 62–3; 60; 50–1; 51; 59.

70. Ibid., p. 50.

71. Ibid., pp. 57–8.

72. Ibid., pp. 53–4.

73. Leonard Woolf and James Strachey, eds., *Virginia Woolf & Lytton Strachey, Letters* (New York: Harcourt, Brace, 1956), p. 73.

74. L2, to LS, 28 Feb. 1916, p. 82.

75. *ND*, pp. 106, 111. The surviving MS of *Night and Day*, in the Berg Collection of the New York Public Library, begins near the end of chapter XI, and is dated 6 Oct. 1916.

76. L2, to LS, 26 Nov. 1919, p. 401.

77. Saxon Sydney-Turner (1880–1962) was a Cambridge friend of Thoby Stephen, Lytton Stratchey and Leonard Woolf, who later worked at the Treasury. He was an enthusiastic musician (Vanessa Bell painted him at the piano, about 1908).

78. L2, to Saxon Sydney-Turner, 25 Jan. 1920, pp. 418, 419, and see *VO*, p. 29 and p. 357, fn. 8; to R. C. Trevelyan, 30 Jan. 1920 (Sussex University archives, and L2, p. 419).

79. D2, 4 Feb. 1920, p. 17; Woolf often used the image of the writer as rider, as Diane F. Gillespie points out in *The Sisters' Arts: The Writing and Painting of Virginia Woolf and Vanessa Bell* (Syracuse, NY: Syracuse University Press, 1988), pp. 1–2.

80. *A Bibliography* (pp. 4, 5) reproduces pages of chapter XVI from the two surviving copies Woolf marked up with her revisions: one (that marked up for Doran) was in the library of F. B. Adams, Jr, but has since been sold to an anonymous buyer (see *Virginia Woolf Bulletin* 9 (Jan. 2002), p. 64); the other is in the University of Sydney Library, Rare Books and Special Collections.

81. *VO*, pp. 42, 74, 112, 113, 72. Elizabeth Heine provides a list of textual variants between the first English and first American editions at the end of her edition of *The Voyage Out*, op. cit., pp. 453–63; compare discussion and list in *The Voyage Out*, eds. C. Ruth Miller and Lawrence Miller (Oxford: Shakespeare Head/Blackwell, 1995), appendix B, 'Textual Variants', pp. 380–407. Madeline Moore entitled her account of 'the Mystical and the Political in the Novels of Virginia Woolf', *The Short Season Between Two Silences* (London: Allen and Unwin, 1984).

82. *A Bibliography*, pp. 3, 6.

83. *Critical Heritage*, pp. 8–9, 86.

84. Clive's spelling is always erratic. Clive Bell to Mary Hutchinson (CB MH43), n.d. [Mar. 1915]; (CB MH46), 29 Mar. 1915 (Harry Ransom Humanities Research Center at Austin, Texas).

85. *Critical Heritage*, p. 139.

86. See *A Bibliography*, pp. 6, 7.

87. See Heine, p. 400.

88. The clearest account of the revision process is that given by Elizabeth Heine – see above, n. 81.

89. 'The Novels of George Meredith', in Leonard Woolf, ed., *Virginia Woolf, Collected Essays* (London: Chatto and Windus, 1966), vol. 1 pp. 225–6, (and *The Common Reader: Second Series*, London: Hogarth Press, 1932); cited by Louise A. DeSalvo, *Virginia Woolf's First Voyage: A Novel in the Making* (London: Macmillan, 1980), p. ix.

Chapter 2

1. *Night and Day*, ed. Julia Briggs (1919; London: Penguin, 1992). Page numbers appearing in square brackets after quotes refer to this edition of the book.

2. *ND*, p. 26, and see David Bradshaw, 'Eugenics: "They should certainly be killed"', in Bradshaw, ed., *A Concise Companion to Modernism* (Oxford: Blackwell, 2003), pp. 49–53.

3. *An Autobiography*, vol. 1, pp. 4–5.

4. Leonard Woolf, *The Wise Virgins* (1914; New York: Harcourt, Brace, 1979), p. 52. Mark Hussey explores the interaction between the Woolfs' early fictions in 'Refractions of Desire: The Early Fiction of Virginia and Leonard Woolf', *Modern Fiction Studies*, 38, 1 (Spring 1992), pp. 127–46.

5. As Woolf would have known, the name 'Katharine' derives from the Greek adjective 'katharos', meaning pure, unspotted.

6. L2, to Janet Case, 19 Nov. 1919, p. 400.

7. *ND*, p. 120.

8. L2, to Lytton Strachey, 28 Oct. 1919, p. 394 (Lytton's letter to her is missing).

9. *Biography*, vol. 1, p. 141 (and see Ch. 1, pp. 20–1, above).

10. Ibid., pp. 131, 144.

11. L1, to Sydney Waterlow, 9 Dec. 1911, pp. 485–6; L1, to Vanessa Bell, 21 July 1911, pp. 469–71.

12. L1, to Violet Dickinson, 4 June 1912, p. 500; L1, to JC, June 1912, p. 501.

13. *An Autobiography*, vol. 1, p. 54.

14. For an influential critique of Leonard's role, see Roger Poole, *The Unknown Virginia Woolf* (1978; 3rd edn., London, NJ: Humanities Press International, 1990).

15. The single surviving MS of *Night and Day*, dated 6 Oct. 1916, and headed 'Dreams and Realities', is in the Berg Collection of the New York Public Library. The phrase 'dreams and realities' had been used by Terence Hewet in *The Voyage Out*, ed. Jane Wheare (1915; London: Penguin, 1992), p.172, and is applied to Ralph in *ND* (p. 120).

16. L4, to Ethel Smyth, 16 Oct. 1930, p. 231.

17. *An Autobiography*, vol. 2, p. 62.

18. Elizabeth Heine, in the Definitive Collected Edition of *The Voyage Out* (London: Hogarth Press, 1990), finds it 'an almost miraculous novel', p. 401.

19. L1, to VD, June 1912, p. 502.

20. See Noel Annan, *Leslie Stephen: The Godless Victorian* (Chicago: University of Chicago Press, 1984), pp. 136–8; Thomas C. Caramagno, *The Flight of the Mind: Virginia Woolf's Art and Manic-Depressive Illness* (Berkeley: University of California Press, 1992), pp. 103–7.

21. D2, 3 Dec. 1923, p. 277.

22. *Sir Leslie Stephen's Mausoleum Book*, intro. Alan Bell (Oxford: Oxford University Press, 1977), p. 92, cited by Caramagno, p. 108; see also Woolf's account of Laura in 'Old Bloomsbury' as 'a vacant-eyed girl whose idiocy was becoming daily more obvious, who could hardly read, who would throw the scissors into the fire, who was tongue-tied and stammered and yet had to appear at table with the rest of us', *MoB*, p. 182; for a more sympathetic account, see Henrietta Garnett, *Anny: A Life of Anne Isabelle Thackeray* (London: Chatto and Windus, 2004), esp. pp. 217, 256.

23. *Biography*, vol. 1, p. 35.

24. Caramagno, pp. 101–3.

25. See Elaine Showalter, *The Female Malady: Women, Madness and English Culture 1830–1980* (London: Virago, 1987), p. 134.

26. Caramagno, p. 11.

27. *An Autobiography*, vol. 2, p. 17.

28. Showalter, pp. 138–9.

29. See Ann J. Lane, ed., *The Charlotte Perkins Gilman Reader: 'The Yellow Wallpaper' and Other Fiction* (London: The Women's Press, 1981).

30. 'A Sketch of the Past', *MoB*, p. 83.

31. 'Old Bloomsbury', *MoB*, p. 182.

32. Ibid., p. 183.

33. Ibid., p. 184.

34. 'A Sketch of the Past', *MoB*, p. 123.

35. L4, to ES, 11 March 1931, p. 298.

36. *Biography*, vol. 1, p. 201.

37. Leonard describes her 'tranquillity and quietude (. . . to some extent superficial)', in *An Autobiography*, vol. 2, p. 14.

38. L2, to LS, 26 Dec. 1912, p. 16.

39. Vanessa Bell to Roger Fry, 24 Dec. 1912, cited in *Biography*, vol. 2, p. 8.

40. *An Autobiography*, vol. 2, pp. 55–6, where Leonard refers to his consul-

tations, in the course of recalling events of 1912 (before his marriage). According to Leonard's diary, he consulted Virginia's doctor, Dr Savage, in March 1912 – see George Spater and Ian Parsons, *A Marriage of True Minds: An Intimate Portrait of Leonard and Virginia Woolf* (London: Jonathan Cape/ Hogarth Press, 1977), p. 59, but consultations with other doctors took place early in 1913 – see also Frederic Spotts, *Letters of Leonard Woolf* (London: Bloomsbury, 1989), pp. 181–2; *Selected Letters of Vanessa Bell*, ed. Regina Marler (London: Bloomsbury, 1993), pp. 134, 137; Hermione Lee, *Virginia Woolf* (London: Chatto and Windus, 1996), pp. 334–5.

41. *Mrs Dalloway*, intro. Elaine Showalter, ed. Stella McNichol (1925; London: Penguin, 1992), p. 109; for detailed accounts of the doctors consulted, see Stephen Trombley, *All That Summer She Was Mad: Virginia Woolf, Female Victim of Male Medicine* (New York: Continuum, 1982).

42. L1, to VD, ? July 1912, p. 506.

43. L2, to VD, ? 9 Oct. 1912, p. 9.

44. L2, to VD, 11 Apr. 1913, p. 23.

45. D2, 2 Jan. 1923, p. 221; L3, to Ethel Sands, 9 Feb. 1927, p. 329.

46. D3, 5 Sept. 1926, p. 107.

47. Jean Thomas to Violet Dickinson, 14 Sept. 1913, cited in *Biography*, vol. 2, p. 16, fn.

48. L2, to Leonard Woolf, 4 Aug. 1913; 5 Aug. 1913, p. 34.

49. 'Regeneration' was the name given to Henry Head's drastic experiments, which involved severing his nerves to observe their properties of recovery (it was adopted by Pat Barker as the title of her trilogy of novels, which includes portraits of Rivers and the poet Siegfried Sassoon).

50. Hermione Lee examines the question of how far the drugs Woolf was given exacerbated her condition, Lee, pp. 184–5.

51. L1, to Lady Robert Cecil, Jan. 1907, p. 278.

52. 'A Sketch of the Past', *MoB*, p. 72.

53. L3, to Gwen Raverat, 1 May 1925, p. 180.

54. *MD*, p. 202.

55. Poole, p. 157, citing Spater and Parsons, p. 69.

56. 'I'm glad you are fat; for then you are warm and mellow and generous and creative. I find that unless I weigh 9½ stones I hear voices and see visions and can neither eat nor sleep', L2, to Jacques Raverat, 10 Dec. 1922, p. 592.

57. D1, 2 Jan. 1915, p. 4; 'Effie' would become 'Katharine' – her name is altered to 'Katharine' on the 22nd leaf of the surviving MS – see Elizabeth Heine, 'Postscript to the *Diary of Virginia Woolf*, Vol.1: "Effie's Story" and *Night and Day*', *Virginia Woolf Miscellany*, 9, Winter (1977), p. 10.

58. D1, 15 Jan. 1915, p. 19.

59. L2, to Molly MacCarthy, 16 Dec. 1914, p. 56.

60. D1, 27 Jan. 1915, p. 29.

61. D1, 31 Jan 1915, p. 32.

62. D1, 30 Jan. 1915, p. 31.

63. D1, 25 Jan. 1915, p. 28.

64. D1, 3 Jan. 1915, p. 5; D1, 4 Jan. 1915, p. 6; D1, 5 Jan. 1915, p. 8; D1, 9 Jan. 1915, p. 13 (and compare the 'maimed file of lunatics' seen by Septimus Smith, *MD*, p. 98).

65. VB to Roger Fry, 25 June 1915, cited in *Biography*, vol. 2, p. 26.

66. *An Autobiography*, vol. 2, p. 111.

67. Ibid., p. 120.

68. Ibid., pp. 105-24, esp. p. 115.

69. Thomas C. Caramagno believes Woolf was suffering from bipolar syndrome (see n. 20 above); for another recent account, see Douglass W. Orr, *Virginia Woolf's Illnesses*, ed. Wayne K. Chapman (Clemson, SC: Clemson University Digital Press, 2004).

70. 'Mrs D. seeing the truth. S.S. seeing the insane truth', entry for 16 Oct. 1922 in the holograph notebook in the Berg Collection (and compare D2, 14 Oct. 1922, p. 207), also cited by Showalter in her introduction to *MD*, p. xxvii.

71. D2, 8 Aug. 1921, p. 125.

72. 'On Being Ill' (1926), *Essays*, vol. 4, p. 317.

73. D2, 8 Aug. 1921, p. 126.

74. D3, 26 Sept. 1929, p. 254.

75. L2, to LS, 22 Oct. 1915, p. 67.

76. L2, to LS, 25 July 1916, p. 107.

77. See Henrietta Garnett's recent biography, n. 22, above.

78. Mitchell A. Leaska, ed., Virginia Woolf, *A Passionate Apprentice: The Early Journals, 1897-1909* (London: Hogarth Press, 1990), 29 Jan. 1897, p. 24. According to the Curator, she visited it again on 29 March 1898 with Vanessa and Hester Ritchie (when they signed the Visitors' Book). Leslie Stephen had been appointed Chairman of the Carlyle's House (Chelsea) Purchase Fund, and on 31 Dec. 1894 he had written a letter to *The Times* appealing for funds (I am grateful to Stuart Clarke for this information). See also David Bradshaw, ed., Virginia Woolf, *Carlyle's House and Other Sketches* [VW's 1909 Notebook] (London: Hesperus, 2003), pp. 3-4; D4, 16 Mar. 1931, p. 13 – for the resulting article, 'Great Men's Houses', published in *Good Housekeeping*, third in a series called 'The London Scene' in March 1932, see Rachel Bowlby, ed., Virginia Woolf, *The Crowded Dance*

of *Modern Life: Selected Essays* (London: Penguin, 1993), vol. 2, pp. 117–22.

79. *ND*, p. 4.

80. *ND*, p. 95; Celia Milvain and Cousin Caroline (*ND*, pp. 96, 99) suggest Mary Fisher and Caroline Emelia Stephen. In 1904 Virginia apparently wrote comic biographies of them, though they have not survived (L1, to VD, 6 Dec. 1904, p. 163).

81. 'A Sketch of the Past', *MoB* (1976 edn.), pp. 150–1 – I quote the earlier text here.

82. 'I'm a little surprised that it gives you the horrors. When I was writing it, I didn't think it was much like our particular Hell – but one never knows.' L2, to VB, 27 Oct. 1919, p. 393.

83. Or so he feared – 'Reminiscences', *MoB*, p. 41.

84. L1, to VD, 25 Aug. 1907, p. 306.

85. This was the quotation from *The Idiot* that Forster had used in his review of *The Voyage Out* (see Ch.1, p. 23).

86. D1, 27 Mar. 1919, p. 259.

87. Ibid.

88. Ibid.

89. L2, to Ka Arnold-Forster (formerly, Ka Cox), 9 Oct. 1919, p. 391.

90. *A Bibliography*, pp. 18–19.

91. D1, 30 Oct. 1919, p. 307.

92. D1, 21 Oct. 1919, p. 307.

93. D1, p. 306, fn. 5.

94. D1, 23, 30 Oct. 1919, p. 307; L2, to VB, 27 Oct. 1919, p. 393; Clive Bell on VW in *The Dial*, Dec. 1924, reprinted in *Critical Heritage*, p. 140.

95. '[D]ialogue was what I was after in this book – so I'm very glad you hit on that: I mean it was one of the things –', L2, to LS, 28 Oct. 1919, p. 394.

96. L2, to JC, 5 Jan. 1920, p. 416 (see also L2, to VB, 2 Jan. 1920, p. 412).

97. D1, 15 Nov. 1919, p. 312.

98. Margaret Llewelyn Davies (1861–1944) was a feminist, a Suffragist and the General Secretary of the Women's Co-operative Guild; she was a loyal friend to the Woolfs and encouraged Leonard's interest in socialist politics.

99. D1, 15 Nov. 1919, pp. 312–13. This essay on Charlotte Brontë was published in the *Times Literary Supplement*, 13 Apr. 1916 (*Essays*, vol. 2, pp. 26–31). A later essay on Brontë for the same publication (*Essays*, vol. 2, pp. 192–5) is more narrowly focused on critical discussions of her work.

100. L2, to Margaret Llewelyn Davies, 16 Nov. 1919, p. 399.

101. Ibid.; the *Times Literary Supplement* reviewer (not identified as such in her letter) twice used the phrase 'common human wisdom' in a review of 30 Oct. 1919, reprinted in *Critical Heritage*, p. 76.

102. Though her reaction at the time had been either ironic or distrustful: 'I saw Miss LL.Davies at a lighted window in Barton St with all the conspirators round her, and cursed under my breath.' L1, to JC, ? Dec. 1910, p. 442 (see Lee, pp. 280–1).

103. *The World* (13 Dec. 1919, p. 25) – this quotation is included in 'Some Press Opinions', printed at the back of the first edition of *Jacob's Room* (London: Hogarth Press, 1922), p. 5 (see Ch. 1, n. 68).

104. Ford Madox Ford's review of *ND* for the *Piccadilly Review*, 23 Oct. 1919, is reprinted in *Critical Heritage*, p. 74. The following comparisons are all cited among 'Some Press Opinions' (as above): the *Westminster Gazette* ('Day and Night', 13 Dec. 1919, p. 12 and 'Some Press Opinions', p. 5) thought her 'much nearer Charlotte Brontë' than Jane Austen; E.A.B., reviewing the novel for *New Commonwealth* (21 Nov. 1919, p. 5 and 'Some Press Opinions', p. 4) thought of George Meredith; Frank Swinnerton in the *Daily Herald* ('Love in a Mist', 24 Dec. 1919, p. 8 and 'Some Press Opinions', p. 6) thought the novel 'had affinities . . . to some of the early novels of Henry James'; P. P. Howe in *The Fortnightly Review* ('Fiction: Autumn 1919', 1 Jan. 1920, pp. 69–70 and 'Some Press Opinions', p. 6) saw no influence 'unless it is that of Dostoevsky', while *The Field* (29 Nov. 1919, p. 732 and 'Some Press Opinions', p. 6) considered it 'a novel which owes nothing to any other'; Katherine Mansfield in the *Athenaeum* thought it 'impossible to refrain from comparing [it] with the novels of Miss Austen' (reprinted in *Critical Heritage*, p. 80).

105. Massingham's review as 'Wayfarer' was published on 29 Nov. 1919, and is quoted in 'Some Press Opinions', p. 4. Woolf referred to Olive Heseltine's reply to Massingham in her diary, D1, 5 Dec. 1919, p. 316.

106. *Critical Heritage*, p. 77; D1, 30 Oct. 1919, p. 308.

107. L2, to LS, 28 Oct. 1919, p. 394.

108. L2, to VD, 16 Nov. 1919, p. 402.

109. *ND*, fn. 3, p. 444.

110. L2, to Clive Bell, 27 Nov. 1919, p. 403.

111. D1, 19 Mar. 1919, p. 257.

112. Mansfield's review in *Critical Heritage*, p. 81.

113. Ibid., p. 80.

114. D1, 28 Nov. 1919, p. 314.

115. D1, 28 Nov. 1919, p. 313; L2, to LS, 26 Nov. 1919, p. 401.

116. Leonard Woolf and James Strachey, eds., *Virginia Woolf & Lytton Strachey, Letters* (New York: Harcourt, Brace, 1956), p. 118, LS to VW, 27 Nov. 1919.

117. *ND*, 'A Note on the Text', pp. xxxix–xli, and see also J. H. Stape, ed.,

Night and Day (Oxford: Shakespeare Head/Blackwell, 1994), p. 421, fn. to p. 56.

118. L2, to LS, 26 Nov. 1919, p. 401 (and see Ch.1, p. 24).

119. D1, 30 Oct. 1919, pp. 307–8.

120. D1, 6 Nov. 1919, p. 311.

121. Ibid., p. 310.

122. Ibid.; 'The Novels of Virginia Woolf', *New Criterion*, April 1926, reprinted in *Critical Heritage*, p. 173.

123. L4, to ES, 16 Oct. 1930, p. 231.

124. D1, 15 Jan. 1915, p. 19.

125. *A Bibliography*, p. 19.

126. *A Bibliography*, pp. 20–1, 23–4.

Chapter 3

1. L2, to Vanessa Bell, 26 Apr. 1917, p. 150.

2. 'Modern Novels', *Times Literary Supplement*, 10 April 1919, reprinted in *Essays*, vol. 3, p. 33.

3. L2, to VB, 26 July 1917, p. 169.

4. L1, to Madge Vaughan, and Violet Dickinson, early Jan. 1905, pp. 173, 174 (the silver-point process involved drawing on specially prepared paper with a silver pencil).

5. *An Autobiography*, vol. 2, pp. 169, 170.

6. L2, to VB, 26 Apr. 1917, p. 150; compare her letter to Margaret Llewelyn Davies, L2, 2 May 1917, p. 151.

7. So it appeared on the flyer – see J. H. Willis, Jr, *Leonard and Virginia Woolf as Publishers: The Hogarth Press 1917–1941* (Charlottesville, VA: University Press of Virginia, 1992), p. 15, and *An Autobiography*, vol. 2, p. 171.

8. L4, to Ethel Smyth, 16 Oct. 1930, p. 231.

9. *CSF*, p. 86, or Virginia Woolf, *Monday or Tuesday* (Richmond: Hogarth Press, 1921), p. 85.

10. Reproduced in Tony Bradshaw, ed., *The Bloomsbury Artists: Prints and Book Design* (Aldershot: Scolar Press, 1999), p. 48. For all four of Carrington's woodcuts (for which she was paid 15 shillings), see Jeremy Greenwood, *Omega Cuts* (Woodbridge: The Wood Lea Press, 1998), p. 41.

11. L2, to VD, May 1917, p. 155, and compare her letter to VB, 8 June 1917 – 'the fascination is extreme' (p. 159).

12. *Essays*, vols. 2 and 3, indicate that Woolf wrote 35 reviews for the *Times Literary Supplement* in 1917, 44 in 1918, and 33 in 1919, as well as 12

for other periodicals; see John Mepham, *Virginia Woolf, A Literary Life* (Basingstoke: Macmillan, 1991), p. 66, which also lists her earnings from journalism. On the Woolfs' political collaboration, see Wayne K. Chapman and Janet M. Manson, 'Carte and Tierce: Leonard, Virginia Woolf, and War for Peace', in Mark Hussey, ed., *Virginia Woolf and War: Fiction, Reality and Myth* (Syracuse, NY: Syracuse University Press, 1991), pp. 58–78.

13. Since 1916 the Woolfs had employed Nelly Boxall as cook and Lottie Hope as housemaid – they had come from Roger Fry's household at Durbins. On the Woolfs' finances, see Mepham, pp. 35–6, 64–6.

14. *A Bibliography*, pp. 13–14.

15. L2, to Clive Bell, 24 July 1917, p. 167.

16. L2, to David Garnett, 26 July 1917, p. 167.

17. L2, to Harriet Weaver, 17 May 1918, p. 242.

18. L2, to VB, 26 Apr. 1917, p. 150.

19. L2, to Lytton Strachey, 25 July 1916, p. 107.

20. Vincent O'Sullivan and Margaret Scott, eds., *Collected Letters of Katherine Mansfield* (Oxford: Oxford University Press, 1984), vol. 1, p. 313, to VW, ? 24 June 1917.

21. See D1, 11 Oct. 1917, p. 58, and compare L2, to VB, 11 Feb. 1917, p. 144.

22. *Collected Letters of KM*, vol. 2, p. 77, to J. M. Murry, 16, 17 Feb. 1918.

23. D1, 30 Nov. 1918, p. 222.

24. D1, 22 Mar. 1919, p. 258.

25. *Collected Letters of KM*, vol. 4, p. 154, to VW, 27 Dec. 1920.

26. D2, 5 June 1920, p. 45 (see also D1, 28 May 1918, p. 150, 'As usual we came to an oddly complete understanding').

27. L2, to Ottoline Morrell, 15 Aug. 1917, p. 174.

28. *Collected Letters of KM*, vol. 1, p. 325, to Ottoline Morrell, 15 Aug. 1917.

29. The typescript is in the Harry Ransom Humanities Research Center at the University of Texas at Austin (see *A Bibliography*, p. 427, and Kathryn N. Benzel, 'Woolf's Early Experimentation with Consciousness: "Kew Gardens," Typescript to Publication, 1917–1919', in Ann Ardis and Bonnie Kime Scott, eds., *Virginia Woolf, Turning the Centuries: Selected Papers from the Ninth Annual Conference on Virginia Woolf* (New York: Pace University Press, 2000), pp. 192–9). My discussion of 'Kew Gardens' is indebted to Alice Staveley's research – see her ' "Kew Will Do": Cultivating Fictions of Kew Gardens', in Diane F. Gillespie and Leslie K. Hankins, eds., *Virginia Woolf and the Arts: Selected Papers from the Sixth Annual Conference on Virginia Woolf* (New York: Pace University Press, 1997), pp. 57–66, and her forthcoming monograph on the subject.

30. *Collected Letters of KM*, vol. 1, p. 327, to VW, *c*.23 Aug. 1917.

31. Ibid. This episode has been discussed by Antony Alpers in *The Life of Katherine Mansfield* (1980; Oxford: Oxford University Press, 1982), pp. 249–52, and others since; the dated typescript at Austin (see n. 29 above) only adds to the puzzle.

32. Virginia Woolf and L. S. Woolf, *Two Stories* (Richmond: Hogarth Press, 1917), p. 6. 'Three Jews' was reprinted in the *Virginia Woolf Bulletin*, 5, September 2000, pp. 4–11. On their outsider status, see Natania Rosenfeld, *Outsiders Together: Virginia and Leonard Woolf* (Princeton, NJ: Princeton University Press, 2000).

33. *Two Stories*, p. 16.

34. *Night and Day*, ed. Julia Briggs (1919; London: Penguin 1992), ch. XXV, pp. 279–88 (see also D1, 26 Nov. 1917, p. 82 '[The orchids] always make me anxious to bring them into a novel').

35. 'Modern Fiction', in *The Common Reader* (London: Hogarth Press, 1925), *Essays*, vol. 4, p. 160.

36. *CSF*, p. 95 (and *Monday or Tuesday*, p. 77).

37. L2, to VB, 15 July 1918, p. 260. This painting was a particular favourite of Roger Fry's, as Frances Spalding points out in her biography, *Roger Fry: Art and Life* (1980; Norwich: Black Dog Books, 1999), pp. 195–6.

38. L2, to VB, 15 July 1918, pp. 259, 260.

39. For Vanessa's woodcuts, see Greenwood, p. 26 (only the tailpiece appears in Bradshaw, p. 43). On the fourfold structure of 'Kew Gardens', see my article 'Writing by Numbers: Aspects of Woolf's Revisionary Practice', in Roger Lüdeke, ed., *Text and Border: the Borders of the Text*, forthcoming.

40. D1, 9 June 1919, p. 279.

41. D1, 10 June 1919, p. 280; the review, published on 12 May, is reprinted in *Critical Heritage*, pp. 66–7.

42. L2, to VB, 18 June 1919, p. 369.

43. L2, to Roger Fry, 10 Sept. 1916, p. 115. On the Omega Workshop, see Isabelle Anscombe, *Omega and After: Bloomsbury and the Decorative Arts* (London: Thames and Hudson, 1981), and Judith Collins, *The Omega Workshops* (London: Secker and Warburg, 1983).

44. Harold Child, reviewing *Monday or Tuesday* for the *Times Literary Supplement*, 1 Dec. 1923, reprinted in *Critical Heritage*, p. 87.

45. 'Orphans is what I say we are – we Georgians': L2, to Janet Case, 21 May 1922, p. 529.

46. Their artistic relationship is examined in depth in Diane F. Gillespie, *The Sisters' Arts: The Writing and Painting of Virginia Woolf and Vanessa Bell*

(Syracuse, NY: Syracuse University Press, 1988); see also Jane Dunn, *A Very Close Conspiracy* (London: Jonathan Cape, 1990).

47. D1, 22 Nov. 1917, p. 80.

48. Roger Fry, 'Art and Life', in *Vision and Design* (1920; London: Phoenix Library/ Chatto and Windus, 1928), pp. 11–12.

49. Clive Bell, *Art* (1914; London: Chatto and Windus, 1915), p. 207.

50. Ibid., p. 28.

51. Roger Fry, 'An Essay in Aesthetics', in *Vision and Design*, p. 29.

52. Fry, 'Art and Life', p. 14.

53. Roger Fry, 'Retrospect', in *Vision and Design*, pp. 295–6.

54. D1, 16 July 1918, p. 168.

55. 'The Royal Academy' (the *Athenaeum*, 22 Aug. 1919), *Essays*, vol. 3, p. 90.

56. Ibid., p. 91.

57. Bell, p. 29.

58. Fry, 'Retrospect', p. 291.

59. 'Character in Fiction' (also published as 'Mr Bennett and Mrs Brown', though distinct from an earlier essay with that title), *Essays*, vol. 3, p. 421; see also Peter Stansky, *On or About December 1910: Early Bloomsbury and Its Intimate World* (Cambridge, MA: Harvard University Press, 1996), and my own essay, ' "This Moment I Stand On": Woolf and the Spaces in Time', Virginia Woolf Society of Great Britain, Occasional Papers, 2001.

60. L2, to Gerald Brenan, 25 Dec. 1922, p. 598.

61. Ibid.

62. Ibid.

63. L2, to HW, 17 May 1918, p. 242.

64. L2, to MLD, 17 Aug. 1919, p. 385.

65. The problems it posed, and the fact that its author, Hope Mirrlees, corrected it during the typesetting are evident from two page proofs marked up by her, and now in the E. J. Pratt Library, Victoria University, Toronto. Woolf later hand-corrected 160 of the 175 copies – D2, 24 Apr. 1920, p. 33. For Mirrlees's poem itself, see my edition of it in *The Gender Complex of Modernism*, ed. Bonnie Kime Scott (Urbana and Chicago, IL: Illinois University Press, forthcoming).

66. D1, 18 Apr. 1918, pp. 139–40.

67. L2, to HW, 17 May 1918, p. 242.

68. L2, to RF, 24 Apr. 1918, p. 234.

69. These reading notes for Woolf's essay 'Modern Novels' appear in a notebook entitled 'Modern Novels (Joyce)', in the Berg Collection of the New York Public Library. Edited by Brenda Silver, they are reprinted in *The Gender*

of Modernism: A Critical Anthology, ed. Bonnie Kime Scott (Bloomington, IN: Indiana University Press, 1990), p. 642.

70. *Essays*, vol. 3, p. 33.

71. 'Notes for "Modern Novels"', in Scott, *Gender of Modernism*, p. 644.

72. Ibid., p. 643.

73. Ibid., p. 644.

74. D1, 3 Jan. 1915, p. 5.

75. D1, 23 Oct. 1918, p. 206.

76. See, for example, L2, to Duncan Grant, 6 March 1917, p. 146, or the notorious anecdote about Lytton, 'Old Bloomsbury', *MoB*, p. 195.

77. D2, 16 Aug. 1922, p. 189 (and see also 6 Sept. 1922, pp. 199–200; 26 Sept. 1922, p. 202).

78. See Leonard's first letter to T. S. Eliot, *Letters of Leonard Woolf*, ed. Frederic Spotts (London: Bloomsbury, 1990), p. 279.

79. D1, 15 Nov. 1918, pp. 218–19.

80. Ibid., p. 219.

81. 'Certainly she "leaves out" with the boldest of them: here is syncopation if you like it. I am not sure that I do', Clive Bell, *Since Cézanne* (New York: Harcourt, Brace, 1922), p. 224 (originally published as 'Plus de Jazz', *New Republic*, 21 Sept. 1921, pp. 92–6).

82. For Woolf's view of Joyce, see D2, 26 Sept. 1922, p. 202.

83. 'It is Miriam Henderson's stream of consciousness going on and on', wrote May Sinclair, 'The Novels of Dorothy Richardson' (*The Egoist*, April 1918, reprinted in Scott, *Gender of Modernism*, p. 444). Richardson herself preferred the term 'interior monologue'.

84. From Woolf's review of *The Tunnel*, the fourth novel in the 'Pilgrimage' sequence, (*Times Literary Supplement*, 13 Feb. 1919, reprinted in *Essays*, vol. 3, p. 11). She also reviewed the seventh novel, *Revolving Lights* (*Nation and Athenaeum*, 19 May 1923; *Essays*, vol. 3, pp. 367–8).

85. '[T]he damned egotistical self; which ruins Joyce & Richardson to my mind' – D2, 26 Jan. 1920, p. 14.

86. *Essays*, vol. 3, p. 12.

87. D1, 28 Nov. 1919, p. 315.

88. D2, 16 Jan. 1923, p. 227.

89. *CSF*, pp. 85–6 (*Monday or Tuesday*, p. 84).

90. *CSF*, p. 118 (*Monday or Tuesday*, p. 50).

91. '[A] random game, like that we play in railway carriages with people who leave us at Putney' – from Woolf's unpublished essay 'Byron and Mr Briggs', *Essays*, vol. 3, p. 485.

92. See 'Freudian Fiction' (*Times Literary Supplement*, 25 Mar. 1920; *Essays*, vol. 3, pp. 195–7).

93. There are two essays with this title, but I am referring to the longer of the two, published separately as the first of a series of 'Hogarth Essays', and reprinted as 'Character in Fiction', *Essays*, vol. 3, pp. 420–36.

94. Woolf made the same point in her introduction to *Mrs Dalloway*: 'it was necessary to write the book first and to invent a theory afterwards', *Essays*, vol. 4, p. 550, and she later told a correspondent, 'a novel is an impression not an argument. The book is written without a theory; later, a theory may be made' (L5, to Harmon H. Goldstone, 16 Aug. 1932, p. 91).

95. Arnold Bennett, 'Neo-Impressionism and Literature', *Books and Persons* (London: Chatto and Windus, 1917), p. 281, and see Beth Rigel Daugherty, 'The Whole Contention between Mr Bennett and Mrs Woolf Revisited', in Elaine K. Ginsberg and Laura Moss Gottlieb, eds., *Virginia Woolf: Centennial Essays* (Troy, NY: Whitston, 1983), p. 270.

96. Rigel Daugherty, pp. 284–5.

97. 'Books and Persons', *Essays*, vol. 2, p. 130.

98. 'Notes for "Modern Novels"', in Scott, *Gender of Modernism*, p. 644 – see n. 69 above (following Daniel Ferrer, I read 'visions', instead of 'versions').

99. In her review of it for the *Athenaeum*, 13 June 1919, reprinted in Clare Hanson, ed., *The Critical Writings of Katherine Mansfield* (Basingstoke: Macmillan, 1987), p. 53.

100. *A Bibliography*, pp. 13–14; see also Willis, pp. 16–18.

101. L2, to VB, 1 July 1918, p. 257; D1, 9 Nov. 1918, p. 216; D1, 21 Nov. 1918, p. 221.

102. *A Bibliography*, pp. 15–16; Kirkpatrick and Clarke add that Leonard made it 170 copies (*An Autobiography*, vol. 2, p. 170). The book is listed for 1919 in J. Howard Woolmer, *A Checklist of the Hogarth Press, 1917–1938* (London: Hogarth Press, 1976), p. 31, and was the fifth production of the Hogarth Press, according to Donna M. Rhein, *The Handprinted Books of Leonard and Virginia Woolf at the Hogarth Press, 1917–1932* (Ann Arbor, MI: UMI Research Press, 1985), p. 151.

103. *Critical Heritage*, p. 67.

104. L2, to CB and VB, 4 June 1919, pp. 364–5; to VB, 6 June 1919, pp. 365–6; D1, 10 June 1919, p. 280; Willis, p. 32.

105. *A Bibliography*, pp. 17, 14.

106. In 'A Society' (*CSF*, p. 134), 'An Unwritten Novel' (*CSF*, p. 112) and 'The String Quartet' (*CSF*, p. 138). David Bradshaw's introduction to his edition of *'The Mark on the Wall' and Other Short Fiction* (Oxford: Oxford University Press, 2001) enlarges on this point, p. xxv.

107. *Critical Heritage*, p. 88; D2, 10 Apr. 1921, p.108.

108. *An Autobiography*, vol. 2, p. 37.

109. Child admired it (*Critical Heritage*, p. 88), as did the reviewer for the *Manchester Guardian*, who found it 'the most brilliant by its gay scepticism' (in 'Some Press Opinions', printed at the end of *Jacob's Room* (London: Hogarth Press, 1922, p. 8)), but Desmond MacCarthy thought it 'not her best' (*Critical Heritage*, p. 91), and Clive Bell thought it 'quite beneath her genius' (*Critical Heritage*, p. 142); Mary Agnes Hamilton, 'Short Stories', *Time and Tide*, vol. II, 13 May 1921, pp. 456–67.

110. D2, 26 Jan. 1920, p. 13; D2, 9 Mar. 1920, p. 24 – George Booth was the son of Charles Booth, a friend of Woolf's parents. The quintet has not been identified, and the story seems to concern a quartet, one of the speakers referring to 'early Mozart' – see Peter Jacob's brief discussion in ' "The Second Violin Tuning in the Ante-room": Virginia Woolf and Music', in Diane F. Gillespie, ed., *The Multiple Muses of Virginia Woolf* (Columbia, MS: University of Missouri Press, 1993), pp. 242–4, and Susan Dick's note on the typescript, which refers to 'a slow movement by Mozart', *CSF*, p. 301, fn. 2. The fifth chapter of E. M. Forster's *Howard's End* (1912) had famously described the effect of hearing Beethoven's Fifth Symphony, going on to discuss the impact of music more generally.

111. L2, to VB, 31 Oct. 1920, p. 445.

112. *A Bibliography*, p. 26; *An Autobiography*, vol. 2, p. 174. For the cover of *Monday or Tuesday*, see Greenwood, p. 29.

113. *Critical Heritage*, p. 88.

114. L2, to VD, 8 Apr. 1921, p. 466.

115. Michael Holroyd, *Lytton Strachey* (1967–8; London: Chatto and Windus, 1994), p. 495; D2, 15 Apr. 1921, p. 110.

116. D2, 8 Apr. 1921, p. 106.

117. *Critical Heritage*, p. 87.

118. D2, 10 Apr. 1921, p. 108.

119. D2, 12, 13 Apr. 1921, pp. 108–10.

120. D2, 15 Apr. 1921, p. 110.

121. D2, 17 Apr. 1921, p. 111.

122. See Willis, pp. 52–4, who notes discrepancies between Virginia Woolf's diary entries on the sales of *Monday or Tuesday* and the account book records.

123. Gillespie, in *The Sisters' Arts* (op. cit.), reproduces many of the pages from it, see pp. 124–36; *A Bibliography*, pp. 17–18.

124. *A Haunted House and Other Short Stories* (London: Hogarth Press, 1943), p. 7.

125. *A Bibliography*, pp. 122–3.

Chapter 4

1. *Jacob's Room*, ed. Sue Roe (1922; London: Penguin, 1992). Page numbers appearing in square brackets after quotes refer to this edition of the book.

2. D1, 27 Aug. 1918, p. 186.

3. Martin Gilbert, *First World War* (London: Weidenfeld and Nicolson, 1994), p. 110. Winifred Holtby, still at school, wrote an eye-witness account of the raid – see Marion Shaw, *The Clear Stream: A Life of Winifred Holtby* (London: Virago, 1999), pp. 28–9. On the significance of Scarborough, see Masami Usui, 'The German Raid on Scarborough in *Jacob's Room*', *Virginia Woolf Miscellany*, 35, 7; David Bradshaw, 'Winking, Buzzing, Carpet-beating: Reading *Jacob's Room*', Virginia Woolf Society of Great Britain, 2003, pp. 12–17.

4. Clare Hanson, ed., *The Critical Writings of Katherine Mansfield* (Basingstoke: Macmillan, 1987), p. 59.

5. Vincent O'Sullivan and Margaret Scott, eds., *The Collected Letters of Katherine Mansfield* (Oxford: Oxford University Press, 1993), vol. 3, p. 82, to J. M. Murry, 10 Nov. 1919.

6. 'The Cinema', *Arts* magazine, New York, 1926, and *Essays*, vol. 4, p. 349.

7. D1, 13 Dec. 1917, p. 92.

8. D1, 7 Mar. 1918, p. 123.

9. 'Mr Sassoon's Poems', *Times Literary Supplement*, 31 May 1917, and *Essays*, vol. 2, p. 120.

10. 'Two Soldier-Poets', *Times Literary Supplement*, 11 July 1918, and *Essays*, vol. 2, p. 270.

11. 'I never think his poetry good enough for him', L2, to Ka Cox, 12 Jan. 1916, p. 75.

12. L2, to KC, 13 Aug. 1918, p. 267.

13. D1, 27 July 1918, p. 172.

14. 'Rupert Brooke', *Times Literary Supplement*, 8 Aug. 1918, and *Essays*, vol. 2, pp. 281–2.

15. 'A Sketch of the Past', *MoB*, p. 71.

16. 'Leslie Stephen', *The Times*, 28 Nov. 1932, and Leonard Woolf, ed., Virginia Woolf, *Collected Essays* (London: Chatto and Windus, 1966), vol. 4, pp. 78, 79.

17. '[We] regard the opposing of violence by violence as a suicidal and hopeless mode of proceeding' – Caroline Stephen, *Quaker Strongholds* (London: Kegan Paul, 1890), quoted by Sybil Oldfield, *Women Against the Iron Fist:*

Alternatives to Militarism, 1900–1989 (Oxford: Basil Blackwell, 1989), pp. 98–9.

18. Regina Marler, ed., *Selected Letters of Vanessa Bell* (London: Bloomsbury, 1993), p. 69.

19. In an unpublished memoir of her nephew, Julian Bell, appendix C in *Biography*, vol. 2, p. 258.

20. Michael Holroyd, *Lytton Strachey* (1967–8; London: Chatto and Windus, 1994), pp. 348–9.

21. *An Autobiography*, vol. 2, pp. 128–9.

22. L2, to Vanessa Bell, 14 Apr. 1916, p. 89; see also Marler, p. 195; according to Frances Spalding, *Vanessa Bell* (London: Weidenfeld and Nicolson, 1983), p. 149, she also worked part-time for the National Council for Civil Liberties.

23. L2, to Duncan Grant, 3 Jan. 1915, p. 57.

24. L2, to DG, 15 Nov. 1915, p. 71.

25. L2, to Margaret Llewelyn Davies, 23 Jan. 1916, p. 76.

26. Lucy Thoumaian proposed this to Sylvia Pankhurst, who considered it 'splendid but impractical' – see Angela Ingram, ' "In Christ's Name – Peace!": Theodora Wilson and Radical Pacifism', in Angela Ingram and Daphne Patai, eds., *Rediscovering Forgotten Radicals: British Women Writers, 1889–1939* (Chapel Hill, NC: University of North Carolina Press, 1993), p. 177.

27. L1, to Janet Case, 1 Jan. 1910, p. 421.

28. L1, to Violet Dickinson, 27 Feb. 1910, p. 422.

29. *Night and Day*, ed. Julia Briggs (1919; London: Penguin 1992), p. 67 (and the whole of ch. VI).

30. D1, 6 Jan. 1918, p. 101.

31. Helena Swanwick, *I Have Been Young* (London: Victor Gollancz, 1935), pp. 233, 239; Anne Wiltsher, *Most Dangerous Women* (London: Pandora, 1985) pp. 22–3; see also Johanna Alberti, *Beyond Suffrage: Feminists in War and Peace, 1914–28* (London: Macmillan, 1989), esp. chs. 2 and 3.

32. Swanwick, p. 247.

33. Introductory Letter to Margaret Llewelyn Davies, ed., *Life As We Have Known It by Co-operative Working Women* (1931; London: Virago, 1977), pp. xxi, xxvii.

34. D1, 18 Sept. 1918, pp. 193, 196.

35. See Ch. 2: The Aftermath, p. 53.

36. Introductory Letter, in Llewelyn Davies.

37. *Three Guineas*, Michèle Barrett, ed., *A Room of One's Own/Three Guineas* (1929, 1938; London: Penguin, 1993), p. 161.

38. D1, 11 Jan. 1918, p. 104.

39. D1, 9 Mar. 1918, p. 125.

40. Hanson, p. 59 (and *Collected Letters of KM*, vol. 3, p .82, to J. M. Murry, 10 Nov. 1919, following her review of *Night and Day* – see above, n. 5).

41. *CSF*, p. 112 (and Ch. 3, n. 106, above).

42. D2, 26 Jan. 1920, pp. 13–14.

43. The opening page of the first MS notebook of *JR* – Edward L. Bishop, ed., *Virginia Woolf's Jacob's Room: The Holograph Draft* (New York: Pace University Press, 1998), p. 1.

44. *Holograph Draft*, pp. 50–3. Woolf later revised and published this episode as 'A Woman's College from Outside' in *Atalanta's Garland* (Edinburgh: Edinburgh University Press, 1926), reproduced as appendix II of Sue Roe's Penguin edition of *Jacob's Room*, pp. 189–92.

45. *Holograph Draft*, pp. 57–8 (I have omitted Woolf's deletions).

46. *ND*, p. 17.

47. This review was discovered too late to be included in the first volume of *Essays* – see B. J. Kirkpatrick, 'Virginia Woolf: Unrecorded TLS Reviews', *Modern Fiction Studies*, 38, 1 (Spring 1992), p. 289.

48. *JR*, p. 104 (and see p. 161, fn. 2). Woolf's use of a range of named characters who put in fleeting appearances to give an impression of the life of the city may owe something to *Ulysses*, as well as to Eliot's early city poems – the impact of the latter is more evident in the holograph draft.

49. D2, 23 June 1922, p. 178.

50. *JR*, pp. 57, 70, 93.

51. *JR*, pp. 83–4, 24, 38.

52. 'A Sketch of the Past', *MoB*, pp. 103–4.

53. By Henry Massingham, writing as 'Wayfarer' in the *Nation*, 29 Nov. 1919 – see D1, 5 Dec. 1919, p. 316, and Ch. 2: The Aftermath, p. 53.

54. Opening page of notebook 1 (*Holograph Draft*, p. 1).

55. *Critical Heritage*, p. 98 – the review was headed 'Middle Aged Sensualists', altered in Woolf's diary to 'An elderly sensualist': D2, 29 Oct. 1922, p. 209.

56. 'Professions for Women' (1931), in *Collected Essays*, vol. 2, pp. 287–8.

57. *Holograph Draft*, p. 123.

58. *Holograph Draft*, p. 267 (and see Ch. 1, p. 17).

59. D2, 13 Nov. 1920, p.75; compare *JR*, p. 90.

60. D2, 8 June 1920, p. 47; compare *JR*, p. 56.

61. D1, 12 Mar. 1919, p. 251 (and L2, to VB, 23 Mar. 1919, p. 341); compare *JR*, pp. 67–8.

62. D2, 26 Sept. 1920, p. 69.

63. Ibid.

64. D2, 1 Oct. 1920, p. 70.

65. *To the Lighthouse*, intro. Hermione Lee, ed. Stella McNichol (1927; London: Penguin, 1992), pp. 94, 173, 174.

66. Woolf's side of this correspondence is reprinted as appendix III to D2, p. 342.

67. Ibid.

68. Ibid., p. 339.

69. D2, 26 Sept. 1920, p. 69. On 13 Feb. 1921, Woolf wrote to Katherine Mansfield, 'Like an idiot I lost my temper with Arnold Bennett for abusing women, and wasted my time writing a foolish violent, I suppose unnecessary satire', though she did not indicate when her satire was actually written – *Congenial Spirits: The Selected Letters of Virginia Woolf*, ed. Joanne Trautmann Banks (London: Hogarth Press, 1989), p. 128.

70. *CSF*, p. 135 (also *Monday or Tuesday*, p. 34).

71. *CSF*, p. 136 (also *Monday or Tuesday*, p. 35).

72. *CSF*, p. 135 (also *Monday or Tuesday*, p. 33).

73. *CSF*, p. 134 (also *Monday or Tuesday*, p. 32).

74. *CSF*, p. 135 (also *Monday or Tuesday*, p. 33).

75. *JR*, pp. 3, 4, 5, 7–9.

76. *JR*, pp. 144, 145–7, 148, 150, 151.

77. Some of the details of this scene in the Cabinet – 'the very centre of the centre . . . a million wireless messages . . . from all over the world . . . – where the fate of armies does more or less hang upon what two or three elderly gentlemen decide' – were suggested by a much later interview with her cousin Herbert Fisher, who brought inside information of the approaching victory, D1, 15 Oct. 1918, p. 204, and (to a lesser extent) by another meeting with him three years later, D2, 18 Apr. 1921, pp. 112–13. Woolf drew a similar contrast between the statues of past leaders and present politicians (for whom 'the transition into marble is unthinkable') in her article ' "This is the House of Commons" ', fifth in a series on 'The London Scene', written for *Good Housekeeping* (1931–2), and reprinted in Rachel Bowlby, ed., *Virginia Woolf, The Crowded Dance of Modern Life: Selected Essays* (London: Penguin, 1993), vol. 2, p. 129.

78. 'Our generation is daily scourged by the bloody war. Even I scribble reviews instead of novels because of the thick skulls at Westminster & Berlin', D2, 29 June 1920, p. 52 (suggesting that she blamed the war for losses in her invested income).

79. 'Strange Meeting', *The Poems of Wilfred Owen*, ed. Jon Stallworthy (London: Hogarth Press, 1985), p. 125.

80. *CSF*, p. 86 (also *Monday or Tuesday*, p. 84).

81. The idea of 'making a whole' is central to Woolf's unpublished essay 'Byron and Mr Briggs', appendix II, *Essays*, vol. 3, p. 482. A different and more material kind of gap is also present in the text itself, where Woolf left spaces between different sections of writing – see Edward L. Bishop, 'Mind the Gap: The Spaces in *Jacob's Room*', *Woolf Studies Annual*, 10 (2004), pp. 31–49.

82. D2, 26 July 1922, p. 186.

83. The three notebooks are in the Berg Collection of the New York Public Library, and are transcribed in *Holograph Draft* (see n. 43, above, for further details); D2, 15 Nov. 1921, pp. 141–2.

84. D2, 8 Aug. 1921, p. 125.

85. D2, 29 Oct. 1922, pp. 209–10.

86. D2, 23 June 1922, p. 178.

87. L2, to VB, 10 Aug. 1922, p. 543.

88. D2, 6 Sept. 1922, p. 199.

89. D2, 14 Oct. 1922, p. 207 (where Carrington's letter is cited in fn. 8); Leonard Woolf and James Strachey, eds., *Virginia Woolf & Lytton Strachey, Letters* (New York: Harcourt, Brace, 1956), p. 144.

90. D2, 14 Oct. 1922, p. 208.

91. *An Autobiography*, vol. 2, p. 235.

92. D2, 4 Oct. 1922, p. 205; L2, to VD, 29 Oct. 1922, p. 574.

93. *An Autobiography*, vol. 2, p. 239. *A Bibliography* records Leonard's selection from Woolf's essays, *Granite and Rainbow* (London: Hogarth Press, 1958), as printed by R. & R. Clark, p. 134.

94. *A Bibliography*, p. 27, and see Tony Bradshaw, ed., *The Bloomsbury Artists: Prints and Book Design* (Aldershot: Scolar Press, 1999), plate 23.

95. *An Autobiography*, vol. 2, p. 241.

96. Ibid., p. 239 (though *A Bibliography*, p. 27, puts the second impression at 2,000); L2, to Ka Arnold-Forster (formerly Ka Cox), 1 Nov. 1922, p. 580 (and see also D2, 29 Oct. 1922, p. 209; L2, to Ottoline Morrell, 1 Nov. 1922, p. 579). J. H. Willis, Jr, in *Leonard and Virginia Woolf as Publishers: The Hogarth Press 1917–1941* (Charlottesville, VA: University Press of Virginia, 1992), finds inconsistencies between the Woolfs' reports of sales and the evidence of the account books (as he had done in the case of *Monday or Tuesday*), p. 61.

97. *An Autobiography*, vol. 2, p. 239.

98. L2, to Roger Fry, 22 Oct. 1922, p. 573 (and see also L2, to Clive Bell, 7 Nov. 1922, p. 581); L2, to C. P. Sanger, 30 Oct. 1922, p. 578; L2, to David Garnett, 20 Oct. 1922, p. 571.

99. *Critical Heritage*, pp. 95, 97.

100. Reprinted ibid., pp. 98, 99, 108. Woolf had anticipated accusations of pretentiousness – D2, 15 Apr. 1920, p. 30.

101. *Critical Heritage*, pp. 107 (*Yorkshire Post*), 105 (*Daily Telegraph*), and see also p. 110 (*Nation*, New York); on 'impressionism', see headnote, p. 99, and p. 15.

102. *Critical Heritage* (*Cassell's Weekly*), p. 113.

103. *Nation and Athenaeum*, 1 Dec. 1923, *Essays*, vol. 3, pp. 384–8.

104. D2, 27 Nov. 1922, p. 214.

Chapter 5

1. D2, 19 July 1922, p. 184.

2. See Ch. 3, n. 94, above.

3. Julia Duckworth Stephen, *Stories for Children, Essays for Adults*, eds. Diane F. Gillespie and Elizabeth Steele (Syracuse, NY: Syracuse University Press, 1987), p. 47. The volume includes *Notes from Sick Rooms* and Julia's stories for children, and reproduces some of her husband's drawings.

4. Vanessa Bell, 'Notes on Virginia's Childhood', *Sketches in Pen and Ink*, ed. Lia Giachero (London: Hogarth Press, 1997), p. 63.

5. 'A Sketch of the Past', *MoB*, pp. 76–7, 79 (where Schulkind points out in a footnote that Vanessa's memoir spells it 'Cle-mente' – see Bell, *Sketches*, p. 59); according to Quentin Bell, *Biography*, vol. 1, p. 28, the first issue of the 'Hyde Park Gate News' would have been on 9 Feb. 1891, shortly after Virginia's ninth birthday.

6. 'A Sketch', *MoB*, p. 95. Madge Symonds, daughter of the writer J. A. Symonds, married Woolf's first cousin, Will Vaughan (see Ch. 6, p. 152 for her relationship with the character 'Sally Seton').

7. 'It was the Elizabethan prose writers I loved first & most wildly, stirred by Hakluyt, which father lugged home for me – I think of it with some sentiment – father tramping over the Library with his little girl sitting at H[yde] P[ark] G[ardens] in mind. He must have been 65; I 15 or 16, then; . . . I used to read it & dream of those obscure adventures', D3, 8 Dec. 1929, p. 271. In 'A Sketch of the Past', Woolf recalled 'writing an essay – the first, the only essay I ever showed father, upon the Elizabethan voyagers', 'A Sketch of the Past', *MoB* (1976), p. 138 (this sentence only occurs in the earlier edition).

8. 'Hours in a Library', *Times Literary Supplement*, 13 Nov. 1916 (*Essays*, vol. 2, p. 56). This essay describes her reading between the ages of 18 and 24 ('the great season for reading'), and provides 'a list of the books that someone read in a past January at the age of twenty, most of them probably for the

first time'. Although this reader was obviously herself, she refers to him throughout as male.

9. Ibid., p. 58.

10. Mitchell A. Leaska, ed., Virginia Woolf, *A Passionate Apprentice: The Early Journals 1897–1909* (London: Hogarth Press, 1990), 'The Country in London', 1903, p. 178.

11. L1, to Violet Dickinson, ? May 1905, p. 190.

12. *CSF*, p. 34; on 'The Journal of Mistress Joan Martyn', see Juliet Dusinberre, *Virginia Woolf's Renaissance: Woman Reader or Common Reader?* (London: Macmillan, 1997), pp. 18–23; Melba Cuddy-Keane, 'Virginia Woolf and the Varieties of Historicist Experience', in Beth Carole Rosenberg and Jeanne Dubino, eds., *Virginia Woolf and the Essay* (London: Macmillan, 1997), pp. 66–8.

13. *CSF*, p. 74. Woolf probably chose the *Cornhill* magazine for its family connections – previous editors had included Thackeray and his son-in-law Leslie Stephen. For a more detailed account of 'Memoirs of a Novelist', see my article 'Virginia Woolf and "The Proper Writing of Lives"', in John Batchelor, ed., *The Art of Literary Biography* (Oxford: Clarendon Press, 1995), pp. 253–4.

14. In his Introduction to *Essays*, vol. 1, p. xii, Andrew McNeillie observes that the *Guardian* was an 'unlikely outlet for even an anonymous daughter of Sir Leslie Stephen', but it had a surprisingly wide readership.

15. Her first review for the *Times Literary Supplement* was 'Literary Geography', 10 Mar. 1905 (*Essays*, vol. 1, pp. 32–5); her last was on 'Congreve's Comedies: Speed, Stillness and Meaning', 25 Sept. 1937 (reprinted in Leonard Woolf, ed., Virginia Woolf, *Collected Essays* (London: Chatto and Windus, 1966), vol. 1, pp. 76–84).

16. From a review of *The Golden Bowl*, *Guardian*, 22 Feb. 1905 (*Essays*, vol. 1, p. 24).

17. 'Men and Women', *Times Literary Supplement*, 18 Mar. 1920 (*Essays*, vol. 3, p. 193).

18. *Jacob's Room*, ed. Sue Roe (1922; London: Penguin, 1992), pp. 91–2; *A Room of One's Own*, Michèle Barrett, ed., *A Room of One's Own/Three Guineas* (1929, 1938; London: Penguin, 1993) pp. 6–7.

19. 'Reading', *Essays*, vol. 3, p. 142.

20. Ibid., p. 141.

21. Ibid., p. 156.

22. 'The Royal Academy', *Athenaeum*, 22 Aug. 1919 (*Essays*, vol. 3, p. 92). See Ch. 14, below, for Woolf's later treatment of 'Englishness', and my article ' "Almost Ashamed of England being so English": Woolf and Ideas of

Englishness', in Robin Hackett, Jane Marcus and Gay Wachman, eds., *Inroads and Outposts, At Home and Abroad in the Empire: British Women in the Thirties* (Gainesville, FL: University of Florida Press, forthcoming).

23. 'Men and Women', *Essays*, vol. 3, p. 193.

24. Quoted in Woolf's response, 'The Plumage Bill', *Woman's Leader*, 23 July 1920 (*Essays*, vol. 3, p. 241).

25. Ibid., p. 243 (and for an earlier example of such substitution, see the discussion of 'A Society', above, Ch. 4, p. 103).

26. Ibid., p. 245.

27. Both sides of the argument are reprinted in Rachel Bowlby, ed., *Virginia Woolf: A Woman's Essays*, vol. 1 (London: Penguin, 1992), p. 31.

28. D2, 19 Dec. 1920, p. 81 (Fry's *Vision and Design* was officially published in January 1921).

29. Woolf's review is reprinted as appendix A of *Roger Fry*, ed. Diane F. Gillespie (Oxford: Shakespeare Head/Blackwell, 1995), pp. 381, 383.

30. D2, 24 Mar. 1922, p. 172, but see also pp. 120, 142 and 170, for 23 May 1921, 15 Nov. 1921 and 12 Mar. 1922, as she winds herself up to begin writing.

31. 'The Elizabethan Lumber Room', *The Common Reader* (London: Hogarth Press, 1925) and *Essays*, vol. 4, p. 59; for 'Byron and Mr Briggs', see appendix 2, *Essays*, vol. 3, pp. 473–99.

32. 'Indiscretions', *Vogue*, Nov. 1924 (*Essays*, vol. 3, pp. 460–4).

33. 'Byron and Mr Briggs', *Essays*, vol. 3, pp. 478–9. He may have been named after John Leech's Mr Briggs, whose adventures the young Stephens followed in their father's old volumes of *Punch*, and imitated in their newspaper, the 'Hyde Park Gate News' (see *Bibliography*, vol. 1, p. 30); Dryden on Shakespeare, in his 'Essay on the Dramatic Poetry of the Last Age'.

34. 'Modern Fiction', *TCR* and *Essays*, vol. 4, p. 160. This passage was added when Woolf revised her 1919 essay 'Modern Novels' for *TCR*, so it may well have been written after 'Byron and Mr Briggs'. For 'gig lamps', see the *Oxford English Dictionary* (Partridge says it was current at Oxford University from 1848, in his *Dictionary of Historical Slang*).

35. 'Byron and Mr Briggs', *Essays*, vol. 3, p. 482. I have simplified the heavily corrected text reproduced in full by Andrew McNeillie by drawing on Edward A. Hungerford's 'clean' version published in *The Yale Review*, vol. LXVIII, no. 3 (March 1979), pp. 333–4.

36. Ibid., p. 482 (and Hungerford, p. 333). The expression that immediately follows this passage, 'The cat is out of the bag', had been used by MacCarthy to refer to Bennett's assertion 'that women are inferior to men in intellectual power' (reprinted in Bowlby, n. 27 above), and from then on, Woolf used it

in contexts where sexual prejudice was being exposed, most famously in *Three Guineas* where 'The odour thickens. . . . The cat is out of the bag; and it is a Tom', *Three Guineas*, Michèle Barrett, ed., *A Room of One's Own/Three Guineas* (1929, 1938; London: Penguin, 1993), p. 174.

37. D2, 17 Aug. 1923, p. 261.

38. Ibid.

39. She recorded conversations in her diary at pp. 252–8, 8, 17 and 22 July 1923; on 28 July, she was reading for 'Mr Conrad: A Conversation' (p. 259), reprinted *Essays*, vol. 3, p. 376. It was published in the *Nation and Athenaeum* at the beginning of September, but by the 5th she was feeling 'slightly dashed' by its reception 'which has been purely negative – No one has mentioned it' (D2, 5 Sept. 1923, p. 265).

40. 'I rejoice to concur with the common reader; for by the common sense of readers uncorrupted by literary prejudices, after all the refinements of subtilty and the dogmatism of learning, must be finally decided all claim to poetical honours', Johnson's life of Gray, *Lives of the English Poets*, cited in TCR (*Essays*, vol. 4, p. 19).

41. Woolf's reading can be followed through her diary, e.g. D2, pp. 156 (3 Jan. 1922); 189 (16 Aug.); 196 (28 Aug.); 205 (4 Oct.); 208 (14 Oct.); 212 (7 Nov.); 225 (7 Jan. 1923), etc.

42. D2, 4 Oct. 1922, p. 205 – 'At forty I am beginning to learn the mechanism of my own brain', she concluded (p. 206); she celebrated her new system in diary entries for D2, 3 Sept. 1922, p. 198; 5 May 1924, p. 301; 21 Dec. 1924, p. 325.

43. D2, 12 Mar. 1922, p. 171.

44. She was still rethinking these issues at the time of her death: notes towards 'Reading at Random', and drafts of 'Anon' and 'The Reader', left unfinished, have been edited by Brenda R. Silver in Bonnie Kime Scott, ed., *The Gender of Modernism* (Bloomington and Indianapolis: Indiana University Press, 1990), pp. 673–701.

45. D2, 3 Aug. 1922, p. 188; 17 Aug. 1923, p. 261.

46. 'The Pastons and Chaucer', TCR (*Essays*, vol. 4, p. 23).

47. Ibid., *Essays*, vol. 4, p. 26.

48. 'Byron and Mr Briggs', *Essays*, vol. 3, pp. 482, 485.

49. Charlotte M. Yonge, *The Daisy Chain or Aspirations: A Family Chronicle* (1856; London: Macmillan, 1896), p. 163.

50. See William Herman, 'Virginia Woolf and the Classics: Every Englishman's Prerogative Transmuted into Fictional Art', in Elaine K. Ginsberg and Laura Moss Gottlieb, eds., *Virginia Woolf: Centennial Essays* (Troy, NY: Whitston Publishing, 1983), pp. 257–68.

51. 'On Not Knowing Greek', *TCR* (*Essays*, vol. 4, p. 48).

52. 'The Elizabethan Lumber Room', *TCR* (*Essays*, vol. 4, pp. 53, 55), and compare 'Reading', *Essays*, vol. 3, pp. 149, 148.

53. D2, 31 Jan. 1921, 16 Feb., 17 Apr. and 26 Nov., pp. 88, 90, 112 and 145.

54. F. M. Dostoevsky, *Stavrogin's Confession and The Plan of The Life of a Great Sinner*, trans. S. S. Koteliansky and Virginia Woolf (London: Hogarth Press, 1922). On Woolf's translations from the Russian, see two articles by Natalya Reinhold: 'Virginia Woolf's Russian Voyage Out', *Woolf Studies Annual*, 9, ed. Mark Hussey (New York: Pace University Press, 2003), pp. 1–27, and ' "A railway accident": Virginia Woolf Translates Tolstoy', in Reinhold, ed., *Woolf Across Cultures* (New York: Pace University Press, 2004), pp. 237–48.

55. 'The Russian Point of View', *TCR* (*Essays*, vol. 4, p. 184).

56. 'Notes on an Elizabethan Play', *TCR* (*Essays*, vol. 4, p. 62). McNeillie notes that the text printed in the *Times Literary Supplement*, 5 March 1925, gives 'rends us', instead of 'reads us', p. 69.

57. L2, to Janet Case, 21 May 1922, p. 529.

58. *Essays*, vol. 3, p. 336; L2, to Gerald Brenan, 25 Dec. 1922, p. 598. This argument is developed in greater detail in my essay ' "This Moment I Stand On": Virginia Woolf and the Spaces in Time', Virginia Woolf Society of Great Britain, 2001.

59. *Cassell's Weekly*, 28 Mar. 1923, reprinted in *Critical Heritage*, p. 113.

60. *Nation and Athenaeum*, 10 Mar. 1923, reprinted ibid., p. 109.

61. D2, 2 Aug. 1924, p. 308; 17 Oct. 1924, p. 317.

62. 'Mr Bennett and Mrs Brown' – *New York Evening Post*, 17 Nov. 1923, *Nation and Athenaeum*, 1 Dec. 1923 (*Essays*, vol. 3, p. 388).

63. D2, 3 Feb. 1924, p. 290.

64. 'Character in Fiction', *Criterion*, July 1924 (*Essays*, vol. 3, p. 421).

65. Ibid., pp. 434, 435, 436 (and compare *A Room of Ones's Own*, p. 94).

66. *Mrs Dalloway*, intro. Elaine Showalter, ed. Stella McNichol (1925; London: Penguin, 1992), p. 8; Virginia Woolf, *'The Hours'*, ed. Helen M. Wussow (New York: Pace University Press, 1996), pp. 194–5.

67. 'Character in Fiction', *Essays*, vol. 3, p. 431.

68. MacCarthy, in his original review of Bennett, had given it as an aphorism that 'Men and women are really more alike than they can believe each other to be; but they ought not to behave to each other as though this were true'; Woolf stated that she did not agree 'that men and women are alike' – Bowlby, *A Woman's Essays*, pp. 30, 38.

69. *A Bibliography*, pp. 274, 32–3 (see also *Essays*, vol. 3, p. 436).

70. *Critical Heritage*, pp. 132, 135, 17. The earlier version of 'Mr Bennett and Mrs Brown' had also been published in the States, first in the *Literary Review* of the *New York Evening Post* (17 Nov. 1923), and later in the Boston literary periodical, *The Living Age* (2 Feb. 1924 – see *A Bibliography*, p. 271 or *Essays*, vol. 3, p. 388).

71. *A Bibliography*, p. 274 (*Essays*, vol. 3, p. 437).

72. 'I open this book [her diary] today merely to note that Miss Eleanor Ormerod, destroyer of insects, promises well for Murry; should he take kindly to my first (Eccentrics: I myself rather liked it)'. D1, 30 Mar. 1919, p. 260. 'The Eccentrics' was published in the *Athenaeum* on 25 April 1919, but 'Miss Ormerod' was first published in *The Dial* in 1924.

73. *A Bibliography*, p. 34.

74. D3, pp. 12, 15.

75. Ibid., pp. 17 (9 May 1925); 25 (1 June); 29 (14 June).

76. Ibid., pp. 32 (18 June); 33 (27 June).

77. Ibid, p. 109 (13 Sept. 1926); Leonard Woolf, Preface to Virginia Woolf, *A Writer's Diary* (London: Hogarth Press, 1953), p. viii. Andrew McNeillie makes the same point in his introduction to *Essays*, vol. 3 (p. xx), citing P. N. Furbank as an example of a critic who thought 'that essay-writing was her proper *métier*'.

78. E. M. Forster, The Rede Lecture 1941, reprinted in *Two Cheers for Democracy* (1951; London: Penguin, 1965), pp. 261–2; for Quentin Bell's impatience with *Three Guineas*, see his essay 'A Room of One's Own and Three Guineas', Appendix 1, *Elders and Betters* (London: John Murray, 1995), pp. 212–26, reprinted in Merry Pawlowski, ed., *Virginia Woolf and Fascism* (Basingstoke: Palgrave, 2001), pp. 13–20; for Nigel Nicolson, see his biography *Virginia Woolf* (London: Weidenfeld and Nicolson, 2000), pp. 132–4, though his views are also apparent in the incidental commentaries provided in the six volumes of Woolf's *Letters*.

Chapter 6

1. *Mrs Dalloway*, intro. Elaine Showalter, ed. Stella McNichol (1925; London: Penguin, 1992). Page numbers appearing in square brackets after quotes refer to this edition of the book.

2. David Hare, *The Hours*, a screenplay, based on the novel by Michael Cunningham (New York: Miramax Books, 2002), pp. 8–9.

3. 'Mrs Dalloway in Bond Street', *CSF*, p. 152 (first published in *The Dial*, July 1923).

4. L1, to Violet Dickinson, Oct./Nov. 1902, p. 60. At this stage, it was to be a play, and she planned to write it with Jack Hills.

5. See 'Modern Fiction', *The Common Reader* (London: Hogarth Press, 1925) (*Essays*, vol. 4, p. 160).

6. Ibid.

7. Ibid.

8. Ibid.

9. To Katherine Mansfield, 13 Feb. 1921, *Congenial Spirits: Selected Letters of Virginia Woolf*, ed. Joanne Trautmann Banks (London: Hogarth Press, 1989), p. 128.

10. L2, to Gerald Brenan, 25 Dec. 1922, p. 598.

11. 'Modern Fiction', *Essays*, vol. 4, p. 161.

12. D2, 26 Jan. 1920, p. 14.

13. 'Modern Fiction', *Essays*, vol. 4, p. 161; and see also Woolf's preliminary notes for this essay, Suzette Henke, 'Virginia Woolf: The Modern Tradition', in Bonnie Kime Scott, ed., *The Gender of Modernism* (Bloomington and Indianapolis: Indiana University Press, 1990), pp. 642–5.

14. E. M. Forster, 'Virginia Woolf' (the Rede Lecture, 1941), in *Two Cheers for Democracy* (1951; London: Penguin, 1965), p. 254.

15. See D3, 27 Apr. 1925, p. 12, quoted in 'The Aftermath', below, p. 157. For a helpful account of Woolf's narrative technique (there described as 'free indirect discourse'), see chapter 3 of Anna Snaith's *Virginia Woolf: Public and Private Negotiations* (London: Macmillan, 2000).

16. The explosion recalled an incident during the War, when Leonard and Virginia were walking down St James's Street – see D1, 1 Feb. 1915, p. 32; on the novelty of sky-writing (invented in August 1922), see Elaine Showalter's introduction to *Mrs Dalloway*, p. xxiv.

17. Notes for 'a possible revision of this book', 16 Oct. 1922, in 3rd holograph notebook for *Jacob's Room*, dated 12 Mar. 1922, and labelled 'Book of scraps of J's R. & first version of The Hours' (p. 153), in the Berg Collection of the New York Public Library, transcribed in Virginia Woolf, *The Hours: the British Museum Manuscript of 'Mrs Dalloway'*, ed. Helen M. Wussow (New York: Pace University Press, 1996), appendix 2, p. 412.

18. For a fuller account of these, see 'The Aftermath', below, p. 156, esp. n. 138, and Ch. 7, pp. 164–5.

19. L2, to Jacques Raverat, 25 Aug. 1922, p. 554.

20. D2, 29 Aug. 1923, p. 262.

21. D2, 29 Sept. 1924, p. 315.

22. D2, 17 Feb. 1922, p. 168.

23. D1, 6 Dec. 1919, p. 316, but 'Really, I am not a good lioness', D3, 14 June

1925, p. 30; on her life in 'society', see D2, 29 Oct. 1922, p. 210; D2, 16 Nov. 1923, p. 275; D2, 3 July 1924, p. 305 and her memoir 'Am I a Snob?', *MoB*, pp. 210–14.

24. The Prime Minister is 'this symbol of what they all stood for, English society' – *MD*, p.189. See also Natania Rosenfeld, *Outsiders Together: Virginia and Leonard Woolf* (Princeton, NJ: Princeton University Press, 2000), p. 103, and Alex Zwerdling, *Virginia Woolf and the Real World* (Los Angeles, CA: University of California Press, 1986), esp. chapters 4 and 5.

25. On Leonard as a candidate, see D2, 26 May 1920, p. 42; on their support for the strikers, 'The "docile herds" . . . are not so deluded after all. They have held the country up for eleven days, I think. We did a little to support them too, & kept one man out on strike who would have gone back without our pound', D1, 7 Oct. 1919, p. 304.

26. 'Character in Fiction', *Criterion*, July 1924 (later published by the Hogarth Press as 'Mr Bennett and Mrs Brown'), *Essays*, vol. 3, p. 422.

27. As she acknowledged, for example in her introduction to Margaret Llewelyn Davies, ed., *Life as We Have Known It by Co-operative Working Women* (London: Hogarth Press, 1931), p. xxi: 'If every reform they demand was granted it would not touch one hair of my comfortable capitalistic head.'

28. D1, 12 May 1919, p. 271. On Clarissa's dismissal of the Armenians, see Trudi Tate, *Modernism, History and the First World War* (Manchester: Manchester University Press, 1998), pp. 155–9; Linden Peach, *Virginia Woolf – Critical Issues* (London: Macmillan, 2000), pp. 104–5.

29. On the significance of the Italian campaign in the novel, see David Bradshaw, ' "Vanished, Like Leaves": The Military, Elegy and Italy in *Mrs Dalloway*', *Woolf Studies Annual*, 8, ed. Mark Hussey (New York: Pace University Press, 2002), pp. 107–25, where he points out that the portrait of Septimus owes something to the experiences of Ralph Partridge (who had fought in Italy), and the temperament of Gerald Brenan (p. 121); Rezia was largely inspired by Lydia Lopokova (Mrs Maynard Keynes) – see D2, 15 Aug. 1924, p. 310.

30. D2, 13 Mar. 1921, p. 100.

31. See 'The Aftermath', below, p. 155.

32. D3, 18 June 1925, p. 32.

33. *MD*, p. 8.

34. *MD*, pp. 133, 134. *The Hours* MS, pp. 194, 195, and compare p. 317: ' "An offering" he murmured . . . the window sill was an altar;' see also end of Ch. 5, above, p. 125.

35. Compare *The Hours* MS, 'that woman's gift, that essential one: making life wherever she happened to be', p. 91.

36. D2, 28 June 1923, p. 250.

37. *MD*, p. 213 (and *The Hours* MS, p. 251), and p. 54, 'It is Clarissa herself, he thought'. Compare Julia Stephen, 'she was the centre; it was herself' in 'A Sketch of the Past', *MoB*, p. 84, and Mrs Ramsay, 'There she sat', *To the Lighthouse*, intro. Hermione Lee, ed. Stella McNichol (1927; London: Penguin, 1992), p. 219.

38. L2, to T. S. Eliot, 14 Apr. 1922, p. 521.

39. *MD*, p. 21 and n. 21, p. 218; p. 134 and n. 53, p. 223; see also p. 187.

40. *The Voyage Out*, ed. Jane Wheare (1915; London: Penguin, 1992), p. 60.

41. 'Mrs Dalloway in Bond Street', *CSF*, p. 153. In the novel, it is Richard Dalloway who is given a modified version of these reflections on Buckingham Palace – see p. 128. Woolf made substantial changes to her portrayals of both Dalloways in the later novel, giving their silliest or most unpleasant traits to other characters. Richard Dalloway is never 'Dick' (as he had been in *The Voyage Out*), is no longer in the Cabinet, but instead sits on committees defending the oppressed. His worst characteristics are taken over by Hugh Whitbread, including the intrusive kiss (Hugh had kissed Sally in the billiard room at Bourton – *MD*, p. 80). Woolf told Philip Morrell, 'I meant Richard Dalloway to be liked. Hugh Whitbread to be hated', L3, 27 July 1925, p. 195. Clarissa's absurd patriotism is given to Millicent Bruton (see *MD*, p. 198).

42. D2, 22 and 25 Aug. 1922, pp. 193 and 195–6.

43. *CSF*, p. 157; on being 'recumbent', see D1, 25 Oct. 1917 (p. 66), 26 Apr. 1918 (p. 144).

44. *CSF*, p. 153.

45. Woolf protested against the limitations imposed on the woman writer by the male reader in 'Professions for Women' (1931), Leonard Woolf, ed., Virginia Woolf, *Collected Essays* (London: Chatto and Windus, 1966), vol. 2, p. 288.

46. *CSF*, pp. 158–9.

47. *CSF*, p. 158.

48. Clarissa quotes from stanza xl of Shelley's 'Adonais' ('From the contagion of the world's slow stain/ He is secure, and now can never mourn/ A heart grown cold, a head grown grey in vain') and the Dirge from *Cymbeline* ('Fear no more the heat o' the sun . . .'), *CSF*, pp. 154, 155, 157–8. In the novel, Woolf abandoned the quotations from Shelley, but kept those from Shakespeare.

49. *The Hours* MS, p. 411 (for full details see above, n. 17).

50. Ibid.; D2, 4 Oct. 1922, p. 205.

51. The club was founded by Leonard as 'a meeting place for people interested in peace and democracy', and much frequented by the Woolfs – see D1, 10 Oct. 1917, p. 57, and many other references.

52. 'The Prime Minister', appendix B, *CSF*, p. 322.

53. D2, 19 June 1923, p. 248. She added, 'But here I may be posing.'

54. 'Miss Kilman would do anything for the Russians, starved herself for the Austrians', *MD*, p. 12.

55. *CSF*, p. 318.

56. *CSF*, p. 323. In the novel, Lady Bruton is expecting Richard Dalloway to write a history of her family – 'all the papers were ready . . . whenever the time came; the Labour Government she meant' (*MD*, p. 121) – as a Conservative MP, Dalloway would then be out of office.

57. *CSF*, p. 321.

58. *CSF*, p. 323.

59. Woolf's comment is more applicable to Stanley Baldwin, Prime Minister in June 1923 (from May 1923 to Jan. 1924, and again from Nov. 1924) than to the white-maned, charismatic Lloyd George, Prime Minister until Oct. 1922, when she began the novel. The uniforms worn by male figures of authority became an important theme in *Three Guineas* (1938).

60. For the importance of Big Ben in the novel, see David Bradshaw's edition of *Mrs Dalloway* (Oxford: Oxford University Press, 2000), pp. xxxiii–iv.

61. D2, 8 Oct. 1922, p. 206 (misdated by Woolf – it was actually 7 Oct.).

62. Woolf described their engagement as 'my first introduction to the passion of love' in '22 Hyde Park Gate', *MoB*, p. 165 (though, as Schulkind notes, she had said much the same of Stella's engagement to Jack Hills).

63. L2, to Margaret Llewelyn Davies, ? 3 Jan. 1920, p. 413; 'Friendship's Gallery', ed. Ellen Hawkes, *Twentieth Century Literature*, 25, 3/4 (Fall/Winter 1979), p. 283.

64. D1, 7 Dec. 1917, pp. 87–9 (see also L2, to Vanessa Bell, 8, 9 Dec. 1917, pp. 201–2); D2, 8 Oct. 1922, p. 206.

65. D2, 14 Oct. 1922, p. 207.

66. 'Introduction to *Mrs Dalloway*', *Essays*, vol. 4, p. 550.

67. Ibid., p. 549.

68. L5, to H. H. Goldstone, 19 Mar. 1932, p. 36; Clarissa's death is, however, suggested in the published novel, first by 'her heart, affected, they said, by influenza' (p. 4), and later imagined by Peter Walsh, as the final stroke of St Margaret's 'tolled for death that surprised in the midst of life, Clarissa falling where she stood, in her drawing-room' (p. 54).

69. D2, 14 Oct. 1922, p. 207.

70. D2, 8 Aug. 1921, p. 125.

71. *The Hours* MS, appendix 2, p. 412.

72. Her words are echoed by Peter Walsh – see n. 68, above.

73. *The Hours* MS, appendix 2, p. 415.

74. D2, 29 June 1920, p. 51.

75. D2, 13 Nov. 1922, p. 212; D2, 3 Dec. 1922, p. 216.

76. D2, 16 Jan. 1923, p. 226.

77. D2, 17 Oct. 1924, p. 317.

78. *The Hours* MS, appendix 2, pp. 420–1.

79. D1, 28 May 1918, pp. 150–1 (see also 21 Nov. 1918, p. 221).

80. *The Hours* MS, pp. 2, 3.

81. *MD*, pp. 18, 78; D2, 13 June 1923, pp. 245–6; Joyce's 'Bloomsday' was Thursday, 16 June 1904, but there is disagreement about Woolf's Wednesday – David Bradshaw argues for an imaginary Wednesday in his edition of *Mrs Dalloway*, pp. 182–3.

82. D2, 13 June 1923, p. 246.

83. D2, 19 June 1923, p. 249.

84. D2, 28 June 1923, p. 250.

85. D2, 2 Jan. 1923, p. 222; 28 June 1923, p. 250.

86. D2, 8 July 1923, p. 251.

87. D2, 15 Oct. 1923, p. 272. The same entry records that Woolf herself had undergone a distressing experience at Rodmell earlier that month, when she had panicked and gone to meet Leonard at the station. Thinking he had failed to return, she bought herself a ticket to London, but then bumped into him, and they returned to Monk's House together (pp. 270–1), an episode radically rewritten in the novel and film, *The Hours*.

88. Woolf's notebooks are transcribed by Helen Wussow in *The Hours* MS.

89. D2, 15 Oct. 1923, p. 272, and see also p. 263, 30 Aug. 1923.

90. *An Autobiography*, vol. 2, pp. 274–9 (the end of the previous chapter, pp. 258–73, considers Virginia's love of parties, their developing social life and the decision to move to London).

91. D2, 9 Jan. 1924, p. 283.

92. D2, 15 Oct. 1923, p. 271; 9 Jan. 1924, p. 283; *MD*, p. 76.

93. D2, 5 Apr. 1924, p. 298.

94. D2, 5 May 1924, p. 301; 17 Oct. 1924, p. 317; 5 Apr. 1924, p. 299; 2 Aug. 1924, p. 307.

95. D2, 7 Sept. 1924, p. 312; 17 Oct. 1924, p. 316.

96. D2, 19 June 1923, p. 248; *The Hours* MS, p. 56 – on the significance of eyesight as a metaphor, see Ch. 5, above, p. 117.

97. Elaine Showalter, *The Female Malady: Women, Madness and English Culture, 1830–1980* (London: Virago, 1987), esp. p. 164, and ch. 7,

pp. 167–94. Showalter contrasts the brutal methods used by Lewis Yealland with those of W. H. R. Rivers.

98. D2, 14 Oct. 1922, p. 207.

99. VO, p. 327; MD, pp. 154, 75.

100. 'Kew Gardens', CSF, p. 92; MD, p. 76.

101. 'Old Bloomsbury', MoB, p.184; MD, pp. 26, 98; D1, 9 Jan. 1915, p. 13.

102. MD, pp. 95–6; D2, 5 May 1924, p. 301; MD, p. 106.

103. See David Bradshaw, ed., Mrs Dalloway, p. xvi.

104. MD, pp. 99, 100, 105–6; veronal, the drug that Woolf took in her 1913 suicide attempt, is mentioned in the manuscript draft (The Hours MS, p. 119).

105. The Hours MS, appendix 2, pp. 423–5.

106. The Hours MS, pp. 130, 132.

107. The Hours MS, p. 133.

108. The Hours MS, appendix 2, p. 412; Forster, 'Virginia Woolf', p. 254.

109. Jacob's Room, ed. Sue Roe (1922; London: Penguin, 1992), p. 56; Mitchell A. Leaska, ed., Virginia Woolf, A Passionate Apprentice: The Early Journals 1897–1909 (London: Hogarth Press, 1990), p. 220; D2, 8 June 1920, p. 47. Roe also refers to the two old women at the gates of Kensington Gardens, whom Woolf remembered from her childhood – one of them sold balloons – see 'A Sketch of the Past', MoB, pp. 75–6.

110. L4, to Quentin Bell, 5 Jan. 1931, p. 276.

111. See J. Hillis Miller, 'Mrs Dalloway: Repetition as the Raising of the Dead', Fiction and Repetition: Seven English Novels (Oxford: Basil Blackwell, 1982), p. 190; Stuart N. Clarke, 'The Old Woman's Song in Mrs Dalloway', Virginia Woolf Bulletin, 17 (Sept. 2004), pp. 50–2. The first two stanzas can be roughly reconstructed from MD, pp. 89–91 and The Hours MS, pp. 96, 98. The final stanza runs as follows: 'On ev'ry grave are flowers all red and golden, / In death's dark valley this is Holy Day. / Come to my arms and let mine arms enfold you, / As once in May, as once in May.'

112. Notably in 'Luriana Lurilee', TTL, pp. 120–1, 129, but this theme is also central to The Waves.

113. The Hours MS, appendix 2, pp. 425–6.

114. See Paul Fussell, The Great War and Modern Memory (1975; Oxford: Oxford University Press, 2000), esp. ch. 8, pp. 270–309.

115. D1, 28 Nov. 1919, p. 315.

116. D2, 2 June 1921, p. 122.

117. D2, 15 Dec. 1922, pp. 216–17; Nigel Nicolson, Portrait of a Marriage (London: Weidenfeld and Nicolson, 1973), p. 185.

118. D2, 15 Sept. 1924, p. 313.

119. D2, 1 Nov. 1924, p. 320.

120. In the second of the three notebooks in the British Museum Library (Add. MSS. 51045), Woolf wrote against the last words of the book, 'Thursday Oct. 9th 1924, 11.15.' (*The Hours* MS, p. 251), see also D2, 17 Oct. 1924, pp. 316–17.

121. D2, 13 Dec. 1924, p. 323.

122. D3, 6 Jan. 1925, p. 4.

123. See L2, to JR, 25 Aug. 1922, pp. 553–5; see also William Pryor, ed., *Virginia Woolf and the Raverats: A Different Sort of Friendship* (Bath: Clear Books, 2003).

124. L3, to JR, 24 Jan. 1925, pp. 155–6.

125. Ibid., p. 154.

126. L3, to JR, 5 Feb. 1925, p. 163.

127. For details, see Glenn P. Wright, 'The Raverat Proofs of *Mrs. Dalloway*', *Studies in Bibliography*, 39 (1986), pp. 241–61.

128. Quoted in D3, 8 Apr. 1925, p. 7, fn. 3.

129. Details of the Raverat proof corrections in Wright's article, p. 260; of the US proofs, in Morris Beja, ed., *Mrs Dalloway* (Oxford: Shakespeare Head/ Blackwell, 1996), pp. 186–7.

130. See Beja, ed., *Mrs Dalloway*, p. 195; Wright, p. 256 (compare 'that insolence & levity', *The Hours* MS, p. 388).

131. Wright, p. 256.

132. See D2, 6 Mar., p. 170; 17 July, p. 182; 22 July, p. 185; 16 Aug., p. 189 (when her doctor advised ' "Equanimity – practise equanimity, Mrs Woolf" ').

133. D3, 18 June 1925, p. 32.

134. Ibid.

135. Muriel Bradbrook, 'Notes on the Style of Mrs. Woolf', *Scrutiny*, 1,1 (1932), pp. 33–8; Suzette Henke, '*Mrs Dalloway*: The Communion of Saints', in Jane Marcus, ed., *New Feminist Essays on Virginia Woolf* (Lincoln, NB: University of Nebraska Press, 1981), pp. 125–47 (p. 144), both cited by Laura A. Smith, 'Who Do We Think Clarissa Dalloway is Anyway? Re-Search Into Seventy Years of Woolf Criticism', in E. Barrett and P. Cramer, eds., *Re:Reading, Re:Writing, Re:Teaching Virginia Woolf: Selected Papers from the Fourth Annual Conference on Virginia Woolf* (New York: Pace University Press, 1995), pp. 217, 218.

136. Tony Bradshaw, ed. *The Bloomsbury Artists: Prints and Book Design* (Aldershot: Scolar Press, 1999), plate 25.

137. D3, 14 May 1925, p. 18.

138. D3, 14 June 1925, p. 29, where she recorded having written '6 little stories'. Six stories, plus 'Mrs Dalloway in Bond Street' were reprinted in *Mrs Dalloway's Party*, ed. Stella McNichol (London: Hogarth Press, 1975). Susan

Dick's first edition of *CSF* (1985) added two more ('Happiness' and 'A Simple Melody'), and an appendix in her second edition (1989) included 'The Prime Minister', the story originally intended to follow 'Mrs Dalloway in Bond Street'.

139. D3, 15 May 1925, p. 21.

140. See D3, 17 May (p. 22); 20 May (p. 24); 16 June (p. 31).

141. Reprinted in *Critical Heritage*, p. 192 ('A Novelist's Experiment', *Times Literary Supplement*, 21 May 1925).

142. *Critical Heritage*, p. 164 (Gerald Bullitt, *Saturday Review*, 30 May 1925, p. 558); p. 165 (P. C. Kennedy, *New Statesman*, 6 June 1925, p, 229).

143. *Critical Heritage*, pp. 171–7, E. M. Forster, 'The Novels of Virginia Woolf', *New Criterion*, Apr. 1926, pp. 277–86; Edwin Muir, 'Virginia Woolf', *Nation and Athenaeum*, 17 Apr. 1926, pp. 70–2.

144. *Critical Heritage*, p. 159, Richard Hughes, 'A Day in London Life', *Saturday Review of Literature* (New York), 16 May 1925, p. 755.

145. From Woolf's notebook, 'Notes for Writing', transcribed by Susan Dick as appendix A, in her edition of *To the Lighthouse: The Original Holograph Draft* (London: Hogarth Press, 1983), pp. 7–8, 10 (notes dated by Woolf 6 and 14 Mar. 1925).

146. D3, 27 Apr. 1925, p. 12.

147. *A Bibliography*, pp. 38, 46; see also D3, 14 June (p. 29), 16 June (p. 31).

148. Larsen's opera, performed in Cleveland in July 1993, is reviewed by Suzanne Ferguson, *Virginia Woolf Miscellany*, 42 (Spring, 1994), pp. 2–3.

149. The film of *Mrs Dalloway* is discussed by Diane F. Gillespie, Howard Harper and Melba Cuddy-Keane, in Laura Davis and Jeanette McVicker, eds., *Virginia Woolf and Her Influences: Selected Papers from the Seventh Annual Conference on Virginia Woolf* (New York: Pace University Press, 1998), pp. 162–75.

150. In the novel, Clarissa says 'I had meant to have dancing' (p. 195), but evidently there was not enough space: 'But talk of dancing! The rooms were packed.'

151. Robin Lippincott, *Mr Dalloway: A Novella* (Louisville, KY: Sarabande Books, 1999).

152. Michael Cunningham, *The Hours* (London: Fourth Estate, 1999).

153. Ibid., p. 211.

Chapter 7

1. *To the Lighthouse*, intro. Hermione Lee, ed. Stella McNichol (1927; London: Penguin, 1992). Page numbers appearing in square brackets after quotes refer to this edition of the book.

2. 'A Sketch of the Past', *MoB*, p. 81.

3. D3, 28 Nov. 1928, p. 208.

4. 'A Sketch of the Past', *MoB*, p. 81.

5. D3, 23 Jan. 1927, p. 123.

6. D3, 20 July 1925, p. 36.

7. 'I keep thinking of sounds I heard as a child – at St Ives mostly', D2, 15 Dec. 1922, p. 217; 'A Sketch of the Past', *MoB*, p. 65.

8. D2, 30 Mar. 1921, p. 105.

9. Mitchell A. Leaska, ed., Virginia Woolf, *A Passionate Apprentice: The Early Journals 1897–1909* (London: Hogarth Press, 1990), p. 282.

10. A letter to Vita says she thinks she may have left 'a diary for the year 1905', as well as other things at Long Barn – L3, 7 Jan. 1926, p. 227 (and see Lee's introduction to *TTL*, p. xxx).

11. D2, 22 Mar. 1921, p. 103; see also Marion Dell, *Peering Through the Escallonia: Virginia Woolf, Talland House and St Ives* (London: Cecil Woolf, 1999). 'A spring day' is probably a metaphor for childhood, since the Stephens visited Talland House during the summer months.

12. D2, 17 Oct. 1924, p. 317.

13. Virginia Woolf, *To the Lighthouse: the Original Holograph Draft*, ed. Susan Dick (London: Hogarth Press, 1983), appendix A, pp. 7–8.

14. *Holograph Draft*, p. 11 (entry dated 'August 6th 1925').

15. D3, 14 May 1925, pp. 18–19.

16. *Holograph Draft*, p. 2.

17. D3, 14 May 1925, p. 19.

18. D3, 14 June 1925, p. 29 – compare D3, 8 Feb. 1926, p. 58: 'a little tired, from having thought too much about To the Lighthouse.'

19. Edited under this title by Stella McNichol (London: Hogarth Press, 1973), and see Ch. 6, 'The Aftermath', p. 156, n. 138.

20. D3, 30 July 1925, p. 38.

21. 'Together and Apart', *CSF*, p. 193.

22. L3, to Vita Sackville-West, 31 Jan., 2 Feb. 1926, p. 237.

23. D3, 27 Feb. 1926, p. 63.

24. 'The New Dress', *CSF*, pp. 170–7, and for Woolf's 'frock consciousness', see D3, 27 Apr. 1925, p. 12 (and D3, 30 June 1926, pp. 90–1).

25. 'The Man who Loved His Kind', *CSF*, pp. 195–200; see D3, 27 June 1925, p. 33, 'I do not love my kind. I detest them', and compare Lily's comment on Charles Tansley, 'how could he love his kind who did not know one picture from another', *TTL*, p. 213.

26. 'A Simple Melody', *CSF*, pp. 204, 206.

27. 'A Summing Up', *CSF*, p. 210.

28. *Holograph Draft*, p. 2 (dated 'August 6th 1925').

29. Woolf 'felt rather queer, to think how much of this there is in To the Lighthouse, & how all these people will read it & recognise poor Leslie Stephen & beautiful Mrs Stephen in it', D3, 24 Feb. 1926, p. 61.

30. First published by the Hogarth Press, and hand-set by Virginia – see above, Ch. 3, p. 62.

31. 'Impassioned Prose', Woolf's essay on De Quincey written the following year, before completing *TTL*, *Essays*, vol. 4, p. 365.

32. D3, 14 Sept. 1925, p. 40.

33. D3, 5 Sept. 1925, p. 39.

34. *Holograph Draft*, pp. 29, 30, 31 – this last page is dated 'Sept. 3rd' in MS, and by the second line, 'Miss Briscoe' has become 'Lily' (a name initially given to Minta – see p. 16). Woolf apparently only completed a further 10 pages between 3 Sept. 1925 and 10 Jan. 1926.

35. *Essays*, vol. 4, p. 319.

36. D3, 27 Nov. 1925, p. 47.

37. D2, 15 Dec. 1922, p. 217.

38. Ibid., p. 216; 19 Feb. 1923, pp. 235–6.

39. D2, 5 July 1924, p. 307. Judd Street, lying between Tavistock Square and St Pancras, was somewhat run down (though Woolf's dressmaker lived there).

40. *Letters of Vita Sackville-West to Virginia Woolf*, ed. Louise DeSalvo and Mitchell Leaska (London: Hutchinson, 1984), 16 July 1924, p. 54.

41. D2, 15 Sept. 1924, p. 313.

42. L3, to VS-W, 23 Sept. 1925, p. 215; 31 Jan. 1927, p. 319. Woolf had earlier used the image of a lighthouse 'besieged by the bodies of lost birds, who were dashed senseless, by the gale, against the glass' in *Night and Day*, ed. Julia Briggs (1919; London: Penguin 1992), p. 334 (compare 'birds dashed against the lamp and the whole place rocking', *TTL*, p. 9).

43. D2, 19 Feb. 1923, p. 235.

44. D2, 1 Nov. 1924, p. 320 (this comment was occasioned by her tea with Mary Hutchinson, see Ch. 6, p. 153).

45. L3, to Jacques Raverat, 24 Jan. 1925, pp. 155–6.

46. D3, 27 Nov. 1925, p. 47.

47. D3, 7 Dec. 1925, p. 48.

48. D3, 21 Dec. 1925, p. 51; L3, to VS-W, 22 Dec. 1925, p. 224.

49. D3, 21 Dec. 1925, pp. 51–2.

50. *Biography*, vol. 2, p. 120.

51. D3, 19 Jan. 1926, p. 57.

52. *Holograph Draft*, p. 3, entry dated 15 Jan. 1926.

53. Ibid.

54. L3, to VS-W, 23 Dec. 1925, p. 225, 'Clive, whose heart is turning to honey, in which the yellow bee blooms', cf. 'The China rose is all abloom/ And buzzing with the yellow bee' (noted by Lee, *TTL*, p. 246, n. 96); the poem, by Charles Elton, had apparently been written down by Philippa Strachey and was first published in Vita Sackville-West and Harold Nicolson, eds., *Another World Than This* (London: Michael Joseph, 1945), p. 108 – and see n. 76, below.

55. L3, to VS-W, 1 Mar. 1925, p. 245.

56. She wrote of her diary, '[i]t is to serve the purpose of my memoirs', D3, 8 Feb. 1926, p. 58; '[i]f I died, what would Leo make of them?', D3, 20 Mar. 1926, p. 67; 'L. taking up a volume the other day said Lord save him if I died first & he had to read through these', D3, 3 Feb. 1927, p. 125.

57. L3, to VS-W, 16 Nov. 1925, p. 221.

58. See, for example, L3, to VS-W, 16 Apr. 1926, p. 256; D3, 9 May 1926, p. 80; D3, 28 Sept. 1926, pp. 111–12 (though each of them appeared to have quite a different cause).

59. D3, 23 Feb. 1926, p. 59 (did VW write 'palette' for 'palate'?)

60. *Vita and Harold: The Letters of Vita Sackville-West and Harold Nicolson, 1910–1962*, ed. Nigel Nicolson (London: Weidenfeld and Nicolson, 1992), 17 Dec. 1925, p. 135.

61. For example L3, to VS-W, 15 Jan. 1926, p. 230; 3 Feb. 1926, p. 238; 17 Feb. 1926, p. 240; 1 Mar. 1926, p. 24.

62. *Letters of VS-W to VW*, 13 Jan. 1926, p. 94; 4 Feb. 1926, p. 107.

63. L3, to VS-W, early Nov.? 1925, p. 220; 22 Dec. 1925, p. 224; 13 Apr. 1926, p. 253; 7 Jan. 1926, p. 227.

64. On 26 July 1926 – see L3, to VS-W, 8 Aug. 1926, pp. 284–5.

65. L3, to VS-W, 26 Jan. 1926, p. 233.

66. D3, 23 Feb. 1926, p. 59.

67. L3, to VS-W, 3 Feb. 1926, p. 238.

68. D3, 3 Mar. 1926, p. 64; *Holograph Draft*, p. 126 (p. 129 dated 5 March).

69. D3, 9 Apr. 1926, p. 73; L3, to VS-W,13 Apr. 1926, p. 254; L3, to Vanessa Bell, 16 Apr. 1926, p. 256. 'Sentimental? Victorian?' she asked of *TTL* in her diary, D3, 5 Sept. 1926, p. 107, and a few days later, 'I go in dread of

"sentimentality"', D3, 13 Sept. 1926, p. 110 (also D3, 20 July 1925, p. 36 and L3, to VS-W, 13 May 1927, p. 374).

70. See also Jane Lilienfeld, 'Where the Spear Plants Grew: the Ramsays' Marriage in *To the Lighthouse*', in Jane Marcus, ed., *New Feminist Essays* (London: Macmillan, 1981), pp. 148–69.

71. For Andrew and Nancy, see *TTL*, pp. 83–4.

72. L3, to VS-W, 13 Apr. 1926, pp. 254–5.

73. *Holograph Draft*, p. 279; E. M. Forster, *A Passage to India* (1924; London: Penguin, 1936), p. 178. Forster's influence on Woolf's work is evident from her first novel onwards; it is reflected in her choice of the name 'Mrs Bast' for the cleaning woman in 'Time Passes', since Leonard Bast is a central (and lower-middle-class) character in *Howards End*. In 1927 Woolf was to publish two articles on Forster, on 'Aspects of the Novel', and the novels themselves – see *Essays*, vol. 4, pp. 457–63, 491–500.

74. D3, 7 Dec. 1925, p. 50.

75. *Holograph Draft*, p. 260.

76. On different occasions, both Virginia and Leonard Woolf responded to enquiries about 'Luriana Lurilee' – Virginia wrote to the *Sunday Times* on 18 May 1930 (see *A Bibliography*, p. 289), and later informed a correspondent that the poem was by Charles Elton (1839–1900), 'a lawyer and historian; he made it in his sleep, together with one upon Sha[v]ing', and that Lytton Strachey used to recite them – L6, 9 Mar. 1939, p. 321. See also *Letters of Leonard Woolf*, ed. F. Spotts (London: Bloomsbury, 1989), p. 488 (and see n. 54 above).

77. '[S]he felt herself like a leaf blowing in at a window'; 'turning leaves, climbing from this to that', *Holograph Draft*, p. 194.

78. *Holograph Draft*, p. 196.

79. D3, entry headed 18 Apr.; actually written 30 Apr. 1926, p. 76.

80. D3, 30 Sept. 1926, p. 113; *Holograph Draft*, p. 3 (see also Woolf's Outline for 'Time Passes', appendix B); 'Mr Bennett and Mrs Brown', *Essays*, vol. 3, p. 422. Peter Stansky, *On or About December 1910* (Cambridge, MA: Harvard University Press, 1996), and above, Ch. 5, p. 125; for further discussion of time and rupture in Woolf, see my essay '"This Moment I Stand On": Woolf and the Spaces in Time', Virginia Woolf Society of Great Britain, 2001.

81. *TTL*, p. 137; *Jacob's Room*, ed. Sue Roe (1922; London: Penguin, 1992), p. 140; George Dangerfield, *The Strange Death of Liberal England* (1935; London: Paladin, 1970), p. 372.

82. See Ch. 1, p. 18. Woolf brought together Clive Bell's injunction to 'reach up to the tall fruit of your imagination and feel it growing warm and ripe' and

a line from *Cymbeline* when she wrote in her diary, 23 Feb. 1926 (D3, p. 59) that she felt she 'was on the right path: & that what fruit hangs in my soul is to be reached there.'

83. 'Impassioned Prose', *Essays*, vol. 4, p. 365. Woolf set *TTL* in the Hebridian islands off the west coast of Scotland, and the thought of 'the destruction of the island and its engulfment in the sea' occurs to Mrs Ramsay (*TTL*, p. 20), and later to Mr Ramsay, who turns 'from the sight of human ignorance and human fate and the sea eating the ground we stand on' (*TTL*, p. 50).

84. In the *Holograph Draft*, the Dreadnought is 'that lean murderous ship' whose black snout will break the mirror, and interrupt 'the dream of harmony and completeness' by bringing 'death, starvation, pain' (p. 222).

85. D3, 30 Sept. 1926, p. 113.

86. L3, to VS-W, 13 May 1927, p. 374. See Kate Flint, 'Virginia Woolf and the General Strike', *Essays in Criticism*, 36 (1986), pp. 319–34.

87. D3, 12 May 1926, p. 85; 11 May 1926, p. 83.

88. D3, 5–11 May 1926, pp. 77–85; L3, to VB, 12 May 1926, p. 260 (where she describes it as 'all unutterably boring and quite unimportant and yet very upsetting'); *Holograph Draft*, appendix A, p. 12.

89. See n. 69, above, for Woolf's views on sentimentality.

90. D3, 20 May 1926, p. 87; 25 May 1926, p. 88.

91. L3, to VS-W, 16 Mar. 1926, p. 247.

92. D3, 5 Sept. 1926, p. 106 – she asked herself 'Could I do it in a parenthesis? so that one had the sense of reading the two things at the same time?', a solution she later adopted in 'Time Passes'.

93. 'Impassioned Prose', *Essays*, vol. 4, p. 365.

94. On 'June 21st 1926', according to *Holograph Draft*, p. 257; D3, 22 July 1926, p. 96; 13 Sept. 1926, p. 109.

95. 'And this last lap, in the boat, is hard, because the material is not so rich as it is with Lily on the lawn', D3, 13 Sept. 1926, p. 109.

96. I owe this point to Hans Gabler. The numbering of the sections is significant throughout – see my essay, 'Writing by Numbers: an Aspect of Woolf's Revisionary Practice', in Roger Lüdeke, ed., *Text and Border: the Borders of the Text*, forthcoming.

97. D3, 23 Feb. 1926, p. 60; *TTL*, p. 56.

98. Woolf examined her capacity for making up scenes in 'A Sketch of the Past', *MoB*, p. 142; Lily's 'tunnelling', *TTL*, p. 188, recalls Woolf's process of digging out 'caves' behind her characters which will connect (D2, 30 Aug. 1923, p. 263); *TTL*, pp. 194, 195.

99. For this passage, included and then removed from the proofs, see *To the Lighthouse*, ed. Susan Dick (Oxford: Shakespeare Head/Blackwell, 1992),

p. 207 (and compare *Holograph Draft*, p. 315). It is also quoted by Hans Gabler, who argues that the passage was removed so that the book would be contained within the standard 20 gatherings in 'A Tale of Two Texts: Or, How One Might Edit Virginia Woolf's *To the Lighthouse*', *Woolf Studies Annual*, 10 (2004), p. 17.

100. D3, 27 June 1925, p. 34.

101. D3, 31 July 1926, p. 103; 15–30 Sept. 1926, pp. 110–13; 23 Nov. 1926, p. 117.

102. In the MS, Woolf is undecided about what Mrs Ramsay is reading to James – at first it is 'the story of the three dwarfs' ('The Three Dwarfs in the Forest'? *Holograph Draft*, p. 73), which becomes 'the story of the Woodman's daughter' ('The Three Bears'? *Holograph Draft*, pp. 96, 101, 103, 104). In the published text she chose the more interesting story of the Flounder, usually known as 'The Fisherman and his Wife', and quoted (*TTL*, pp. 62–3, 67–8) from Margaret Hunt's translation of *Grimms' Household Tales* in Bohn's Standard Library Edition (London: George Bell, 1884) – see Lee's note, *TTL*, p. 236. Browne's 'The Sirens' Song' (not referred to in the MS) and Shakespeare's 98th sonnet (not identified by number in the MS) are both reprinted in Woolf's favourite bedside reading, *The Oxford Book of English Verse 1250–1900*, ed. Sir Arthur Quiller-Couch (Oxford: Oxford University Press, 1900) – see Susan Dick's note in her Shakespeare Head edition of *TTL*, p. 187. Tolstoy's *Anna Karenina* (*TTL*, p. 117) replaces *War and Peace* in the dinner table discussion, though now with a different significance (*Holograph Draft*, p. 179, and see p. 172 and n. 72, above).

103. D3, 23 Jan. 1927, pp. 123–5.

104. *Holograph Draft*, p. 138 (cited by Lee, *TTL*, p. 242). Tansley's words recur to Lily throughout the novel, usually linked to anxieties about her own art (e.g. *TTL*, pp. 54, 94, 99, 173, 213). On Woolf's struggles with misogyny, see above, Ch. 4, pp. 101–3; Ch. 5, pp. 113, 116. In 'The Lighthouse', Lily thinks that 'the war had drawn the sting of her femininity' (*TTL*, p. 174), apparently meaning what we would call her feminism.

105. *Holograph Draft*, p. 136.

106. Clive Bell, *Art* (1914; London: Chatto and Windus, reprinted 1923), p. 210.

107. Mr Paunceforte has made it fashionable 'to see everything pale, elegant, semi-transparent', p. 23 (see also pp. 54, 59).

108. See Tom Cross, *The Shining Sands: Artists in Newlyn and St Ives, 1880–1930* (Tiverton: West Country Books/Cambridge: The Lutterworth Press, 1994), especially pp. 86, 92–3, 160–1 and 105.

109. *TTL*, p. 226; see Roger Fry's 'An Essay in Aesthetics', *Vision and Design*

(1920; Phoenix Library, 1928), pp. 31, and 33–4 for the five qualities: vision is what Lily has, design what she does.

110. L3, to Roger Fry, 27 May 1927, p. 385 and fn. 2.

111. 'Such a successive unity is of course familiar to us in literature and music', Fry, *Vision and Design*, p. 33; Fry's letter, quoted in L3, p. 385, fn. 2.

112. Retold in several places, including *A Bibliography*, p. 48.

113. D3, 28 Feb. 1927, p. 129; 21 Mar. 1927, p. 132.

114. D3, 5 May 1927, p. 134; *Times Literary Supplement* review reprinted in *Critical Heritage*, pp. 193–4.

115. Bennett reviewed *TTL* for the *Evening Standard* (*Critical Heritage*, p. 200); Edwin Muir reviewed it for Leonard's *Nation and Athenaeum* (*Critical Heritage*, pp. 209–10); Taylor reviewed it for *The Spectator* (*Critical Heritage*, p. 199).

116. Mauron translated a version of 'Time Passes' that stands between the holograph draft and the printed text. This, as Susan Dick points out in her Shakespeare Head edition of the novel, 'is of special interest since it is the only intermediate version of any part of the novel that has survived' (p. xxviii). She reproduces it as Appendix C in her edition (pp. 212–29). Both the typescript and Mauron's translation are included in James M. Haule, '"Le Temps passe" and the Original Typescript: an Early Version of the "Time Passes" Section of *To the Lighthouse*', *Twentieth Century Literature*, 29, 3 (Fall 1983), pp. 267–311. Full publication details of Mauron's translation, and others, in *A Bibliography*, p. 330.

117. Both are reprinted in *Critical Heritage*, p. 213 and pp. 215–18, 220–1.

118. Ibid., pp. 196–7; 208.

119. Publication details in *A Bibliography*, p. 49. Susan Dick's Shakespeare Head edition of *TTL* sets out the problem (pp. xxx–xxxiv) and lists variants (pp. 192–211), adopting the corrected US proofs, now at Smith College, as copy text. McNichol's Penguin edition also lists variants, while adopting a different approach – see pp. 260–8. See also Gabler, 'A Tale of Two Texts', and my own article, 'Between the Texts: Virginia Woolf's Acts of Revision', in W. Speed Hill and Edward M. Burns, eds., *TEXT*, vol. 12 (Ann Arbor, MI: University of Michigan Press, 1999), pp. 143–65.

120. Reproduced in Tony Bradshaw, *The Bloomsbury Artists: Prints and Book Design* (Aldershot: Scolar Press, 1999), plate 25. A 'fountain of joy' is experienced by Cam in *TTL*, p. 205, echoing the 'fountain of white water' seen from the shore, p. 25, and Mrs Ramsay's self-transformation into 'a column of spray', p. 42 (and compare p. 72, where the light from the lighthouse makes her feel flooded with delight).

121. *Selected Letters of Vanessa Bell*, ed. Regina Marler (London: Blooms-

bury, 1993), 11 May 1927, p. 317. Vanessa wrote, 'I suppose I'm the only person in the world who can have those feelings, at any rate to such an extent'. Meanwhile, Woolf, who had not yet received this, had written Vanessa a hilarious letter of reproach – L3, 15 May 1927, pp. 375–6. As Gabler notes in his article (p. 18), page 86 of *TTL* (where Vanessa has 'only got to') actually includes an account of Vanessa (as Lily), painting.

122. D3, 16 May, 6 June 1927, pp. 136–7; L3, to RF, 27 May, p. 385; D3, 11 May 1927, p. 135.

123. *A Bibliography*, p. 48; D3, 6 June 1927, p. 137; *Letters of Leonard Woolf*, 12 Nov. 1965, p. 541; 11 Jan. 1969, p. 572.

124. *A Bibliography*, pp. 58, 59.

125. BBC TV in association with Colin Gregg Films – the screenplay was by Hugh Stoddart, and the cast included Rosemary Harris, Michael Gough, Suzanne Bertish, Lynsey Baxter, Pippa Guard and T. P. McKenna.

126. D3, 23 July 1927, p. 147. On Woolf and motoring, see Melba Cuddy-Keane, Natasha Aleksiuk, Kay Li, Morgan Love, Chris Rose and Andrea Williams, 'The Heteroglossia of History, Part One: The Car' in Beth Rigel Daugherty and Eileen Barrett, eds., *Texts and Contexts: Selected Papers from the Fifth Annual Conference on Virginia Woolf* (New York: Pace University Press, 1996); Makiko Minow-Pinkney, 'Virginia Woolf and the Age of Motor Cars' in Pamela Caughie, ed., *Virginia Woolf in the Age of Mechanical Reproduction* (New York and London: Garland, 2000), pp. 159–82.

Chapter 8

1. *Orlando: The Holograph Draft*, ed. S. N. Clarke (London: S. N. Clarke, 1993), p. 287.

2. *Essays*, vol. 4, pp. 523, 519. 'The Sun and the Fish' has affinities with other imaginative essays of this period, in particular 'On Being Ill' (1926), *Essays*, vol. 4, p. 317; 'Street Haunting: A London Adventure' (1927), *Essays*, vol. 4, p. 480; 'Evening over Sussex: Reflections in a Motor Car', Leonard Woolf, ed., Virginia Woolf, *Collected Essays* (London: Chatto and Windus, 1966), vol. 2, p. 290 (undated, but Makiko Minow-Pinkney assigns it to 'the late summer of 1927' – it is clearly connected with the final chapter of *Orlando*, as she points out in 'Virginia Woolf and the Age of Motor Cars', in Pamela Caughie, ed., *Virginia Woolf in the Age of Mechanical Reproduction* (New York and London: Garland, 2000), p. 163); and 'Flying Over London', *Collected Essays*, vol. 4, p. 167.

3. D3, 30 June 1927, p. 142; *Letters of Vita Sackville-West to Virginia Woolf,* ed. Louise DeSalvo and Mitchell Leaska (London: Hutchinson, 1984), p. 234. The new aquarium had opened on 7 Apr. 1924 – see Woolf's paragraph, 'Aesthetically speaking, the new aquarium . . .', *Essays*, vol. 3, p. 404.

4. *Letters of VS-W to VW*, 8 Feb. 1928, p. 269.

5. The passage continues, 'I hold the conviction that such connections will to a very large extent cease to be regarded as merely unnatural, and will be understood far better, . . . it will be recognized that many more people of my type do exist than under the present-day system of hypocrisy is commonly admitted.' A first step might be 'the reconstruction of the system of marriage'. It appears in Vita's unpublished account of her love affair with Violet Trefusis, reprinted as part III of Nigel Nicolson's *Portrait of a Marriage* (1973; London: Weidenfeld and Nicolson, 1990), pp. 101–2.

6. D2, 15 Dec. 1922, p. 217; on Vita's motherly side, she 'so lavishes on me the maternal protection which . . . I have always most wished from everyone', D3, 21 Dec. 1925, p. 52.

7. D3, 30 Sept. 1926, p. 113 (see also entries for 15 and 28 Sept.)

8. 'After Lighthouse I was I remember nearer suicide, seriously, than since 1913', D4, 17 Oct. 1934, p. 253; she was also depressed when correcting the proofs of *Orlando* –'the worst time of all. It makes me suicidal', D3, 20 June 1928, p. 186.

9. Victoria Glendinning, *Vita: The Life of Vita Sackville-West* (New York: Alfred Knopf, 1983), p. 168; 'I'd like to come if you're alone, sometime,' L3, to Vita Sackville-West, 19 Oct. 1926, p. 300; 'a miracle of discretion – one letter in another . . . compare this 19th Nov – with last, and you'll admit there's a difference', L3, to VS-W, 19 Nov. 1926, p. 302.

10. L3, to VS-W, 30 Dec. 1926, p. 313; *Letters of VS-W to VW*, 2 Jan. 1927, p. 174.

11. *Letters of VS-W to VW*, 2 Jan. 1927, p. 175; 28 Jan. 1927, p. 179.

12. Ibid., 31 Jan. 1927, p. 183.

13. L3, to VS-W, 6 Mar. 1927, p. 342.

14. D3, 14 Mar. 1927, p. 131.

15. For 'Jessamy', see the *Oxford English Dictionary*, entry (4). The Ladies of Llangollen were Lady Eleanor Butler (1739–1829) and Sarah Ponsonby (1755–1831); diarists and letter writers, their rejection of marriage and preference for 'romantic friendship' has been subjected to different interpretations. In 1936 Mary Gordon published an account of them with the Hogarth Press entitled *The Chase of the Wild Goose*, and the wild goose appears on the last page of *Orlando*, but the connection remains as elusive as the chase – see Danell Jones, 'The Chase of the Wild Goose: The Ladies of Llangollen and *Orlando*', in Vara Neverow-Turk and Mark Hussey, eds., *Themes and*

Variations: Selected Papers from the Second Annual Conference on Virginia Woolf (New York: Pace University Press, 1993), pp. 181–9.

16. *Essays*, vol. 4, p. 352.

17. L3, to VS-W, 19 Nov. 1926, p. 302.

18. *Challenge* was printed by Collins and ready for binding in 1920, but Vita withdrew it, publishing it only in New York with George Doran in 1924 (it was eventually published by Collins with an introduction by Nigel Nicolson, in 1974); see Glendinning, pp. 93, 109, 176.

19. Ibid., pp. 95, 99.

20. *Letters of VS-W to VW*, 11 June 1927, p. 229; L3, to VS-W, 14 June 1927, p. 391.

21. Mary Hutchinson became 'the oyster' – see L3, to VS-W, 4 July 1927, p. 395 (also 18 July, 5 and 7 Aug., pp. 398, 407 and 409) and *Letters of VS-W to VW*, 8 July 1927, p. 236.

22. Glendinning, pp. 179–80; L3, to VS-W, 4 July, 7 Aug. 1927, pp. 395, 408.

23. L3, to Lytton Strachey, 3 Sept. 1927, p. 418.

24. *Biography*, vol. 2, p. 132.

25. 'The New Biography', *Essays*, vol. 4, pp. 475, 473, 478.

26. D3, 20 Sept. 1927, pp. 157–8; 5, 22 Oct. 1927, p. 161.

27. L3, to VS-W, 9 Oct. 1927, pp. 428–9.

28. *Letters of VS-W to VW*, 11 Oct. 1927, p. 252. This letter ends, 'I am Virginia's good puppy, beating my tail on the floor, responsive to a kind pat' (p. 253).

29. See, for example, L3, to VS-W, 21 Oct., 23 Oct., 30 Oct., 4 Nov., 6 Nov., 11 Nov., 16 Nov., 22 Nov., 5 Dec. 1927, pp. 433–6, 441–2.

30. Glendinning, p. 103.

31. L3, to VS-W, 13 Oct. 1927, p. 431.

32. L3, to VS-W, 23 Sept. 1927, p. 214.

33. D2, 3 Dec. 1923, p. 277.

34. The early life of Vanessa is reprinted as 'Reminiscences' in *MoB*, pp. 28–59; her lives of Caroline Stephen and Mary Fisher have been lost – see *Biography*, vol. 1, p. 93. Woolf's play, *Freshwater*, is close in mood to ch. V of *Orlando*: written in 1923 and performed in a revised version in 1935, it is a farce about her great-aunt, the photographer Julia Margaret Cameron, featuring such eminent Victorians as the poet Tennyson, the painter Frederick Watts and his young bride Ellen Terry (who later runs away with a sailor) – see *Freshwater*, ed. Lucio P. Ruotolo (New York: Harcourt, Brace Jovanovich, 1976), pp. 59–60; introduction to *Victorian Photographs of Famous Men and Fair Women* by Julia Margaret Cameron (London: Hogarth Press, 1926), reprinted *Essays*, vol. 4, pp. 375–83.

35. 'Friendship's Gallery', ed. Ellen Hawkes, *Twentieth Century Literature*, 25, 3/4 (Fall/Winter 1979), pp. 270–302, and see also L1, to Violet Dickinson, ? Aug. 1907, p. 303; 'Memoirs of a Novelist', *CSF*, pp. 69–79.

36. See *Holograph Draft* – the second page begins 'Suggestions for short pieces. / A Biography. / This is to tell a persons life from the year 1500 to 1928. / Changing its sex. / taking different aspects of the character in different / Centuries. the theory being that character goes / on underground before we are born; & / leaves something afterwards also.' A few more notes follow. The third page is dated 8 Oct. 1927 and headed, '*Orlando. a biography*'. See also diary entries at n. 26 above.

37. *Holograph Draft*, p. 145; an Elizabethan verse translation of *Orlando Furioso* by Sir John Harington was published in 1591.

38. Glendinning, p. 127.

39. *Orlando*, intro. Sandra Gilbert, ed. Brenda Lyons (1928; London: Penguin Books, 1993). Page numbers appearing in square brackets after quotes refer to this edition of the book.

40. The first chapter was begun on 8 Oct. and the second on 29 Oct., *Holograph Draft*, pp. 3, 48; 'extraordinarily unwilled', D3, 20 Dec. 1927, p. 168; 'happiest autumn', D3, 20 Nov. 1927, p. 164 (and reasserted 30 Nov., 20 Dec. pp. 165, 168). 'I write so quick I can't get it typed before lunch', D3, 20 Nov. 1927, p. 164 (though elsewhere Woolf seems to have typed out her handwritten drafts after, rather than before, lunch).

41. D3, 23 Jan. 1927, p. 125.

42. Holleyman and Treacher, *Catalogue of Books from The Library of Leonard and Virginia Woolf* (Brighton: Holleyman and Treacher, 1975) lists a 1926 reprint of *Knole and the Sackvilles*, inscribed 'Virginia from Vita/ Knole/ Jan. 19th 1927' (V/s, section II, p. 2). Vita had already given her a copy, at her own request, when they first met ('I should never have dared to dun you if I had known the magnificence of the book'), L3, 3 Jan. 1923, p. 1.

43. See, for example, O, pp. 49–50, 75–6.

44. D3, 8 Dec. 1929, p. 271.

45. Woolf's early volumes of *An English Garner* have since been lost, though volumes 3 to 7, rebound by Virginia herself, survive in the library of Leonard and Virginia Woolf, now at Washington State University – for further details see Alan Isaac, *Virginia Woolf, the Uncommon Bookbinder* (London: Cecil Woolf, 2000), pp. 15, 17.

46. T. S. Eliot, *Little Gidding* (1942), section 1, lines 1, 3, 6.

47. D3, 20 Sept. 1927, p. 157.

48. Glendinning, p. 107 (for *Challenge*, see n. 18 above).

49. Glendinning, pp. 26, 32; L3, to VS-W, 13 [14] Oct. 1927, p. 430; 17 Feb. 1926, p. 240.

50. O, pp. 19, 37; *Holograph Draft*, p. 40; O, p. 41; *Othello*, V. ii. 99–101.

51. Leonard reported her two-day coma in *An Autobiography*, vol. 2, pp. 52, 124.

52. The misery of the Stephen children at that time is shared by James and Cam Ramsay in *To the Lighthouse*, where Lily Briscoe sympathizes with them, pp. 162–3.

53. Harold Nicolson, *Some People* (1927; London: Constable, 1931), p. 187.

54. This passage is discussed in greater detail in my essay, ' "This Moment I Stand On": Woolf and the Spaces in Time', Virginia Woolf Society of Great Britain, 2001, pp. 3, 15–16.

55. *Letters of VS-W to VW*, 9 Feb. 1927, p. 189; L3, to VS-W, 23 Mar. 1927, p. 351; Vita Sackville-West, *Passenger to Teheran* (London: Hogarth Press, 1926), p. 9. Woolf professed herself impressed by *Passenger*, and felt 'I have picked up a good many things I had missed in private life. What are they, I wonder, the very intimate things, one says in print?' L3, to VS-W, 15 Sept. 1926, p. 291 – see Ian Blyth, 'A Little "Einsteinian" Confusion', *Virginia Woolf Bulletin*, 9 (Jan. 2002), pp. 29–33. Woolf produced a comparably displaced present moment in *Orlando* by announcing its publication date, 11 October 1928, as 'the present moment', though this was not the moment she wrote it, nor the moment it would be read by others, except for Vita.

56. *As You Like It*, III. ii. 328–9; O, pp. 38, 142–4; 212.

57. O, p. 69; 'Now is life very solid, or very shifting? I am haunted by the two contradictions', D3, 4 Jan. 1929, p. 218.

58. According to Woolf's earliest notes, 'taking different aspects of the character in different centuries' (*Holograph Draft*, p. 2). The book attributes different characteristics to different centuries in such an exaggerated way as to imply self-mockery.

59. O, p. 74 – this corresponds to Vita's account in *Knole and the Sackvilles* (1922), pp. 95–6, except that she lists 365 rooms, rather than bedrooms.

60. Vita's father, the third Baron Sackville, died at Knole on 28 Jan. 1928, during the writing of the book – see Glendinning, pp. 188–9.

61. Constantinople has always stood as a meeting point between Europe and Asia, and between Christianity and Islam, but in the 1920s, under Ataturk's energetic modernization, it combined Turkish nationalism and Western secular values in ways that further complicated its dual identity – see my article, 'Constantinople: Virginia Woolf at the Crossroads of the Imagination', in Natalya Reinhold, ed., *Woolf Across Cultures* (New York: Pace University Press, 2004), pp. 179–89.

62. 'Dreams of golden domes' were envisaged by 'The Jessamy Brides' (see n. 14 above). For the 1906 visit, see Mitchell A. Leaska, ed., *Virginia Woolf, A Passionate Apprentice: The Early Journals 1897–1909* (London: Hogarth Press, 1990), p. 347. Constantinople was the furthest east that Woolf ever travelled.

63. See *To the Lighthouse*, intro. Hermione Lee, ed. Stella McNichol (1927; London: Penguin, 1992), pp. 54, 186, and especially p. 81. Lyndall Gordon sees Constantinople as a central element in Woolf's imagination, in *Virginia Woolf: A Writer's Life* (1984; New York: W. W. Norton, 2000), pp. 111–12.

64. 'Such a view over the Golden Horn, and the sea, and Santa Sophia! . . . I find it lovely', Glendinning, p. 69; O, p. 84.

65. Leslie Stephen was offered the KCB in 1902 (when he was already terminally ill). Vita was later to write an account of her gipsy grandmother, in *Pepita* (London: Hogarth Press, 1937). This is one of the many places in which *Orlando* alludes to Vita's family or her personal experiences – her lawsuit (O, pp. 119, 176–7) would be another key example.

66. The masque for King James in the holograph is vaguely described as 'by . . . Jonson, Shakespeare, or another'; the passage continues, 'Something was already being said about the Chariot of love' (*Holograph Draft*, pp. 39–40) which suggests that Woolf was thinking of the poem 'See the chariot at hand here of Love' from Jonson's *A Celebration of Charis* (not a masque but a sequence of poems describing a triumphal procession). In her own masque, Woolf follows the Jonsonian masque structure surprisingly closely, having apparently identified its key elements. Ten years earlier, Lady Strachey had read Virginia 'Ben Jonson's masques. They are short & in between she broke off to talk a little . . . I enjoyed it', D1, 18 Jan. 1918, p. 106. For Milton's *Comus* ('Sabrina fair' is quoted in *The Voyage Out*), see *Holograph Draft*, p. 102.

67. O, pp. 95–7; *Holograph Draft*, p. 72.

68. Woolf may have attributed some of her own adolescent fantasies to Katharine Hilbery in *Night and Day*, including 'the taming of wild ponies . . . or the conduct of a vast ship in a hurricane round a black promontory of rock' – 'much of the furniture of this [inner] world was drawn directly from the past, and even from the England of the Elizabethan age', *Night and Day*, ed. Julia Briggs (1919; London: Penguin, 1992), pp. 34, 116, and see p. xxviii; 'nothing is known . . .', *A Room of One's Own*, Michèle Barrett, ed., *A Room of One's Own/Three Guineas* (1929, 1938; London: Penguin, 1993), p. 42.

69. *Between the Acts*, intro. Gillian Beer, ed. Stella McNichol (1941; London, Penguin, 1992), pp. 73–4.

70. See earlier discussions of *The Voyage Out* (Ch. 1, p. 9) and *Jacob's Room*

(Ch. 4, pp. 100–1, above); D3, 20 Dec. 1927, p. 167 – 'her clients' is ambiguous but surely refers to Nell's. For a full analysis of this passage, see my article 'The Conversation Behind the Conversation: Speaking the Unspeakable in Virginia Woolf', in Catherine Bernard and Christine Reynier, eds., *Études Anglaises*, forthcoming.

71. '[T]he relationship so secret & private compared with relations to men' – D2, 1 Nov. 1924, p. 320.

72. Woolf would reuse the idea of 'all girls together' in *A Room of One's Own*, pp. 74, 100.

73. O, pp. 19, 175, 205; L3, to VS-W, 5 Dec. 1927, p. 443; D3, 14 March 1927, p. 131.

74. *Holograph Draft*, p. 171. Orlando's disappointment corresponds to Virginia's with Thoby's intellectual friends from Cambridge. She had felt 'intolerably bored' with them since 'there was no physical attraction between us' ('Old Bloomsbury', *MoB*, p. 194 – cited by Clarke in a footnote). Without recognizing their interest in one another, she had found the atmosphere subtly misogynist – as Orlando finds that of Addison, Pope and Lord Chesterfield (the first draft had added Arnold Bennett, Desmond MacCarthy and Orlo Williams, her old adversaries (see Ch. 5, p. 116) for good measure – see *Holograph Draft*, p. 169).

75. 'Full circle' since the novel's opening sentence.

76. D3, 11, 18 Feb. 1928, pp. 174–5; *Orlando* as 'empty; & too fantastic', D3, 11 Feb., p. 175; 'too long for a joke, & too frivolous for a serious book', 22 Mar., p. 177; 'a freak', 21 Apr., p. 180.

77. D3, 18 Feb. 1928, p. 175; 'all about death' only in the *Holograph Draft*, p. 201 (but compare O, p. 164); the tingling finger links writing (uneasily) with marriage in O, pp. 165–6.

78. O, pp. 174–5, 181. For Woolf being married in a thunderstorm, see L2, to Ottoline Morrell, 17 Aug. 1912, and to Janet Case, 17 Aug. 1912, p. 3.

79. As Gay Wachman points out, '*Orlando* and *A Room of One's Own* are not merely subjected to censorship; censorship is also, ironically and satirically, their *subject*', *Lesbian Empire: Radical Crosswriting in the Twenties* (New Brunswick, NJ: Rutgers University Press, 2001), p. 214, fn. 103, and for details of Joynson-Hicks's activities, see pp. 162–4.

80. O, pp. 207, 211–12 (but the make of car is supplied from *Holograph Draft*, pp. 267, 272), 227–8.

81. Mrs Percy Bartholomew, according to a footnote in D3, p. 104, 'cooked for the Woolfs at Monk's House when Nelly was not there' – she first appears in *Orlando*, on p. 161; the boat on the Serpentine (O, p. 199) suggests the loss and recovery of Virginia's toy boat in Kensington Gardens, in 'A Sketch

of the Past', *MoB*, p. 77; for the third edition of *Kew Gardens*, see *A Bibli-ography*, pp. 17–18 (for 'Kew Gardens' see Ch. 3, above).

82. *L3*, to VS-W, 24 June 1927, p. 394; Vita thought Roger Fry's Omega Workshop furniture 'horrible' (Glendinning, p. 88), and had not got on with him at a dinner party on 19 Dec. 1924 (see *D3*, 21 Dec. 1924, p. 325).

83. *O*, pp. 203–4; 'Thursday, March the 20th' – in fact 20 March fell on a Tuesday in 1928, and Woolf announced the end of *Orlando* on both the 17th and the 22nd in her diary (*D3*, 18, 22 Mar., pp. 176–7) and in a letter to Vita, probably dated 20 March, she tells her that it was finished on the 17th (*L3*, ? 20 Mar. 1928, p. 474), but the link with the October conception ('begun on 8th October', *D3*, p. 177) makes this the obvious sense. *Orlando* is full of very precise dates of the year, scattered through the text – some of these are 'present moments', dates when she actually wrote a particular passage (e.g. the Kew passage includes 'the second of March' (*O*, p. 203), when she was probably writing that section), but others have not yet been satisfactorily explained.

84. *D3*, 20 Dec. 1927, p. 167; 8 Aug. 1928, p. 189.

85. Gillian Beer, 'The Body of the People: *Mrs Dalloway* to *The Waves*' in *Virginia Woolf: The Common Ground* (Edinburgh: Edinburgh University Press, 1996), p. 58; *D3*, 21 Apr. 1928, p. 181 – it continues, 'Once I get the wheels spinning in my head, I don't want money much, or dress, or even a cupboard, a bed at Rodmell or a sofa'.

86. For 'Evening over Sussex', see n. 2, above; *O*, pp. 212–13; *L3*, to VS-W, 6 Mar. 1928, p. 469, 'You are driving down to Knole, and as you go, you exhibit the most profound and secret side of your character'.

87. See, for example, Glendinning, p. 141: 'She herself lived with fantasy versions of herself – Julian and her "Spanish gypsy" self, and the self that was for ever master of Knole'.

88. Suzanne Raitt points out both Woolf's fondness for 'Life' (with a capital 'L') and the letter in which she describes herself and Clive, walking and talking 'of Vita Vita Vita as the new moon rises and the lambs huddle on the downs' (*L3*, to VS-W, 23 Dec. 1925, p. 225) – in *Vita & Virginia: The Work and Friendship of V. Sackville-West and Virginia Woolf* (Oxford: Oxford University Press, 1993), p. 34. In the holograph, Woolf defines the meaning of life as 'the sudden [splash?]; the violent spurt of joy' (*Holograph Draft*, p. 246), with a partial echo of *To the Lighthouse*.

89. *Holograph Draft*, p. 287, and see n. 15, above, and Sandra Gilbert, introduction to *O*, p. xxxviii. Birds promising imminent revelation are charac-teristic of the poetry of W. B. Yeats, whose recent volume, *The Tower*, Woolf had been reviewing as she finished *Orlando* (it was published on 21 April

1928 – see *Essays*, vol. 4, pp. 544–5). As Orlando finally reaches Knole in the holograph, she leaves the footman 'to bring after her the smelts, the sheets, then a basket of figs, the complete works of Mr Yeats' (*Holograph Draft*, p. 274, where Clarke's footnote refers us to her essay).

90. *Holograph Draft*, pp. 250–1; O, p. 83.

91. Nicolson, *Portrait of a Marriage*, p. 186.

92. For Vita's reaction, see below, n. 102; for Leonard's, see D3, 31 May 1928, p. 185.

93. L3, to VS-W, ? 20 Mar. 1928, p. 474.

94. D3, 7 July 1928, p. 187.

95. D3, 22 Sept. 1928, p. 197; to Vita, Woolf wrote 'I am melancholy and excited in turn. You see, I would not have married Leonard had I not preferred living with him to saying goodbye to him', L3, 16 Sept. 1928, p. 531.

96. Glendinning, pp. 200–2; L3, to LW, 24, 25, 26 ('We have decided that we had better get back on Monday afternoon instead of Tuesday'), 27, 28 Sept. 1928, pp. 533–9; Woolf wrote to Harold Nicolson, 'we had a perfect week, . . . It went like a flash', L3, 7 Oct. 1928, p. 541; Vita wrote to him that though it was 'very nice . . . I like doing expeditions with you', *Vita and Harold: The Letters of Vita Sackville-West and Harold Nicolson 1910–1962*, ed. Nigel Nicolson (London: Weidenfeld and Nicolson, 1992), 25 Sept. 1928, p. 204.

97. D3, 10 Sept. 1928, p. 196; 8 Aug. 1928, p. 189.

98. *ROO*, p. 94; 'The New Biography', *Essays*, vol. 4, p. 478.

99. The photographs and original dust-jacket are reproduced in Brenda Lyons' edition of *Orlando*, which includes 'A Note on the Illustrations', pp. xlvii–xlix, and see *Holograph Draft*, Appendix D: the illustrations, pp. 35–6. J. H. Stape gives the history of the painting of Sackville on the dust-jacket in ' "The Man at Worthing" and the Author of "The Most Insipid Verse She Had Ever Read": Two Allusions in *Orlando*', *Virginia Woolf Miscellany*, 50 (Fall 1997), pp. 5–6.

100. See *A Bibliography*, p. 62; 'The Manuscript', pp. 10–12, *Holograph Draft*, and *A Bibliography*, p. 425 (item G12).

101. *Letters of VS-W to VW*, 11 Oct. 1928, pp. 304, 306.

102. Vita's letter to Harold of 12 Oct. 1928, the first passage cited by Madeline Moore, in *The Short Season Between Two Silences: The Mystical and Political in the Novels of Virginia Woolf* (Boston: Allen and Unwin, 1984), p. 107, the second by Glendinning, p. 204.

103. The passage, which begins 'Let us go, then, exploring . . .' (O, p. 188), was reproduced in Vita Sackville-West and Harold Nicolson, *Another World Than This* (London: Michael Joseph, 1945), p. 131; Vita's broadcast ('Virginia

Woolf and *Orlando*') was reprinted in *The Listener*, 27 Jan. 1955, pp. 157–8 (and there is a British Library recording of her reading from the MS of *Orlando* from 1954).

104. See O, p. 245, fn. 37.

105. D3, 22 Sept. 1928, p. 198.

106. *An Autobiography*, vol. 2, p. 292.

107. D3, 7 Nov. 1928, p. 203; L6, to VS-W, 14 May 1936, p. 40–1; *Bibliography*, pp. 63–4, 61.

108. D3, 27 Oct. 1928, p. 200.

109. Conrad Aiken, writing in *The Dial*, called it a 'jeu d'esprit' and wrote of 'Mrs Woolf's general air of high spirits; of having a lark; of going, as it were, on an intellectual spree' (*Critical Heritage*, pp. 235, 236), and Arnold Bennett called it 'a high-brow lark' (*Critical Heritage*, p. 232); J. C. Squire, who thought it 'a trifle', and lacking in high spirits, made the point about 'English literature and the English people' (*Critical Heritage*, pp. 229, 228).

110. D3, 7 Nov. 1928, p. 201; L3, to VS-W, 22 Oct. 1928, pp. 547–8; D3, 7 Nov. 1928, p. 201.

111. Helen MacAfee, *Critical Heritage*, p. 237; Aiken on the last few pages, *Critical Heritage*, p. 235; Cleveland B. Chase for the *New York Times*, on 'these last thirty-odd pages' and on Einstein, *Critical Heritage*, pp. 231, 230.

112. On the variants, see Alison M. Scott, ' "Tantalising Fragments": The Proofs of Virginia Woolf's *Orlando*', *Publications of the Bibliographical Society of America*, 88, 3 (September 1994), pp. 279–351; Brenda Lyons's Appendix, *Orlando*, pp. 265–73.

113. *A Bibliography*, pp. 64–5. In 1960, the initial printing of *Orlando* in Signet Classics was over 60,000, followed by further substantial print runs in 1963 and 1965, a fact that contradicts Regina Marler's claim in *Bloomsbury Pie* (London: Virago, 1997) that in the early 1960s, 'The vogue for *Orlando* was still years away, and it sold only a few hundred copies in England each year and was out of print in America' (p. 37) – in fact it has remained an established favourite. Bowen's essay is reprinted in *The Mulberry Tree: Writings of Elizabeth Bowen*, ed. Hermione Lee (London: Virago, 1996; Vintage, 1999), pp. 131–6.

114. Marler, esp. pp. 185–91, and Brenda R. Silver in *Virginia Woolf Icon* (Chicago: University of Chicago Press, 1999), esp. pp. 222–35, both give interesting accounts of the reception and rewritings of *Orlando* in recent years; Marler quotes from Heilbrun, p. 131. The blank page in the *Holograph Draft* is p. 228 (verso); see also *ROO*, pp. 88–9, 93–4.

115. On Edna O'Brien's *Virginia*, see Marler, pp. 188–91; on Atkins's *Vita and Virginia*, see Marler, pp. 228, 252, and Silver, pp. 182–3.

116. On Robert Wilson's *Orlando*, see Silver, pp. 223, 230, and *Robert Wilson* by Franco Quadri, Franco Bertoni and Robert Stearns (Paris: Editions Plume, 1997), pp. 50–3; 140–3; on Robin Brooks' *Orlando*, Silver, pp. 223, 231; on Ulrike Ottinger's *Freak Orlando*, Silver, pp. 223, 231–3; on Sally Potter's film *Orlando*, Silver, pp. 223, 225–34, and Marler, pp. 4, 259; Jane Marcus in 'A Tale of Two Cultures', *Women's Review of Books*, January 1994, p. 11, is cited by Silver, p. 228.

117. L4, to Clive Bell, 19 Jan. 1931, p. 279.

118. Carter's dig at *Orlando* (cited by Marler, p. 185) was part of her commentary for Tom Paulin's programme, *J'Accuse* (produced by Jeff Morgan, Fulmar Productions for Channel Four, London, 29 Jan. 1991), and her *Orlando* libretto is reprinted in *The Curious Room: Collected Dramatic Works* (London: Chatto and Windus, 1996), pp. 155–82. Jeanette Winterson discusses *Orlando* in 'A Gift of Wings', *Art Objects: Essays on Ecstasy and Effrontery* (London: Jonathan Cape, 1995), pp. 61–77.

Chapter 9

1. D3, 31 May 1929, p. 231.

2. D3, 13 Apr. 1929, pp. 221–2.

3. *A Room of One's Own/Three Guineas*, ed. Michèle Barrett (1929, 1938; London: Penguin, 1993). (Page numbers appearing in square brackets after quotes refer to this edition of the book.) From another point of view, *ROO* and *To the Lighthouse* are antithetical – see D3, 3 Sept. 1928, p. 195, where Woolf considers 'this tyranny of mother over daughter': 'And then, they ask, why women dont write poetry. Short of killing Mrs W[oolf]. nothing could be done. Day after day one's life would be crumpled up like a bill for 10 pen[ce] 3 farthings. Nothing has ever been said of this.' But she herself had more to say about this in her essay 'Professions for Women', reprinted as Appendix II to *ROO*, pp. 356–61.

4. 'Satire is to be the main note – satire & wildness', D3, 14 Mar. 1927, p. 131.

5. Later published as 'A Woman's College from Outside' in *Atalanta's Garland* (Edinburgh: Edinburgh University Press, 1926), pp. 11–16, in *CSF* and as appendix 2 to *Jacob's Room*, ed. Sue Roe (1922; London: Penguin Books, 1992).

6. D3, 18 Feb. 1928, p. 175.

7. This report was by Elsie Phare (later, Elsie Duncan-Jones), who had originally invited Woolf; it appeared in *Thersites* (Michaelmas Term, 1928), p. 87

– see Jane Marcus, *Virginia Woolf, Cambridge and A Room of One's Own: 'The Proper Upkeep of Names'* (London: Cecil Woolf, 1996), p. 39. Marcus cites other memories of the occasion from *A Newnham Anthology* (1979), pp. 41–2.

8. Carrington wrote to Dorelia John in February 1928, relating her plans for the decoration of Rylands' grand but rather empty set of rooms, which she painted as classical pastiches, in delicate colours inspired by his collection of Crown Derby china – see Jane Hill, *The Art of Dora Carrington* (London and New York: Thames and Hudson, 1994), pp. 126–7, which includes a black-and-white photograph of his room.

9. D3, 27 Oct. 1928, pp. 201, 200. Recalling Woolf's visit to Girton with Vita in her autobiography, *The Land Unknown* (1975), the poet Kathleen Raine described them as 'the two most beautiful women I had ever seen' – see Marcus, *VW, Cambridge*, pp. 32, 35; Queenie Roth Leavis and Muriel Bradbrook were also present at Woolf's lecture.

10. D3, 7 Nov. 1928, p. 203.

11. D3, 15 May 1929, p. 227; 13 May 1929, p. 226; 28 Nov. 1928, p. 209.

12. D3, 28 Mar. 1929, p. 218.

13. D3, 16 Sept. 1929, p. 253.

14. 'The Moths' was Woolf's initial title for *The Waves* (see Ch. 10), D3, 16 Sept. 1929, p. 254 (and compare D3, 16 Feb. 1930, p. 286: 'If I could stay in bed another fortnight . . . I believe I should see the whole of The Waves').

15. L4, to Ka Arnold-Forster, 13 Feb. 1929, p. 22.

16. 'Desmond destroyed our Saturday walk; he is now mouldy & to me depressing . . . And the egotism of men surprises & shocks me even now', she wrote, comparing MacCarthy's behaviour that afternoon (3 Nov.) with that of 'the girls at Newnham or Girton. They are far too spry; far too disciplined. None of that self-confidence is their lot', D3, 7 Nov. 1928, p. 203–4. Though personally fond of him, Woolf had already crossed swords with MacCarthy over his anti-feminism (see above, Ch. 4, p. 101), and *ROO* twice cites his condescending sentence, 'female novelists should only aspire to excellence by courageously acknowledging the limitations of their sex' (although it continued, 'Jane Austen and in our own time Mrs Virginia Woolf have demonstrated how gracefully this gesture can be accomplished'), *ROO*, pp. 68, 100. The offending sentence had first appeared in MacCarthy's journal, *Life and Letters*, August 1928. Woolf taxed him with it on 5 September (see 3D, 10 Sept. 1928, p. 195), an episode also referred to in *ROO* (p. 32), where 'Z [i.e. MacCarthy], most humane, most modest of men' resents Rebecca West's critique of men.

17. D3, 31 Aug. 1928, p. 193; L6, to Roger Fry, 16 Oct. 1928, p. 524.

18. D3, 10 Nov. 1928, pp. 206–7. A copy of Woolf's deposition as a witness is in the Morris Ernst Collection, Harry Ransom Research Center at the University of Texas at Austin (see *A Bibliography*, p. 421).

19. L4, to Quentin Bell, 20 Mar. 1929, p. 34.

20. 'Women and Fiction', Leonard Woolf, ed., Virginia Woolf, *Collected Essays* (London: Chatto and Windus, 1966), vol. 2, p. 148. In her diary, Woolf recorded that 'the thinking had been done & the writing stiffly & unsatisfactorily 4 times before' (D3, 13 Apr. 1929, pp. 221–2) but this essay is the sole version that survives.

21. *Women & Fiction: The MS Versions of A Room of One's Own*, ed. S. P. Rosenbaum (Oxford: Shakespeare Head/Blackwell, 1992), pp. 55–6; 143–4.

22. Marcus, *VW, Cambridge*, p. 49. See also the opening of her essay 'Taking the Bull by the Udders: Sexual Difference in Virginia Woolf – A Conspiracy Theory', and the close of 'Sapphistry: Narration as Lesbian Seduction in *A Room of One's Own*', both in Jane Marcus, ed., *Virginia Woolf and the Languages of Patriarchy* (Bloomington and Indianapolis: Indiana University Press, 1987).

23. This distinction was first drawn by Winifred Holtby (author of the first full-length study of Woolf, published in 1932) in a letter to the *Yorkshire Post*, reprinted in *Time and Tide* (6 Aug. 1926, pp. 714–15) – see Marion Shaw, *The Clear Stream: A Life of Winifred Holtby* (London: Virago, 2000), p. 145.

24. The significance of 'But' is emphasized by its frequent repetition in the text, often at the beginning of sentences – see *ROO*, p. 90; *Women & Fiction*, pp. 153, 157, 186, 189.

25. *ROO*, p. 90. Woolf's strategy of interruption is discussed by Peggy Kamuf, 'Penelope at Work: Interruptions in *A Room of One's Own*', reprinted in Rachel Bowlby, ed., *Virginia Woolf: Longman Critical Readers* (London: Longman, 1992), pp. 180–95.

26. See *ROO*, pp. 74, 82–3.

27. See Genesis 3.24.

28. *ROO*, pp. 35, 102 – but the 'gentleman, which Milton recommended for my perpetual adoration' (presumably the God of *Paradise Lost*), has become 'Milton's bogey' by the final paragraph.

29. 'But partridges various? I don't think there could be more than one kind of partridge', Rylands objected, adding that, 'as always with Virginia it is the idealized, the romantic fantasy of what should have been and what it was to her' – see Jean Russell Noble, ed., *Recollections of Virginia Woolf* (1972; London: Sphere Books, 1989), p. 175.

30. These are reportedly the last words of the painter, Thomas Gainsborough (1727–88).

31. *Women & Fiction*, p. 14 (Freudian theory does appear in *ROO*, but not until p. 28); Woolf's review of Huxley's novel, 'Cleverness and Youth', appeared in the *Times Literary Supplement* on 5 Feb. 1920 (*Essays*, vol. 3, p. 177).

32. *ROO*, p. 11; 'the emotion, the vibration of love', *To the Lighthouse*, intro. Hermione Lee, ed. Stella McNichol (1927; London: Penguin, 1992), pp. 106, 110, and see also *JR*: 'But something is always impelling one to hum vibrating, like the hawk moth, at the mouth of the cavern of mystery . . .' (p. 61). This image sequence – sex, humming/vibrating, moths – may be connected with Fabre's experiments with moths, and his discovery of the effects of pheromones – see Ch. 10, pp. 241–2.

33. See 'Mr Bennett and Mrs Brown' (as 'Character in Fiction'), *Essays*, vol. 3, p. 421; *Women & Fiction*, pp. 20, 151; *ROO*, pp. 89, 14.

34. See above, Ch. 8, p. 204, esp. n. 74; Strachey and Keynes had been close friends since undergraduate days. *ROO* links homosexuality with misogyny in an ironic passage about Oscar Browning (pp. 48–9), explicated by Marcus, *Patriarchy*, pp. 181–5.

35. *Women & Fiction*, p. 23; *ROO*, p. 15.

36. 'Friendship's Gallery', ed. Ellen Hawkes, *Twentieth Century Literature*, 25, 3/4 (Fall/Winter 1979), pp. 275–302; *Women & Fiction*, p. 23 (the passage is slightly different in *ROO*, p. 15).

37. *Women & Fiction*, p. 23.

38. On Harrison and women's degrees, see Sandra J. Peacock, *Jane Ellen Harrison: The Mask and the Self* (New Haven, CT: Yale University Press, 1988), pp. 118–23; Woolf visited Harrison in Mecklenburgh Street in February 1928, a visit she recalled on hearing of Jane's death from her friend, Hope Mirrlees, D3, 17 Apr. 1928, p. 180 (and see D3, 18 Feb. 1928, p. 176 for Woolf's visit).

39. *Women & Fiction*, p. 24. In *The Invention of Jane Harrison* (Cambridge, MA: Harvard University Press, 2000), p. 8, Mary Beard notes that Woolf's lectures at Newnham and Girton were given only days before Gilbert Murray's Memorial Lecture for Harrison, on 27 Oct. 1928 (though we do not know for certain whether Harrison figured in the original lectures). Although Harrison is not named in full at this stage (as if to emphasize her spiritual power), her books on Greek archaeology appear in *ROO*, p. 72 as an example of women's developing range as writers.

40. *ROO*, pp. 28–32. See also notes, *Women & Fiction*, p. 49 ('Anger: / desire to be superior. / importance to have / some one inferior'). Woolf's

response to misogyny or 'sex antagonism' is recorded in a diary entry for 22 June 1927, D3, p. 140: 'Women haters depress me, & both Tolstoi and Mrs Asquith hate women.'

41. Mrs Ramsay 'had the whole of the other sex under her protection for reasons she could not explain, for their chivalry and valour, for the fact that they negotiated treaties, ruled India, controlled finance', *TTL*, p. 10.

42. Imagery of food plays an important part in *A Room of One's Own*: women suffer from malnutrition, both physically and intellectually; also, as Catherine Stimpson observes, 'Men need women to feed their psychic appetites' ('Woolf's Room, Our Project: The Building of Feminist Criticism', in Bowlby, p. 168).

43. *ROO*, p. 42. For 'The Journal of Mistress Joan Martyn', see *CSF*, pp. 33–62.

44. Winifred Holtby, *Virginia Woolf: A Critical Memoir* (1932; Chicago: Academy Press, 1978), p. 161. Holtby discusses the two together in her final chapter, 'Two in a Taxi'.

45. *Orlando*, intro. Sandra Gilbert, ed. Brenda Lyons (1928; London: Penguin Books, 1993), p. 188 – a reference earlier in the paragraph to thinking 'of a gamekeeper' suggests D. H. Lawrence's *Lady Chatterley's Lover*, published in Florence in 1928, which Vita read in July (see Victoria Glendinning, *Vita: The Life of Vita Sackville-West* (New York: Alfred Knopf, 1983), p. 199). Lawrence reappears as Mr A. in *ROO*, pp. 89–90.

46. *To the Lighthouse: The Original Holograph Draft*, ed. Susan Dick (London: Hogarth Press, 1983), p. 136.

47. *ROO*, pp. 42–4; *O*, pp. 95–7 (Shakespeare's appearances in *Orlando* at pp. 16, 56, 215).

48. *Women & Fiction*, p. 74. At this stage, the 'Shakespeare woman' has not yet become Shakespeare's sister, but is 'Mary Arden', Shakespeare's mother's name, linking her with the other 'Maries', the women speakers in the text, named from the traditional ballad of Mary Hamilton, 'Mary Seton, Mary Beton, Mary Carmichael and me'. For Vita's 'gallivanting', see L3, to Vita Sackville-West, 9 Oct. 1927, p. 429.

49. Another avatar of the lost or silenced sister was Angela Williams, the woman undergraduate who shadowed Jacob Flanders, but was subsequently cut out of *Jacob's Room* (see n. 5 above).

50. Compare 'Let us not take it for granted that life exists more fully in what is commonly thought big than what is commonly thought small', 'Modern Fiction', *Essays*, vol. 4, p. 161.

51. *ROO*, p. 74; on 'Reddin', see Glendinning, pp. 119–21: 'Chloe, in the manuscript, resented love's slavery, but felt lost without it . . .'

52. *ROO*, p. 76; *Women & Fiction*, p. 116 (by p. 117, it has become 'that vast unlighted chamber'); for 'the Cave of Harmony', see Marcus, *Patriarchy*, p. 167.

53. *Women & Fiction*, p. 114.

54. This moment recalls Orlando's meeting with Nell and her friends, which is similarly dramatized ('but hist again – is that not a man's step on the stair?' – *O*, p. 152), and similarly re-creates women's intimacy and exclusive bonding. Joynson-Hicks and Bodkin appear in *ROO*, pp. 78, 100 (Bodkin possibly lurking in a linen cupboard).

55. *Women & Fiction*, p. 71.

56. *Women & Fiction*, pp. 139, 142, 143.

57. *ROO*, p. 94. The British text has 'art', the US text has 'act'. The typescript has 'art of creation' (*Women & Fiction*, appendix 3, p. 191), but in chapter II, Woolf had asked, 'what is the state of mind that is most propitious to the act of creation?' (*ROO*, p. 46).

58. Just as there are at least two different openings, in the first few pages, there are at least three distinguishable endings, rather like musical codas. The first is here (*ROO*, p. 94); the second announces 'Here I would stop, but the pressure of convention decrees that every speech must end with a peroration' (p. 99). Almost the final words of the text are 'poverty and obscurity', the defining characteristics of women according to the old order (p. 103).

59. Compare Castalia's fear in 'A Society' that 'we shall perish beneath the fruits of [men's] unbridled activity; and not a human being will survive to know that there once was Shakespeare!', *CSF*, p. 135.

60. *ROO*, p. 39 – Woolf was quoting from G. M. Trevelyan's recent *History of England* (London: Longman, 1926), pp. 260–1.

61. Compare the penultimate verse of Revelation, 'Even so, come Lord Jesus' (22.20). At the end of *To the Lighthouse*, Lily Briscoe says, 'He has landed, . . . It is finished' of Mr Ramsay, later modified to 'It was done; it was finished', of her painting (and the book – *TTL*, pp. 225, 226) – compare John 19.30, 'he said, It is finished'.

62. L4, to VS-W, 15 Feb. 1929, p. 23.

63. *Women & Fiction*, pp. 37, 174.

64. D3, 19 Aug. 1929, p. 242, and see p. 233, 12 May 1929; proof-correcting is recorded on pp. 233, 234, 235, 237, 239 – 15, 16, 23, 30 June and 5 Aug. 1929.

65. D3, 28 Mar. 1929, pp. 219–20. For Woolf's original intention to use the upstairs room of the extension as a bedroom, see Sarah Bird Wright, *Staying at Monk's House: Echoes of the Woolfs* (London: Cecil Woolf, 1995), pp. 19–20.

66. D3, 29 Apr. 1929, p. 222; L4, to Vanessa Bell, 7, 24 Apr. 1929, pp. 37, 41.

67. The extension was built on the south-facing wall of Monk's House. On 1 Sept. 1930, ill in bed, she told Ethel Smyth, 'I am lying in my room looking at the apple tree' (L4, p. 206). In mid-September, she told Ethel that she was sleeping downstairs, 'for we've changed your bedroom into a sitting room, and I sleep and dress in full view of the garden; and having to change certain monthly articles t'other day, found the benign face of the gardener on me' (L4, p. 214). See also D3, pp. 257, 265–8, 270, 274, 295.

68. D3, 23 Oct. 1929, p. 262. 'Feminine' here means 'feminist', as when the narrator of To the Lighthouse observes that 'the war had drawn the sting of [Lily's] femininity', TTL, p. 174, and Ch. 7, n. 104.

69. These two reviews, and extracts from Vita's broadcast as reprinted in The Listener, are included in Critical Heritage: the Times Literary Supplement review, p. 256; Arnold Bennett, p. 259; Vita Sackville-West, p. 258.

70. Rebecca West, 'Autumn and Virginia Woolf', in Ending in Earnest: A Literary Log (New York: Doubleday, Doran, 1931), pp. 211, 213, 212. Marcus discusses West's review in Patriarchy, pp. 136–7.

71. William Empson on Virginia Woolf, originally in Scrutinies by Various Writers, ed. Edgell Rickword (1931), reprinted in Critical Heritage, p. 306.

72. Tony Bradshaw, The Bloomsbury Artists: Prints and Book Designs (Aldershot: Scolar Press, 1999), plate 26; L4, to VB, ? 20 Aug. 1929, p. 81 (see also L4, to VB, 24/5 June 1929, p. 68).

73. L4, to VS-W, 5 Apr. 1929, p. 36.

74. These details from A Bibliography, pp. 71, 72–3; see also D3, 5 Nov. 1929, p. 264, 'it sells, I think', and 14 Dec. 1929, p. 272, 'the sales of A Room are unprecedented'.

75. ROO, p. 94, and see above, n. 57.

76. See British first edition of A Room of One's Own, p. 168. This change provides the starting point for my article 'Between the Texts: Virginia Woolf's Acts of Revision', in W. Speed Hill and Edward M. Burns, eds., TEXT 12 (Ann Arbor, MI: University of Michigan Press, 1999), pp. 143–65.

77. There are several accounts of Woolf's reception in the US in the 1970s – see, for example, Ellen Bayuk Rosenman, A Room of One's Own: Women Writers and the Politics of Creativity (New York: Twayne, 1995), pp. 19–21, or my essay, 'The Story So Far . . .', in Julia Briggs, ed., Virginia Woolf: Introductions to the Major Works (London: Virago, 1994), pp. xvii–xxi.

78. Nancy Topping Bazin, Virginia Woolf and the Androgynous Vision (New Brunswick, NJ: Rutgers University Press, 1973); Carolyn Heilbrun, Towards a Recognition of Androgyny: Aspects of Male and Female in Literature (London: Gollancz, 1973); Elaine Showalter, A Literature of their Own:

British Women Novelists from Brontë to Lessing (Princeton, NJ: Princeton University Press, 1978).

79. Toril Moi, *Sexual/Textual Politics: Feminist Literary Theory* (London: Methuen, 1985), pp. 8–9; Makiko Minow-Pinkney, *Virginia Woolf and the Problem of the Subject: Feminine Writing in the Major Novels* (Brighton: Harvester Press, 1987); Rachel Bowlby, *Virginia Woolf: Feminist Destinations and Further Essays* (Edinburgh: Edinburgh University Press, 1997) (though Bowlby's and Minow-Pinkney's discussions are not limited to *A Room of One's Own*).

Chapter 10

1. 'These 9 weeks give one a plunge into deep waters' – D3, 28 Sept. 1926, p. 112.
2. L4, to Ethel Smyth, 28 Sept. 1930, p. 223.
3. D3, 23 June 1929, p. 236; 19 Aug. 1929, p. 243 – see also 'the only exciting life is the imaginary one', D3, 21 Apr. 1928, p. 181.
4. *The Voyage Out*, ed. Jane Wheare (1915; London: Penguin, 1992), p. 204.
5. D3, 15, 28 Sept. 1926, pp. 110, 111.
6. D3, 4 Sept. 1927, p. 153.
7. D3, 18 Dec. 1928, p. 212; *An Autobiography*, vol. 2, pp. 291–2 (the discrepancy between their accounts is discussed by Hermione Lee, *Virginia Woolf* (London: Chatto and Windus, 1996), pp. 560–1).
8. D3, 30 Sept. 1926, p. 113. As she completed the first and second drafts of *The Waves*, Woolf's thoughts reverted to her initial vision (see D3, 29 Apr. 1930, p. 302; D4, 7 Feb. 1931, p. 10). The episode of the puddle occurs in *The Waves*, ed. Kate Flint (1931; London: Penguin, 1992), pp. 47, 120, and see also 'A Sketch of the Past', *MoB*, p. 78.
9. D3, 30 Sept. 1926, p. 113; 28 Sept. 1926, p. 111 – and see also D3, 15 June 1929, p. 233, for 'what I call the sense of "Where there is nothing"'; 23 June 1929, p. 235, 'I shall make myself face the fact that there is nothing – nothing for any of us'.
10. D3, 14 Mar. 1927, p. 131; 22 Sept. 1928, p. 198.
11. D3, 21 Feb. 1927, p. 128; this essay was first published in the *New York Herald Tribune*, 14 and 21 Aug. 1927 (see *Essays*, vol. 4, pp. 428–39). Leonard retitled it 'The Narrow Bridge of Art' in *Granite and Rainbow* (*Essays*, vol. 4, p. 440).
12. *Essays*, vol. 4, pp. 431, 429, 435, 439.
13. *Selected Letters of Vanessa Bell*, ed. Regina Marler (London: Bloomsbury,

1993), pp. 314–15 (3 May 1927) (and see *W*, p. 99, for 'the bestial and beautiful passion of maternity').

14. *L3*, to Vanessa Bell, 8 May 1927, p. 372. A moth-hunt (linked for Woolf with the sound of a tree falling – see *W*, p. 153) is described in detail in her essay on 'Reading' (*Essays*, vol. 3, pp. 150–2), as well as in *Jacob's Room* (ed. Sue Roe (1922; London: Penguin, 1992)), p. 17. Woolf also wrote a virtuoso account of 'The Death of the Moth' (reprinted by Leonard as the opening essay in the collection of that title, published by the Hogarth Press in 1942).

15. *D3*, 16 Feb. 1930, p. 287 – 'Something happens in my mind . . . It becomes chrysalis . . . Then suddenly something springs . . . this is I believe the moth shaking its wings in me.' She was considering the effect of illness on the creative process, arguing that illness might help with the composition of *The Waves* – for the value of illness, see also *D3*, p. 254 (16 Sept. 1929), p. 295 (1 Mar. 1930), p. 317 (8 Sept. 1930), and see Ch. 9, p. 220. For the moth hunt in *Jacob's Room*, see *JR*, p. 61, and for the hum of sexual attraction, *A Room of One's Own* (*A Room of One's Own/Three Guineas*, ed. Michèle Barrett (1929, 1938; London: Penguin, 1993), p.11.

16. *D3*, 18 June 1927, p. 139; Woolf refers to her book as a 'playpoem' elsewehere, for example *D3*, 7 Nov. 1928, p. 203.

17. *D3*, 28 Nov. 1928, p. 209; compare, 'I do a little work on it in the evening when the gramophone is playing late Beethoven sonatas', *D3*, 18 June 1927, p. 139.

18. *D3*, 28 May 1929, p. 229.

19. *D3*, 23 June 1929, p. 236; 28 May 1929, p. 229 (Woolf may simply mean that she intended to entitle it 'Autobiography', rather as she had subtitled *Orlando* 'A Biography'); see 'A Sketch of the Past', *MoB*, esp. pp. 65, 71, 78 for memories recalling episodes in *The Waves*. Woolf's fiction tended to draw on her own earliest memories, though most self-consciously and deliberately in *To the Lighthouse*.

20. Virginia Woolf, *The Waves: The Two Holograph Drafts*, ed. J. W. Graham (Toronto and Buffalo: University of Toronto Press, 1976), pp. 3, 5 (the 'moody fitful little girl' and the name 'Jinny' are separated, but are the first references to a female character), and 6; *D3*, 23 June 1929, p. 236.

21. 'A Sketch of the Past', *MoB*, pp. 64–5.

22. *Holograph Drafts*, pp. 1, 2.

23. Ibid., pp. 6, 9; Woolf had earlier wondered whether 'she might see things happen' in the leaves of a plant – see *D3*, 28 May 1929, p. 229.

24. *Holograph Drafts*, p. 6 (left-hand margin), pp. 2, 9.

25. Ibid., p. 6.

26. Ibid., pp. 6, 7. This vision might have been suggested by a painting she

had seen: Léon Frédéric's *La Source* (1890–99), a secular triptych painted with a lush surface realism, shows a crowd of naked babies and small children welling from a stream. This large and disturbing work was exhibited at the Paris Expo of 1900, and subsequently hung in the Musées Royaux des Beaux-Arts at Brussels, though there does not seem to have been an obvious occasion for Woolf to have seen it (Vanessa visited Paris for a week in April 1900). It is the first plate in Robert Rosenblum *et al.*, *1900: Art at the Crossroads* (London: Royal Academy of Arts, 2000).

27. *Holograph Drafts*, p. 7; 'such as the first garden must have been', p. 73; 'Death; the branch of the apple tree against the moon', p. 4 (and compare 'A Sketch of the Past', *MoB*, p. 71); W, pp. 17, 3 (and compare Genesis 1:1–8).

28. *Holograph Drafts*, pp. 7, 12–15, 16. In the very first version of this story, 'Susie' goes down to the cellar (an image of abjection), and Archie follows her (pp. 7, 8).

29. Page numbers appearing in square brackets after quotes refer to Kate Flint's 1992 Penguin edition of the *The Waves*; compare *Holograph Drafts*, pp. 12–17.

30. *Holograph Drafts*, p. 16.

31. In a brilliant Freudian reading of *The Waves*, Daniel Ferrer links Woolf's earliest memories with the primal scene, though he does not include this sequence in his analysis – see his *Virginia Woolf and The Madness of Language*, trans. G. Bennington and R. Bowlby (London: Routledge, 1990), esp. pp. 71–2. I am grateful to Hans Gabler for pointing out the connection between these two draft episodes.

32. *Holograph Drafts*, p. 16; for Blo' Norton and Virginia's walk with Thoby, see Mitchell A. Leaska, ed., Virginia Woolf, *A Passionate Apprentice: The Early Journals 1897–1909* (London: Hogarth Press, 1990), p. 310; for Susan's 'home ground', *Holograph Drafts*, p. 184. For the possibility that Elvedon might have been inspired by 'Fairyland' (a wood near St Ives), see Ch. 13, p. 350.

33. See Sonya Rudikoff, *Ancestral Houses: Virginia Woolf and the Aristocracy* (Palo Alto, CA: Society for the Promotion of Science and Scholarship, 1999), p. 200.

34. For post-colonial readings, see Jane Marcus, 'Britannia Rules *The Waves*' in her *Hearts of Darkness: White Women Write Race* (New Brunswick, NJ and London: Rutgers University Press, 2004), pp. 59–85; Patrick McGee, 'The Politics of Modernist Form: or, Who Rules *The Waves*?' *Modernist Fiction Studies*, 38, 3 (Autumn, 1992), pp. 631–50. Linden Peach discusses the contemporary context in *Virginia Woolf: Critical Issues* (London: Macmillan, 2000), esp. pp. 162–3; and see also Kathy Phillips, *Virginia Woolf*

Against Empire (Knoxville, TN: University of Tennessee Press, 1994), pp. 253–83.

35. For example, *W*, pp. 55, 81–2.

36. *W*, pp. 168, 175; and see *Orlando*, intro. Sandra Gilbert, ed. Brenda Lyons (1928; London: Penguin, 1993), p. 206. Susan Dick discusses Woolf's use of 'Literary realism in . . . *The Waves*' in Sue Roe and Susan Sellers, eds., *The Cambridge Companion to Virginia Woolf* (Cambridge: Cambridge University Press, 2000), see esp. p. 68.

37. 'The Mark on the Wall', *CSF*, p. 86.

38. On the politics of India, see D3, 20 and 22 Dec. 1930, pp. 338, 339; D4, 26 Jan. 1931, p. 8; on an impending crash, D4, 15 Aug. 1931, p. 39.

39. D3, 19 Aug. 1929, p. 243; 30 Sept. 1926, p. 113.

40. D3, 28 Sept. 1926, p. 112; 19 Aug. 1929, p. 243 ('These are the great events & revolutions in one's life'); 21 Sept, 1929, p. 255 – and compare '& then go down step by step into that queer region', 5 Aug. 1929, p. 239. On p. 235 (23 June 1929), she wrote of 'sinking down, down. And as usual, I feel that if I sink further I shall reach the truth', which is that 'there is nothing'.

41. D3, 11 Oct. 1929, p. 259, and compare 13 Oct. 1929, p. 262, 'Nature is having her revenge, & is now making me write one word an hour', 5 Nov. 1929, p. 264. It was 'nothing like the speed & certainty of The Lighthouse', 22 Aug. 1929, p. 248.

42. For 'I don't know', see D3, 31 May 1928, p. 185 ('Something abstract poetic next time – I don't know'), p. 236 (23 June 1929), p. 268 (30 Nov. 1929, twice), p. 285 (26 Jan. 1930); p. 298, 28 Mar. 1930, has both phrases together. For 'there is something there', see p. 264 (5 Nov. 1929).

43. D3, 26 Dec. 1929, p. 275.

44. D3, 30 Sept. 1929, p. 113; 7 Nov. 1928, p. 203.

45. Roger Fry, 'Retrospect', *Vision and Design* (1920; London: Chatto and Windus, 1928), p. 302.

46. 'A Sketch of the Past', *MoB*, p. 72.

47. D3, 11 Oct. 1929, p. 260, and see Mark Hussey, *The Singing of the Real World: The Philosophy of Virginia Woolf's Fiction* (Columbus, OH: Ohio State University Press, 1986).

48. *Holograph Drafts*, pp. 6, 9, 39, 60, 69.

49. Ibid., p. 4, is particularly close to the 'flowerbed' sequences of 'Kew Gardens'; D3, 25 Sept. 1929, p. 257, and compare 11 Oct. 1929, p. 259, 'is there some radical fault in my scheme?' She was still asking herself whether 'the structure is wrong' as she finished the first draft, D3, 29 Apr. 1930, p. 302.

50. *Holograph Drafts*, pp. 41, 42, 58 (verso).

51. Ibid., p. 60, and compare D3, 16 Sept. 1929, p. 254 – 'But that wont be the name', 25 Sept. 1929, p. 257, 'that wont be its title', 23 Oct. 1929, p. 262, 'The Moths; but I think it is to be waves, is trudging along'.

52. *Holograph Drafts*, p. 63.

53. Ibid., pp, 67, 68, and see Gillian Beer's introduction to her edition of *The Waves* (Oxford: Oxford University Press, 1992), p. xxxvi.

54. Pirandello's play under this title was written in 1921 and translated into English in 1923. Woolf is likely to have known it, and may even have read it in Italian, since she wrote to Janet Case about a season of his plays on at the New Oxford Theatre: 'Everybody in London is going to hear Pirandello, and I have actually stumbled through a play in Italian' (she doesn't say which) – L3, to Janet Case, 23 June 1925, pp. 191–2. Edwin Muir briefly compared *The Waves* with *Six Characters . . .* , which he thought 'much overpraised' (*Critical Heritage*, p. 291). Although *The Waves* destabilizes narrative conventions, the published text never explicitly admits that its characters are fictional, though in the second draft, Bernard, at the farewell party, says, 'How foolish we should think the most inspired novelist who tried to make a story of us. How we escape definition', *Holograph Drafts*, p. 553.

55. On 'natural happiness', see above, Ch. 7, p. 171 and W, pp. 99, 131–2, 146, 154.

56. In the first draft, Bernard and Susan are lovers – see *Holograph Drafts*, pp. 345, 348, 'It was Susan who first taught me the pleasures of love', but in the published text, Jinny replaces Susan as Bernard's lover (W, p. 194).

57. W, p. 79, and see pp. 71–2, 168; Louis and Rhoda are 'conspirators with [their] hands on the cold urn' – pp. 107, 174, 176 – and for a while lovers, but she leaves him because she 'feared embraces', p. 157.

58. *Holograph Drafts*, p. 11 refers to Louis's 'dreams, those pre-natal meditations' – 'For he had existed endlessly'; 'the boy whose . . . belief it was that he had lived say a million years in other capacities', p. 49.

59. See n. 9 above, and W, p. 171 ('where I have nothing. I have no face'), and compare pp. 31, 98 ('I have no face'), and p. 47 ('We are nothing').

60. W, pp. 41–2 – Rhoda's question, 'Present it! – oh! to whom?' is the final line of Shelley's poem 'The Question', and Rhoda is particularly linked with quotations from Shelley, including the words from 'The Indian Serenade', 'I faint, I fail'. Woolf shared Rhoda's habit of quoting from Shelley to express melancholy feelings – see D3, 7 Dec. 1925, p. 48; 4 Sept. 1927, p. 153. Through the figure of Persephone, Woolf evokes familiar seasonal myths, as she does later, when Percival, the sun hero, falls to earth after the sun reaches its zenith.

61. D3, 4 Jan. 1929, p. 218.

62. 'I am convinced that I am right to seek for a station whence I can set my people against time & the sea', D3, 5 Nov. 1929, p. 264. By 9 Apr. 1930 (p. 300), Woolf thought it 'possible that I have got my statues against the sky.'

63. See n. 8, above.

64. W, p. 13; 'half in love with the typewriter and the telephone', p. 127, also pp. 128–9; 'slinking cats', p. 155 – see such early Eliot poems as 'Preludes' or 'Rhapsody on a Windy Night' for comparable details; Louis at a cheap restaurant, pp. 68–9, and compare the last lines of Eliot's 'A Cooking Egg'. Louis's account of his own 'prim and supercilious gait' at p. 154 recalls 'How unpleasant to meet Mr Eliot!' ('Five-Finger Exercises' (v)).

65. W, pp. 47, 78–80, 95, 97; for the nightingale, p. 135 (Woolf had commented on Eliot's nightingale in 'Poetry, Fiction and the Future', Essays, vol. 4, p. 433). Jinny is linked with the nightingale (Philomela), Rhoda with the swallow (Procne); 'like crabs', p. 121.

66. Holograph Drafts, p. 565 (written shortly after 23 Oct. 1930); compare D3, 18 Oct. 1930, p. 324, 'Home now, & find ... Tom's new edition of Johnson'.

67. D2, 20 Sept. 1920, pp. 67–8 (also recounted by Leonard, An Autobiography, vol. 2, p. 266).

68. T. S. Eliot, Selected Essays (London: Faber and Faber, 1969), p. 287; 'Quick now ...' is the ending of 'Burnt Norton' (v) (1935).

69. D3, 28 Nov. 1928, p. 209–10.

70. D3, 27 Oct. 1928, p. 201 – 'forgetting Mary & Tom & how we went to be read aloud to', and see Leonard's longer account of this occasion in his An Autobiography, vol. 2, pp. 266–7. The Ash Wednesday epigraphs were from Dante – on the impact of reading Dante, see D3, 30 Aug. 1930, p. 313.

71. Holograph Drafts, pp. 208–11.

72. D3, 11 Oct. 1929, p. 260.

73. Holograph Drafts, p. 104; Percival first appears in a portion of the MS written in about the third week of October 1929, and so connected with the diary entry in n. 72 – see the 'Collation of Dates' with MSS pages at the end of Holograph Drafts, Appendix D, p. 69.

74. W, p. 116. One possible source for the name might be John Percival, the famous headmaster of Clifton, the public school attended by Roger Fry and, later, Thoby Stephen, though Clifton is unlikely to have been the school represented in The Waves (the crucifixes worn by the masters suggest the Oxford Movement). Stuart N. Clarke believes Woolf was thinking of Giggleswick School, where her cousin Will Vaughan was headmaster in 1906, when she stayed there. The chapel was a great feature, and in 1906 the school

could well have had a portrait of Queen Alexandra (W, pp. 16, 23, 24, but anachronistic in terms of the novel's time scheme).

75. 'Impressions at Bayreuth', *The Times*, 21 Aug. 1909 (*Essays*, vol. 1, p. 290) – see also L1, to VB, 8, 12 Aug. 1909, pp. 404, 406 ('a very mysterious emotional work, unlike any of the others'; 'I felt within a space of tears').

76. The farewell party is 'our festival' (W, pp. 91, 105), a version of the Last Supper with Percival as the doomed Messiah, bringing order: 'sitting together here we love each other and believe in our own endurance' (p. 92), and later 'We are drawn into this communion by some deep, some common emotion . . . Shall we say "love of Percival" . . . ?' (p. 95); see also Bernard's summing up, p. 183. The dinner party at the end of the first section of *To the Lighthouse* has comparable religious undertones – see Ch. 7, p. 173.

77. W, pp. 216–17, though the association of the boy's voice with the dove might also be linked with the popular aria, 'O, for the wings of a dove', sung by boy sopranos. The French quotation is the last line of Paul Verlaine's sonnet on *Parsifal*, quoted by T. S. Eliot in 'The Fire Sermon', *The Waste Land* (iii).

78. 'The sense of this came acutely about a week ago on beginning to write the Phantom party', D3, 12 Jan. 1930, p. 282; *Holograph Drafts*, p. 214, dated Jan 3rd – see p. 203 verso for a reference to 'The phantom Conversation'.

79. D3, 12 Jan. 1930, p. 282.

80. W, pp. 173, 207, and compare D3, 11 Oct. 1929, p. 260, 'when I wake early I say to myself, Fight, fight'. Woolf linked this to 'the sense that comes to me of being bound on an adventure' (for which, see the reference to Dante's and Tennyson's Ulysses on p. 255), and D4, 11 Apr. 1931, p. 17.

81. W, pp. 115, 116, 187.

82. W, p. 114 (and see John 8:12); Jane Harrison, *Themis: A Study of the Social Origins of Greek Religion* (1912; London: Merlin Press, 1989), especially p. xviii and chs. 5 and 8. Gillian Beer's edition of *The Waves*, p. 253, cites Jane Harrison's work in connection with Rhoda's vision of a procession, near the end of the farewell party.

83. *Holograph Drafts*, pp. 560–1, though Woolf almost immediately redrafted these two pages so that the molehill (unlikely in India?) became part of a wider argument: 'We deserve to be tripped up by molehills', pp. 562–3. In the first draft, 'He died of an accident soon after taking up his post', p. 242.

84. Thomas Hardy, 'Hap', and see above, Ch. 1, pp. 12–13.

85. D3, 22 Dec. 1930, p. 339; T. S. Eliot, 'East Coker' (v); D3, 26 Dec. 1929, p. 275. For W. B. Yeats, 'The innocent and the beautiful / Have no enemy but time' ('In Memory of Eva Gore-Booth and Con Markiewicz', October 1927).

86. D3, 21 Feb. 1930, p. 290. Woolf was still pained over Vita's infidelities,

and found Ethel 'discriminating . . . – judging Vita & her secondrate women friends shrewdly', p. 291.

87. 'Honesty is her quality: & the fact that she made a great rush at life; friendships with women interest me', D1, 28 Nov. 1919, p. 315 – Woolf reviewed Smyth's *Streaks of Life* for the *New Statesman* in 1921 (*Essays*, vol. 3, pp. 297–300); 'two letters daily', D3, 16 June 1930, p. 306; 'But dear me I am not in love with Ethel. And oh yes – her experience', D3, 25 Aug. 1930, p. 314. Virginia quarrelled with Leonard about Ethel (28 Mar. 1930, p. 298) (Ethel drove him 'frantic'); Ethel defended herself 'in a speech which lasted 20 minutes by my watch', D4, 7 July 1931, p. 34.

88. D3, 25 Aug. 1930, p. 313.

89. L4, to Quentin Bell, 14 May 1930, p. 171.

90. D3, 31 May 1929, p. 230 – compare her account of her failing sight later that year, 16 Sept. 1929, p. 254.

91. *Holograph Drafts*, pp. 383–4.

92. D3, 29 Apr. 1930, p. 302.

93. D3, 1 May 1930, p. 303.

94. L4, to ES, 28 Aug. 1930, p. 204; see also D3, 2 Sept. 1930, p. 316, 'I say I am writing The Waves to a rhythm not to a plot', a rhythm 'in harmony with the painters', and 30 Dec. 1930, p. 343.

95. *Holograph Drafts*, p. 400; the earlier episodes are also numbered differently, although their sequence is that of the final version, with two chapters on 'The garden' (presumably the first consisted of the material that became the first interlude).

96. D3, 6 Aug. 1930, p. 312, although it is clear from the holograph that she had arrived at her method of presenting the soliloquies from half-way through the first draft, with the 'Conversation' of the farewell party.

97. D3, 6 Aug. 1930, p. 311: 'The rain pelts – look at it (as the people in The Waves are always saying) now.' Six weeks later, she told Hugh Walpole that she had just written ' "Listen," she said, "Look" ' (L4, 27 Sept. 1930, p. 221) – these are Rhoda's words at the farewell party in the second draft: *Holograph Drafts*, p. 540, and compare W, p. 101.

98. The choruses, identified by Graham in *Holograph Drafts*, occur at W, pp. 93, 101 (Rhoda's 'Look . . . listen' opens the second), 109, 172, 175; Daniel Ferrer explores the problems of where the speakers are speaking from (op. cit., esp. pp. 65–6, 91–6), and James Naremore suggests that they 'inhabit a kind of spirit realm from which, in a sad, rather world-weary tone, they comment on their time-bound selves below' in *The World Without a Self: Virginia Woolf and the Novel* (New Haven, CT: Yale University Press, 1973), p. 173.

99. D3, 2 Sept. 1930, p. 315.

100. D3, 8 Sept. 1930, p. 317; 22 Dec. 1930, p. 339. On 'the theme effort', see J. W. Graham, 'Manuscript Revision and the Heroic Theme of *The Waves*', *Twentieth Century Literature*, 29, 3 (Fall 1983), pp. 312–32.

101. D4, 7 Feb. 1931, p. 10. The fin (for an early version of which, see D2, 15 Oct. 1923, p. 270) appeared to Woolf in the late summer of 1926 – D3, 30 Sept., p. 113 and see W, pp. 139, 145, 210, and n. 121, below.

102. *Holograph Drafts*, introduction, p. 38.

103. D4, 7 Jan. 1931, p. 4.

104. D4, 13 May 1931, p. 25 (as she had done in the case of *Mrs Dalloway* – see Ch. 6, The Aftermath, p. 154 above).

105. W, pp. 18, 21, 38, 141.

106. W, pp. 56, 73, 127.

107. W, p. 202; D4, 30 May 1931, p. 28; *Holograph Drafts*, p. 582 (verso).

108. Compare Matthew 26.26, 'Take, eat: this is my body'.

109. W, pp. 60, 222, and compare p. 212, 'I do not altogether know who I am'; see also O, pp. 212–14 and Ch. 8, p. 208 above; on life as 'a many-sided substance . . . a many-faceted flower', see W, pp. 175–6.

110. 'A Sketch of the Past', *MoB*, p. 73; L4, to G. Lowes Dickinson, 27 Oct. 1931, p. 397 – 'I'm getting old myself – I shall be fifty next year; and I come to feel more and more how difficult it is to collect oneself into one Virginia; . . . I wanted to give the sense of continuity'.

111. *ROO*, p. 94.

112. W, pp. 61, 65, 96, 99, 155.

113. For Woolf's early schemes, see the fragment probably written during the summer of 1928, and reprinted in *Holograph Drafts*, appendix A, pp. 63–4, 'She was tired of all this . . .', or D3, 28 May 1929, pp. 229–30, 'But who is she?'; W, p. 183. Makiko Minow-Pinkney, in an incisive analysis which also draws on the holograph drafts, sees a conflict between the masculine 'symbolic order' and the Kristevan *chora*, the early, unstructured language associated with the mother – *Virginia Woolf and the Problem of the Subject: Feminine Writing in the Major Novels* (Brighton: Harvester, 1987), pp. 152–86.

114. W, pp. 219, 221 (the eclipse was, of course, that of 1927 which she had watched with Vita – see above, Ch. 8, p. 187).

115. W, pp. 222–3, 225, 228.

116. D4, 23 June 1931, p. 30; 7 July 1931, p. 34. For Mabel's role, see D3, 12 Dec. 1930, p. 336. J. W. Graham discusses Woolf's typing arrangements, and the sequence and nature of these changes in his introduction to the *Holograph Drafts*, pp. 35–6.

117. In her diary for 13 Apr. 1930 (D3, p. 300), Woolf recorded reading

Shakespeare, though probably not the sonnets – she used a characteristic Shakespearean syntactic structure – 'my wildest tumult & utmost press of mind', and declared that 'This is not "writing" at all. Indeed. I could say that Sh[akespea]re surpasses literature altogether, if I knew what I meant'. Mrs Ramsay reads a Shakespeare sonnet in *To the Lighthouse*, intro. Hermione Lee, ed. Stella McNichol (1927; London: Penguin, 1992), pp. 131–2.

118. W, p. 215; a diary entry for 26 Jan. 1930 discusses the importance of the interludes as transitions, and to 'give a background – the sea; insensitive nature', D3, p. 285.

119. J. H. Willis, Jr, *Leonard and Virginia Woolf as Publishers: The Hogarth Press, 1917–41* (Charlottesville, VA: University Press of Virginia, 1992), p. 198.

120. D4, 19 July 1931, p. 36.

121. The fin appears in section 7 (which approximates to Woolf's age in 1926), W, pp. 139, 145, and reappears in the final episode, where the draining experience is characterized by its absence – 'Now there is nothing', p. 218. In the first draft, the loss of selfhood occurs in September (*Holograph Drafts*, p. 387), as it had done for Woolf; finally, she 'netted that fin', D4, 7 Feb. 1931, p. 10, and see n. 101 above.

122. D4, 30 Sept. 1931, p. 46; 15 Sept., p. 43; 16 Sept., p. 44; 22 Sept., p. 45.

123. D4, 5 Oct. 1931, p. 47; *Critical Heritage*, p. 266.

124. D4, 9 Oct. 1931, p. 47; for the dust-jacket, see Tony Bradshaw, *The Bloomsbury Artists: Prints and Book Design* (Aldershot: Scolar Press, 1999), plate 30; for details of print runs, see *A Bibliography*, pp. 81–2; D4, 14 Oct. 1931, pp. 47–8.

125. D4, 29 Dec. 1931, p. 57 and 26 Feb. 1932, p. 79.

126. D3, 14, 17 Oct. 1931, pp. 48, 49, and compare L4, to Vita Sackville-West, 8 Oct. 1931, p. 387: 'I'm sending The Waves, but I don't much think you'll like it.' For Vanessa's response, see *Selected Letters of VB*, p. 367, ? 15 Oct. 1931; for Dickinson's letter, see *Critical Heritage*, p. 271.

127. *Critical Heritage*, pp. 284, 264, 267, 274, 275; among its critics were Frank Swinnerton for the *Evening News*, pp. 267–8, and Louis Kronenberger for the *New York Times Book Review*, pp. 273–5; admirers included A. S. McDowall for the *Times Literary Supplement*, p. 263, Storm Jameson for the *Fortnightly Review*, p. 277, and Edwin Muir for *The Bookman*, p. 294.

128. D4, 16 Nov. 1931, p. 52; 17 Oct. 1931, p. 49.

129. D4, 16 Nov. 1931, p. 53.

130. D4, 3 Jan. 1933, p. 140; see also L5, to Virginia Isham, 4 Jan. 1933, p. 145.

131. Mark Hussey, *Virginia Woolf A to Z: A Comprehensive Reference* (New York: Facts on File, 1995), p. 362.

132. *Letters of Leonard Woolf*, ed. F. Spotts (London: Bloomsbury, 1990), 24 May, 29 May 1941, pp. 259–60.

133. Ibid., 3 June 1966, p. 566.

Chapter 11

1. *The Pargiters*, ed. Mitchell A. Leaska (London: Hogarth Press, 1978), p. xxxv, which reprints Vera Brittain's weekly column in the *Nation and Athenaeum* for that week. Woolf, in her turn, apparently read Brittain's column – indeed, she referred to Brittain's account of her 'cold, gloomy, ground-floor bedroom, which faced due north and was overrun with mice' at Cambridge in the speech she made that night (*Pargiters*, pp. xxxiv–v and compare p. 166), and would later use it in *Three Guineas* (Michèle Barrett, ed., *A Room of One's Own/Three Guineas* (1929, 1938; London: Penguin, 1993)), at chapter 1, fn. 18, p. 280. With a quotation from Keynes from an article in the same edition of the *Nation and Athenaeum* (17 Jan. 1931), this is the earliest dateable quotation from a periodical to appear in *Three Guineas*, as Naomi Black points out in her introduction to her edition (Oxford: Shakespeare Head/Blackwell, 2001), p. xxi.

2. *Pargiters*, p. xxxv, and for further details, see *The Memoirs of Ethel Smyth*, ed. Ronald Crichton (London: Viking, 1987), p. 345.

3. *Pargiters*, p. xliv – an abbreviated and revised version of Woolf's talk was published as 'Professions for Women' by Leonard Woolf in *The Death of a Moth* (1942), and subsequently in Leonard Woolf, ed., Virginia Woolf, *Collected Essays* (London: Chatto and Windus, 1966), vol. 2, pp. 284–9. *The Pargiters* prints both the longer, 25-page typescript, here cited, and a shorter typescript that looks like notes for the longer one (Appendix, pp. 163–7). The former is probably closer to what Woolf read that evening. On the relationship between the two typescripts and the published text of 'Professions for Women', see Black's edition of *TG*, pp. xxxviii–xxxix, xl–xlii.

4. The speaker dismisses the Angel in the House by throwing the inkpot at her – thus staining her purity and simultaneously asserting the power of the pen (*Collected Essays*, vol. 2, p. 286; *Pargiters*, p. xxxii.

5. *Pargiters*, pp. xxxvii–viii, xl.

6. Ibid., xlii–iii. The list was inspired by a list of professions in the 1930 report of the Junior Council of the National Society for Women's Service, then (as now) in the Women's Library – see Black's edition of *TG*, pp. xlii; fn.7, xlviii.

For Woolf's substantial use of the Library, see Merry M. Pawlowski, 'The Virginia Woolf and Vera Douie Letters: Woolf's Connections to the Women's Service Library', in Mark Hussey, ed., *Woolf Studies Annual*, vol. 8 (New York: Pace University Press, 2002), pp. 3–62.

7. D4, 20, 23 Jan. 1931, p. 6.

8. Woolf had quoted her aunt Anny Ritchie's joke about the younger generation knocking on the door in *Night and Day*, ed. Julia Briggs (1919; London: Penguin, 1992), p. 78. But, as Black's introduction suggests (p. xxxix), she may be referring to the previous paragraph, which ended 'Men too can be emancipated' – *Pargiters*, p. xliv (reading corrected by Alex Zwerdling, *Virginia Woolf and the Real World* (Los Angeles, CA: University of California Press, 1986), p. 348, fn.18).

9. L4, to Clive Bell, 21 Feb. 1931, p. 294; *ND*, pp. 124–5.

10. 'Aurora Leigh', included in *The Common Reader: Second Series* (London: Hogarth Press, 1932), and *Collected Essays*, vol.1, pp. 209–18, esp. p. 218.

11. L5, to Ottoline Morrell, 23 Feb. 1933, pp. 161–2; L4, to Helen McAfee, 2 July 1931, p. 351. It is not clear at what point between October 1930 and late June 1931 Woolf actually saw Besier's play (see L4, to Vita Sackville-West, 1 Oct. 1930, p. 224; to Ethel Smyth, 27 June 1931, p. 349).

12. See D4, 19 July 1931, p. 36; the notebook was to become the first of eight that contain the MS draft of *The Years* (five pages have been cut out, and the notebook then begins '11 October 1932'). The second notebook, dated 21 July 1931, contains 19 pages of the first MS draft of the opening chapter of *Flush*; both are in the Berg Collection of the New York Public Library.

13. D4, 10, 16 Aug. 1931, pp. 38, 40.

14. D4, 8 Oct., 16 Nov. 1931, pp. 47, 52–3.

15. L5, to John Lehmann, 31 July 1932, p. 83, to OM, 23 Feb. 1933, p. 162, and to David Garnett, 8 Oct. 1933, p. 232 – perhaps by way of an excuse.

16. L4, to Lytton Strachey, 10 Dec. 1931, p. 412.

17. D4, 27 Dec. 1931, 1 Jan., 18 Jan. 1932, pp. 56, 61–2, 64.

18. D4, 18 Jan., 22 Jan. 1932, pp. 64–5.

19. D4, 12 Mar. 1932, pp. 81–3.

20. D4, 29 Dec. 1931, p. 57. 'The appalling novel' might also be 'The Tree' (see the entry for 14 Oct. 1931, p. 48).

21. D4, 8 Feb. 1932, p. 74.

22. D4, 3 Sept. 1931, p. 42; 11, 16 Feb. 1932, pp. 75, 77. The phrase 'Men are like that' was her half-sister Stella's, when commenting on her brothers' disapproval of Jack Hills visiting too often – 'Reminiscences', *MoB*, p. 50. The phrase 'enough powder to blow up St Pauls' is echoed in 'The Duchess and the Jeweller', where the Jeweller sees his diamonds as 'Gunpowder enough

to blow up Mayfair', *CSF*, p. 250. According to Susan Dick (*CSF*, p. 308), Woolf could have been working on its predecessor, 'The Great Jeweller', in February 1932.

23. D4, 3, 13 June 1932, pp. 107–8, 109.

24. D4, 8 Feb. 1932, p. 74.

25. D4, 11 July 1932, p. 115.

26. D4, 8 July 1932, p. 115.

27. *Flush*, ed. Alison Light (1933; London: Penguin, 2000). Page numbers appearing in square brackets after quotes refer to this edition of the book. See Light's introduction, for a fuller account of the novel's genesis and concerns.

28. On 5 Jan. 1933 (D4, p. 141), Woolf recorded 'the third time of writing that Whitechapel scene'. Of the seventy or so substantive variants between the UK and the US editions, the great majority occur in this chapter – see *Flush*, ed. Elizabeth Steele (Oxford: Shakespeare Head/Blackwell, 1999), appendix C, pp. 106–23.

29. *The Voyage Out*, ed. Jane Wheare (1915; London: Penguin, 1992), pp. 68, 312–13.

30. *Good Housekeeping*, Dec. 1931, Jan., Mar., May, Oct., Dec. 1932; five of the six essays are reprinted in Rachel Bowlby, ed., Virginia Woolf, *The Crowded Dance of Modern Life: Selected Essays* (London: Penguin, 1993), pp. 107–32.

31. *Essays*, vol. 4, pp. 480–91.

32. See *An Autobiography*, vol. 2, p. 297 and many diary entries, e.g. D4, pp. 172, 246 (cited in the text, p. 289, and see n. 76).

33. D4, 5 Jan. 1933, p. 142; 25 May 1932, p. 102.

34. L5, to ES, 1 Apr. 1932, p. 40; D4, 13 July 1932, p. 115; 2 Oct. 1932, p. 125.

35. *Pargiters*, p. 5.

36. D4, 2 Nov. 1932, p. 129.

37. *Pargiters*, pp. 5, 8, 9, 11.

38. Unlike Delia, Ethel actually got to Germany. Rose's career as a suffragette also recalls Ethel's experiences (including being imprisoned in Holloway), while Digby's wife, Eugenié, is named after the ex-Empress, widow of Napoleon III, who befriended and supported the young Ethel (see *Memoirs of ES*, esp. pp. 56, 293–301). Leonard also encountered the Empress Eugenié in Sri Lanka (at that time called Ceylon), *An Autobiography*, vol. 1, pp. 221–6.

39. *Pargiters*, pp. 28, 30; 29, 31, but note that Leaska's division of the episodes into numbered and alternating 'chapters' and 'essays' is his own addition. In the MS notebook, the first chapter is numbered '56' (as part of an imaginary

family history running from '1800 to the year 2032', p. 9), but thereafter, different episodes begin on new pages, and are headed with ink-blots with lines radiating out from them (reproduced by Leaska), a figure drawn by Eleanor several times during the course of the novel – see *The Years*, ed. Jeri Johnson (1937; London: Penguin, 1998), pp. 66, 129–30, 158, 269, and her introduction (pp. xxiv, xxxiii). On the holograph notebooks, see Grace Radin, *Virginia Woolf's* The Years: *The Evolution of a Novel* (Knoxville, TN: University of Tennessee Press, 1981).

40. *Pargiters*, pp. 37, 38.

41. Ibid., pp. 43, 48; *VO*, pp. 68, 312–13; for Woolf's childhood terrors, see 'A Sketch of the Past', *MoB*, p. 123. Quentin Bell, in *Biography*, vol. 1, p. 35, noted that this scene was 'based on experience . . . a man who hung around Hyde Park and was seen by both Vanessa and Virginia'. In the MS notebook, this episode has been written very fast and fluently, and with few corrections. See also D4, 10 Nov. 1932, p. 130, which also refers to her article on her father ('my LS'), drafted on the first twenty pages of the second MS notebook but then cut out (she had begun writing *The Pargiters* in that notebook on 28 Nov. 1932).

42. *Pargiters*, pp. 48, 51.

43. Ibid., pp. 51, 53–4.

44. Ibid., pp. 131–49.

45. Ibid., p. 154, and more generally, pp. 150–9; see also diary entry for 13 July 1932 (D4, pp. 115–16).

46. As Jane Marcus originally pointed out – see *Pargiters*, p. xiv. Woolf may also have known the further sense of 'pargeting' – that is, 'to cover or decorate with ornamental work of any kind' (*Oxford English Dictionary*). While a pargeter or plasterer is spelled with an 'e', the Woolfs also knew a man named 'Pargiter', a railway signalman near Rodmell. Initially, Woolf used both spellings interchangeably in her MS. The scene of Colonel Pargiter's visit to Mira was begun on 9 Mar. 1933 (notebook 3), after the rest of the 1880 episode had been drafted, though it would later come first.

47. D4, 19 Dec. 1932, p. 132; 2 Nov. 1932, pp. 129–30; *Pargiters*, p. 9.

48. D4, 5, 15, 19 Jan. 1933, pp. 141–3.

49. D4, 13, 25 Apr. 1933, pp. 150, 151–2.

50. D4, 2 Nov. 1932, p. 129. The essay/letter is reprinted in *The Death of the Moth*, and *Collected Essays*, vol. 2, pp. 196–203.

51. L5, to VS-W, 16 Aug. 1933, p. 214, and see the previous day's letter to Quentin, 15 Aug. 1933, as she sent him *Ordinary Families* (which she admired), and Antonia White's *Frost in May* (which she did not); D4, 2 Sept. 1933, p. 177.

52. D1, 15 Jan. 1915, p. 19.

53. D4, 19 Dec. 1932, p. 133; *Pargiters*, p. 9.

54. 'Mr Bennett and Mrs Brown', *Essays*, vol. 3, p. 427; see also diary entry, D4, 31 May 1933, p. 161: 'I mean how give ordinary waking Arnold Bennett life the form of art?'

55. D4, 2 Oct. 1935, p. 346.

56. At the time of its publication, Woolf thought a great deal of *The Years* 'very feeble – the scene in the college still makes me blush', D5, 14 Mar. 1937, p. 68.

57. D4, 2 Feb. 1933, p. 146; Magdalena and Elvira are first mentioned in a diary entry for 17 Dec. 1932, D4, p. 132; see also 31 Dec. 1932, p. 134.

58. *Pargiters*, p. 7.

59. D4, 25 Mar. 1933, pp. 147–8 – see also entry for 28 March, 'No, thank Heaven, I need not emerge from my fiction in July to have a tuft of fur put on my head'; 'A Dance in Queen's Gate', in Mitchell A. Leaska, ed., *Virginia Woolf, A Passionate Apprentice: The Early Journals 1897–1909* (London: Hogarth Press, 1990), p. 164.

60. 'We cannot help each other, [North] thought, we are all deformed', Y, p. 278. See also D4, 28 Apr. 1935, p. 307, 'What is the use of trying to preach when human nature is so crippled?', and her letter to Stephen Spender, L6, 30 Apr. 1937, p. 122: 'Eleanor's experience was meant to be all right . . . the others were crippled in one way or another – though I meant Maggie and Sara to be outside that particular prison.'

61. D4, 6 Apr. 1933, p. 149 (she added optimistically, 'Four months should finish the first draft . . .'). She was revising it on 30 Dec. 1934, p. 266 ('with what excitement I wrote it! And now hardly a line of the original left'), and again on 5 Sept. 1935, p. 338, and 26 Sept., p. 344, when she asked herself 'Why is this – . . . [scene] the most difficult I have ever written?' (though other scenes from 1914, 1917 and the 'Present Day' were also to give problems).

62. Though these scenes are repetitive, and would be difficult to transcribe, they are among the most interesting of Woolf's unpublished writings – see Radin's account, pp. 49–55. The suffragette slogan, 'Every patriarch has his prostitute', is later remembered by Kitty at her dinner-party (see Radin, p. 86); 'time is but a roseleaf' echoes an observation attributed to Sir James Jeans in Woolf's diary for 30 Jan. 1932 (D4, p. 65): 'Civilisation is the thickness of a postage stamp on the top of Cleopatra's needle; & time to come is the thickness of postage stamps as high as Mont Blanc'. In 'twice twelve thousand years', a man of the future, 'looking in at this window will hold his nose and say Pah they stink' (compare Y, p. 139). For the source of the postage stamp/ Cleopatra's needle analogy in James Jeans's *The Universe Around Us*, see

Holly Henry, *Virginia Woolf and the Discourse of Science* (Cambridge: Cambridge University Press, 2003), p. 48. The exclamation 'Pah! They stink' was originally made by Jacques Raverat (in part the model for Rennie), as Frances Spalding notes, in *Gwen Raverat: A Biography* (London: Harvill, 2001), p. 208.

63. Page numbers appearing in square brackets after quotes refer to Johnson's 1998 Penguin edition of the *The Years*.

64. Woolf's Introductory Letter to Margaret Llewelyn Davies, ed., *Life as We Have Known It*, by Co-operative Working Women (London: Hogarth Press, 1931), p. xxxiv (reprinted as 'Memories of a Working Women's Guild' in Rachel Bowlby, ed., *Virginia Woolf: A Woman's Essays* (London: Penguin 1992), p. 143).

65. Ibid., pp. xxi, xxviii (or Bowlby, *A Woman's Essays*, pp. 135, 139).

66. See 'Mr Bennett and Mrs Brown', *Essays*, vol. 3, pp. 421, 433, 436.

67. D4, 25 Mar. 1932, p. 86; 'the Nelly question', 18 Feb. 1934, p. 202.

68. D3, 16 Sept. 1929, p. 254; 31 May 1929, p. 230.

69. 'Mr Bennett and Mrs Brown', *Essays*, vol. 3, p. 422.

70. D3, 15 Dec. 1929, p. 274.

71. D3, 12 Nov. 1930, p. 333; 8 Aug. 1929, p. 240; 5 Sept. 1926, p. 107; 18 May, 16 June 1930, pp. 304–5; 8 Sept. 1930, p. 317; D4, 17 Feb. 1931, p. 12.

72. D4, 16, 20 Feb. 1934, pp. 202–3; 19, 26, 27 Mar. 1934, pp. 205–6; L5, to ES, 29 Mar. 1934, p. 284.

73. L6, to ES, 12 Jan. 1941, p. 460.

74. D5, 18 Mar. 1936, p. 18.

75. D4, 30 Sept. 1934, p. 245; 31 Dec. 1932, p. 135.

76. D4, 'in full flood', 13, 20 June, 20 July 1933, pp. 162, 165, 168; 16 Jan., 18 June 1934, pp. 199, 222; 'an exciting book to write' – 26 July 1933, p. 170 (compare 'I don't think I have ever been more excited . . .', 2 Sept. 1934, p. 241); 12 Aug. 1933, p. 172; 2 Oct. 1934, p. 246.

77. For the visit to Herbert Fisher, see D4, 4 Dec. 1933, pp. 191–2; the Parnell biography, 15 Jan. 1933, p. 143; Andrew Marvell, 16 Jan. 1934, p. 199; Leonard and Virginia visited Ireland in May 1934, where they stayed with Elizabeth Bowen at Bowen's Court, and met Mr Rowlands, who became the model for Delia's husband Patrick, D4, 2 May 1934, pp. 211–12; 'Writings chalked up all over the walls. "Don't fight for foreigners. Briton [*sic*] should mind her own business." Then a circle with a symbol in it. Fascist propaganda, L. said', D4, 4 Sept. 1935, p. 337.

78. 'This last chapter must equal in length & importance & volume the first book; & must in fact give the other side, the submerged side of that', D4,

22 May 1934, p. 221. See entries for 2, 7 Aug. 1934 (pp. 234, 236), 2, 30 Sept. (pp. 241, 245), and 5 Oct. (p. 249), all concerned with the problems of ending.

79. D4, 28 July 1934, pp. 232–3; on the ending, and the pleasures of writing, see entries for 7, 17 Aug., 2 Sept. 1934, pp. 236, 237–8, 241.

80. D4, 12 Sept, 17 Oct. 1934, pp. 242, 253, and for 'late afternoon', see L5, to Julian Bell, 9 Sept. 1934, p. 329; Woolf ended 1934 asking herself 'am I to write about [Roger]?', D4, 30 Dec. 1934, p. 267, and see 31 Oct., 12 Nov. 1934, pp. 258, 260.

81. D4, 'Here & Now' – 2 Sept. 1933, p. 176; 'Music, or Dawn' – 17 Aug., 2 Sept. 1934; 'Sons and Daughters' – 30 Sept. 1934, p. 246; 'Ordinary People' – 30 Dec. 1934, 1 Jan., 8 Feb. 1935, pp. 266, 271, 279; 'The Caravan' – 11 Jan. 1935, p. 274; 'Other People's Houses' – 22 Aug. 1935; 'The Years – thats what its to be called –' 5 Sept 1935, p. 338, and see 7, 12, 13 and esp. 15 Sept. 1935, pp. 339–42. The MS notebooks also include lists of possible titles: the fourth notebook (begun on 18 June 1933) is entitled 'The Pargiters or Time Passes or Here and Now or In the Flesh'; the eighth notebook (begun 27 Sept. 1934) is entitled 'The Pargiters, Here & Now, Brothers & Sisters, Dawn, Uncles & Aunts, Time [deleted], Ordinary People, Sons & Daughters.'

82. These galley proofs, like the eight MS notebooks, are in the Berg Collection. The first mention in her diary of the book that became *Three Guineas* (as opposed to the impulse from which both *The Years* and *Three Guineas* sprang) was on 1 Jan. 1935, while she was revising her first draft ('now I want to write On being despised'), D4, p. 271, though she had been keeping scrapbooks of 'Opinions that one now pastes in a book labelled cock-a-doodle-dum' (*A Room of One's Own*, Michèle Barrett, ed., *A Room of One's Own/Three Guineas* (1929, 1938; London: Penguin, 1993), p. 51) since the early 1930s (three bound volumes are among the Monk's House Papers at Sussex University Library (MH/B16.f.)).

83. D4, 14 Apr. 1935, p. 300 (corresponding to a draft in the eighth notebook for 14 Apr. 1935) – I read 'clean', instead of 'clear'.

84. D4, 11 Mar. 1935, p. 287, though it was not the end of their relationship, as some letters discovered ten years ago indicate – see Joanne Trautmann Banks, 'Four Hidden Letters', *Virginia Woolf Miscellany*, 43, Special Summer Issue, 1994, pp. 1–2.

85. D4, 27 Oct. 1935, p. 348, and see also ? 28 Nov., 10 Dec. 1935, p. 356; 13 June 1935, p. 321.

86. D4, 17 Apr. 1934, p. 207; 26 Feb. 1935, p. 282 (see also entries for 1 Nov. 1934, p. 258; 13 June 1935, p. 321; 16 Oct. 1935, p. 347; 18 Nov. 1935, p. 353); 'My idea . . .', D4, 30 Dec. 1934, p. 266.

87. The treatment of the city clocks here, as a kind of chorus, is reminiscent of *Mrs Dalloway*.

88. *Y*, pp. 198–9, and see my essay ' "This Moment I Stand On": Woolf and the Spaces in Time', Virginia Woolf Society of Great Britain, 2001.

89. *The Waves*, ed. Kate Flint (1931; London: Penguin, 1992), p. 183 (see also pp. 196, 227); Woolf had worried from an early stage about 'intellectual argument in the form of art', D4, 31 May 1933, p. 161.

90. D4, 21 Nov. 1935, pp. 353–4 (compare 'how to make the transition from the colloquial to the lyrical, from the particular to the general?', 7 Aug. 1934, p. 236).

91. Sara was 'very like her mother – except when she laughed' (*Y*, p. 169); Eugenié's characteristic gesture of flinging out her hands (pp. 89, 103) seems to be echoed by Maggie ('something about her gesture', p. 178), and poorly imitated by Eleanor (p. 112). In the 'Present Day' section, Nicholas, Eleanor and Sara perform similar gestures (pp. 236, 242, 249), as does Julia Stephen in 'A Sketch of the Past', *MoB*, p. 135.

92. For the gilt-clawed chairs, see *Y*, pp. 93, 96, 106, 121, 210, 229, and for the walrus, pp. 25, 160, 312 – on both, see Johnson's discussion of Woolf's use of repetition (p. xxxi), and the page listings provided in her notes.

93. For newspapers, see *Y*, pp. 5, 56–8 (1880); 82 (1891); 108–11 (including the Colonel's collection of newspaper cuttings – 1908); 118, 130, 140 (1910); 147 (1911); 161 (1913); 172, 182 (1914); 362, 364–6, 371–2 (in the excised section of 1914); 205 (1917); 382–4, 388, 395–9 (in the excised 1921 section); 242 ('Present Day').

94. The stage direction is from *The Tempest*, Act I scene 2. Early twentieth-century 'complete works' of Shakespeare followed the order of the first folio, in which *The Tempest* was printed first – editorial stage directions of this kind were regularly added to Victorian editions (as Johnson notes, *Y*, p. 354); D4, 30 Dec. 1935, p. 361; *Y*, p. 281.

95. *Y*, p. 318, and *ROO*, p. 87 (as Radin observes, p. 9).

96. Woolf had problems ending her novel (see D4, 30 Sept. 1934, p. 245) – the eighth MS notebook shows that, though the caretaker's children appear at the end, their singing was a slightly later addition, made on 4 Oct. 1934 – pp. 18–20: 'the words had a distorted likeness to real words . . . But there was something terrible, hideous & strange about the outcry'.

97. The 'Two Enormous Chunks' cut from the novel survive in galley proofs, and are reprinted as an appendix to the Penguin edition, pp. 361–401. Woolf met Yeats on 25 Oct. 1934 (see diary entry for 26 Oct., D4, pp. 255–7).

98. 'Shall I ever write a long book again – a long novel that has to be held in

the brain, at full stretch – for close on 3 years?' she wondered, D4, 28 Dec. 1935, p. 360; D5, 16, 20 Mar. 1936, pp. 17, 19 – these mood swings indicate the beginning of her breakdown.

99. D5, 24 Nov. 1936, 1, 2, 14 Mar. 1937, pp. 35, 63, 64, 68 and note also 'horrid heats & slumbers', 3 Nov. 1936, p. 30 (Woolf was 54 at the beginning of 1936), though she also told Ethel Smyth on 25 July 1936 that it 'came and passed, as gently and imperceptibly as a lamb, 2 years ago', L6, p. 60.

100. D5, 11 Mar. 1936, p. 15.

101. D5, 9 Apr. 1936, p. 22. The correction of galley proofs as a convenient mode of revision was more typical of the nineteenth century (before the advent of the typewriter), than the twentieth.

102. 'We had a terrifying time with *The Years* in 1936' – Leonard would describe what happened next in his *Autobiography*, vol. 2, pp. 299–302.

103. D5, 23 June 1936, p. 25; 10 Nov. 1936, pp. 31–2; 14 Mar. 1937, p. 67. A precise narrative of events during the summer and autumn of 1936 is difficult to establish as Leonard's account in his *Autobiography* is partly based on Virginia's diary, which is itself incomplete. Letters suggest that she had hoped to finish her revisions before September so that it could be published before Christmas (L6, to ES, 26 Aug. 1936, p. 67), but missed the deadline through 'another headache' (p. 68). By September she was much better at first, but as the month wore on, she wrote herself out again (letters of 2, 4, 15, 18 Sept.). In October she took time off – 'I must have a break before reading that vast shuffle of exhausted sentences' (22 Oct.), and on 1 Nov. she 'started to read the proofs' (D5, p. 29).

104. D4, 13 Sept. 1935, p. 341, and see also, 'the change of scene is whats so exhausting: the catching people plumb in the middle . . . Every beginning seems lifeless –', D5, 16 Mar. 1936, p. 17: between the galley proofs and the page proofs printed at the beginning of 1937, Woolf wrote almost all of the evocative passages that open or link sections of her text (see Radin, pp. 116, 126–30, who comments, 'it is remarkable that the preludes and interludes were added so late in the evolution of *The Years*, since they seem to be such an important structural device', p. 127).

105. D5, 3, 4, 5 Nov. 1936, pp. 29–30.

106. Ibid.

107. '[I] altogether muffed the proportions: which should have given a round not a thin line' – L6, to SS, 7 Apr. 1937, p. 116. The first of these two 'chunks' was mistakenly ascribed to the 1917 section, but, as Karen Levenback has pointed out in 'Placing the First "Enormous Chunk" Deleted from *The Years*', *Virginia Woolf Miscellany* 42 (Spring 1994), pp. 8–9, it actually takes place

in the early days of the war, when mobilization was in full swing, and the blackout had not begun, in September 1914 (thus concluding the 1914 section). The second 'chunk' (which should begin 'The sun was shining . . .'), is the whole of the 1921 section, subsequently cut out in its entirety (it includes a possible vignette of Leonard in the printing shop – Y, p. 390, though it is questionable whether Leonard was capable of 'dissing' (distributing) the type, because of his hand tremor). Like *Mrs Dalloway*, *The Years* was designed to have a twelve-part structure, with the first eight sections culminating in the Great War (1880, 1891, 1907, 1908, 1910, 1911, 1913, 1914 (divided into a May and September sequence)), and four sections thereafter (1917, 1918 – a short section, in which Crosby learns that the war has ended – 1921 (excised), and 'Present Day'). The cutting of the second part of 1914 and the whole of 1921 leaves a less balanced eleven sections. As 'The Aftermath' indicates (p. 301), Woolf herself also had second thoughts about their omission.

108. D5, 30 Nov. 1936, p. 39; 30 Dec. 1936, p. 44; 20 Feb. 1937, p. 58. The diary entry for 30 December begins 'There in front of me lie the proofs – the galleys – to go off today'. The Berg Collection holds a partly marked-up set of page proofs for the 1917 section, dated 15 Dec. 1936. These were further revised before publication, so it seems odd that she was still looking at galley proofs at the end of December (since galley proofs precede page proofs – Radin notes this difficulty in fn. 16, p. 131), but presumably Woolf was revising the galleys section by section, and receiving page proofs by return; these must therefore have been the galleys of the 'Present Day' section.

109. D4, 13 Oct. 1932, p. 128; L5, to VS-W, 18 Oct. 1932, p. 111.

110. D4, 2 Oct., 16 Sept. 1932, pp. 125, 123–4; 24 Mar. 1932, p. 85.

111. *A Bibliography*, pp. 89–90; *An Autobiography*, vol. 2, p. 293 (his figures are a little different from hers).

112. D4, 2 Oct. 1932, p. 181. Spelled 'Pinker', his name almost puns on 'Flush', though Steele argues that the dog in the dust-jacket photo is anonymous, in her edition for the Shakespeare Head Press, p. xxvii.

113. For Woolf's 'Middlebrow' essay, see above, p. 282, and n. 50; the *Daily Mail*'s announcement is cited by Alison Light in her account of the novel's reception, *Flush*, pp. xxvii–xxx, esp. p. xxix; Leonard's figures, from *An Autobiography*, vol. 2, p. 293 (and compare *A Bibliography*, pp. 93–5); L5, to Hugh Walpole, 23 Aug. 1933, p. 219; *Flush*, p. xxix.

114. D4, 6 Oct. 1933, p. 184; West (in the *Daily Telegraph*, 6 Oct.), Grigson (in the *Morning Post*, 6 Oct.) and Garnett (in the *New Statesman*, 7 Oct.) are all cited in footnotes 9, 10, 13 to D4, pp. 184–5; 29 Oct. 1933, p. 187.

115. D4, 20 Oct. 1933, p. 186; L5, to HW, 15 Apr. 1933, p. 177 ('only a

joke'); to VS-W, 7 Oct. 1933, p. 229 ('only a silly little joke'); to Lady Cecil, 5 Feb. 1934, p. 274 ('rather ashamed of my joke').

116. D5, 7 Mar. 1937, p. 65; for the date of publication as 11 March, see D5, fn 5, p. 67; 14 Apr. 1937, p. 79.

117. D5, 12 Mar. 1937, p. 67; Basil de Sélincourt 'has pounced on some of the key sentences', 14 Mar., p. 68; 15 Mar., p. 69. The review for the *Times Literary Supplement*, Theodora Bosanquet's review for *Time and Tide*, and Basil de Sélincourt's review for the *Observer* are reprinted in *Critical Heritage*, pp. 368-70, 367-8 and 371-5.

118. D5, 19 Mar. 1937, p. 70: ' "they" say almost universally that The Years is a masterpiece. The Times says so'; 2 Apr., p. 75; 31 Mar., pp. 74-5; 19 Mar., p. 70. Her diary lists those who were 'in favour of Years', 25 Mar., p. 71, and those for and against, 14 Apr., p. 80, as if such opinion polls might help her to decide. Muir's review for *The Listener*, Garnett's for the *New Statesman* and Howard Spring's for the *Evening Standard* are reprinted in *Critical Heritage* at pp. 386-8, 382-5, 376-8; for Keynes, see D5, 4 Apr., p. 77.

119. L6, to SS, 30 Apr. 1937, p. 123; *A Bibliography*, pp. 99-101.

120. *An Autobiography*, vol. 2, pp. 301, 294-5, 401-2.

121. D5, 7, 12, 17 Mar. 1937, pp. 65, 67, 70; L6, to SS, 7 Apr. 1937, p. 116. Early in *A Room of One's Own*, Woolf had suggested some secret design, and that 'if you look carefully you may find it for yourselves in the course of what I am going to say', *ROO*, p. 5.

Chapter 12

1. 'We must attack Hitler in England', Woolf told E. M. Forster, D5, 24 May 1938, p. 142.

2. Freema Gottlieb refers to 'the genteel anti-Semitism which afflicted Chamberlain's England in the years immediately preceding the Second World War' in her essay, 'Leonard Woolf's attitude to his Jewish Background and to Judaism', *Transactions of the Jewish Historical Society of England*, 1973-75, p. 28, quoted by Phyllis Lassner in her article, ' "The Milk of Our Mother's Kindness Has Ceased to Flow": Virginia Woolf, Stevie Smith and the Representation of the Jew', in Bryan Cheyette, ed., *Between 'Race' and Culture: Representations of 'the Jew' in English and American Literature* (Stanford, CA: Stanford University Press, 1996), p. 134.

3. *The Years*, ed. Jeri Johnson (1937; London: Penguin, 1998), pp. 248-50; this scene is discussed by (among others) Lassner, pp. 134-5, by David

Bradshaw, 'Hyams Place: *The Years*, the Jews and the British Union of Fascists', in Maroula Joannou, ed., *Women Writers of the 1930s: Gender, Politics and History* (Edinburgh: Edinburgh University Press, 1999), pp. 179–89, and by Maren Linett, 'The Jew in the Bath: Imperiled Imagination in Woolf's *The Years*', *Modern Fiction Studies*, 48, 2 (Summer 2002), pp. 341–57.

4. Compare *Three Guineas*, *A Room of One's Own/Three Guineas*, ed. Michèle Barrett (1929, 1938; London: Penguin, 1993), pp. 218–19; Linett, pp. 351–6.

5. Sara's ' "Polluted City, unbelieving city, city of dead fish and worn-out frying pans" ' (*Y*, p. 249) echoes Eliot's 'Unreal City' in *The Waste Land*, as Johnson points out in her edition of *The Years* (p. 354, fn. 19). North's repeated 'Pah' recalls Jacques Raverat's exclamation, 'Pah! They stink' (applied to Jews and others) – Frances Spalding, *Gwen Raverat: A Biography* (London: Harvill, 2001), p. 208.

6. E.g. Bradshaw, p. 182.

7. 'The Duchess and the Jeweller', *CSF*, pp. 248–53, 308–9; D5, 17 Aug. 1937, p. 107.

8. Page numbers appearing in square brackets after quotes refer to Barrett's 1993 Penguin edition of *Three Guineas*.

9. *CSF*, p. 252; D3, 23 Nov. 1926, p. 117 (and compare 'pearl hung', 'pearl necklaces', D3, 21 Dec. 1925, p. 52); D3, 21 Apr. 1928, p. 180 – see also Victoria Glendinning, *Vita: The Life of Vita Sackville-West* (New York: Alfred Knopf, 1983), pp. 192–3; on Lady Sackville-West's obsession with fake jewellery, see Suzanne Raitt, 'Fakes and Femininity: Vita Sackville-West and her mother', in Isobel Armstrong, ed., *New Feminist Discourses* (London: Routledge, 1992), pp. 113–18, esp. 116.

10. *CSF*, p. 249.

11. *Carlyle's House and Other Sketches*, ed. David Bradshaw (London: Hesperus, 2003), pp. 14–15.

12. L1, to Violet Dickinson, 4 June 1912, p. 500, to Janet Case, June 1912, p. 501; L4, to Ethel Smyth, 2 Aug. 1930, pp. 195–6. Cynthia Ozick explored some of these aspects of the Woolfs' relationship in her essay 'Mrs Virginia Woolf: A Madwoman and Her Nurse', *What Henry James Knew and Other Essays on Writers* (London: Jonathan Cape, 1993), pp. 141–76.

13. See the description of the cemetery-keeper's nose in 'Three Jews' (London: Hogarth Press, 1917), p. 11 (reprinted in *Virginia Woolf Bulletin*, 5 (Sept. 2000), p. 7): 'a nose, by Jove, Sir, one of the best, one of those noses, white and shiny . . . immensely broad, curving down, like a broad high-road from between the bushy eye-brows down over the lips. And side face, it was colossal;

it stood out like an elephant's trunk with its florid curves and scrolls'; the end of chapter III of *The Wise Virgins* (1914; New York: Harcourt, Brace Jovanovich, 1979), pp. 51-2.

14. D5, 1 Nov. 1937, p. 117 (and 30 Oct. 1938, p. 182). In the sixth MS notebook of *The Years*, the Jew is named 'Isaac', so is quite literally Abraham's son, while Sara was the name of Abraham's wife (as it was of Mrs Ramsay – see *To the Lighthouse*, intro. Hermione Lee, ed. Stella McNichol (1927; London: Penguin, 1992), p. 258, fn. 37).

15. E. M. Forster, 'Virginia Woolf', in *Two Cheers for Democracy* (London: Penguin, 1965), p. 261.

16. For example, the demonstrators against nuclear arms at the American base at Greenham Common in the 1980s (and see Naomi Black's introduction to her edition of *Three Guineas* (Oxford: Shakespeare Head/Blackwell, 2001), p. liv).

17. *Y*, p. 98, and see *TG*, pp. 206-7, 257-8, 266, 269, 302-3 (fn. 39, 40).

18. D5, 19 July 1937, pp. 102-3; her last visit, 2 Apr. 1937, p. 76, and compare Mitchell A. Leaska, ed., Virginia Woolf, *A Passionate Apprentice: The Early Journals 1897-1909* (London: Hogarth Press, 1990), pp. 181-4. Woolf's obituary for Janet Case is reprinted in *Twentieth Century Literature*, 28, 3 (Fall 1982), pp. 298-300.

19. 'The Mark on the Wall', *CSF*, p. 88; 'A Society', *CSF*, pp. 124-36, esp. 135.

20. *Jacob's Room*, ed. Sue Roe (1922; London: Penguin, 1992), p. 153; D4, 11 Jan. 1935, p. 274; *TG*, pp. 183-7, 191, 194, 228.

21. D4, 20 Apr. 1935, p. 303; D5, 12 Oct. 1937, p. 112.

22. D4, 1 Jan. 1935, p. 271; D5, 3 June 1938, p. 148; D4, 6 Jan. 1935, p. 273; 26 Feb. 1935, p. 282.

23. D4, 16 Feb. 1932, p. 77; 9 Apr. 1935, pp. 297-8 (Mrs Green was the wife of the historian J. R. Green, and a writer herself); 17 Apr. 1935, p. 302 – see also 28 Apr. 1935, p. 307 (where a discussion about war sends her back to 'my Professions book').

24. D4, 12 Apr. 1935, p. 298; *An Autobiography*, vol. 2, p. 325; D4, 22 Apr. 1935, p. 304.

25. *An Autobiography*, vol. 2, pp. 325-8, 330; D4, 6, 9, 12 May 1935, pp. 309, 311, 312; 20 June 1935, p. 324; L5, to Victoria Ocampo, 21 June 1935, p. 405 (the first Spanish translation would be that of Jorge Luis Borges, in the following year).

26. *A Room of One's Own*, *A Room of One's Own/Three Guineas*, ed. Michèle Barrett (1929, 1938; London: Penguin, 1993), pp. 32, 28; *TG*, pp. 254-5. Woolf apparently borrowed the term from Grenstead's appendix

to *The Ministry of Women* report of the Archbishop's Commission (p. 314, fn. 30), later asserting that 'Society was a father, and afflicted with the infantile fixation too' (*TG*, p. 263), but as Michèle Barrett observes, 'it is not clear exactly what she means by it' (*TG*, p. 330, fn f).

27. D4, 20 Jan. 1931, p. 6.

28. L. C. B. Seaman, *Post-Victorian Britain, 1902–1951* (London: Methuen, 1966), pp. 253–4; D5, 13 Mar., 11 Nov., 17 Nov. 1936, pp. 17, 33, 34.

29. D4, 29 Apr. 1933, p. 153; *TG*, p. 235: 'The small boy struts and trumpets outside the window: implore him to stop; he goes on; say nothing; he stops'; D4, 20 Apr. 1935, p. 303.

30. D4, 2 Oct. 1935, p. 345; 15 Oct., 27 Oct. 1935, pp. 346, 348.

31. On white feathers, see *TG*, chapter 3, fn. 35, p. 316; 'Another procession, without banners, was blocking Long Acre' refers to this meeting, *JR*, p.153, and see Ch. 4, pp. 90–1; *Y*, p. 307, and see *TG*, p. 129: 'finally because she used force, sent her to prison, and would very likely still keep her there, had it not been, paradoxically enough, that the help she gave her brothers when they used force at last gave her the right to call herself . . . a stepdaughter of England'; D4, 15, 27 Oct., 21 Nov. 1935, pp. 346, 348, 354.

32. See Barbara Brothers, 'British Women Write the Story of the Nazis: A Conspiracy of Silence', in Angela Ingram and Daphne Patai, eds., *Rediscovering Forgotten Radicals: British Women Writers 1889–1939* (Chapel Hill, NC: University of North Carolina Press, 1993), pp. 244–64, and Phyllis Lassner, *British Women Writers of World War II: Battlegrounds of Their Own* (Basingstoke: Macmillan, 1997), which carefully distinguishes between the different attitudes of various writers; Marion Shaw, *The Clear Stream: A Life of Winifred Holtby* (London: Virago, 1999), esp. pp. 227–32; Daphne Patai, 'Imagining Reality: The Utopian Fiction of Katharine Burdekin', in Ingram and Patai, op. cit., pp. 226–43; Keith Williams, 'Back from the Future: Katharine Burdekin and Science Fiction in the 1930s', in Joannou, op. cit., pp. 151–64; Loretta Stec, 'Dystopian Modernism vs Utopian Feminism: Burdekin, Woolf, and West Respond to the Rise of Fascism', in Merry Pawlowski, ed., *Virginia Woolf and Fascism: Resisting the Dictators' Seduction* (London: Palgrave, 2001), pp. 178–93; D4, 20 Apr. 1935, p. 303.

33. D4, 30 Dec. 1935, p. 361; D5, 3, 4 Jan. 1936, pp. 3, 4; 18 Mar., p. 18; 9 Apr., p. 22; 3 Nov., p. 28.

34. Fourth MS notebook of *The Years*, p. 27 (Berg Collection) (though these words are partly crossed out); the guinea coin, as the *Oxford English Dictionary* explains, was originally minted from African gold, for African trade, and is thus implicated in the colonial exploitation of the seventeenth and eighteenth centuries.

35. D5, 24 Nov. 1936, 'Began 3 Gs. yesterday. & liked it.', p. 35; 17 Nov. 1936, pp. 33–5. Robert Cecil was President of the League of Nations Union and Honorary President of the London and National Society for Women's Service.

36. D5, 28 Jan. 1937, p. 52; 18 Feb. 1937, p. 55; 24 Feb., p. 62. Diane F. Gillespie discusses Woolf's equestrian imagery in *The Sisters' Arts: The Writing and Painting of Virginia Woolf and Vanessa Bell* (Syracuse, NY: Syracuse University Press, 1988), pp. 1–2. Woolf's riding metaphors may also pun on her standard diary abbreviation for it as '3 Gs.' ('gee' being both a word of command to a horse, and the horse itself) – see entries in D5 for 24 Feb., 7, 10, 17 Mar., 14 Apr., 12 Oct. 1937, pp. 61, 65, 66, 69, 79, 112.

37. *The Pargiters*, ed. Mitchell A. Leaska (London: Hogarth Press, 1978), p. 9.

38. *A Room of One's Own* refers to 'Opinions that one now pastes in a book labelled cock-a-doodle-dum and keeps for reading to select audiences on summer nights', *ROO*, p. 51; 'history in the raw' is Woolf's term for the daily newspapers, *TG*, p. 121; 'if you want to know any fact about politics you must read at least . . . three different versions of the same fact, and come in the end to your own conclusion', *TG*, pp. 220–1.

39. See Elaine Gualtieri, '*Three Guineas* and the Photograph: The Art of Propaganda', in Joannou, esp. pp. 166–7, and appendix 1 to *TG*, pp. 335–55; Brenda R. Silver, *Virginia Woolf's Reading Notebooks* (Princeton, NJ: Princeton University Press, 1983), pp. 255–314; the notebooks, edited by Vara Neverow and Merry Pawlowski, are themselves online at http://www. csub.edu/woolfcenter.

40. *TG*, chapter 3, fn. 1, p. 304 – this note comments not only on the appeals and requests for pledges addressed to 'Private people of no political training', but also notices how political debate has shifted from the private to the public sphere. Accounts of Woolf herself as a non-joiner need to be revised in the light of *A Bibliography*, E17–20, pp. 408–9, and Anna Snaith, 'Wide Circles: The *Three Guineas* Letters', *Woolf Studies Annual*, vol. 6 (New York: Pace University Press, 2000), pp. 7–8.

41. Woolf refers simply to an unnamed women's college, and 'a society to help the daughters of educated men to obtain employment in the professions (*TG*, pp. 151, 163). She identifies their 'honorary treasurers' as (rhetorical) 'sisters', amused to be writing of two actual sisters (as Barrett observes, *TG*, fn. b, p. 328). For a detailed account of the twelve letters, see Naomi Black's introduction to her edition, pp. xv–xviii.

42. See also *TG*, pp. 142, 202; *Pargiters*, p. 31.

43. *TG*, pp. 149–50, chapter 1, fn. 23, p. 283; *Pargiters*, pp. 28, 33 (and see *ROO*, p. 18); *TG*, pp. 154, 157.

44. *TG*, pp. 128–32; chapter 1, fn.16, p. 279 (MacCardie's comments were among the earliest of Woolf's newspaper cuttings, dating from November 1931); p. 138.

45. *TG*, p. 236.

46. *TG*, p. 270 and chapter 2, fn. 39, pp. 302–3; pp. 190, 212; compare D5, 28 Aug. 1938, p. 164: 'A single step in Cheko Slovakia – like the Austrian Archduke in 1914 & again its 1914'; *TG*, pp. 123, 153, 167, 181, 197, 231, 237. More hopefully, Woolf also observes that 'The years change things' (p. 151), deliberately echoing Kitty in *The Years*, at a key moment of transition, her train journey of May 1914: 'The years changed things; destroyed things; heaped things up', *Y*, p. 198.

47. *TG*, 'the procession', pp. 134–7, 142 (and facing photograph), 183–7 (including photograph), 191, 194, 228; 'the bridge', pp. 130–1, 133, 199; 'the mulberry tree', pp. 181, 190, 199, 224 (and for a further Blakean echo, see p. 175, 'The caterpillar on a leaf / Repeats to thee thy mother's grief', *Auguries of Innocence* (cited by Black in her edition, p. 192)); significant examples of three dots occur at pp. 118, 156, 162, 166, 216, 218, 246.

48. See Gualtieri, in Joannou, esp. pp. 167–73; L6, to Julian Bell, 16 Nov. 1936, p. 85; *TG*, p.162.

49. At an early stage (16 Feb. 1932: D4, p. 77), Woolf had considered 'Men Are Like That' as a possible title – see above, Ch. 11, n. 22; 'A Sketch of the Past', *MoB*, p. 140.

50. *Y*, p. 242.

51. Alice Staveley identified the photographs in 'Name That Face', *Virginia Woolf Miscellany*, 51 (Spring 1998), pp. 4–5; before Hitler, there had been a non-military German youth movement, *Der Wandervogel* – see D3, Rodmell, 1926, p. 104.

52. For *Jacob's Room*, see above, n. 31; *Mrs Dalloway*, intro. Elaine Showalter, ed. Stella McNichol (1925; London: Penguin, 1992), p. 188; *TG*, pp. 170–1, 195, and chapter 2, fn. 19, p. 295.

53. *TG*, p. 123, chapter 1, fn. 7, p. 275; *An Autobiography*, vol. 2, pp. 287–8, 344; for Woolf's presence, see D4, 8 Mar. 1932, p. 80, and Stuart N. Clarke, 'The Lord Chief Justice and the Woolfs', *Virginia Woolf Bulletin*, 14 (Sept. 2003), pp. 12–25.

54. *TG*, p. 227 (introducing the ceremony of burning the word 'feminist'); on Lang's 'Commission on the Ministry of Women', see pp. 246–55. Woolf's allusive discussion of Lang with H. G. Wells, as she began work on *Three Guineas*, turned on what was perceived as his sexual hypocrisy – D5, 28 Jan. 1937, p. 53.

55. For this point, see Staveley, n. 51 above; for Woolf's account of the

abdication crisis, see D5, 10–13 Dec. 1936, pp. 40–4; *Three Guineas*, chapter 1, fn. 11, p. 276.

56. In his pamphlet *War Mongers*, published by the Peace Pledge Union, and quoted by Peter Stansky and William Abrahams, *Journey to the Frontier: Two Roads to the Spanish Civil War* (1966; London: Constable, 1994), p. 396; Julian Bell had initially shared his parents' pacifism (editing and publishing the memoirs of First World War pacifists in *We Did Not Fight*, 1935), but his views gradually changed, as Stansky and Abrahams record.

57. D5, 12 Feb., 14, 15 Mar., 15, 21 Apr. 1937, pp. 54, 68–9, 79–80.

58. Woolf's memoir of Julian (which includes an account of their last evening together and her 'unexpressed certainty' that he would be killed) is appendix C of Quentin Bell's *Biography*, vol. 2, p. 258; D5, 11 June, 11 July, 6, 25 Aug., 13 Oct. 1937, pp. 93, 101, 104–5, 109, 113–14; see also Stansky and Abrahams, p. 412.

59. D5, 11 Aug. 1937, p. 106; 6 Aug., p. 105; 30 Nov., p. 119; 17 Aug., p. 108.

60. D5, 17 Aug. 1937, p. 107; 26 Sept., p.111; 29 Aug., p. 109; 12 Oct., pp. 112–13.

61. D5, 17 Aug. 1937, p. 108; 13 Oct., p. 114.

62. D5, 13 Oct. 1937, p. 114 – Quentin Bell notes the inconsistency of this diary entry, in appendix 1, '*A Room of One's Own* and *Three Guineas*', to his *Elders and Betters* (London: John Murray, 1995), p. 219 (though Woolf may be partly quoting Philip Hart, rather than giving her own opinion); 28 Feb. 1939, p. 206.

63. 'The Artist and Politics' (Leonard Woolf, ed., Virginia Woolf, *Collected Essays* (London: Chatto and Windus, 1966), vol. 2, p. 231), originally 'Why Art To-Day Follows Politics', published in the *Daily Worker*, 14 Dec. 1936; D5, 13 Mar. 1936, p. 17.

64. Woolf turned down an invitation to give the Clark Lectures at Cambridge (D4, 29 Feb. 1932, pp. 79–80 – 'a time serving pot hunter if I accepted'), an honorary degree at Manchester University (D4, 25 Mar. 1933, pp. 147–8) and becoming a Companion of Honour (D4, 15 May 1935, p. 314); *TG*, p. 219; D5, 22 June 1937, p. 96.

65. Woolf bracketed Jameson with Hugh Walpole, Compton Mackenzie and Philip Guedalla as 'the old Prostitutes' – D5, 31 May 1938, p. 147; *TG*, pp. 216–17; for Woolf's advantages, see her introduction to Margaret Llewelyn Davies, ed., *Life As We Have Known It, by Co-operative Working Women* (1931; London: Virago, 1977), especially pp. xxi, xxvii–viii (and Ch. 11, p. 286 and n. 65). These issues are explored in chapter 4, 'Class and Money', of Alex Zwerdling's *Virginia Woolf and the Real World* (Berkeley,

CA: University of California Press, 1986), pp. 87–119, and from a very different standpoint by Jane Marcus in ' "No More Horses": Virginia Woolf on Art and Propaganda', in *Art and Anger: Reading Like a Woman* (Columbus, OH: Ohio State University Press, 1988), pp. 101–21.

66. Leonard Woolf, *Quack! Quack!* (London: Hogarth Press, 1935), pp. 201, 197.

67. On Mosley, see Bradshaw, 'Hyams Place'; the B.U.F. symbol is seen by North on his way to visit Sara in *The Years* (Y, p. 227), and had been seen by Woolf herself on 4 Sept. 1935, in the midst of the Abyssinian crisis: 'Fascist propaganda, L[eonard]. said. Mosley again active' (D4, p. 337); on the plight of German women, see Marie-Luise Gattens, '*Three Guineas*, Fascism, and the Construction of Gender', in Pawlowski, *Fascism*, pp. 21–38, and for a comment on Italian women, see Lia Giachero, 'Seduced by Fascism: Benedetta Cappa Marinetti, the Woman Who Did Not Write *Three Guineas*', ibid., p. 161.

68. D5, 22 Oct. 1937, p. 115; 9 Jan. 1938, p. 125.

69. D5, 28 June 1937, p. 100 (and see D4, 25 Apr. 1935, p. 303, for further doubts about her reasoning capacity: 'not a good ratiocinator, Lytton used to say. Do I instinctively keep my mind from analysing, which would impede its creativeness? I think there's something in that').

70. Alex Zwerdling cites from the proofs an angry passage on male egotism (Zwerdling, p. 263), and see L6, to May Sarton, 2 Feb. 1939, p. 314, and to Elizabeth Bowen, 28 Feb. 1939, p. 319.

71. D5, 4 Feb., 10 Mar. 1938, pp. 127, 128 (but see also 12 Apr., p. 133, 'I didn't get so much praise from L[eonard]. as I hoped'); galley proofs were sent back on 26 Mar., p. 131; page proofs due, 12 Apr., p.133; on its serialization, see Naomi Black's article ' "Women Must Weep": The Serialization of *Three Guineas*', in James M. Haule and J. H. Stape, eds., *Editing Virginia Woolf: Interpreting the Modernist Text* (Basingstoke: Palgrave, 2002), pp. 74–90.

72. D5, 12 Apr. 1938, p. 134; *Three Guineas*, American additions to chapter 1, fn. 23, p. 283; fn. 34, p. 289; chapter 2, fn. 41, p. 304; chapter 3, fn. 47, p. 321 – listed as appendix III, pp. 364–5; D5, 3, 7 Feb. 1938, pp. 127, 128 (and 'my Outsider papers', 26 Mar., p. 132).

73. D5, 12 Mar. 1938, pp. 129–30; 26 Mar., p. 132; *TG*, chapter 2, fn. 3, p. 290 records ' "Nazis now control the whole of Austria" (Daily paper, March 12th, 1938)', though chapter 3, fn. 20, p. 313 is dated 'March 28th, 1938'.

74. D5, 28 Apr. 1938, pp. 136, 137; L6, to Vanessa Bell, 11 Mar. 1938, p. 218.

75. D5, 4 Feb. 1938, p. 127; 12 Apr., p. 133, and later in the same entry, 'Am

I right though in thinking that it has some importance ... as a point of view ... ?', D5, p. 134.

76. D5, 22, 28 Aug. 1938, pp. 163, 163–4.

77. D5, 4 Apr. 1937, p. 77; 3 June 1938, p. 148.

78. D5, 23 Aug. 1938, p. 163; 17 July, p. 156; 22 Nov., pp. 188–9, and see also 14 Sept. 1938, p. 170 ('[I] am not to care if its ... made my friends hostile').

79. D5, 28 May 1938, pp. 145–6; 3 June, p. 148 (the *Times Literary Supplement* review is reprinted in *Critical Heritage*, pp. 400–1); 5 June, p. 149; 14 Sept., p. 170; 3 June, p. 148.

80. D5, 3 June 1938, p. 148, fn. 1; 1 Sept., p. 166: 'Oh Queenie was at once cancelled by a letter from Jane Walker [an eminent woman doctor] – a thousand thanks ... 3 Gs ought to be in the hands of every English speaking man & woman &c.' For Walker's letter, see Snaith, pp. 73–4; Q. D. Leavis's article for *Scrutiny*, Sept. 1938, is reprinted in *Critical Heritage*, see esp. pp. 412–13, 417.

81. Letters from all those named except Ethel Smyth are reprinted by Snaith, pp. 17, 21–2; 20–1; 23; 26; 29–30 (and see also pp. 49–50, 62–3, 103–4, 157–163); 28; 31; 35; 40–2, 48–9; 42–4; 64; 'A note of ecstasy from Ethel [Smyth]' is recorded in D5, 5 June 1938, p. 149, but not included among the other *Three Guineas* letters; letters from strangers cited included Gladys Rossiter, p. 38; Dorothy Soden, p. 73; Geraldine Ostle, p. 18.

82. D5, 22 Sept. 1938, p. 173; Snaith, p. 50; Ernest Huxley's letters, Snaith, pp. 114–34, 135–50; Agnes Smith's letters, Snaith, pp. 98–103, 105–6, and see Snaith's introduction, esp. pp. 3–4, which points out that the letters disprove Q. D. Leavis's accusation that *Three Guineas* was 'a conversation between [Woolf] and her friends'.

83. D5, 19 Dec. 1938, p. 193.

84. Brenda R. Silver, '*Three Guineas* Before and After: Further Answers to Correspondents', in Jane Marcus, ed., *Virginia Woolf: A Feminist Slant* (Lincoln, NB: University of Nebraska Press, 1983), pp. 270–1; D5, 8 Dec. 1939, p. 249, and fn. 4; 'Thoughts on Peace in an Air Raid', *New Republic*, New York (21 Oct. 1940), *Collected Essays*, vol. 4, pp. 173–7 (and perhaps D5, 12 June 1940, p. 295, fn. 10).

85. D5, 11 June 1938, p. 149 – Judith Stephen's letter is reprinted by Snaith, p. 24; D5, 30 Oct. 1938, p. 182; Woolf interpreted Gardner's words as a response to Vita's criticism: 'Now Vita never contemplated that quality in 3 Gs'. A copy of Mann's lecture remained in the Woolfs' library – see Holleyman and Treacher, *Catalogue of Books from the Library of Leonard and Virginia Woolf* (Brighton: Holleyman and Treacher, 1975), section 2, p. 39.

86. Nigel Nicolson, *Virginia Woolf* (London: Weidenfeld & Nicolson, 2000), pp. 133, 135; *Biography*, vol. 2, p. 204, and Bell, *Elders and Betters*, appendix 1, p. 14; D5, 14 Nov. 1938, p. 186; Lassner, pp. 47–9.

87. *An Autobiography*, vol. 2, pp. 204–5; D5, 15 May 1940, p. 285; Hermione Lee, *Virginia Woolf* (London: Chatto & Windus, 1996), p. 693, cites a later letter to Woolf from Agnes Smith (8 Nov. 1940, Lee, fn. 94, p. 859) urging her to continue writing about politics in her own way – 'After all, *A Room of One's Own* and *Three Guineas* WERE politics'.

Chapter 13

1. *An Autobiography*, vol. 2, p. 300 – the Schubert song occurs, appropriately enough, in *Schwanengesang* (Swan Songs), and Leonard roughly translated Heine's poem from memory. For Woolf's visit in August 1905, see Mitchell A. Leaska, ed., Virginia Woolf, *A Passionate Apprentice: The Early Journals 1897–1909* (London: Hogarth Press, 1990), p. 282: 'We hung there like ghosts in the shade of the hedge, & at the sound of footsteps we turned away'. Woolf returned to St Ives at intervals through her life, in actuality and, finally, in imagination.

2. D5, 29 June 1939, p. 222 ('What a dream life is to be sure – that he should be dead, & I reading him').

3. D4, 17 Oct. 1934, p. 254 ('it is right to have lives – What a pity that it should all be lost').

4. D4, 5 Apr. 1935, p. 296 (also 20 June 1935, p. 324) – see also D5, 19 Feb. 1940, p. 269, as her Fry biography came to an end: 'Lytton is hinted as my next task'.

5. See D4, 31 Oct., 1, 12 Nov. 1934, pp. 258, 260; 29 Aug., p. 336; L6, to Sibyl Colefax, 14 Aug. 1940, p. 415; L6, to Ethel Smyth, 6 June 1936, p. 44. On 12 July 1935, Woolf gave the opening lecture for the Roger Fry Memorial Exhibition held at Bristol – see D4, 15 July 1935, p. 330, and for the lecture itself, Leonard Woolf, ed., Virginia Woolf, *Collected Essays* (London: Chatto and Windus, 1966), vol. 4, pp. 88–92.

6. D4, 17 Oct. 1935, p. 253; 31 Oct., 12 Nov., 21 Nov. 1935, pp. 258, 260, 262.

7. *CSF*, pp. 33–62.

8. 'Lady Hester Stanhope' (*Times Literary Supplement*, 20 Jan. 1910, reprinted *Essays*, vol. 1, pp. 325–9); essays on Miss Ormerod, Miss Mitford and Mrs Pilkington appear in *The Common Reader* (1925), see *Essays*, vol. 4, pp. 131–40; 190–95; 127–31; Dorothy Osborne (and essays on Mary

Wollstonecraft and Dorothy Wordsworth) in *The Second Common Reader* (1932) and in *Essays*, vol. 4, pp. 553–8. Woolf's interest in early women's writing in some respects anticipates our own, though her accounts of them are more biographically focused, and thus closer to an earlier tradition of exemplary women's lives – see Alison Booth, 'Those Well-lit Corridors of History', in Ann Ardis and Bonnie Kime Scott, eds., *Turning the Centuries, Papers from the Ninth Annual Conference on Virginia Woolf* (New York: Pace University Press, 2000), pp. 24–34.

9. In the early days of her friendship with Ethel Smyth, Woolf wrote her a number of autobiographical letters, in particular those of 22 June, 15 Aug. and 16 Oct. 1930, L4, pp. 180, 199–200, 231. Woolf's contributions to the Memoir Club are reprinted in *MoB*, pp. 164–220.

10. 'How I interest myself!' – D5, 2 Apr. 1937, p. 75. On 7 Oct. 1919, Woolf observed of her diary that 'all writing, even this unpremeditated scribbling, has its form, which one learns' (D1, p. 304), and on 28 Dec. 1919, that it had 'grown a person, with almost a face of its own' (D1, p. 317). On writing to 'old Virginia', see, for example D1, 20 Jan. 1919, p. 234; D2, 3 May 1921, p. 117; 17 Oct. 1924, p. 320; later, Woolf saw her diary as providing material for her memoirs: 'At 60 I am to sit down & write my life', D3, 8 Feb. 1926, p. 58; for this and for Leonard as reader, see D3, 3 Feb. 1927, p. 125 (and also 20 Mar. 1926, p. 67).

11. On 3 Nov. 1936, Woolf 'thought of a scheme for another book – it should be told in the first person. – Would that do as a form for Roger? (D5, p. 30), but in the event she siphoned off her autobiographical impulse into 'A Sketch of the Past'. On the two different versions of 'A Sketch', see 'The Aftermath', pp. 367, 369.

12. 'The Art of Biography', *Atlantic Monthly*, April 1939, reprinted *Collected Essays*, vol. 4, p. 222.

13. 'Memoirs of a Novelist' in *CSF*, pp. 69–79; D4, 12 Nov. 1934, p. 260 – she goes on 'but M[argery Fry]. hesitates: I have heard nothing from her; & rather suspect she wants to do it herself.'

14. L6, to Vita Sackville-West, 3 May 1938, p. 226.

15. 'The arts of painting and writing lay close together, and Roger Fry was always making raids across the boundaries . . . And many of his theories held good for both arts', *Roger Fry: A Biography*, ed. Diane F. Gillespie (1940; Oxford: Shakespeare Head/Blackwell, 1995), pp. 193–4. My account is indebted to this edition. For Woolf's dissatisfaction with the discourse of art history, see her review of *Vision and Design*, reprinted as appendix A to *Roger Fry*, p. 383 ('pictures either hold much less than books, or . . . the language for expressing what they hold has still to be invented'); for Fry's, see

'Words Wanted in Connection with Art', reprinted in *A Roger Fry Reader*, ed. Christopher Reed (Chicago: University of Chicago Press, 1996), pp. 424–6.
16. Roger Fry to Virginia Woolf, 18 Oct. 1918; RF to VW, 3 Dec. 1928 (both in the University of Sussex Library), cited by Frances Spalding, *Roger Fry: Art and Life* (1980; Norwich: Black Dog Books, 1999), pp. 198, 244–5; L3, to Roger Fry, 27 May 1927, p. 385.

17. D5, 9 Feb. 1940, p. 266; D4, 30 Dec. 1935, p. 361.

18. L6, to Vanessa Bell, 8 Oct. 1938, p. 285; D5, 25 July 1940, p. 305; Leonard's response, D5, 20 Mar. 1940, p. 271.

19. See *The Pargiters*, ed. Mitchell A. Leaska (London: Hogarth Press, 1978), esp. pp. xxxviii–xl.

20. *Roger Fry*, pp. xxxi–ii, see also p. 28.

21. D5, 6 Jan. 1940, p. 256. Woolf discussed some of these issues in correspondence with Katharine Furse, daughter of J. A. Symonds, who was writing a life of her (gay) father – see Rowena Fowler, 'Virginia Woolf and Katharine Furse: An Unpublished Correspondence', *Tulsa Studies in Women's Literature*, 9 (Fall 1990), pp. 201–28.

22. D5, 7 July 1938, p. 155; 12, 13 Apr. 1938, pp. 133, 134; 3 May 1938, p. 138.

23. D5, 7 July 1938, p. 155; 7 Aug. 1938, p. 160; 20, 30 May 1938, pp. 141, 146.

24. D5, 7 Aug., 17 Aug. 1938, pp. 160, 161; 22 Aug. 1938, pp. 162–3 (referred to in the opening of *Between the Acts*).

25. D5, 31 Aug. 1938, p. 165 (see also 17, 28 Aug., pp. 162, 163, 164).

26. D5, 10 Sept. 1938, p. 167.

27. D5, 13, 14, 16 Sept. 1938, pp. 169, 170; Woolf's dreams, D5, 17 Sept. 1938, p. 172; 30 Sept. 1938, p. 177; 29, 30 Sept., 1 Oct. 1938, pp. 175–7 on their meeting and its outcome (see also R. A. C. Parker, *Chamberlain and Appeasement: British Policy and the Coming of the Second World War* (Basingstoke: Macmillan, 1993), esp. ch. 8, pp. 156–81).

28. D5, 1 Oct. 1938, pp. 177–8; for similar responses to storms, see Woolf's letter to Christabel McLaren, 11 May? 1930: 'I do hope you've been nice to Dotty today, & the storms of the air dont symbolise you & her at Penns', 'Letters to Christabel McLaren', ed. Stephen Barkway, *Virginia Woolf Bulletin*, 15 (Jan. 2004), p. 41, and 'the sudden profuse shower one night . . . wh[ich]. made me think of all men & women weeping', D5, 24 Mar. 1940, p. 274.

29. D5, 20, 22 Oct. 1938, pp. 181–2, and see also 14, 15, 24 Nov., 1, 11 Dec. 1938, pp. 186, 189, 190, 191, where her generosity continues to annoy her. For 'Lappin and Lapinova', see *CSF*, pp. 261–8; for 'The Art of Biography', *Collected Essays*, vol. 4, pp. 221–8, esp. p. 227.

30. *Collected Essays*, vol. 4, pp. 226, 227.

31. D5, 18 Jan. 1939, p. 200; 15 Nov. 1938, p. 186; 24 Nov. 1938, p. 189; 19 Dec. 1938, p. 192; L6, to VS-W, 25 Dec. 1938, p. 307; D5, 5, 9 Jan. 1939, pp. 197, 198 (and see also *An Autobiography*, vol. 2, pp. 325–6).

32. D5, 26 Apr. 1938, p. 135; 25, 26 May 1938, pp. 142–3.

33. D5, 9 Jan. 1939, p. 198; W. H. Auden, 'In Memory of W. B. Yeats', *Collected Shorter Poems, 1927–1957* (London: Faber and Faber, 1969), p. 141; D5, 29 Jan. 1939, p. 202, and *An Autobiography*, vol. 2, pp. 311–12.

34. D5, 11 Mar. 1939, pp. 207–8; 20 Sept. 1938, p. 173; in a footnote to chapter 6, Woolf explained Helen's illness as the result of 'an incurable thickening of the bone of the skull' (*Roger Fry*, p. 118), the explanation that Margery Fry had given her (see D5, 19 Feb. 1940, p. 269). According to Frances Spalding, Fry's more recent biographer, 'Helen suffered from schizophrenia and was probably the victim of inherited syphilis', Spalding, *Fry*, fn. 14, p. 264 (Spalding could be much more open about Fry's love affairs than Woolf felt able to be).

35. Boris Anrep's mosaics on the landing of the National Gallery include a recognizable portrait of Woolf as Clio, the muse of history; *Roger Fry*, p. xiv.

36. As Regina Marler points out in *Bloomsbury Pie* (London: Virago, 1998), pp. 212–15, Frances Spalding is almost single-handedly responsible for the re-assessment of Fry's paintings. The catalogue of the Courtauld exhibition, *Art Made Modern: Roger Fry's Vision of Art*, ed. Christopher Green (London: Merrell Holberton, 1999), focuses on Fry's achievements as a critic rather than as a painter, as most accounts tend to do.

37. D5, 20 Mar. 1940, p. 272; scenes from *Roger Fry* at pp. 119–20, 137–8, 230, 243–4. On 28 Sept. 1938, in the middle of the Munich crisis, Woolf visited the National Gallery to look 'at Renoir, Cézanne &c: tried to see through Roger's eyes', D5, p. 174, and compare her letter to Ruth Fry – L6, 16 Mar. 1941, p. 479 – where she claimed that her favourite review had 'said that Roger Fry was there and not V.W., which was what I wanted'; D5, 20 Mar. 1940, p. 272.

38. D5, 24, 29, 31 Jan. 1939, pp. 201, 202, 203; 28 Feb. 1939, p. 206; 16 Mar. 1939, p. 208; 15 Apr. 1939, p. 215.

39. 'A Sketch of the Past', *MoB*, pp. 64–5.

40. 'A Sketch of the Past', *MoB*, p. 134, and compare *The Waves*, ed. Kate Flint (1931; London: Penguin, 1992), p. 11 (see Ch. 10, p. 245, for another explanation of 'Elvedon').

41. D5, 9 June 1940, p. 293 (and compare 24 July 1940, p. 304: '[t]here's no standard to write for: no public to echo back').

42. Entitled '22 Hyde Park Gate' and 'Old Bloomsbury', these are reprinted in *MoB*.

43. 'A Sketch of the Past', *MoB*, p. 64; D5, 17 Aug. 1938, p. 162, and on 29 June 1939, p. 222, she wonders 'if I shall ever read this again. Perhaps if I go on with my memoirs, . . . I shall make use of it.'

44. 'A Sketch of the Past', *MoB*, pp. 64, 75.

45. Ibid., p. 75; D3, 'Rodmell. 1926', p. 102; *To the Lighthouse*, intro. Hermione Lee, ed. Stella McNichol (1927; London: Penguin, 1992), p. 209.

46. 'A Sketch of the Past', *MoB*, p. 67; here she talks about 'the feeling of ecstasy, . . . the feeling of rapture', while distinguishing between the two emotions on the previous page.

47. Ibid., pp. 68, 69, and compare L6, to ES, 12 Jan. 1941, p. 460, 'I still shiver with shame at the memory of my half brother, standing me on a ledge, aged about 6, and so exploring my private parts. Why should I have felt shame then?'

48. 'A Sketch of the Past', *MoB*, p. 69.

49. Ibid., p. 70 – Woolf had been reading Helena Swanwick's autobiography, *I Have Been Young* (1935), as Schulkind's note explains.

50. 'A Sketch of the Past', *MoB*, pp. 71, 72.

51. Ibid., p. 71; the abandoned introduction to *The Common Reader* was 'Byron and Mr Briggs' (*Essays*, vol. 3, pp. 474–99), discussed in Ch. 5 above, esp. pp. 116–18; preface to *The Common Reader*, *Essays*, vol. 4, p. 19; 'A Sketch of the Past', *MoB*, p. 72.

52. 'A Sketch of the Past', *MoB*, pp. 72, 73; Woolf's essay, 'Anon', searches for the expression of a 'common life' in literature – 'certain emotions always in being: felt by people always' – see Brenda R. Silver, 'Virginia Woolf: Cultural Critique', in Bonnie Kime Scott, ed., *The Gender of Modernism* (Bloomington and Indianapolis: Indiana University Press, 1990), pp. 674, 679–93, esp. p. 692; 'A Sketch of the Past', *MoB*, p. 73.

53. 'A Sketch of the Past', *MoB*, pp. 65, 80. A few months later, Woolf was thinking about inner voices as 'Censors. How visionary figures admonish us . . .', D5, 7 Aug. 1939, p. 229.

54. In 1936, Woolf dined with Karin and Adrian, and enjoyed a conversation about psychoanalysis (D5, 11 Nov. 1936, p. 32); on 8 Mar. 1939, she attended the 25th anniversary dinner of the British Psycho-Analytical Society, where she met Melanie Klein and invited her to dinner ('A woman of character & force' – D5, 11, 16 Mar. 1939, pp. 208, 209) – see Elizabeth Abel, *Virginia Woolf and the Fictions of Psychoanalysis* (Chicago: University of Chicago Press, 1989), pp. 19–20; Woolf's essay 'Freudian Fiction' ('The triumphs of science are beautifully positive'), *Times Literary Supplement*, 25 Mar. 1920,

and *Essays*, vol. 3, pp. 195-7; Roger Fry, *The Artist and Psycho-Analysis*, Hogarth Essays, First Series, no. 2 (London: Hogarth Press, 1924), reprinted in *A Roger Fry Reader*, pp. 351-65.

55. 'Began reading Freud last night', D5, 2 Dec. 1939, p. 248, and thereafter she read with great excitement – see D5, pp. 249, 250, 252, and into 1940 (pp. 266, 299), although this passage cited from 'A Sketch of the Past', *MoB*, p. 81, was written earlier, between 2 and 15 May 1939.

56. 'A Sketch of the Past', *MoB*, pp. 81, 82, 83; Daniel Ferrer analyses Woolf's earliest memories of her mother in his account of *The Waves*, *Virginia Woolf and the Madness of Language*, trans. G. Bennington and R. Bowlby (London: Routledge, 1990), pp. 68-73.

57. Vanessa Bell, 'Notes on Virginia's Childhood', *Sketches in Pen and Ink*, ed. Lia Giachero (London: Pimlico, 1998), p. 60.

58. 'A Sketch of the Past', *MoB*, pp. 85-91, and esp. p. 84 – Peter Walsh's exclamation about Clarissa Dalloway, 'For there she was' (*Mrs Dalloway*, intro. Elaine Showalter, ed. Stella McNichol (1925; London: Penguin, 1992), p. 213) and Prue's about Mrs Ramsay, 'That's my mother . . . That is the thing itself . . . as if there were only one person like that in the world' (*TTL*, p. 126), reflect Woolf's feelings about her mother.

59. 'A Sketch of the Past', *MoB*, pp. 92, 93; *TTL*, p. 54; 'A Sketch of the Past', *MoB*, pp. 93, 92, 95.

60. 'A Sketch of the Past', *MoB*, p. 98; D5, 14, 25 May 1939, pp. 218, 219: 'Shall we end our lives looking in that great peaceful garden; in the sun? I hope so'; 'A grim thought struck me; wh[ich]. of these rooms shall I die in?', D5, 13 July 1939, p. 226, and 25 July for her unwritten 'reflections'(p. 226); on 'the unreality of force', see 3, 6 Sept. 1939, p. 234 – 'any idea is more real', p. 235.

61. D5, 2 Aug. 1939, p. 229, Woolf was trying to cut down smoking; on 28 July 1939, p. 227, she reread her diary; 'Knitting is also a help', 29 Mar. 1940, p. 277, and see 27 June 1940, p. 299, 'too many cigarettes, . . . incessant knitting', with the Battle of Britain imminent; L6, to VB, 8 Oct. 1938, p. 285 (and compare 'Perhaps it is more interesting to describe "The Crisis" than R.'s love affairs', D5, 25 Aug. 1939, p. 230); the German–Soviet pact, D5, 25 Aug. 1939, p. 231.

62. D5, 25 Aug. 1939, pp. 230-1; 3 Sept. 1939, p. 233.

63. D5, 6 Sept. 1939, pp. 234-5; 25 Sept. 1939, p. 239; 31 Jan. 1940, p. 263 (for the horrors of the London blackout, see 11 Sept., 22 Oct. 1939, pp. 236, 242-3); on writing articles, 6, 7 Oct. 1939, pp. 240, 241; on returning to her memoir, 25 Oct., 30 Nov. 1939, 19 Feb. 1940, pp. 243, 248, 269, and a reference to it, 25 Apr. 1940, p. 281.

64. D5, 9 Feb. 1940, p. 266, and 3,19, 20, 30 Jan. 1940, pp. 255, 257, 259, 262 and editor's note, p. 252; VB to VW, 13 Mar. 1940, *Selected Letters of Vanessa Bell*, ed. Regina Marler (London: Bloomsbury, 1993), p. 461; D5, 20 Mar. 1940, pp. 271–2.

65. D5, 20 Mar. 1940, p. 271, but Woolf had already been thinking about 'what are the interesting things . . . what I should like to read here [in her diary] in 10 years time . . . Perhaps literal facts. The annal, not the novel', D5, 29 Apr. 1939, pp. 216–17, and she would later agree with Leonard that Fry's biography was 'one of my failures . . . patches of an[n]al; too much quotation; sometimes its cramped & poky', D5, 10 June 1940, p. 293; on balconies as viewpoints, see the openings of her short stories 'The Searchlight' and 'The Symbol', *CSF*, pp. 269, 288. For an alternative reading of 'anal', see Panthea Reid Broughton, ' "Virginia Is Anal": Speculations on Virginia Woolf's Writing *Roger Fry* and Reading Sigmund Freud', *Journal of Modern Literature*, 14, 1 (Summer 1987), pp. 151–7.

66. D5, 29 Mar. 1940, p. 276; 2 Feb. 1940, p. 263; 24 Mar. 1940, p. 274; 6 May 1940, p. 282 – it did last: Angelica was to marry David Garnett, and tell her own version of events in *Deceived with Kindness: A Bloomsbury Childhood* (London: Chatto and Windus, 1984).

67. D5, 6 May 1940, p. 283; 13 May 1940, p. 284 (and on 15 May, the Woolfs argued over whether Leonard should join the Home Guard – 'Gun & uniform to me slightly ridiculous'); on the evacuation of Dunkirk, and Harry West (a Rodmell neighbour)'s experience of it, 12, 20 June 1940, pp. 294, 297; 14, 20 June, pp. 296, 297 – Woolf, completing 'Pointz Hall', felt a (Yeatsian) 'gaiety & recklessness' was called for – D5, 22 June 1940, p. 298.

68. 'A Sketch of the Past', *MoB*, p. 100; p. 70 (see also pp. 64, 85, 98, 100).

69. D5, 15 May 1940, pp. 284–5; 7, 9 June 1940, pp. 292–3 (see also *An Autobiography*, vol. 2, pp. 383, 404); 'The Black Book' (1940), compiled by Walter Schellenberg (*Sonderfahndungsliste G.B.*) (London: Imperial War Museum, 1989), p. 222; D5, 20 June 1940, p. 297; 15 May 1940, p. 285; 22, 27 June 1940, pp. 298, 299.

70. 'A Sketch of the Past', *MoB*, p. 98 – these were Woolf's thoughts from the previous summer, from a sequence dated 19 July 1939.

71. Ibid., pp. 96, 105.

72. Ibid., p. 107; D5, 25 Apr. 1940, p. 281; 'A Sketch of the Past', *MoB*, pp. 108 (see also D5, 8 Dec. 1939, p. 249), 114, 116, 118, 119, 122–4.

73. D5, 16 Aug. 1940, p. 311 (see also 19, 28, 31 Aug. 1940, pp. 312, 313, 314); 'Thoughts on Peace in an Air Raid', *Collected Essays*, vol. 4, pp. 173, 174–6.

74. D5, 10 Sept. 1940, p. 316; 13, 18 Sept. 1940, pp. 319, 322.

75. D5, 17, 20, 22 Oct. 1940, pp. 329, 330–1, 332 (she made a further visit on 29 Oct. 1940, D5, p. 334).

76. 'A Sketch of the Past', *MoB*, pp. 126, 136, 138; Bell, 'Notes on Virginia's Childhood', p. 57.

77. 'A Sketch of the Past', *MoB*, pp. 142, 143, 144, 150; 'somehow ridiculous', p. 147; 158.

78. 'Elsewhere' – i.e., in her Memoir Club essays, '22 Hyde Park Gate' and 'Old Bloomsbury', reprinted in *MoB*, pp. 177, 182, 183. The revised typescript of 'A Sketch of the Past' refers to George's 'crude wish to dominate . . . some jealousy, of Jack [Hills] . . . and, as became obvious later, some sexual urge' (p. 154), and to 'the sexual jealousy that fermented in his depths' (p. 156).

79. D5, 1 Nov. 1940, p. 335; 2 Oct. 1940, pp. 326–7; 23 Nov. 1940, pp. 340–1, for the end of 'P. H.' and 'thinking of taking my mountain top – that persistent vision – as a starting point' ('The Symbol', *CSF*, pp. 288–90); 16 Dec. 1940, p. 343 for 'Reading at Random'.

80. D5, 29 Nov. 1940, p. 342 (she even included the generous Octavia Wilberforce among the 'leeches'); 16, 19 Dec. 1940, pp. 343, 344.

81. D5, 16 Dec. 1940, p. 343; 2 Sept. 1940, p. 315 – Giles also recognizes how vulnerable the landscape is in *Between the Acts*, intro. Gillian Beer, ed. Stella McNichol (London: Penguin, 1992), p. 34; 24 Dec. 1940, p. 346 – and compare 31 Jan. 1940, p. 262: 'I cling to my tiny philosophy: to hug the present moment'.

82. D5, 25 July 1940, p. 305; *A Bibliography*, pp. 110–11; D5, 24 July 1940, p. 303; 26 July 1940, p. 306, and fn. 13; 28 July 1940, pp. 307–8.

83. D5, 1, 2 Aug. 1940, p. 308; 4 Aug. 1940, p. 309; 6, 10 Aug. 1940, p. 310 (Forster's review is reprinted in *Critical Heritage*, pp. 423–5); D5, 10, 16 Aug. 1940, p. 311, and *A Bibliography*, p. 111; D5, 23 Aug. 1940, p. 312.

84. Read's review is reprinted in *Critical Heritage*, pp. 420–2; Forster, ibid., p. 425; 'Sketch of the Past', *MoB*, p. 146.

85. Responding to congratulatory letters, Woolf wrote to Clive Bell, L6, 6 Aug. 1940, pp. 410–11; to R. C. Trevelyan, 12 Aug. 1940, p. 412; to Sibyl Colefax, 14 Aug. 1940, pp. 415–16; to W. J. H. Sprott, 15 Aug. 1940, p. 416; to Sir William Rothenstein, 15 Aug. 1940, pp. 416–17; to Ethel Smyth, 16 Aug. 1940, pp. 417–18; to Dora Sanger, 24 Aug. 1940, p. 422; to Ruth Fry, 28 Aug. 1940, pp. 423–4; to Mrs Easdale, 3 Sept. 1940, p. 425; to Mrs R. C. Trevelyan, 4 Sept. 1940, pp. 425–6; to David Cecil, 4 Sept. 1940, pp. 426–7 and to Violet Dickinson, 8 Sept. 1940, pp. 428–9. Woolf's reply to Ben Nicolson quotes from his letter, L6, 13 Aug. 1940, pp. 413–15, esp. p. 413 – see also draft and typescript of further letters to Nicolson, L6, 24 Aug. 1940, pp. 419–22, and D5, 7 Sept. 1940, p. 316, and fn. 3.

86. *Roger Fry*, p. xxxix, and *A Room of One's Own* (*A Room of One's Own/ Three Guineas*, ed. Michèle Barrett (1929, 1938; London: Penguin, 1993)), p. 25; for details of Spalding's book, see n.16; *A Bibliography*, p. 113.

87. See Editor's Note, 'A Sketch of the Past', *MoB* (1976 edition), pp. 71–3, and compare *MoB* (1985 edition), pp. 61–3; the portrait of her father runs in *MoB*, pp. 107–16 (1985 edition), and is followed by a description of 22 Hyde Park Gate – it is dated 19 June 1940 (though see also D5, 25 Apr. 1940, p. 281). See Katherine C. Hill-Miller, 'Leslie Stephen revisited: a new fragment of Virginia Woolf's "A Sketch of the Past" ', in Alice Kessler-Harris and William McBrien, eds., *Faith of a (Woman) Writer* (Westport, CT: Greenwood Press, 1988), pp. 279–83 (a paper originally given in 1982).

88. See n. 55.

Chapter 14

1. *Three Guineas* (*A Room of One's Own/Three Guineas*, ed. Michèle Barrett (1929, 1938; London: Penguin, 1993)), p. 234; Karl Marx and Friedrich Engels, *Selected Works* (London: Lawrence and Wishart, 1950), vol. 1, p. 44; 'Sketch of the Past', *MoB*, p. 65.

2. *TG*, p. 203; L6, to Ethel Smyth, 12 Jan. 1941, p. 460; for literature as 'common ground', see 'The Leaning Tower', an essay read to the Brighton Workers' Educational Association on 27 April 1940, Leonard Woolf, ed., *Virginia Woolf, Collected Essays* (London: Chatto and Windus, 1966), vol. 2, p. 181; after lunch in *Between the Acts*, the relative merits of English literature and painting are discussed – see *Between the Acts*, intro. Gillian Beer, ed. Stella McNichol (1941; London: Penguin, 1992), p. 35.

3. 'The Years', Fourth Notebook, p. 56 (Berg Collection, New York Public Library); *The Years*, ed. Jeri Johnson (1937; London: Penguin, 1998), pp. 146, 151, 152 (and compare 'This is my England', *Pointz Hall: The Earlier and Later Typescripts of* Between the Acts, ed. Mitchell A. Leaska (New York: State University of New York Publications, 1983), p. 49, or 'that is England', in L6, to ES, 12 Jan. 1941, p. 460). The 1911 section of *The Years* includes further anticipations of *Between the Acts*, such as buying fish (Y, p. 142), and 'travellers' joy' (Y, p. 143) – see my essay ' "Almost ashamed of England being so English": Woolf and ideas of Englishness', in Robin Hackett, Jane Marcus and Gay Wachman, eds., *Inroads and Outposts: British Women in the Thirties* (Gainesville, FL: University of Florida Press, forthcoming).

4. D5, 12 Apr. 1938, p. 133 (although the first page of the earlier typescript is dated '2nd April 1938', *Pointz Hall*, p. 33); D5, 26 Apr. 1938, p. 135.

5. *BA*, pp. 7, 21; D5, 29 Apr., 9 May 1938, pp. 137, 139.

6. *Pointz Hall*, p. 33; *The Waves*, ed. Kate Flint (1931; London: Penguin, 1992), p. 3; L6, to Stephen Spender, 30 Apr. 1937, p. 122.

7. *Pointz Hall*, pp. 33, 36; *BA*, pp. 119, 117; 'Unity' and 'Dispersion' first appear in a speech of Richard Dalloway's, in *The Voyage Out*, ed. Jane Wheare (1915; London: Penguin, 1992), p. 55.

8. Page numbers appearing in square brackets after quotes refer to McNichol's 1992 Penguin edition of *Between the Acts*; *Pointz Hall*, p. 81.

9. *Pointz Hall*, p. 171; *BA*, pp. 104 ('Mrs Swithin . . . was off . . . one-making'), 114 – the phrase 'scraps, orts and fragments' derives from Troilus's grief at Cressida's sexual betrayal in Shakespeare's *Troilus and Cressida*:

> 'The fractions of her faith, orts of her love,
> The fragments, scraps, the bits, and greasy relics
> Of her o'er-eaten faith, are bound to Diomed.' (V. ii. 155–7)

It becomes a repeated expression for disintegration – see also *BA*, pp. 26, 73, 111, 112, 127.

10. Leonard Woolf, *Barbarians at the Gate* (London: Victor Gollancz, 1939), pp. 74–5; D5, 8 Dec. 1938, p. 249, 'I dislike this excitement. yet enjoy it. Ambivalence as Freud calls it. (I'm gulping up Freud)', and see also entries for 9 Dec., p. 250, and 17 Dec., p. 252, 'I read Freud on Groups' – she took notes on *Group Psychology* – see Brenda R. Silver, *Virginia Woolf's Reading Notebooks* (Princeton, NJ: Princeton University Press, 1983), pp. 115–16; 'Nothing is any longer one thing', *Orlando*, intro. Sandra Gilbert, ed. Brenda Lyons (1928; London: Penguin, 1993), p. 210.

11. '31 pages' – see *Pointz Hall*, p. 51; D5, 20 Sept. 1938, p. 172, 6 Oct., p. 179; 19 Dec. 1938, p. 193; 29, 30 May 1940, pp. 289, 290.

12. For Leaska's account of the typescripts, see *Pointz Hall*, pp. 17–21, 25–9, and on Woolf typing her letters, p. 25; L6, to ES, 15 July 1938, p. 255, and further apologies for typing, L6, to Vanessa Bell, 1 Oct. 1938, p. 275 (other typed letters to VB on 3 Oct., pp. 279–81, 8 Oct., pp. 284–8, 24 Oct, pp. 294–6, 2 Nov., pp. 298–300); to Ling Su-Hua, 15 Oct. 1938, p. 289; to Quentin Bell (without apologies), 18 Oct. 1938, pp. 291–3, and to Shena, Lady Simon, 'Forgive this typing, but my hand is getting worse and worse and worse', 21 Nov. 1938, p. 303; for further details of writing problems during the winter of 1940, see Epilogue, n. 4; D5, 26 Apr. 1938, p. 135.

13. *Pointz Hall*, pp. 33–6.

14. *Pointz Hall*, pp. 38–40. Byron and Thomas, linked by their good looks and early deaths (and so, perhaps, antecedents of Rupert Haines), were also linked through Byron's love lyric, 'So, we'll go no more a-roving', here quoted

by Bart Oliver (*BA*, p. 6). It echoes a traditional song whose refrain – 'I'll go no more a-roving with you, fair maid' – would also become the refrain of Thomas's second 'Old Song': *Collected Poems of Edward Thomas*, ed. R. G. Thomas (1978; Oxford: Oxford University Press, 1983), p. 20. Woolf herself quoted this refrain in her talk on 'Craftsmanship' (broadcast on 29 Apr. 1937) in the course of discussing the 'miscegenation' of the English language (*Collected Essays*, vol. 2, p. 250), as well as in a teasing letter to Vita – L6, to Vita Sackville-West, 19 Feb. 1939, p. 318.

15. The phrase 'a passion . . .' from Woolf's essay on Thomas's *A Literary Pilgrim*, 'Flumina Amem Silvasque', in the *Times Literary Supplement*, 11 Oct. 1917, *Essays*, vol. 2, p. 161; for 'the shop in the High Street' see *Pointz Hall*, p. 38.

16. 'Old Man', Thomas, *Collected Poems*, p. 9. It may be Woolf, rather than Isa, who misremembers the poem and the plant – which becomes 'Old Man's Beard' for the rest of the novel, though the earlier typescript contrasts the Byron legend 'that hung like a wreath of Traveller's Joy' with 'the little bare sprig of Old Man's Beard' that is Thomas's poetry (*Pointz Hall*, p. 39).

17. Thomas, *Collected Poems*, p. 28; D5, 26 Apr. 1938, p. 135.

18. The notion of 'passing' (and its links with 'the past') had figured in Woolf's talk on 'Craftsmanship', where she played upon the words of the underground announcement, 'Passing Russell Square' (*Collected Essays*, vol. 2, p. 245).

19. 'Reading', *Essays*, vol. 3, p. 142 – 'bushes of verbena and southernwood yield a leaf as one passes to be crushed and smelt. If we could see also what we can smell – if, at this moment crushing the southernwood, I could go back . . . I should come in the end . . . to . . . Queen Elizabeth herself', p. 145.

20. See Ch. 5, pp. 113–14, above.

21. *BA*, pp. 13, 15; 'wanted a . . . whiff', *Pointz Hall*, p. 54 (perhaps continuing the metaphor of sniffing an aromatic leaf, as well as of being given gas at the dentist) – the nature of Isa's 'raging' (or 'aching') tooth is clearer in the earlier typescript; the guardsmen's rape was first reported in *The Times* at the end of June 1938, a year earlier than the novel supposedly takes place, but at the same time as she actually wrote the earliest version of this scene. The rape first appears at the end of 'The Library' section (dated as 'Begun May 20th'); the following section, entitled 'The Dining Room', is dated 3 July (*Pointz Hall*, pp. 54, 55, 58, 60), although the Woolfs only returned from holiday in Scotland on 2 July. See Stuart N. Clarke, 'The Horse with a Green Tail', *Virginia Woolf Miscellany*, 34 (Spring 1990), pp. 3–4. As first written, 'A certain pleasure mingled with [Isa's] disgust' as she reads of it, *Pointz Hall*, p. 54.

22. 'The Mark on the Wall', *CSF*, p. 89; *BA*, pp. 8, 9–10 (George's vision of the flower recalls her own early memory, described in 'A Sketch of the Past',

MoB, p. 71), 13, 15, and 127–8, echoing Isa's earlier question, 'Did the plot matter? . . . The plot was only there to beget emotion. There were only two emotions; love; and hate . . . Peace was the third emotion', *BA*, pp. 56–7.

23. As in 'Time Passes', *To the Lighthouse*, intro. Hermione Lee, ed. Stella McNichol (1927; London: Penguin, 1992), pp. 142, 145, 150; 138, 144–5 (compare *Pointz Hall*, p. 87, 'like one of those capricious beams that passing cars send over ceilings').

24. In 'Time Passes', the house itself is left 'like a shell on a sandhill to fill with dry salt grains now that life had left it' (*TTL*, p. 149), and at the end of *Between the Acts*, the room becomes a shell once more – pp. 127, 128; at an early stage of planning, *The Waves* was to be 'an endeavour at something mystic, spiritual; the thing that exists when we aren't there', D3, 30 Oct. 1926, p. 114; near the end of *The Waves*, Bernard asks, 'But how describe the world seen without a self? There are no words' (*W*, p. 221).

25. In *To the Lighthouse* Andrew explains Mr Ramsay's interest in 'Subject and object and the nature of reality' to Lily Briscoe: 'Think of a kitchen table then . . . when you're not there' (*TTL*, p. 28), Mr Ramsay himself has promised 'to talk to the young men of Cardiff about Locke, Hume, Berkeley' – *TTL*, p. 51 – also fn. 25, p. 232 (which refers to the debate on the cow in the quad in E. M. Forster's *The Longest Journey*, 1907), and fn. 46, p. 236 (which cites Noel Annan on Leslie Stephen's revaluation of the English empiricists, Locke, Berkeley and Hume, in *Leslie Stephen: The Godless Victorian* (Chicago: University of Chicago Press, 1984), p. 223); *BA*, p. 118, and see Alan J. Friedman and Carol C. Donley, *Einstein as Myth and Muse* (Cambridge: Cambridge University Press, 1985), pp. 141, 146 – who note the influence of Heisenberg's Uncertainty Principle on *The Waves*: 'Woolf, like many other modern writers, recognized the necessity to create literary form which could carry the concepts of relativity, uncertainty and complementarity.'

26. *Pointz Hall*, pp. 61–2; 'A Sketch of the Past', *MoB*, p. 72.

27. *Pointz Hall*, p. 284 (and compare *BA*, p. 24) – here and generally, the later typescript is often close to the published text; John Keats, 'Ode on a Grecian Urn': 'Thou still unravished bride of quietness, / Thou foster-child of silence and slow time'; T. S. Eliot, 'Burnt Norton', v: 'Only by the form, the pattern, / Can words or music reach / The stillness, as a Chinese jar still / Moves perpetually in its stillness'.

28. For Hewet's novel, *The Voyage Out*, ed. Jane Wheare (1915; London: Penguin, 1992), p. 204; *BA*, pp. 12, 13, 25, and note that the portrait of the lady 'drew them down the paths of silence' (p. 29) into 'the heart of silence' (p. 32); the empty bedroom and cot, *BA*, pp. 44, 45; the empty barn, pp. 61, 62; the empty stage, pp. 48, 51, 73, 84, 104, 105.

29. *BA*, pp. 28–9, and see 'The Fascination of the Pool', *CSF*, pp. 226–7 (apparently a description of the pool at Charleston – both the pool and the barn suggest that Woolf had in mind some of the features of Charleston in describing Pointz Hall); compare, in the earlier typescript, 'The pond . . . hoarded silence, deep silence' (*Pointz Hall*, p. 67), emphasizing its relation to the silent dining room. Woolf noted in her diary, 'I cant unstring my mind after trying to write about a lily pool. P. H. is to be a series of contrasts', D5, 4 Aug. 1938, p. 159.

30. *BA*, pp. 27, 28; in the earlier typescript, 'a spring of feeling bubbled up in [Mrs Manresa] from mud that was millions of years old . . . Perhaps poetry grew from mud' (*Pointz Hall*, p. 69), linking her with 'a voice bubbling up . . . the voice of an ancient spring', in *Mrs Dalloway*, intro. Elaine Showalter, ed. Stella McNichol (1925; London: Penguin, 1992), pp. 88–90.

31. For Bernard's 'little language', see the last section of *The Waves*, esp. pp. 183, 196, 199, 227; 'English voices murmuring', *TG*, p. 234 and n. 1, above; for 'the mulberry bush', see above, Ch. 12, p. 322; for these two nursery rhymes in *Between the Acts*, see pp. 70, 71, 74, 106, 107–8, 110.

32. On 'PH poetry', D5, 28 Aug. 1940, p. 313 – Woolf recorded writing 'lots of little poems to go into P. H.: as they may come in handy' (D5, 14 Oct. 1938, p. 180) – see *Pointz Hall*, appendix D, pp. 557–61 for examples; 'mellay', *BA*, p. 57; Lucy Swithin on ancestors, *BA*, p. 43; for 'the scars', *BA*, p. 5, and see also Brenda R. Silver's edition of ' "Anon" and "The Reader": Virginia Woolf's Last Essays', *Twentieth Century Literature*, 25, 3/4 (Fall/Winter 1979), pp. 356–441, pp. 405–6, fn 12 (also reprinted in Brenda R. Silver, 'Virginia Woolf: Cultural Critique', in Bonnie Kime Scott, ed., *The Gender of Modernism: A Critical Anthology* (Bloomington and Indianapolis: Indiana University Press, 1990), p. 694, fn. 6).

33. D5, 18 Jan. 1939, p. 200 – Woolf continued, 'That was by the way the best criticism I've had for a long time: that I poetise my inanimate scenes, stress my personality, dont let the meaning emerge from the matiere –'; D5, 17 Nov. 1940, p. 339 – she broke up 'the rhythm of PH' by reading her notes for 'A Sketch of the Past' which were 'far freer & looser'; *BA*, p. 12.

34. Woolf used this image of the fish in water in 'A Sketch of the Past' (see above, Ch, 13, p. 354 and n. 53), but in the unfinished 'Reading at Random', she renamed that 'stream of influences', social forces and pressures 'Nin, Crot and Pully' – see Silver, 'Anon', p. 403, fn. 4 (or *The Gender of Modernism*, p. 694, fn. 2).

35. The mingling of villagers and gentry points to a possible breakdown of class barriers (though it doesn't actually happen); the barn was inspired by that of Charleston, but the combination of a huge old barn, a village mummers'

play and a rape suggests Thomas Hardy, whose poetry appeared in the earlier typescript (*Pointz Hall*, p. 47).

36. Silver, 'Anon', lines 411–12, p. 392; on Communist pageants, see Raphael Samuel, *Theatres of Memory*, vol. 1 (London: Verso, 1994), p. 207; on Edith Craig's suffragette pageants, Nina Auerbach, *Ellen Terry: Player in Her Time* (London: J. M. Dent, 1987), p. 427, and on Woolf's pageant, Marlowe A. Miller, 'Unveiling "the dialectic of Culture and Barbarism" in British Pageantry: Virginia Woolf's *Between the Acts*', *Papers on Language and Literature*, XXXIV, 2 (Spring 1998), pp. 134–61.

37. *The Abinger Pageant* is reprinted in Forster's *Abinger Harvest* (1936; London: Penguin, 1967), pp. 369–84 – its epilogue demanded, 'Are [houses] man's final triumph? Or is there another England, green and eternal, which will outlast them?' For *England's Pleasant Land* (London: Hogarth Press, 1940), see D5, 17 July 1938, p. 156, and L6, to R. C. Trevelyan, 5 July 1938, p. 255, to ES, 15 July 1938, p. 258. Blake's 'Jerusalem' in Parry's setting is traditionally sung at the end of Women's Institute meetings, and on the last night of the Proms (John Lucas notes that it was broadcast at the end of the 1926 General Strike, *The Radical Twenties: Writing, Politics, Culture* (Nottingham: Five Leaves, 1997), p. 220).

38. E. F. Benson, *Mapp and Lucia* (London: Hodder and Stoughton, 1935); for E. L. Delafield and Jan Struther, see Alison Light, *Forever England: Femininity, Literature and Conservatism Between the Wars* (London: Routledge, 1991), esp. pp. 115–23; L6, to Margaret Llewelyn Davies, 6 Apr. 1940, p. 391; for 'Tracy', see deletions recorded in *Pointz Hall*, pp. 78, 79, 82.

39. *Pointz Hall*, p. 504 (and see p. 558, for another version).

40. *BA*, pp. 59–60 – compare the speaker at the end of the pageant, 'if we don't jump to conclusions, if you think, and I think, perhaps one day, thinking differently, we shall think the same?', p. 118; Woolf's theories in 'Reading at Random' (also referred to as 'Turning the Page') are in part a reworking of T. S. Eliot's 'dissociation of sensibility', as described in his essay 'The Metaphysical Poets' (1921), reprinted in T. S. Eliot, *Selected Essays* (London: Faber and Faber, 1969), p. 288; see n. 32 above for details of 'Anon' and 'The Reader', the surviving drafts of 'Reading at Random'.

41. Dodge's reaction, *BA*, pp. 57–8; 'All that fuss about nothing' is the comment of a voice that responds to the play as if it were real, p. 84; illusion fails twice, pp. 84, 107 (and compare 'I remember the sudden profuse shower one night just before the war wh[ich]. made me think of all men & women weeping', D5, 24 Mar. 1940, p. 274 – probably the storm of 1 Oct. 1938, D5, pp. 177–8).

42. Woolf felt that 'smash and splinters' characterized the writing of her

generation, and wrote to Gerald Brenan, 'The best of us catch a glimpse of a nose, a shoulder, something turning away, always in movement', L2, 25 Dec. 1922, p. 598; Woolf wrote on Lewis Carroll for the *New Statesman*, 9 Dec. 1939 (*Collected Essays*, vol. 1, pp. 254–5).

43. *Between the Acts* finally acquired its title on 26 Feb. 1941 – D5, p. 356; Giles's 'actions', *BA*, pp. 61, 89–90; 'A Sketch of the Past', *MoB*, p. 98.

44. *BA*, pp. 30, 34, 74, 91 –'The glass is falling' may echo the last lines of Louis MacNeice's 'Bagpipe Music' (1938), where it stands for the deteriorating political situation: 'The glass is falling hour by hour, the glass will fall for ever, / But if you break the bloody glass you won't hold up the weather' (Woolf's familiarity with his poetry is apparent from her essay 'The Leaning Tower', *Collected Essays*, vol. 2, p. 181).

45. *BA*, pp. 118, 111, 113–14.

46. 'Words copulated', *Pointz Hall*, p. 177; 'another play', *BA*, p. 40; 'the wall of civilization', *BA*, p. 108; Mrs Swithin's 'Outline History', *BA*, pp. 8, 129.

47. Freud, *Civilization and Its Discontents* (1930), Penguin Freud Library vol. 12, 'Civilization, Society and Religion' (London: Penguin, 1991), p. 256 – Woolf was reading this on 9 Dec. 1939, D5, p. 250, fn. 5.

48. *Pointz Hall*, pp. 431, 440 (and see *BA*, pp. 124, 130).

49. D5, 9, 27 June 1940, 26 Feb. 1941, pp. 293, 299, 357.

50. *BA*, pp. 118, 128; *Y*, p. 271

51. *Pointz Hall*, pp. 173, 178, 184 (in the earlier typescript, Isa confides in William Dodge that she loves 'Haines; he's married to a dull woman in a coat and skirt . . . It's not true, you know, that a woman only needs her children', *Pointz Hall*, p. 121).

52. *Pointz Hall*, pp. 434, 435 – in the later typescript, when Lucy Swithin talks of the children, 'Giles looked up from his newspaper; Isa became a mother again, and also a wife', *Pointz Hall*, p. 438 (and compare *BA*, pp. 126, 128); for Giles's invitation to Mrs Manresa, see *Pointz Hall*, pp. 370, 390, and also p. 525, and the late addition at p. 563.

53. Compare *Pointz Hall*, pp. 439–40.

54. *VO*, p. 251; *Night and Day*, ed. Julia Briggs (1919; London: Penguin, 1992), p. 432; *Y*, pp. 284, 301 – Woolf also used the phrase in her last essay to describe the Elizabethan dramatists: 'Off the stage, they lived in the heart of darkness', Silver, 'Anon', p. 396, line 595 (or *The Gender of Modernism*, p. 691).

55. Joseph Conrad, *Heart of Darkness* in *'Youth'*, *'Heart of Darkness'*, *and 'The End of the Tether': Three Stories* (London: J. M. Dent, 1967), pp. 45–162, Marlow's words, p. 48; for savages in *BA*, see pp. 13, 20, 30, 61, 75 and 118.

56. D5, 23 Nov. 1940, p. 340; 'copying PH', 24 Dec. 1940, p. 346, 9 Jan. 1941, p. 352 (and see Leaska's appendix E, 'Holograph Revisions Later Than November 23, 1940', *Pointz Hall*, pp. 562–5); D5, 26 Feb. 1941, p. 356.

57. To John Lehmann, 3 Apr. 1941, to Donald Brace, 6 Apr. 1941, *Letters of Leonard Woolf*, ed. F. Spotts (London: Bloomsbury, 1989), pp. 255, 256.

58. L6, to John Lehmann, 20 Mar. 1941, p. 482, ? 27 Mar. 1941, p. 486; to John Lehmann, 28 Mar. 1941, *Letters of LW*, p. 250 (the situation was further complicated by the fact that Lehmann had already jumped the gun by announcing the novel's publication in the *New Statesman*).

59. Silver, 'Anon', p. 429, lines 97–8 (or *The Gender of Modernism*, p. 699).

60. *A Bibliography*, pp. 114, 115; Tony Bradshaw, *The Bloomsbury Artists: Prints and Book Design* (Aldershot: Scolar Press, 1999), p. 72, plate 134; *BA*, p. 3; Cecil's review for the *Spectator*, 18 July 1941, p. 64, reprinted in *Critical Heritage*, p. 437.

61. F. R. Leavis, 'After *To the Lighthouse*', *Scrutiny*, 10, 3 (January 1942), p. 295; Kronenberger in *Nation* (New York), reprinted in *Critical Heritage*, pp. 452, 450; 'perhaps the most complete . . .', from Edwin Muir's review for *The Listener*, *Critical Heritage*, p. 444; *Times Literary Supplement* reviewer, *Critical Heritage*, pp. 439, 441; David Cecil, *Critical Heritage*, p. 437; Muir, *Critical Heritage*, p. 445.

62. Bowen's review of *BA* first appeared in the *New Statesman*, 19 July 1941, and was reprinted in her *Collected Impressions* (London, New York, Toronto: Longmans, Green, 1950), p. 74.

63. Ibn Hassan in *Paracriticisms* (1975), quoted in *A Reader's Guide to Contemporary Literary Theory*, eds. Raman Selden and Peter Widdowson (Hemel Hempstead: Harvester, 1993), p. 177; for *Between the Acts* as a postmodern text, see Pamela L. Caughie, *Virginia Woolf and Postmodernism: Literature in Quest and Question of Itself* (Urbana and Chicago: University of Illinois Press, 1991), pp. 51–7; Beth Rigel Daugherty, 'Face to Face with "Ourselves" in Virginia Woolf's *Between the Acts*', *Themes and Variations: Selected Papers from the Second Conference on Virginia Woolf*, eds. Vara Neverow-Turk and Mark Hussey (New York: Pace University Press, 1993), pp. 76–82.

Epilogue

1. 'Point Shirley' (*The Colossus*, 1960; Sylvia Plath, *The Collected Poems* (New York: Harper & Row, 1981)), p. 110.

2. D5, 26 Jan. 1941, p. 354; on her projected book, see diary entries for 23

Nov., 16 Dec., 20 Dec. 1940, 1 Jan. 1941, pp. 340, 343, 345, 351 (and earlier, 12 Sept. 1940, p. 318), L6, to Ethel Smyth, 1 Feb. 1941, p. 466, and as 'a new Common reader', L6, to ES, 1 Mar. 1941, p. 475. The surviving fragments were edited by Brenda R. Silver in '"Anon" and "The Reader": Virginia Woolf's Last Essays', *Twentieth Century Literature*, 25, 3/4 (Fall/Winter 1979), pp. 356–441 (and as 'Virginia Woolf: Cultural Critique', in Bonnie Kime Scott, ed., *The Gender of Modernism* (Bloomington and Indianapolis: Indiana University Press, 1990), pp. 679–701); for Woolf's proposed book on reading, see above, Ch. 5, pp. 117, 119.

3. D5, 26 Feb. 1941, p. 357, and compare 'Its difficult, I find, to write. No audience. No private stimulus, only this outer roar', L6, to Elizabeth Robins, 13 Mar. 1941, p. 479. Octavia Wilberforce also wrote to Elizabeth Robins, about her meetings with Woolf in a series of letters reprinted by Herbert Marder as an appendix to his *The Measure of Life: Virginia Woolf's Last Years* (Ithaca, NY: Cornell University Press, 2000). An undated letter to Robins reports that Woolf 'has no power over words and can't write' (Octavia advised Woolf, 'every true genius has to lie fallow'), p. 351, and another (22 Mar. 1941), reports Woolf as saying, 'I can't write. I've lost the art', p. 357.

4. On 'The Symbol', see D5, 23 Nov. 1940, p. 341: 'I think of taking my mountain top – that persistent vision – as a starting point' (*CSF*, pp. 288–90, and notes, pp. 311–13 – this story is also about the pain of a woman writing); for her 'frozen claw', L6, to Desmond MacCarthy, 22 Feb. 1941, p. 468, and 'like the cramped claw of an aged fowl', L6, to Mary Hutchinson, 10 Feb. 1941, p. 471 – Octavia Wilberforce reports clasping Woolf's 'icy cold' hand, to Elizabeth Robins, 27 Mar. 1941 (Marder, p. 359). See also D5, 24 Dec. 1940, p. 346, 'I note with some dismay that my hand is becoming palsied'.

5. Woolf teasingly referred to Octavia as 'a new lover, a doctor, a Wilberforce, a cousin', L6, to Vita Sackville-West, 19 Jan. 1941, p. 462, and L6, to ES, 1 Feb. 1941, p. 465; Octavia to Elizabeth Robins, undated (Marder, p. 351), and see Wayne K. Chapman and Evelyn Haller, 'Octavia's Story', in Wayne K. Chapman and Janet Manson, eds., *Women in the Milieu of Virginia Woolf* (New York: Pace University Press, 1998), pp. 239–42.

6. L6, to ES, 12 Jan. 1941, p. 460; D5, 9 Jan. 1941, p. 352; 19 Dec. 1940, p. 344.

7. L6, to ES, 12 Jan. 1941, p. 460; D5, 1 Jan 1941, p. 351; for the origins of *The Voyage Out* in the streets between the Strand and the river, see Ch. 1, p. 1; D5, 15 Jan., p. 352 (and L6, to VS-W, 19 Jan. 1941, p. 462: 'Lord, what chaos in the Temple! All my lovely squares gone').

8. D5, 8 Mar. 1941, p. 358; 9 Jan. 1941, p. 351, fn. 2 – the phrase is from Walter de la Mare's 'Fare Well', in his *Motley and Other Poems* (London: Constable, 1918), p. 75 – Woolf reviewed it for the *Times Literary Sup-*

plement, 30 May 1918 (and *Essays*, vol. 2, pp. 252–5 – her review ended by quoting these words).

9. D5, 15 Jan. 1941, pp. 352–3 (for Harriet Weaver's visit, see D1, 18 Apr. 1918, pp. 139–40); Yeats 'became his admirers' in W. H. Auden's 'In Memory of W. B. Yeats', *Collected Shorter Poems, 1927–1957* (London: Faber and Faber, 1969).

10. D5, 26 Jan. 1941, p. 355, and compare 'one cant lift a fringe of the future . . . the blank space in front', L6, to MH, 10 Feb. 1941, p. 472.

11. L6, to ES, 1 Mar. 1941, p. 475; L6, to Lady Cecil, 21 Mar. 1941, p. 483, and compare 'this phase of the war is rather like waiting in the ante room of a Dr. or dentist's', quoted by Octavia Wilberforce to Elizabeth Robins, 28 Feb. 1941 (Marder, p. 354).

12. See Ch. 13, pp. 345, 360; L6, to ES, 1 Mar. 1941, p. 475; D5, 7 June 1940, p. 293; in *King Lear*, the Fool's mysterious last line is 'And I'll go to bed at noon' (III. vi. 92).

13. For 'The Reader', see Silver, ' "Anon" and "The Reader" ', p. 429 (or *The Gender of Modernism*, p. 698). Octavia Wilberforce referred to Woolf's plan to 'do a sketch of her', to Elizabeth Robins, 28 Feb. 1941 (Marder, p. 354), see also Wilberforce's letter to Robins of 22 Mar. 1941 (Marder, p. 357) and the resulting fragment, 'English Youth', in *CSF*, p. 338; Woolf's own letters to Octavia Wilberforce, L6, 4 Mar. 1941, p. 477, to Elizabeth Robins, L6, 13 Mar. 1941, p. 479, and her final diary entry, D5, 24 Mar. 1941, p. 359: 'Octavia's story. Could I englobe it somehow? English youth in 1900'; for Janet Vaughan's contribution to *A Room of One's Own*, see S. P. Rosenbaum, ed., *Women & Fiction: The Manuscript Versions of 'A Room of One's Own'* (Oxford: Shakespeare Head/Blackwell, 1992), p. 213 (note to p. 114). She also contributed to the character of Peggy in *The Years*.

14. Octavia Wilberforce to Elizabeth Robins, 27 Mar. 1941 (Marder, p. 358, and compare 'During part of the last war was when she lost hold . . . she's a bit scared this may happen again', OW to ER, 14 Mar. 1941, Marder, pp. 356–7); Wilberforce made the same point in a letter to Leonard of 29 Mar. 1941, reprinted in *Letters of Leonard Woolf*, ed. F. Spotts (London: Bloomsbury, 1990), pp. 251–2.

15. 'A Sketch of the Past', *MoB*, p. 72 – Woolf's phrasing here anticipates that of T. S. Eliot's *Dry Salvages*, v (February 1941):

> For most of us, there is only the unattended
> Moment, . . . or music heard so deeply
> That it is not heard at all, but you are the music
> While the music lasts.

16. D5, 25 Sept. 1939, p. 239; 'A Sketch of the Past', *MoB*, p. 85 (and D5, 14 May 1939, p. 219); Gertler died on 23 June (at 5 Grove Terrace, a house later lived in by the present writer); Woolf talked to Vanessa and Duncan about Gertler's death two days later, D5, 26 June 1939, p. 221.

17. Woolf cites Toller in D4, 20 Apr. 1935, p. 303. Sybil Oldfield quotes Toller's words in connection with Woolf's 'As a woman my country is the whole world' (from *Three Guineas*), in *Women Against the Iron Fist: Alternatives to Militarism (1900–1989)* (Oxford: Basil Blackwell, 1989), p. 119.

18. On 9 Mar. 1936, Woolf had replied to an invitation from Zweig to send a public birthday card to Sigmund Freud for his eightieth birthday – see *A Bibliography*, p. 401, and Joanne Trautmann Banks, 'Some New Woolf Letters', *Modern Fiction Studies*, 30, 2 (Summer 1984), p. 184.

19. L6, to Leonard Woolf, ? 18 Mar. 1941, p. 481, to Vanessa Bell, ? 23 Mar. 1941, p. 485, to LW, 28 Mar. 1941, pp. 486–7. The traditional dating of these letters is challenged by Panthea Reid, in appendix D, 'A Redating of Virginia Woolf's Suicide Letters', *Art and Affection: A Life of Virginia Woolf* (New York: Oxford University Press, 1996), pp. 471–7; '[Terence] said, "No two people have ever been happier than we have been. No one has ever loved as we have loved."' *The Voyage Out*, ed. Jane Wheare (1915; London: Penguin, 1992), p. 334.

20. L6, to VB, ? 23 Mar. 1941, p. 485; *An Autobiography*, vol. 2, p. 434.

21. Louie Everest began working at Monk's House in 1934, and continued until Leonard's death in 1969; she and her husband lived in a cottage that Leonard had bought (D5, 31 Mar. 1937, fn, 22). She seems to have had a happier relationship with Woolf than previous servants – no doubt, her living out helped. For her account (as Louie Mayer), see Joan Russell Noble, ed., *Recollections of Virginia Woolf by her Contemporaries* (1972; London: Sphere Books, 1989), p. 195.

22. On 17 Aug. 1938, Woolf recorded the deaths by drowning in the Ouse of 'The old woman who lived up at Mt Misery', as well as another unidentified woman – D5, pp. 161–2. Her own body was recovered on 18 April, by Southease bridge, where PC Collins recorded that her watch had stopped at 11.45 (Hermione Lee, *Virginia Woolf* (London: Chatto and Windus, 1996), p. 764); 'Thoughts on Peace in an Air Raid', first published in *New Republic* (New York, 21 Oct. 1940), Leonard Woolf, ed., Virginia Woolf, *Collected Essays* (London: Chatto and Windus, 1966), vol. 4, p. 176 (Woolf was quoting from Sir Thomas Browne's *The Garden of Cyrus*, chapter 5, which she is likely to have known at first hand, though this passage was reprinted in Logan Pearsall Smith, *A Treasury of English Prose*, p. 71, a book she had reviewed – see *Essays*, vol. 3, p. 171).

Index

Abbreviations used for VW's works: BA, *Between the Acts*; JR, *Jacob's Room*; MD, *Mrs Dalloway*; MoB, *Moments of Being*; MT, *Monday or Tuesday*; ND, *Night and Day*; O, *Orlando*; RF, *Roger Fry*; ROO, *A Room of One's Own*; TCR, *The Common Reader*; TG, *Three Guineas*; TTL, *To the Lighthouse*; VO, *The Voyage Out*; W, *The Waves*; Y, *The Years*.